Pride and Prejudice

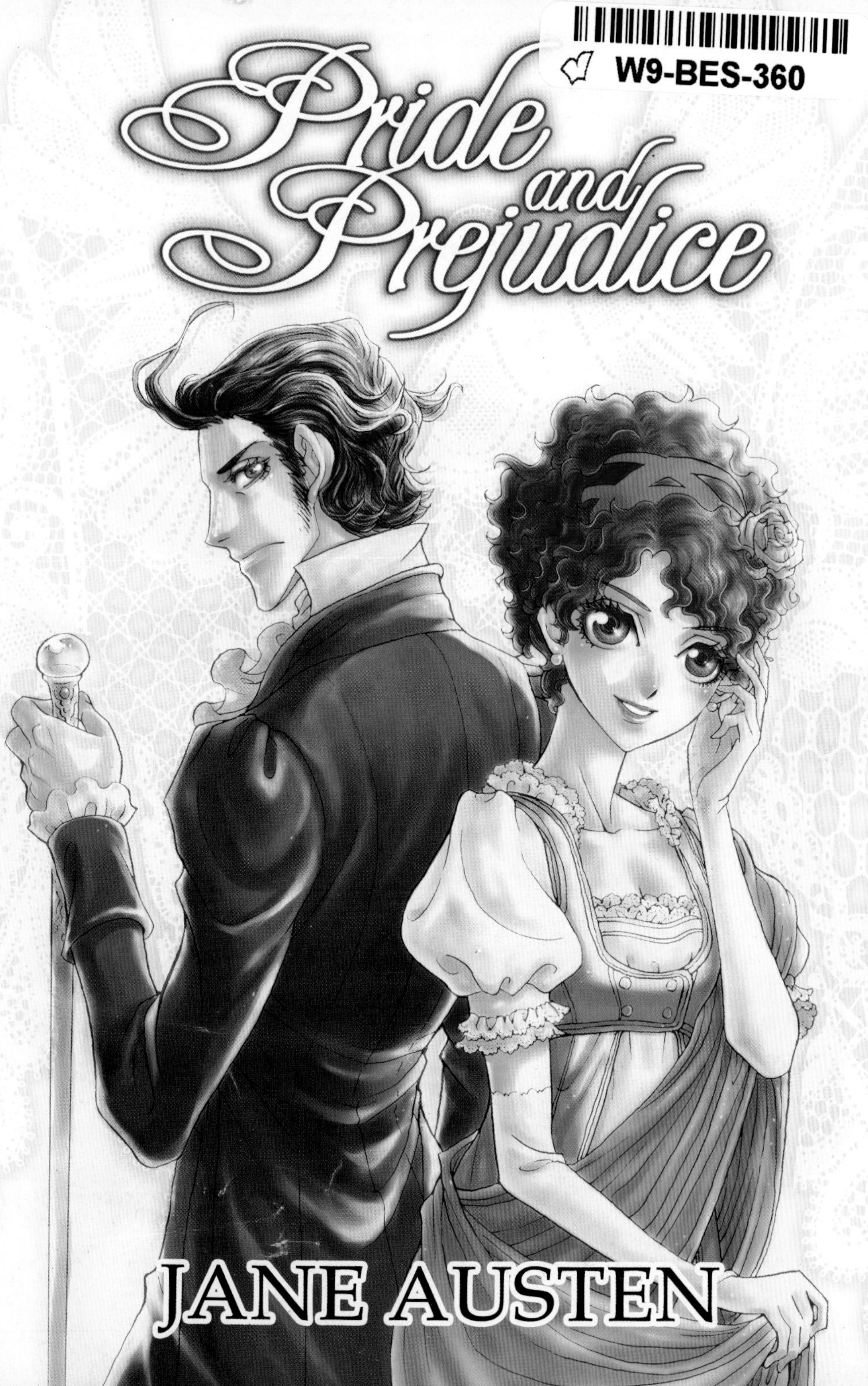

JANE AUSTEN

HOW TO READ MANGA!

Hello there, and welcome to **Manga Classics**! "Manga" is a style of comic book originating in **Japan**.

A manga book is read from **right-to-left,** which is **backwards** from the normal books you know. This means that you will find the first page where you expect to find the last page! It also means that each page begins in the top right corner.

START HERE!

If you have never read a manga book before, here is a helpful guide to get you started!

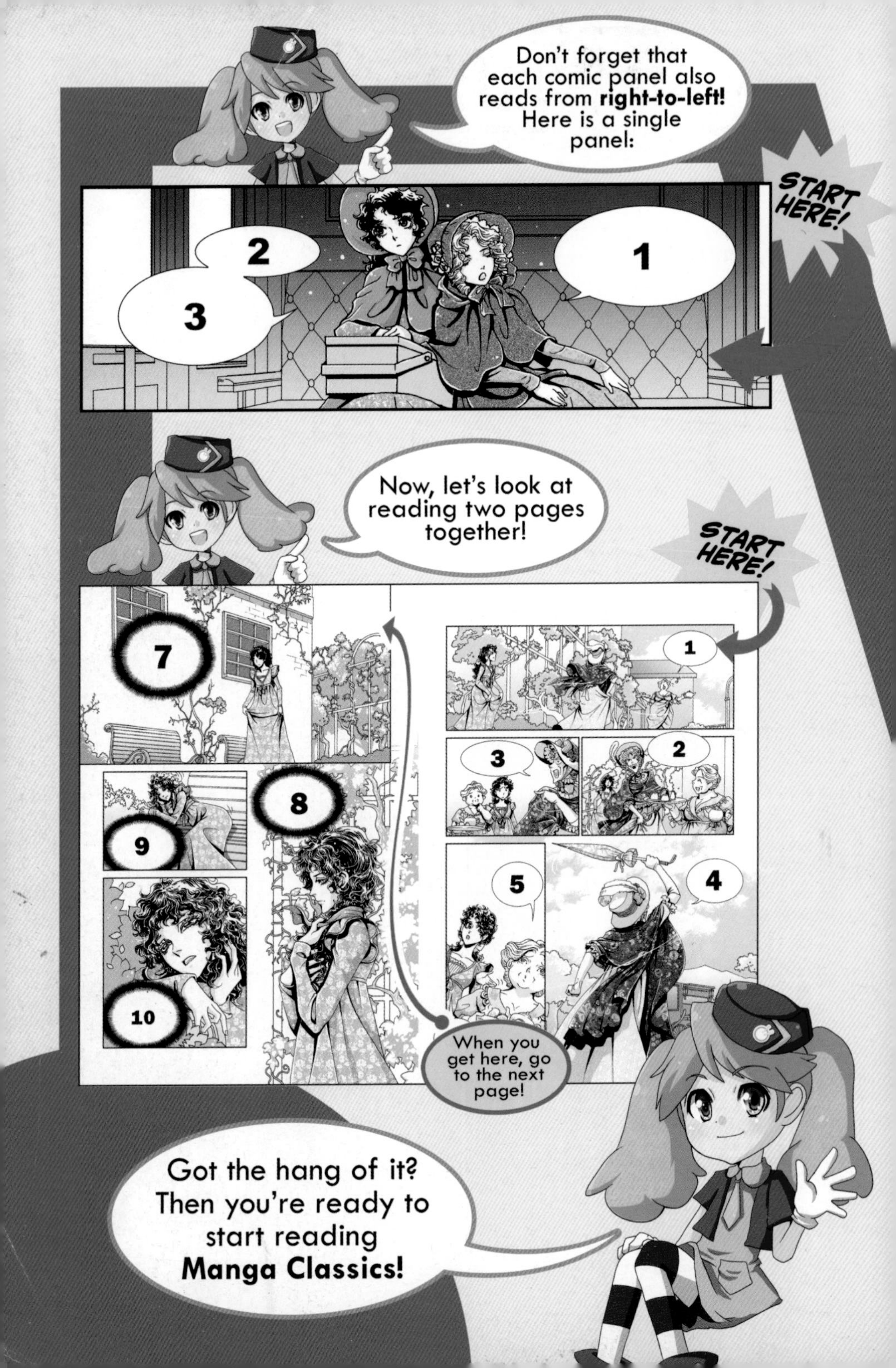

Don't forget that each comic panel also reads from **right-to-left!** Here is a single panel:
START HERE!
1
2
3
Now, let's look at reading two pages together!
START HERE!
1
2
3
4
5
When you get here, go to the next page!
7
8
9
10
Got the hang of it? Then you're ready to start reading **Manga Classics!**

CONTENTS:

Chapter 1:	P.5
Chapter 2:	P.40
Chapter 3:	P.55
Chapter 4:	P.75
Chapter 5:	P.103
Chapter 6:	P.166
Chapter 7:	P.131
Chapter 8:	P.144
Chapter 9:	P.163
Chapter 10:	P.177

Chapter 11:	P.196
Chapter 12:	P.215
Chapter 13:	P.233
Chapter 14:	P.253
Chapter 15:	P.273
Chapter 16:	P.289
Chapter 17:	P.306
Chapter 18:	P.325
Chapter 19:	P.341
Afterwords:	P.369

Chapter 1

It is a truth universally acknowledged that a single man with a good fortune must be in want of a wife. Whether he knows it or not...

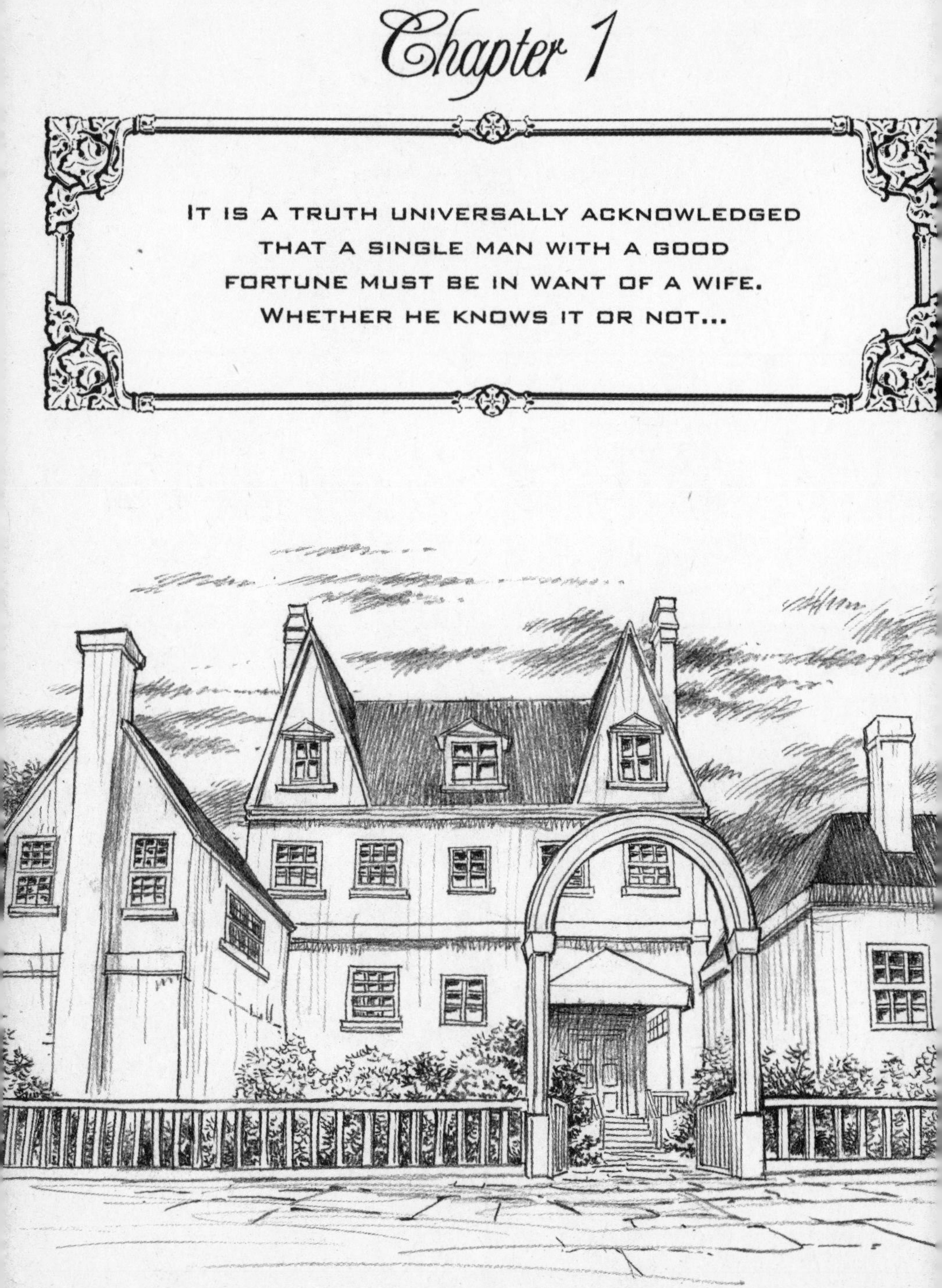

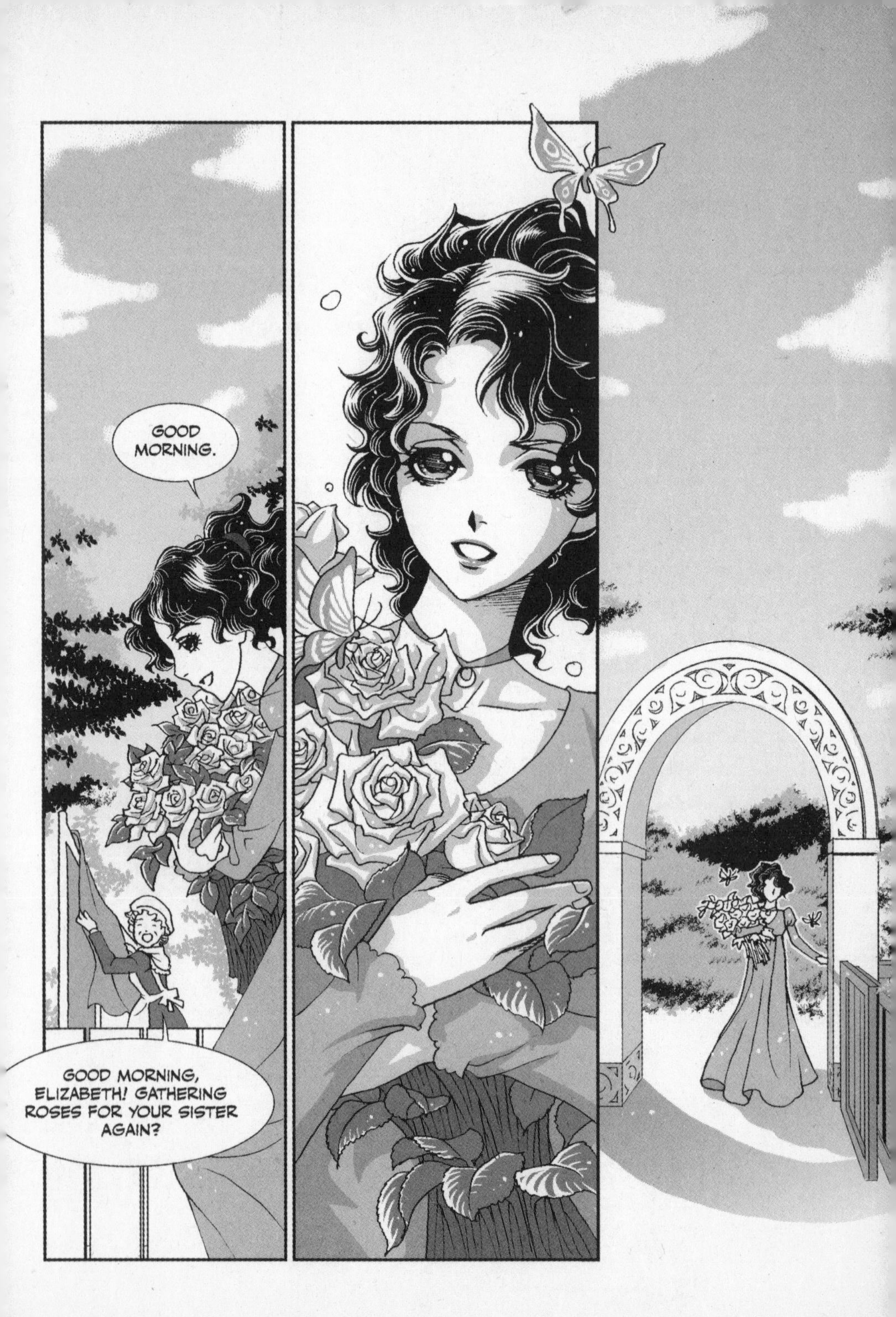
GOOD MORNING.
GOOD MORNING, ELIZABETH! GATHERING ROSES FOR YOUR SISTER AGAIN?

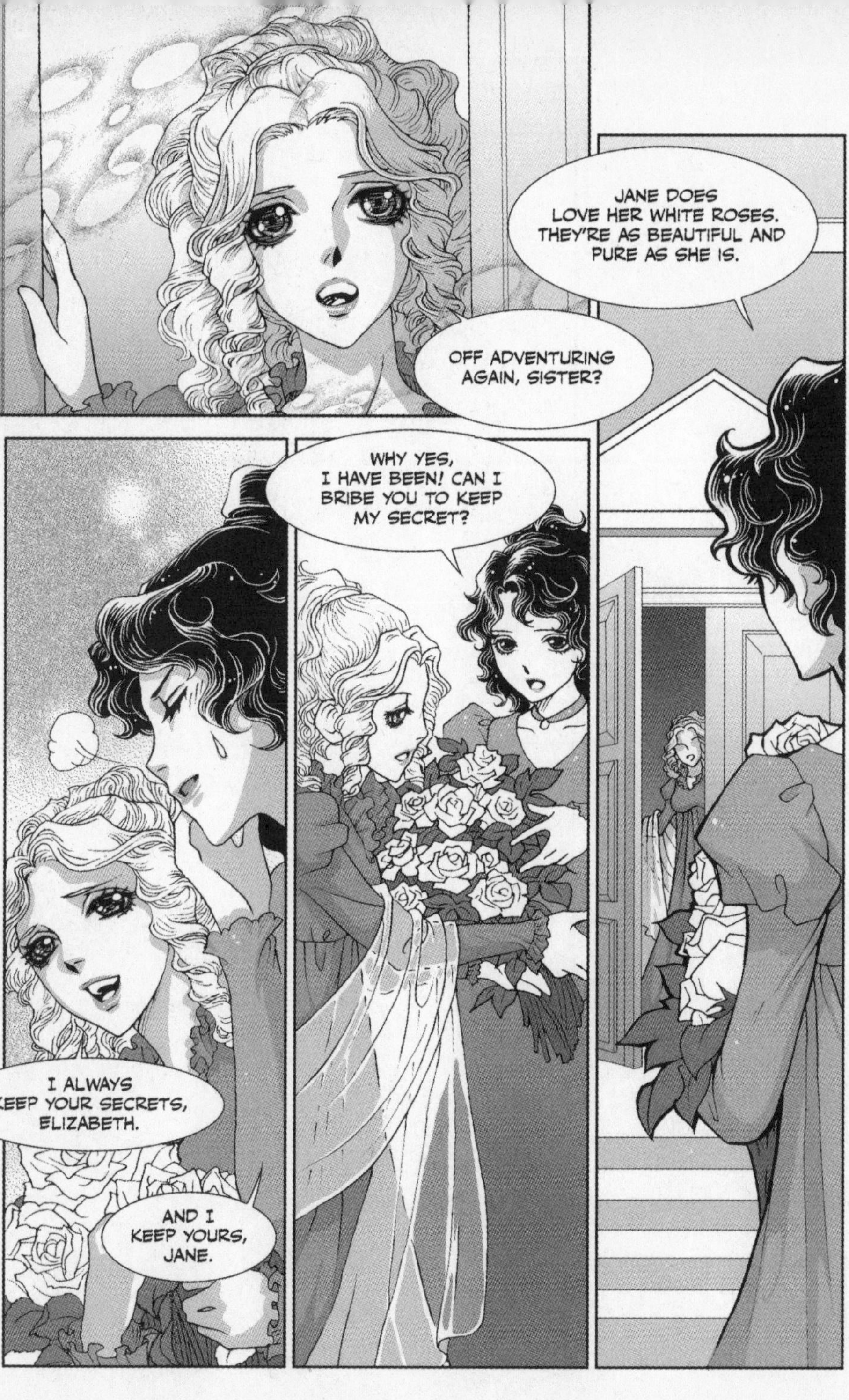
JANE DOES LOVE HER WHITE ROSES. THEY'RE AS BEAUTIFUL AND PURE AS SHE IS.
OFF ADVENTURING AGAIN, SISTER?
WHY YES, I HAVE BEEN! CAN I BRIBE YOU TO KEEP MY SECRET?
I ALWAYS KEEP YOUR SECRETS, ELIZABETH.
AND I KEEP YOURS, JANE.

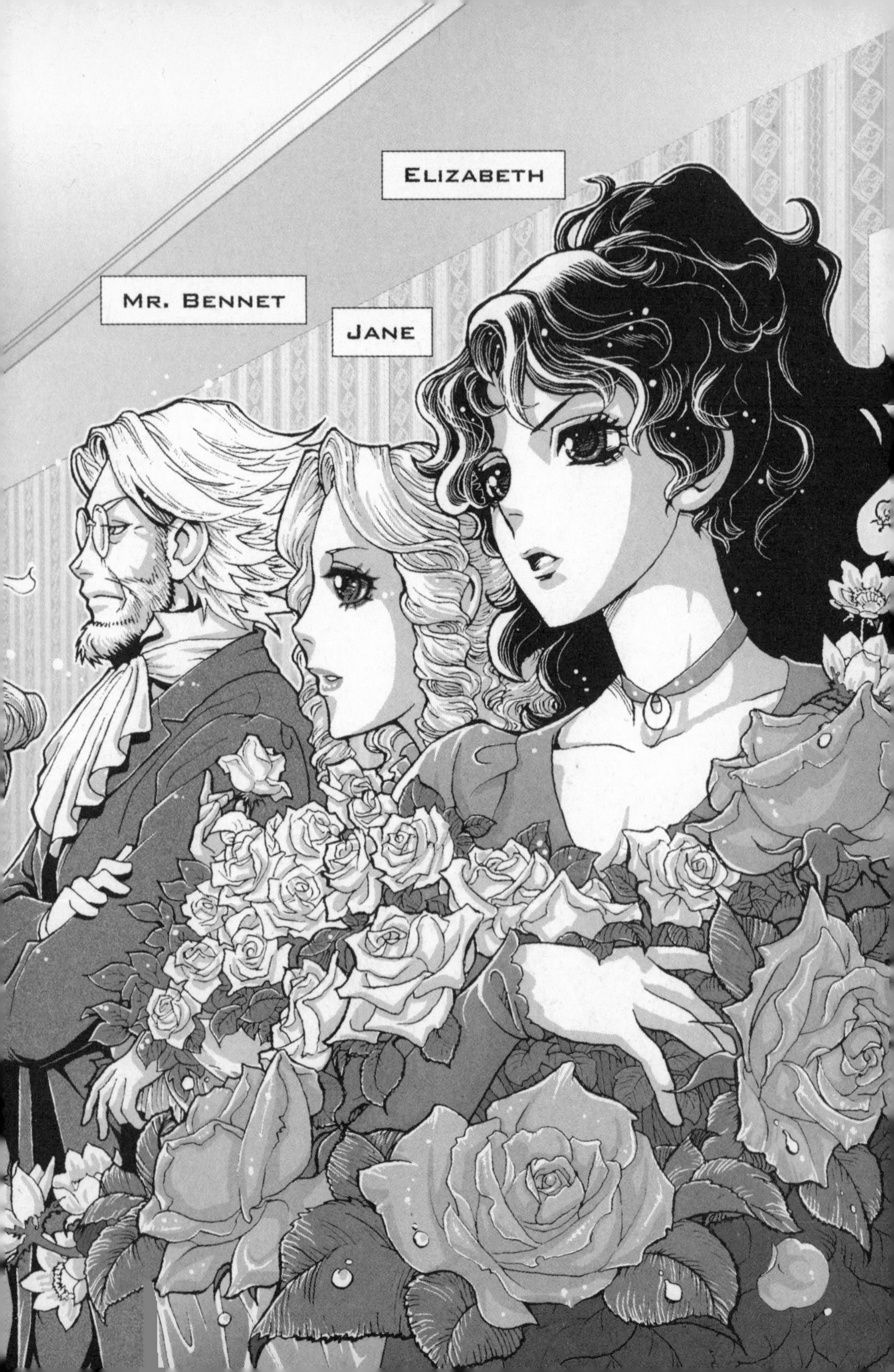
ELIZABETH
JANE
MR. BENNET

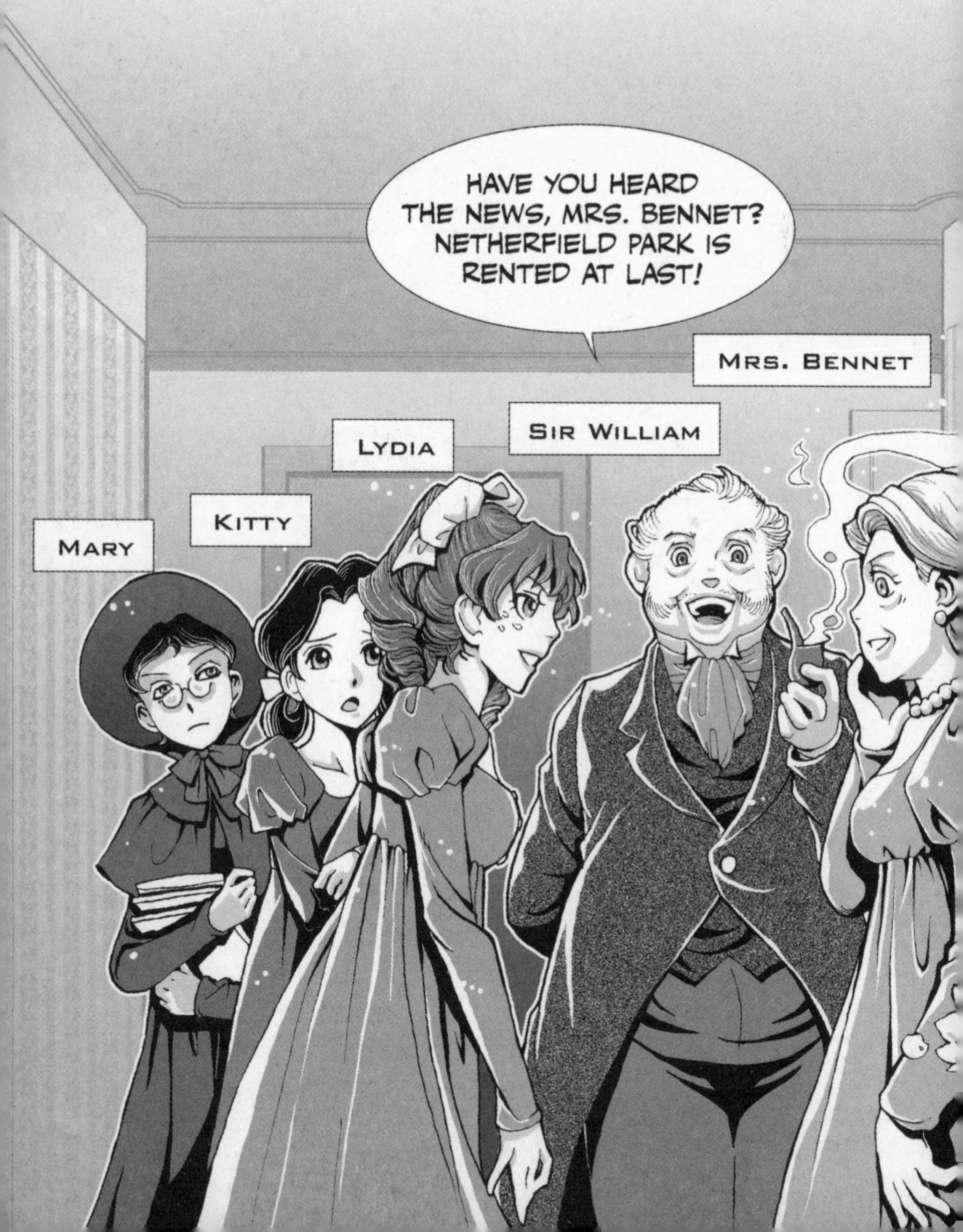
HAVE YOU HEARD THE NEWS, MRS. BENNET? NETHERFIELD PARK IS RENTED AT LAST!
MRS. BENNET
SIR WILLIAM
LYDIA
KITTY
MARY

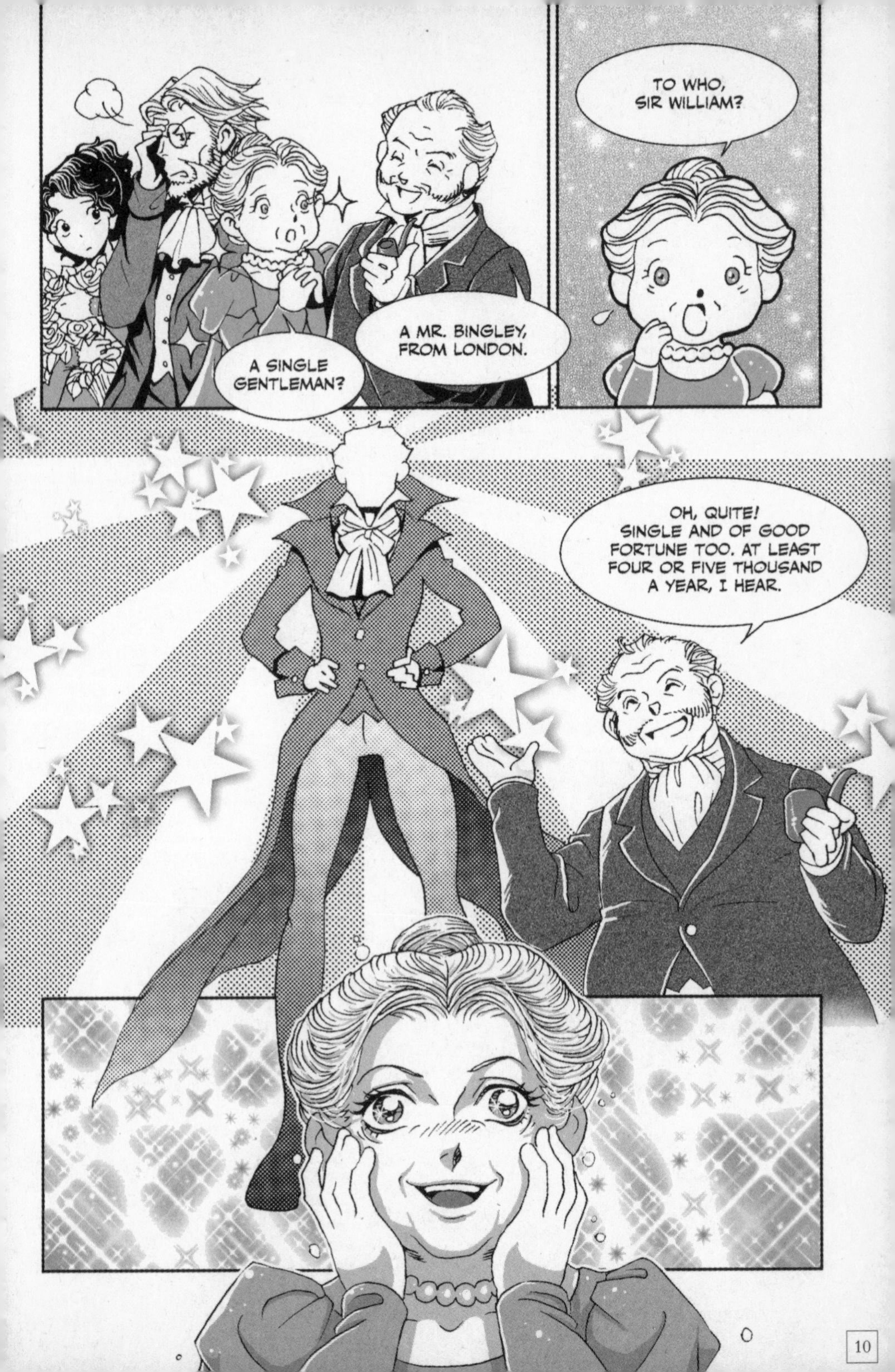
TO WHO, SIR WILLIAM?
A MR. BINGLEY, FROM LONDON.
A SINGLE GENTLEMAN?
OH, QUITE! SINGLE AND OF GOOD FORTUNE TOO. AT LEAST FOUR OR FIVE THOUSAND A YEAR, I HEAR.

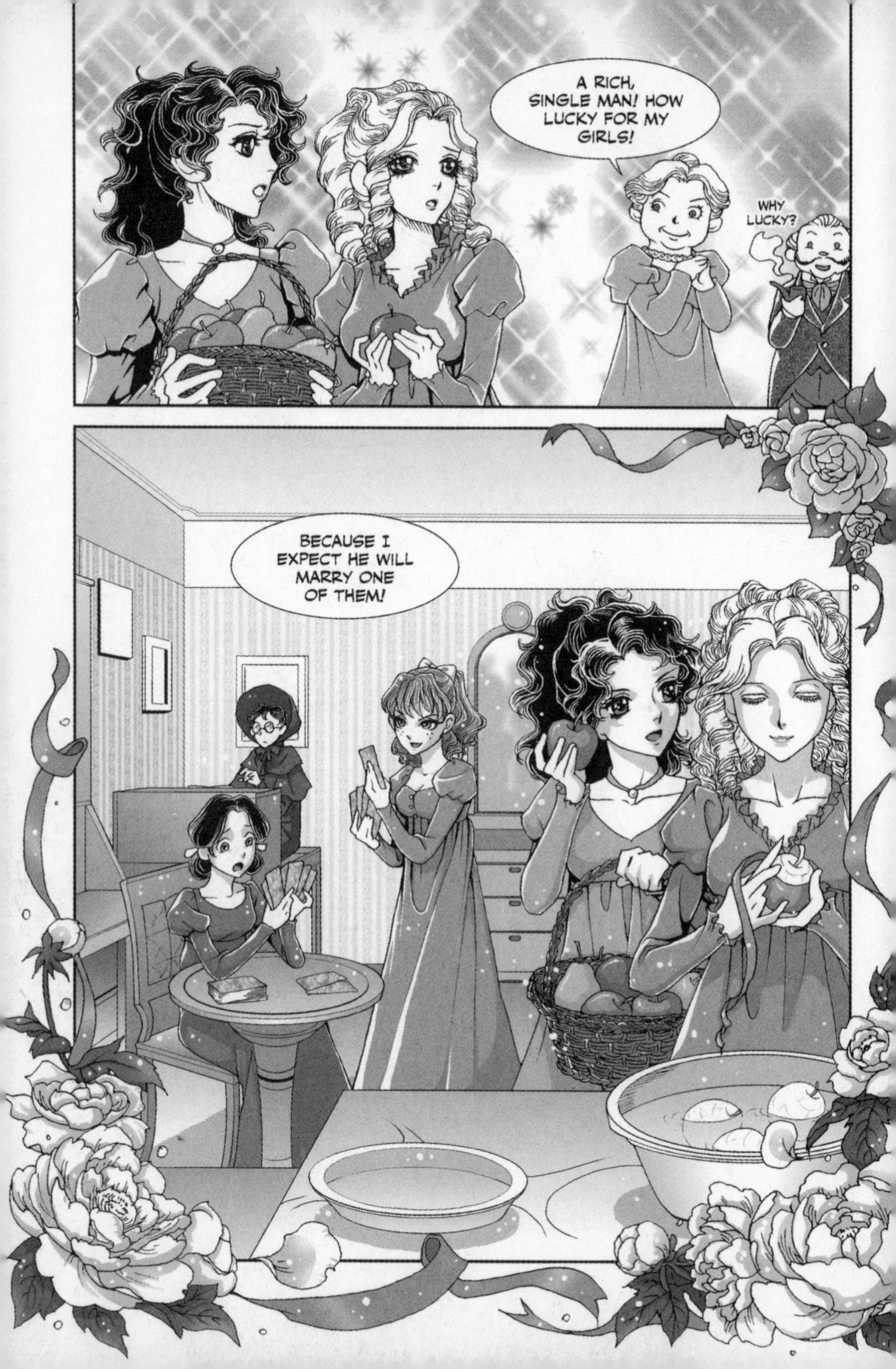
A RICH, SINGLE MAN! HOW LUCKY FOR MY GIRLS!
WHY LUCKY?
BECAUSE I EXPECT HE WILL MARRY ONE OF THEM!

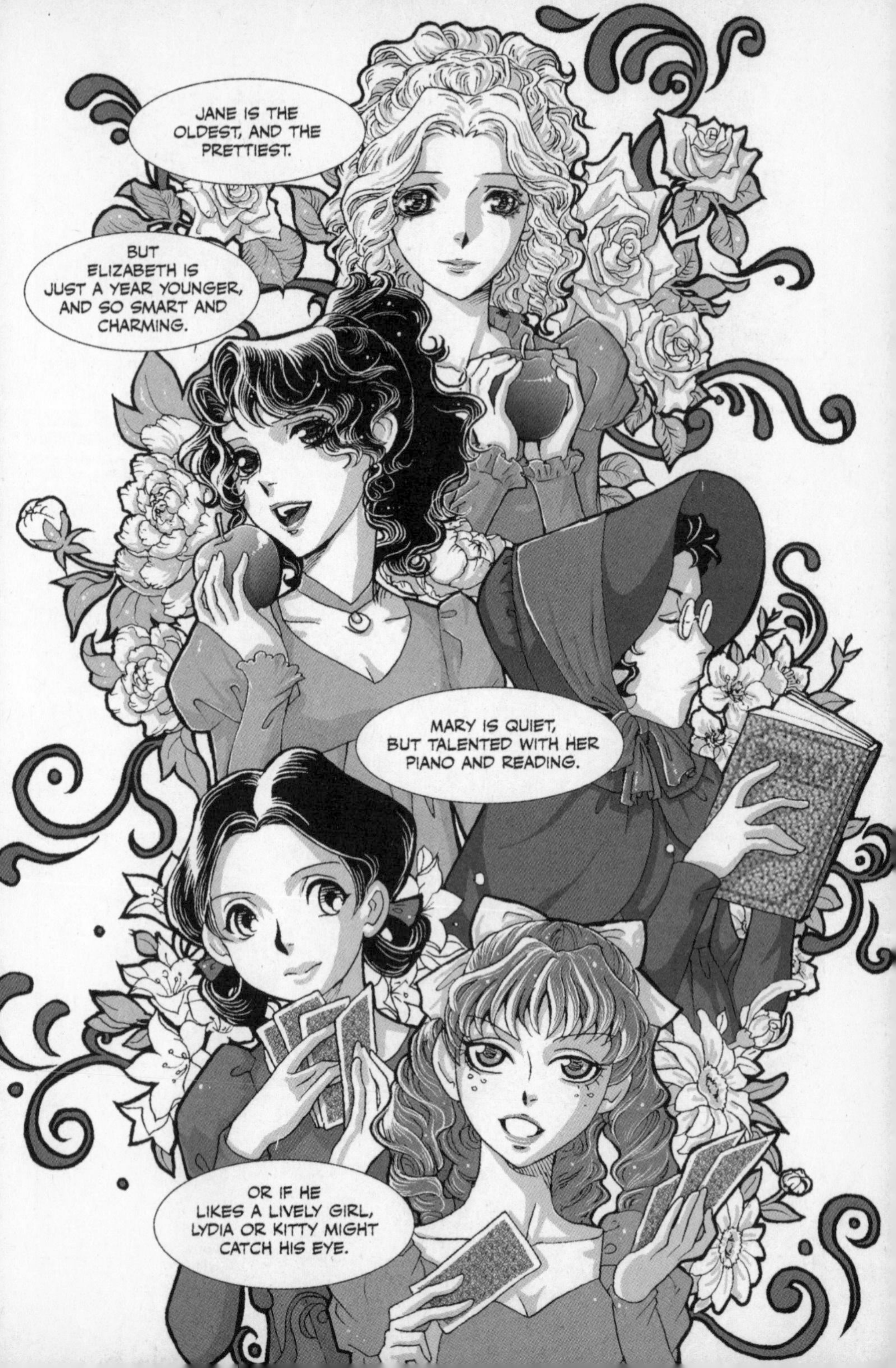
JANE IS THE OLDEST, AND THE PRETTIEST.
BUT ELIZABETH IS JUST A YEAR YOUNGER, AND SO SMART AND CHARMING.
MARY IS QUIET, BUT TALENTED WITH HER PIANO AND READING.
OR IF HE LIKES A LIVELY GIRL, LYDIA OR KITTY MIGHT CATCH HIS EYE.

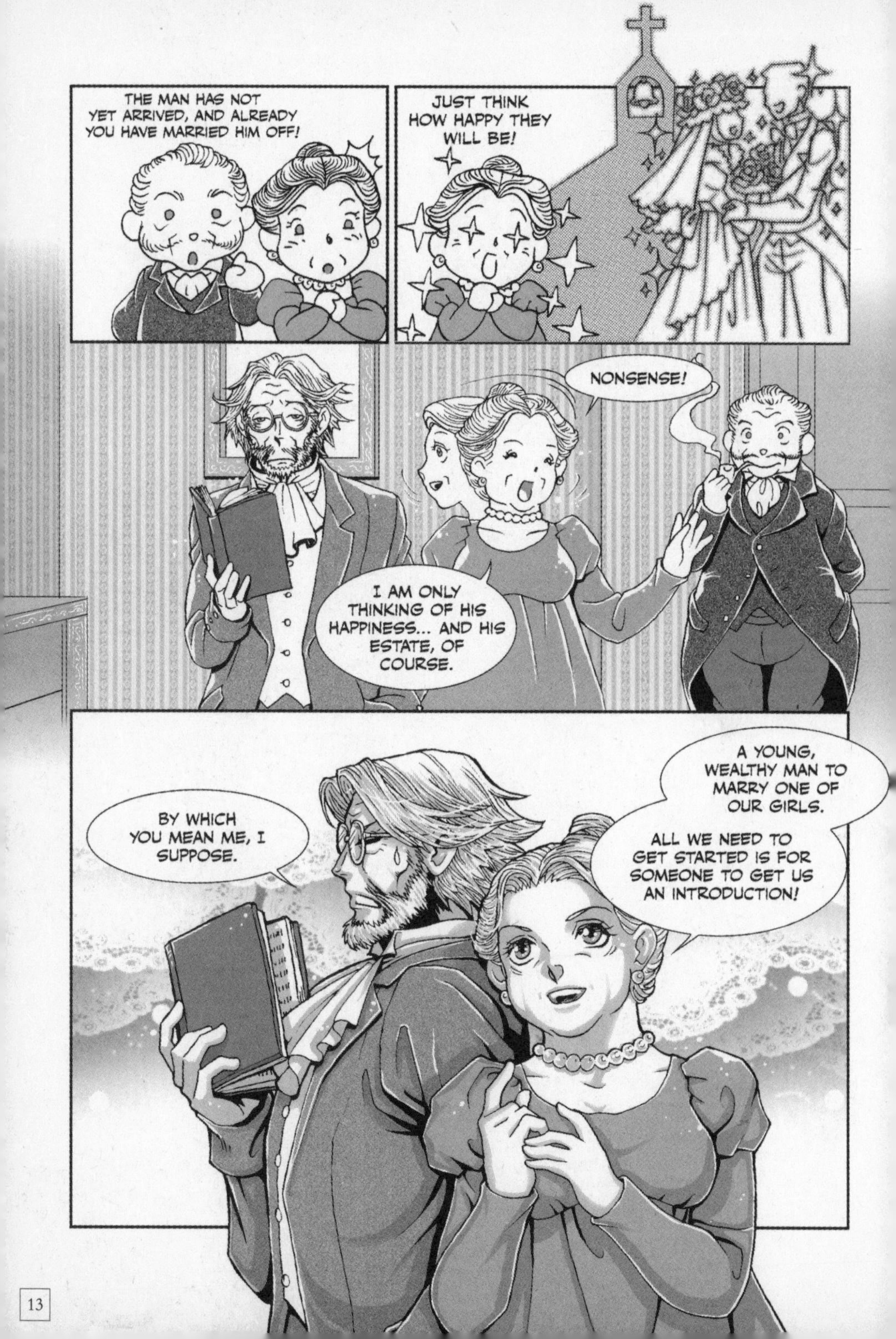
JUST THINK HOW HAPPY THEY WILL BE!
THE MAN HAS NOT YET ARRIVED, AND ALREADY YOU HAVE MARRIED HIM OFF!
NONSENSE!
I AM ONLY THINKING OF HIS HAPPINESS... AND HIS ESTATE, OF COURSE.
A YOUNG, WEALTHY MAN TO MARRY ONE OF OUR GIRLS.
ALL WE NEED TO GET STARTED IS FOR SOMEONE TO GET US AN INTRODUCTION!
BY WHICH YOU MEAN ME, I SUPPOSE.

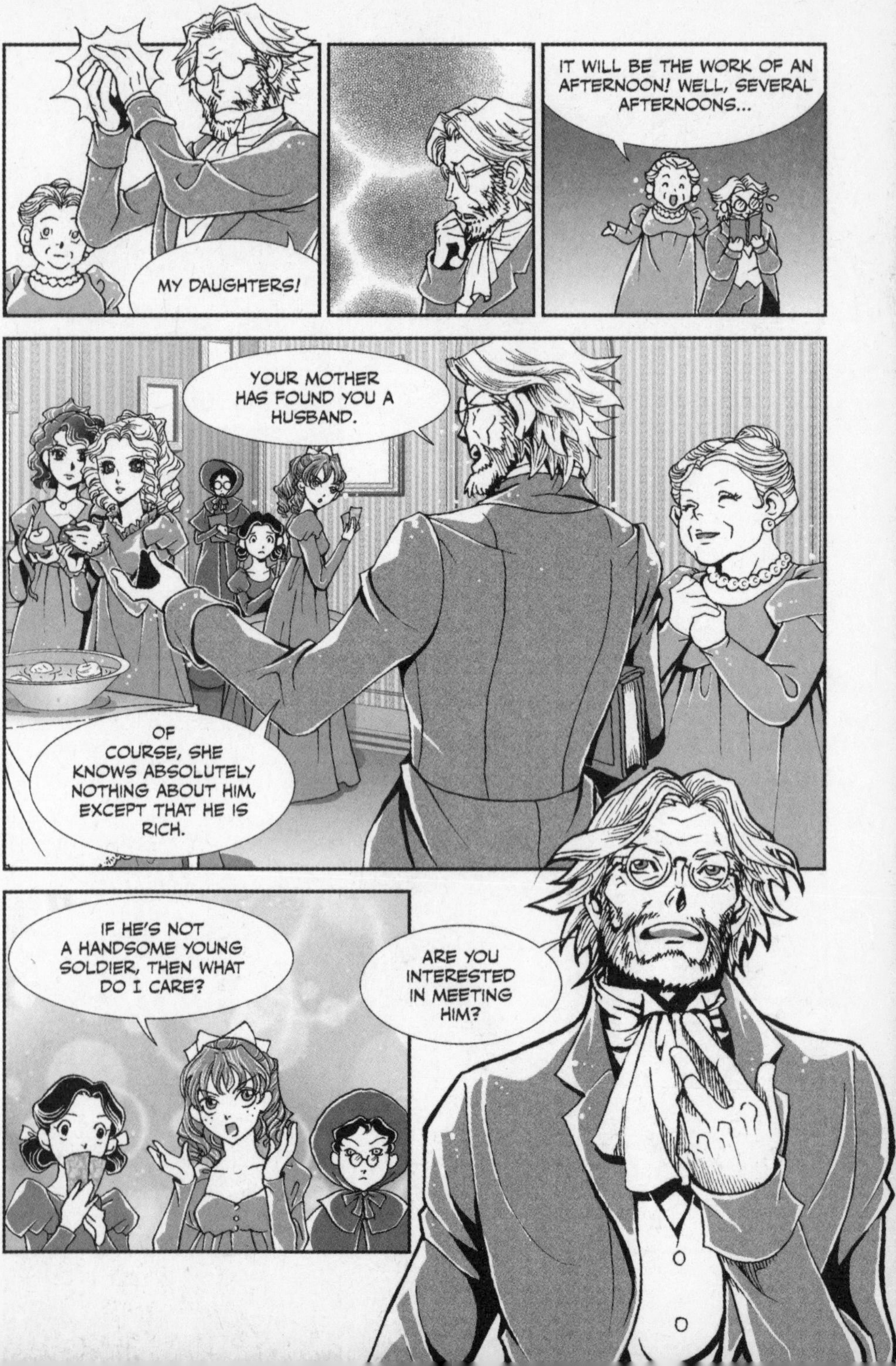
IT WILL BE THE WORK OF AN AFTERNOON! WELL, SEVERAL AFTERNOONS...
MY DAUGHTERS!
YOUR MOTHER HAS FOUND YOU A HUSBAND.
OF COURSE, SHE KNOWS ABSOLUTELY NOTHING ABOUT HIM, EXCEPT THAT HE IS RICH.
ARE YOU INTERESTED IN MEETING HIM?
IF HE'S NOT A HANDSOME YOUNG SOLDIER, THEN WHAT DO I CARE?

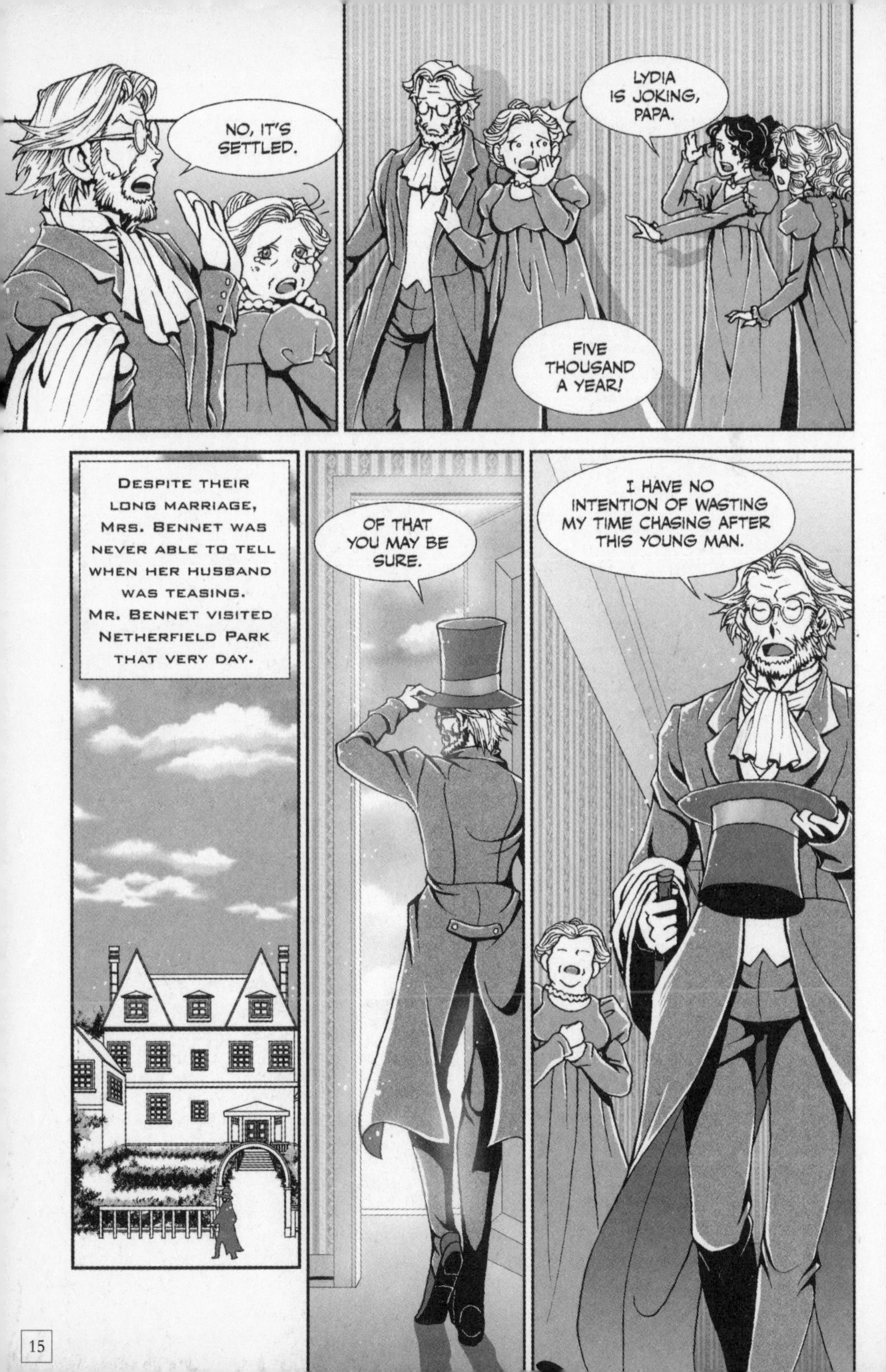
LYDIA IS JOKING, PAPA.
FIVE THOUSAND A YEAR!
NO, IT'S SETTLED.
I HAVE NO INTENTION OF WASTING MY TIME CHASING AFTER THIS YOUNG MAN.
OF THAT YOU MAY BE SURE.
DESPITE THEIR LONG MARRIAGE, MRS. BENNET WAS NEVER ABLE TO TELL WHEN HER HUSBAND WAS TEASING. MR. BENNET VISITED NETHERFIELD PARK THAT VERY DAY.

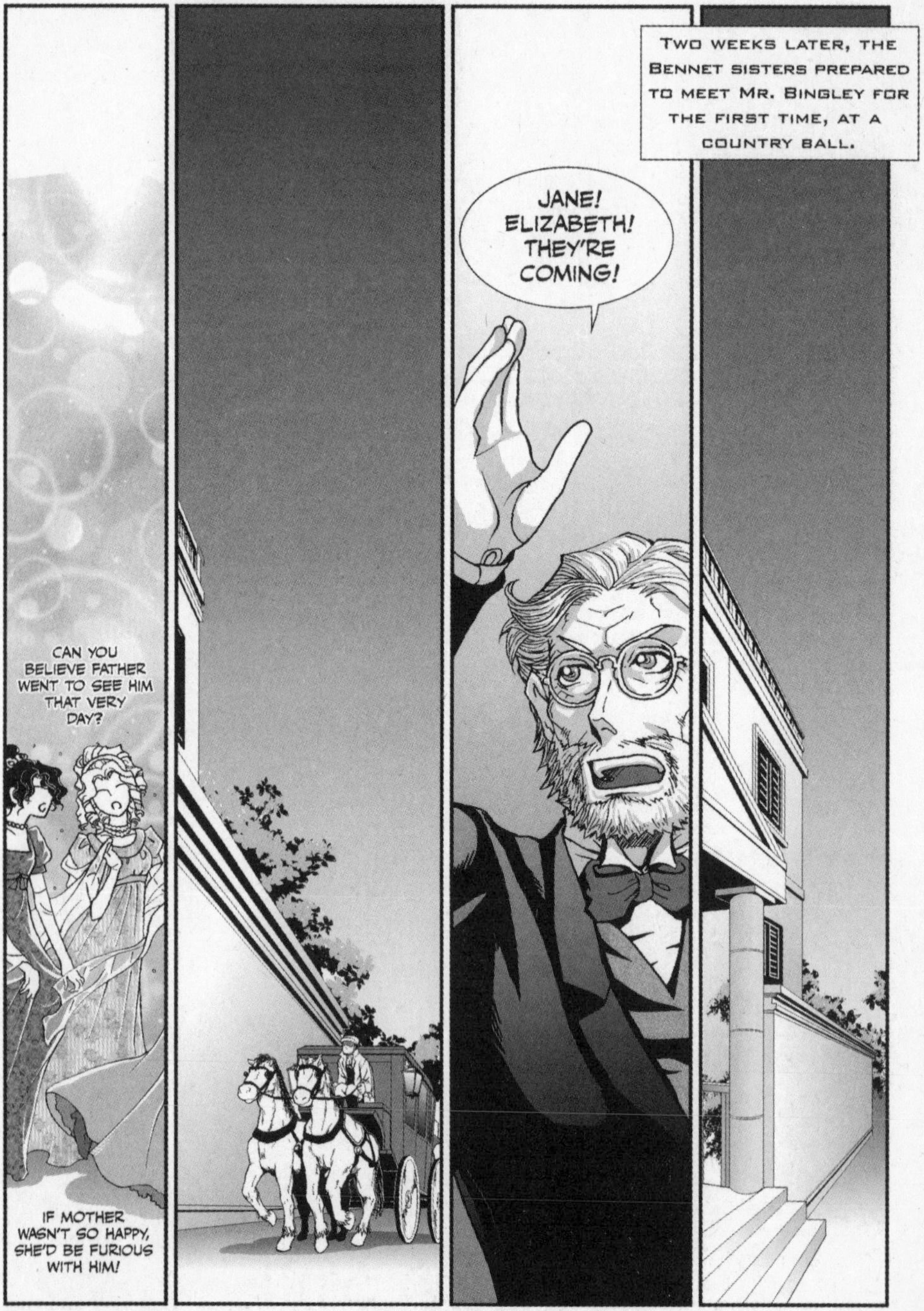
TWO WEEKS LATER, THE BENNET SISTERS PREPARED TO MEET MR. BINGLEY FOR THE FIRST TIME, AT A COUNTRY BALL.
JANE! ELIZABETH! THEY'RE COMING!
CAN YOU BELIEVE FATHER WENT TO SEE HIM THAT VERY DAY?
IF MOTHER WASN'T SO HAPPY, SHE'D BE FURIOUS WITH HIM!

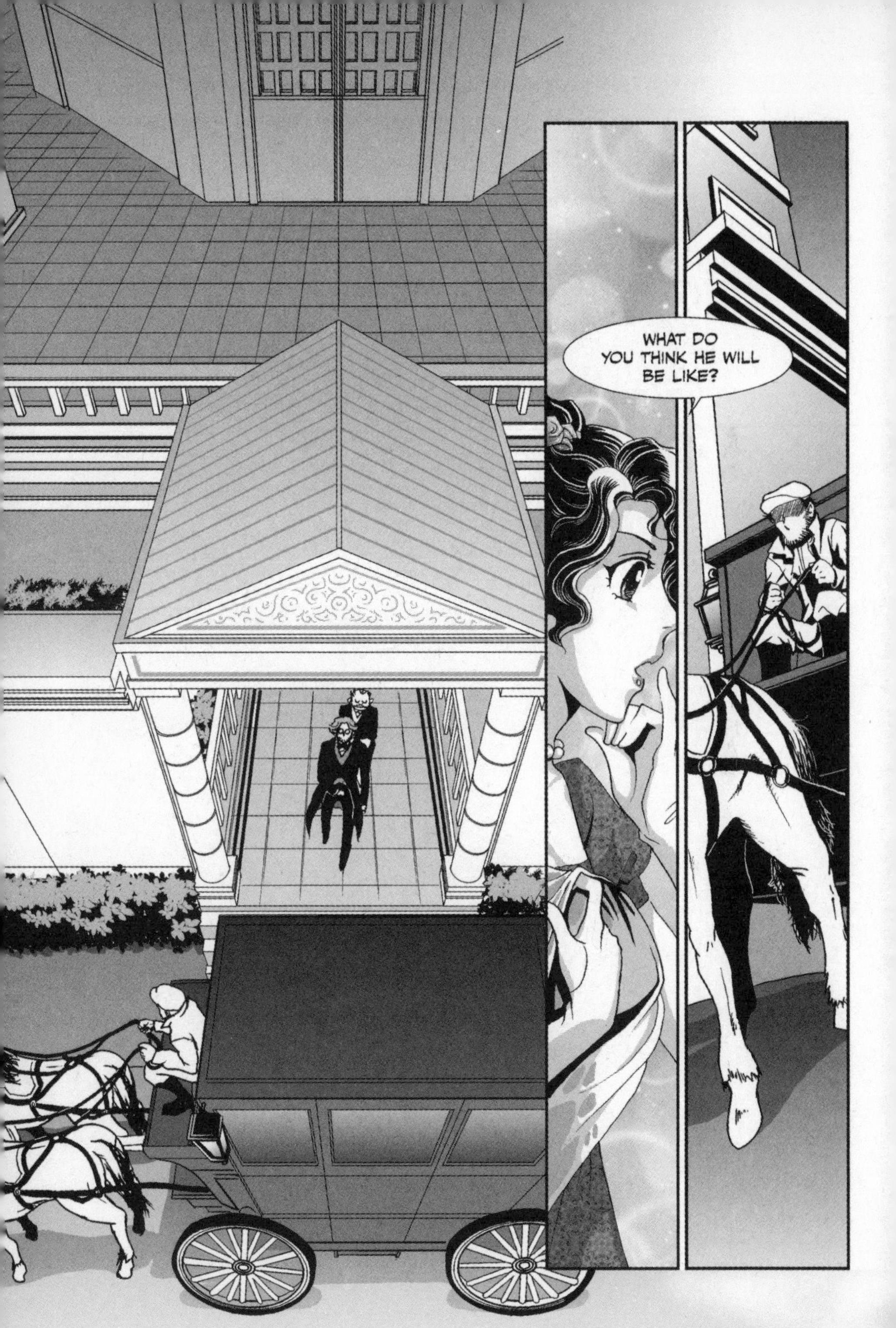
WHAT DO
YOU THINK HE WILL
BE LIKE?

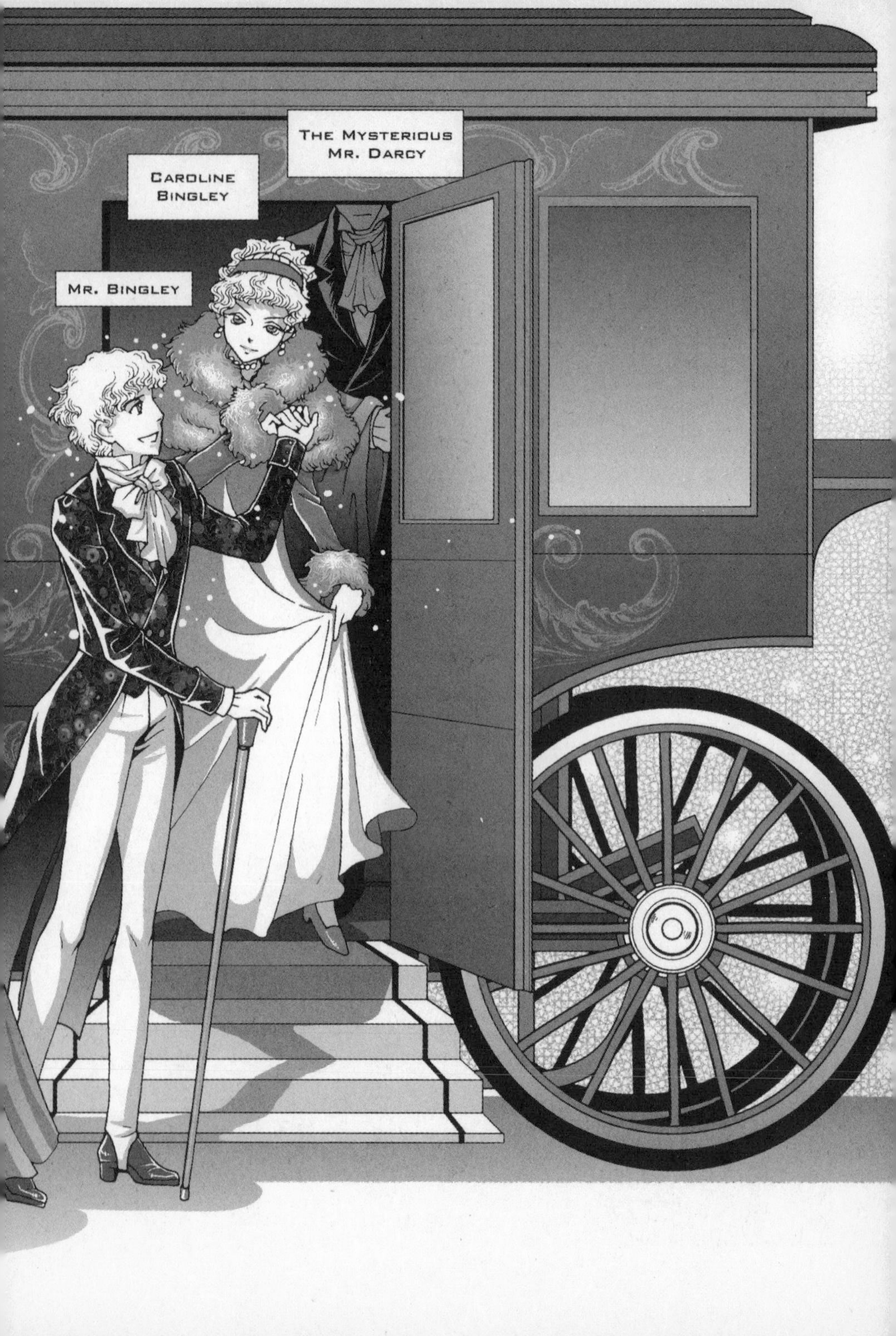
THE MYSTERIOUS MR. DARCY
CAROLINE BINGLEY
MR. BINGLEY

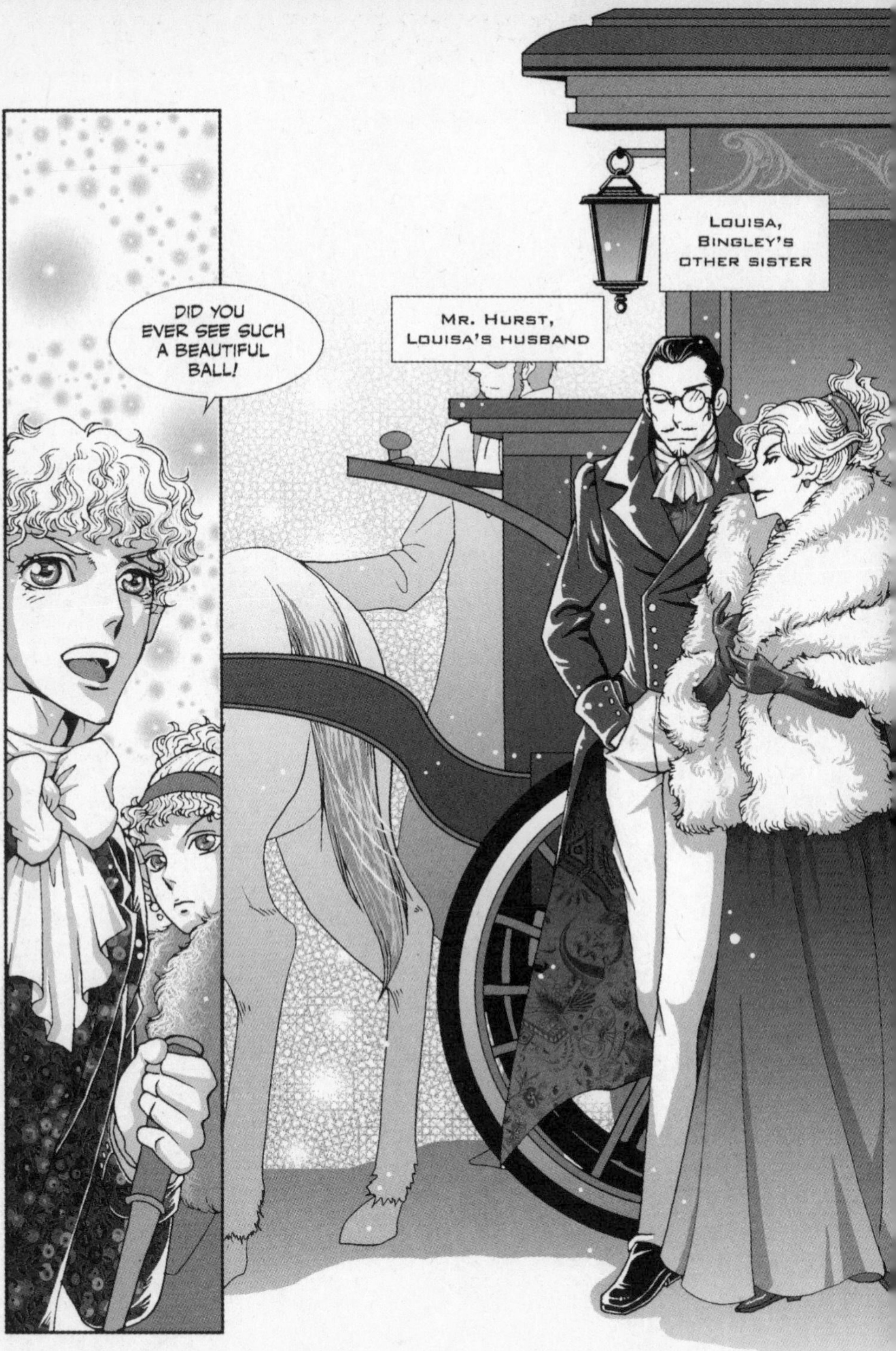

LOUISA, BINGLEY'S OTHER SISTER
MR. HURST, LOUISA'S HUSBAND
DID YOU EVER SEE SUCH A BEAUTIFUL BALL!

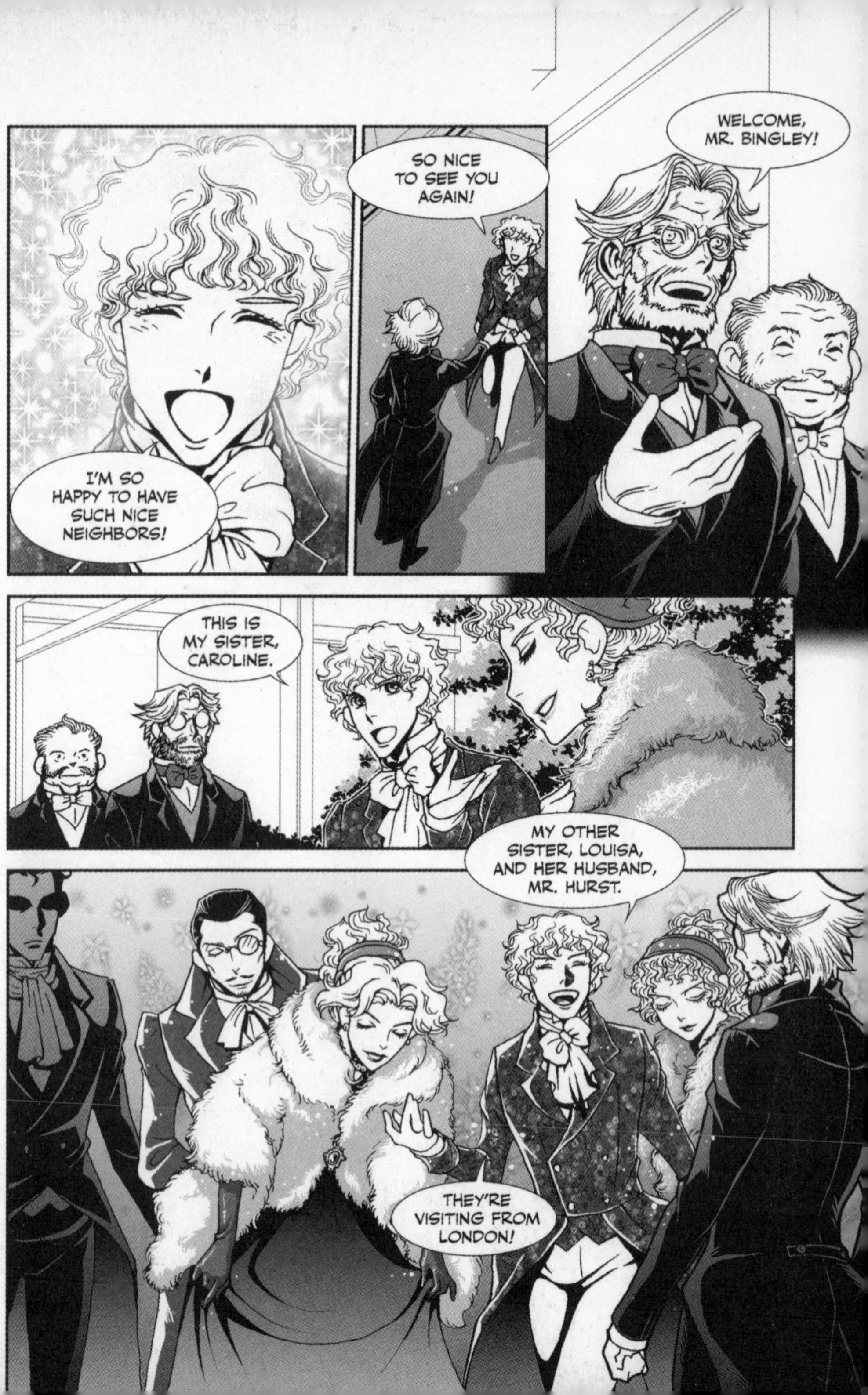
WELCOME, MR. BINGLEY!
SO NICE TO SEE YOU AGAIN!
I'M SO HAPPY TO HAVE SUCH NICE NEIGHBORS!
THIS IS MY SISTER, CAROLINE.
MY OTHER SISTER, LOUISA, AND HER HUSBAND, MR. HURST.
THEY'RE VISITING FROM LONDON!

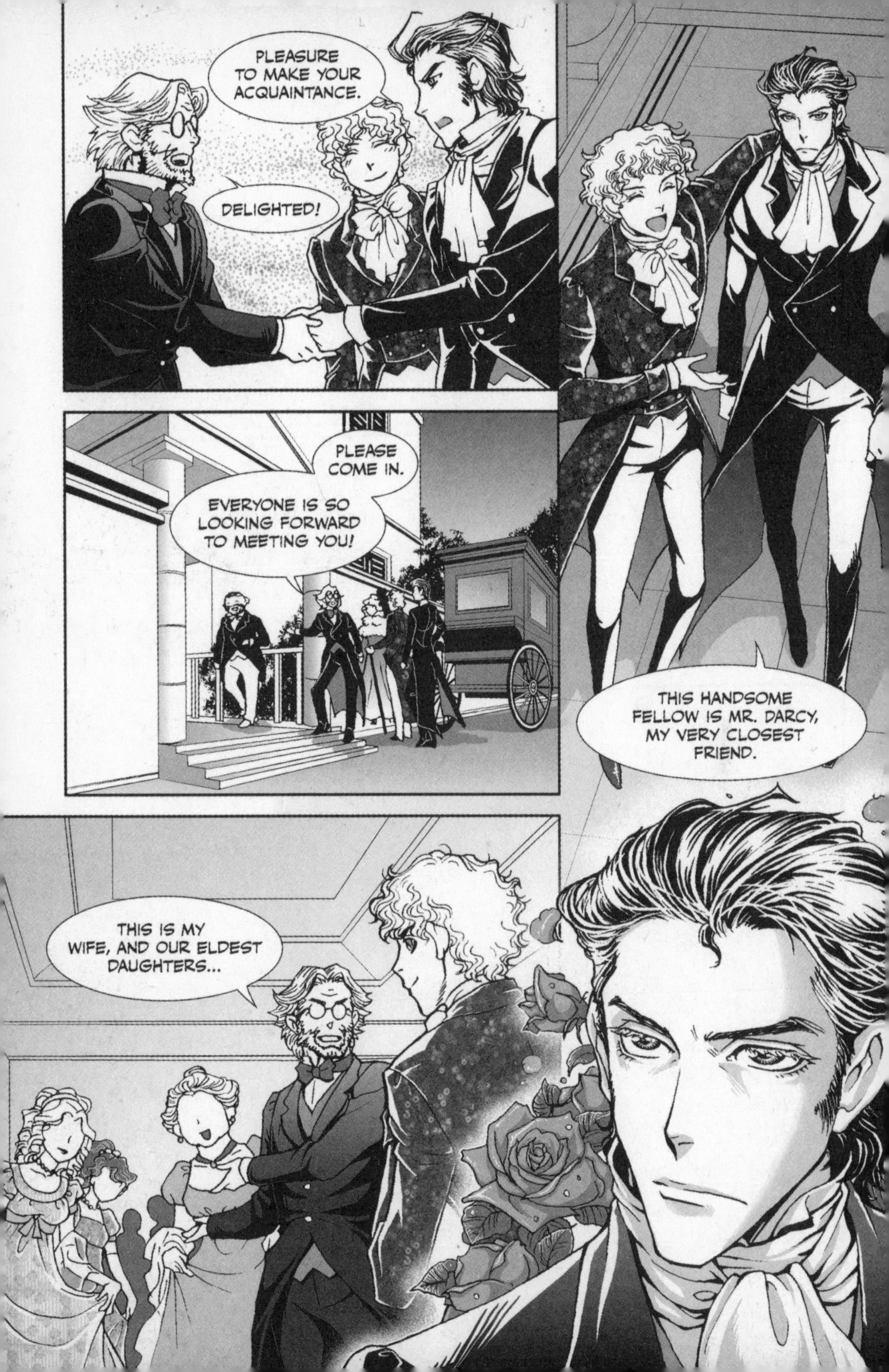
THIS HANDSOME FELLOW IS MR. DARCY, MY VERY CLOSEST FRIEND.
PLEASURE TO MAKE YOUR ACQUAINTANCE.
DELIGHTED!
PLEASE COME IN.
EVERYONE IS SO LOOKING FORWARD TO MEETING YOU!
THIS IS MY WIFE, AND OUR ELDEST DAUGHTERS...

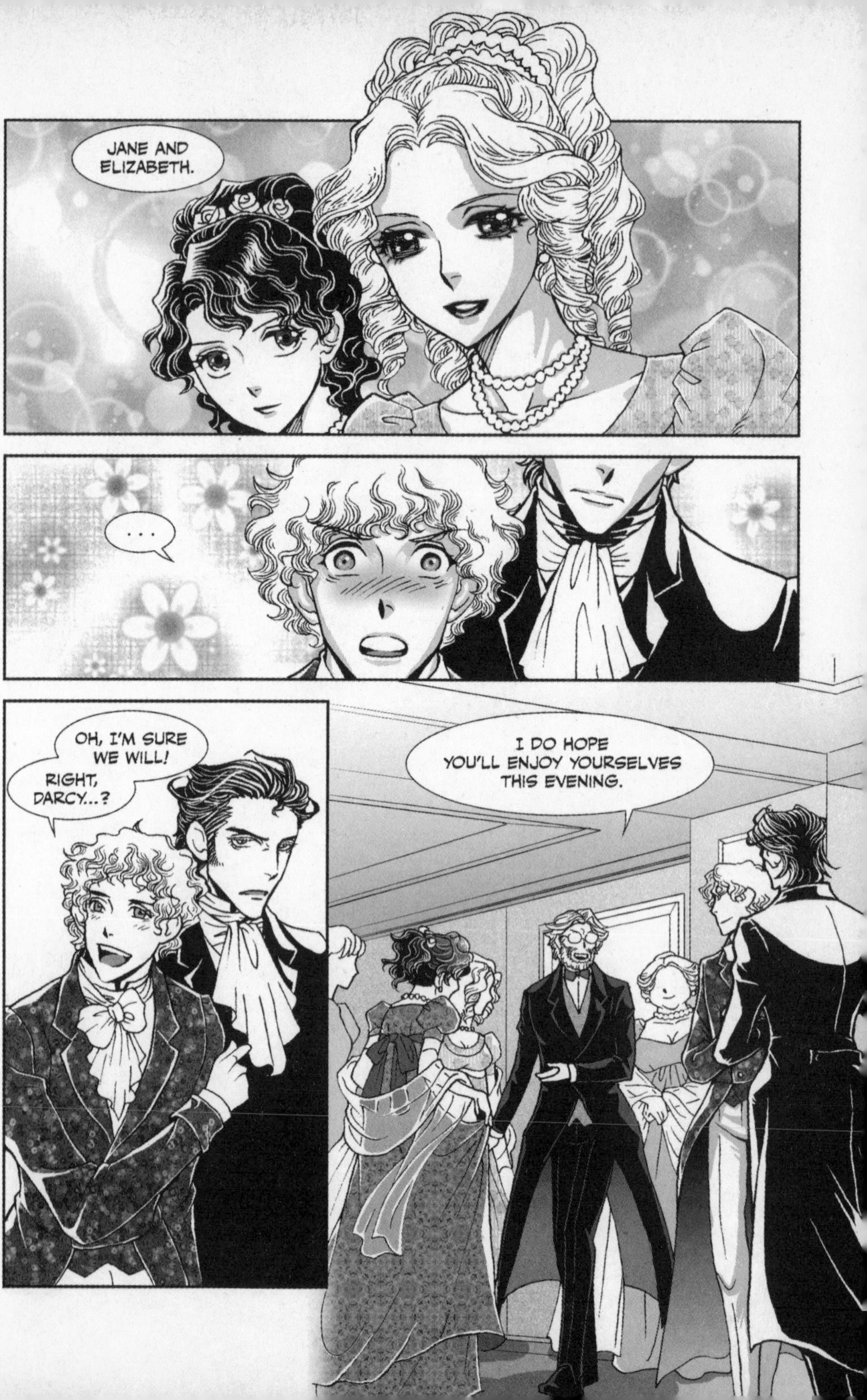
JANE AND ELIZABETH.
...
I DO HOPE YOU'LL ENJOY YOURSELVES THIS EVENING.
OH, I'M SURE WE WILL!
RIGHT, DARCY...?

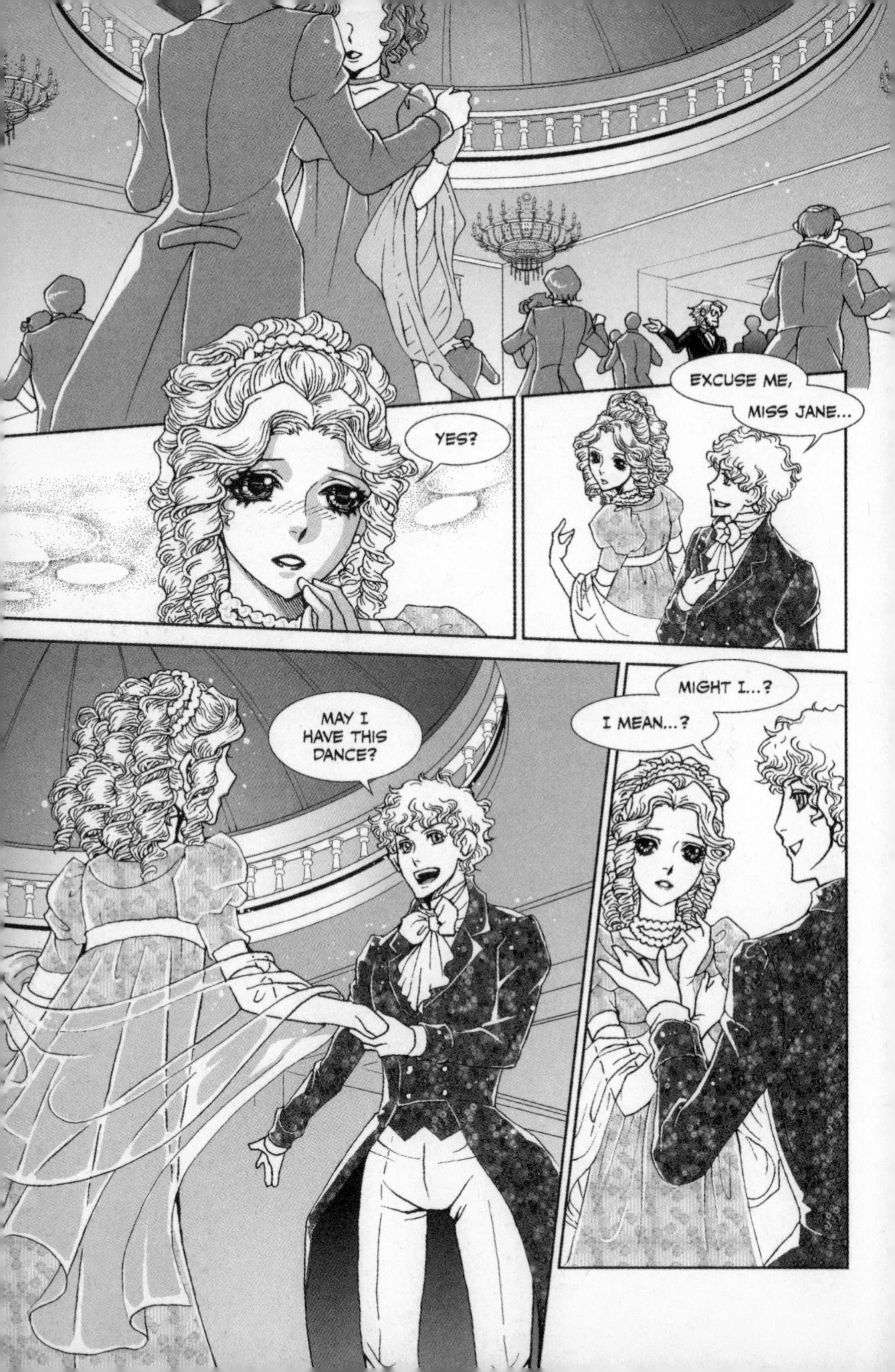
EXCUSE ME, MISS JANE...
YES?
MIGHT I...?
I MEAN...?
MAY I HAVE THIS DANCE?

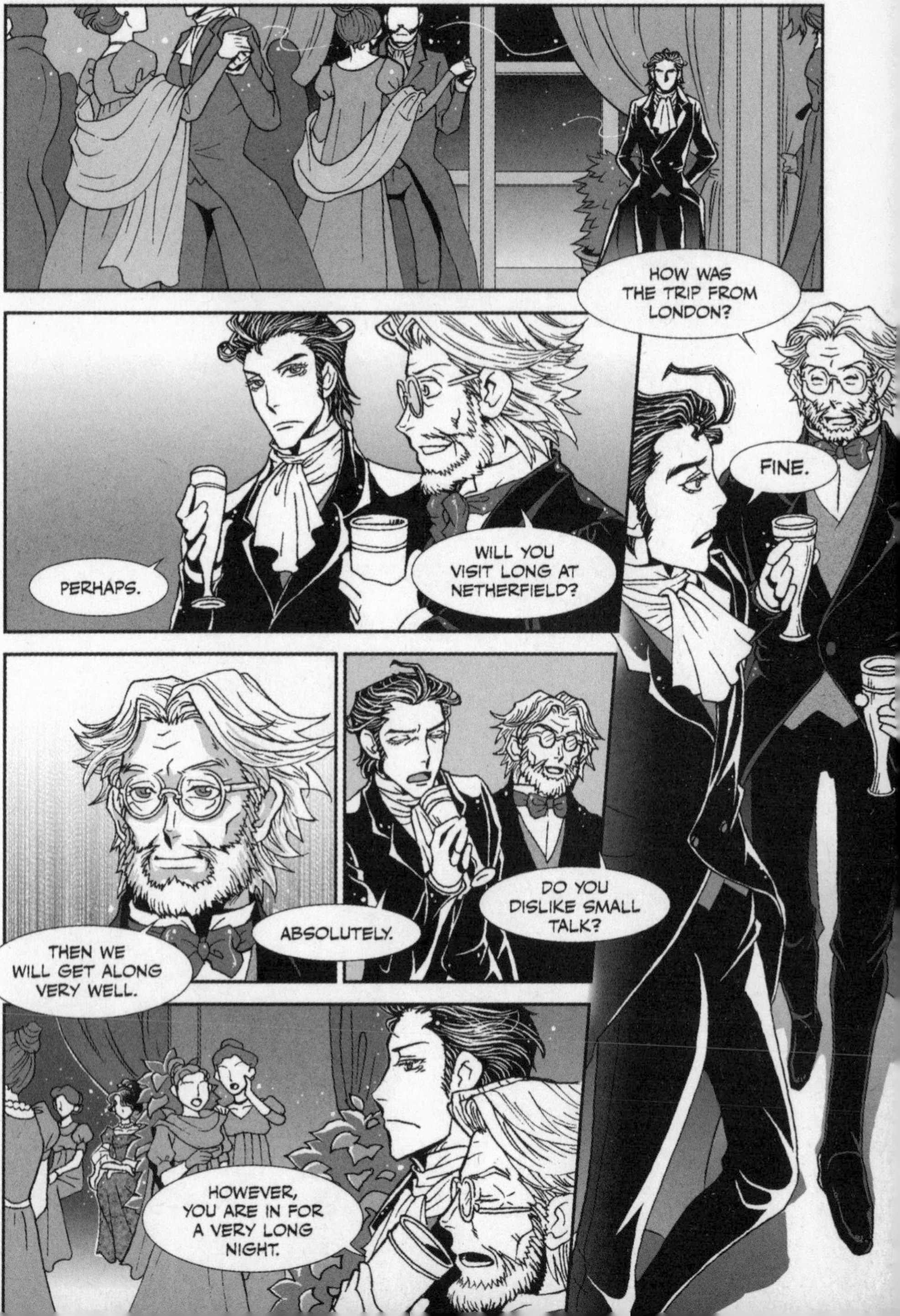
HOW WAS THE TRIP FROM LONDON?
FINE.
WILL YOU VISIT LONG AT NETHERFIELD?
PERHAPS.
DO YOU DISLIKE SMALL TALK?
ABSOLUTELY.
THEN WE WILL GET ALONG VERY WELL.
HOWEVER, YOU ARE IN FOR A VERY LONG NIGHT.

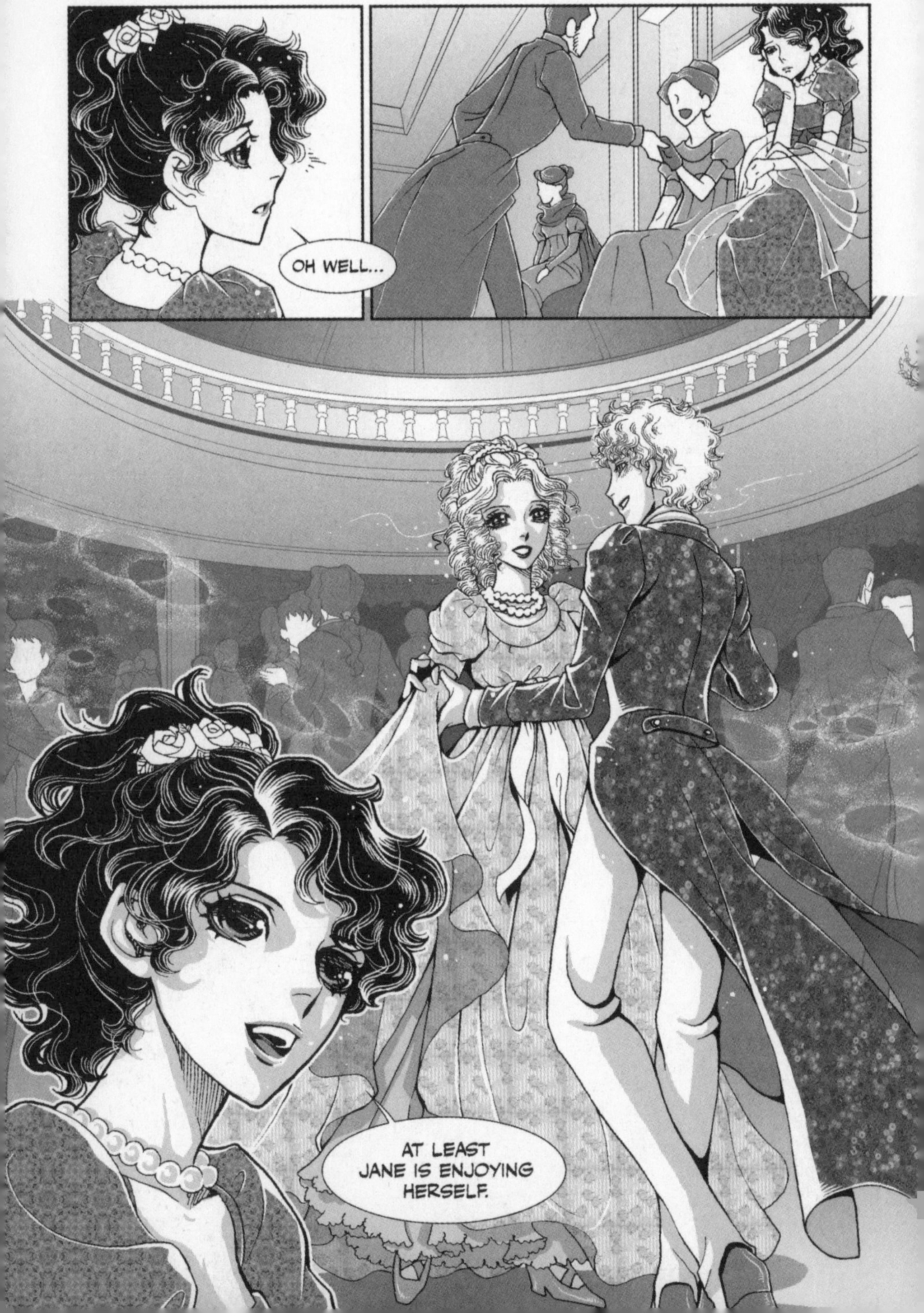
OH WELL...
AT LEAST JANE IS ENJOYING HERSELF.

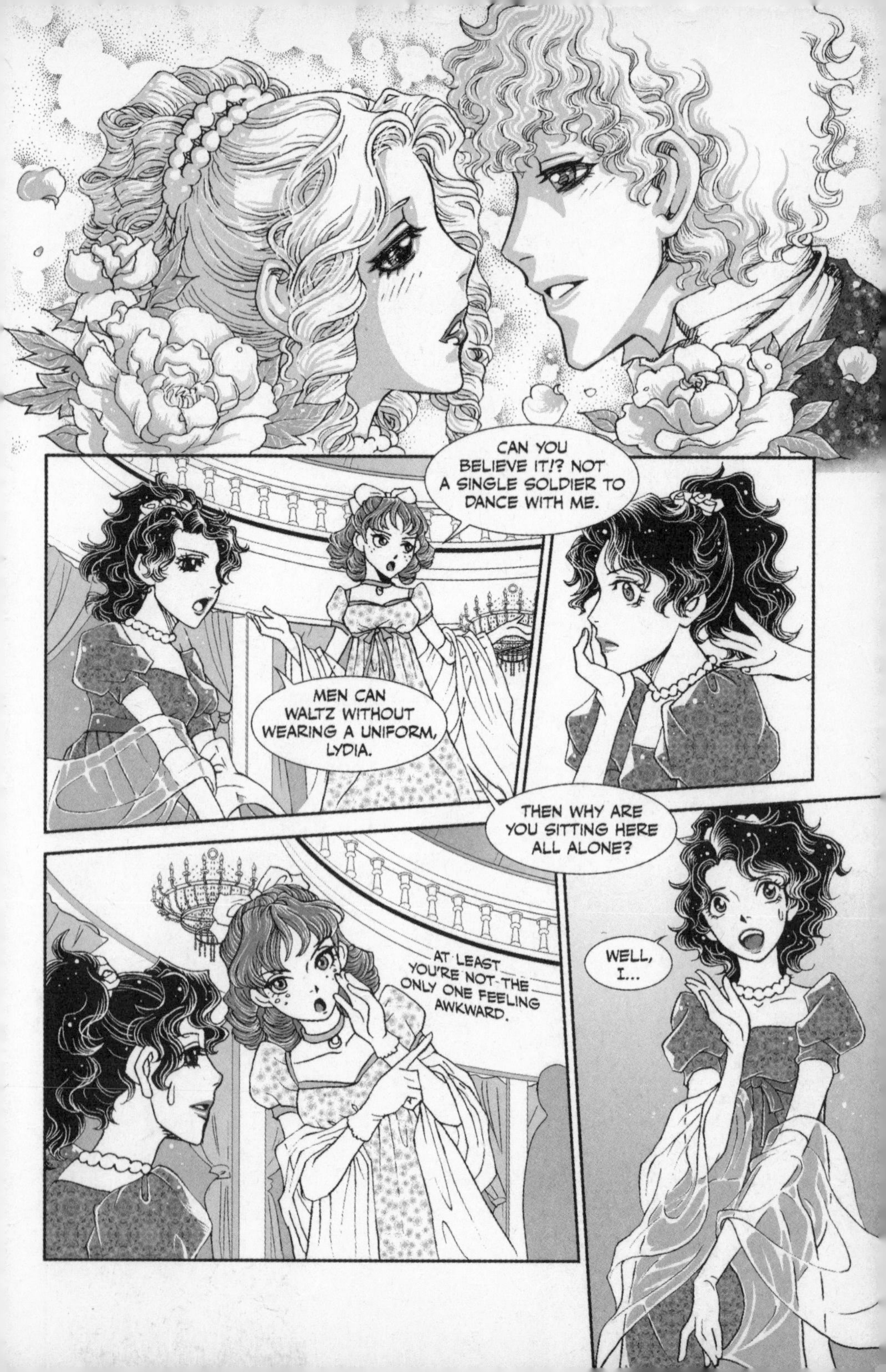
CAN YOU BELIEVE IT!? NOT A SINGLE SOLDIER TO DANCE WITH ME.
MEN CAN WALTZ WITHOUT WEARING A UNIFORM, LYDIA.
THEN WHY ARE YOU SITTING HERE ALL ALONE?
WELL, I...
AT LEAST YOU'RE NOT THE ONLY ONE FEELING AWKWARD.

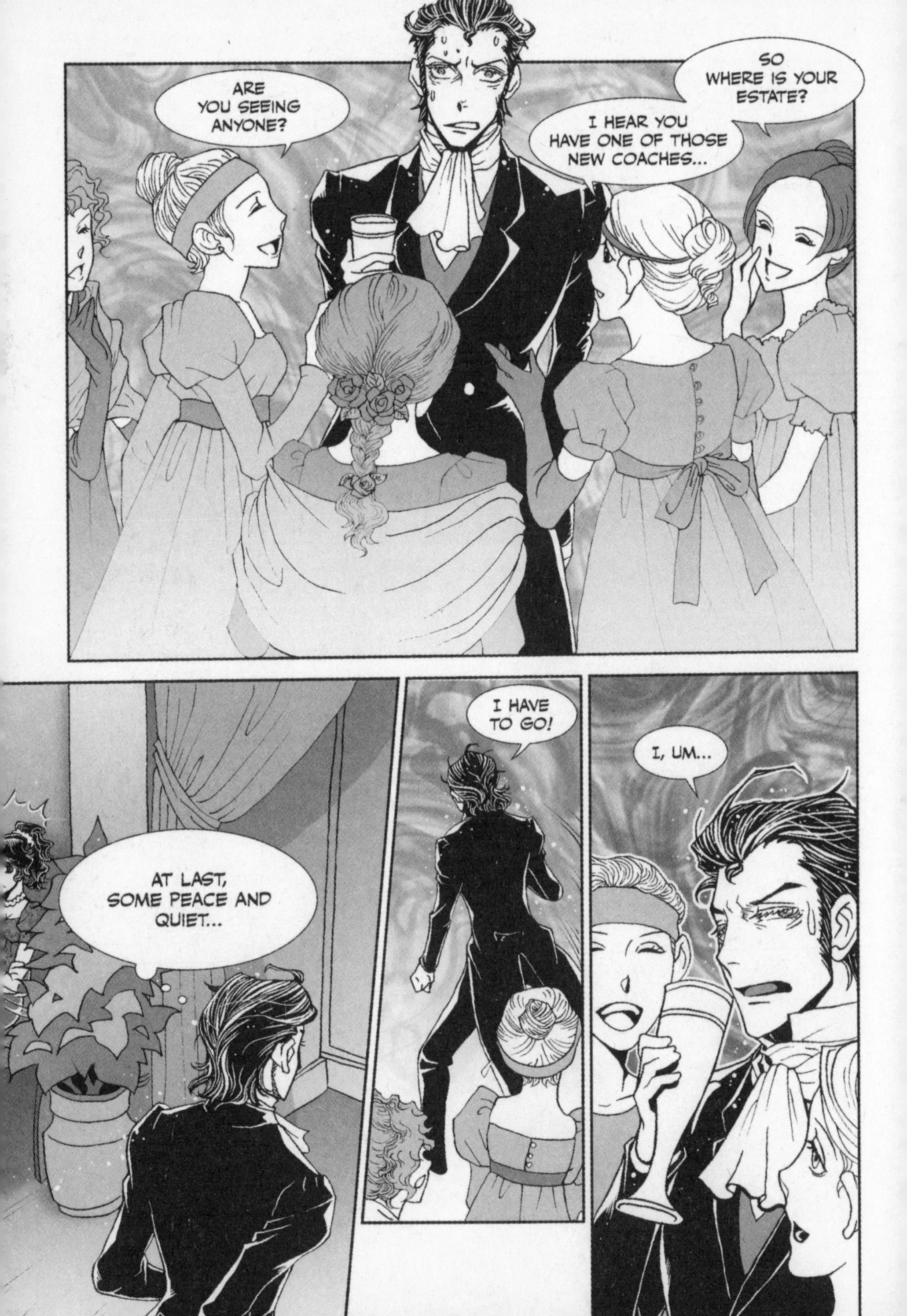
SO WHERE IS YOUR ESTATE?
I HEAR YOU HAVE ONE OF THOSE NEW COACHES...
ARE YOU SEEING ANYONE?
I, UM...
I HAVE TO GO!
AT LAST, SOME PEACE AND QUIET...

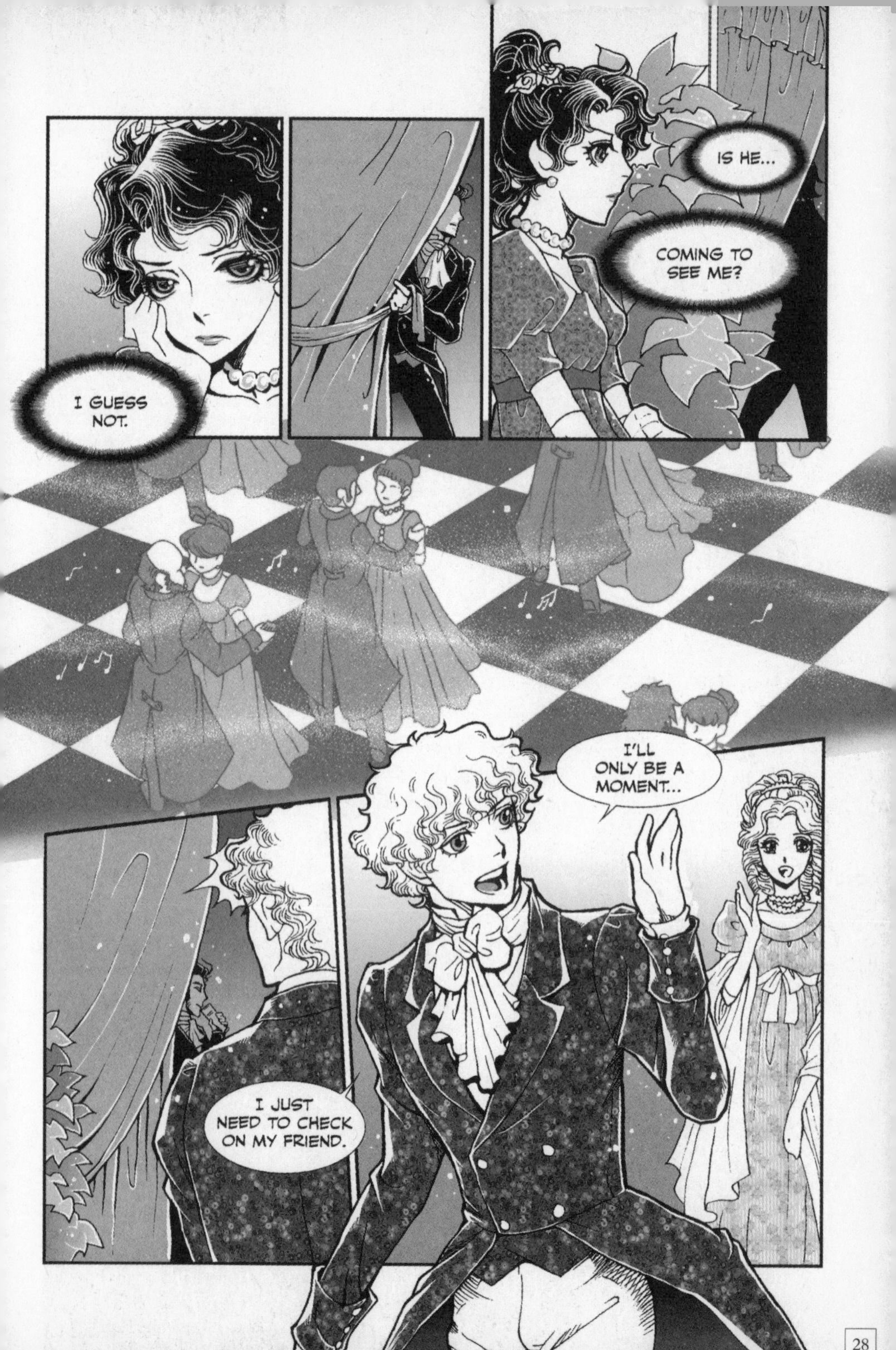
IS HE...
COMING TO SEE ME?
I GUESS NOT.
I'LL ONLY BE A MOMENT...
I JUST NEED TO CHECK ON MY FRIEND.

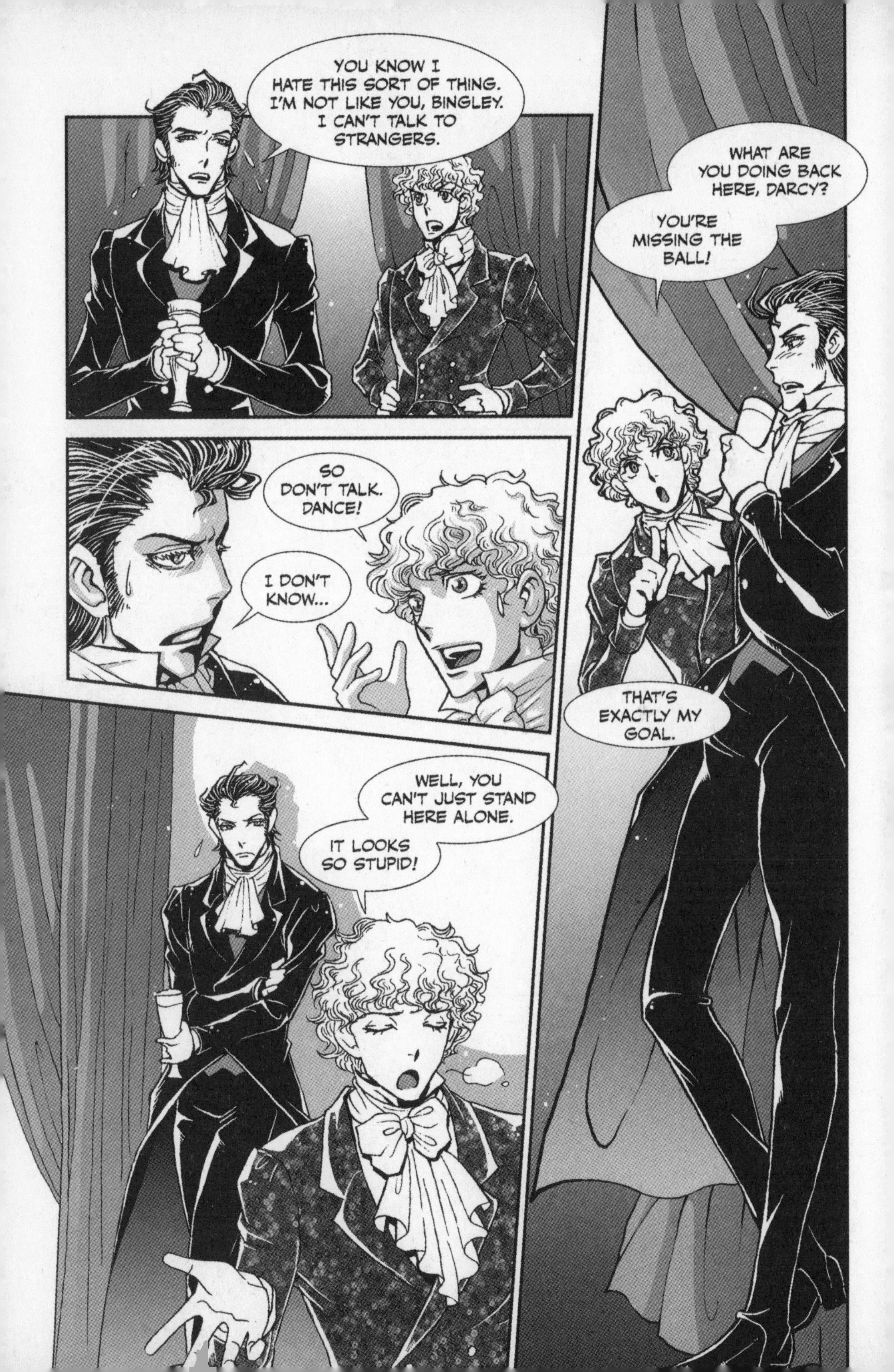

WHAT ARE YOU DOING BACK HERE, DARCY?
YOU'RE MISSING THE BALL!
THAT'S EXACTLY MY GOAL.
YOU KNOW I HATE THIS SORT OF THING. I'M NOT LIKE YOU, BINGLEY. I CAN'T TALK TO STRANGERS.
SO DON'T TALK. DANCE!
I DON'T KNOW...
WELL, YOU CAN'T JUST STAND HERE ALONE.
IT LOOKS SO STUPID!

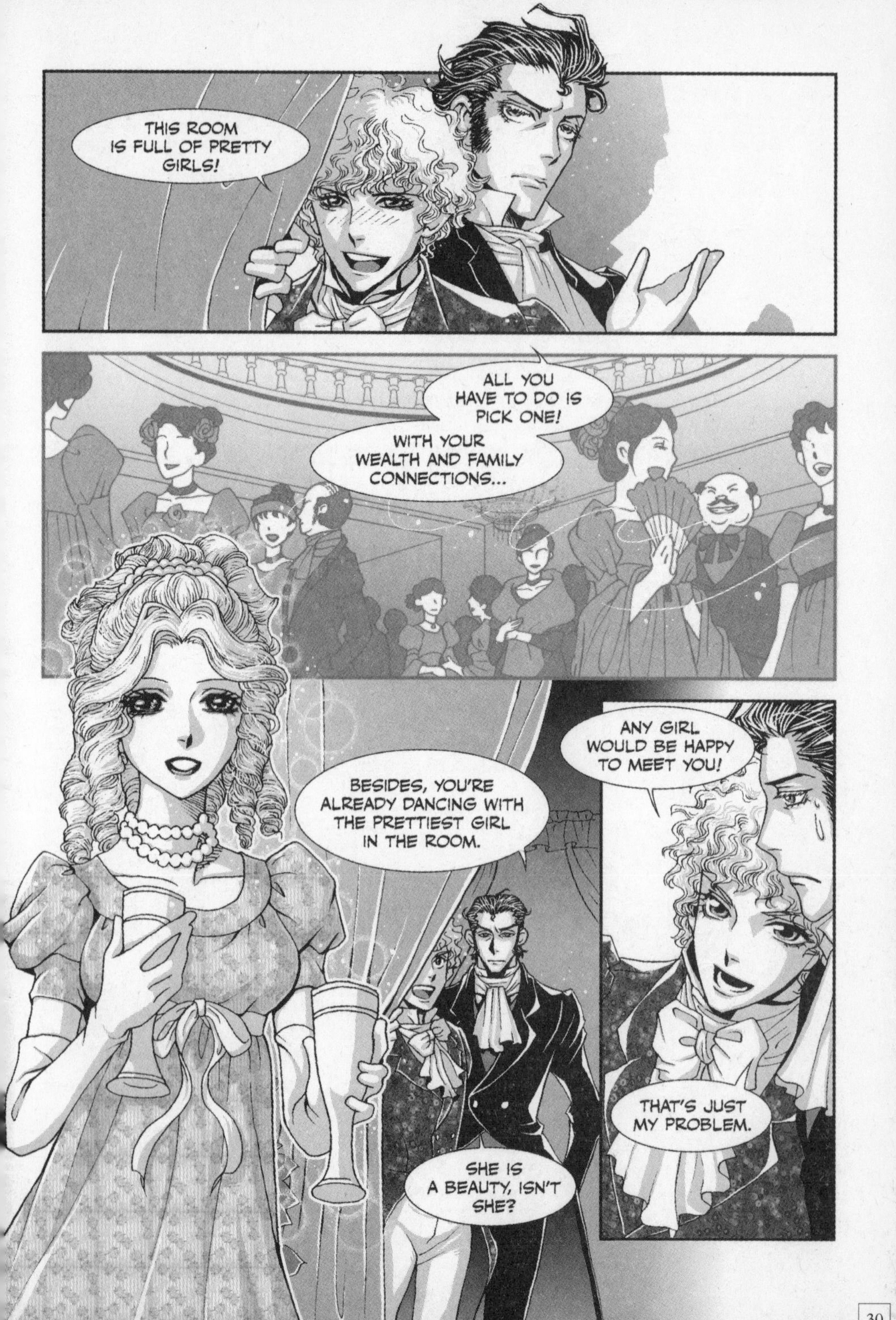
THIS ROOM IS FULL OF PRETTY GIRLS!
ALL YOU HAVE TO DO IS PICK ONE!
WITH YOUR WEALTH AND FAMILY CONNECTIONS...
ANY GIRL WOULD BE HAPPY TO MEET YOU!
THAT'S JUST MY PROBLEM.
BESIDES, YOU'RE ALREADY DANCING WITH THE PRETTIEST GIRL IN THE ROOM.
SHE IS A BEAUTY, ISN'T SHE?

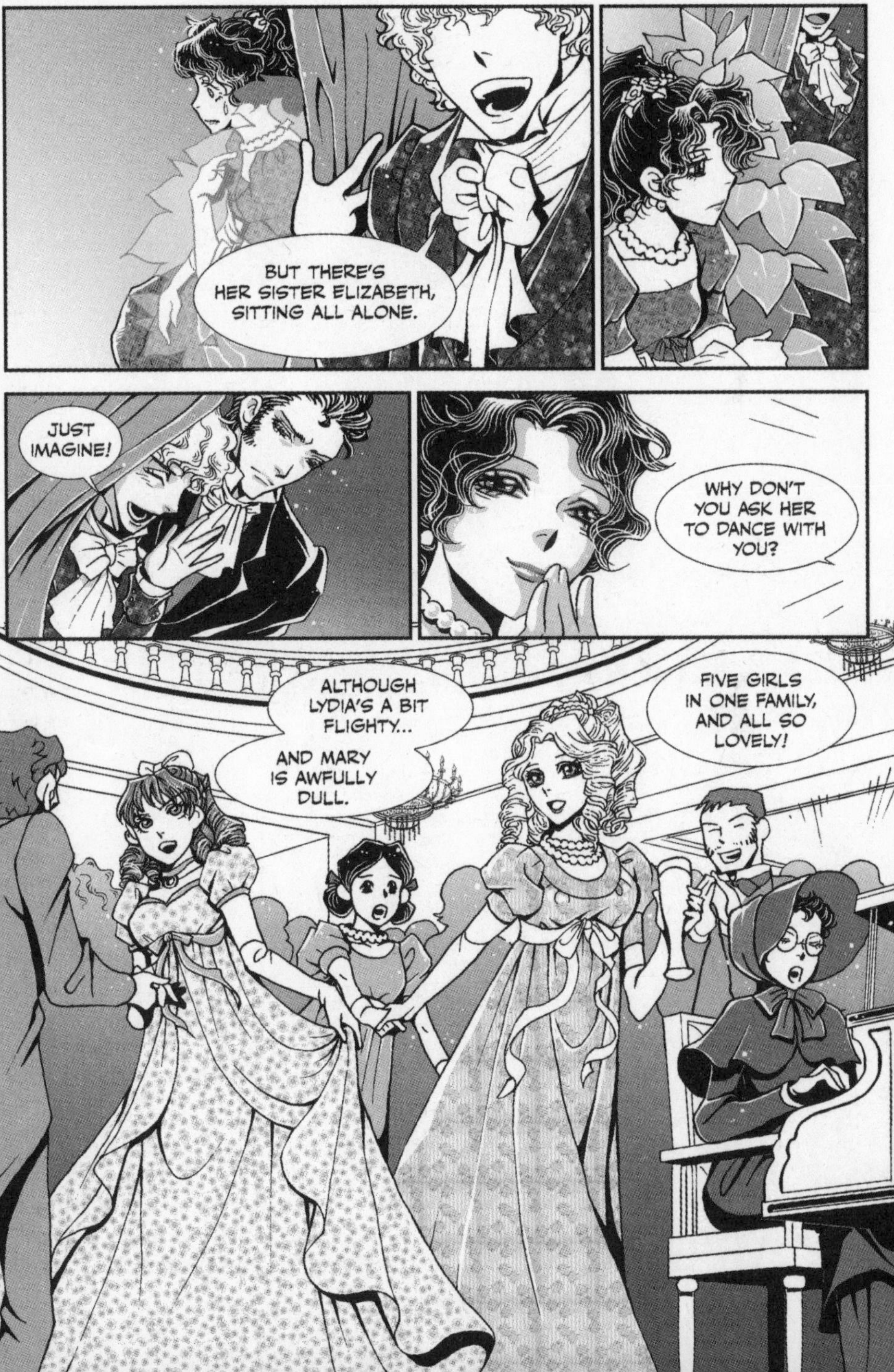
BUT THERE'S HER SISTER ELIZABETH, SITTING ALL ALONE.
WHY DON'T YOU ASK HER TO DANCE WITH YOU?
JUST IMAGINE!
FIVE GIRLS IN ONE FAMILY, AND ALL SO LOVELY!
ALTHOUGH LYDIA'S A BIT FLIGHTY...
AND MARY IS AWFULLY DULL.

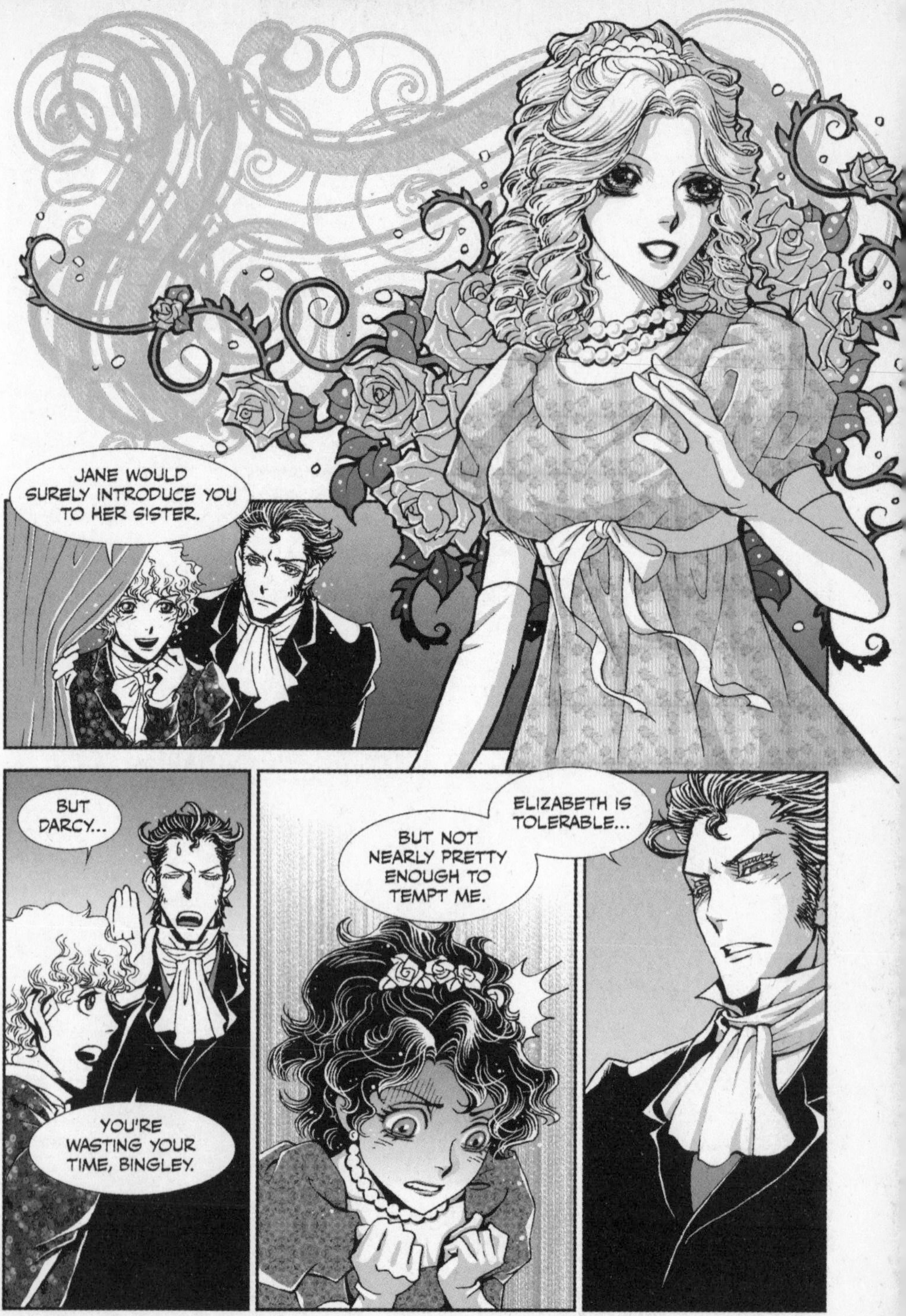
JANE WOULD SURELY INTRODUCE YOU TO HER SISTER.
ELIZABETH IS TOLERABLE...
BUT NOT NEARLY PRETTY ENOUGH TO TEMPT ME.
BUT DARCY...
YOU'RE WASTING YOUR TIME, BINGLEY.

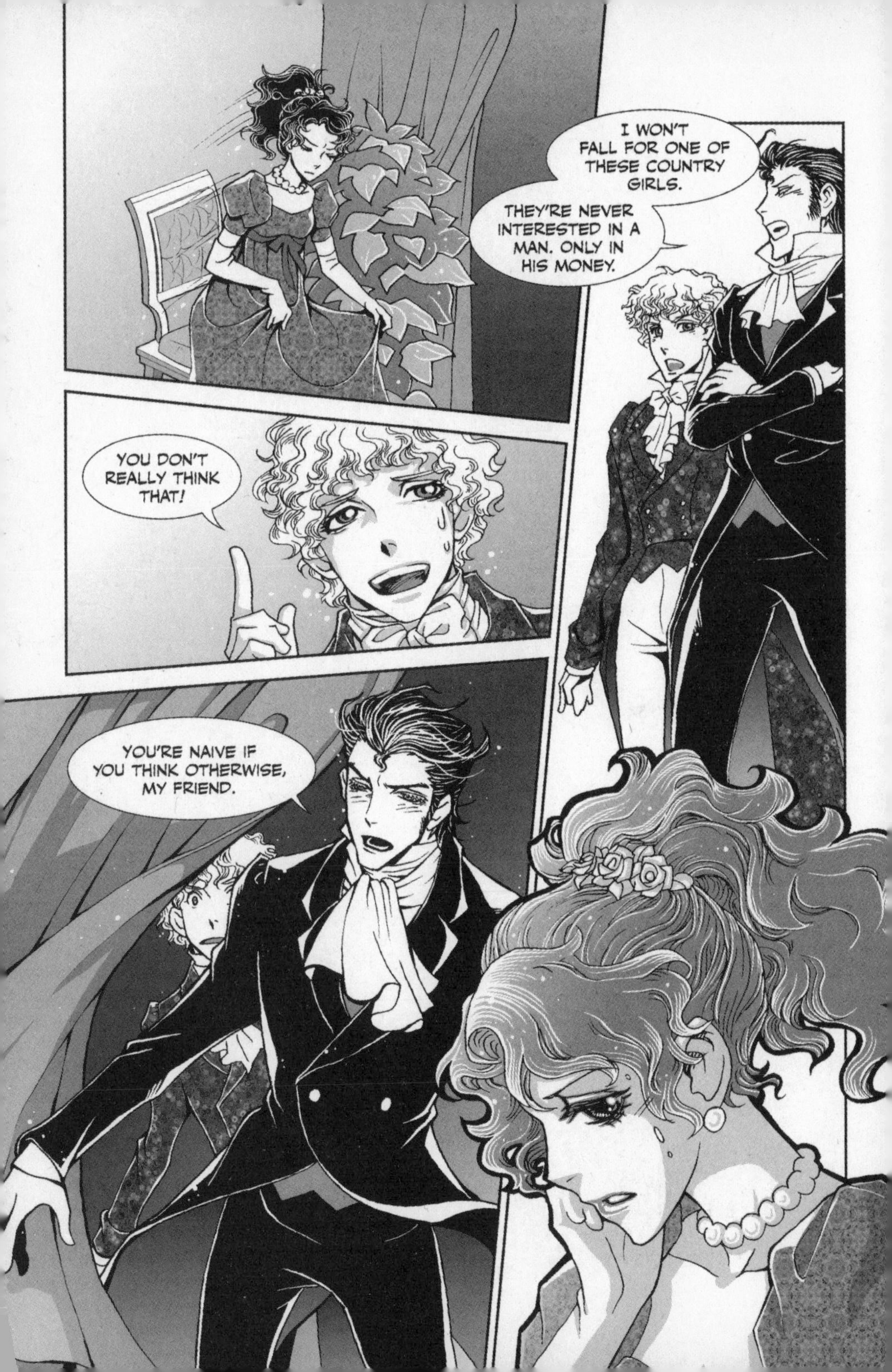
I WON'T FALL FOR ONE OF THESE COUNTRY GIRLS.
THEY'RE NEVER INTERESTED IN A MAN. ONLY IN HIS MONEY.
YOU DON'T REALLY THINK THAT!
YOU'RE NAIVE IF YOU THINK OTHERWISE, MY FRIEND.

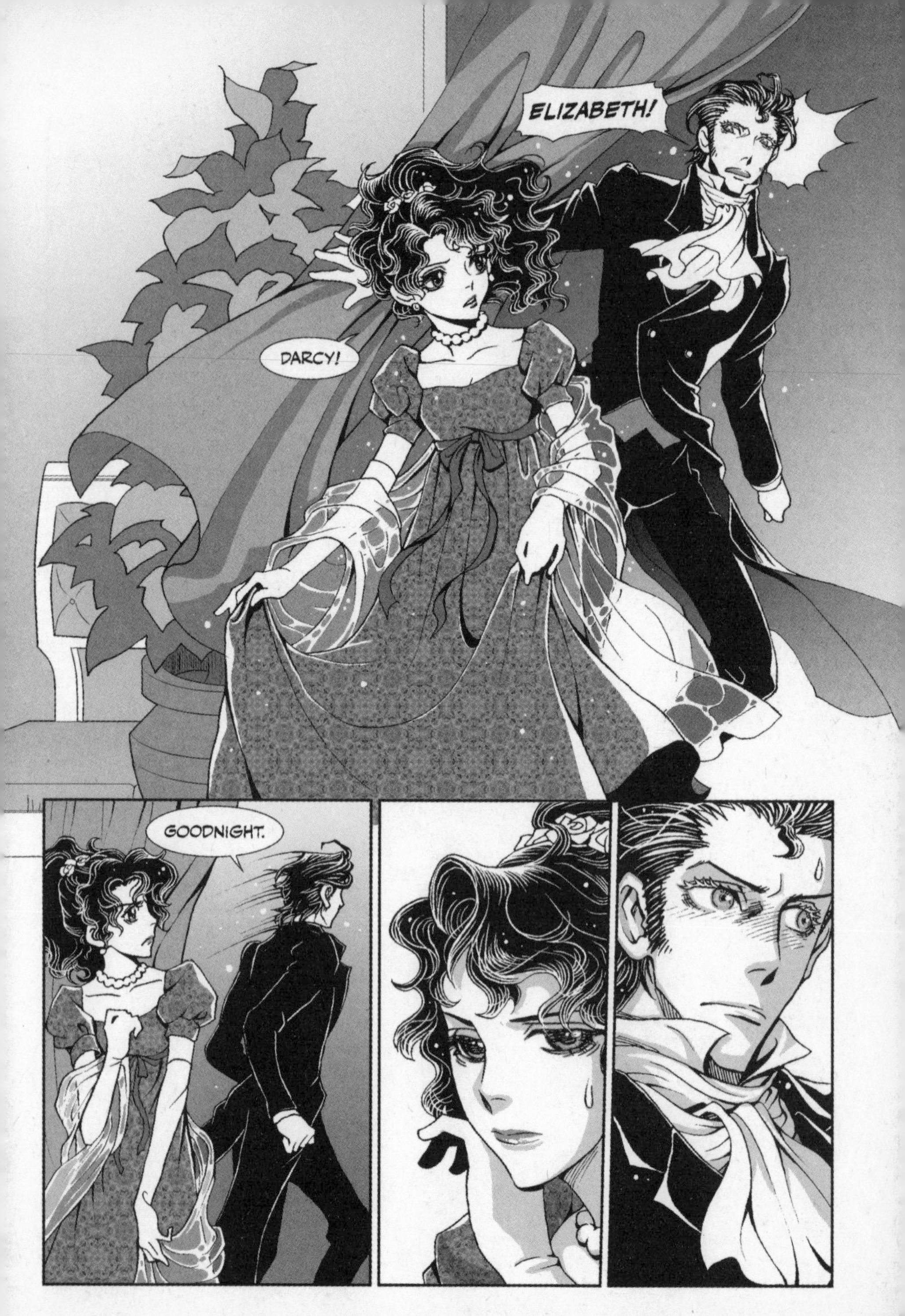
ELIZABETH!
DARCY!
GOODNIGHT.

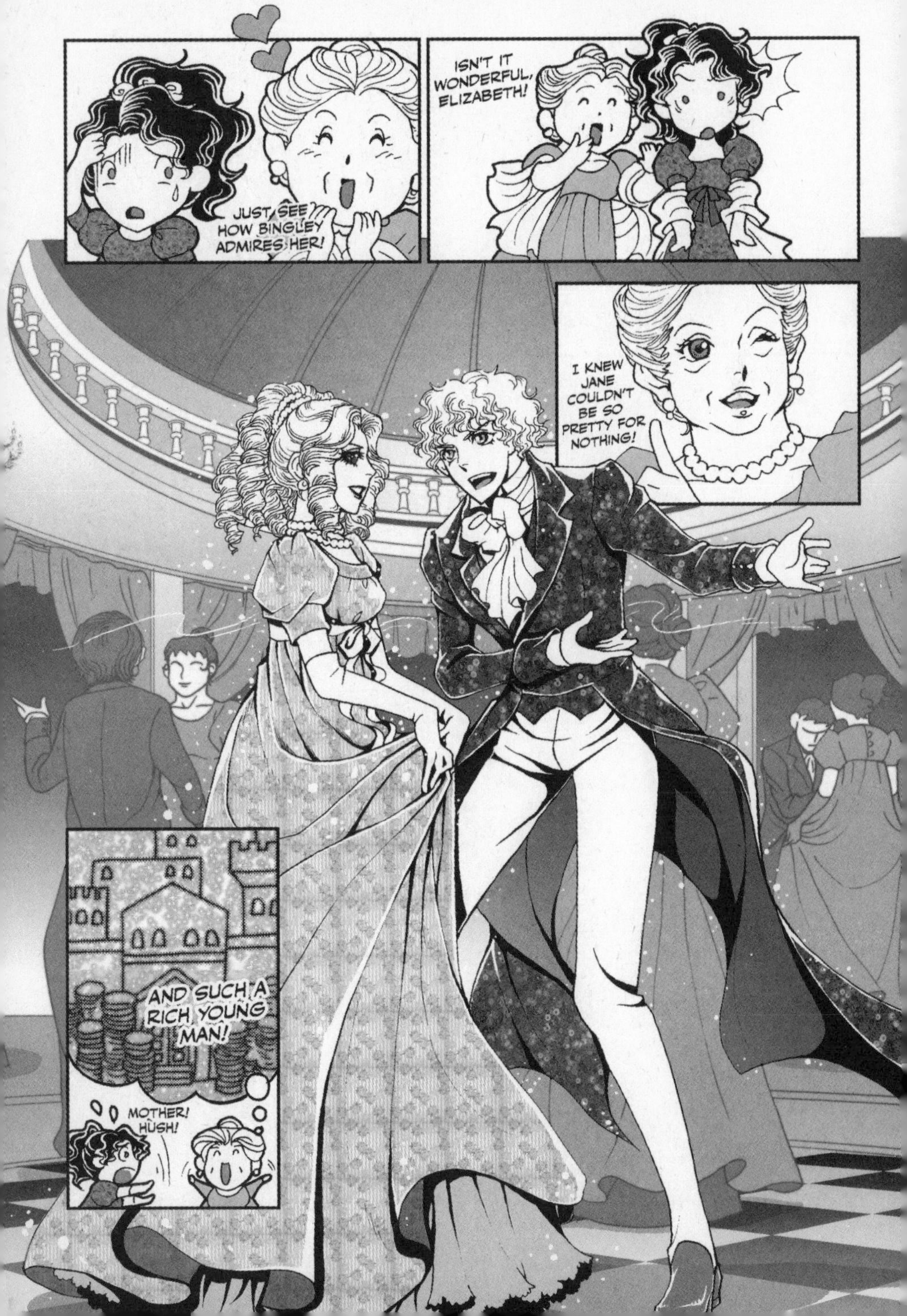
ISN'T IT WONDERFUL, ELIZABETH!
JUST SEE HOW BINGLEY ADMIRES HER!
I KNEW JANE COULDN'T BE SO PRETTY FOR NOTHING!
AND SUCH A RICH YOUNG MAN!
MOTHER! HUSH!

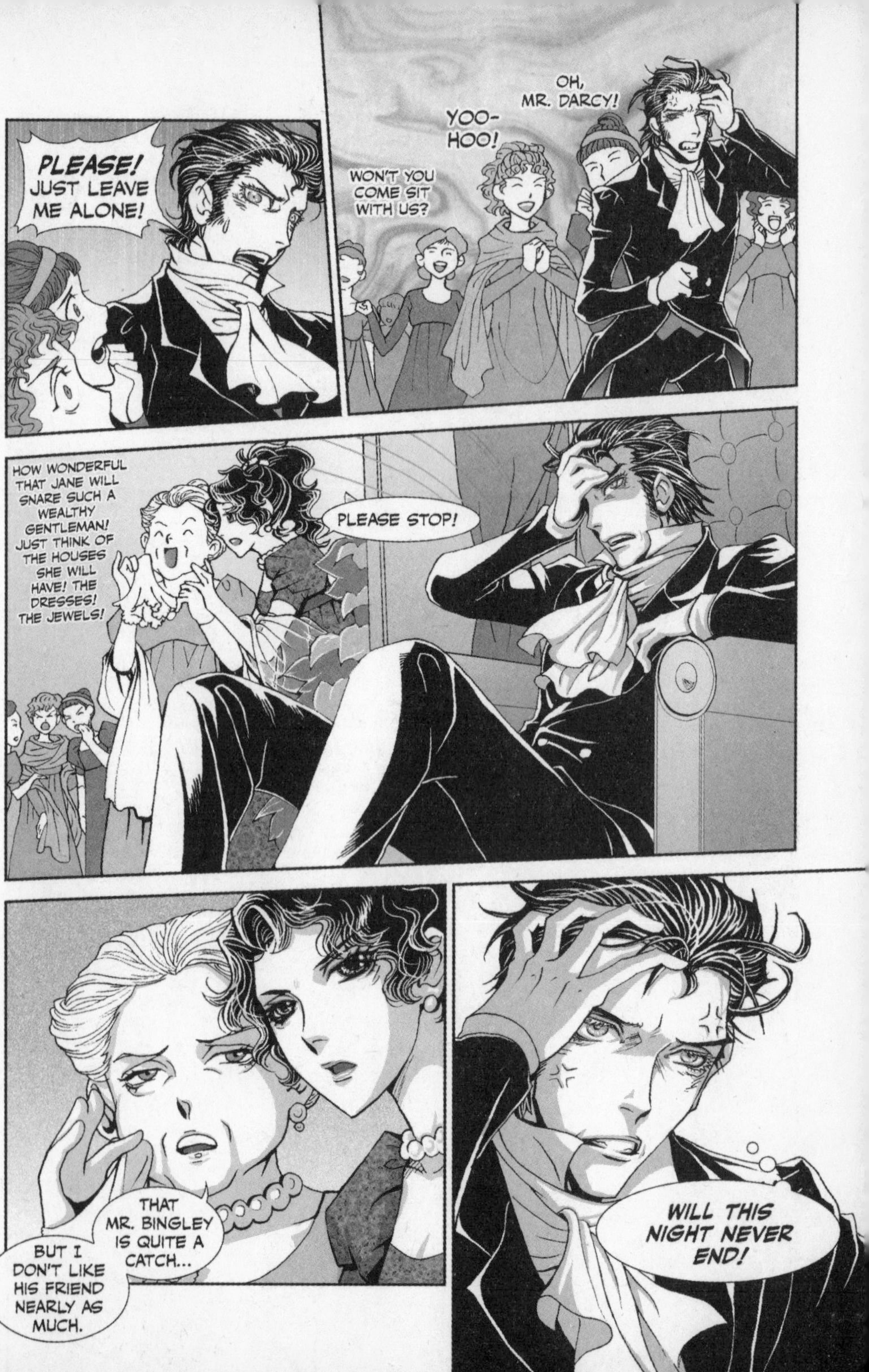
OH, MR. DARCY!
YOO-HOO!
WON'T YOU COME SIT WITH US?
PLEASE! JUST LEAVE ME ALONE!
HOW WONDERFUL THAT JANE WILL SNARE SUCH A WEALTHY GENTLEMAN! JUST THINK OF THE HOUSES SHE WILL HAVE! THE DRESSES! THE JEWELS!
PLEASE STOP!
WILL THIS NIGHT NEVER END!
THAT MR. BINGLEY IS QUITE A CATCH...
BUT I DON'T LIKE HIS FRIEND NEARLY AS MUCH.

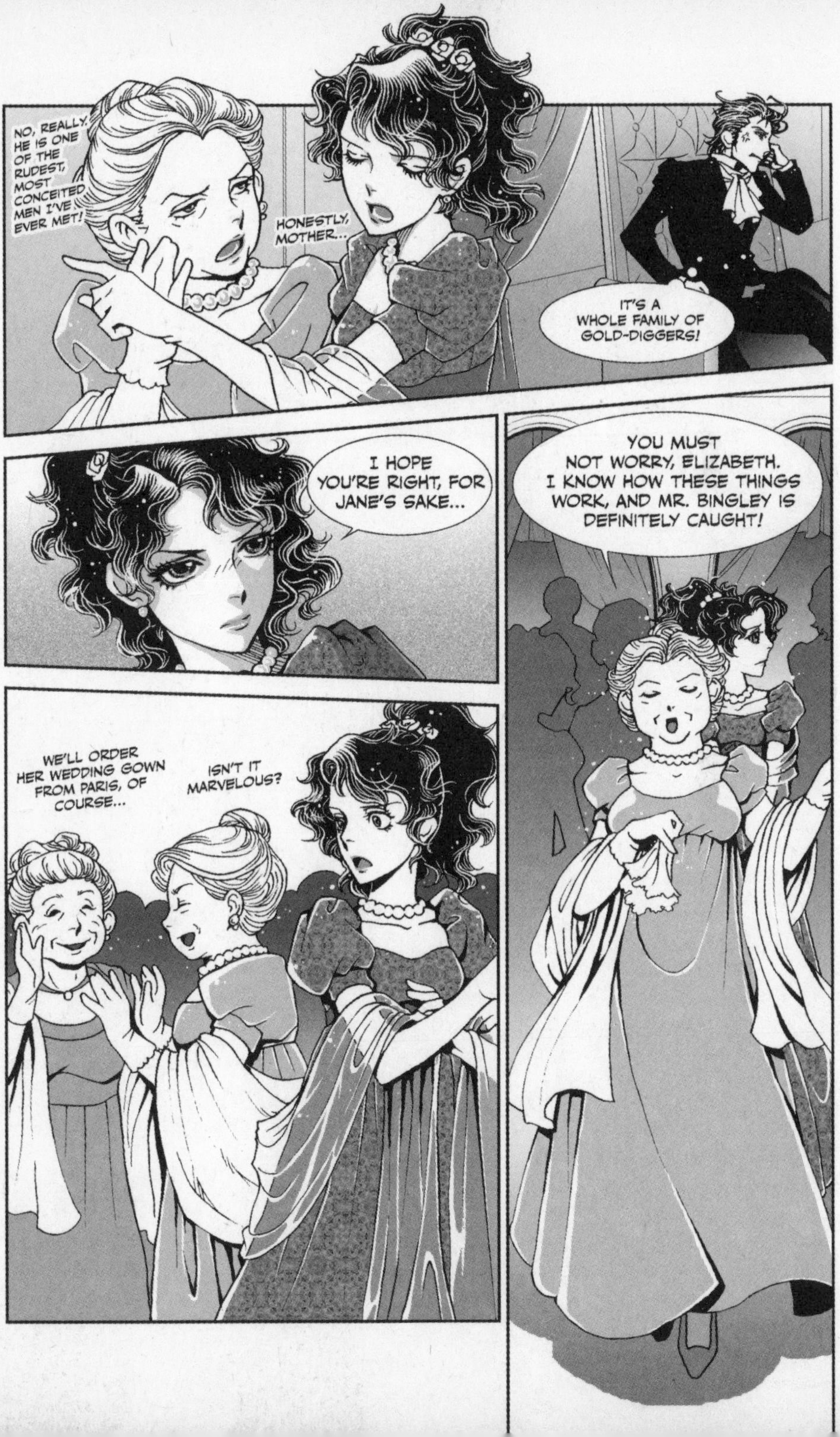
IT'S A WHOLE FAMILY OF GOLD-DIGGERS!
NO, REALLY, HE IS ONE OF THE RUDEST, MOST CONCEITED MEN I'VE EVER MET!
HONESTLY, MOTHER...
YOU MUST NOT WORRY, ELIZABETH. I KNOW HOW THESE THINGS WORK, AND MR. BINGLEY IS DEFINITELY CAUGHT!
I HOPE YOU'RE RIGHT, FOR JANE'S SAKE...
ISN'T IT MARVELOUS?
WE'LL ORDER HER WEDDING GOWN FROM PARIS, OF COURSE...

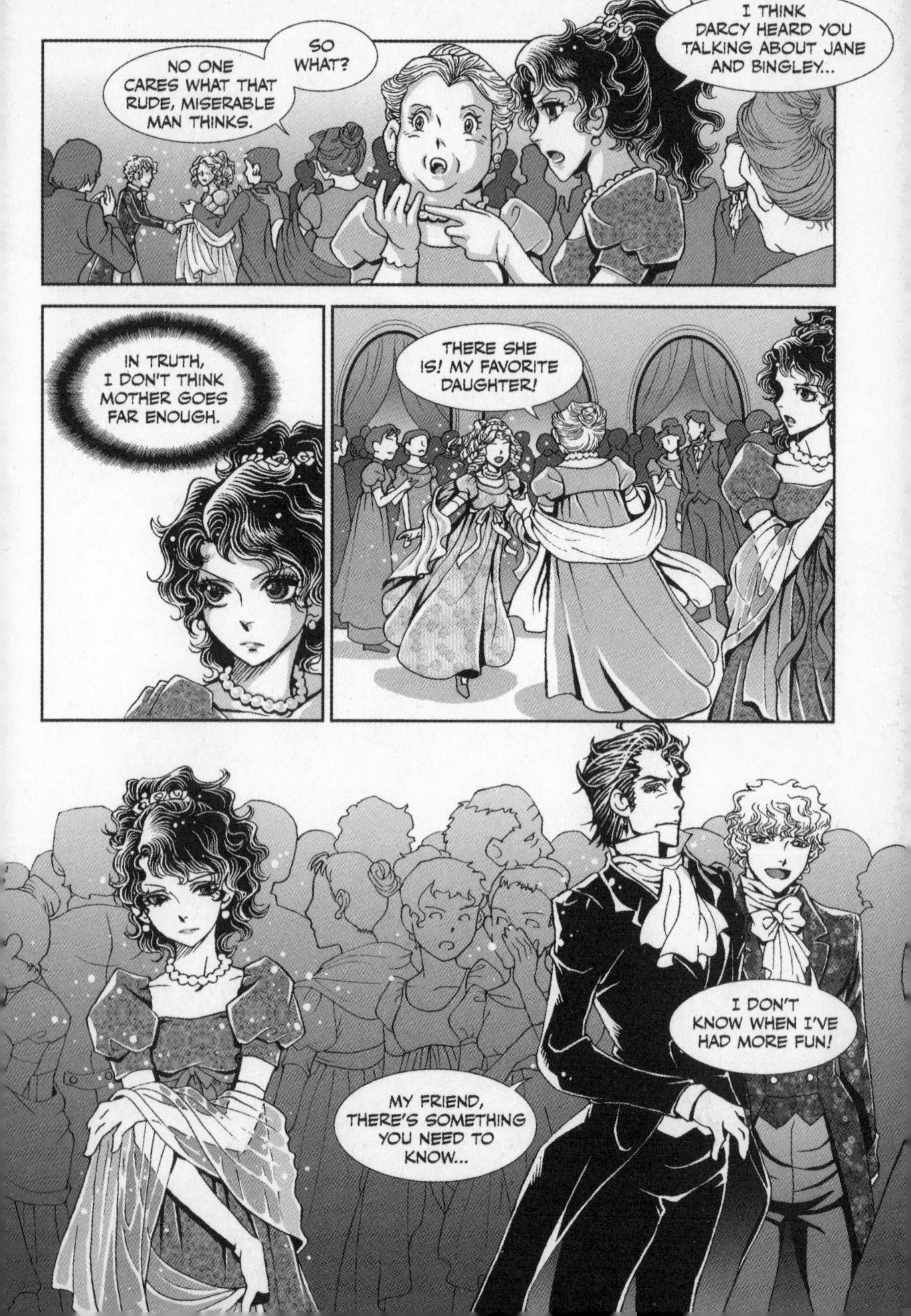
I THINK DARCY HEARD YOU TALKING ABOUT JANE AND BINGLEY...
SO WHAT?
NO ONE CARES WHAT THAT RUDE, MISERABLE MAN THINKS.
THERE SHE IS! MY FAVORITE DAUGHTER!
IN TRUTH, I DON'T THINK MOTHER GOES FAR ENOUGH.
I DON'T KNOW WHEN I'VE HAD MORE FUN!
MY FRIEND, THERE'S SOMETHING YOU NEED TO KNOW...

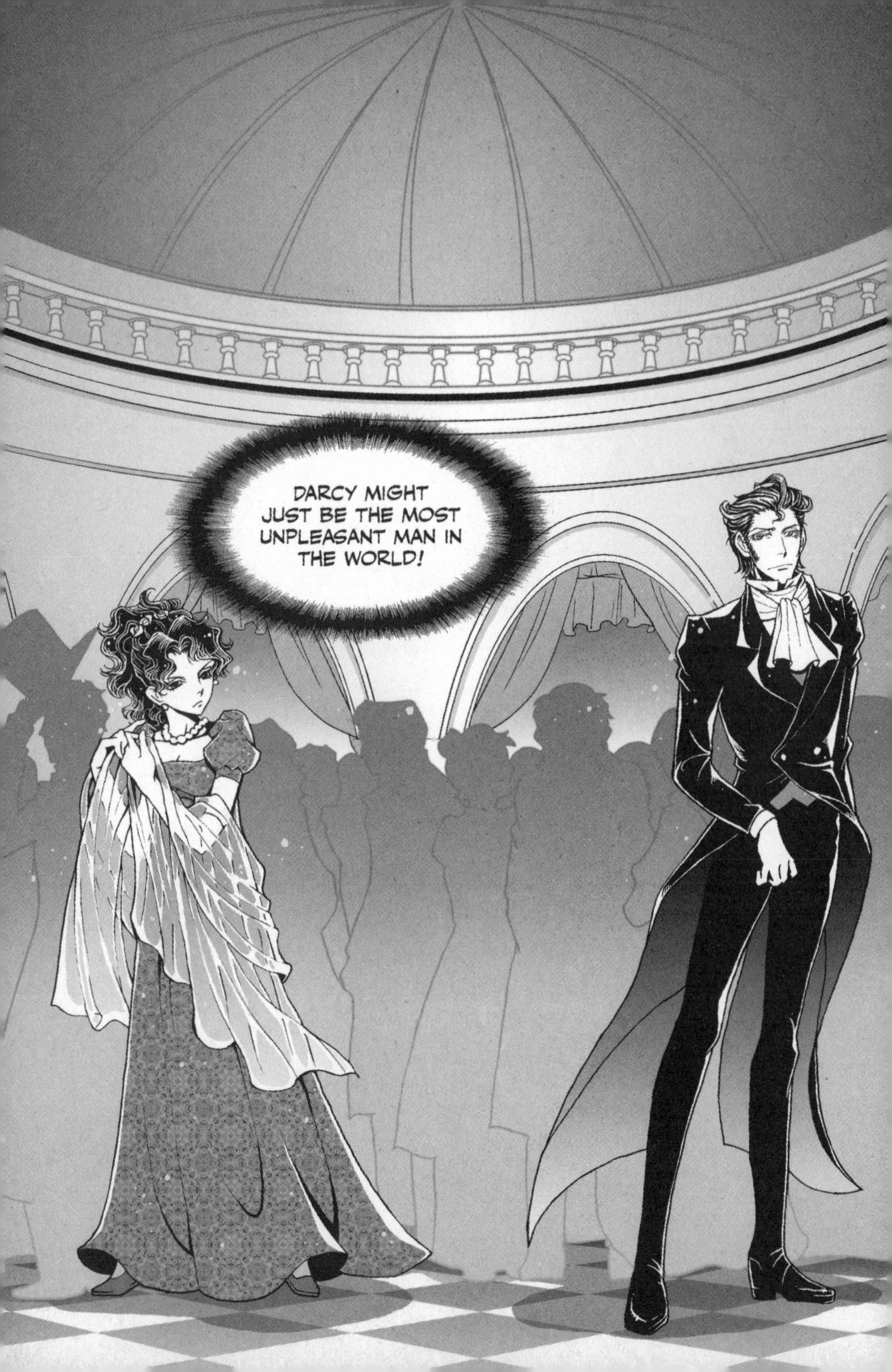
DARCY MIGHT JUST BE THE MOST UNPLEASANT MAN IN THE WORLD!

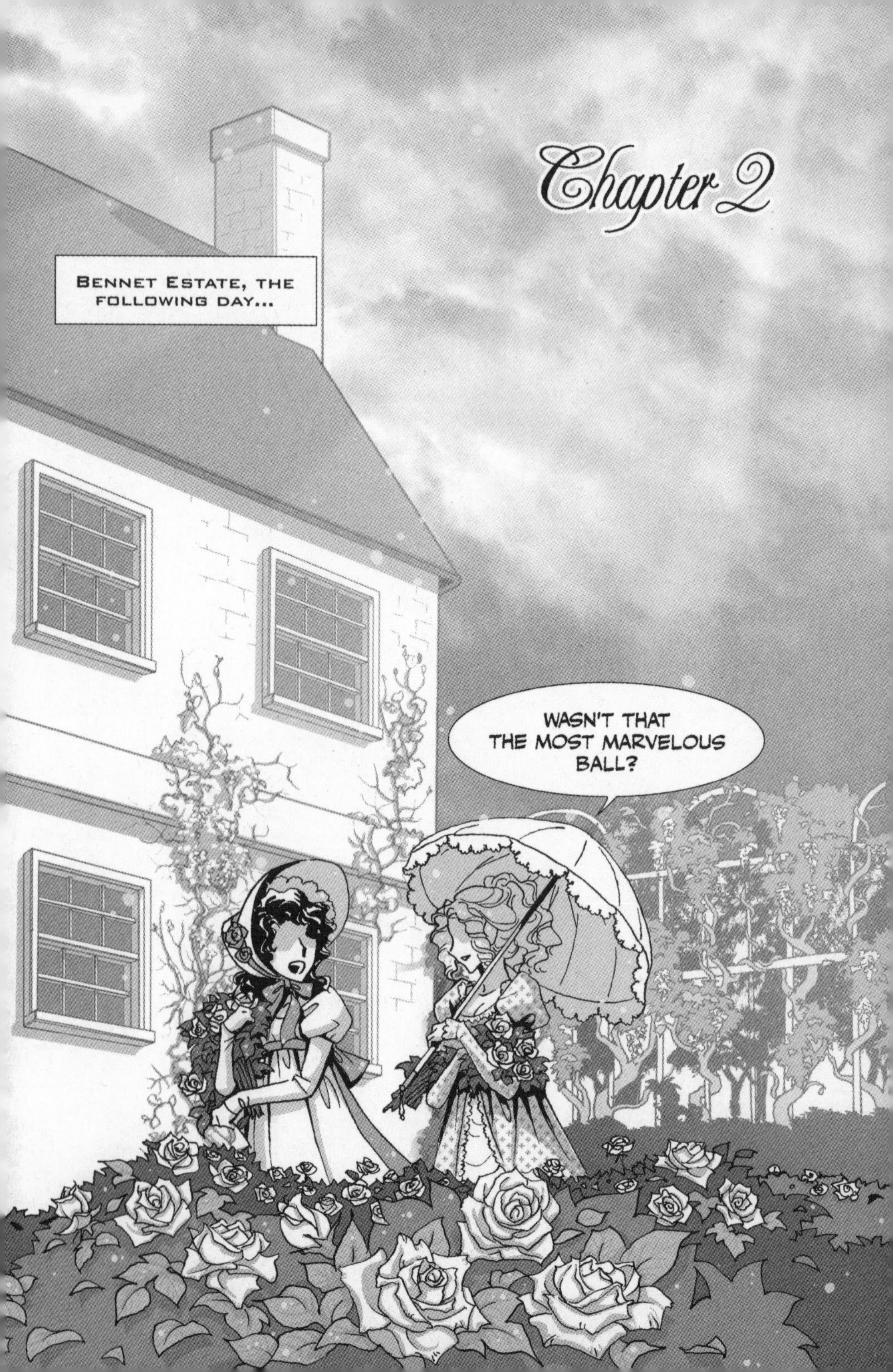

Chapter 2
BENNET ESTATE, THE FOLLOWING DAY...
WASN'T THAT THE MOST MARVELOUS BALL?

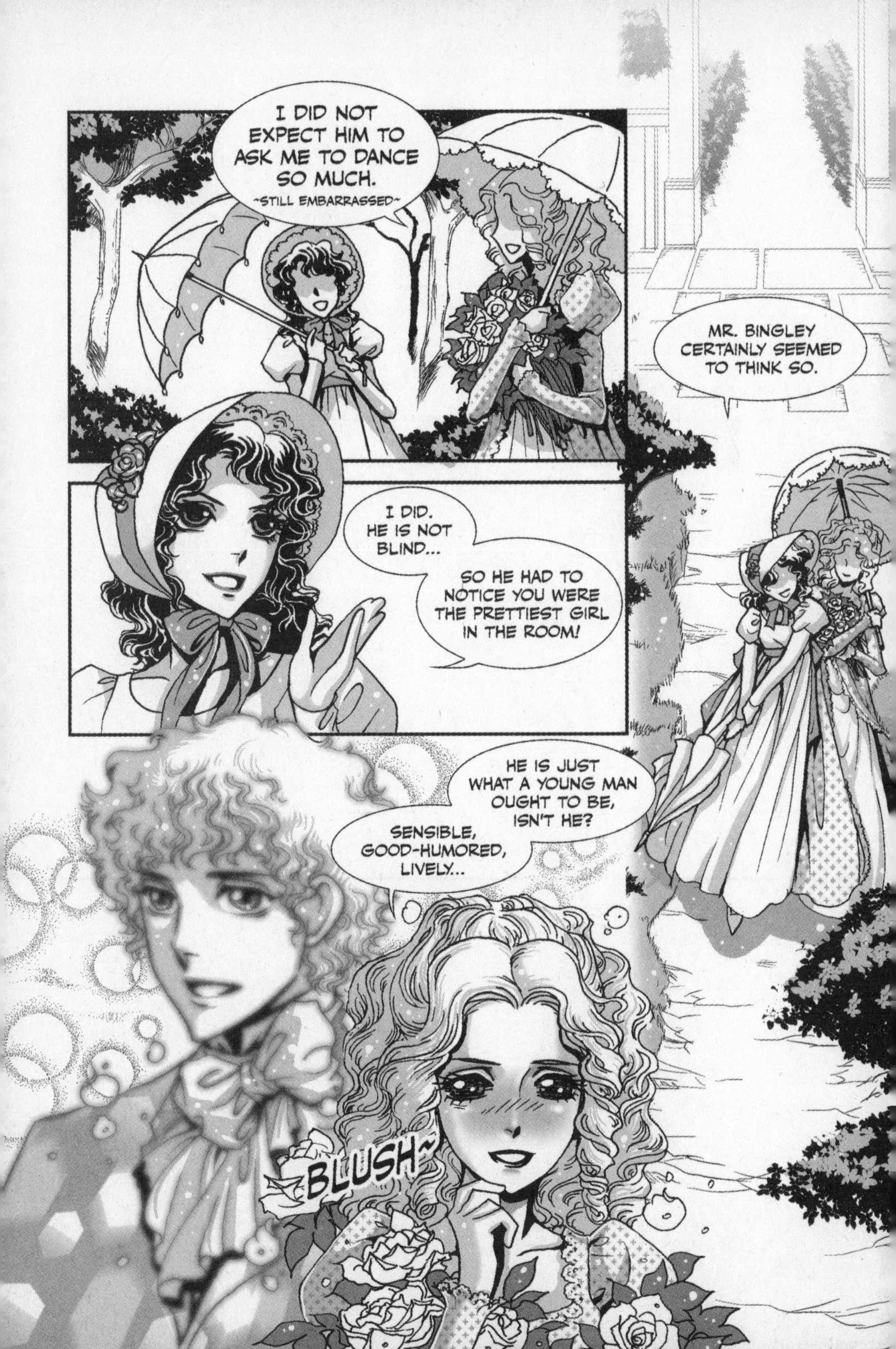
MR. BINGLEY CERTAINLY SEEMED TO THINK SO.
I DID NOT EXPECT HIM TO ASK ME TO DANCE SO MUCH.
~STILL EMBARRASSED~
I DID. HE IS NOT BLIND...
SO HE HAD TO NOTICE YOU WERE THE PRETTIEST GIRL IN THE ROOM!
HE IS JUST WHAT A YOUNG MAN OUGHT TO BE, ISN'T HE?
SENSIBLE, GOOD-HUMORED, LIVELY...
~BLUSH~

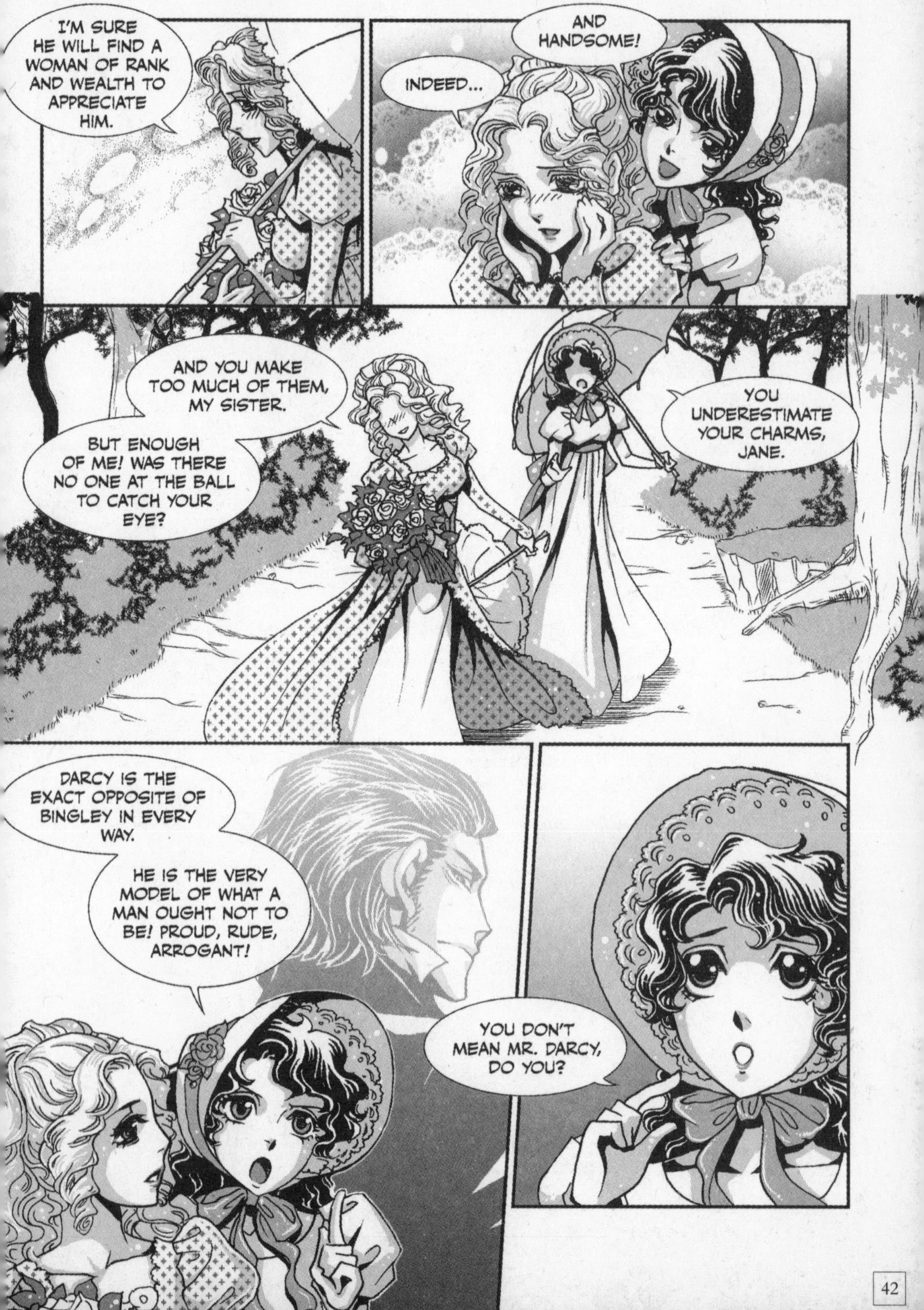
AND HANDSOME!
INDEED...
I'M SURE HE WILL FIND A WOMAN OF RANK AND WEALTH TO APPRECIATE HIM.
YOU UNDERESTIMATE YOUR CHARMS, JANE.
AND YOU MAKE TOO MUCH OF THEM, MY SISTER.
BUT ENOUGH OF ME! WAS THERE NO ONE AT THE BALL TO CATCH YOUR EYE?
YOU DON'T MEAN MR. DARCY, DO YOU?
DARCY IS THE EXACT OPPOSITE OF BINGLEY IN EVERY WAY.
HE IS THE VERY MODEL OF WHAT A MAN OUGHT NOT TO BE! PROUD, RUDE, ARROGANT!

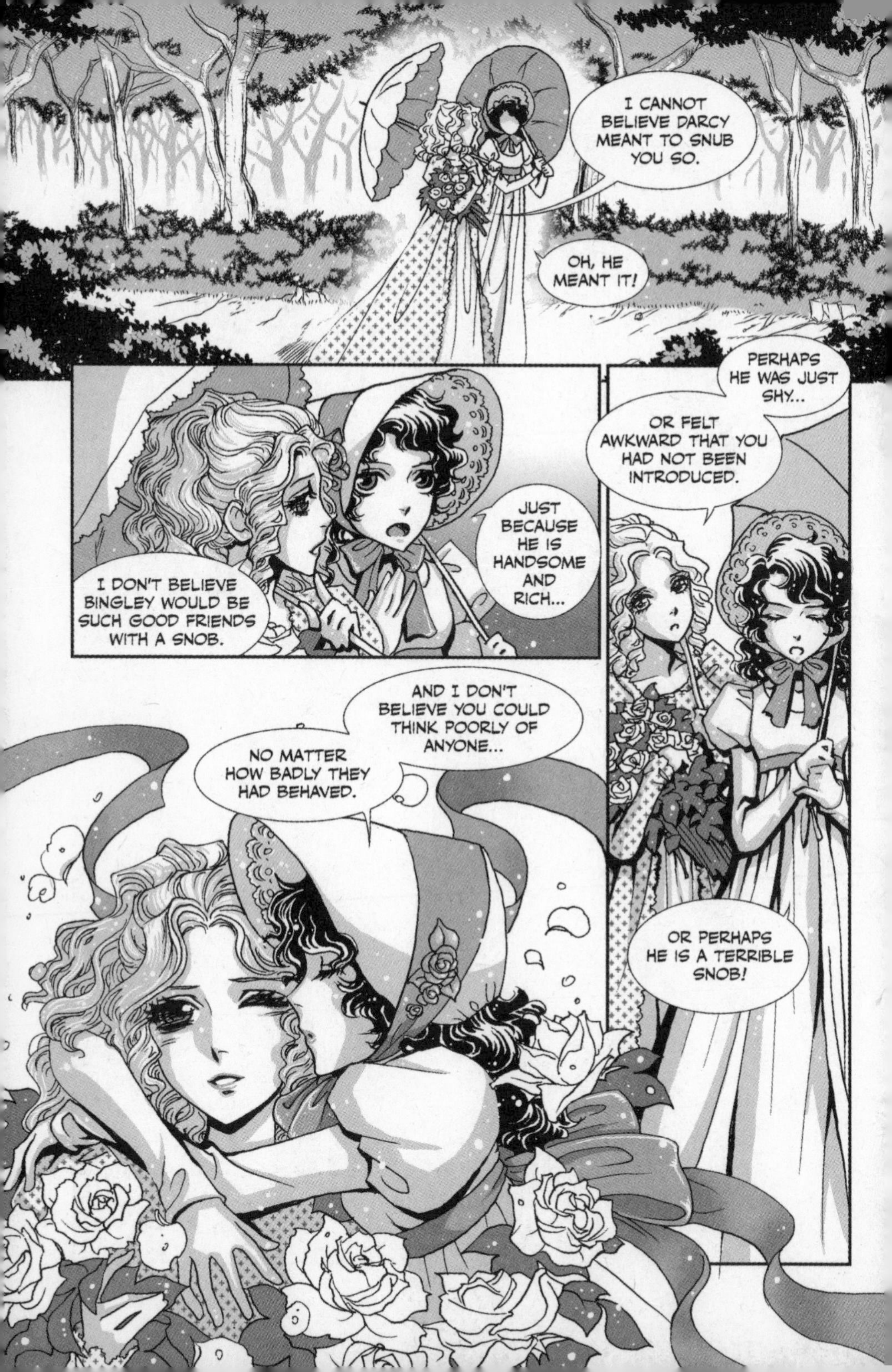
I CANNOT BELIEVE DARCY MEANT TO SNUB YOU SO.
OH, HE MEANT IT!
PERHAPS HE WAS JUST SHY...
OR FELT AWKWARD THAT YOU HAD NOT BEEN INTRODUCED.
OR PERHAPS HE IS A TERRIBLE SNOB!
JUST BECAUSE HE IS HANDSOME AND RICH...
I DON'T BELIEVE BINGLEY WOULD BE SUCH GOOD FRIENDS WITH A SNOB.
AND I DON'T BELIEVE YOU COULD THINK POORLY OF ANYONE...
NO MATTER HOW BADLY THEY HAD BEHAVED.

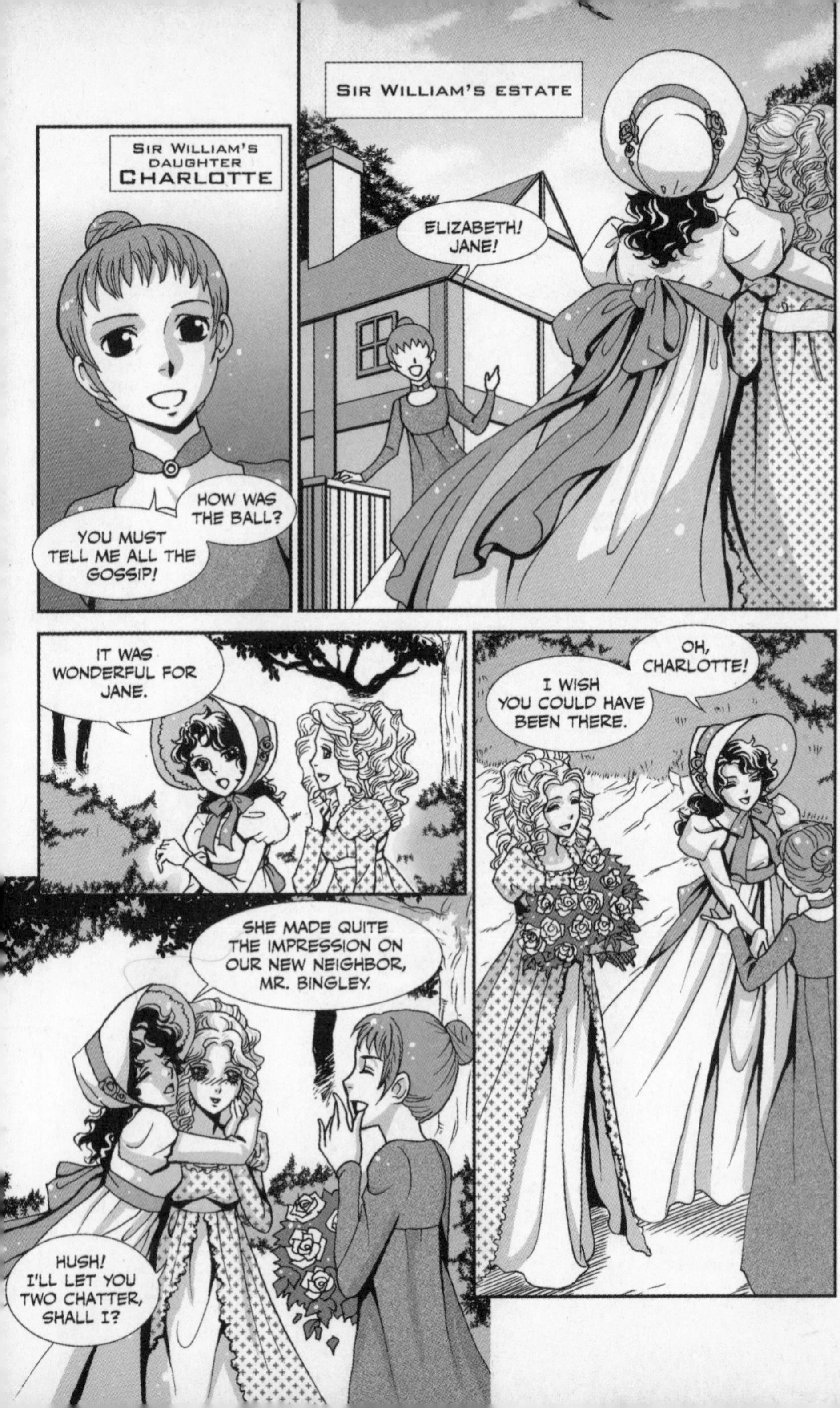
SIR WILLIAM'S ESTATE
ELIZABETH! JANE!
SIR WILLIAM'S DAUGHTER CHARLOTTE
HOW WAS THE BALL?
YOU MUST TELL ME ALL THE GOSSIP!
OH, CHARLOTTE!
I WISH YOU COULD HAVE BEEN THERE.
IT WAS WONDERFUL FOR JANE.
SHE MADE QUITE THE IMPRESSION ON OUR NEW NEIGHBOR, MR. BINGLEY.
HUSH! I'LL LET YOU TWO CHATTER, SHALL I?

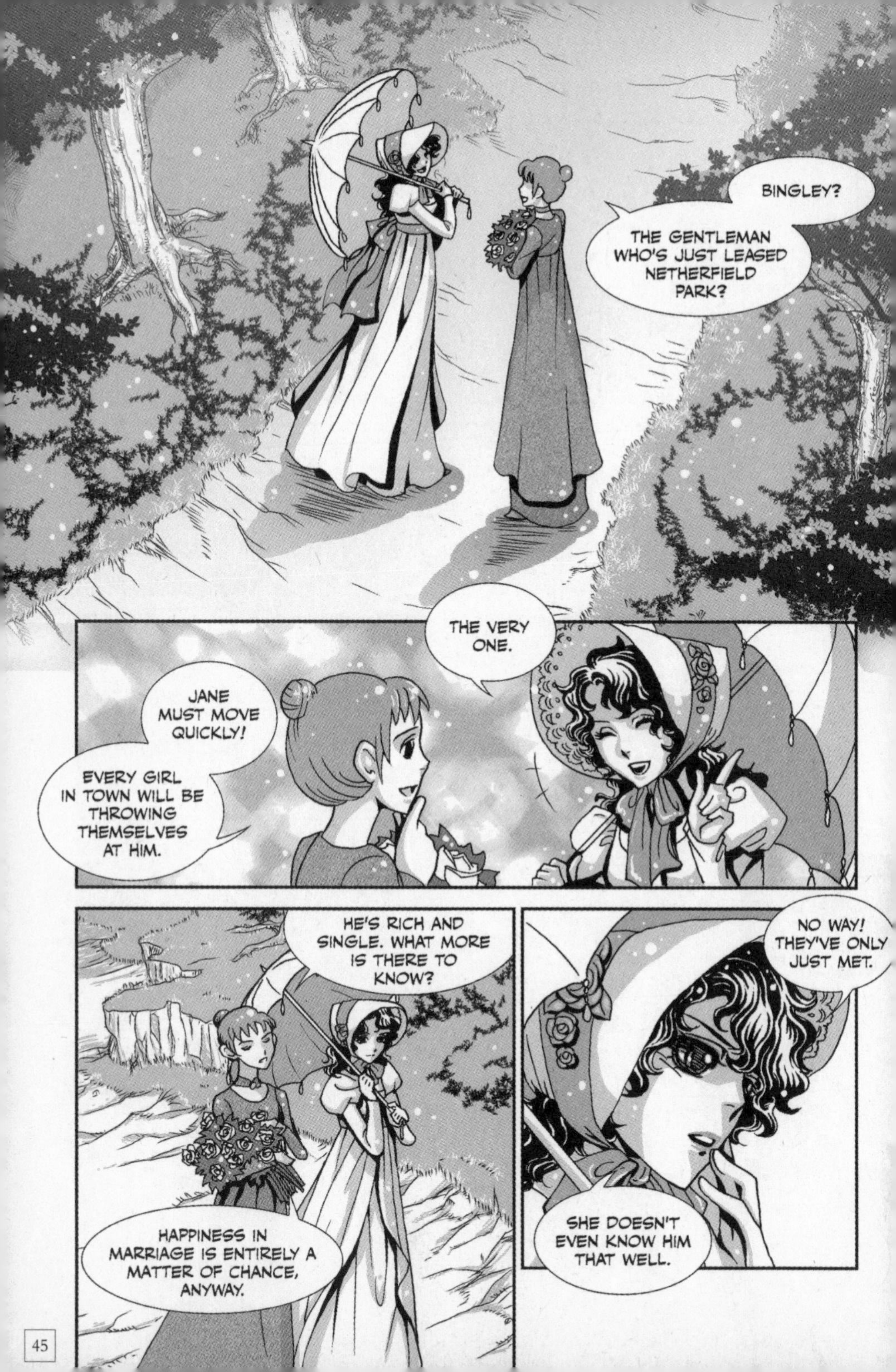
BINGLEY?
THE GENTLEMAN WHO'S JUST LEASED NETHERFIELD PARK?
THE VERY ONE.
JANE MUST MOVE QUICKLY!
EVERY GIRL IN TOWN WILL BE THROWING THEMSELVES AT HIM.
NO WAY! THEY'VE ONLY JUST MET.
SHE DOESN'T EVEN KNOW HIM THAT WELL.
HE'S RICH AND SINGLE. WHAT MORE IS THERE TO KNOW?
HAPPINESS IN MARRIAGE IS ENTIRELY A MATTER OF CHANCE, ANYWAY.

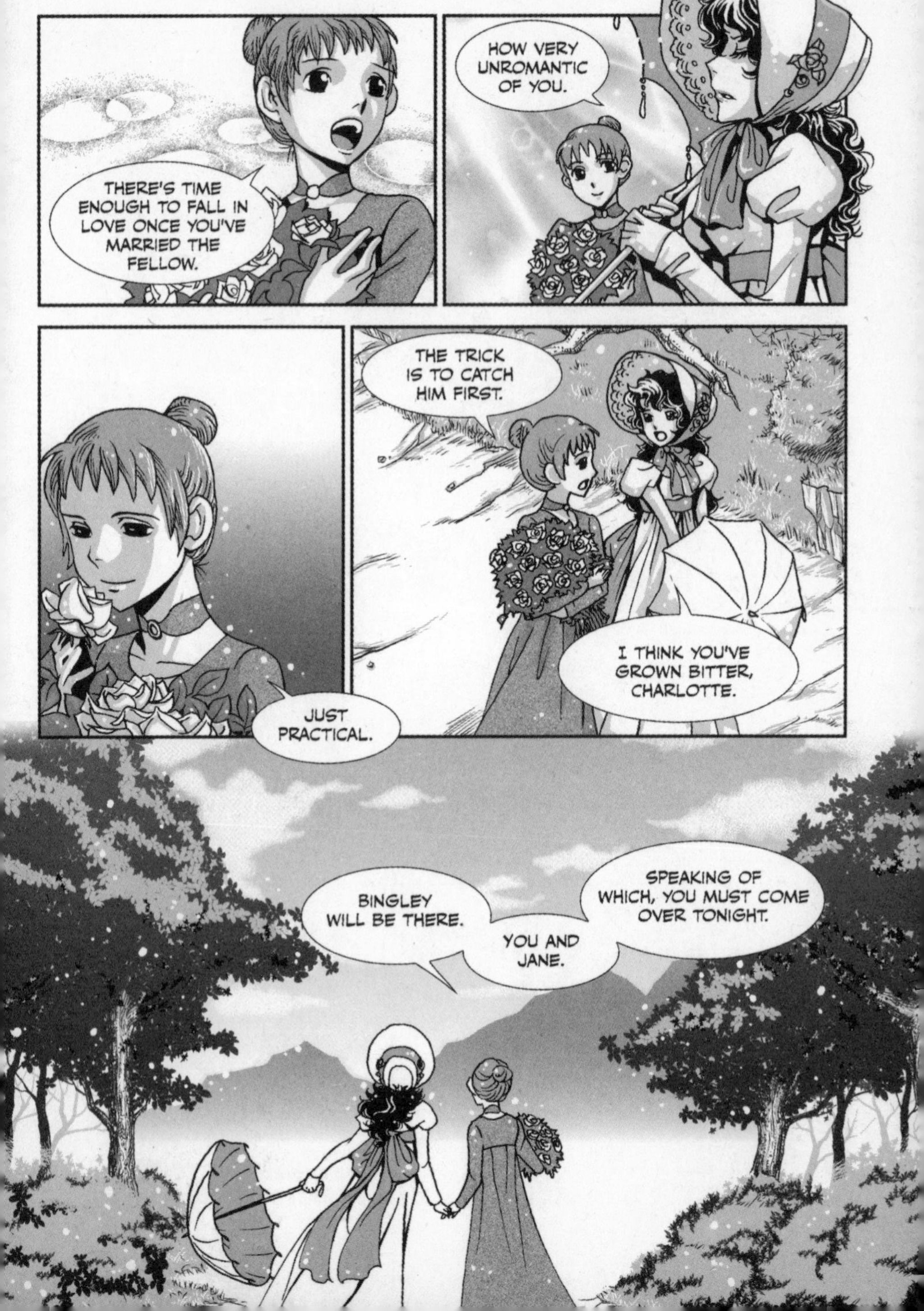
THERE'S TIME ENOUGH TO FALL IN LOVE ONCE YOU'VE MARRIED THE FELLOW.
HOW VERY UNROMANTIC OF YOU.
JUST PRACTICAL.
THE TRICK IS TO CATCH HIM FIRST.
I THINK YOU'VE GROWN BITTER, CHARLOTTE.
SPEAKING OF WHICH, YOU MUST COME OVER TONIGHT.
YOU AND JANE.
BINGLEY WILL BE THERE.

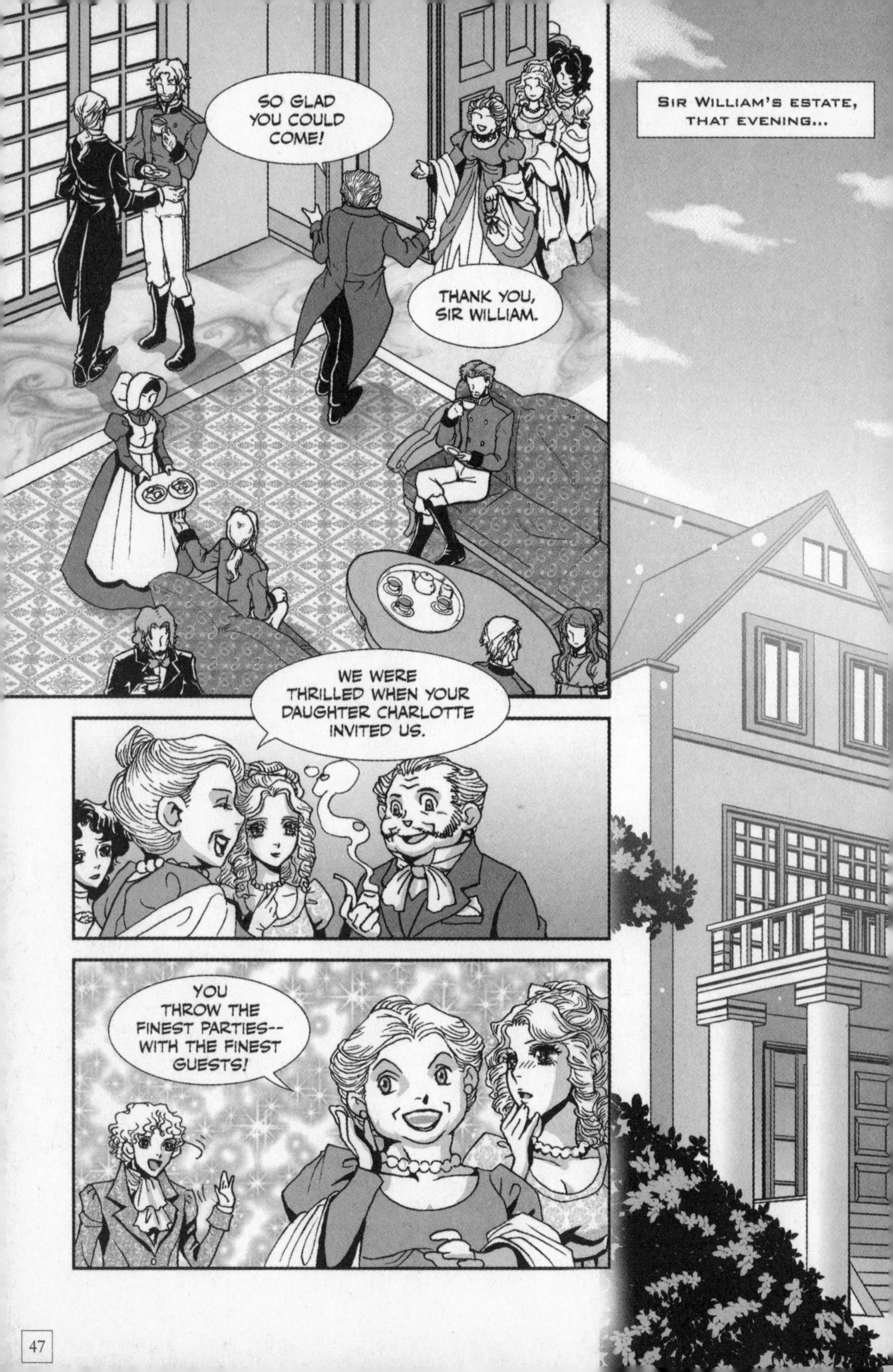

SIR WILLIAM'S ESTATE, THAT EVENING...
SO GLAD YOU COULD COME!
THANK YOU, SIR WILLIAM.
WE WERE THRILLED WHEN YOUR DAUGHTER CHARLOTTE INVITED US.
YOU THROW THE FINEST PARTIES-- WITH THE FINEST GUESTS!

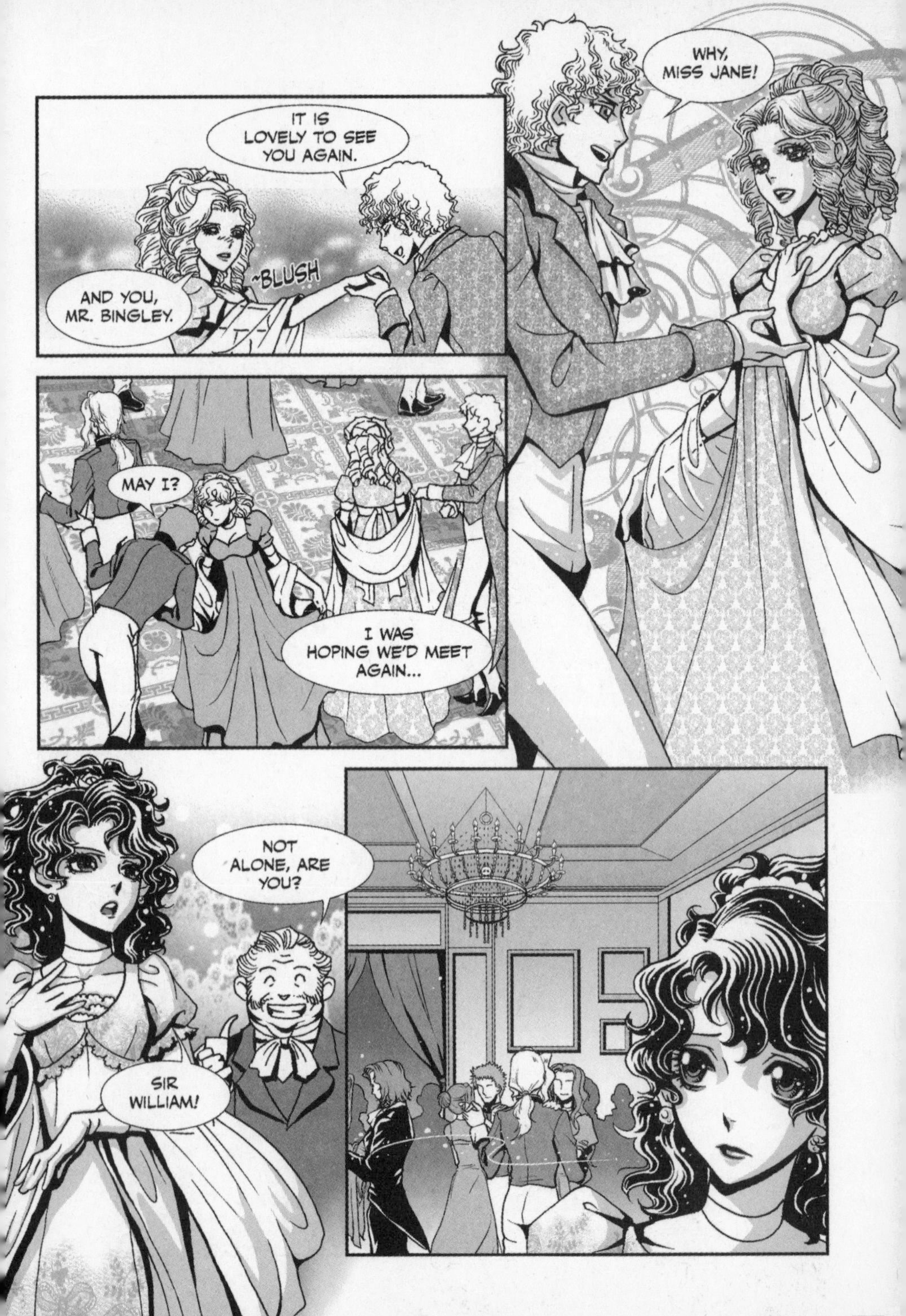
WHY, MISS JANE!
IT IS LOVELY TO SEE YOU AGAIN.
~BLUSH
AND YOU, MR. BINGLEY.
MAY I?
I WAS HOPING WE'D MEET AGAIN...
NOT ALONE, ARE YOU?
SIR WILLIAM!

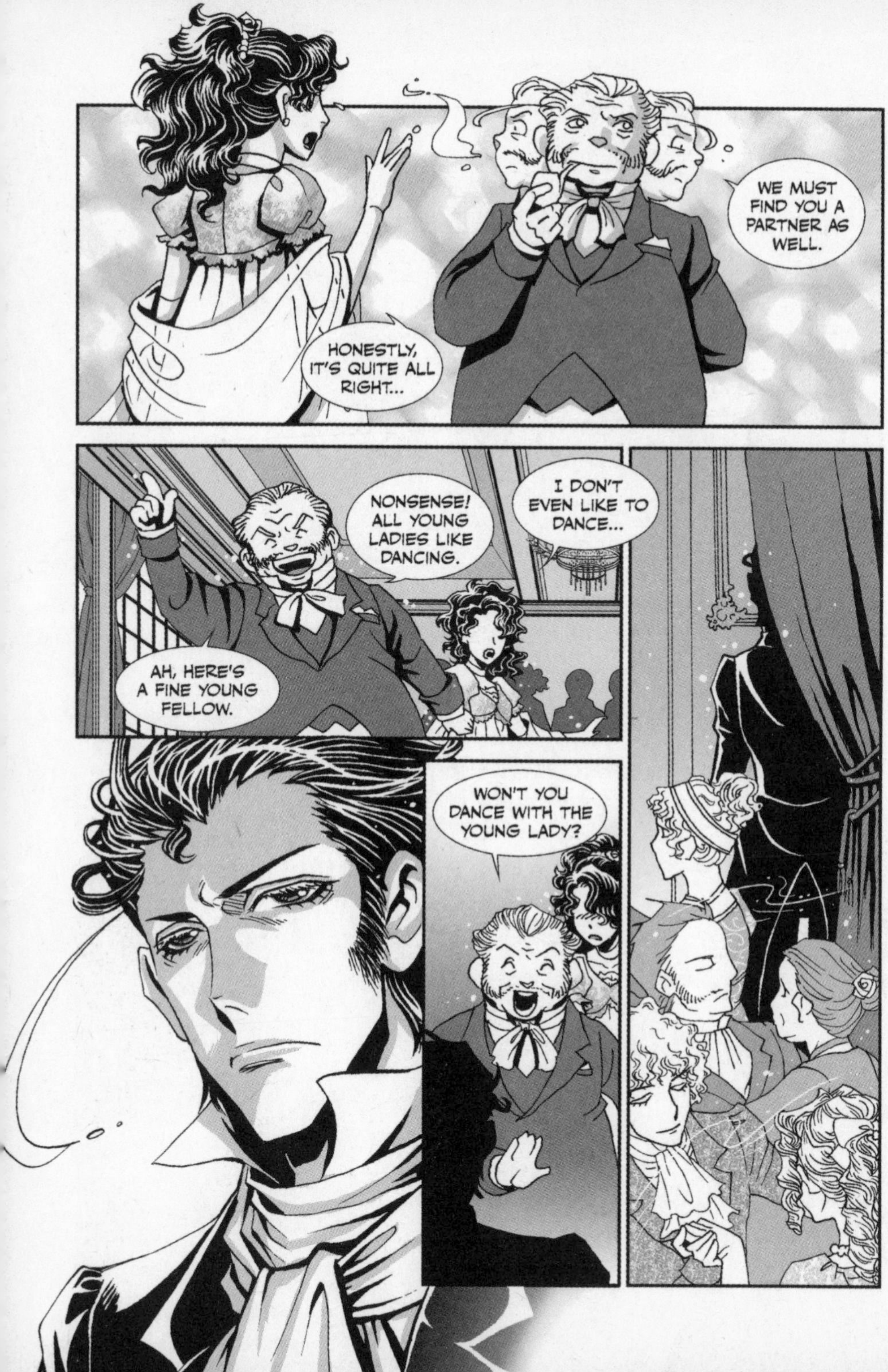
WE MUST FIND YOU A PARTNER AS WELL.
HONESTLY, IT'S QUITE ALL RIGHT...
I DON'T EVEN LIKE TO DANCE...
NONSENSE! ALL YOUNG LADIES LIKE DANCING.
AH, HERE'S A FINE YOUNG FELLOW.
WON'T YOU DANCE WITH THE YOUNG LADY?

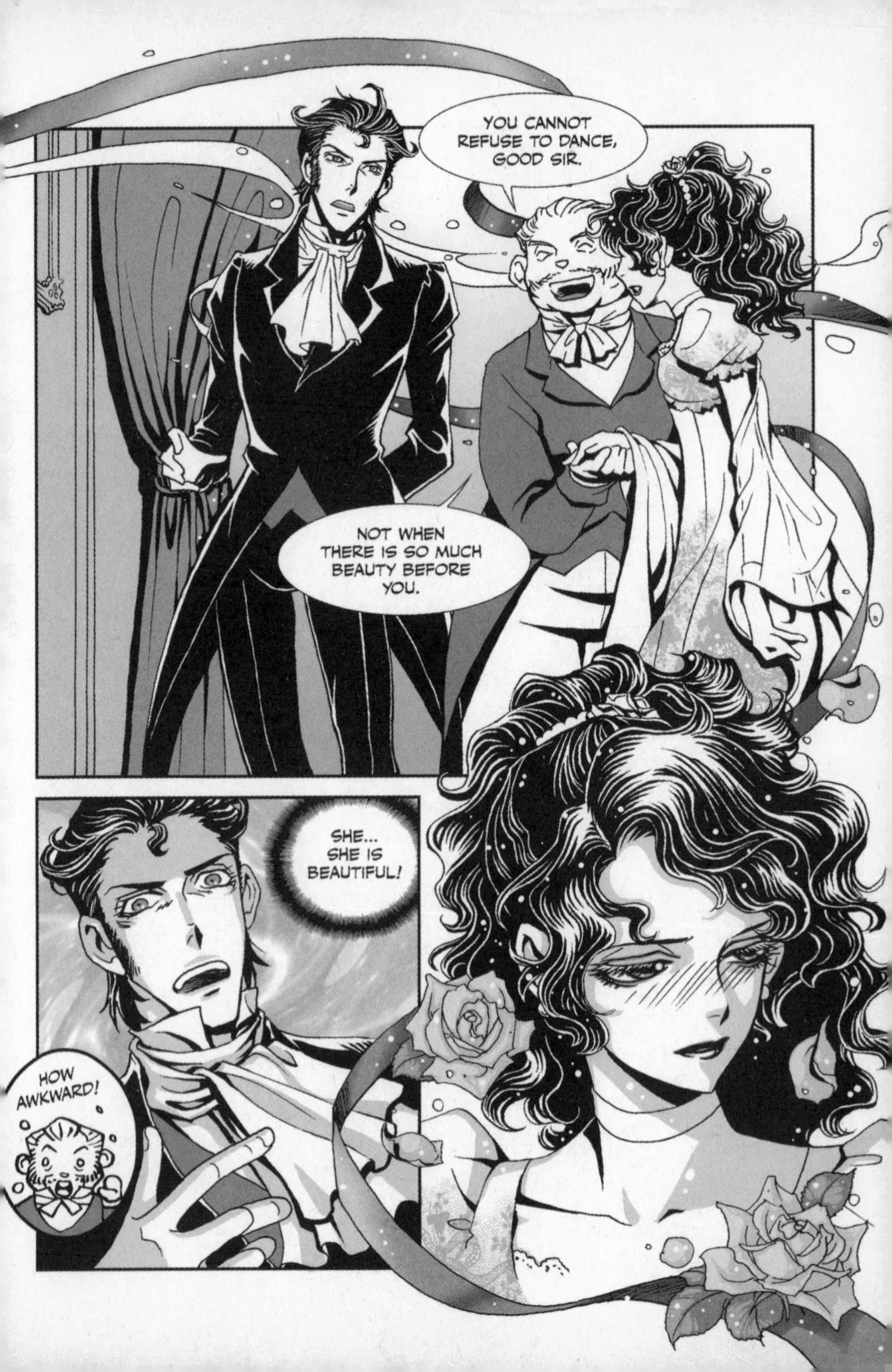
YOU CANNOT REFUSE TO DANCE, GOOD SIR.
NOT WHEN THERE IS SO MUCH BEAUTY BEFORE YOU.
SHE... SHE IS BEAUTIFUL!
HOW AWKWARD!

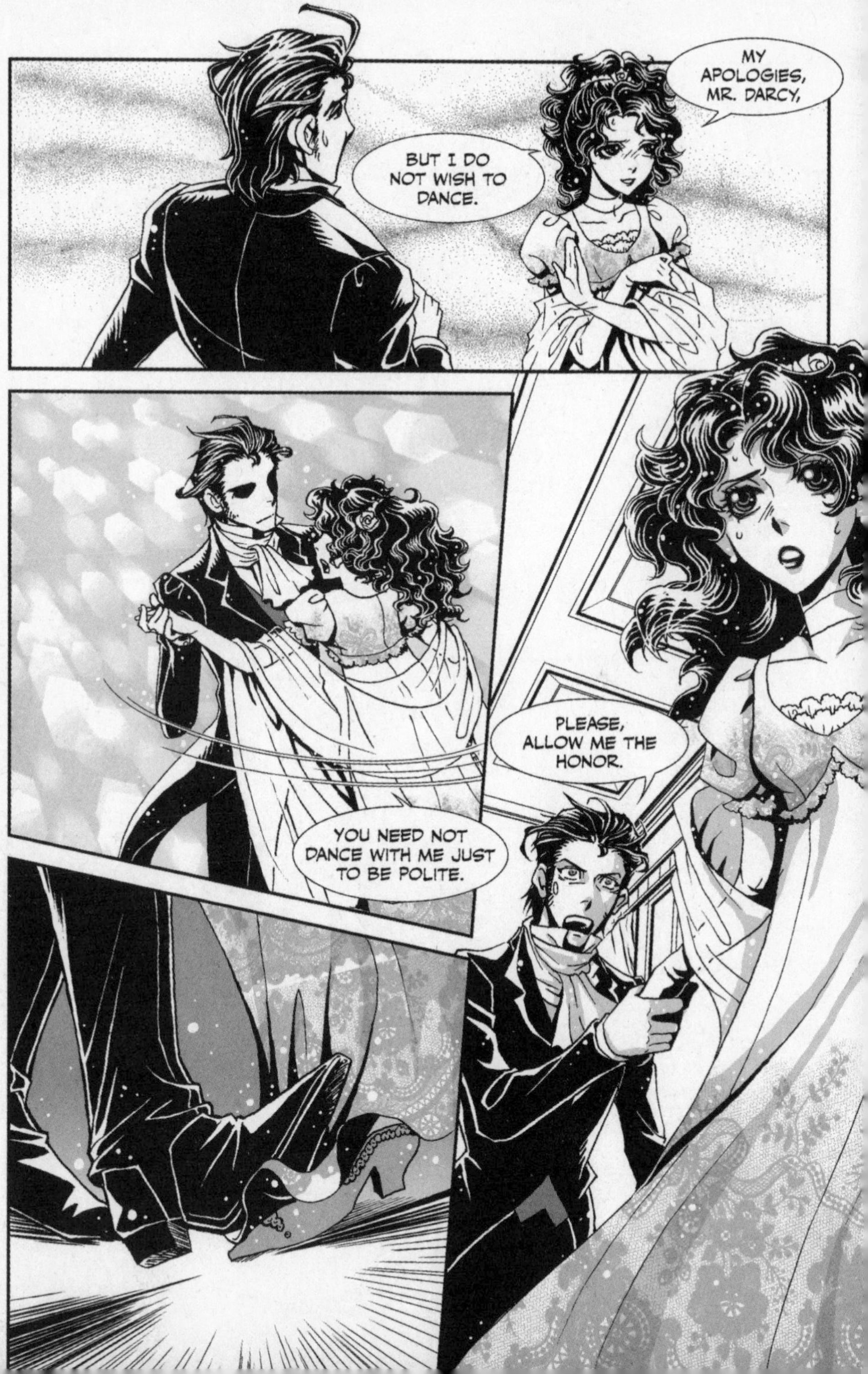
MY APOLOGIES, MR. DARCY,
BUT I DO NOT WISH TO DANCE.
PLEASE, ALLOW ME THE HONOR.
YOU NEED NOT DANCE WITH ME JUST TO BE POLITE.

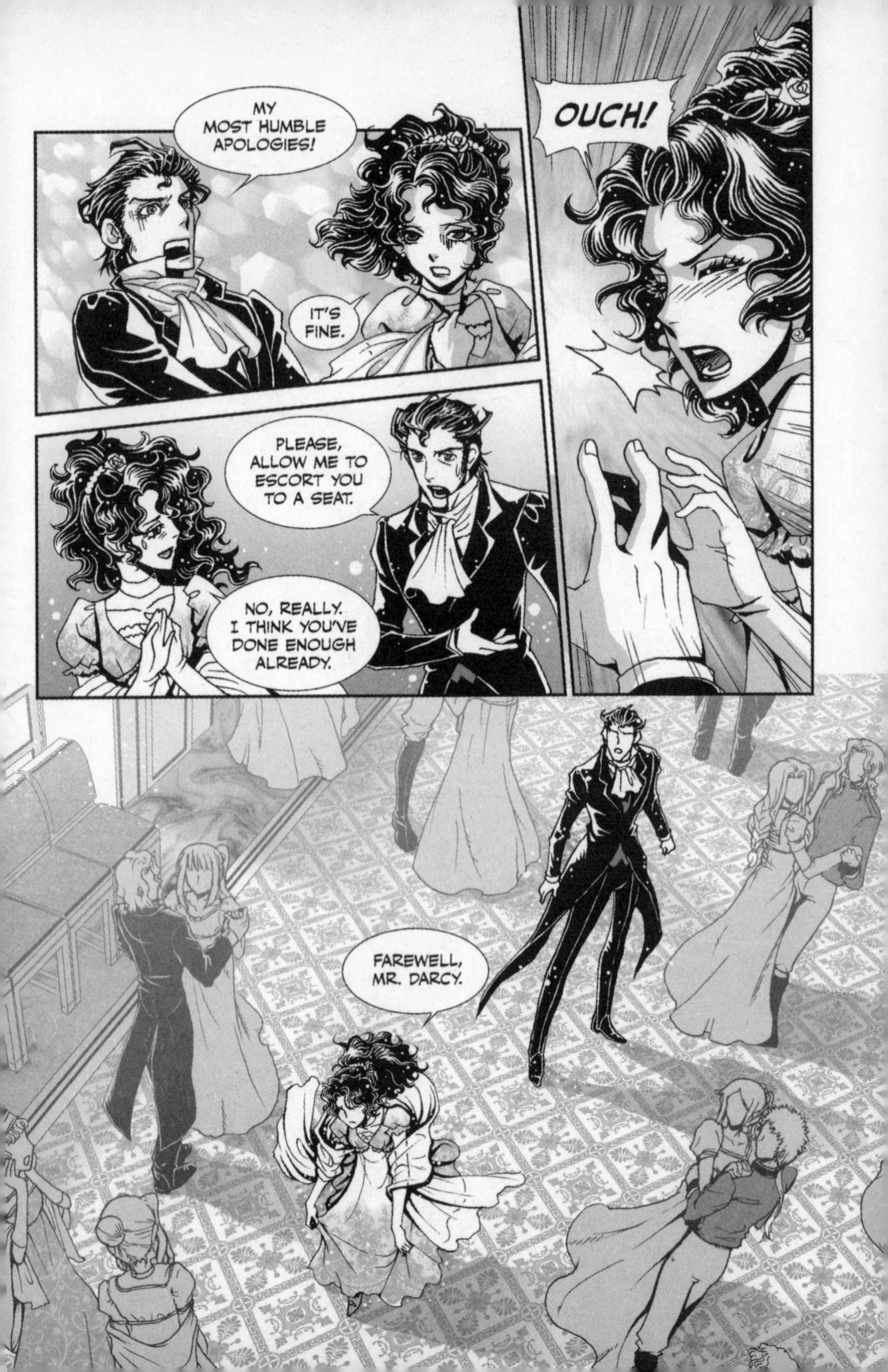
OUCH!
MY MOST HUMBLE APOLOGIES!
IT'S FINE.
PLEASE, ALLOW ME TO ESCORT YOU TO A SEAT.
NO, REALLY. I THINK YOU'VE DONE ENOUGH ALREADY.
FAREWELL, MR. DARCY.

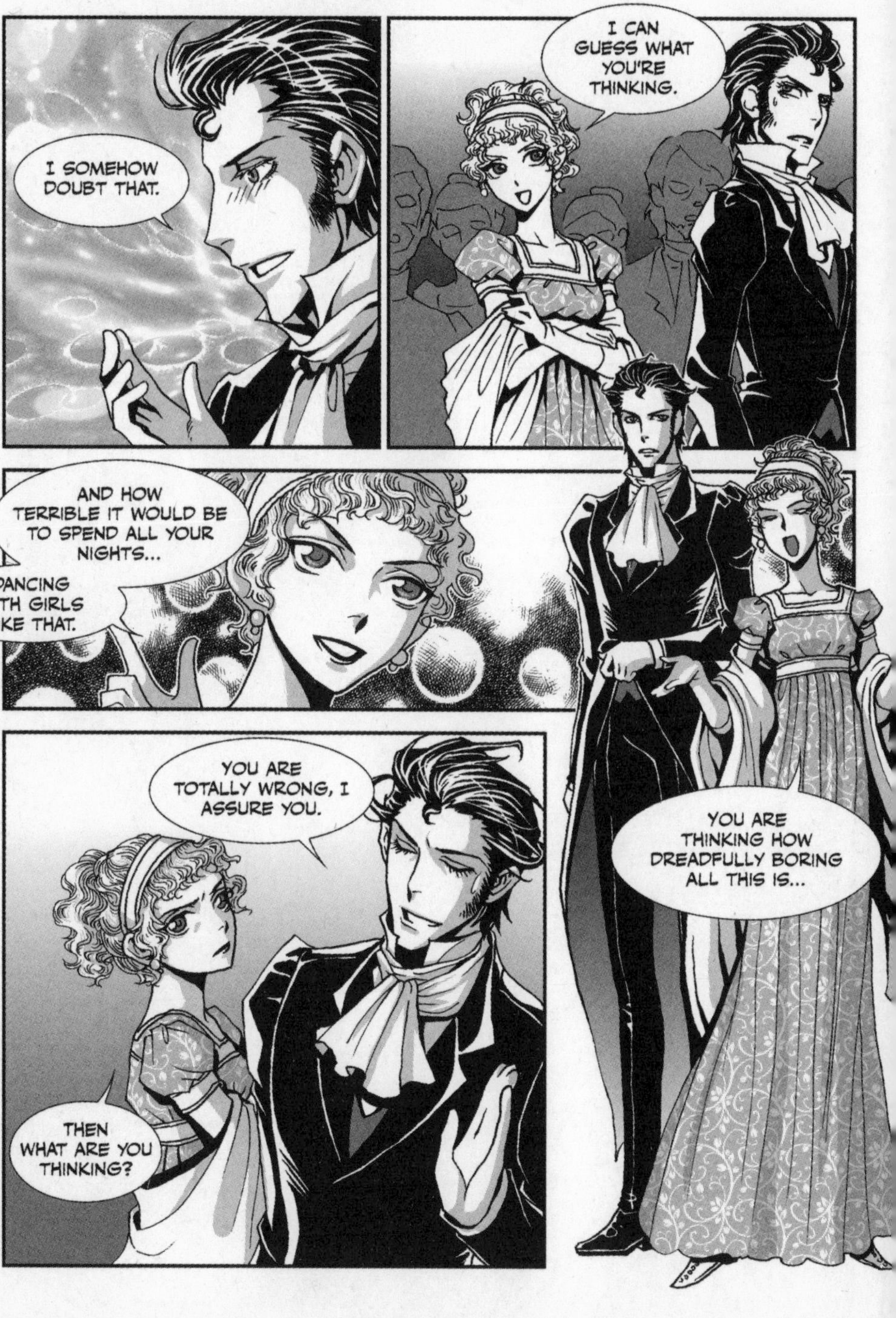
I CAN GUESS WHAT YOU'RE THINKING.
I SOMEHOW DOUBT THAT.
YOU ARE THINKING HOW DREADFULLY BORING ALL THIS IS...
AND HOW TERRIBLE IT WOULD BE TO SPEND ALL YOUR NIGHTS...
DANCING WITH GIRLS LIKE THAT.
YOU ARE TOTALLY WRONG, I ASSURE YOU.
THEN WHAT ARE YOU THINKING?

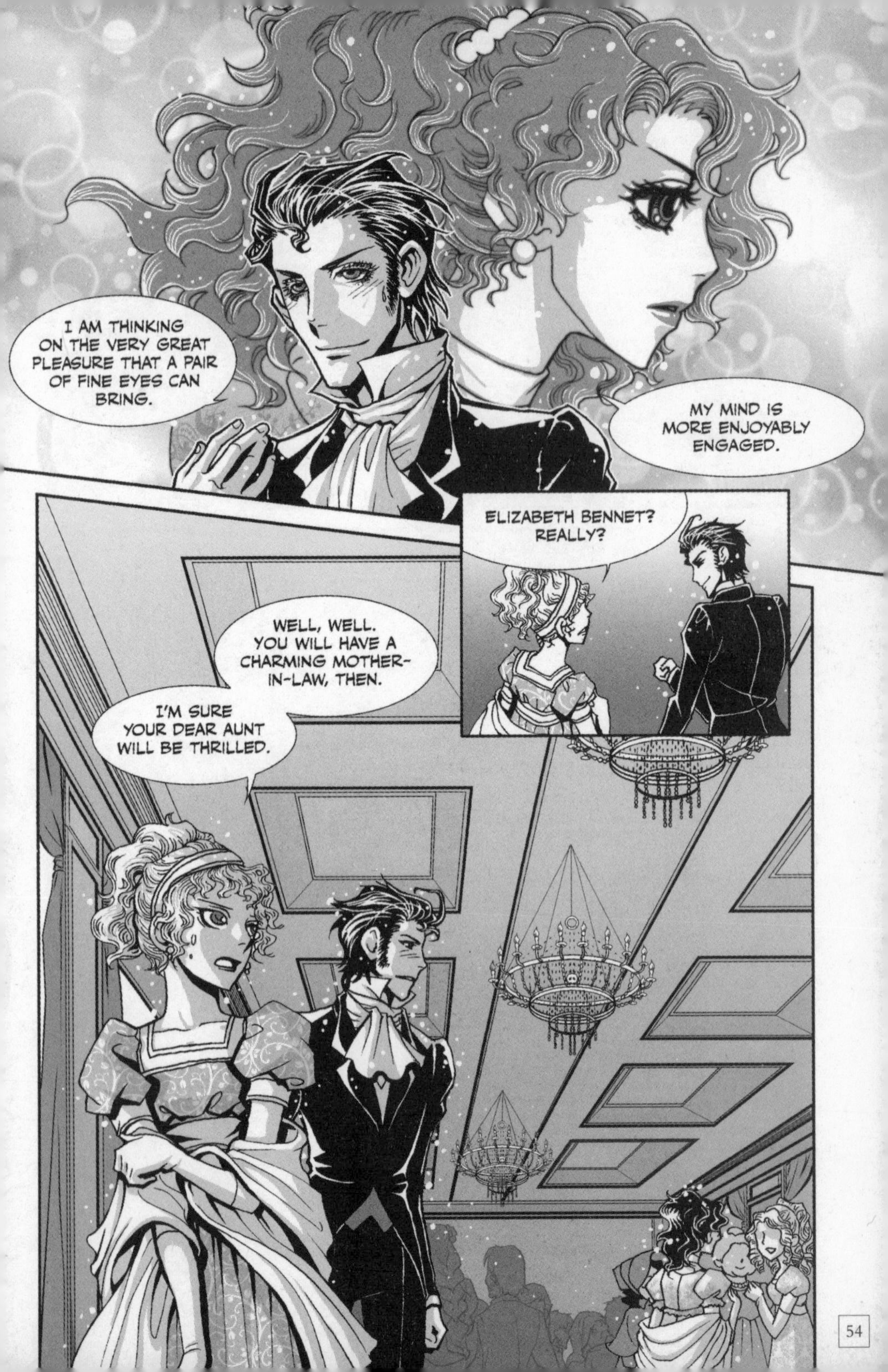
MY MIND IS MORE ENJOYABLY ENGAGED.
I AM THINKING ON THE VERY GREAT PLEASURE THAT A PAIR OF FINE EYES CAN BRING.
ELIZABETH BENNET? REALLY?
WELL, WELL. YOU WILL HAVE A CHARMING MOTHER-IN-LAW, THEN.
I'M SURE YOUR DEAR AUNT WILL BE THRILLED.

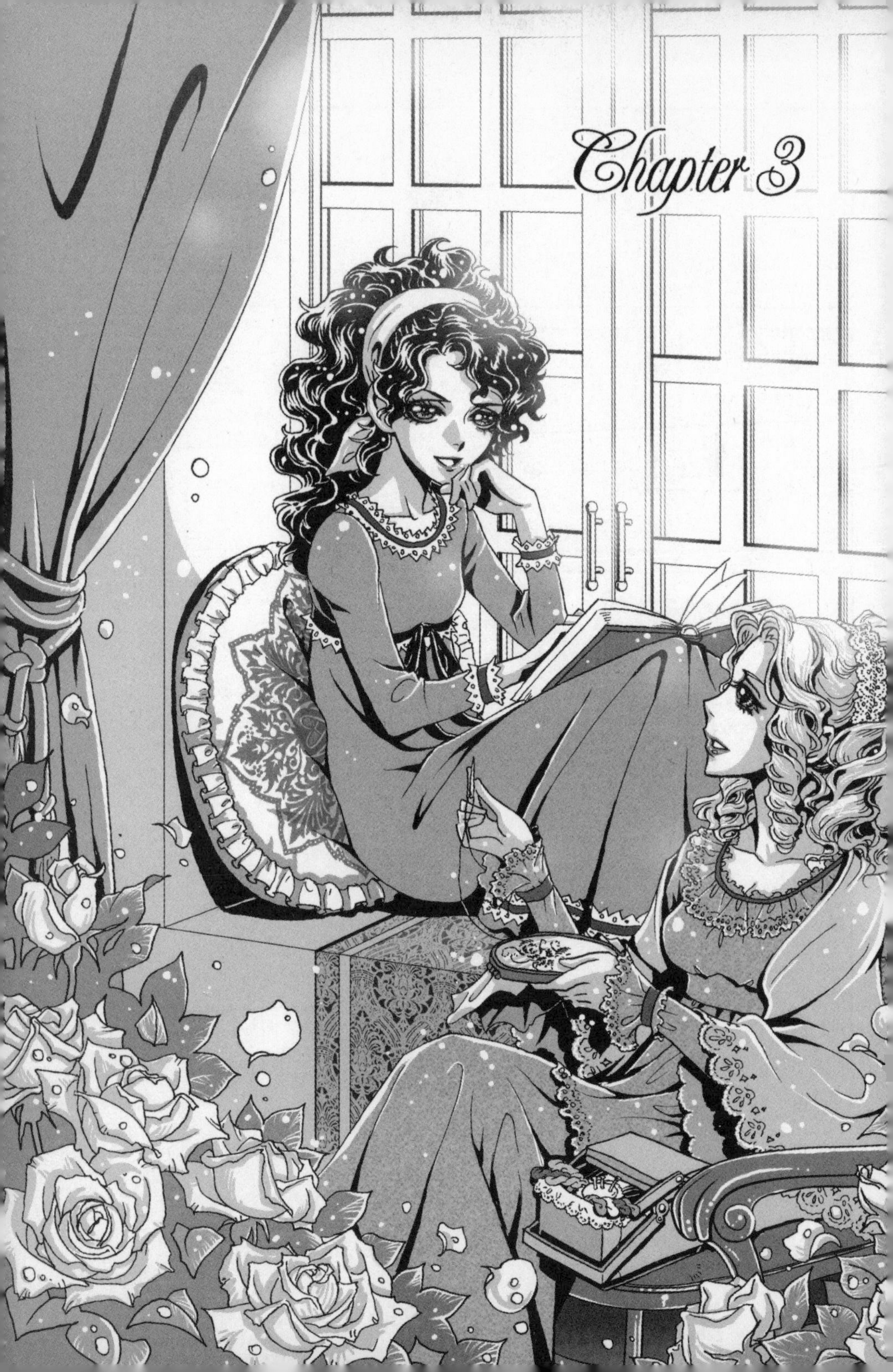
Chapter 3

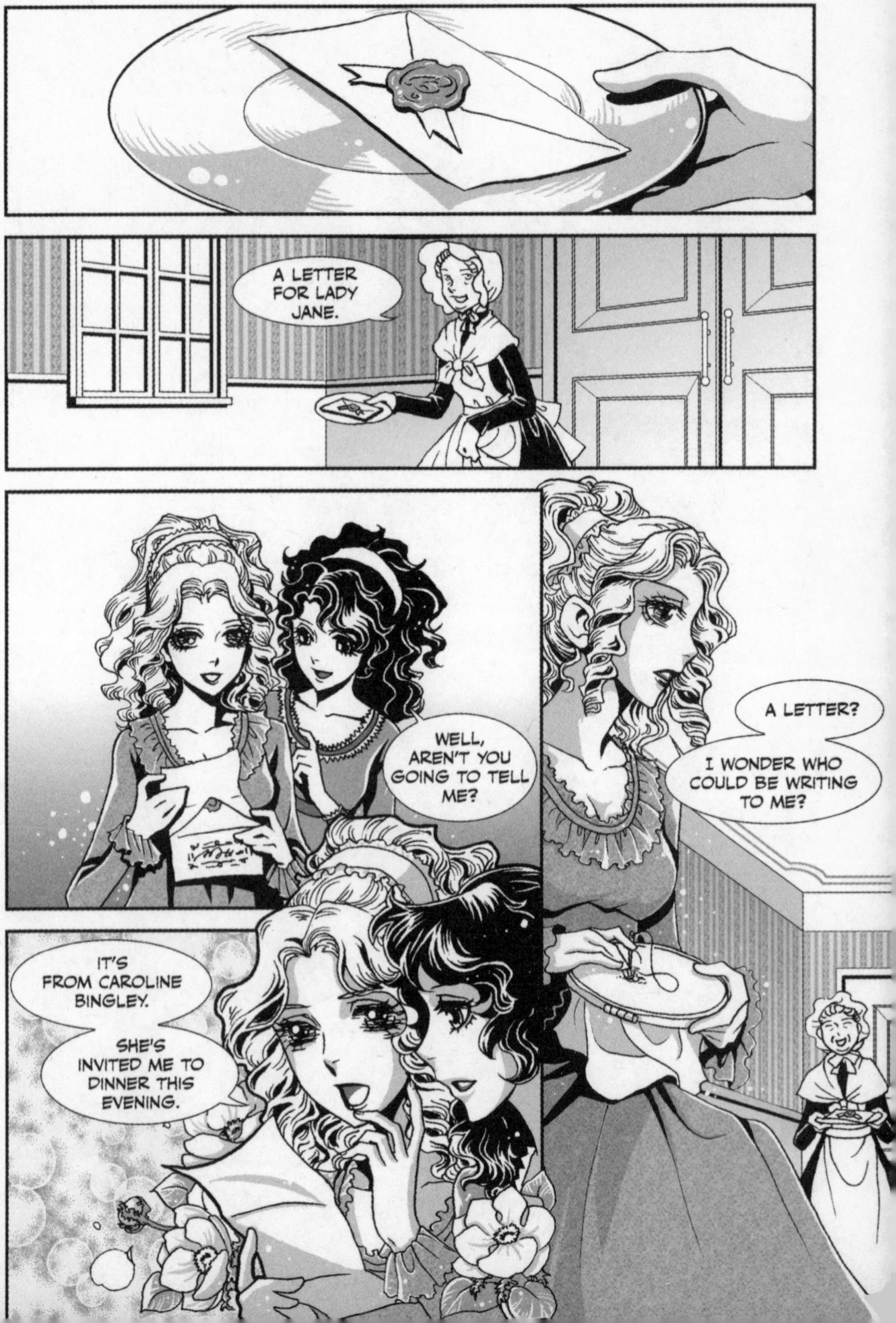
A LETTER FOR LADY JANE.
A LETTER?
I WONDER WHO COULD BE WRITING TO ME?
WELL, AREN'T YOU GOING TO TELL ME?
IT'S FROM CAROLINE BINGLEY.
SHE'S INVITED ME TO DINNER THIS EVENING.

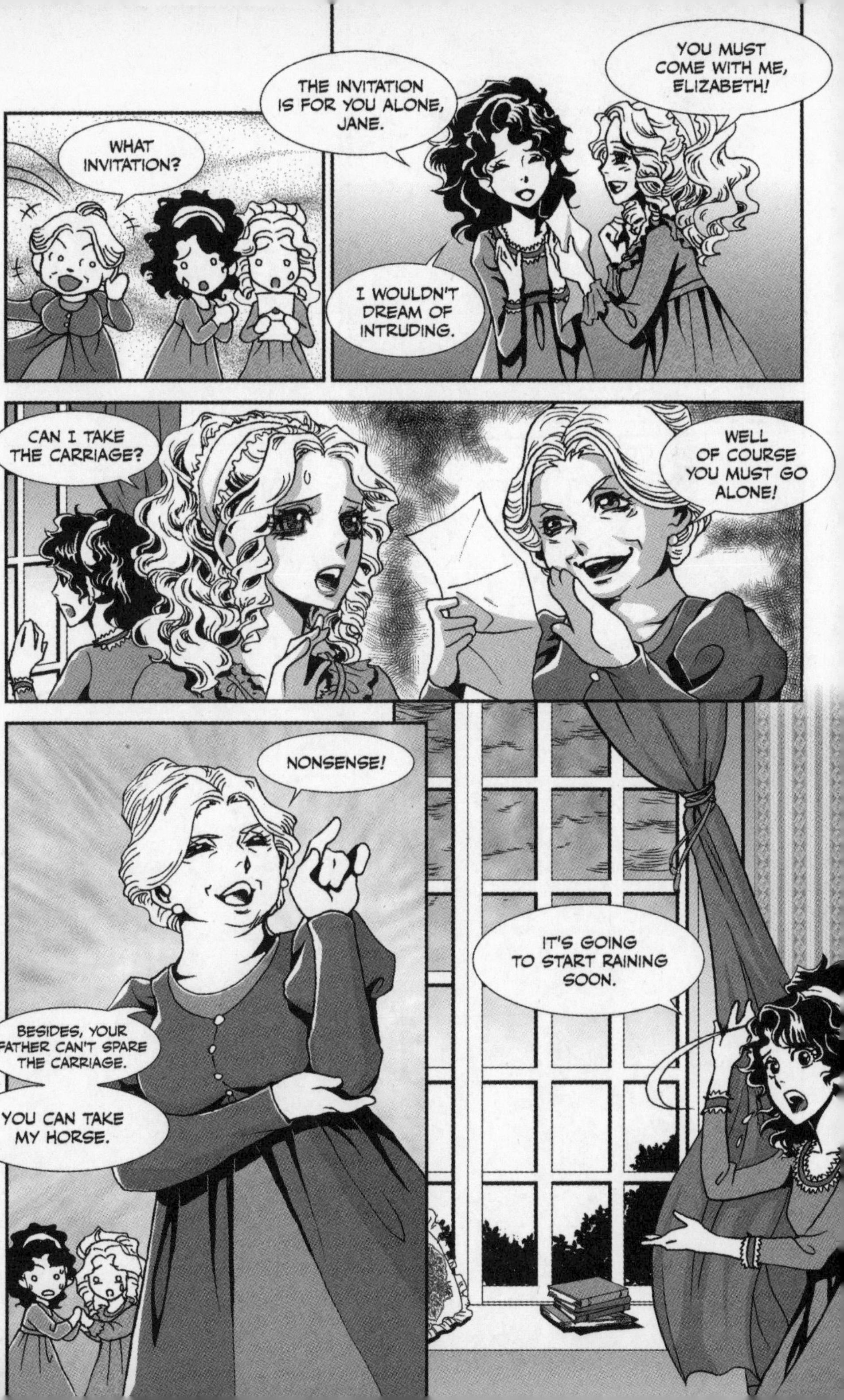
YOU MUST COME WITH ME, ELIZABETH!
THE INVITATION IS FOR YOU ALONE, JANE.
I WOULDN'T DREAM OF INTRUDING.
WHAT INVITATION?
WELL OF COURSE YOU MUST GO ALONE!
CAN I TAKE THE CARRIAGE?
IT'S GOING TO START RAINING SOON.
NONSENSE!
BESIDES, YOUR FATHER CAN'T SPARE THE CARRIAGE.
YOU CAN TAKE MY HORSE.

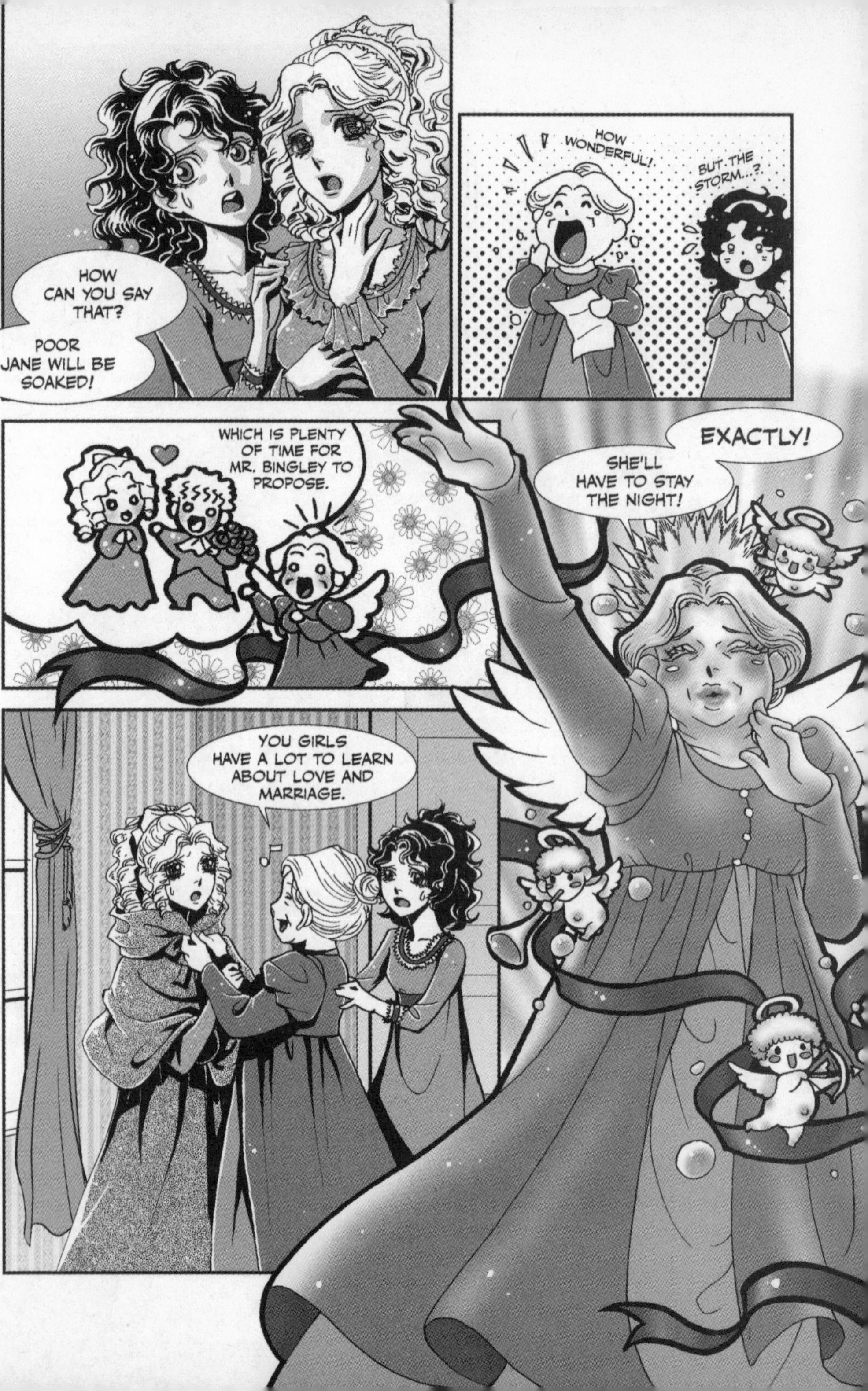
HOW WONDERFUL!
BUT THE STORM...?
HOW CAN YOU SAY THAT?
POOR JANE WILL BE SOAKED!
EXACTLY!
SHE'LL HAVE TO STAY THE NIGHT!
WHICH IS PLENTY OF TIME FOR MR. BINGLEY TO PROPOSE.
YOU GIRLS HAVE A LOT TO LEARN ABOUT LOVE AND MARRIAGE.

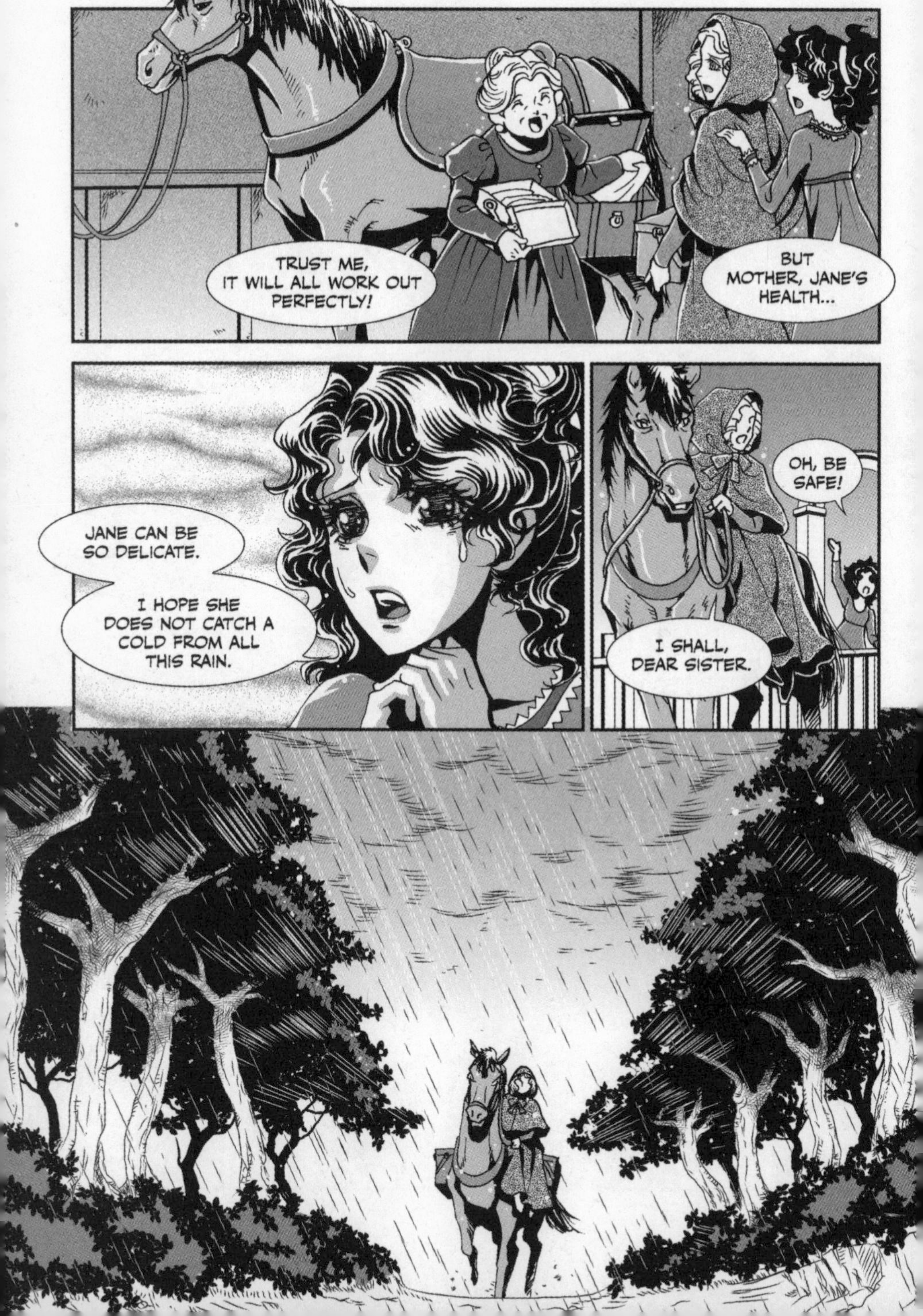
BUT MOTHER, JANE'S HEALTH...
TRUST ME, IT WILL ALL WORK OUT PERFECTLY!
OH, BE SAFE!
I SHALL, DEAR SISTER.
JANE CAN BE SO DELICATE.
I HOPE SHE DOES NOT CATCH A COLD FROM ALL THIS RAIN.

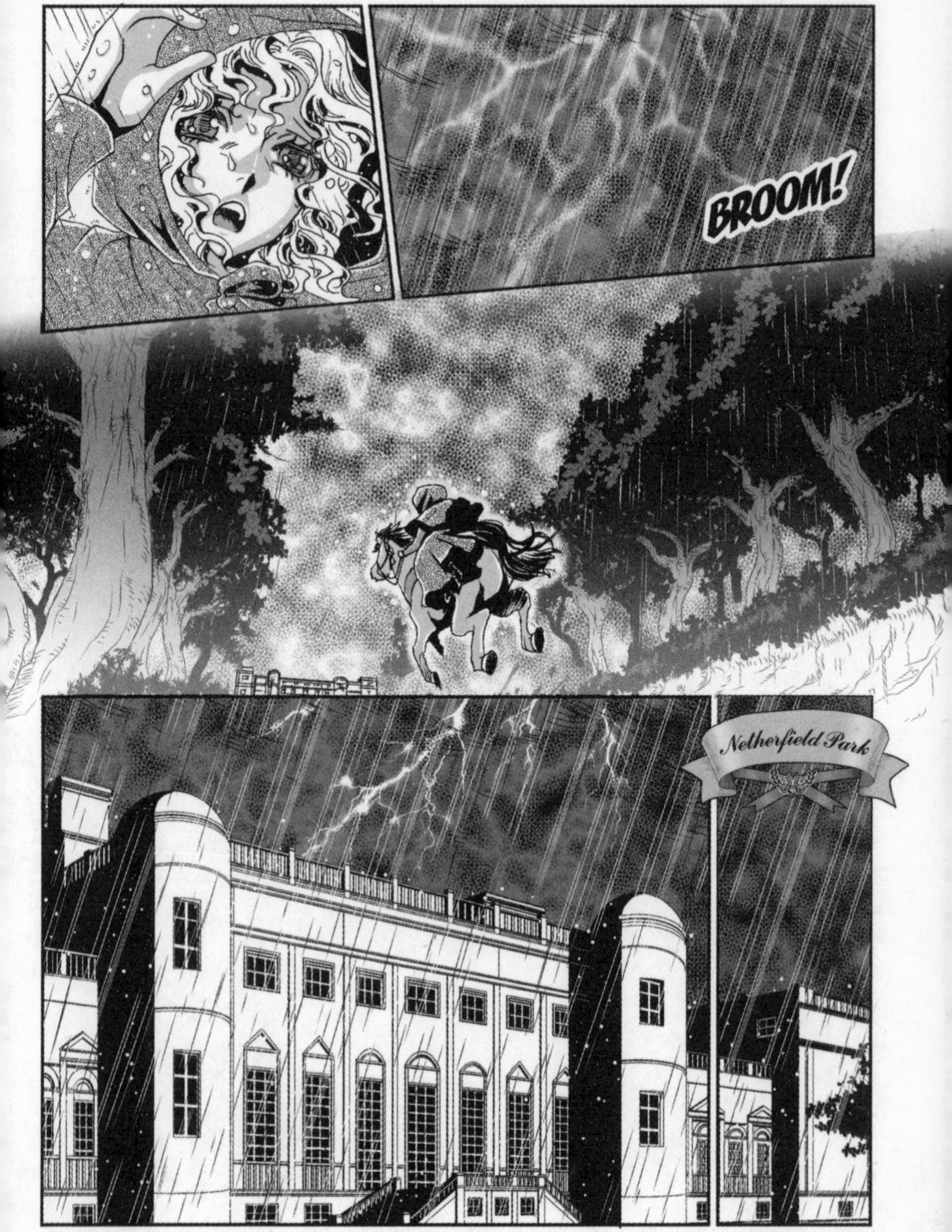
BROOM!
Netherfield Park

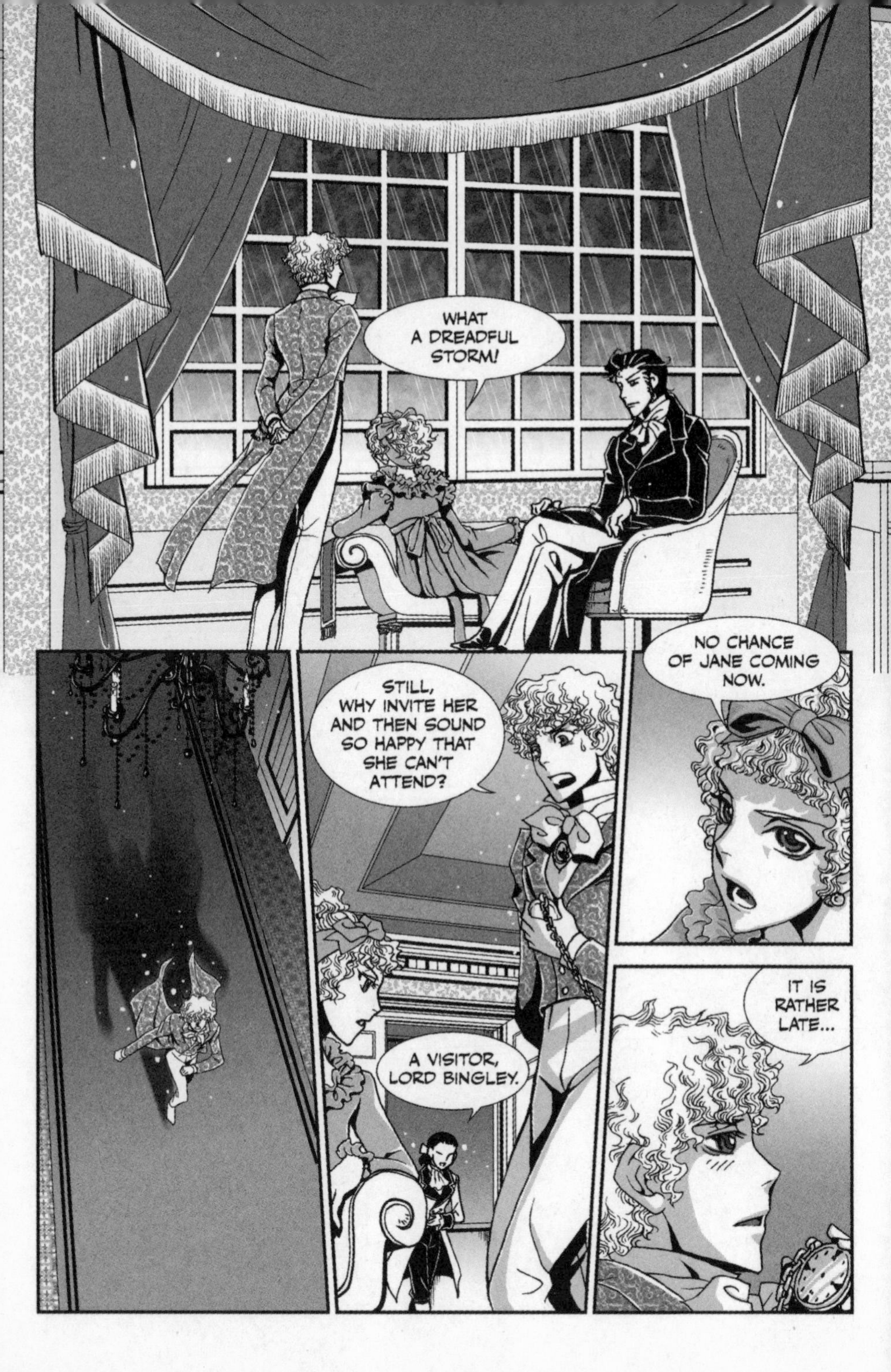
WHAT A DREADFUL STORM!
NO CHANCE OF JANE COMING NOW.
IT IS RATHER LATE...
STILL, WHY INVITE HER AND THEN SOUND SO HAPPY THAT SHE CAN'T ATTEND?
A VISITOR, LORD BINGLEY.

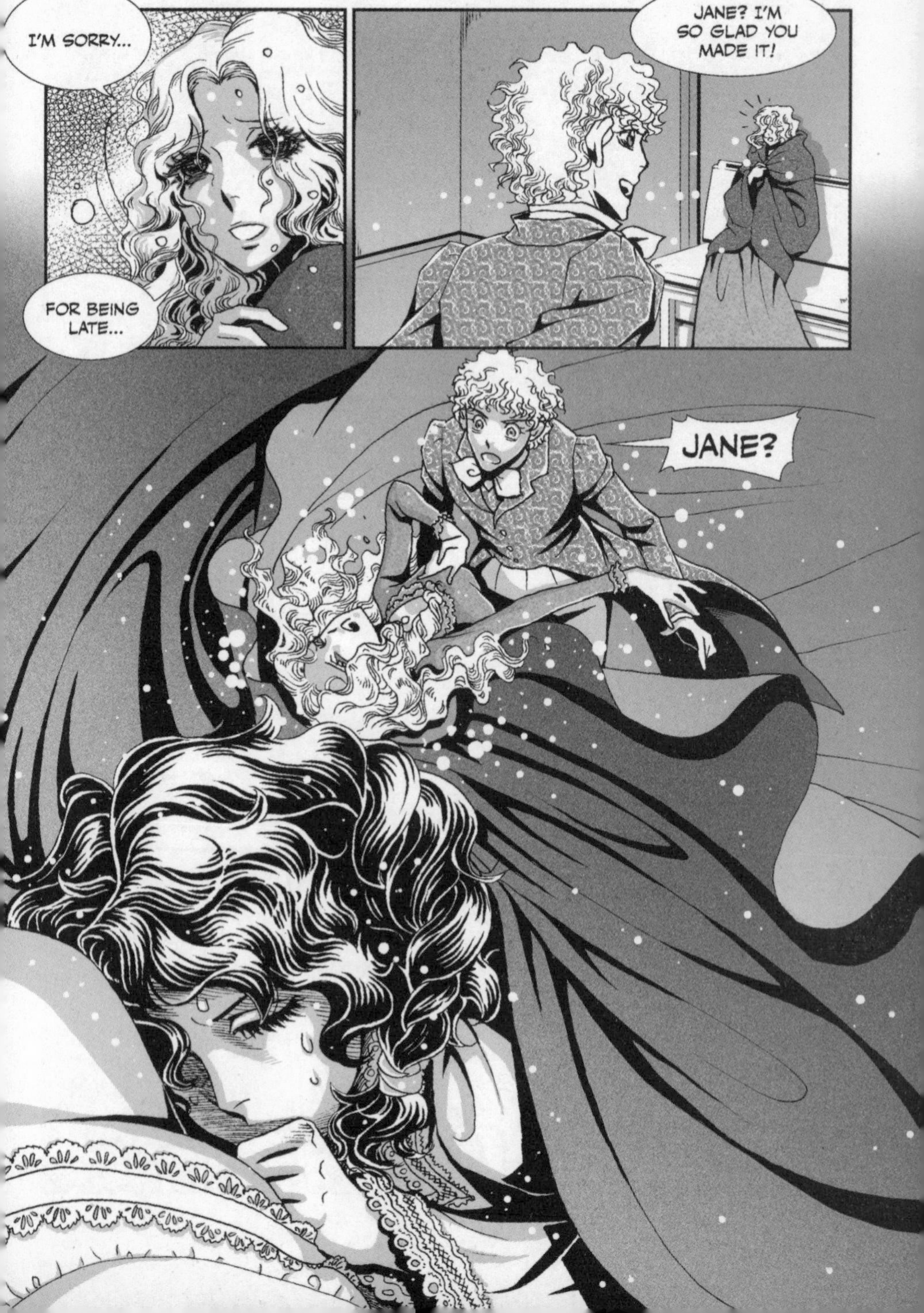
JANE? I'M SO GLAD YOU MADE IT!
I'M SORRY...
FOR BEING LATE...
JANE?

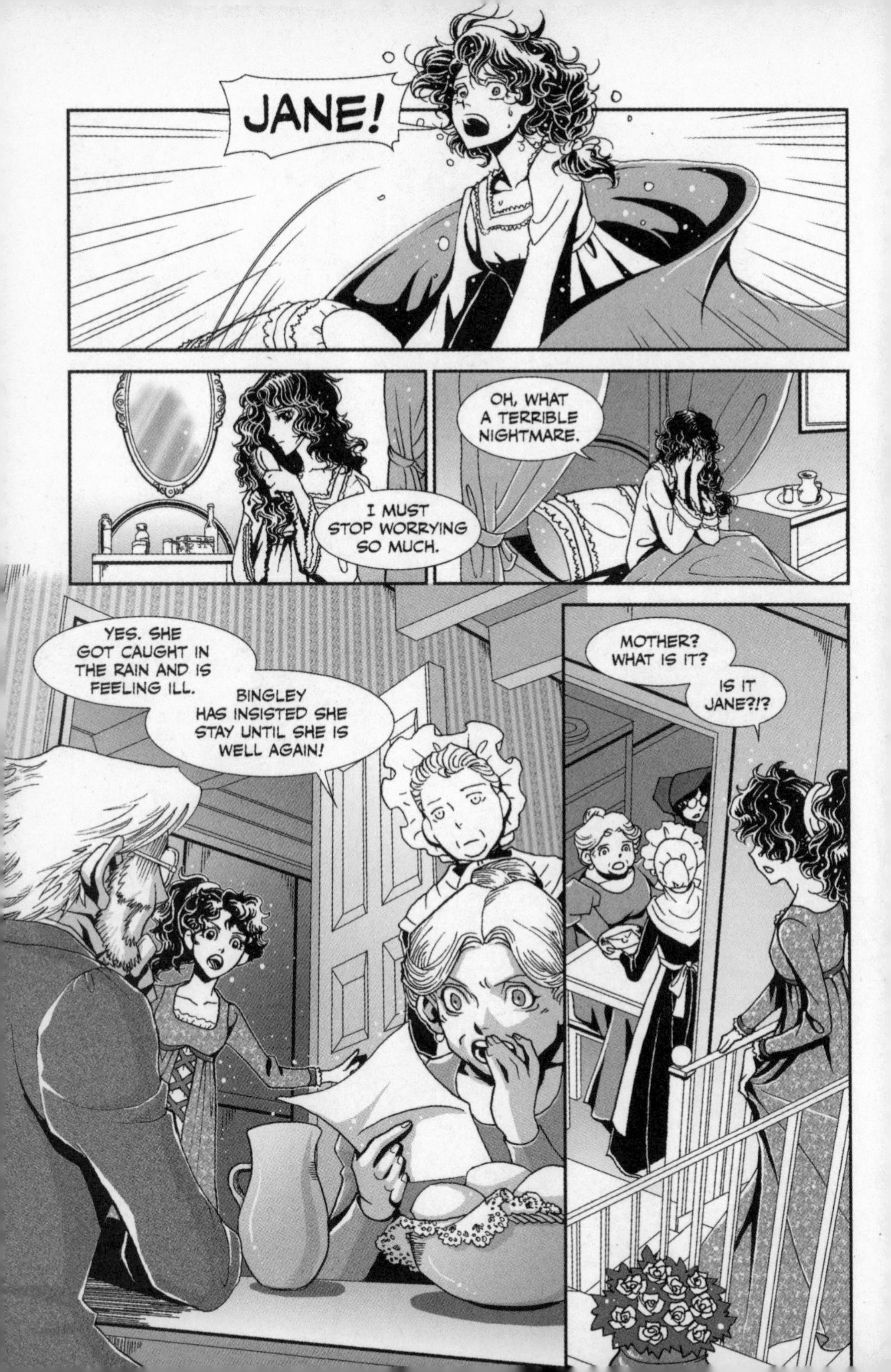
JANE!
OH, WHAT A TERRIBLE NIGHTMARE.
I MUST STOP WORRYING SO MUCH.
MOTHER? WHAT IS IT?
IS IT JANE?!?
YES. SHE GOT CAUGHT IN THE RAIN AND IS FEELING ILL.
BINGLEY HAS INSISTED SHE STAY UNTIL SHE IS WELL AGAIN!

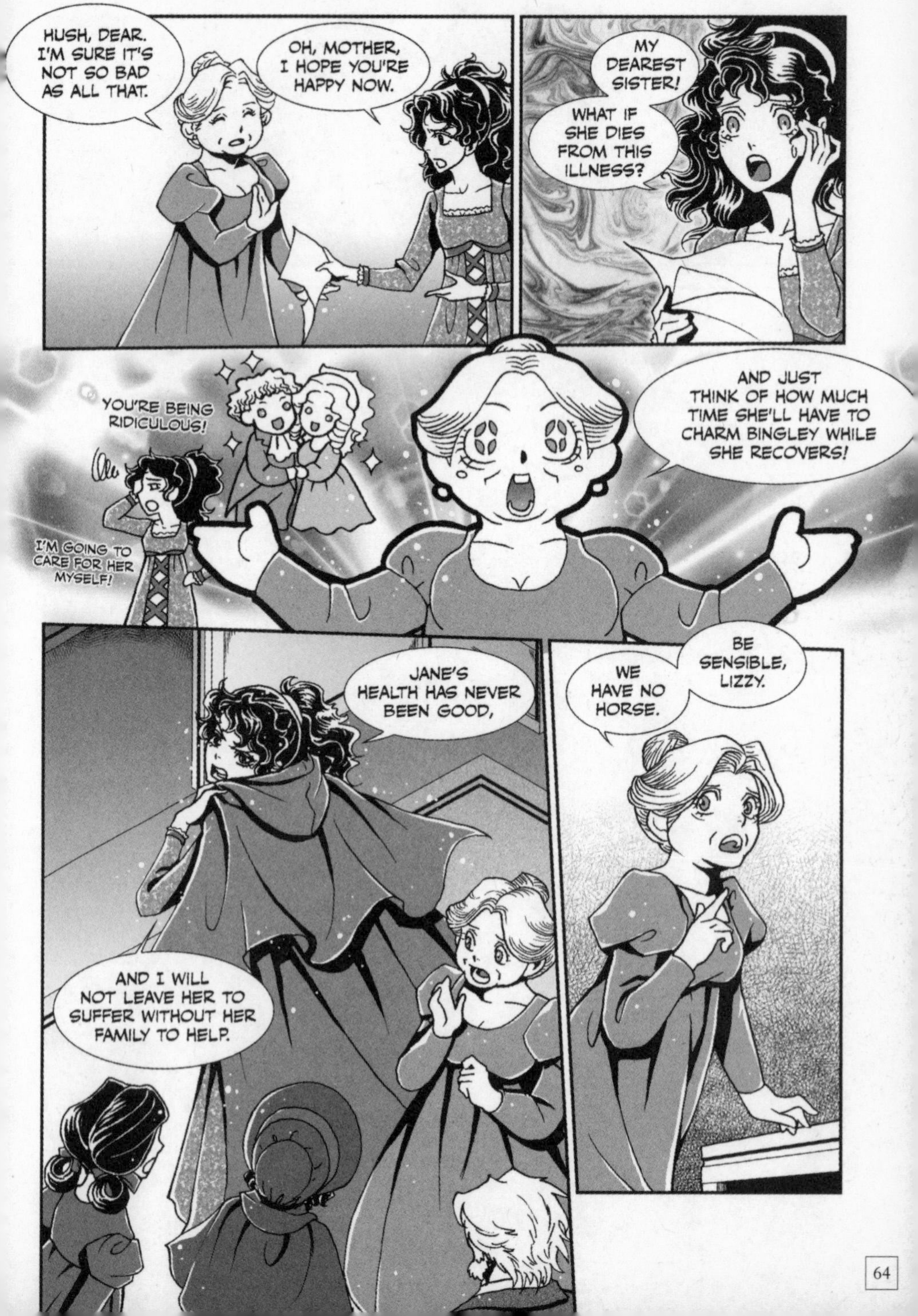
MY DEAREST SISTER!
WHAT IF SHE DIES FROM THIS ILLNESS?
OH, MOTHER, I HOPE YOU'RE HAPPY NOW.
HUSH, DEAR. I'M SURE IT'S NOT SO BAD AS ALL THAT.
AND JUST THINK OF HOW MUCH TIME SHE'LL HAVE TO CHARM BINGLEY WHILE SHE RECOVERS!
YOU'RE BEING RIDICULOUS!
I'M GOING TO CARE FOR HER MYSELF!
BE SENSIBLE, LIZZY.
WE HAVE NO HORSE.
JANE'S HEALTH HAS NEVER BEEN GOOD,
AND I WILL NOT LEAVE HER TO SUFFER WITHOUT HER FAMILY TO HELP.

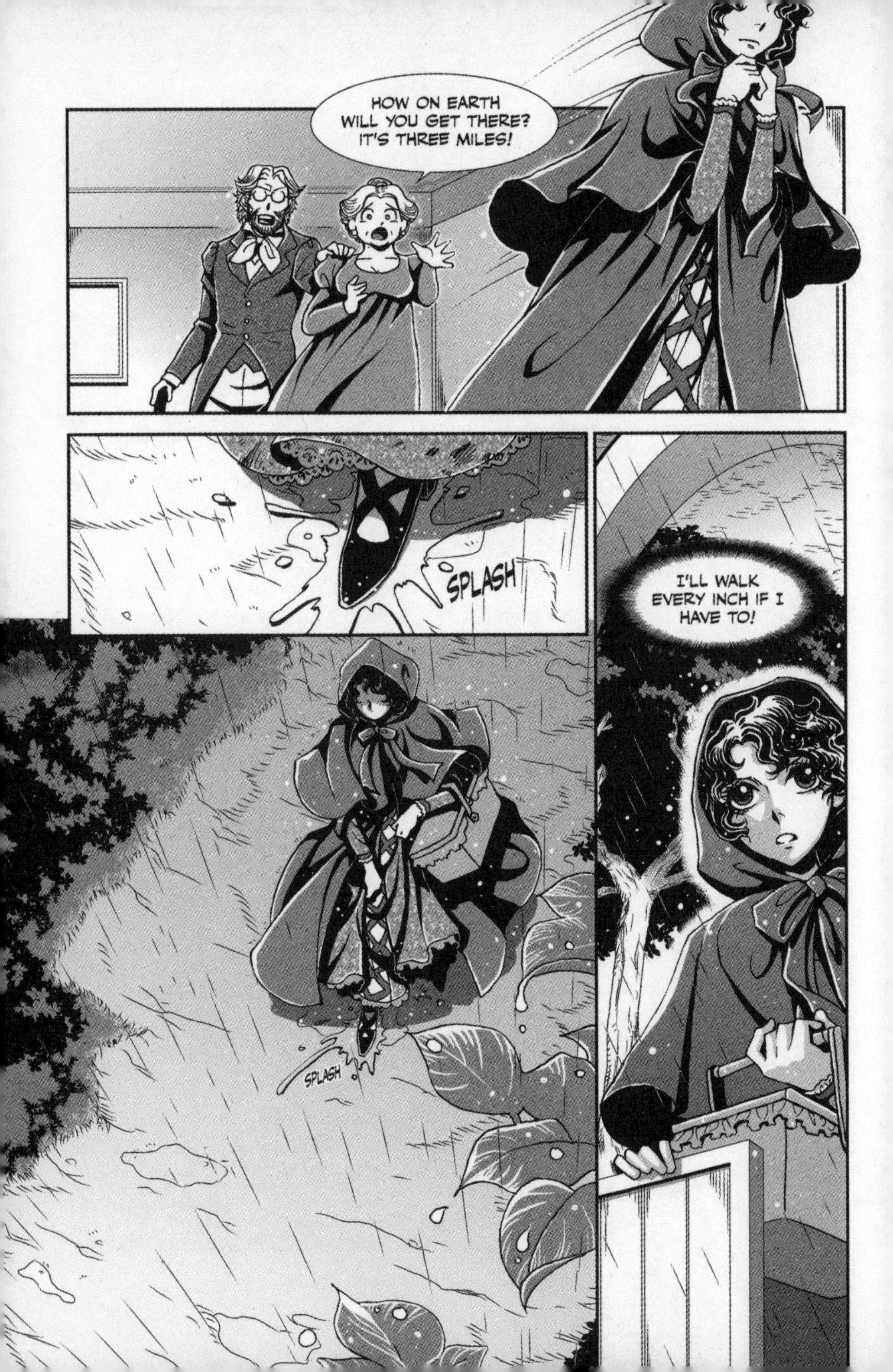
HOW ON EARTH WILL YOU GET THERE? IT'S THREE MILES!
I'LL WALK EVERY INCH IF I HAVE TO!
SPLASH
SPLASH

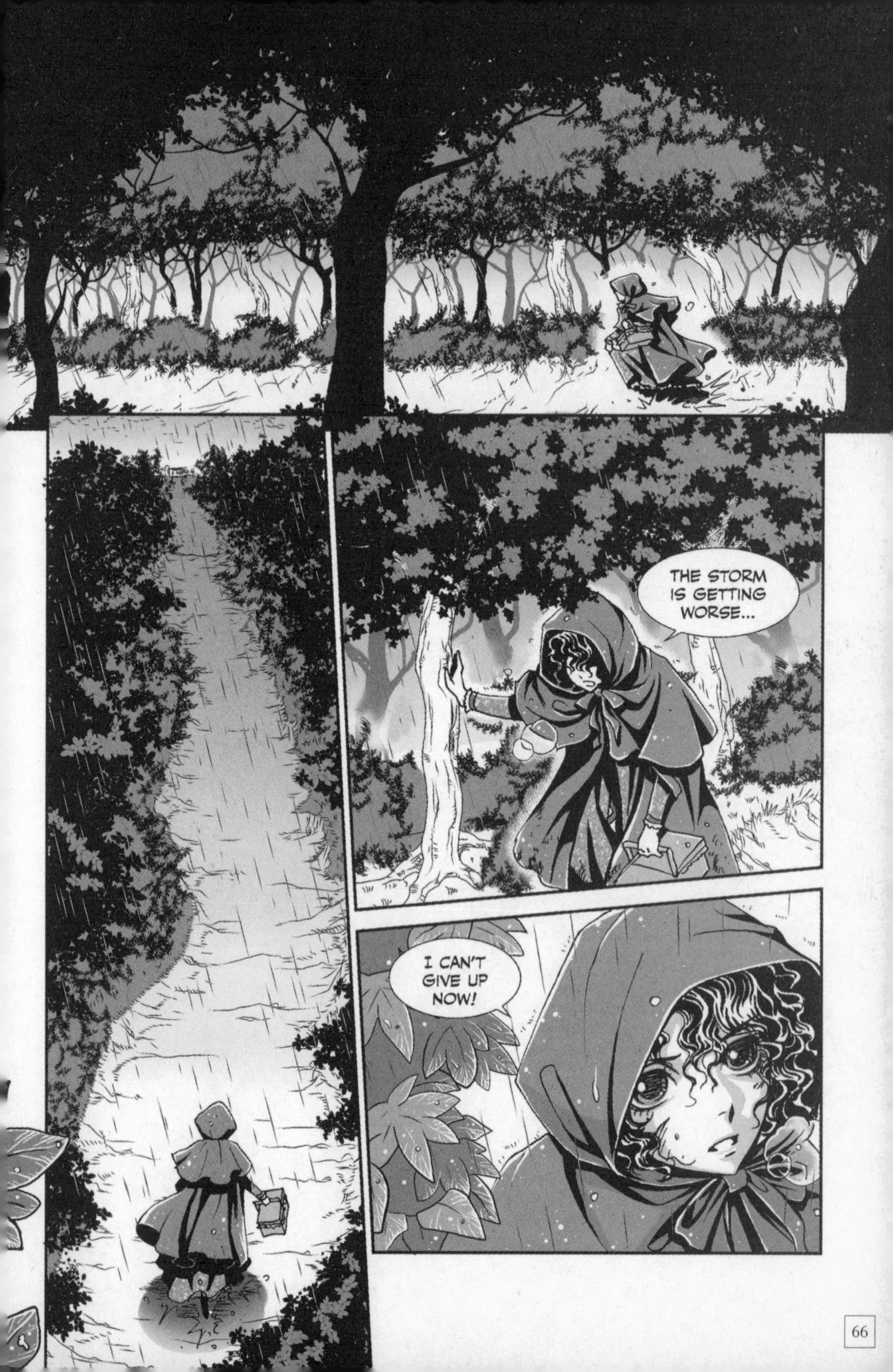
THE STORM IS GETTING WORSE...
I CAN'T GIVE UP NOW!

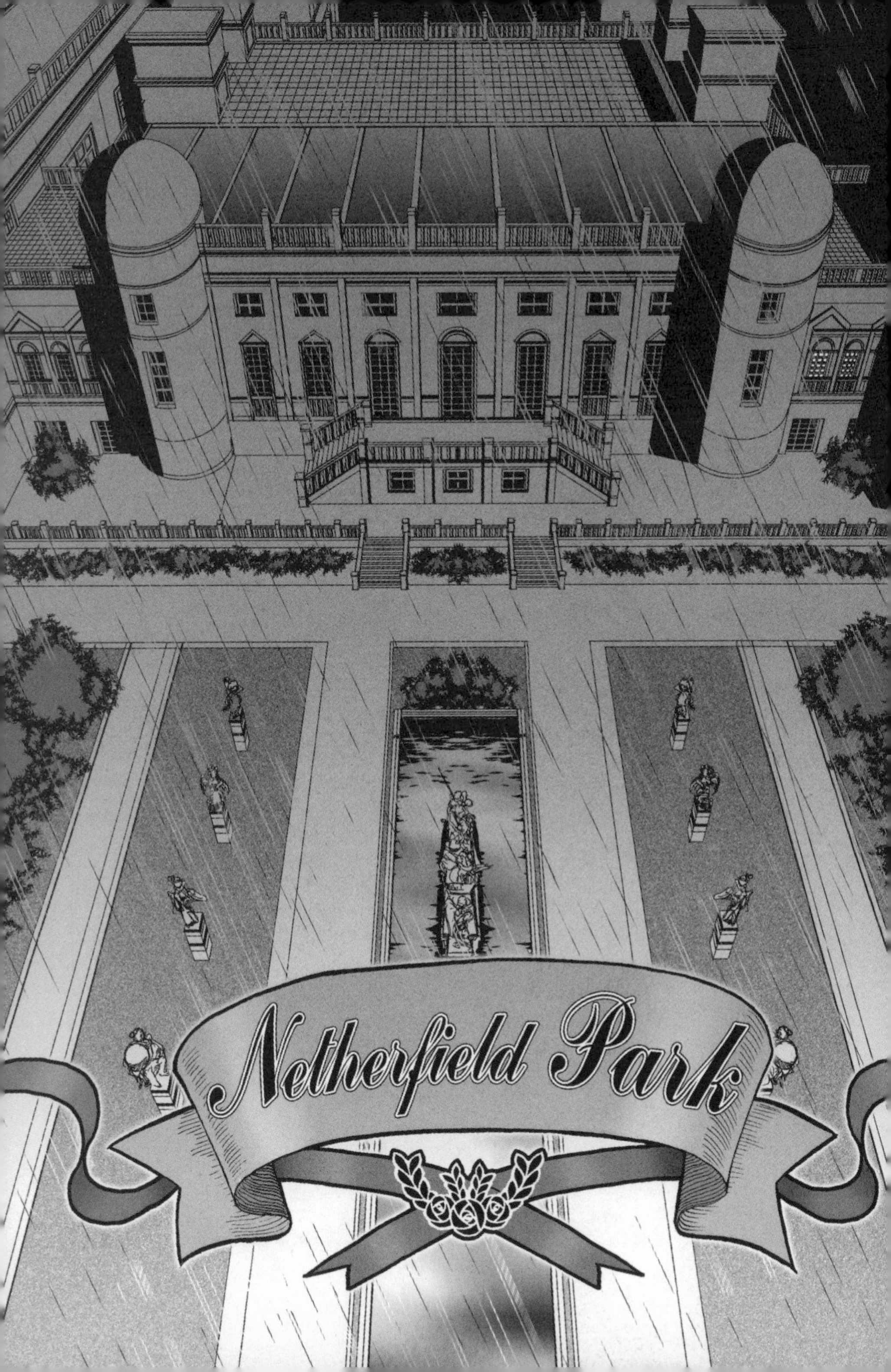
Netherfield Park

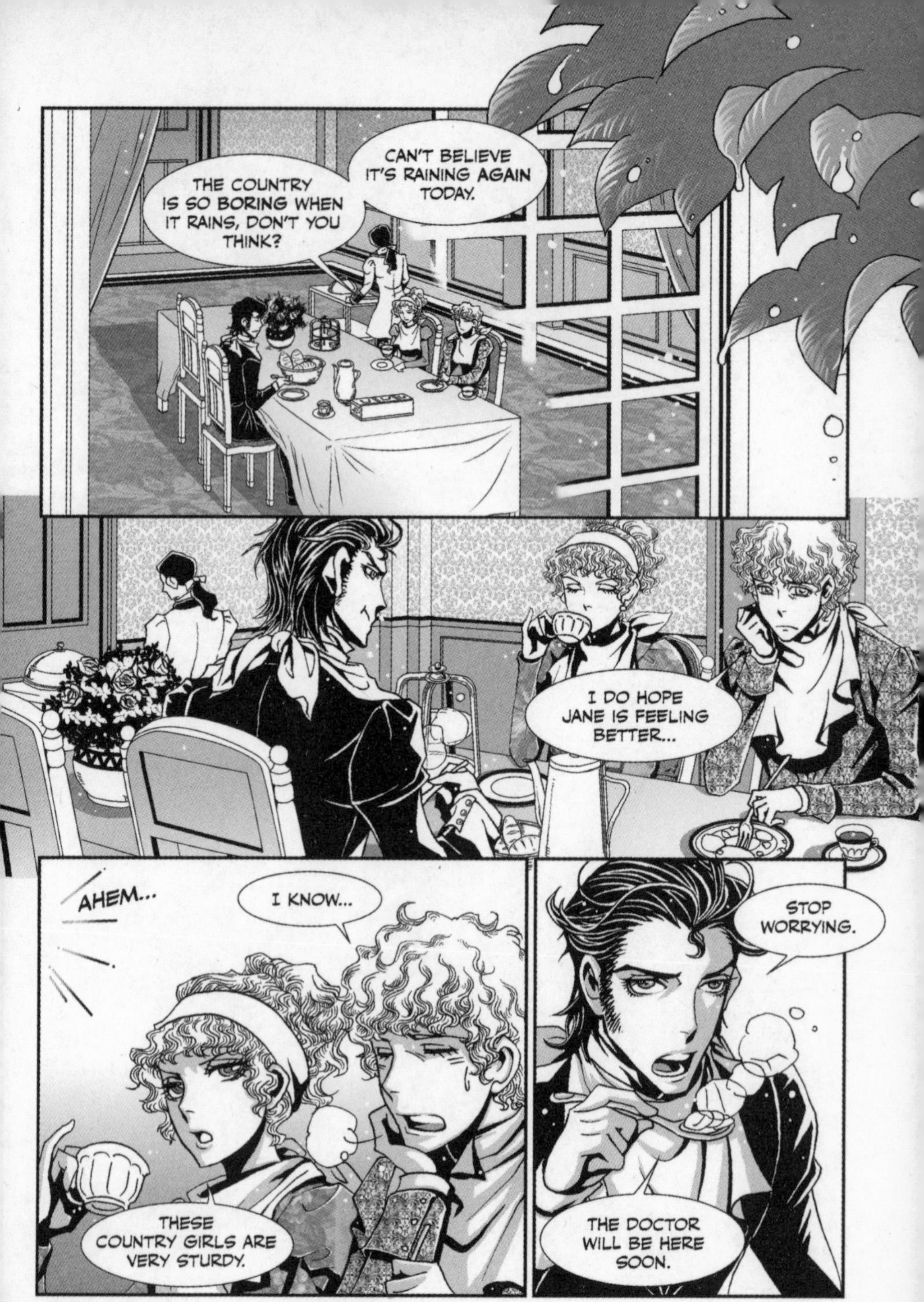
CAN'T BELIEVE IT'S RAINING AGAIN TODAY.
THE COUNTRY IS SO BORING WHEN IT RAINS, DON'T YOU THINK?
I DO HOPE JANE IS FEELING BETTER...
STOP WORRYING.
THE DOCTOR WILL BE HERE SOON.
I KNOW...
AHEM...
THESE COUNTRY GIRLS ARE VERY STURDY.

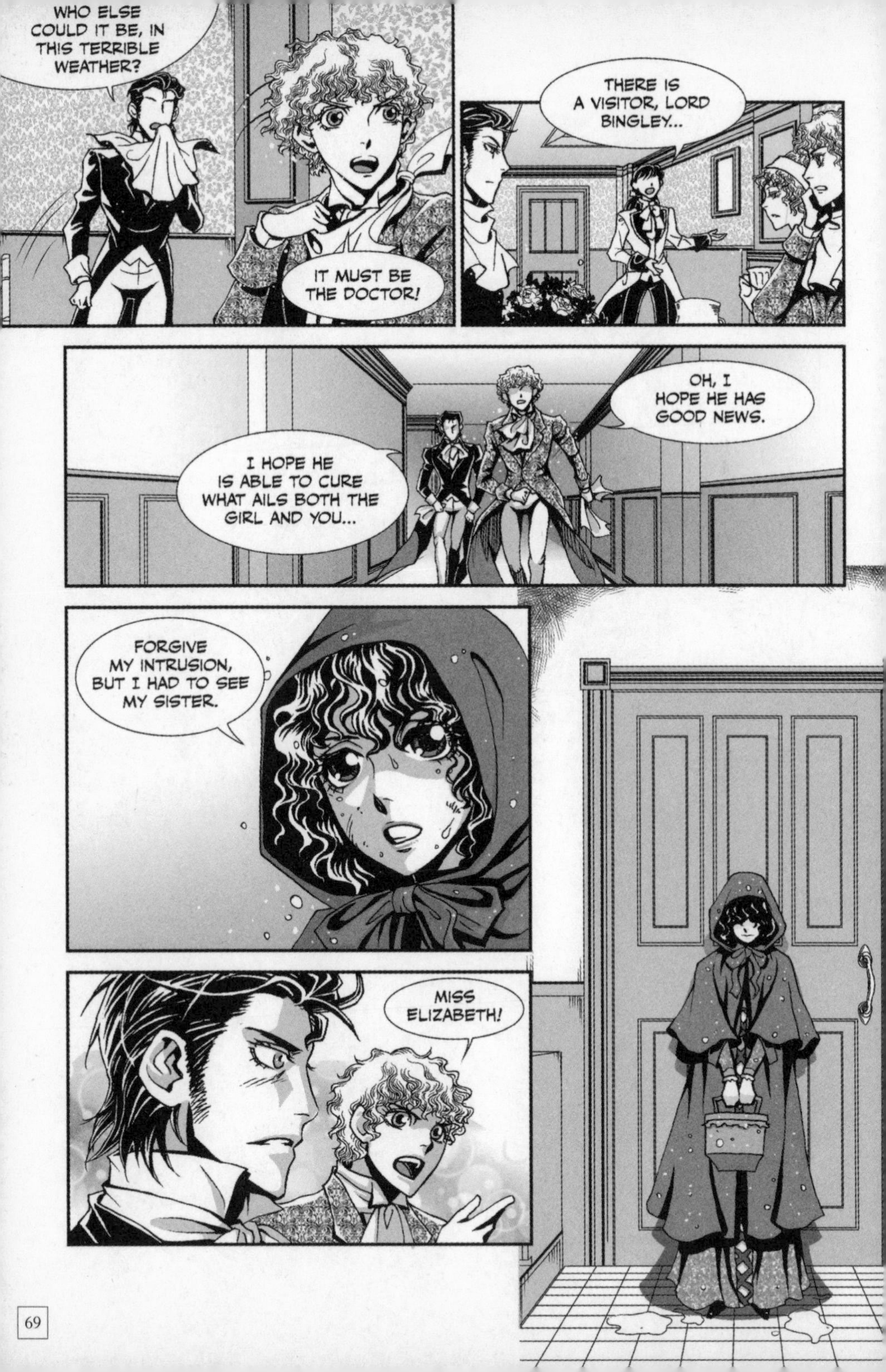
THERE IS A VISITOR, LORD BINGLEY...
WHO ELSE COULD IT BE, IN THIS TERRIBLE WEATHER?
IT MUST BE THE DOCTOR!
OH, I HOPE HE HAS GOOD NEWS.
I HOPE HE IS ABLE TO CURE WHAT AILS BOTH THE GIRL AND YOU...
FORGIVE MY INTRUSION, BUT I HAD TO SEE MY SISTER.
MISS ELIZABETH!

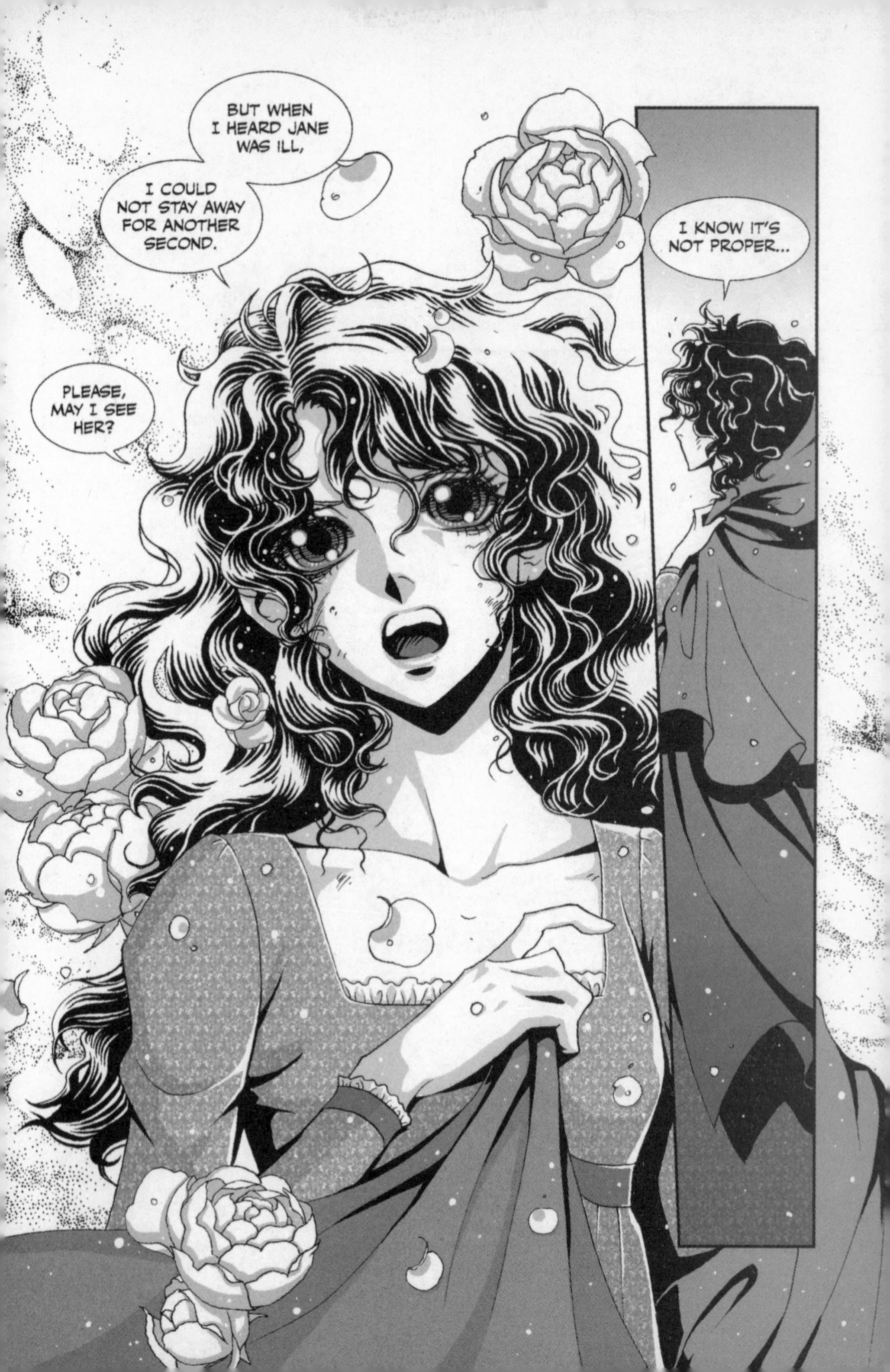
I KNOW IT'S NOT PROPER...
BUT WHEN I HEARD JANE WAS ILL,
I COULD NOT STAY AWAY FOR ANOTHER SECOND.
PLEASE, MAY I SEE HER?

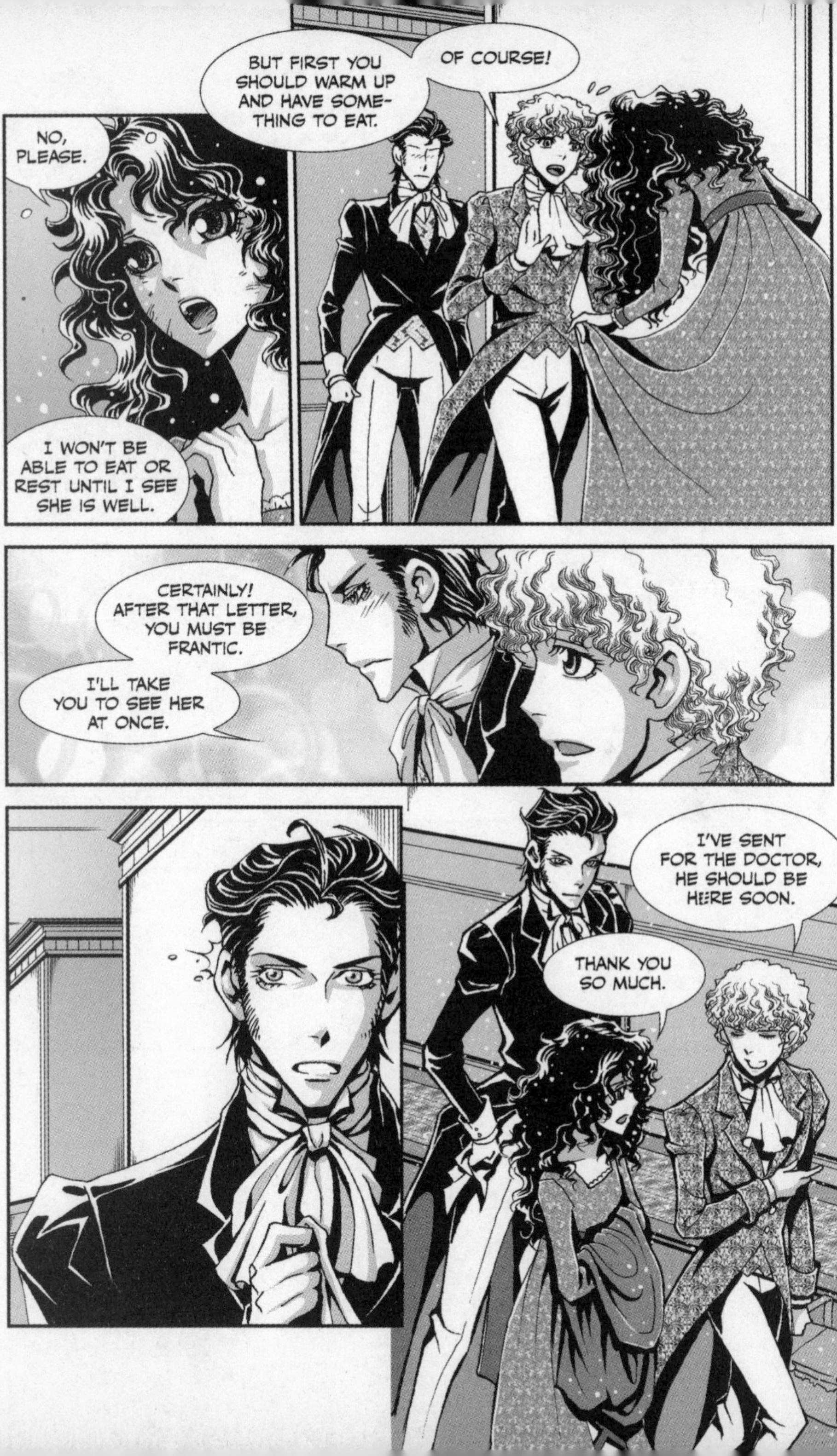
OF COURSE!
BUT FIRST YOU SHOULD WARM UP AND HAVE SOME-THING TO EAT.
NO, PLEASE.
I WON'T BE ABLE TO EAT OR REST UNTIL I SEE SHE IS WELL.
CERTAINLY! AFTER THAT LETTER, YOU MUST BE FRANTIC.
I'LL TAKE YOU TO SEE HER AT ONCE.
I'VE SENT FOR THE DOCTOR, HE SHOULD BE HERE SOON.
THANK YOU SO MUCH.

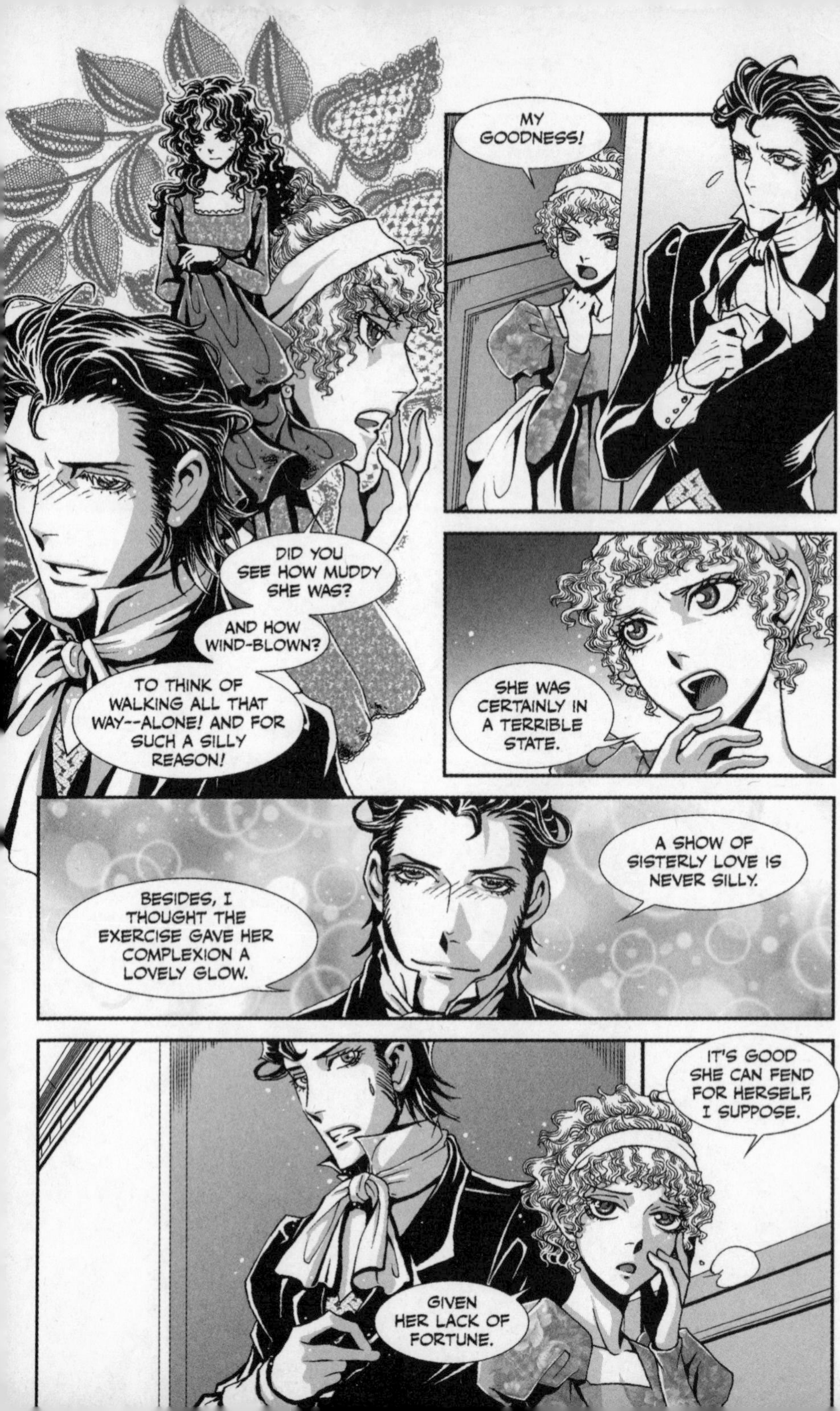
MY GOODNESS!
SHE WAS CERTAINLY IN A TERRIBLE STATE.
DID YOU SEE HOW MUDDY SHE WAS?
AND HOW WIND-BLOWN?
TO THINK OF WALKING ALL THAT WAY--ALONE! AND FOR SUCH A SILLY REASON!
A SHOW OF SISTERLY LOVE IS NEVER SILLY.
BESIDES, I THOUGHT THE EXERCISE GAVE HER COMPLEXION A LOVELY GLOW.
IT'S GOOD SHE CAN FEND FOR HERSELF, I SUPPOSE.
GIVEN HER LACK OF FORTUNE.

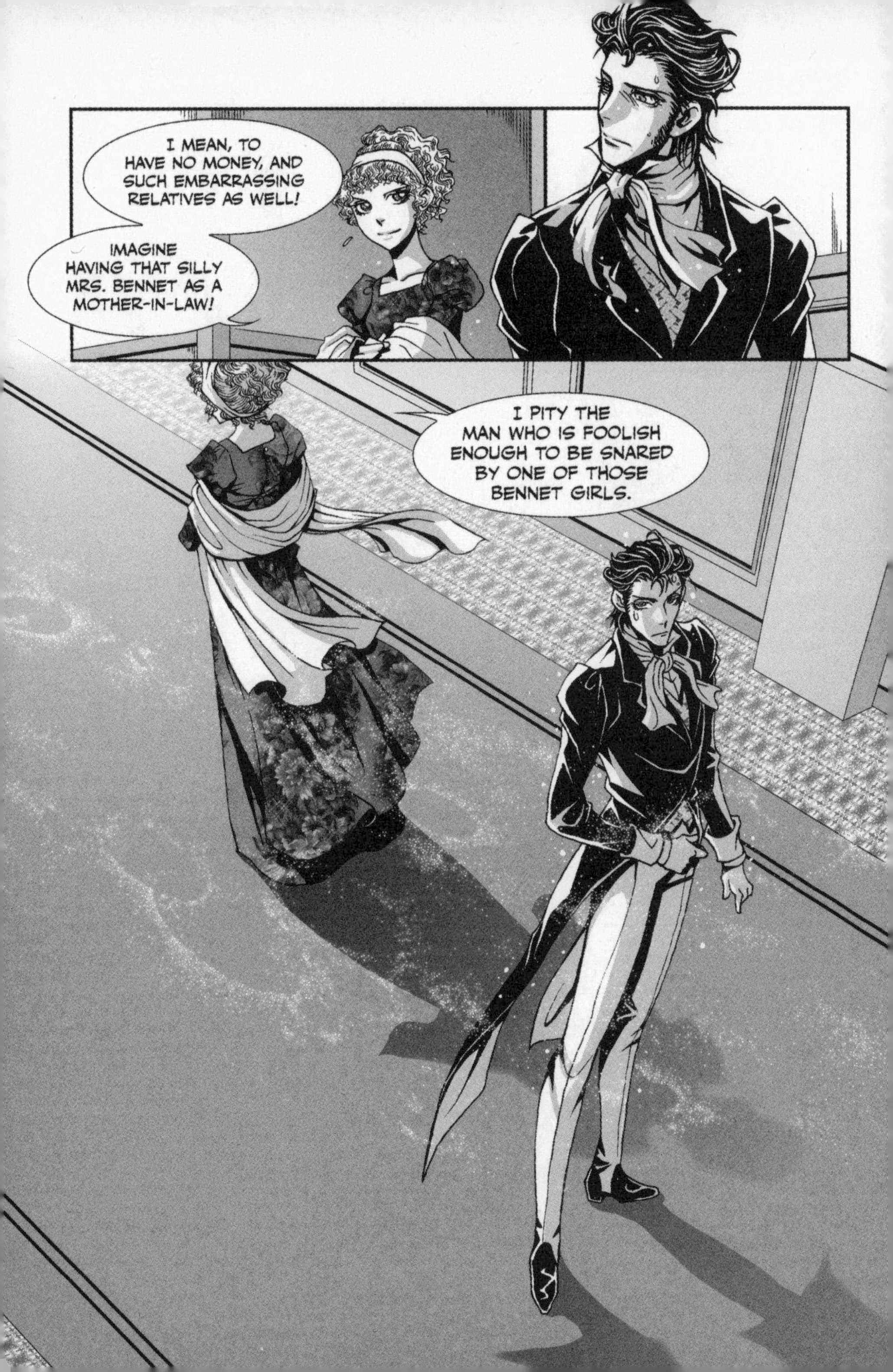
I MEAN, TO HAVE NO MONEY, AND SUCH EMBARRASSING RELATIVES AS WELL!
IMAGINE HAVING THAT SILLY MRS. BENNET AS A MOTHER-IN-LAW!
I PITY THE MAN WHO IS FOOLISH ENOUGH TO BE SNARED BY ONE OF THOSE BENNET GIRLS.

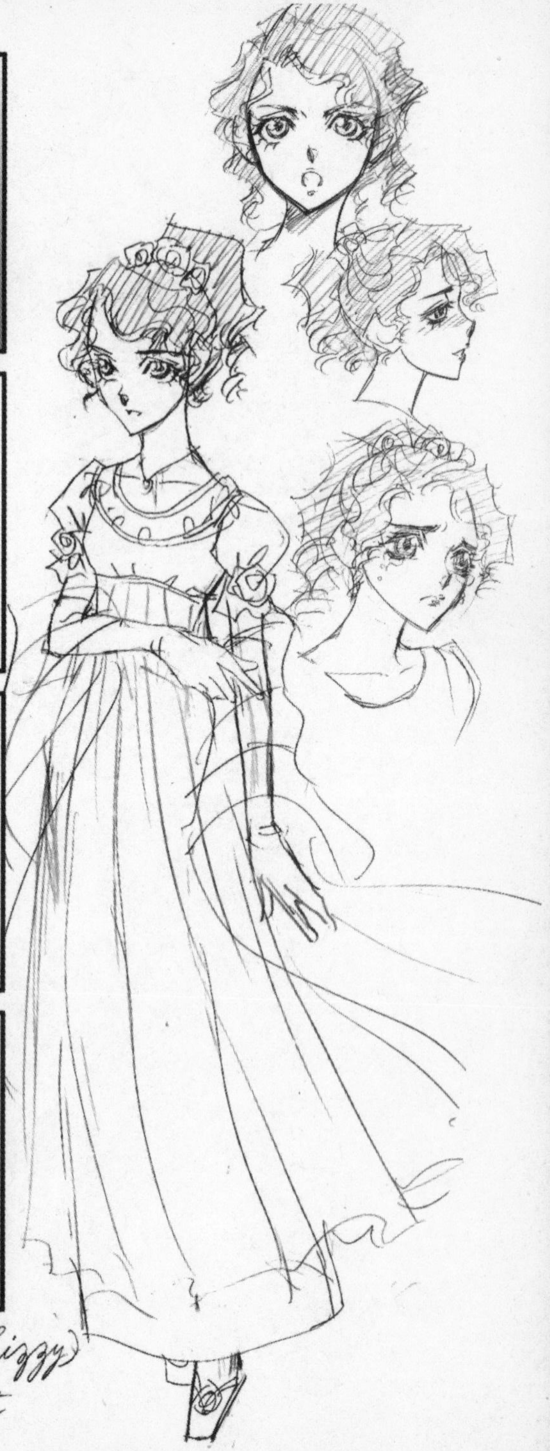

Elizabeth (Lizzy) Bennet

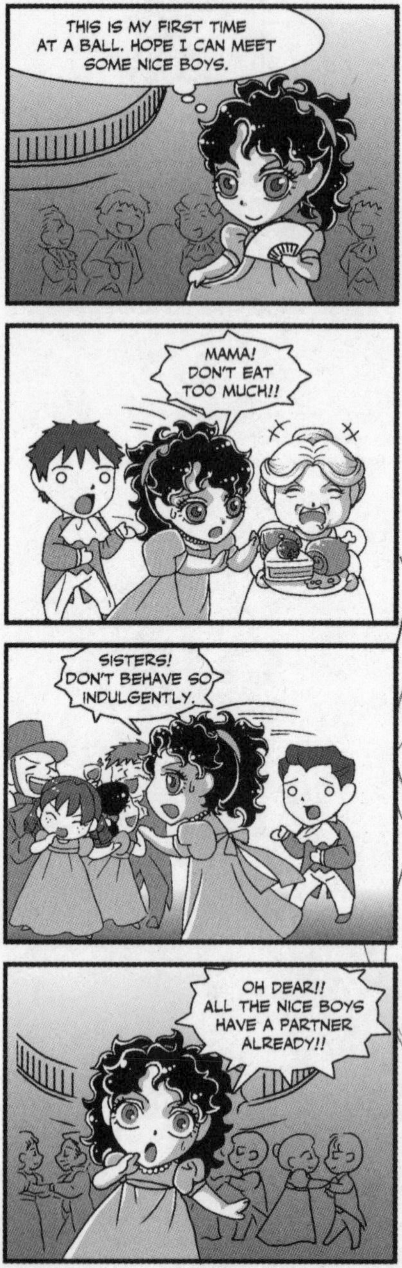

THIS IS MY FIRST TIME AT A BALL. HOPE I CAN MEET SOME NICE BOYS.
MAMA! DON'T EAT TOO MUCH!!
SISTERS! DON'T BEHAVE SO INDULGENTLY.
OH DEAR!! ALL THE NICE BOYS HAVE A PARTNER ALREADY!!

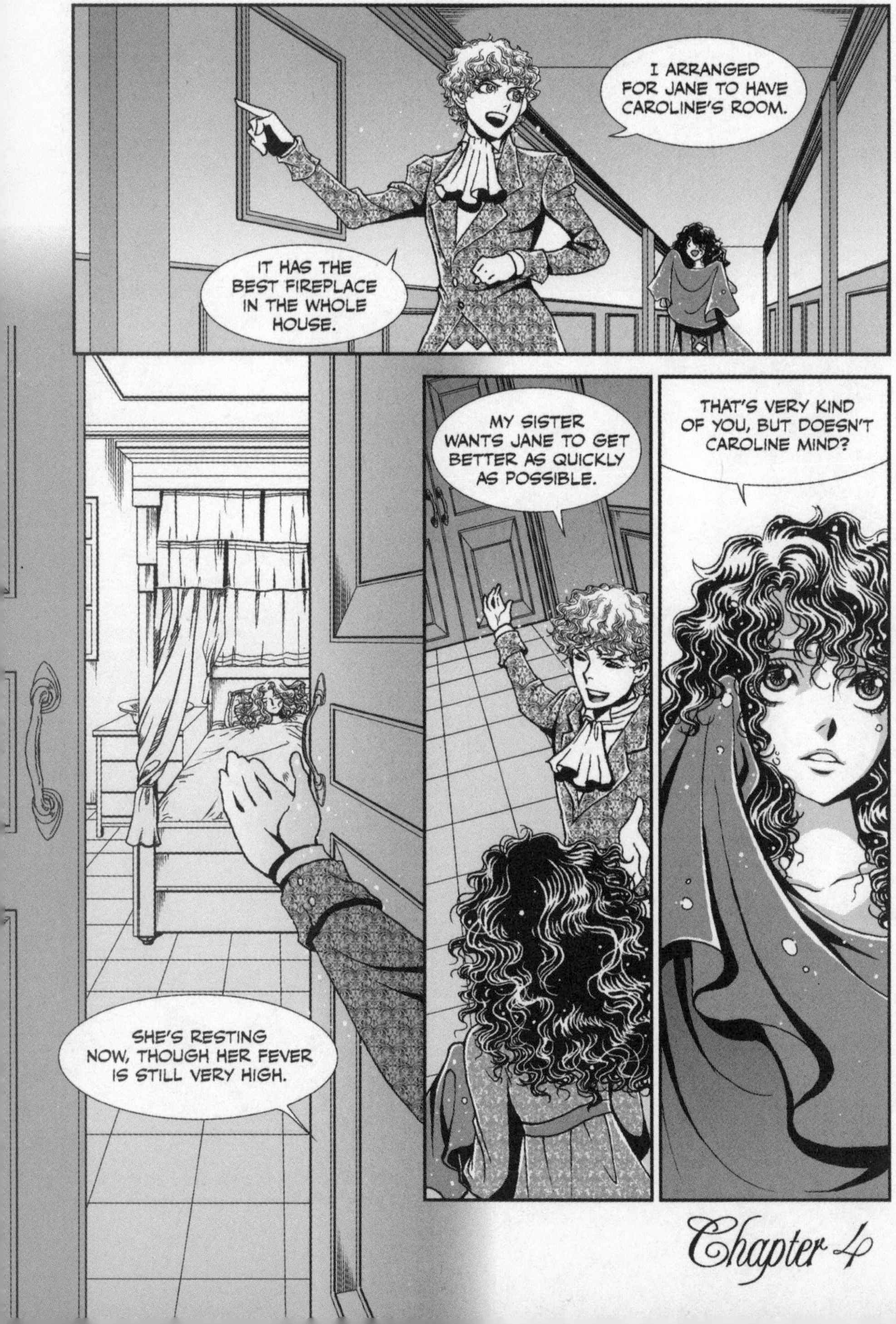
I ARRANGED FOR JANE TO HAVE CAROLINE'S ROOM.
IT HAS THE BEST FIREPLACE IN THE WHOLE HOUSE.
THAT'S VERY KIND OF YOU, BUT DOESN'T CAROLINE MIND?
MY SISTER WANTS JANE TO GET BETTER AS QUICKLY AS POSSIBLE.
SHE'S RESTING NOW, THOUGH HER FEVER IS STILL VERY HIGH.

Chapter 4

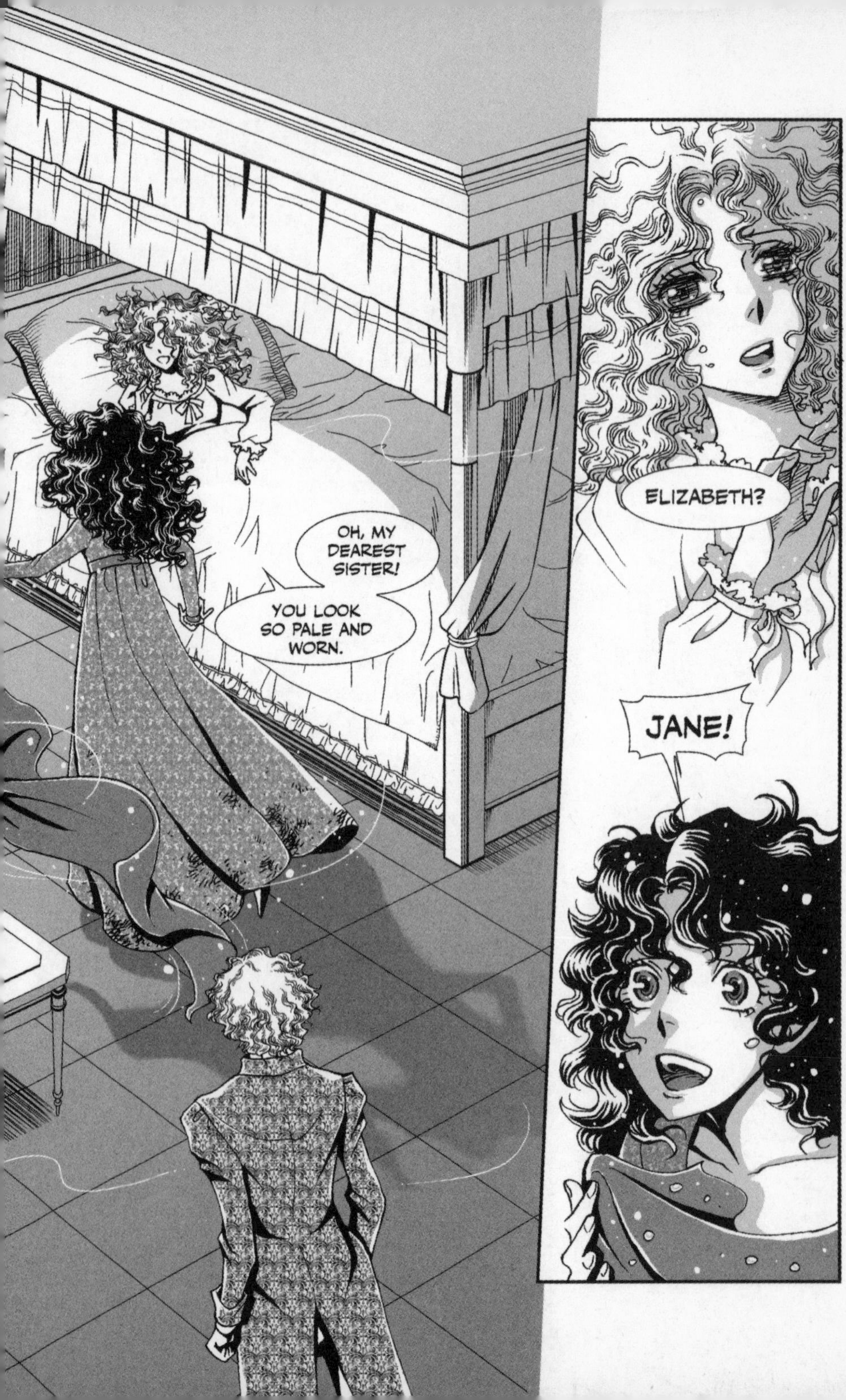
ELIZABETH?
JANE!
OH, MY DEAREST SISTER!
YOU LOOK SO PALE AND WORN.

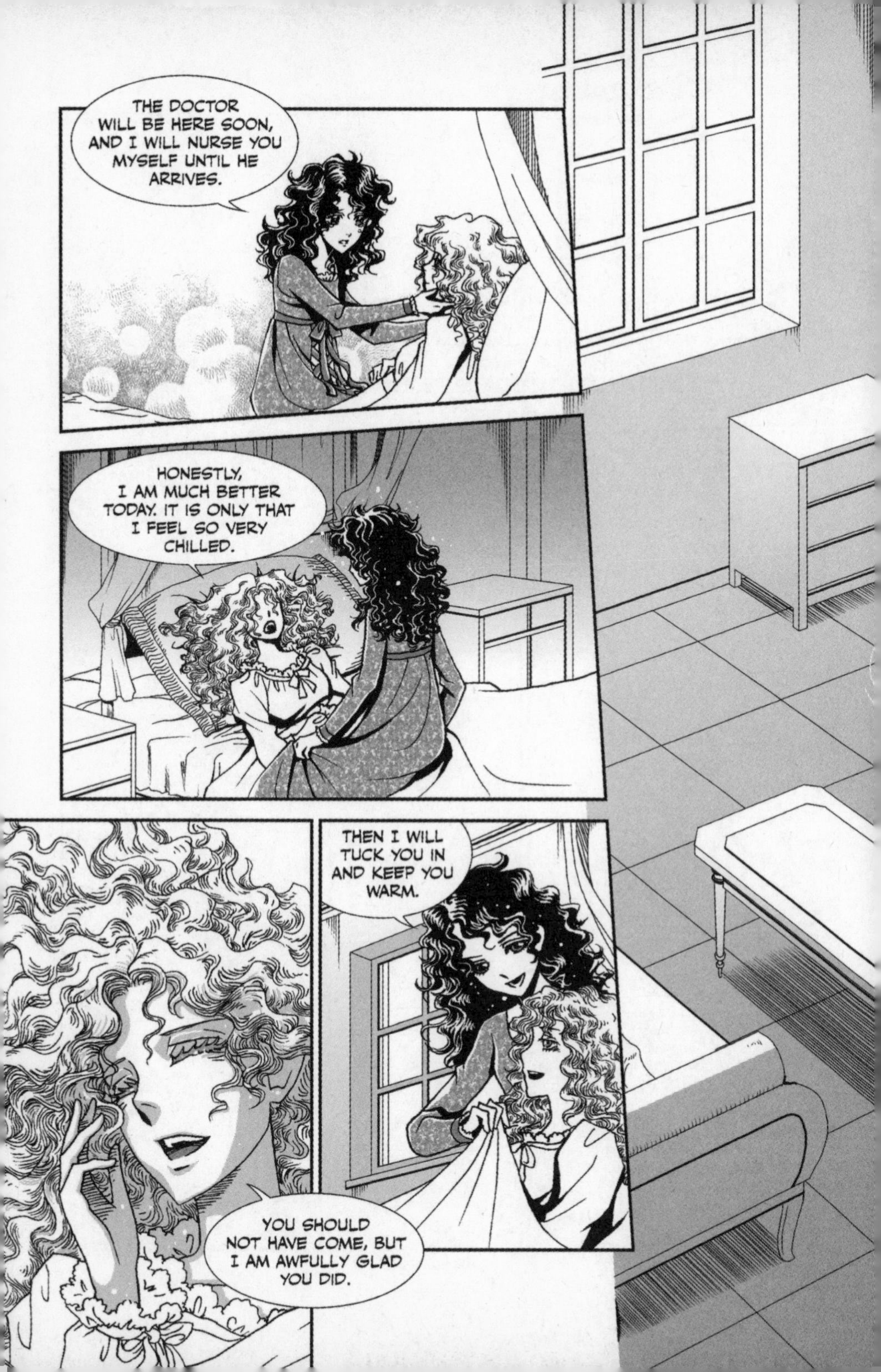
THE DOCTOR WILL BE HERE SOON, AND I WILL NURSE YOU MYSELF UNTIL HE ARRIVES.
HONESTLY, I AM MUCH BETTER TODAY. IT IS ONLY THAT I FEEL SO VERY CHILLED.
THEN I WILL TUCK YOU IN AND KEEP YOU WARM.
YOU SHOULD NOT HAVE COME, BUT I AM AWFULLY GLAD YOU DID.

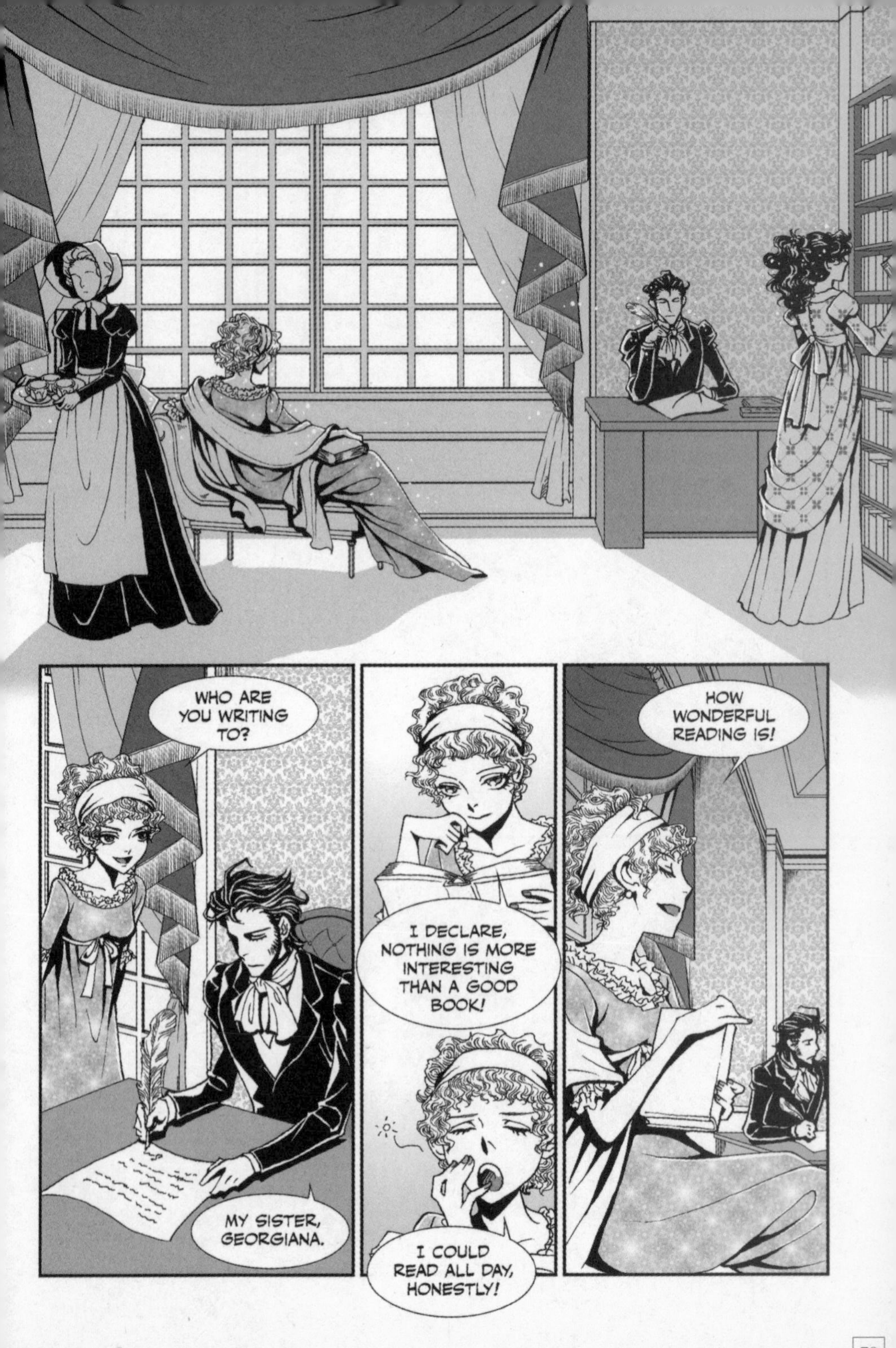
WHO ARE YOU WRITING TO?
MY SISTER, GEORGIANA.
I DECLARE, NOTHING IS MORE INTERESTING THAN A GOOD BOOK!
I COULD READ ALL DAY, HONESTLY!
HOW WONDERFUL READING IS!

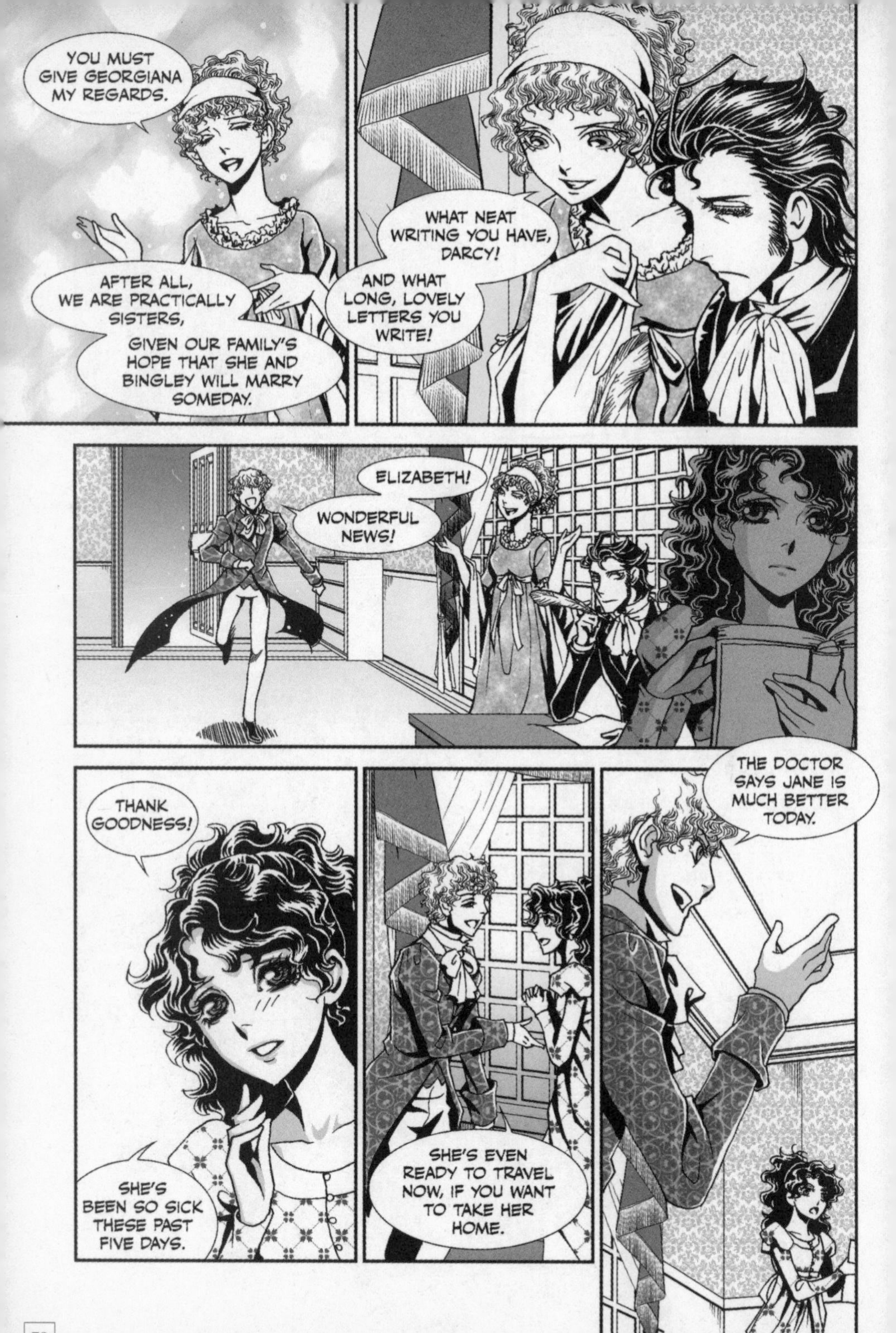
WHAT NEAT WRITING YOU HAVE, DARCY!
AND WHAT LONG, LOVELY LETTERS YOU WRITE!
YOU MUST GIVE GEORGIANA MY REGARDS.
AFTER ALL, WE ARE PRACTICALLY SISTERS,
GIVEN OUR FAMILY'S HOPE THAT SHE AND BINGLEY WILL MARRY SOMEDAY.
ELIZABETH!
WONDERFUL NEWS!
THE DOCTOR SAYS JANE IS MUCH BETTER TODAY.
SHE'S EVEN READY TO TRAVEL NOW, IF YOU WANT TO TAKE HER HOME.
THANK GOODNESS!
SHE'S BEEN SO SICK THESE PAST FIVE DAYS.

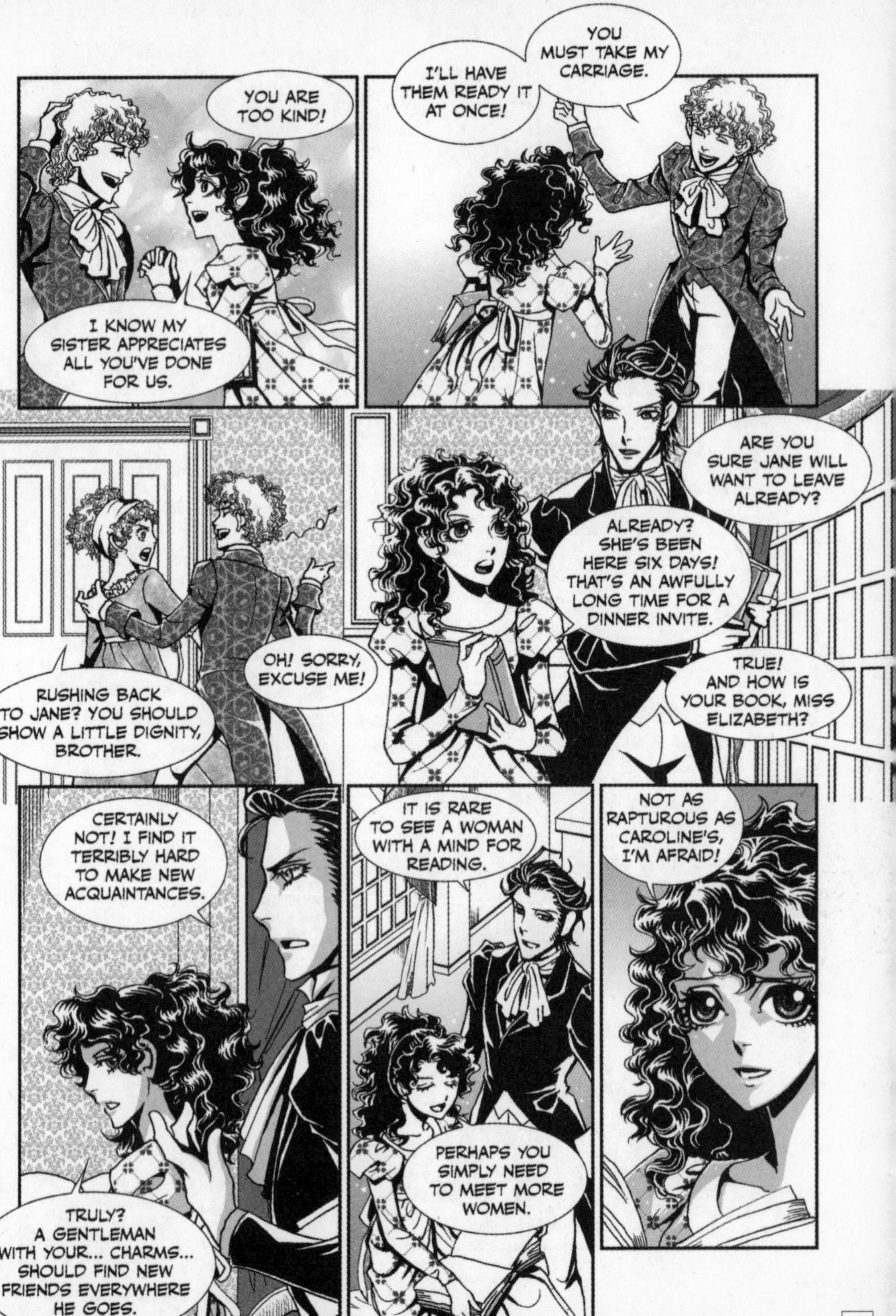
YOU MUST TAKE MY CARRIAGE.
I'LL HAVE THEM READY IT AT ONCE!
YOU ARE TOO KIND!
I KNOW MY SISTER APPRECIATES ALL YOU'VE DONE FOR US.
ARE YOU SURE JANE WILL WANT TO LEAVE ALREADY?
ALREADY? SHE'S BEEN HERE SIX DAYS! THAT'S AN AWFULLY LONG TIME FOR A DINNER INVITE.
TRUE! AND HOW IS YOUR BOOK, MISS ELIZABETH?
OH! SORRY, EXCUSE ME!
RUSHING BACK TO JANE? YOU SHOULD SHOW A LITTLE DIGNITY, BROTHER.
NOT AS RAPTUROUS AS CAROLINE'S, I'M AFRAID!
IT IS RARE TO SEE A WOMAN WITH A MIND FOR READING.
PERHAPS YOU SIMPLY NEED TO MEET MORE WOMEN.
CERTAINLY NOT! I FIND IT TERRIBLY HARD TO MAKE NEW ACQUAINTANCES.
TRULY? A GENTLEMAN WITH YOUR... CHARMS... SHOULD FIND NEW FRIENDS EVERYWHERE HE GOES.

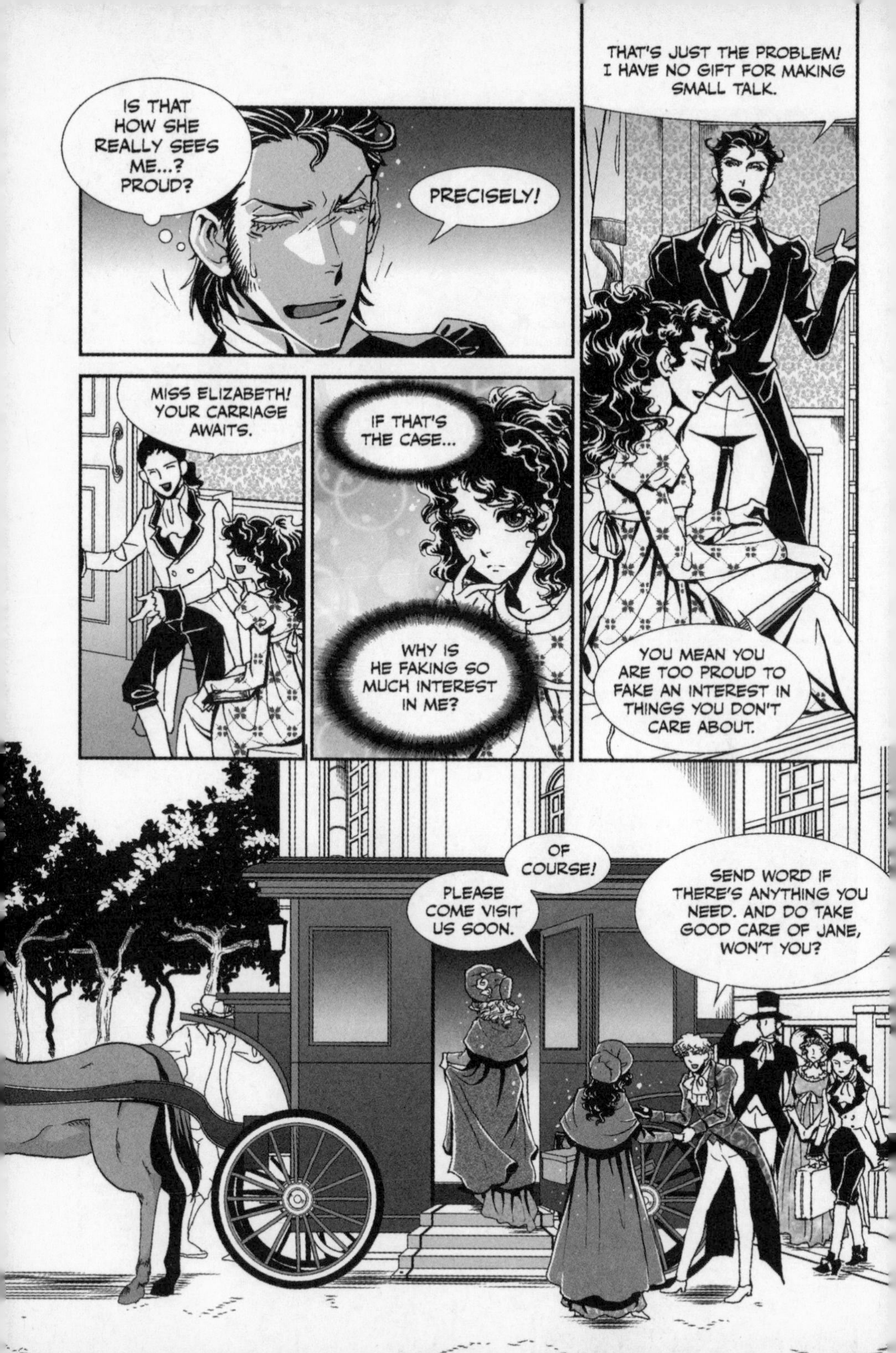
THAT'S JUST THE PROBLEM! I HAVE NO GIFT FOR MAKING SMALL TALK.
YOU MEAN YOU ARE TOO PROUD TO FAKE AN INTEREST IN THINGS YOU DON'T CARE ABOUT.
IS THAT HOW SHE REALLY SEES ME...? PROUD?
PRECISELY!
IF THAT'S THE CASE...
WHY IS HE FAKING SO MUCH INTEREST IN ME?
MISS ELIZABETH! YOUR CARRIAGE AWAITS.
SEND WORD IF THERE'S ANYTHING YOU NEED. AND DO TAKE GOOD CARE OF JANE, WON'T YOU?
OF COURSE!
PLEASE COME VISIT US SOON.

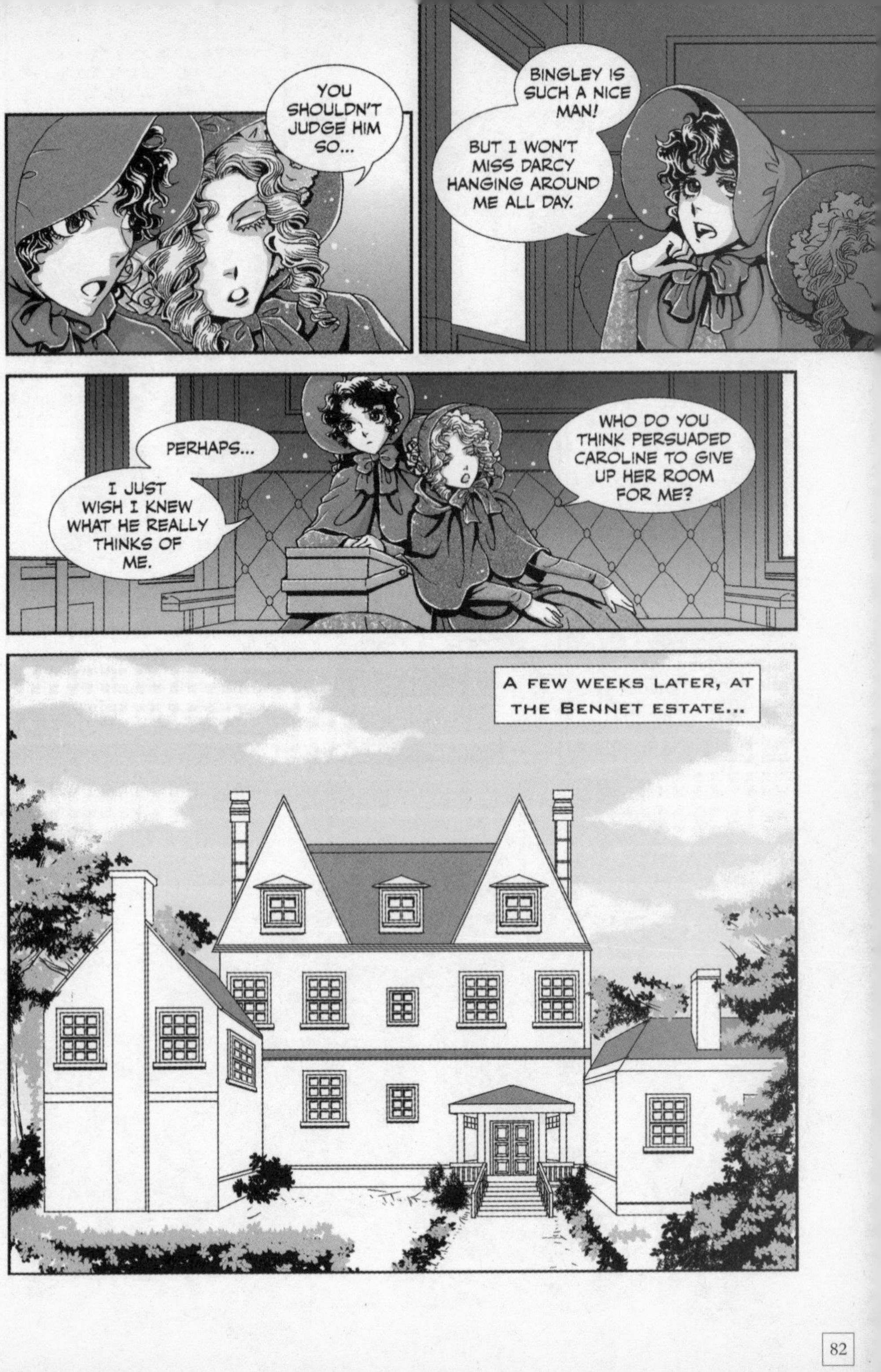
BINGLEY IS SUCH A NICE MAN!
BUT I WON'T MISS DARCY HANGING AROUND ME ALL DAY.
YOU SHOULDN'T JUDGE HIM SO...
WHO DO YOU THINK PERSUADED CAROLINE TO GIVE UP HER ROOM FOR ME?
PERHAPS...
I JUST WISH I KNEW WHAT HE REALLY THINKS OF ME.
A FEW WEEKS LATER, AT THE BENNET ESTATE...

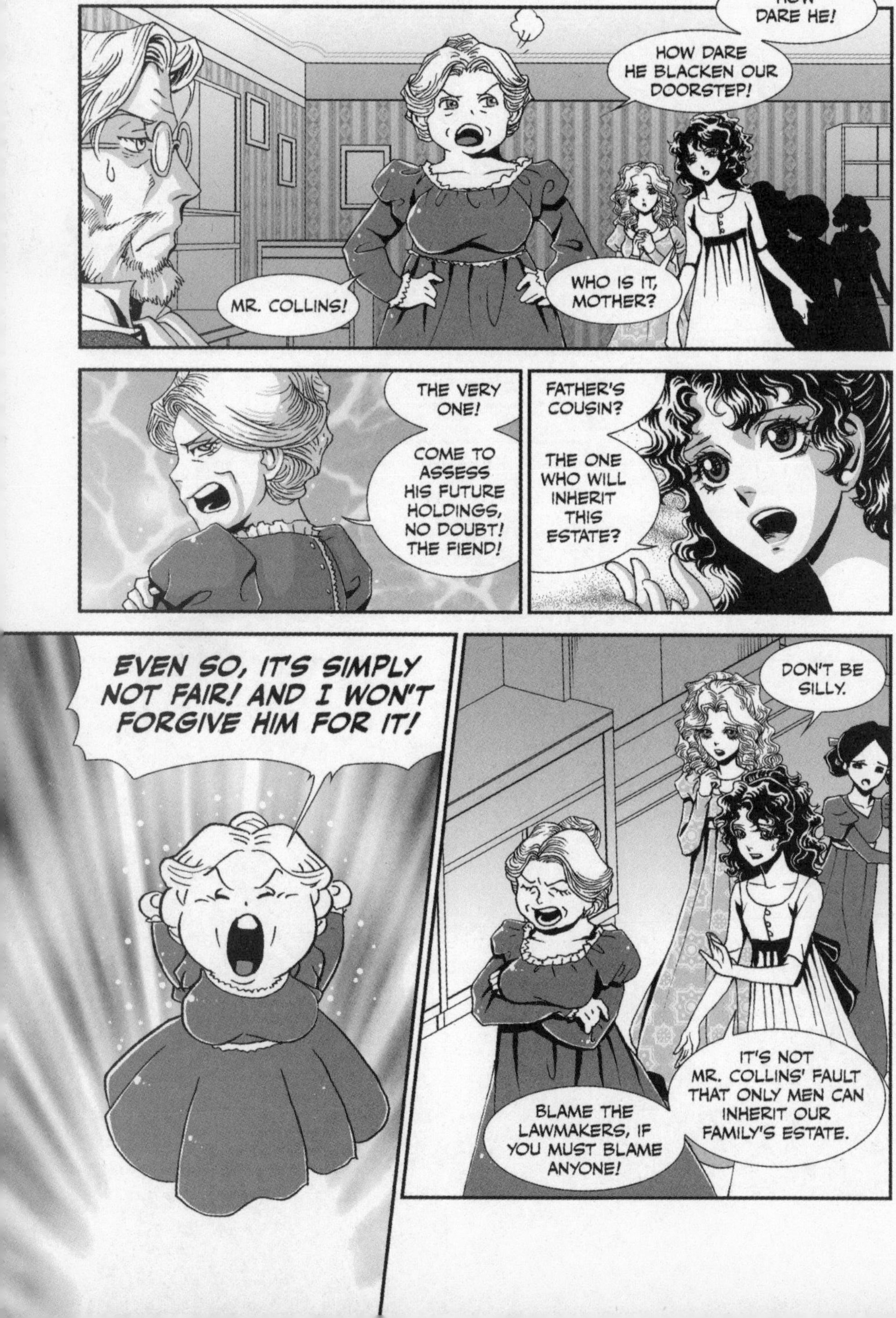
HOW DARE HE!
HOW DARE HE BLACKEN OUR DOORSTEP!
WHO IS IT, MOTHER?
MR. COLLINS!
FATHER'S COUSIN?
THE ONE WHO WILL INHERIT THIS ESTATE?
THE VERY ONE!
COME TO ASSESS HIS FUTURE HOLDINGS, NO DOUBT! THE FIEND!
DON'T BE SILLY.
IT'S NOT MR. COLLINS' FAULT THAT ONLY MEN CAN INHERIT OUR FAMILY'S ESTATE.
BLAME THE LAWMAKERS, IF YOU MUST BLAME ANYONE!
EVEN SO, IT'S SIMPLY NOT FAIR! AND I WON'T FORGIVE HIM FOR IT!

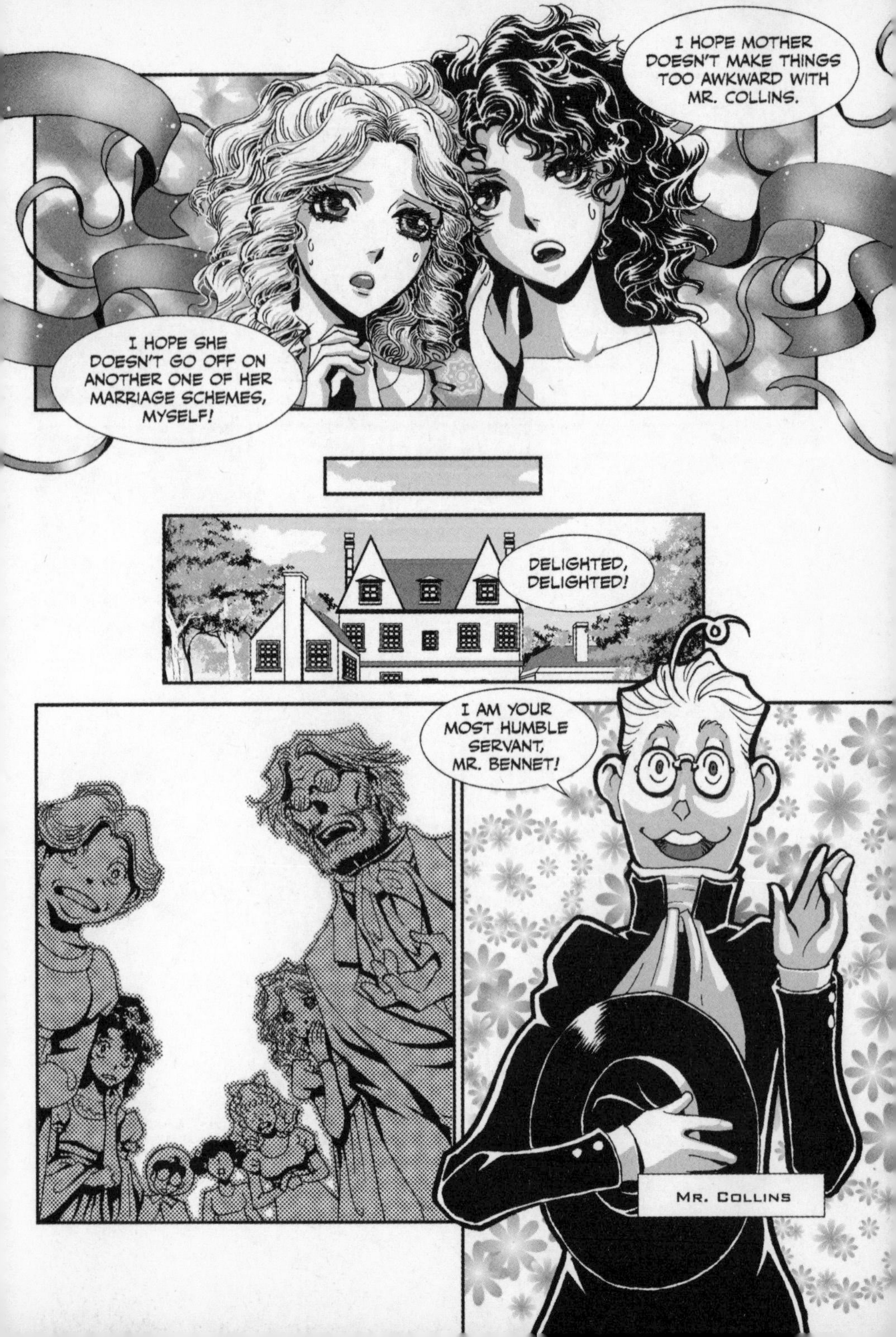
I HOPE MOTHER DOESN'T MAKE THINGS TOO AWKWARD WITH MR. COLLINS.
I HOPE SHE DOESN'T GO OFF ON ANOTHER ONE OF HER MARRIAGE SCHEMES, MYSELF!
DELIGHTED, DELIGHTED!
I AM YOUR MOST HUMBLE SERVANT, MR. BENNET!
MR. COLLINS

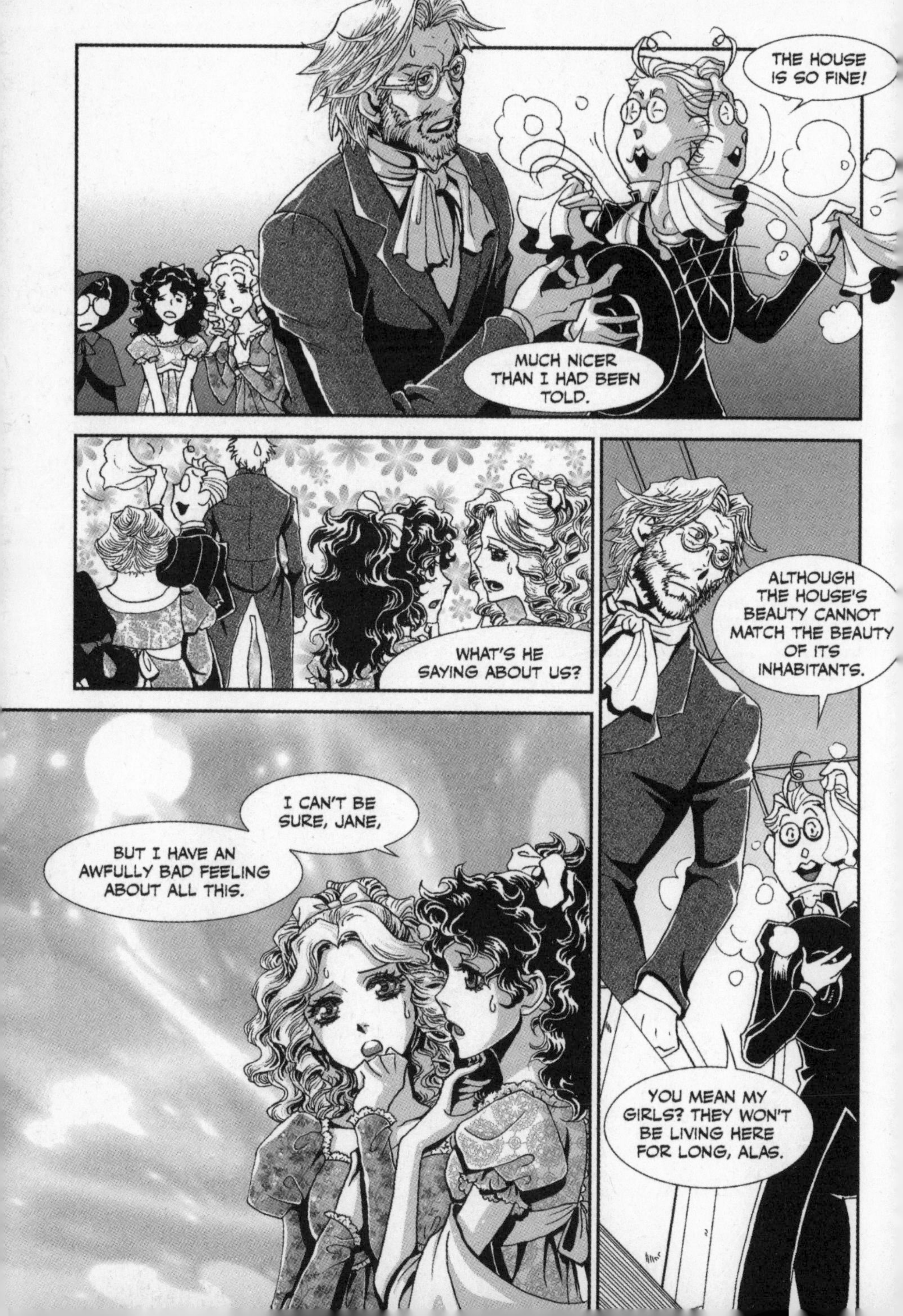
THE HOUSE IS SO FINE!
MUCH NICER THAN I HAD BEEN TOLD.
ALTHOUGH THE HOUSE'S BEAUTY CANNOT MATCH THE BEAUTY OF ITS INHABITANTS.
YOU MEAN MY GIRLS? THEY WON'T BE LIVING HERE FOR LONG, ALAS.
WHAT'S HE SAYING ABOUT US?
I CAN'T BE SURE, JANE,
BUT I HAVE AN AWFULLY BAD FEELING ABOUT ALL THIS.

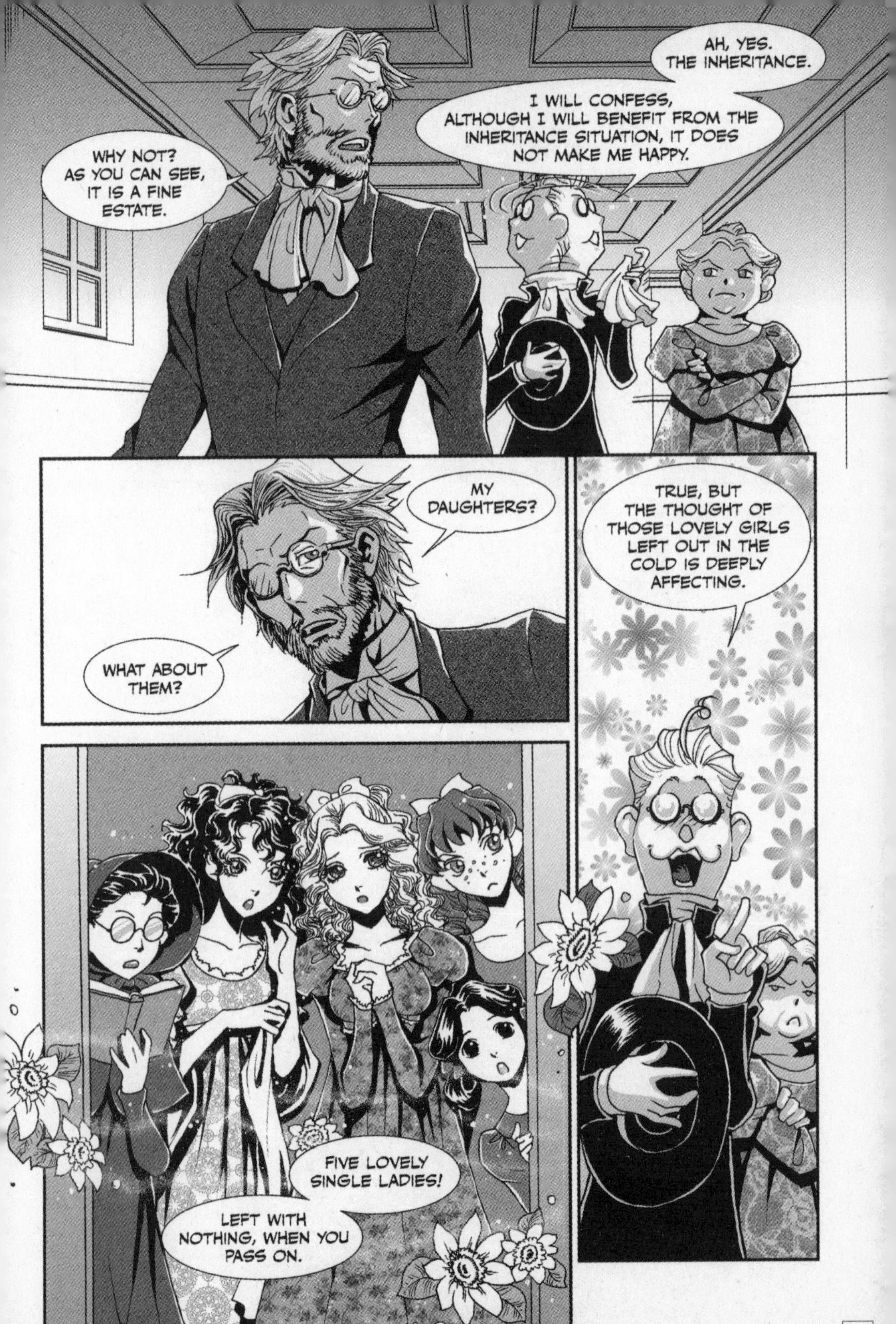
AH, YES. THE INHERITANCE.
I WILL CONFESS, ALTHOUGH I WILL BENEFIT FROM THE INHERITANCE SITUATION, IT DOES NOT MAKE ME HAPPY.
WHY NOT? AS YOU CAN SEE, IT IS A FINE ESTATE.
TRUE, BUT THE THOUGHT OF THOSE LOVELY GIRLS LEFT OUT IN THE COLD IS DEEPLY AFFECTING.
MY DAUGHTERS?
WHAT ABOUT THEM?
FIVE LOVELY SINGLE LADIES!
LEFT WITH NOTHING, WHEN YOU PASS ON.

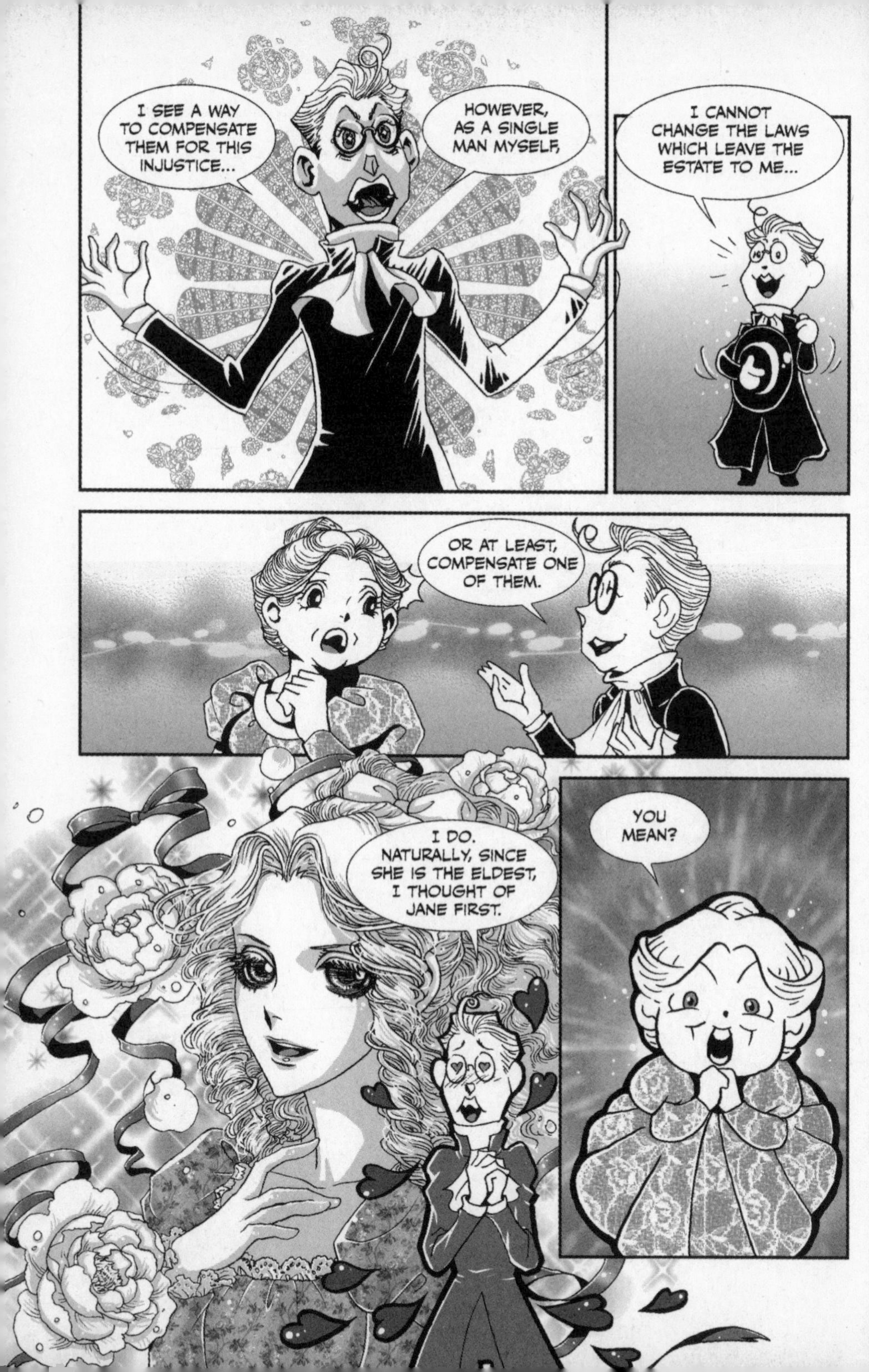
I CANNOT CHANGE THE LAWS WHICH LEAVE THE ESTATE TO ME...
HOWEVER, AS A SINGLE MAN MYSELF,
I SEE A WAY TO COMPENSATE THEM FOR THIS INJUSTICE...
OR AT LEAST, COMPENSATE ONE OF THEM.
YOU MEAN?
I DO. NATURALLY, SINCE SHE IS THE ELDEST, I THOUGHT OF JANE FIRST.

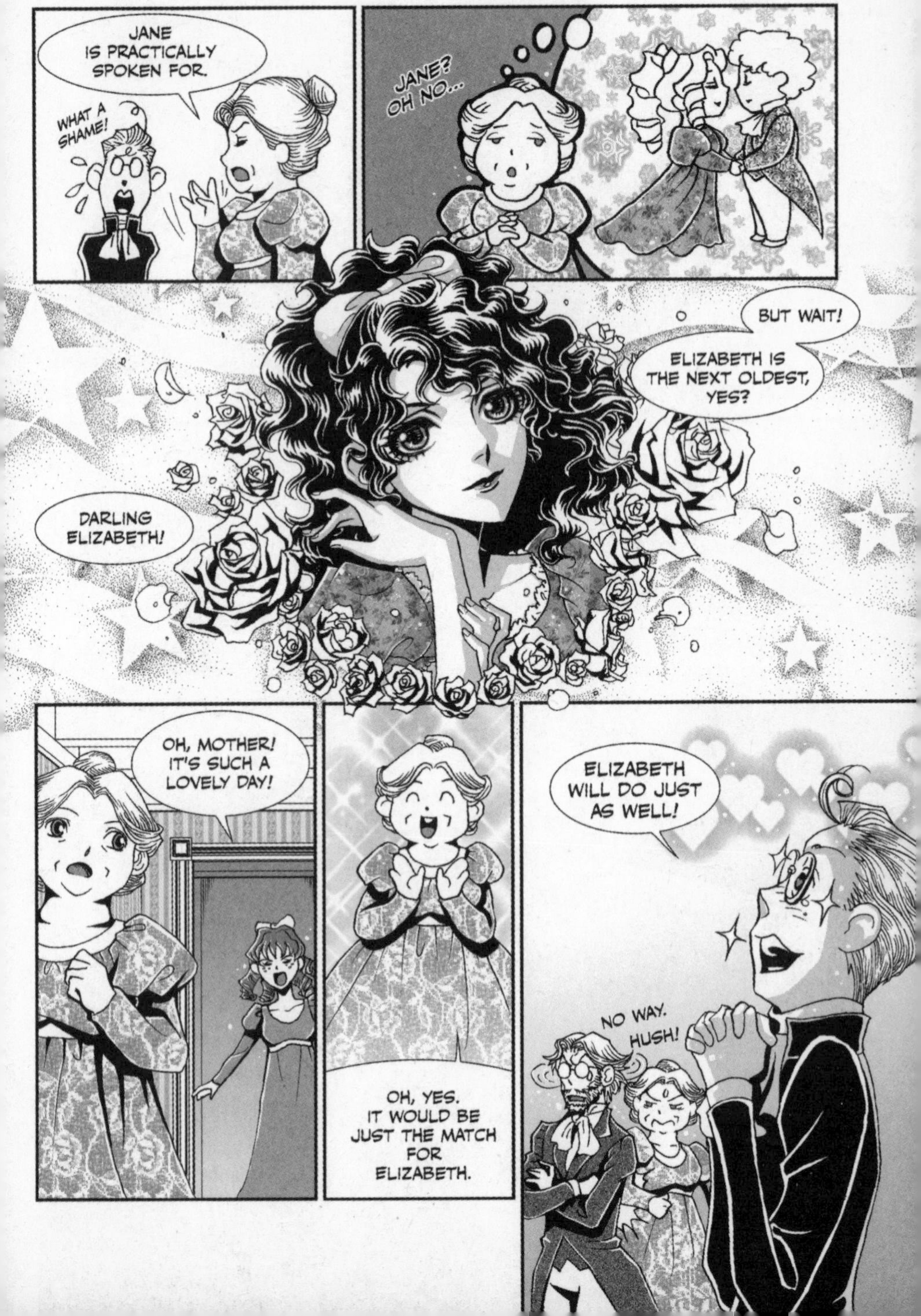
JANE? OH NO...
JANE IS PRACTICALLY SPOKEN FOR.
WHAT A SHAME!
BUT WAIT!
ELIZABETH IS THE NEXT OLDEST, YES?
DARLING ELIZABETH!
ELIZABETH WILL DO JUST AS WELL!
NO WAY.
HUSH!
OH, YES. IT WOULD BE JUST THE MATCH FOR ELIZABETH.
OH, MOTHER! IT'S SUCH A LOVELY DAY!

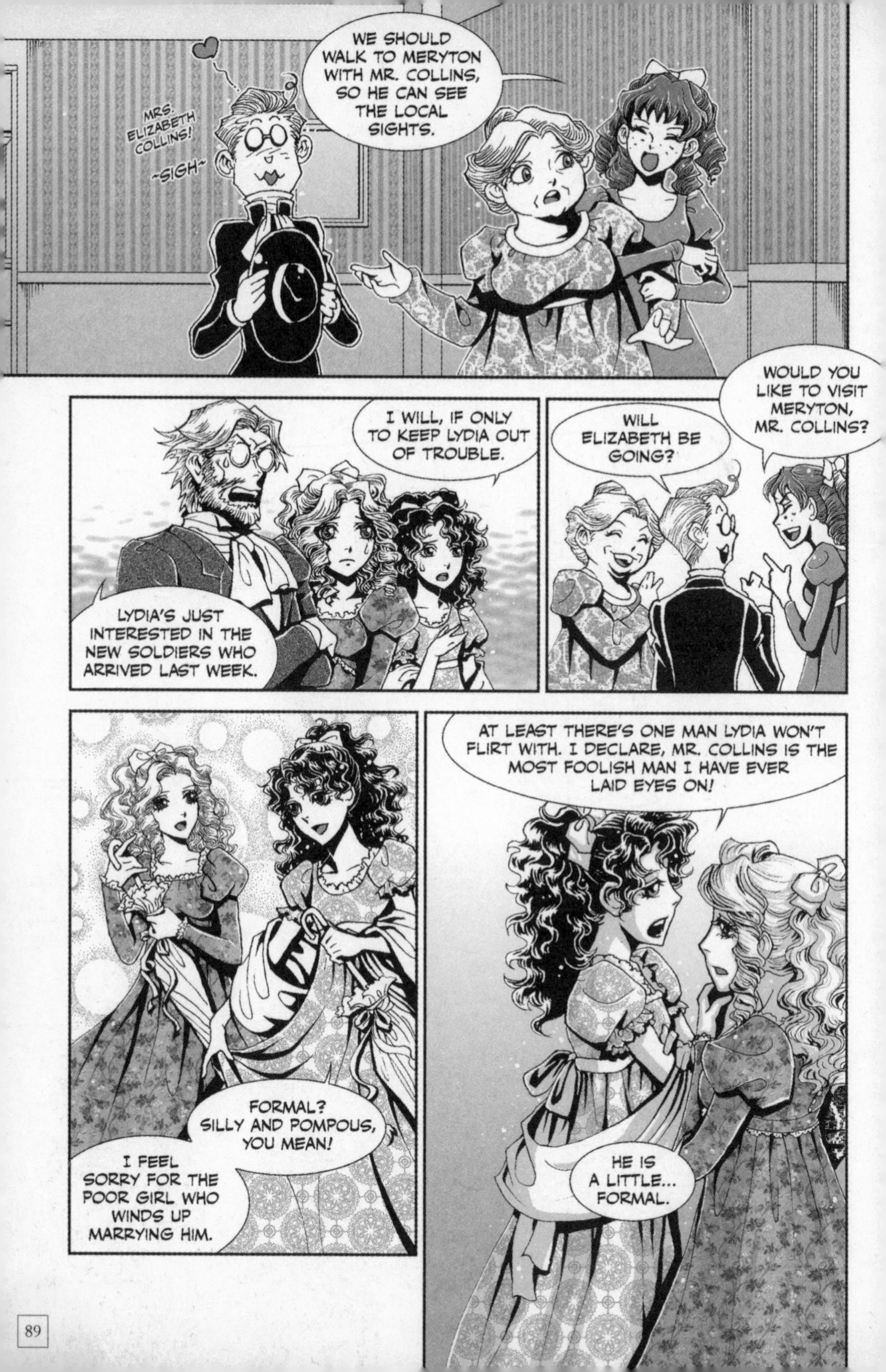
WE SHOULD WALK TO MERYTON WITH MR. COLLINS, SO HE CAN SEE THE LOCAL SIGHTS.
MRS. ELIZABETH COLLINS!
~SIGH~
WOULD YOU LIKE TO VISIT MERYTON, MR. COLLINS?
WILL ELIZABETH BE GOING?
I WILL, IF ONLY TO KEEP LYDIA OUT OF TROUBLE.
LYDIA'S JUST INTERESTED IN THE NEW SOLDIERS WHO ARRIVED LAST WEEK.
AT LEAST THERE'S ONE MAN LYDIA WON'T FLIRT WITH. I DECLARE, MR. COLLINS IS THE MOST FOOLISH MAN I HAVE EVER LAID EYES ON!
HE IS A LITTLE... FORMAL.
FORMAL? SILLY AND POMPOUS, YOU MEAN!
I FEEL SORRY FOR THE POOR GIRL WHO WINDS UP MARRYING HIM.

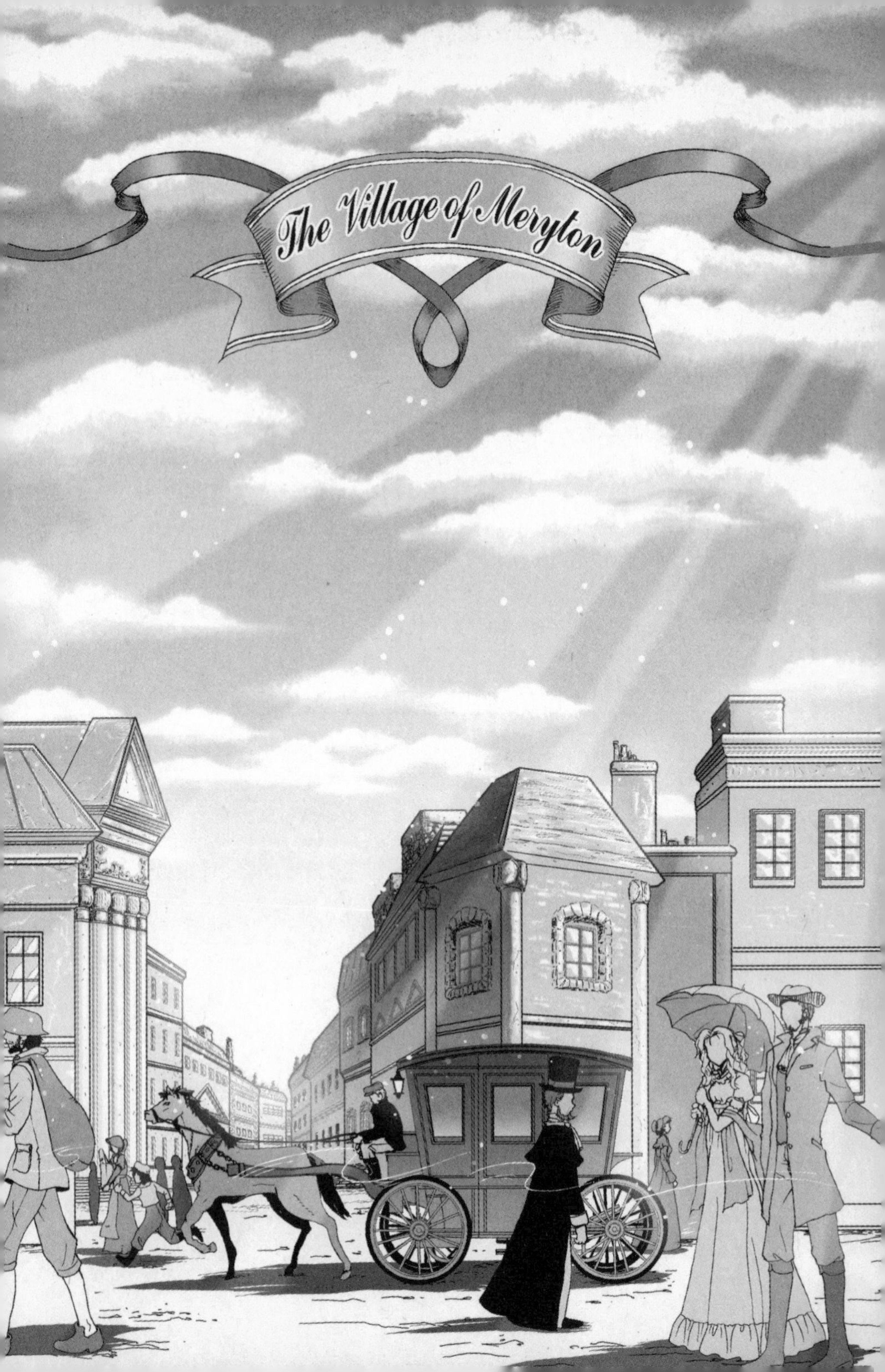
The Village of Meryton

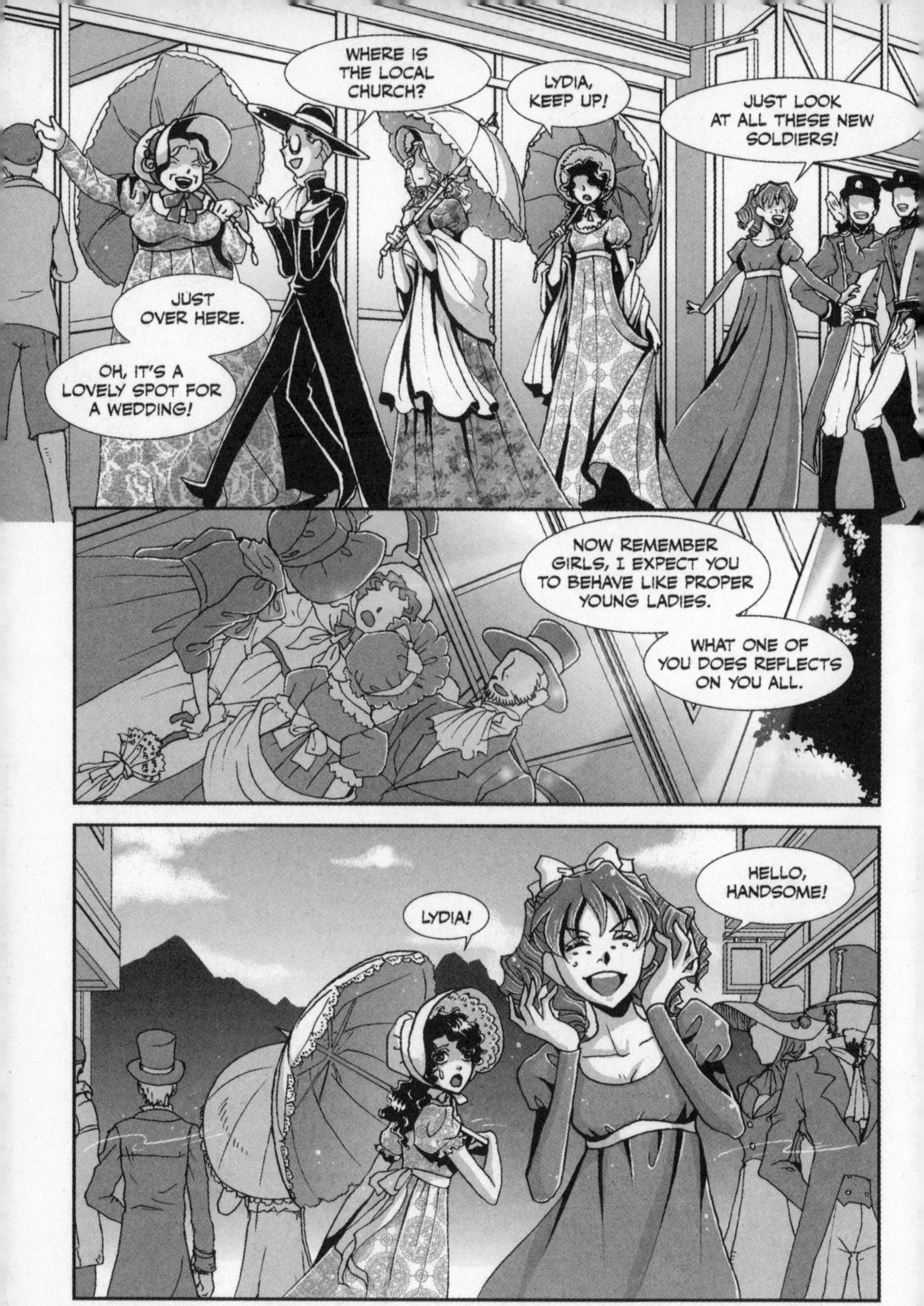
JUST LOOK AT ALL THESE NEW SOLDIERS!
LYDIA, KEEP UP!
WHERE IS THE LOCAL CHURCH?
JUST OVER HERE.
OH, IT'S A LOVELY SPOT FOR A WEDDING!
NOW REMEMBER GIRLS, I EXPECT YOU TO BEHAVE LIKE PROPER YOUNG LADIES.
WHAT ONE OF YOU DOES REFLECTS ON YOU ALL.
HELLO, HANDSOME!
LYDIA!

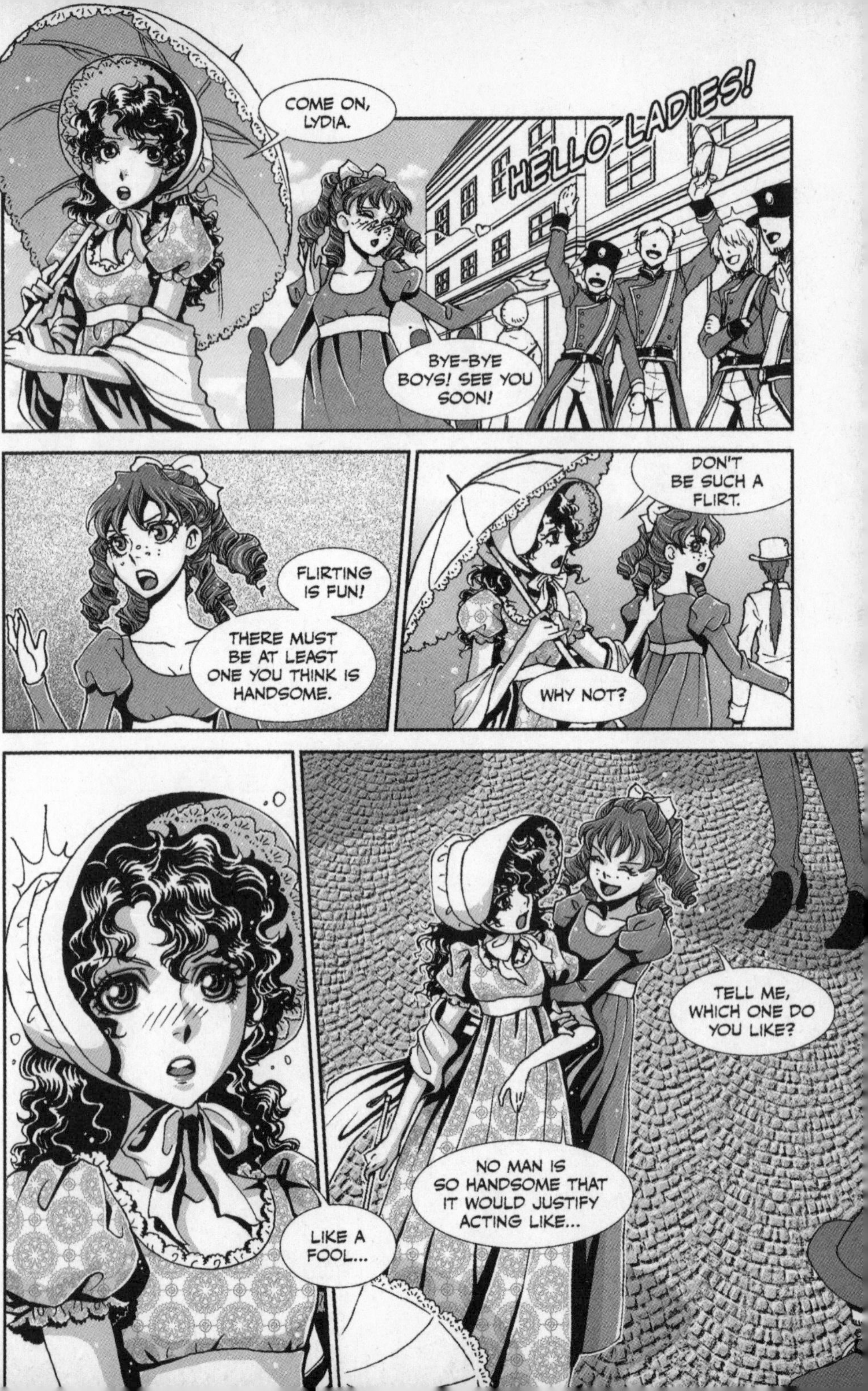
HELLO LADIES!
COME ON, LYDIA.
BYE-BYE BOYS! SEE YOU SOON!
DON'T BE SUCH A FLIRT.
WHY NOT?
FLIRTING IS FUN!
THERE MUST BE AT LEAST ONE YOU THINK IS HANDSOME.
TELL ME, WHICH ONE DO YOU LIKE?
NO MAN IS SO HANDSOME THAT IT WOULD JUSTIFY ACTING LIKE...
LIKE A FOOL...

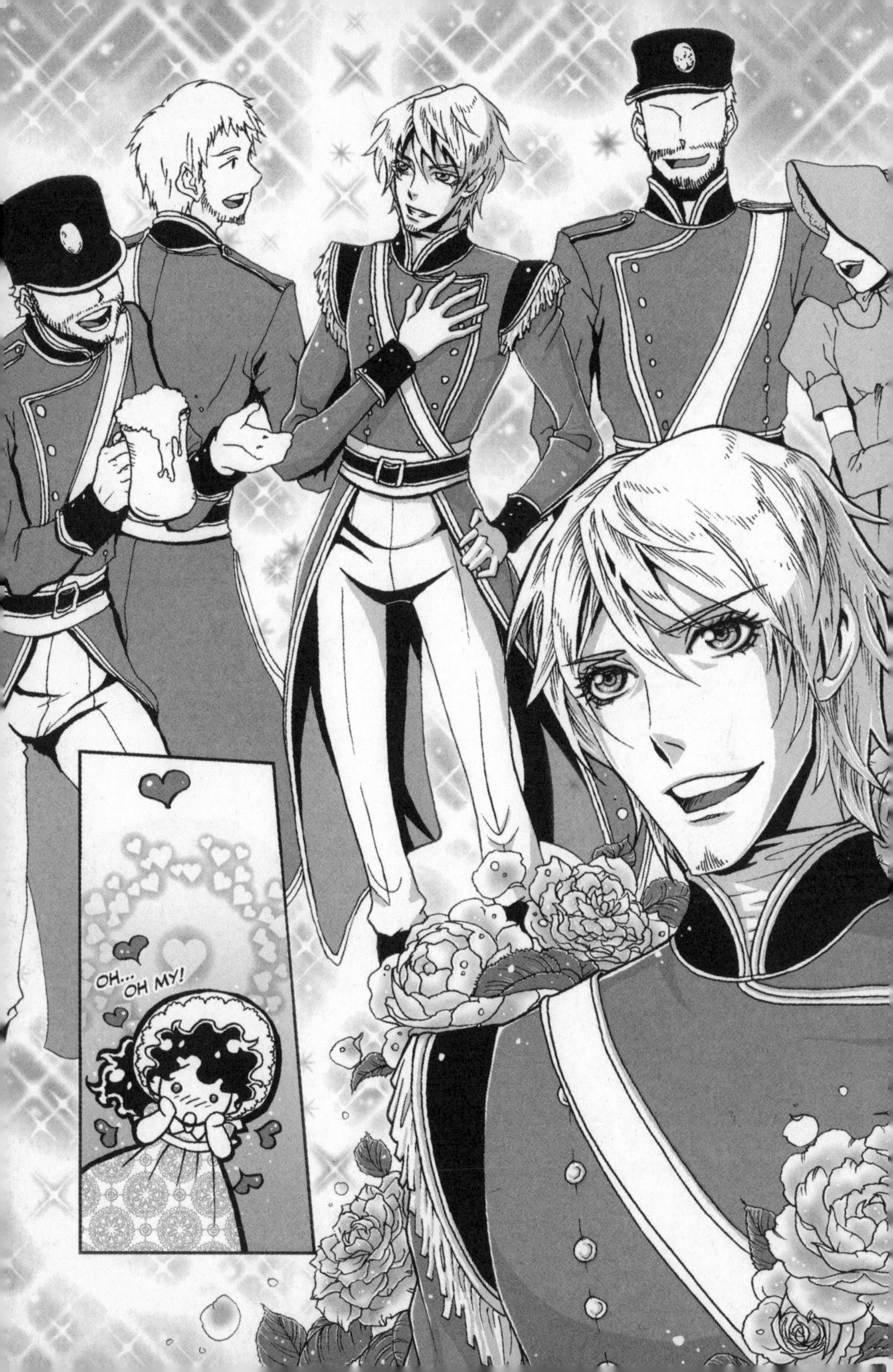
OH... OH MY!

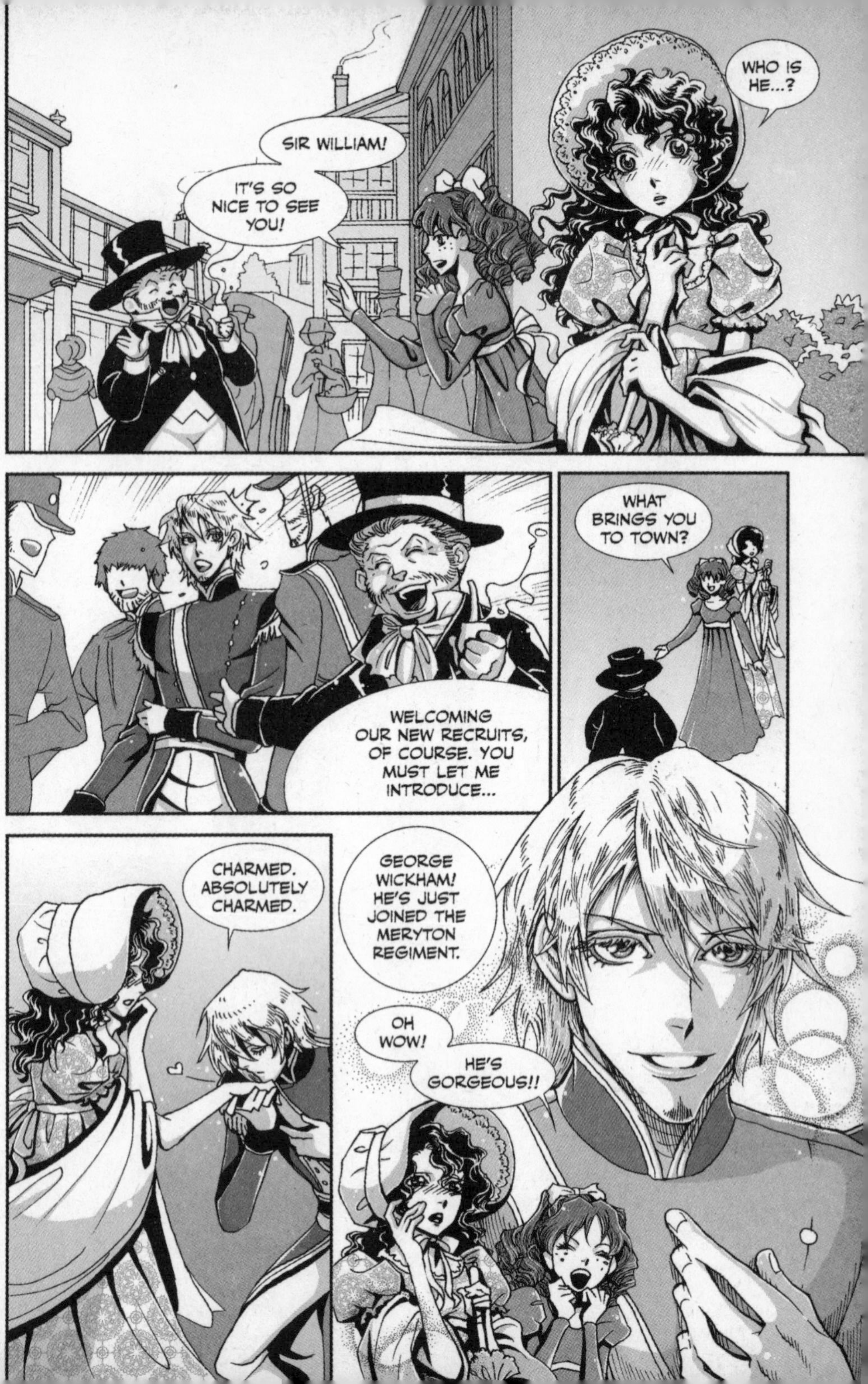
WHO IS HE...?
SIR WILLIAM!
IT'S SO NICE TO SEE YOU!
WHAT BRINGS YOU TO TOWN?
WELCOMING OUR NEW RECRUITS, OF COURSE. YOU MUST LET ME INTRODUCE...
GEORGE WICKHAM! HE'S JUST JOINED THE MERYTON REGIMENT.
OH WOW!
HE'S GORGEOUS!!
CHARMED. ABSOLUTELY CHARMED.

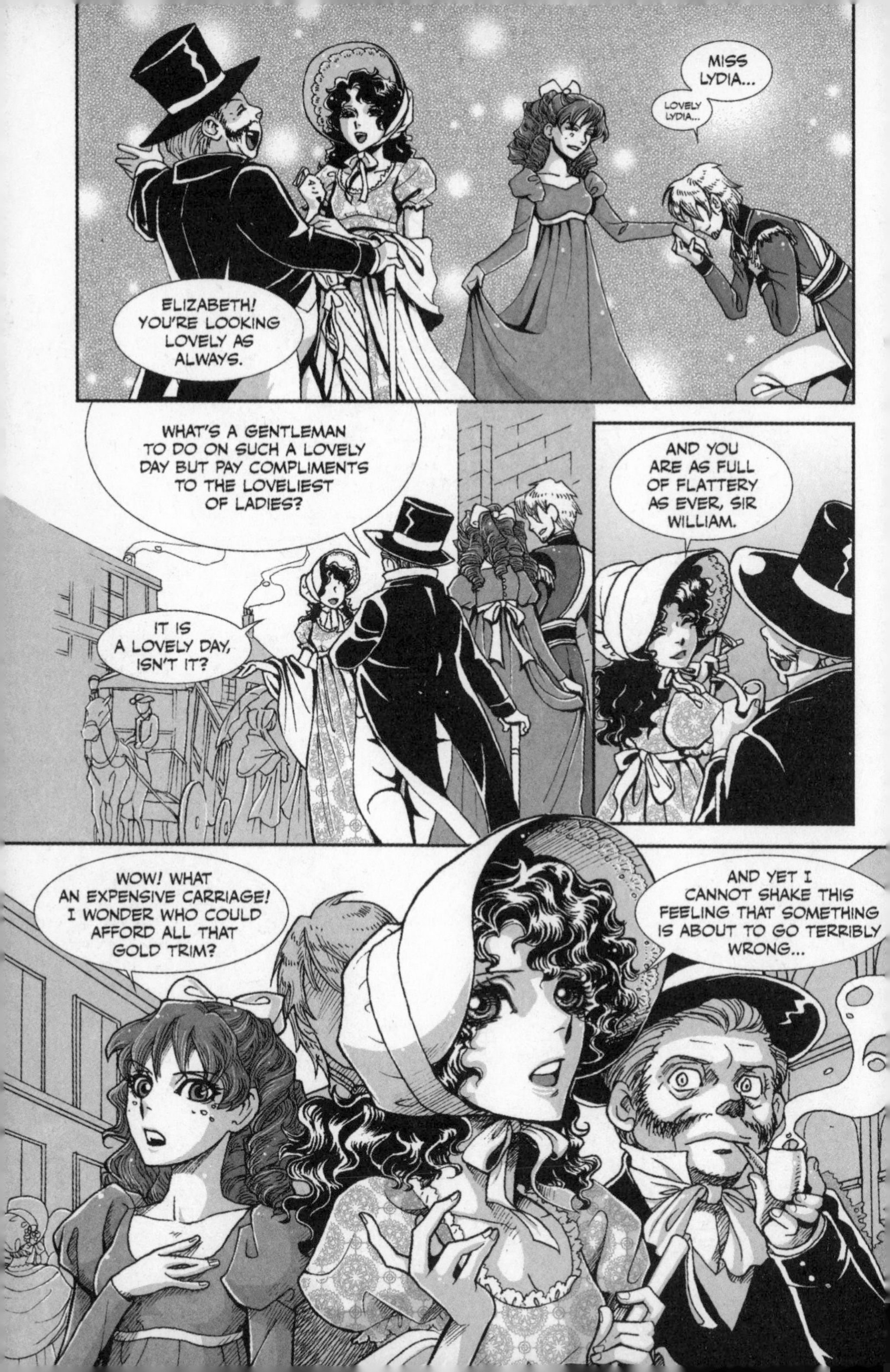
ELIZABETH! YOU'RE LOOKING LOVELY AS ALWAYS.
MISS LYDIA...
LOVELY LYDIA...
WHAT'S A GENTLEMAN TO DO ON SUCH A LOVELY DAY BUT PAY COMPLIMENTS TO THE LOVELIEST OF LADIES?
IT IS A LOVELY DAY, ISN'T IT?
AND YOU ARE AS FULL OF FLATTERY AS EVER, SIR WILLIAM.
WOW! WHAT AN EXPENSIVE CARRIAGE! I WONDER WHO COULD AFFORD ALL THAT GOLD TRIM?
AND YET I CANNOT SHAKE THIS FEELING THAT SOMETHING IS ABOUT TO GO TERRIBLY WRONG...

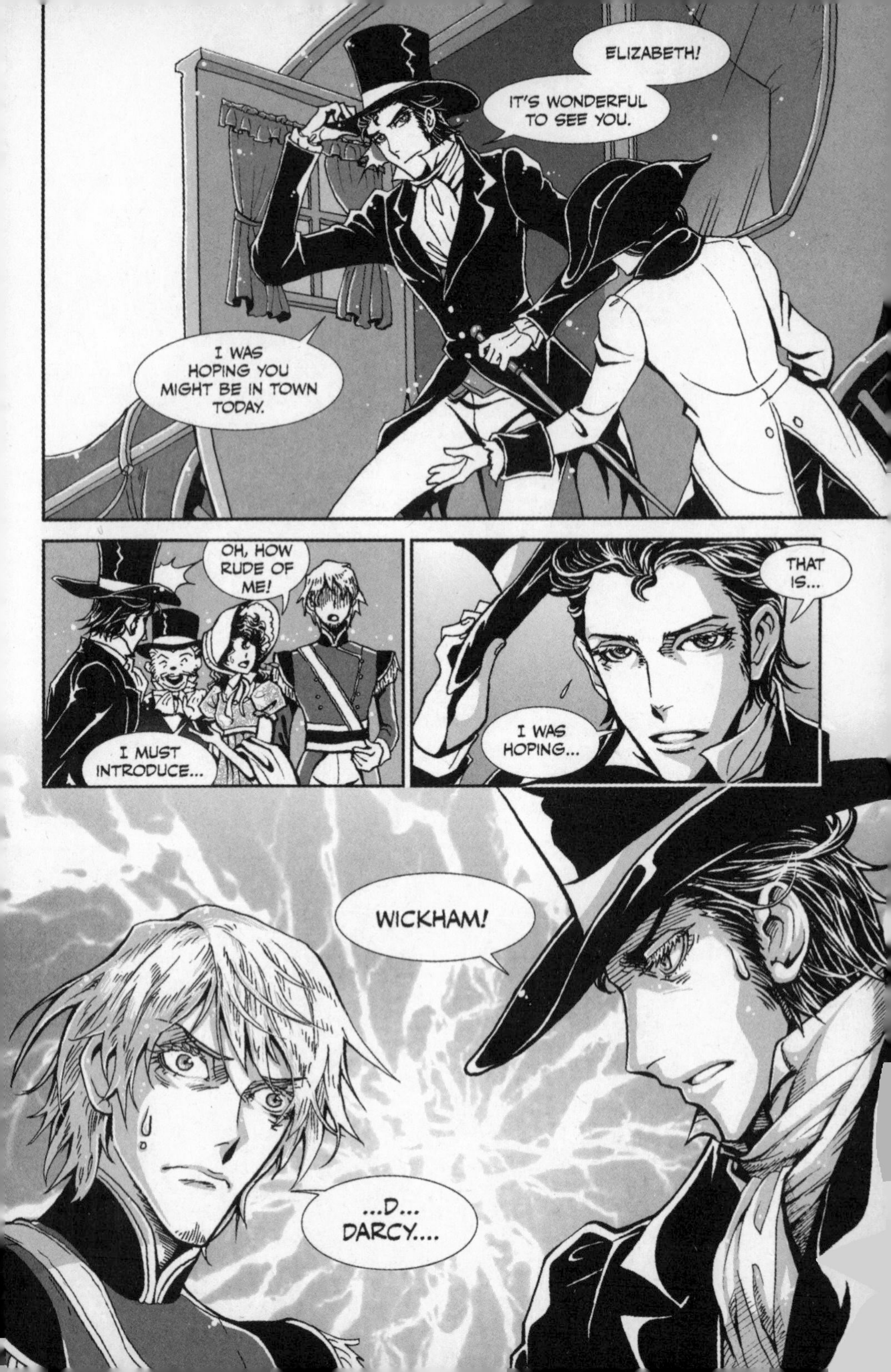
ELIZABETH!
IT'S WONDERFUL TO SEE YOU.
I WAS HOPING YOU MIGHT BE IN TOWN TODAY.
THAT IS...
I WAS HOPING...
OH, HOW RUDE OF ME!
I MUST INTRODUCE...
WICKHAM!
...D... DARCY....

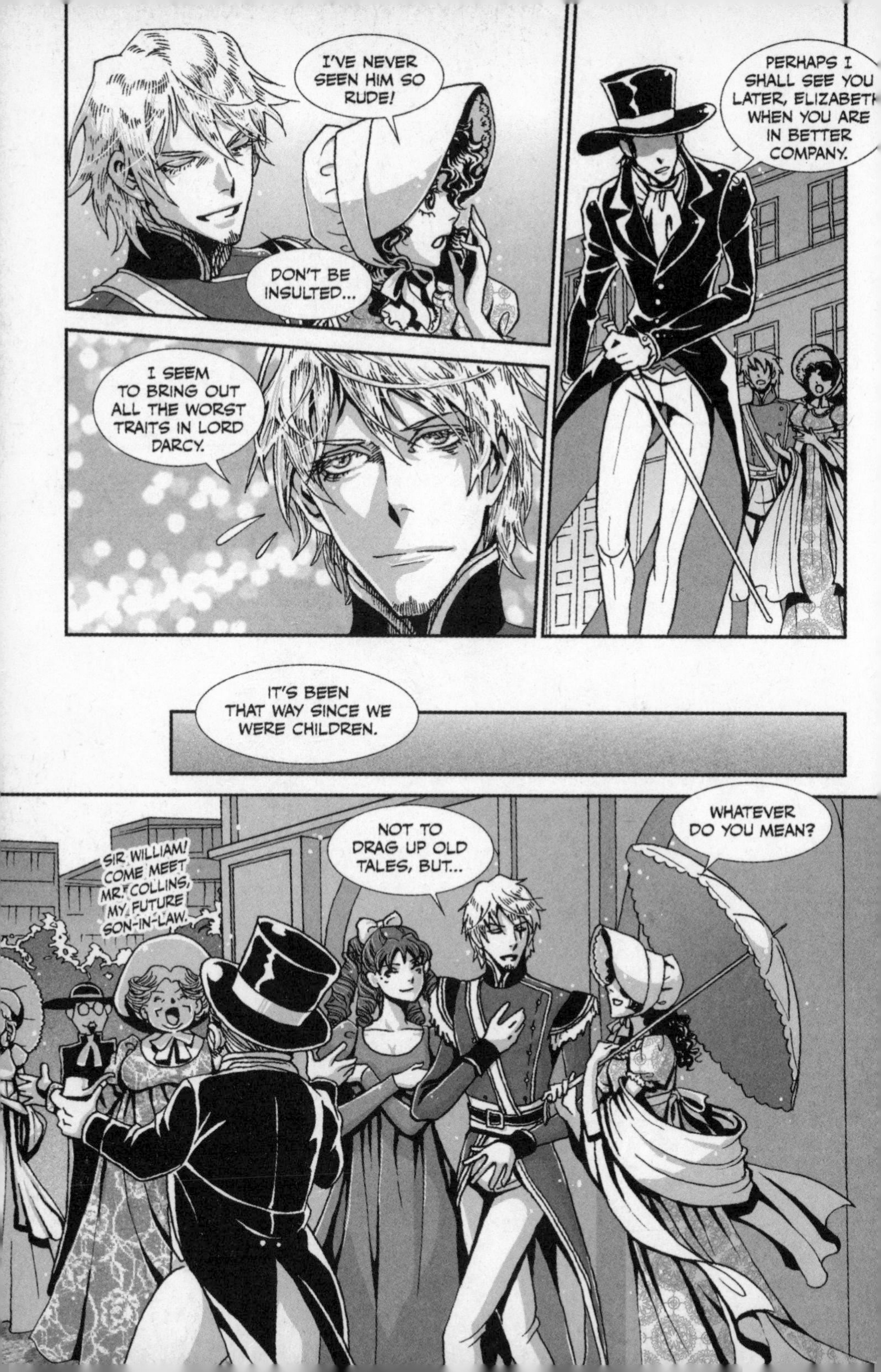
PERHAPS I SHALL SEE YOU LATER, ELIZABETH WHEN YOU ARE IN BETTER COMPANY.
I'VE NEVER SEEN HIM SO RUDE!
DON'T BE INSULTED...
I SEEM TO BRING OUT ALL THE WORST TRAITS IN LORD DARCY.
IT'S BEEN THAT WAY SINCE WE WERE CHILDREN.
WHATEVER DO YOU MEAN?
NOT TO DRAG UP OLD TALES, BUT...
SIR WILLIAM! COME MEET MR. COLLINS, MY FUTURE SON-IN-LAW.

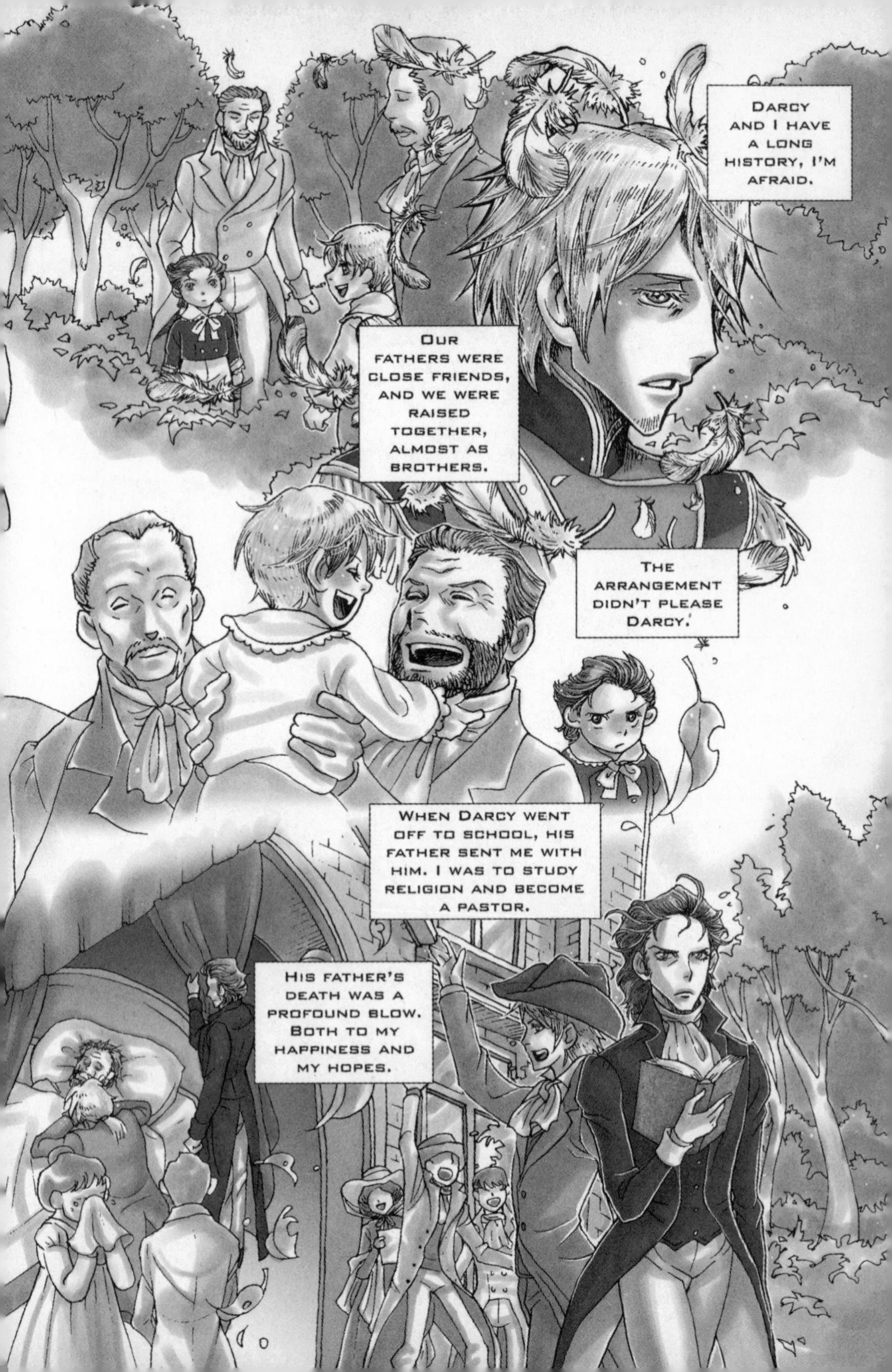
DARCY AND I HAVE A LONG HISTORY, I'M AFRAID.
OUR FATHERS WERE CLOSE FRIENDS, AND WE WERE RAISED TOGETHER, ALMOST AS BROTHERS.
THE ARRANGEMENT DIDN'T PLEASE DARCY.
WHEN DARCY WENT OFF TO SCHOOL, HIS FATHER SENT ME WITH HIM. I WAS TO STUDY RELIGION AND BECOME A PASTOR.
HIS FATHER'S DEATH WAS A PROFOUND BLOW. BOTH TO MY HAPPINESS AND MY HOPES.

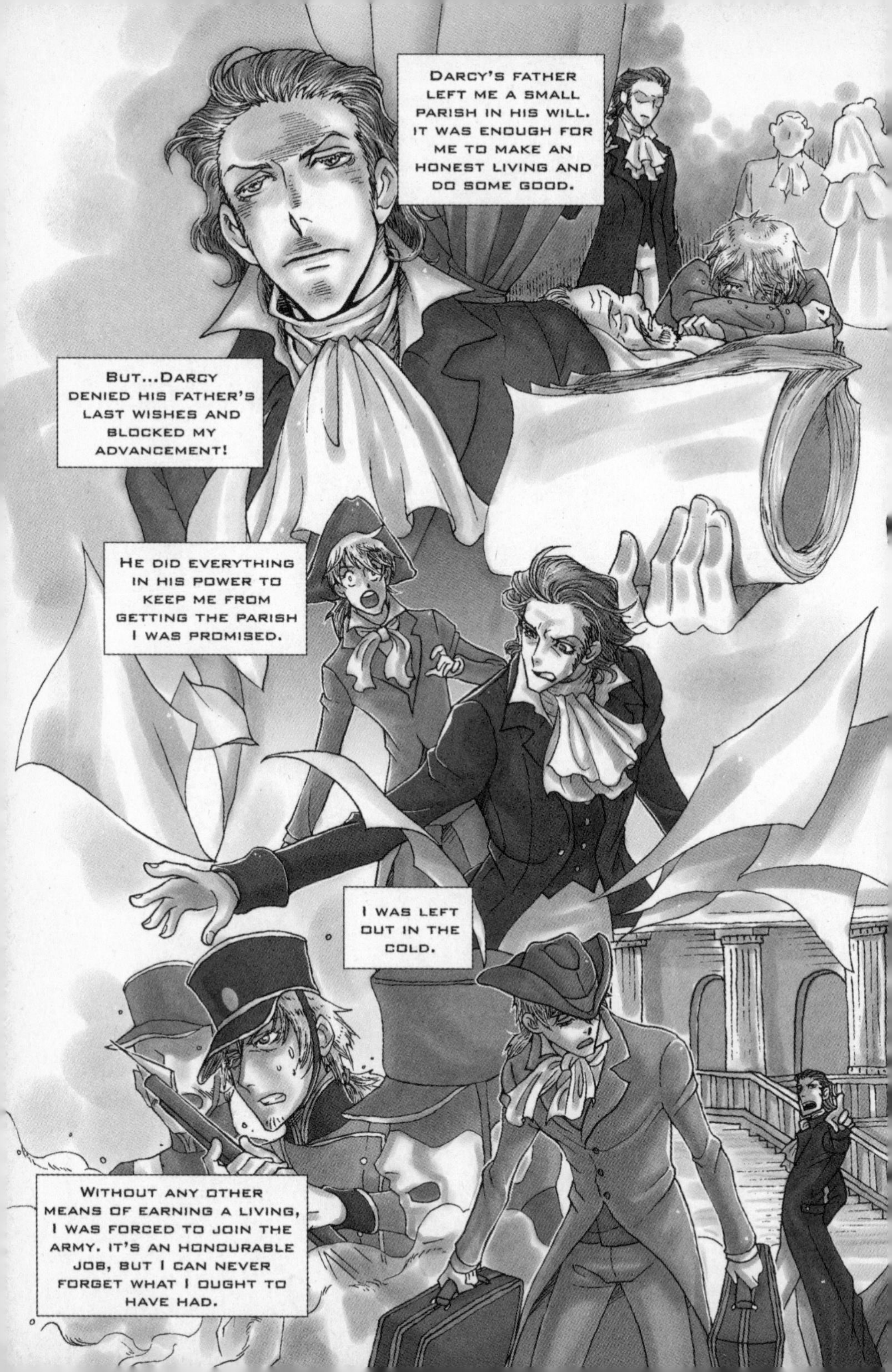

Darcy's father left me a small parish in his will. It was enough for me to make an honest living and do some good.
But...Darcy denied his father's last wishes and blocked my advancement!
He did everything in his power to keep me from getting the parish I was promised.
I was left out in the cold.
Without any other means of earning a living, I was forced to join the army. It's an honourable job, but I can never forget what I ought to have had.

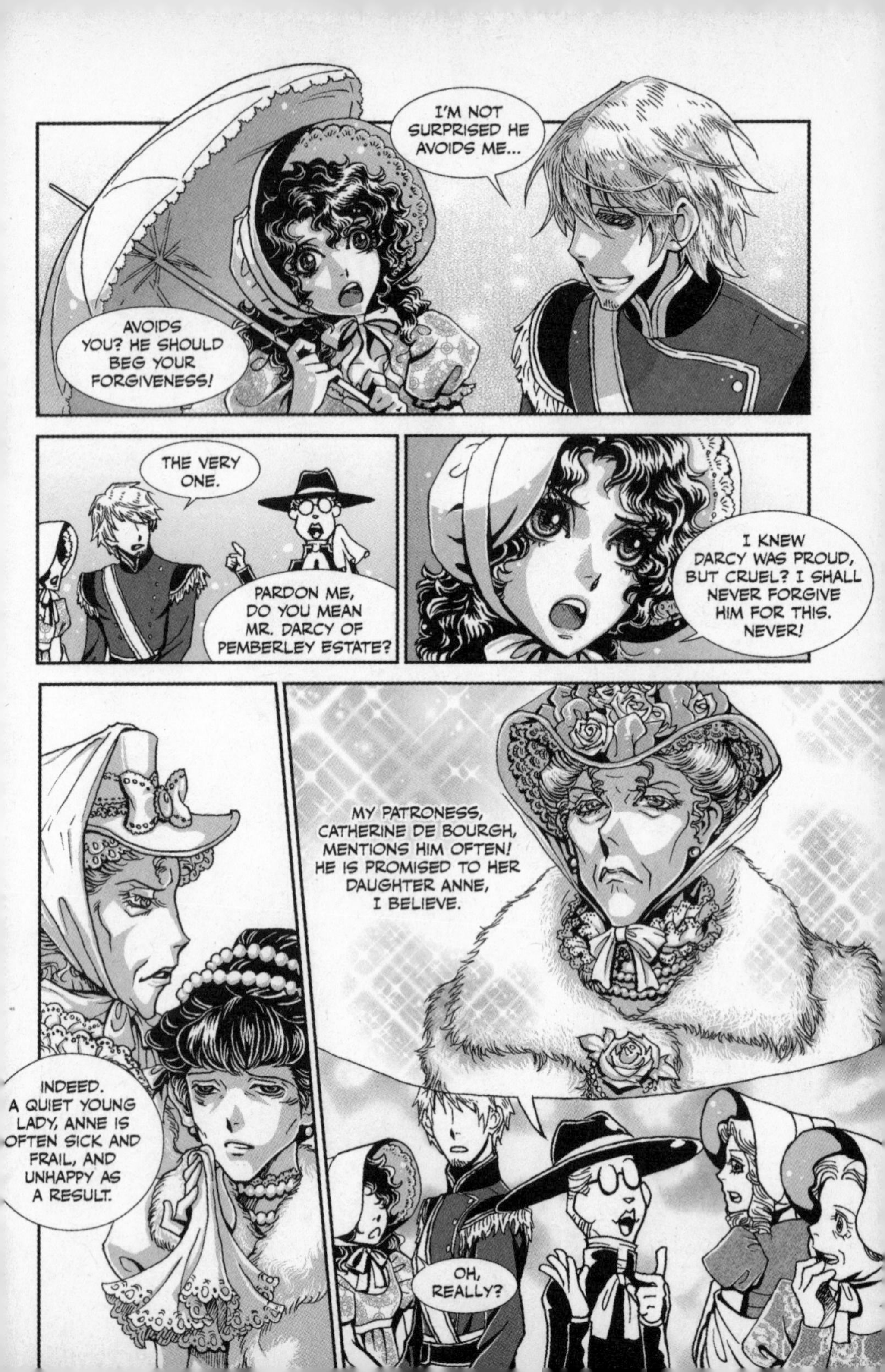
I'M NOT SURPRISED HE AVOIDS ME...
AVOIDS YOU? HE SHOULD BEG YOUR FORGIVENESS!
I KNEW DARCY WAS PROUD, BUT CRUEL? I SHALL NEVER FORGIVE HIM FOR THIS. NEVER!
THE VERY ONE.
PARDON ME, DO YOU MEAN MR. DARCY OF PEMBERLEY ESTATE?
MY PATRONESS, CATHERINE DE BOURGH, MENTIONS HIM OFTEN! HE IS PROMISED TO HER DAUGHTER ANNE, I BELIEVE.
OH, REALLY?
INDEED. A QUIET YOUNG LADY, ANNE IS OFTEN SICK AND FRAIL, AND UNHAPPY AS A RESULT.

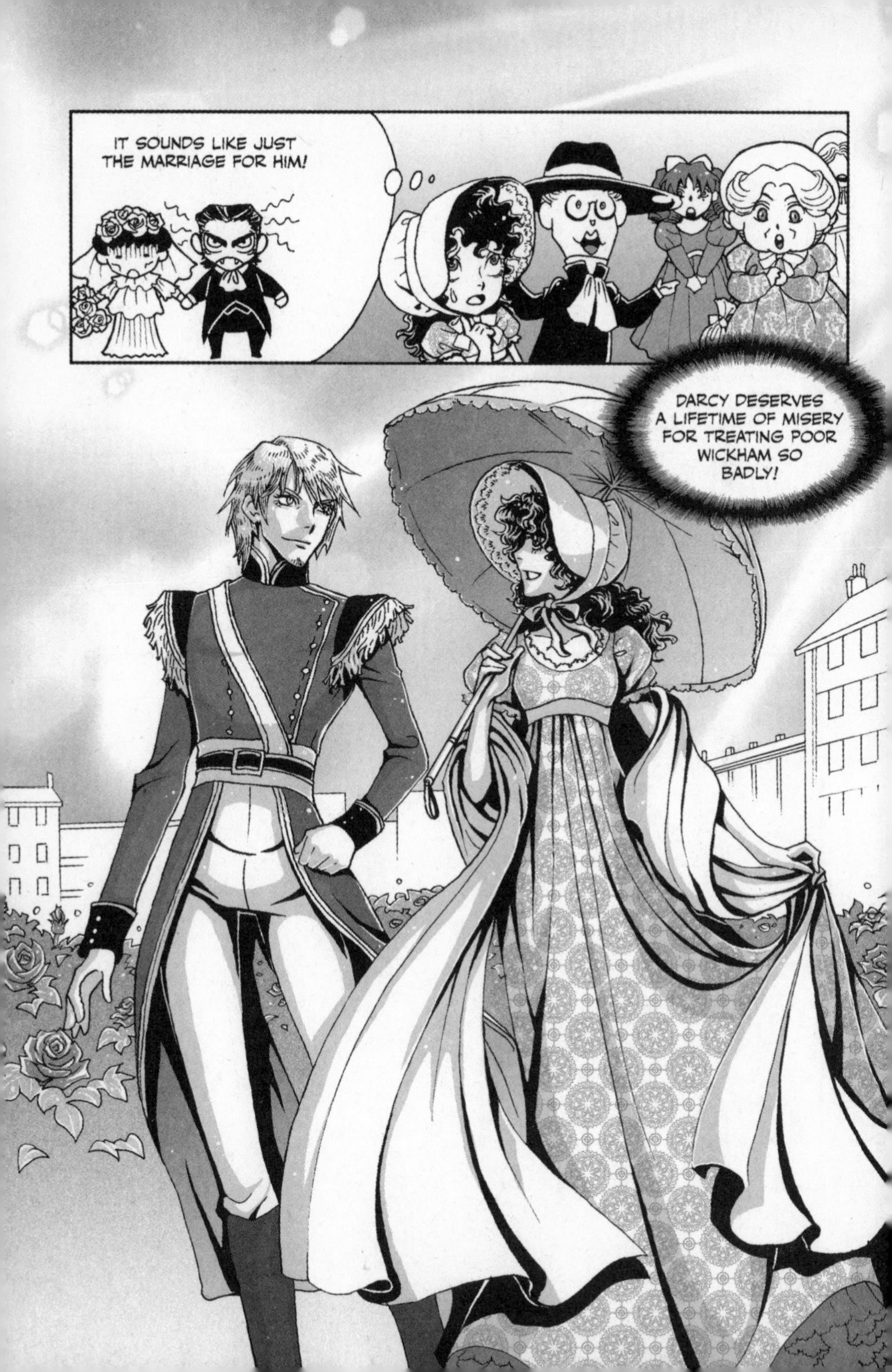
IT SOUNDS LIKE JUST THE MARRIAGE FOR HIM!
DARCY DESERVES A LIFETIME OF MISERY FOR TREATING POOR WICKHAM SO BADLY!

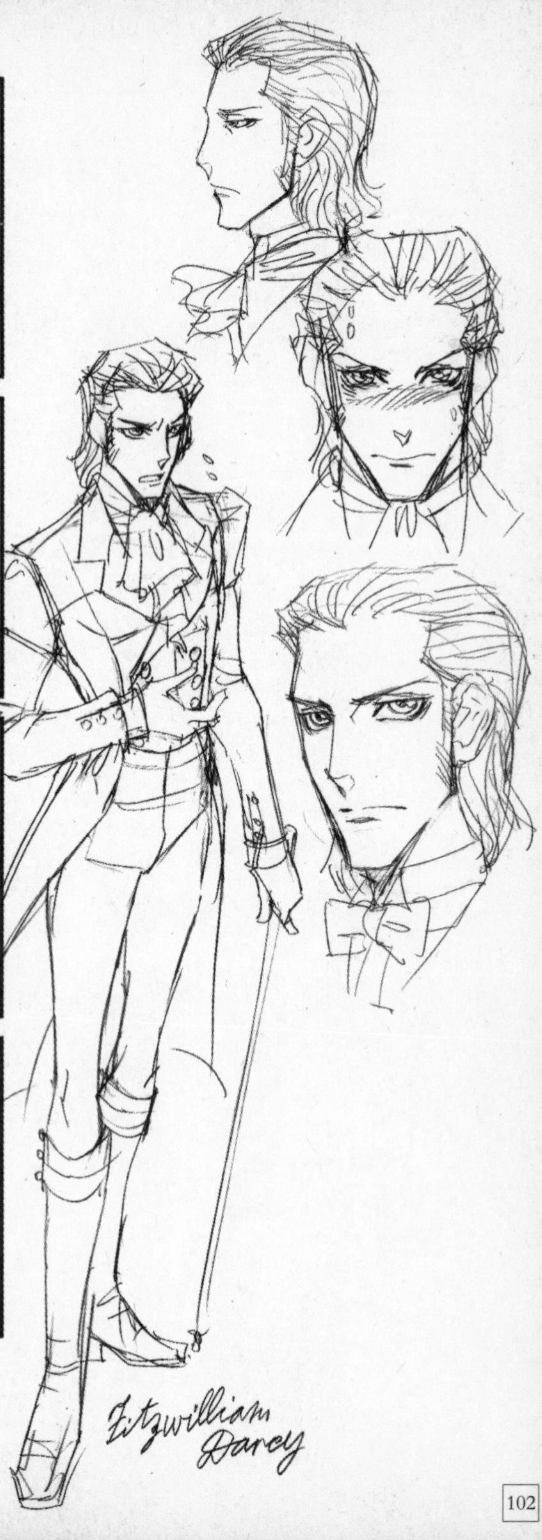
Fitzwilliam Darcy

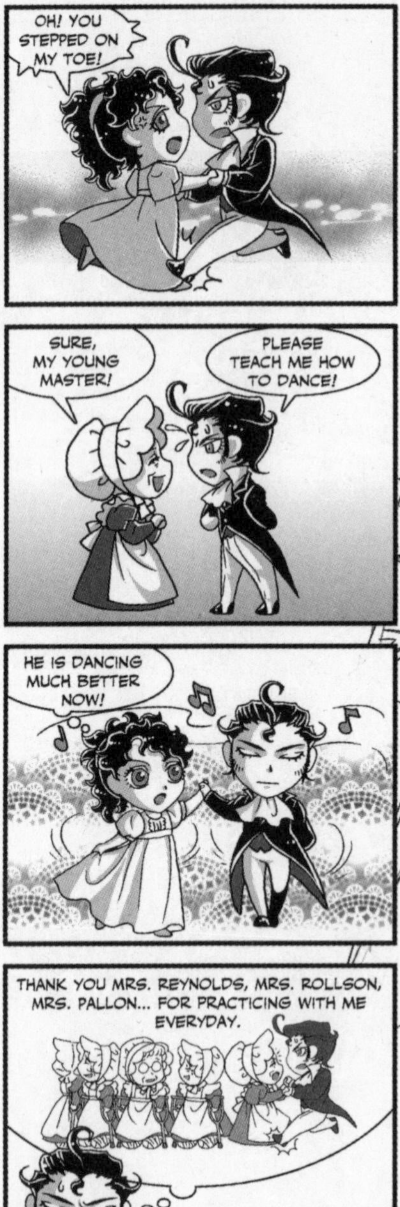
OH! YOU STEPPED ON MY TOE!
PLEASE TEACH ME HOW TO DANCE!
SURE, MY YOUNG MASTER!
HE IS DANCING MUCH BETTER NOW!
THANK YOU MRS. REYNOLDS, MRS. ROLLSON, MRS. PALLON... FOR PRACTICING WITH ME EVERYDAY.

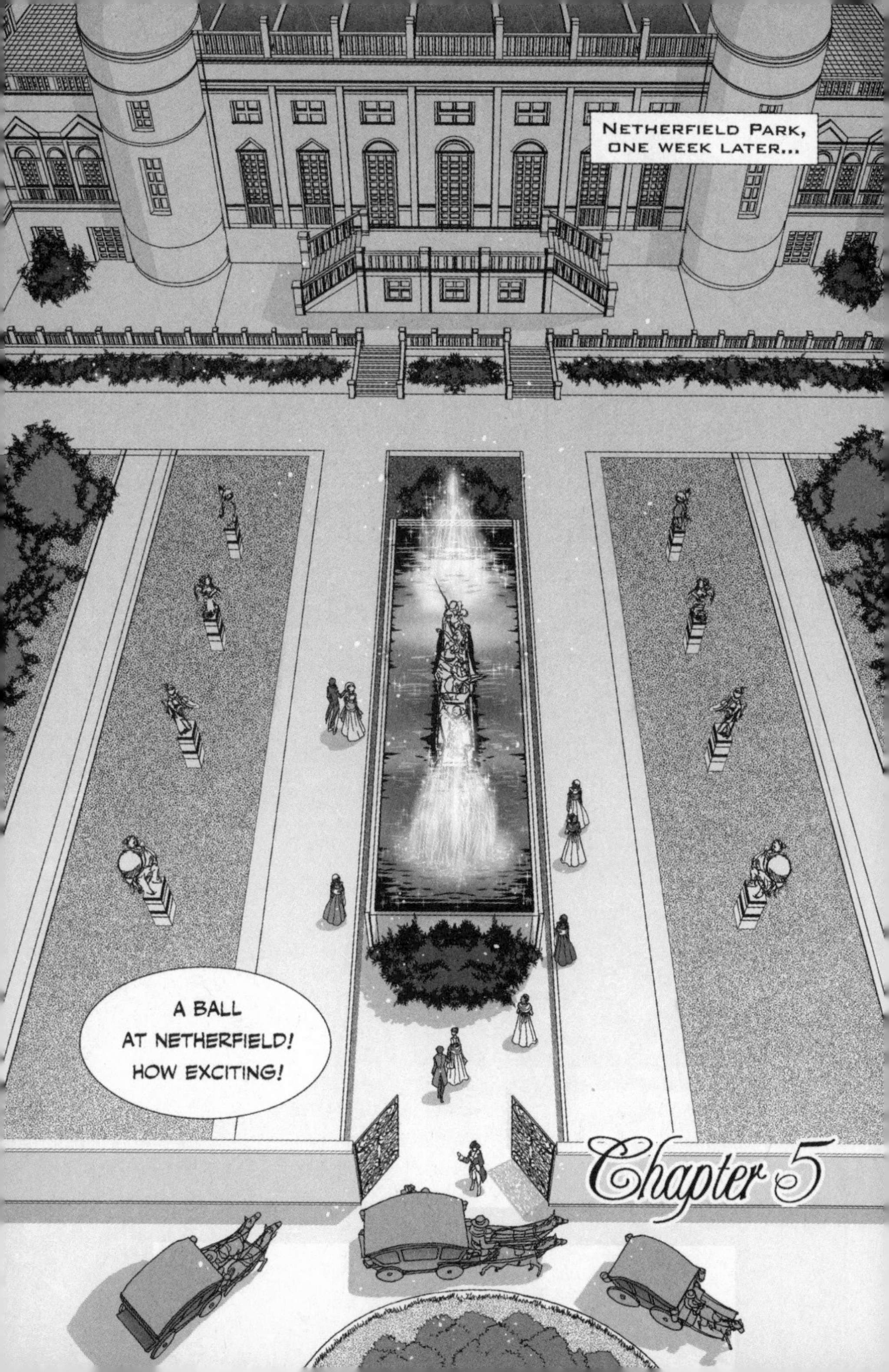
NETHERFIELD PARK, ONE WEEK LATER...
A BALL AT NETHERFIELD! HOW EXCITING!
Chapter 5

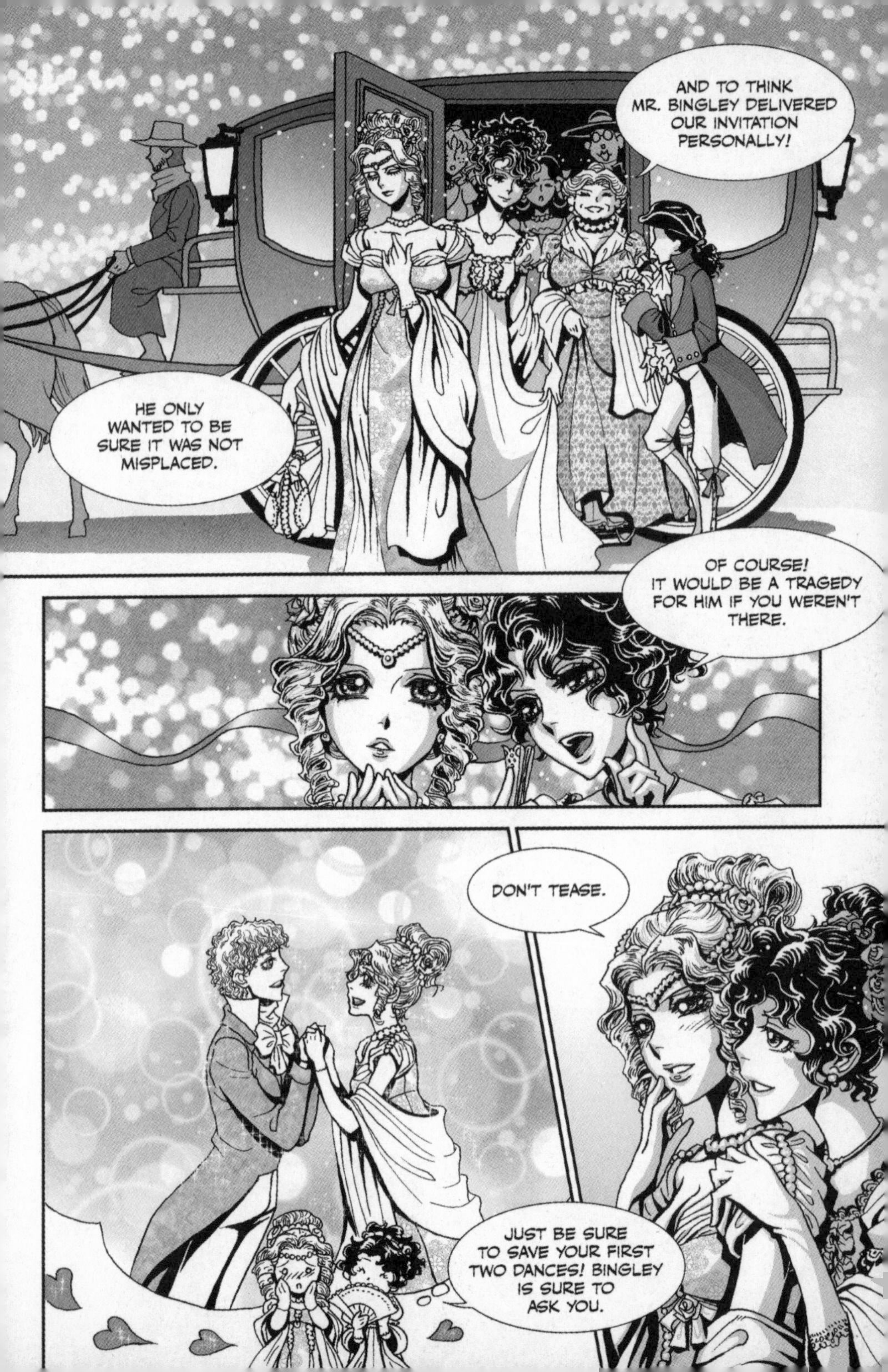
AND TO THINK MR. BINGLEY DELIVERED OUR INVITATION PERSONALLY!
HE ONLY WANTED TO BE SURE IT WAS NOT MISPLACED.
OF COURSE! IT WOULD BE A TRAGEDY FOR HIM IF YOU WEREN'T THERE.
DON'T TEASE.
JUST BE SURE TO SAVE YOUR FIRST TWO DANCES! BINGLEY IS SURE TO ASK YOU.

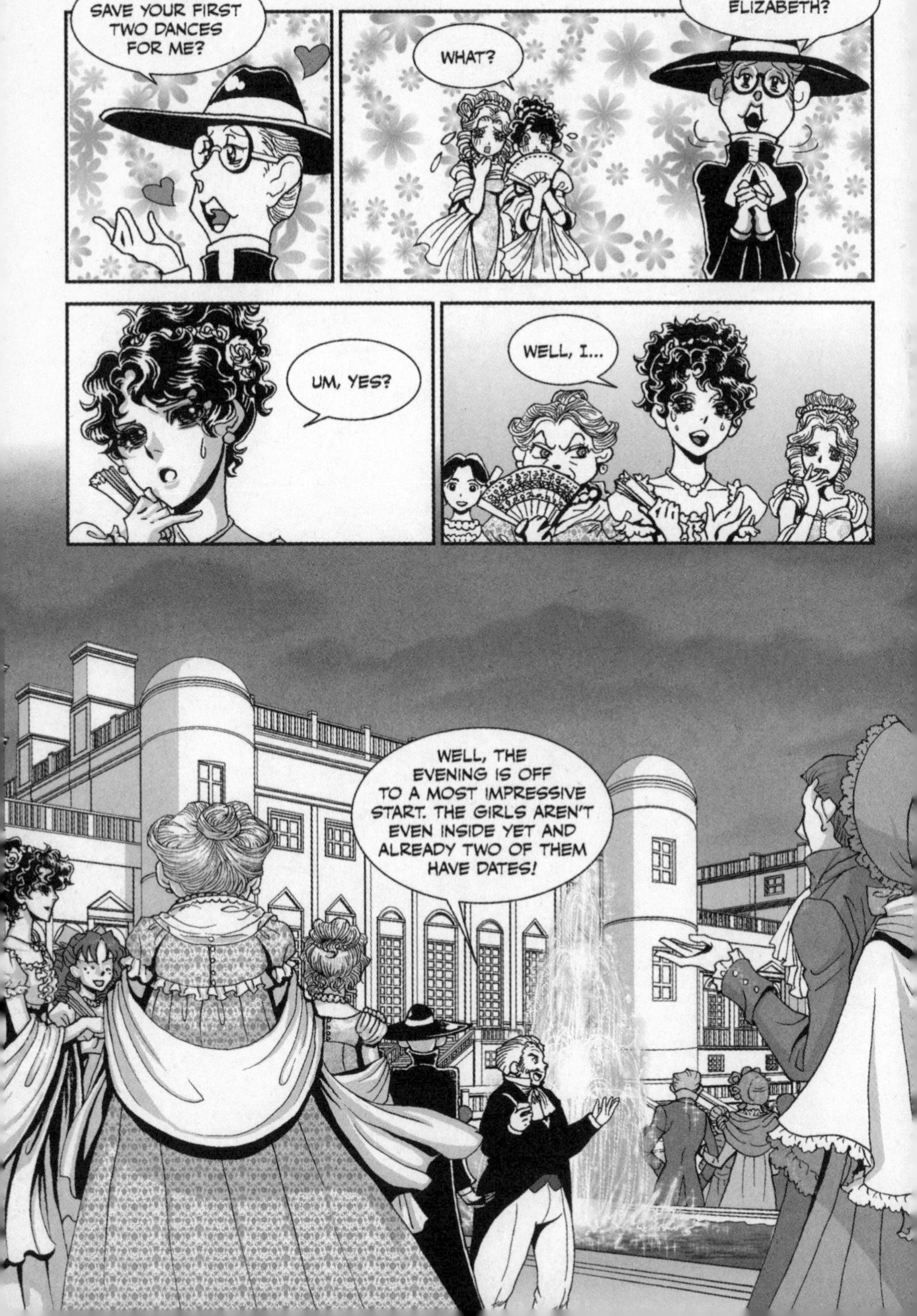
WILL YOU SAVE YOUR FIRST TWO DANCES FOR ME?
WHAT?
AND YOU, ELIZABETH?
UM, YES?
WELL, I...
WELL, THE EVENING IS OFF TO A MOST IMPRESSIVE START. THE GIRLS AREN'T EVEN INSIDE YET AND ALREADY TWO OF THEM HAVE DATES!

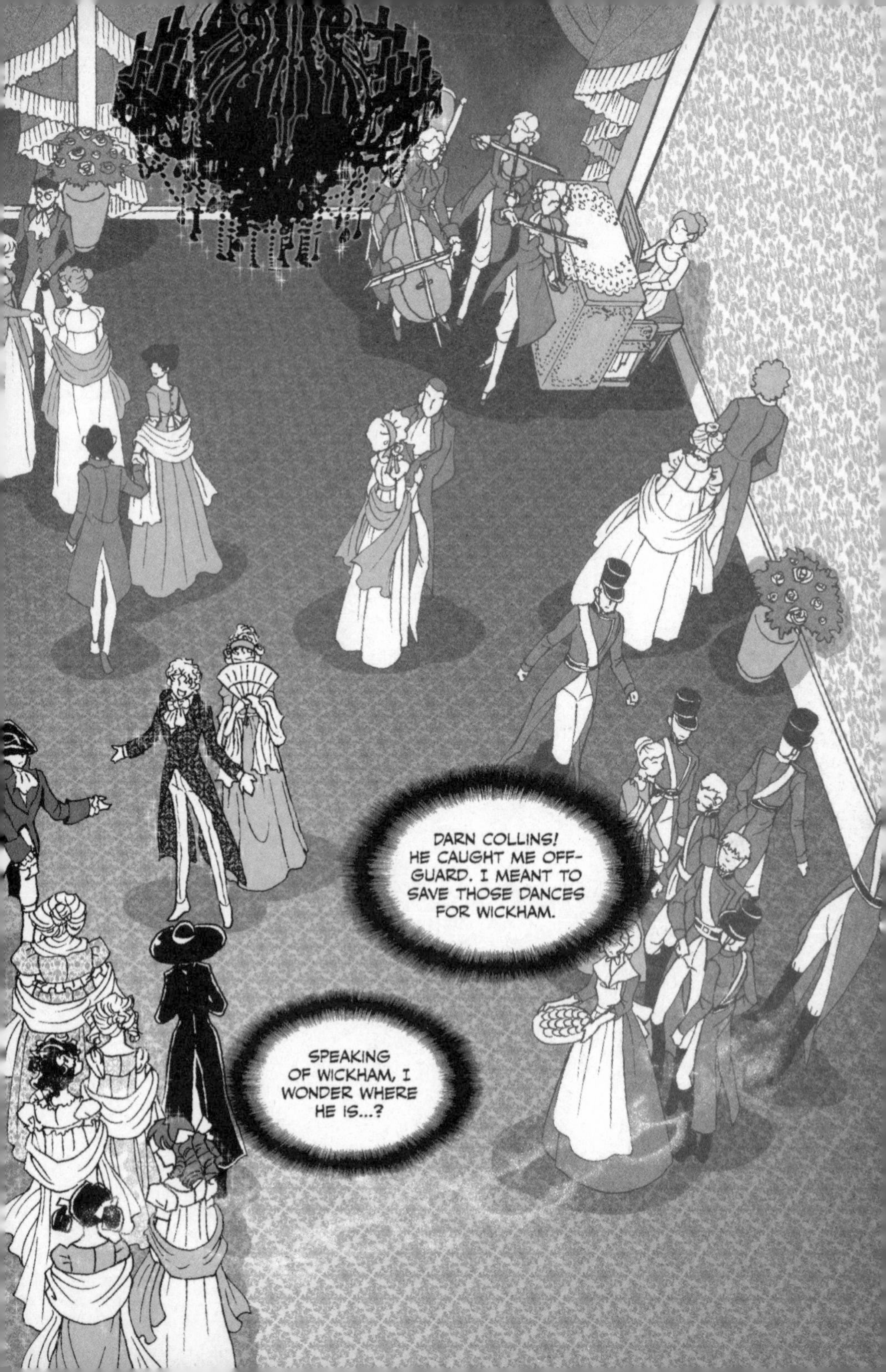
DARN COLLINS! HE CAUGHT ME OFF-GUARD. I MEANT TO SAVE THOSE DANCES FOR WICKHAM.
SPEAKING OF WICKHAM, I WONDER WHERE HE IS...?

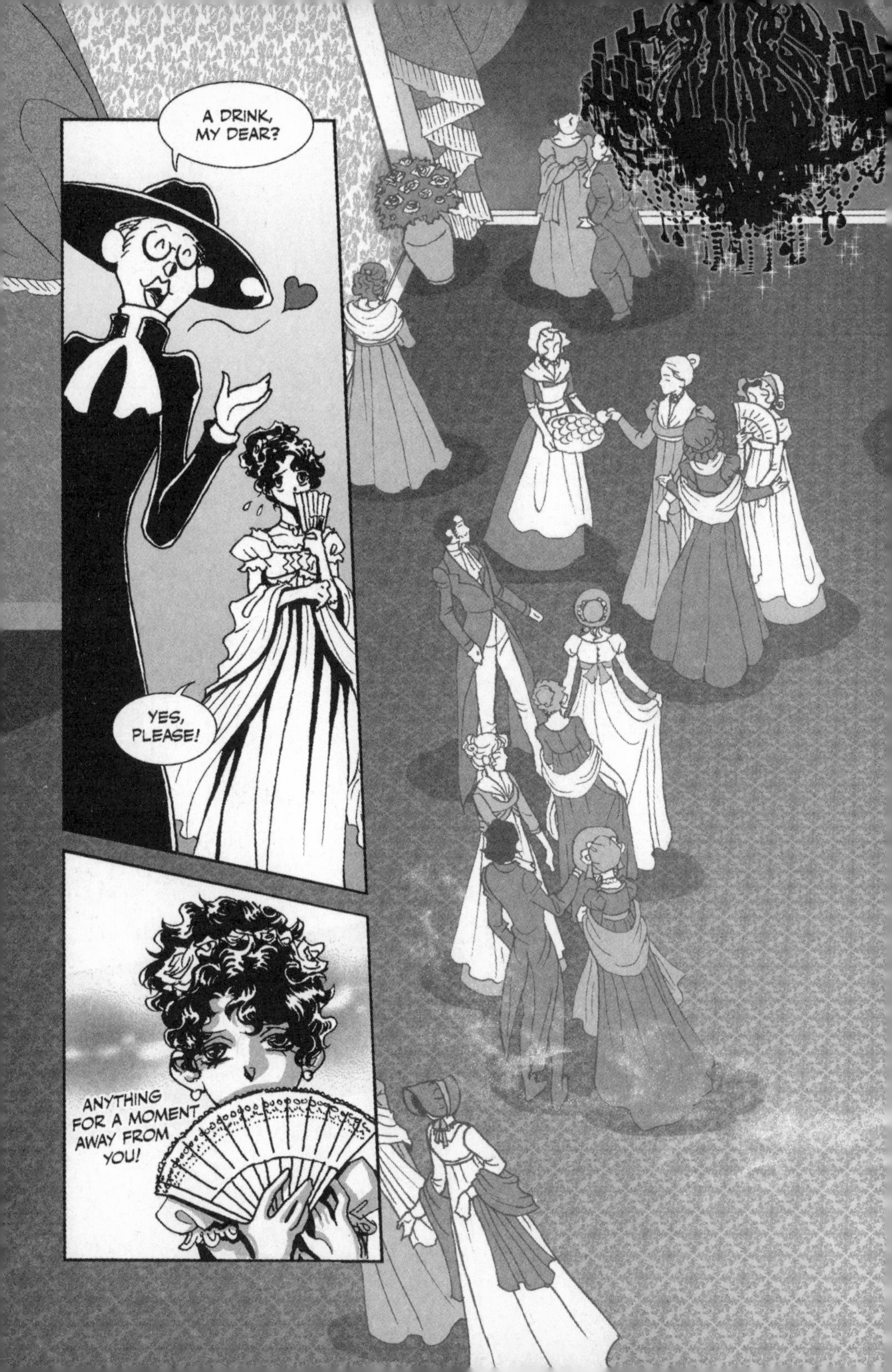
A DRINK, MY DEAR?
YES, PLEASE!
ANYTHING FOR A MOMENT AWAY FROM YOU!

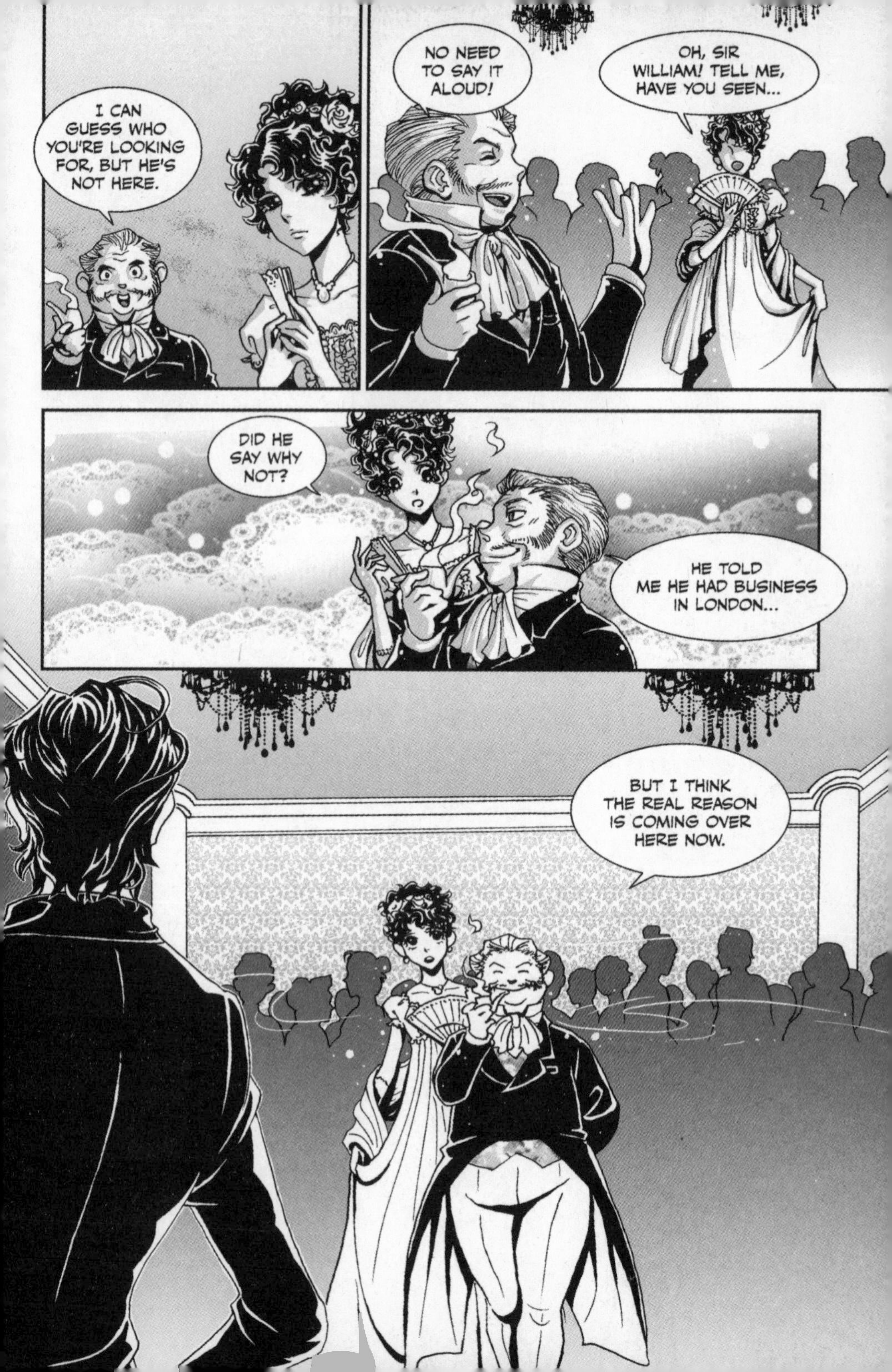
OH, SIR WILLIAM! TELL ME, HAVE YOU SEEN...
NO NEED TO SAY IT ALOUD!
I CAN GUESS WHO YOU'RE LOOKING FOR, BUT HE'S NOT HERE.
DID HE SAY WHY NOT?
HE TOLD ME HE HAD BUSINESS IN LONDON...
BUT I THINK THE REAL REASON IS COMING OVER HERE NOW.

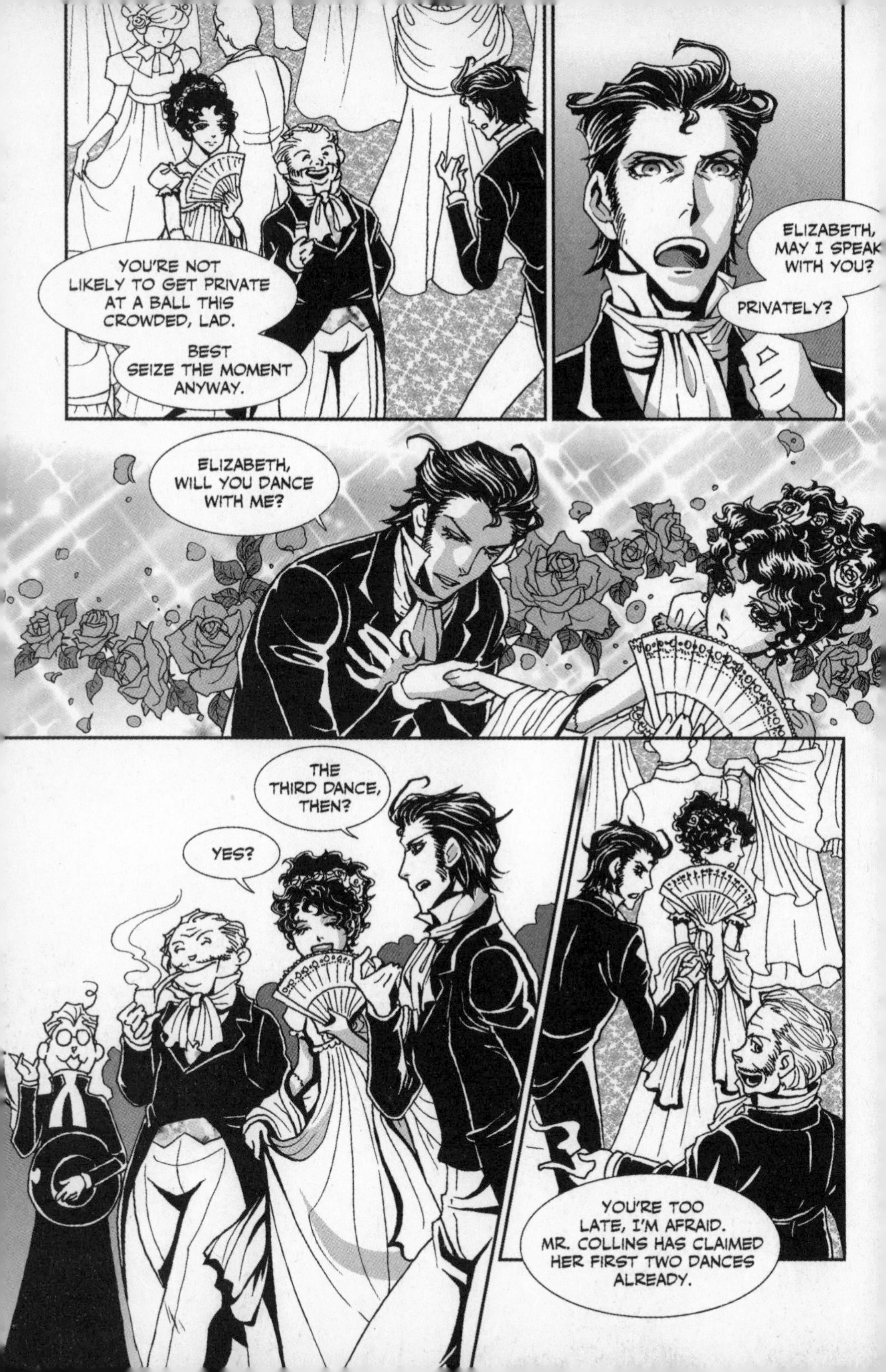
ELIZABETH, MAY I SPEAK WITH YOU?
PRIVATELY?
YOU'RE NOT LIKELY TO GET PRIVATE AT A BALL THIS CROWDED, LAD.
BEST SEIZE THE MOMENT ANYWAY.
ELIZABETH, WILL YOU DANCE WITH ME?
YOU'RE TOO LATE, I'M AFRAID. MR. COLLINS HAS CLAIMED HER FIRST TWO DANCES ALREADY.
THE THIRD DANCE, THEN?
YES?

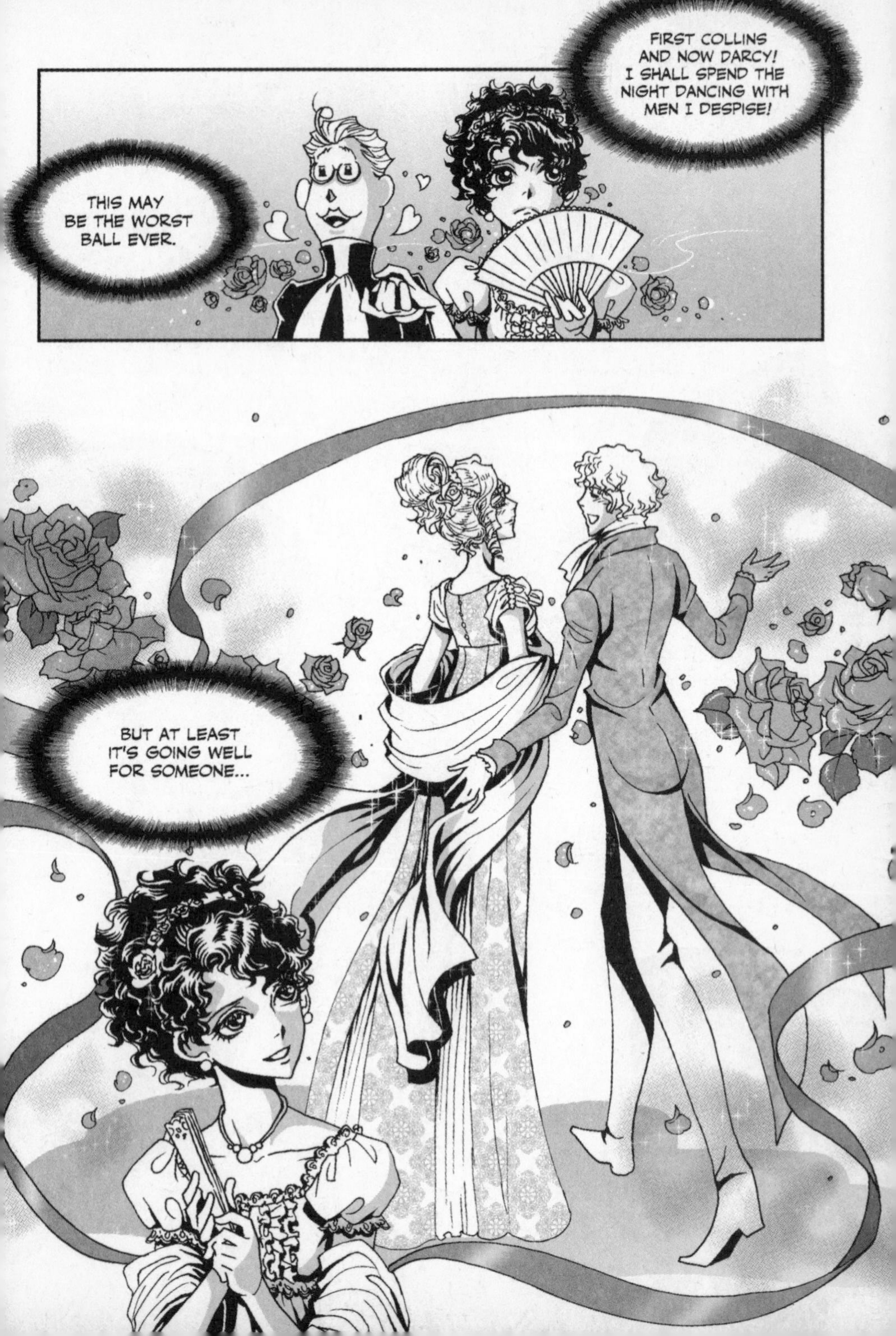
FIRST COLLINS AND NOW DARCY! I SHALL SPEND THE NIGHT DANCING WITH MEN I DESPISE!
THIS MAY BE THE WORST BALL EVER.
BUT AT LEAST IT'S GOING WELL FOR SOMEONE...

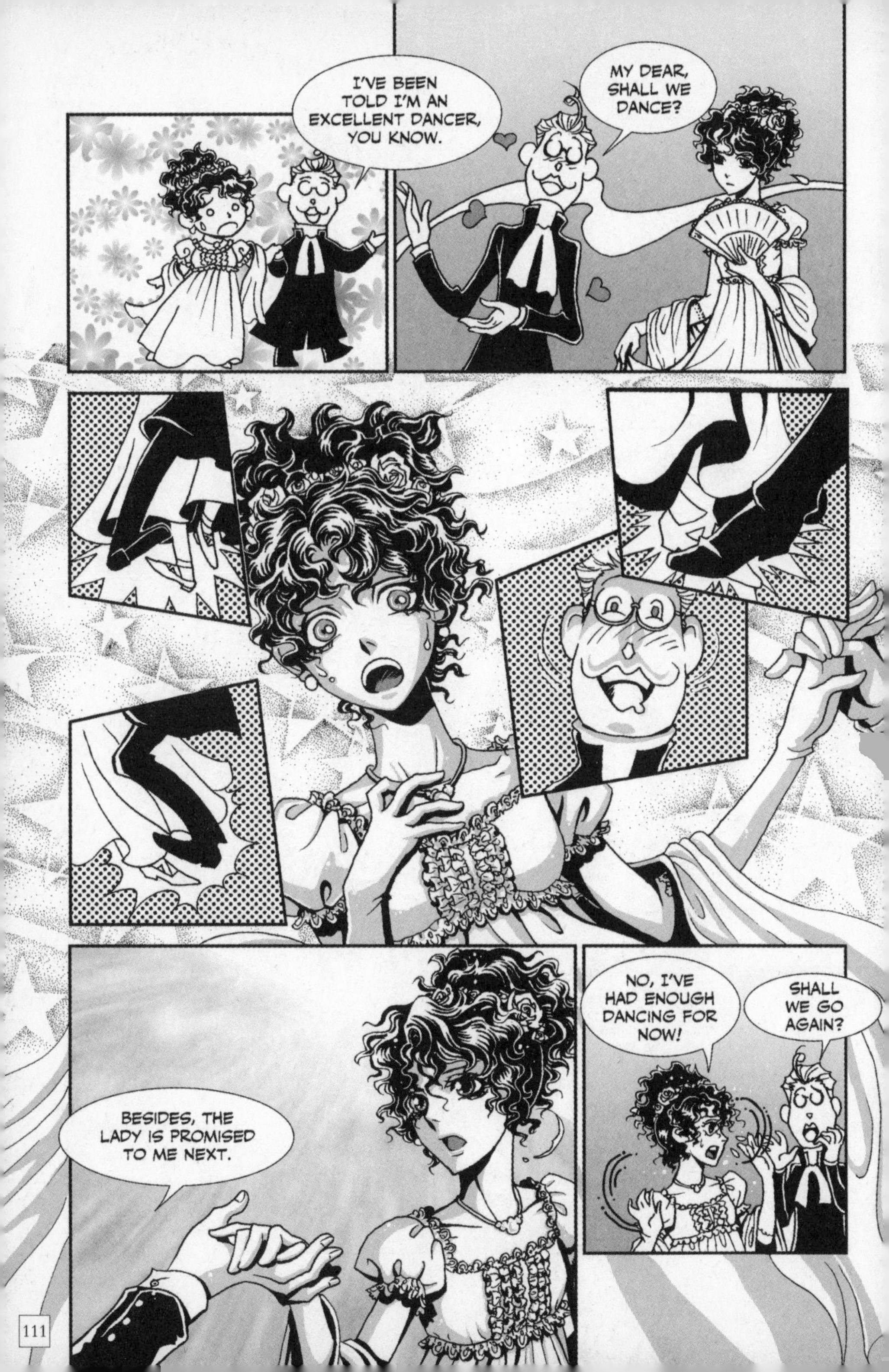
MY DEAR, SHALL WE DANCE?
I'VE BEEN TOLD I'M AN EXCELLENT DANCER, YOU KNOW.
SHALL WE GO AGAIN?
NO, I'VE HAD ENOUGH DANCING FOR NOW!
BESIDES, THE LADY IS PROMISED TO ME NEXT.

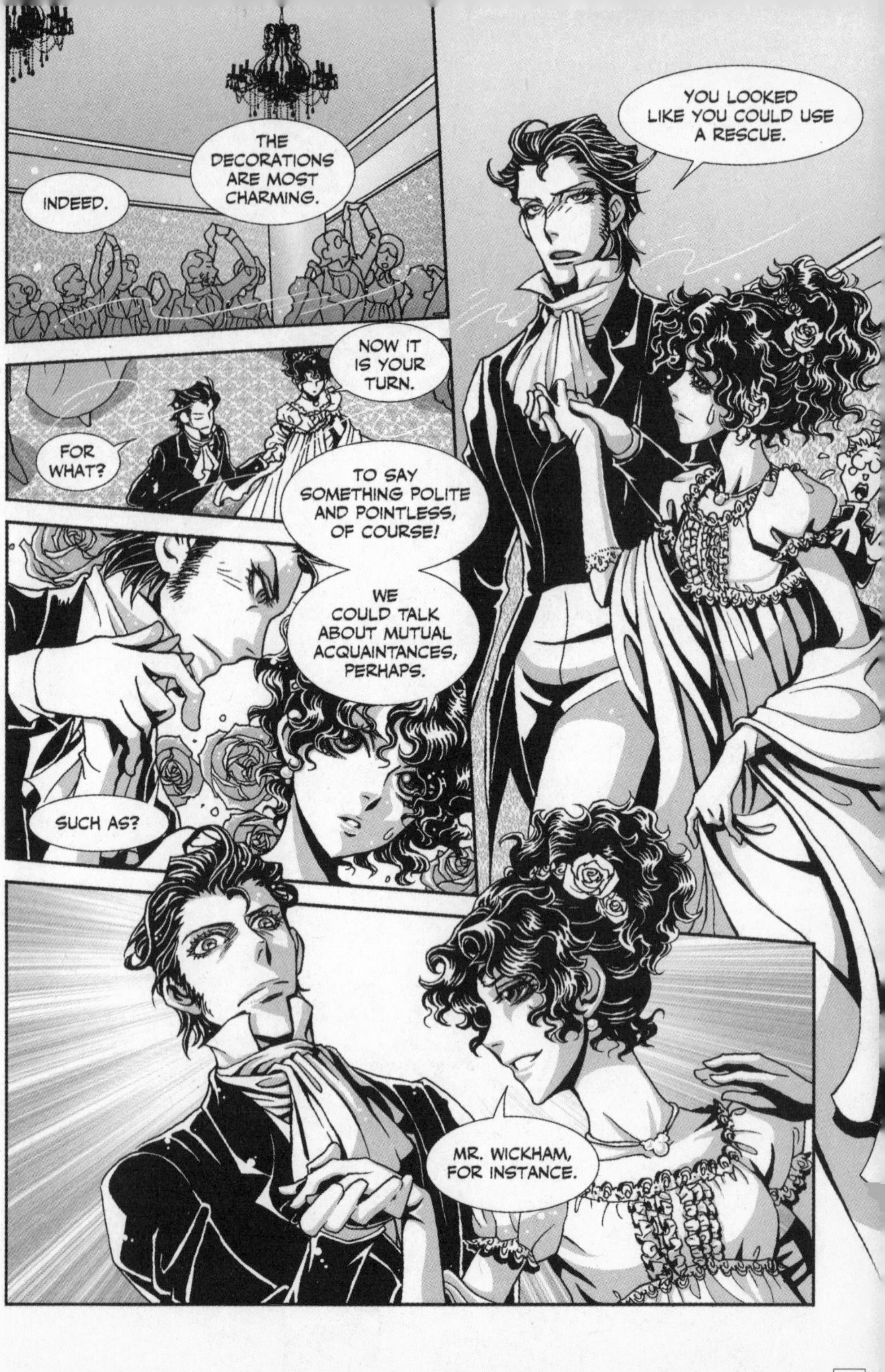
YOU LOOKED LIKE YOU COULD USE A RESCUE.
THE DECORATIONS ARE MOST CHARMING.
INDEED.
NOW IT IS YOUR TURN.
FOR WHAT?
TO SAY SOMETHING POLITE AND POINTLESS, OF COURSE!
WE COULD TALK ABOUT MUTUAL ACQUAINTANCES, PERHAPS.
SUCH AS?
MR. WICKHAM, FOR INSTANCE.

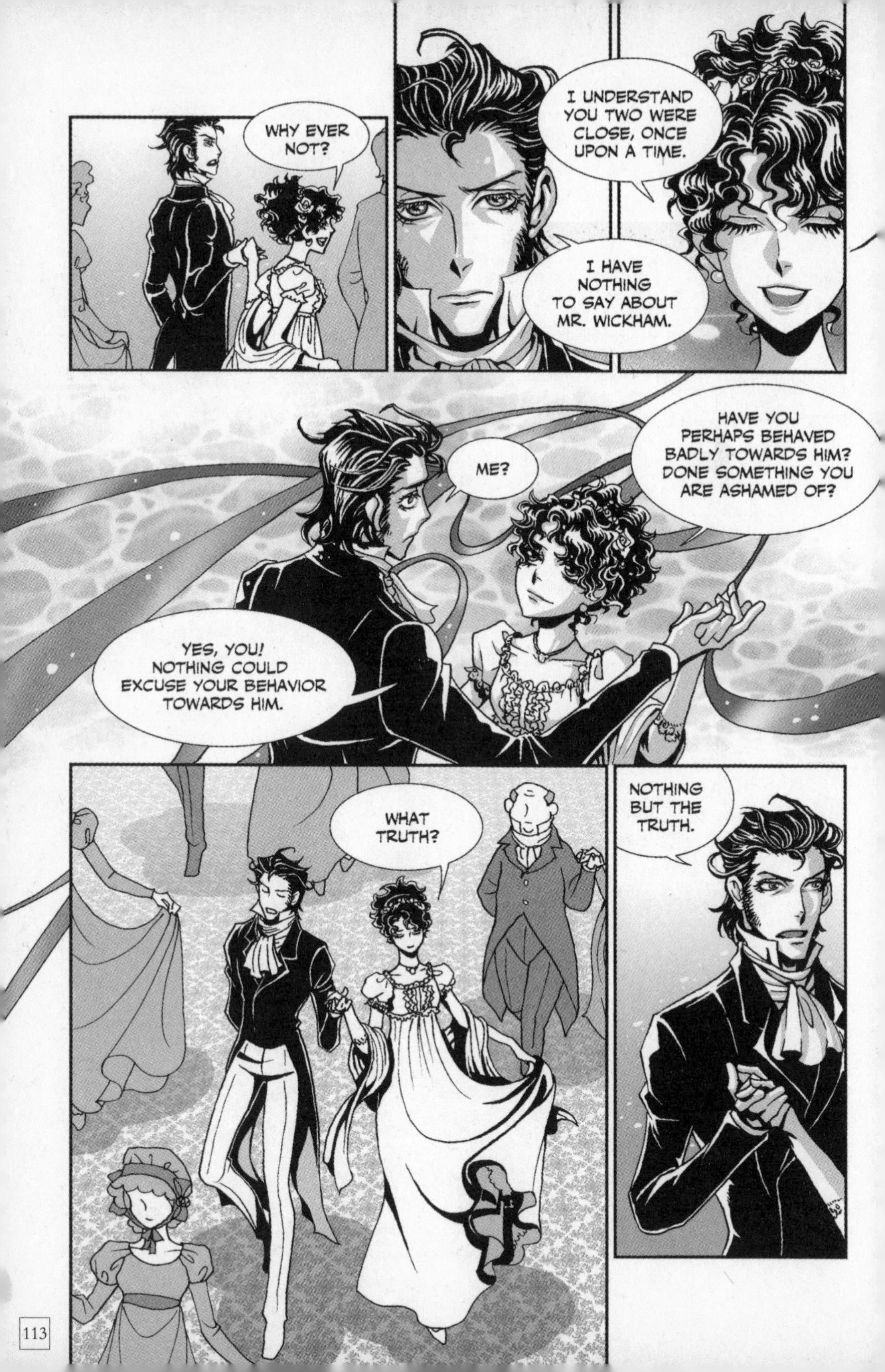
I UNDERSTAND YOU TWO WERE CLOSE, ONCE UPON A TIME.
I HAVE NOTHING TO SAY ABOUT MR. WICKHAM.
WHY EVER NOT?
HAVE YOU PERHAPS BEHAVED BADLY TOWARDS HIM? DONE SOMETHING YOU ARE ASHAMED OF?
ME?
YES, YOU! NOTHING COULD EXCUSE YOUR BEHAVIOR TOWARDS HIM.
NOTHING BUT THE TRUTH.
WHAT TRUTH?

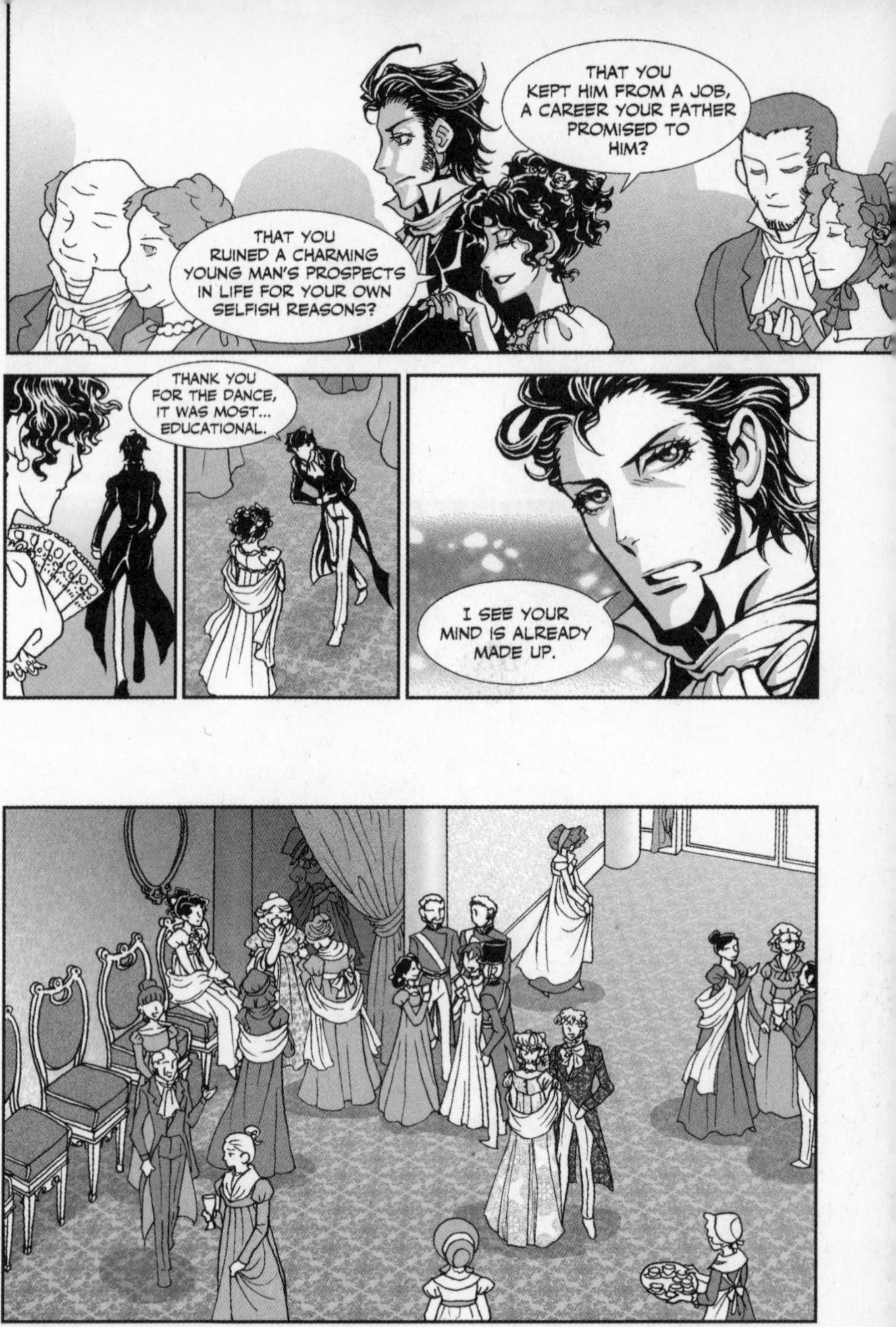
THAT YOU KEPT HIM FROM A JOB, A CAREER YOUR FATHER PROMISED TO HIM?
THAT YOU RUINED A CHARMING YOUNG MAN'S PROSPECTS IN LIFE FOR YOUR OWN SELFISH REASONS?
I SEE YOUR MIND IS ALREADY MADE UP.
THANK YOU FOR THE DANCE, IT WAS MOST... EDUCATIONAL.

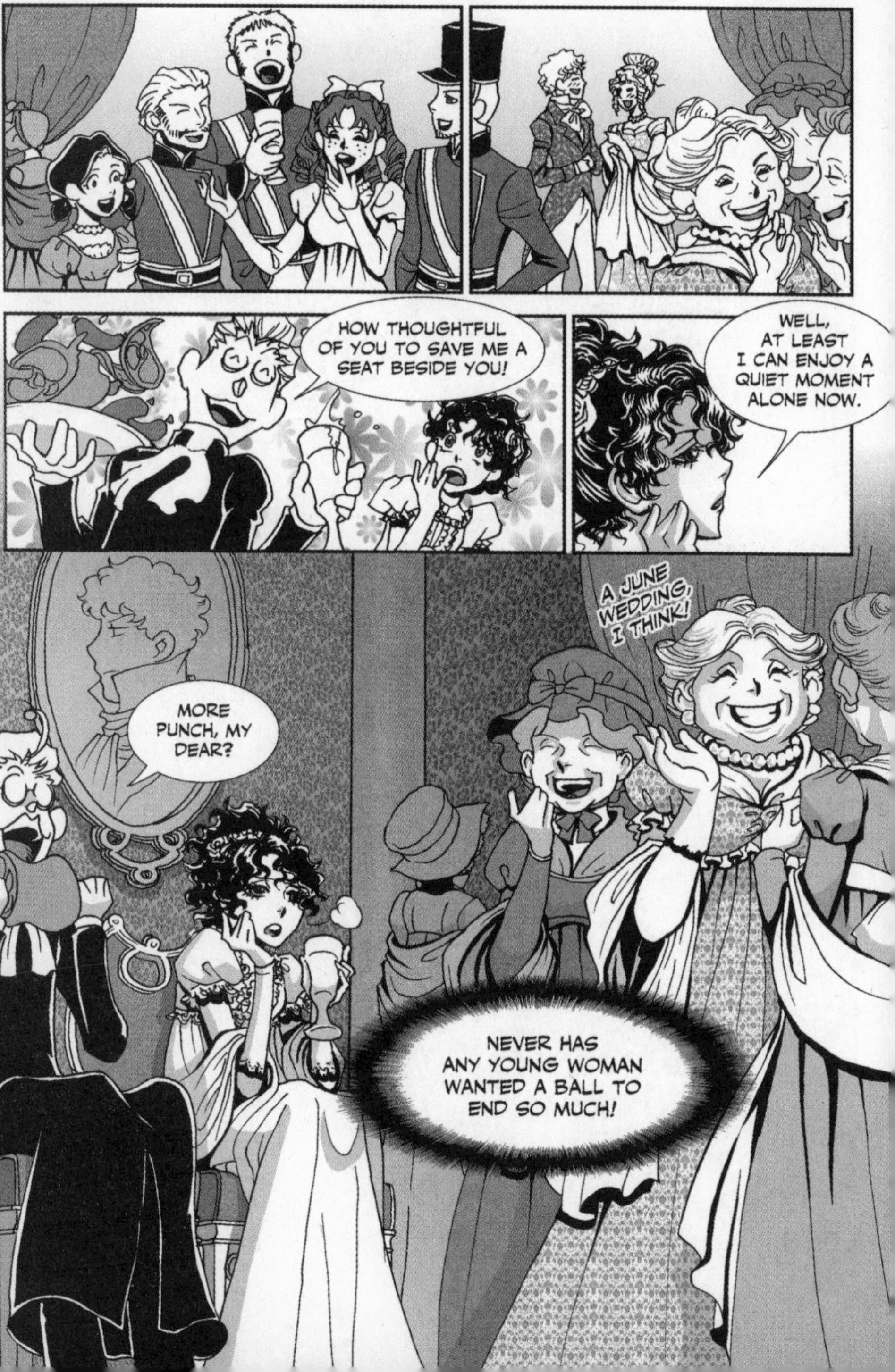
WELL, AT LEAST I CAN ENJOY A QUIET MOMENT ALONE NOW.
HOW THOUGHTFUL OF YOU TO SAVE ME A SEAT BESIDE YOU!
A JUNE WEDDING, I THINK!
MORE PUNCH, MY DEAR?
NEVER HAS ANY YOUNG WOMAN WANTED A BALL TO END SO MUCH!

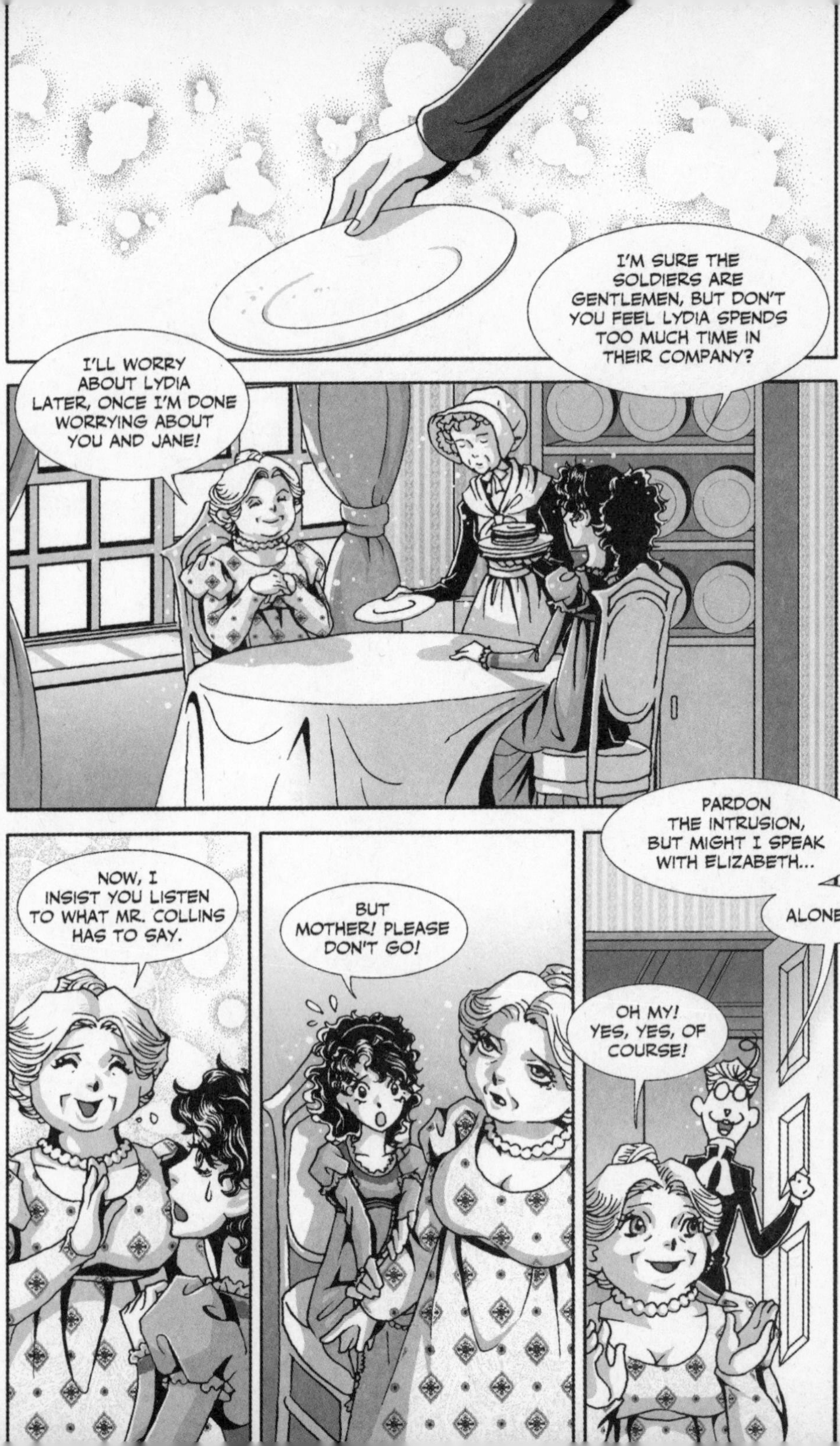
I'M SURE THE SOLDIERS ARE GENTLEMEN, BUT DON'T YOU FEEL LYDIA SPENDS TOO MUCH TIME IN THEIR COMPANY?
I'LL WORRY ABOUT LYDIA LATER, ONCE I'M DONE WORRYING ABOUT YOU AND JANE!
PARDON THE INTRUSION, BUT MIGHT I SPEAK WITH ELIZABETH...
ALONE?
OH MY! YES, YES, OF COURSE!
BUT MOTHER! PLEASE DON'T GO!
NOW, I INSIST YOU LISTEN TO WHAT MR. COLLINS HAS TO SAY.

Chapter 6

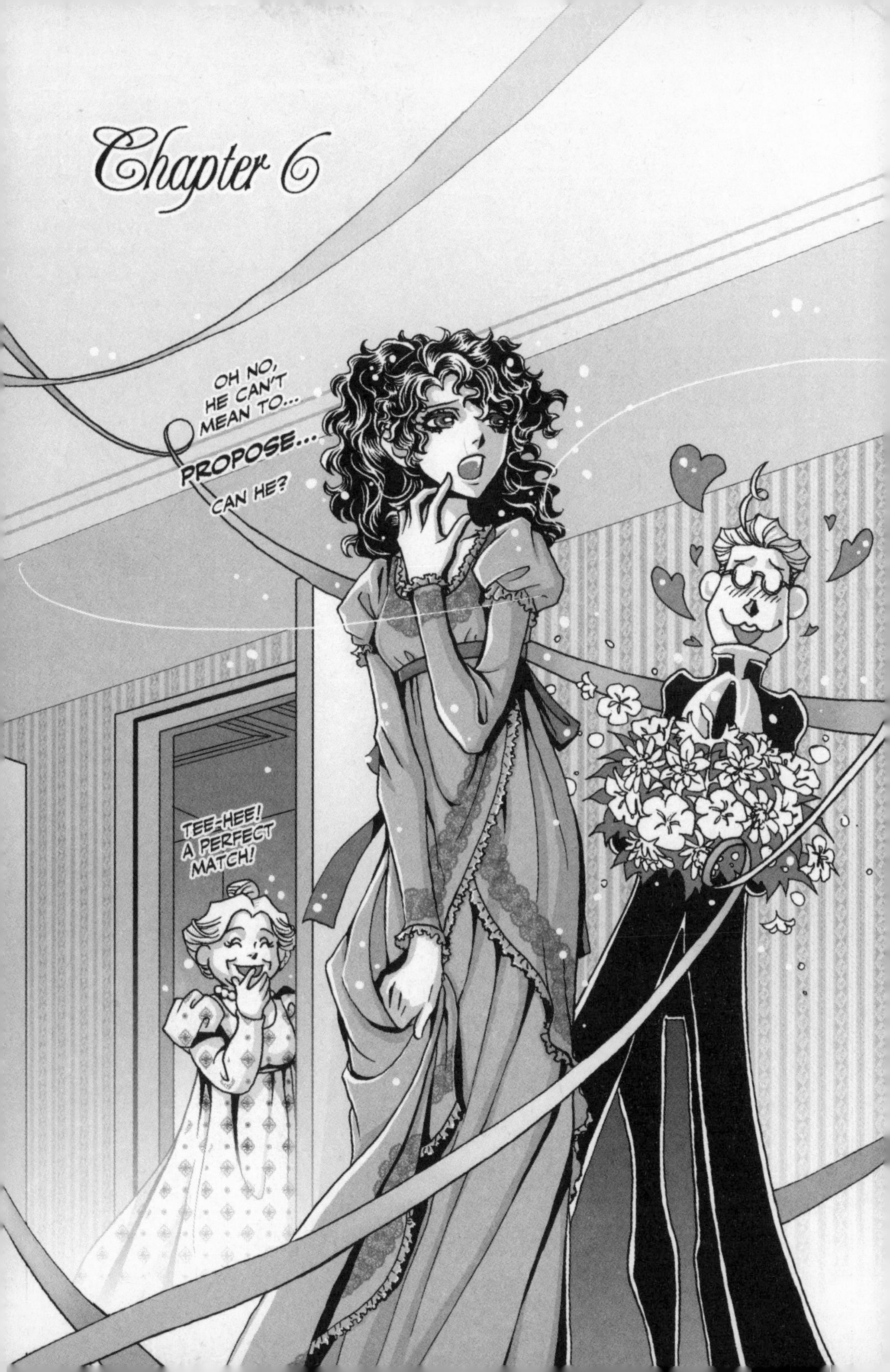
OH NO, HE CAN'T MEAN TO... PROPOSE... CAN HE?
TEE-HEE! A PERFECT MATCH!

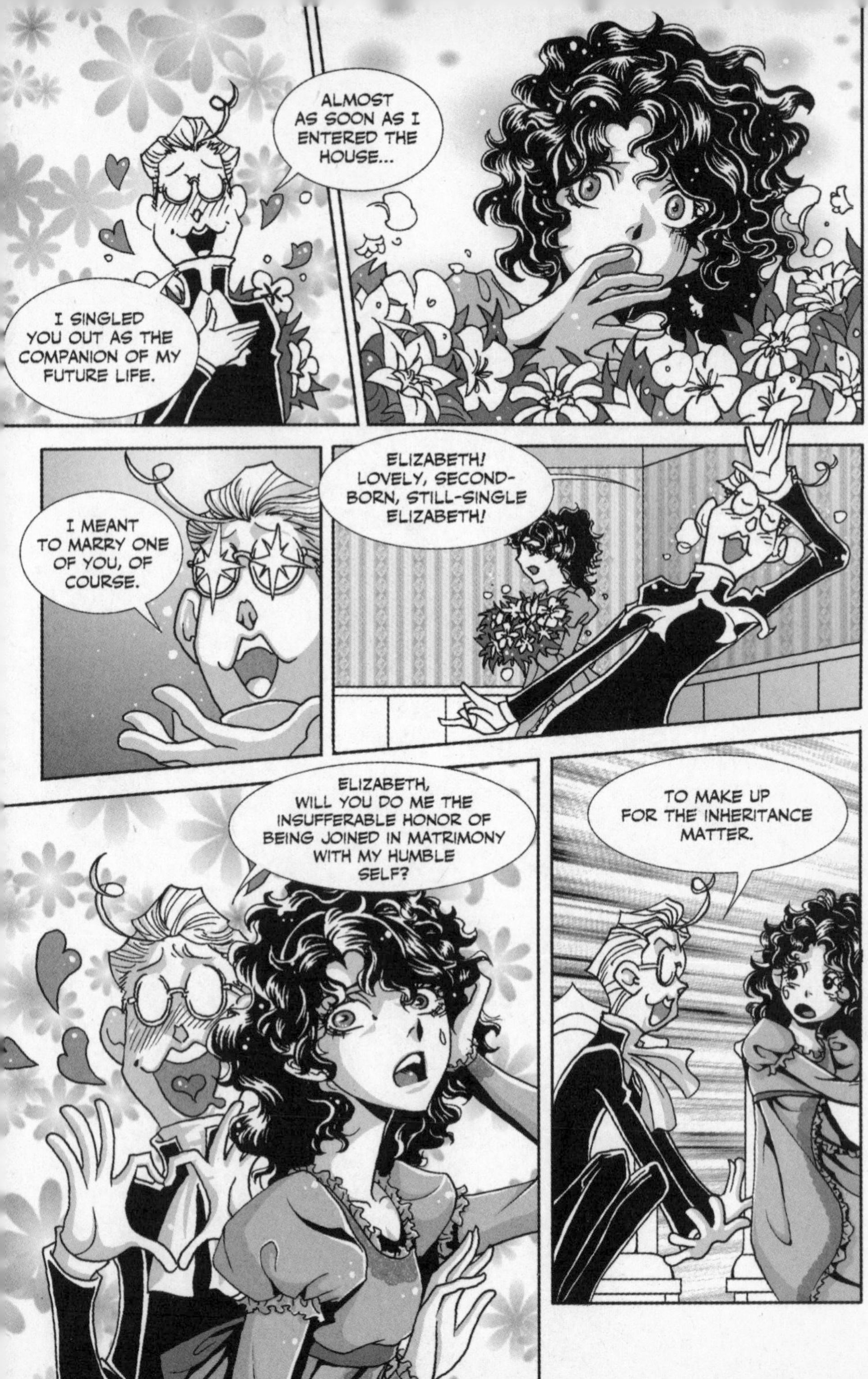
ALMOST AS SOON AS I ENTERED THE HOUSE...
I SINGLED YOU OUT AS THE COMPANION OF MY FUTURE LIFE.
ELIZABETH! LOVELY, SECOND-BORN, STILL-SINGLE ELIZABETH!
I MEANT TO MARRY ONE OF YOU, OF COURSE.
TO MAKE UP FOR THE INHERITANCE MATTER.
ELIZABETH, WILL YOU DO ME THE INSUFFERABLE HONOR OF BEING JOINED IN MATRIMONY WITH MY HUMBLE SELF?

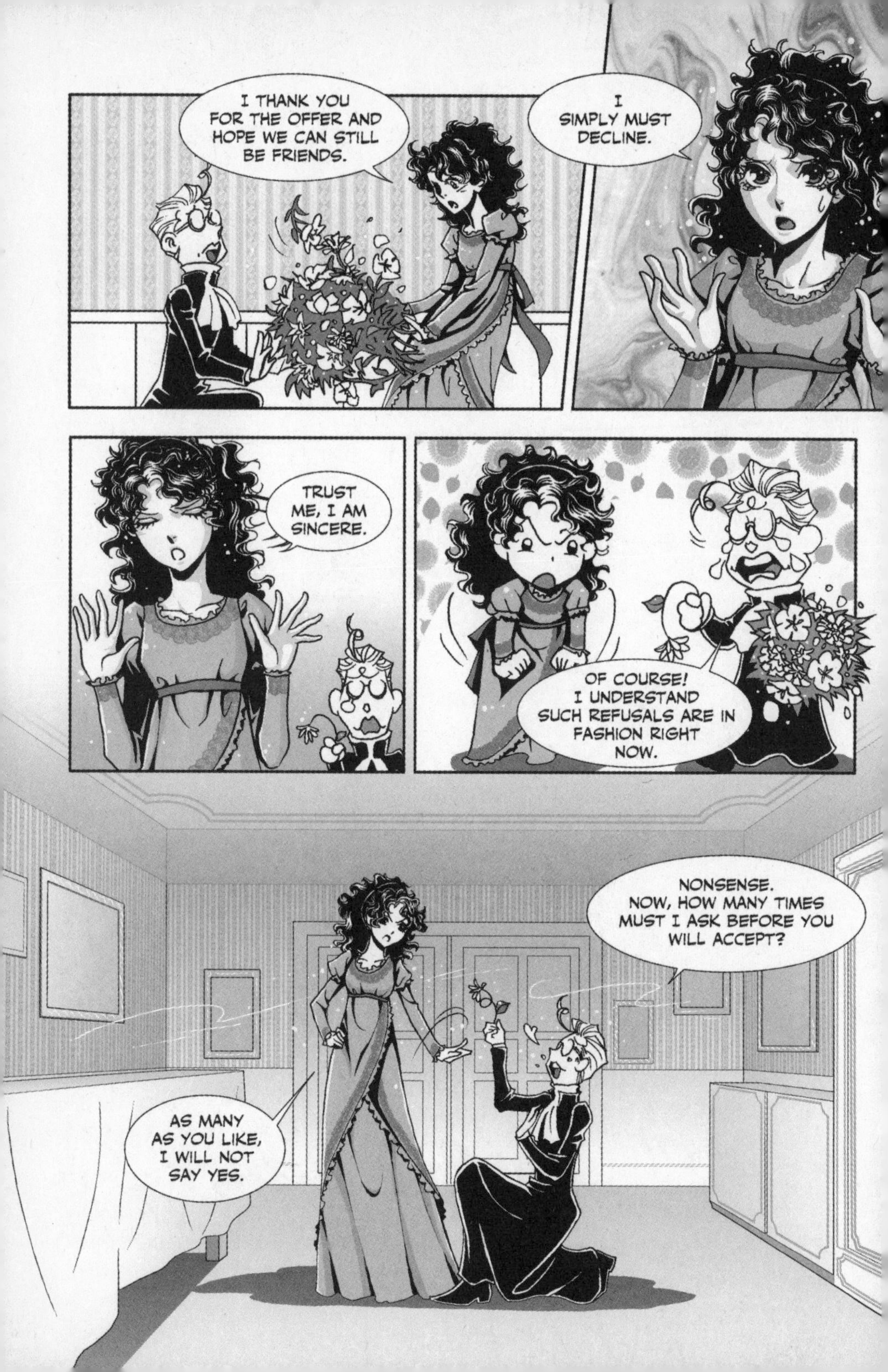
I SIMPLY MUST DECLINE.
I THANK YOU FOR THE OFFER AND HOPE WE CAN STILL BE FRIENDS.
OF COURSE! I UNDERSTAND SUCH REFUSALS ARE IN FASHION RIGHT NOW.
TRUST ME, I AM SINCERE.
NONSENSE. NOW, HOW MANY TIMES MUST I ASK BEFORE YOU WILL ACCEPT?
AS MANY AS YOU LIKE, I WILL NOT SAY YES.

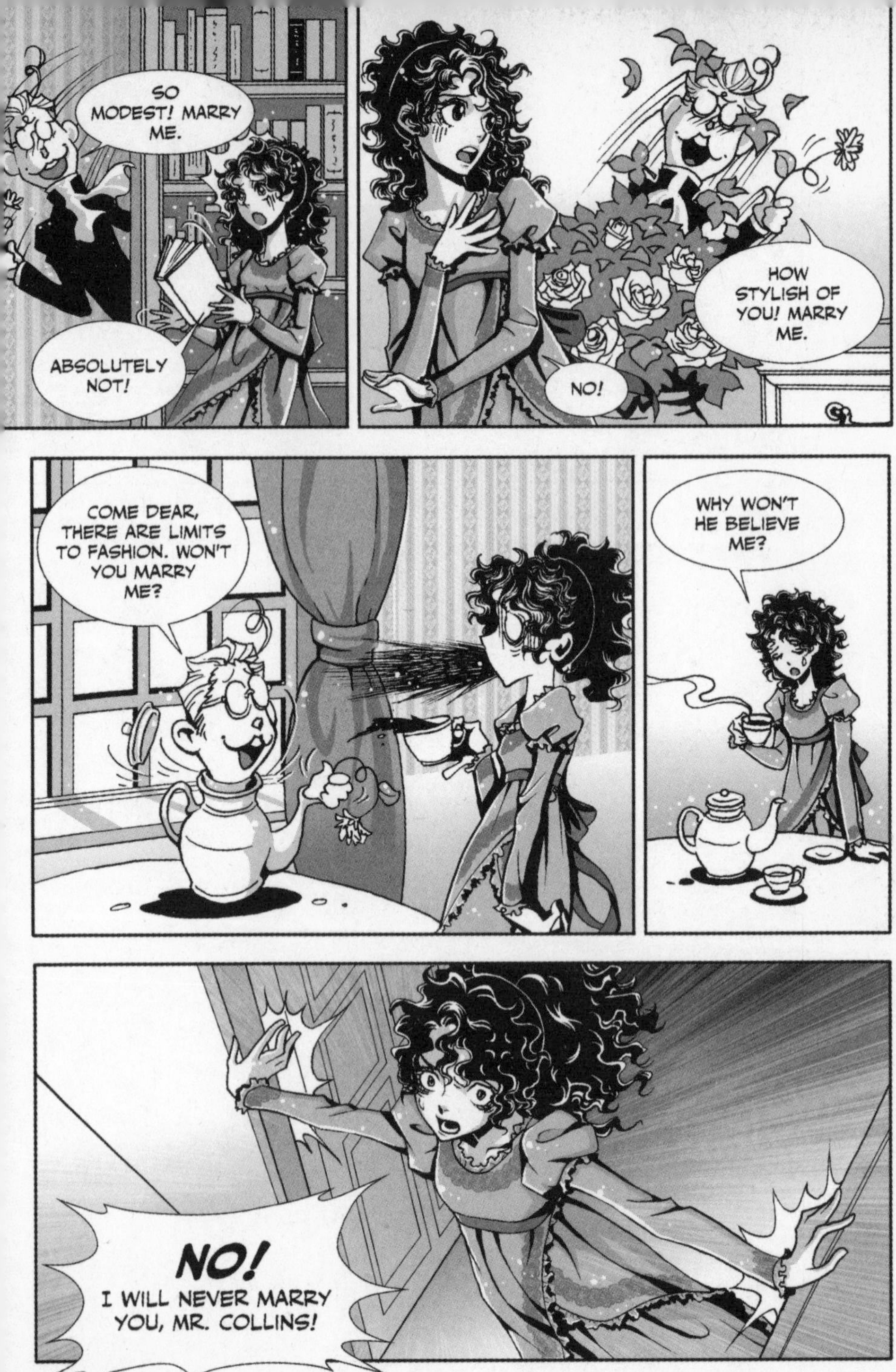
HOW STYLISH OF YOU! MARRY ME.
NO!
SO MODEST! MARRY ME.
ABSOLUTELY NOT!
WHY WON'T HE BELIEVE ME?
COME DEAR, THERE ARE LIMITS TO FASHION. WON'T YOU MARRY ME?
NO! I WILL NEVER MARRY YOU, MR. COLLINS!

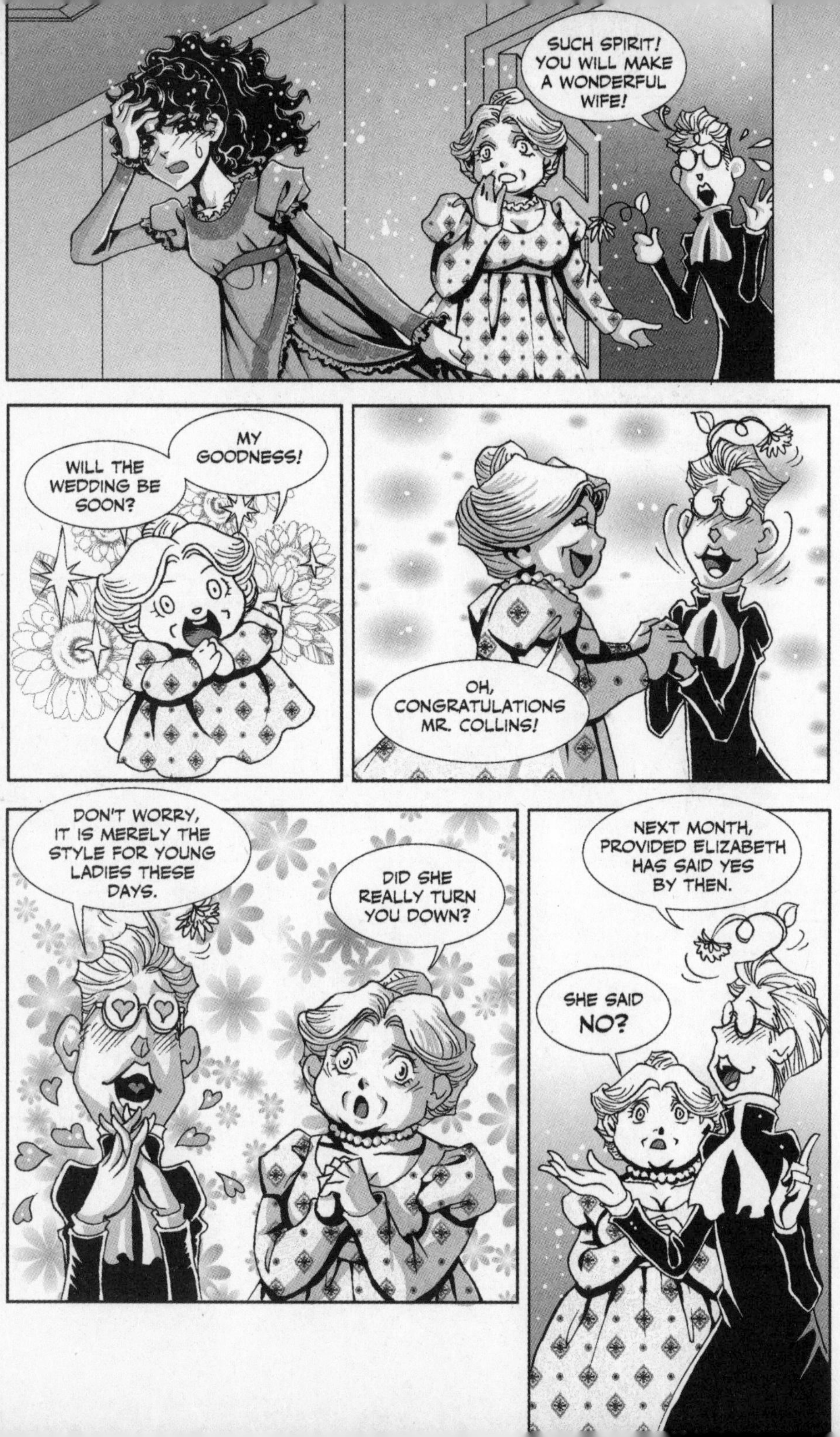
SUCH SPIRIT! YOU WILL MAKE A WONDERFUL WIFE!
OH, CONGRATULATIONS MR. COLLINS!
MY GOODNESS!
WILL THE WEDDING BE SOON?
NEXT MONTH, PROVIDED ELIZABETH HAS SAID YES BY THEN.
SHE SAID NO?
DID SHE REALLY TURN YOU DOWN?
DON'T WORRY, IT IS MERELY THE STYLE FOR YOUNG LADIES THESE DAYS.

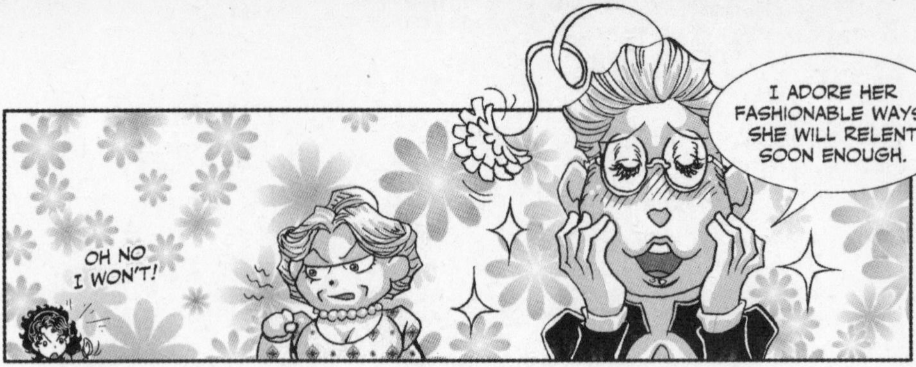
I ADORE HER FASHIONABLE WAYS! SHE WILL RELENT SOON ENOUGH.
OH NO I WON'T!

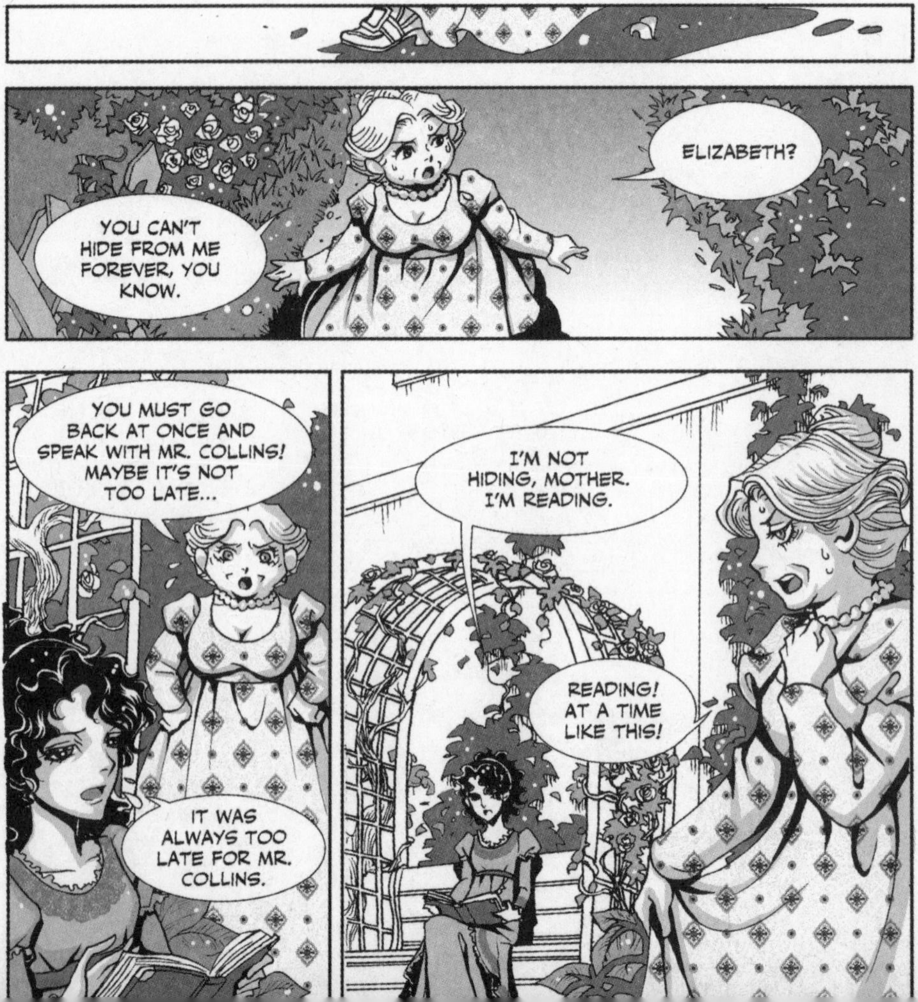
ELIZABETH?
YOU CAN'T HIDE FROM ME FOREVER, YOU KNOW.
I'M NOT HIDING, MOTHER. I'M READING.
READING! AT A TIME LIKE THIS!
YOU MUST GO BACK AT ONCE AND SPEAK WITH MR. COLLINS! MAYBE IT'S NOT TOO LATE...
IT WAS ALWAYS TOO LATE FOR MR. COLLINS.

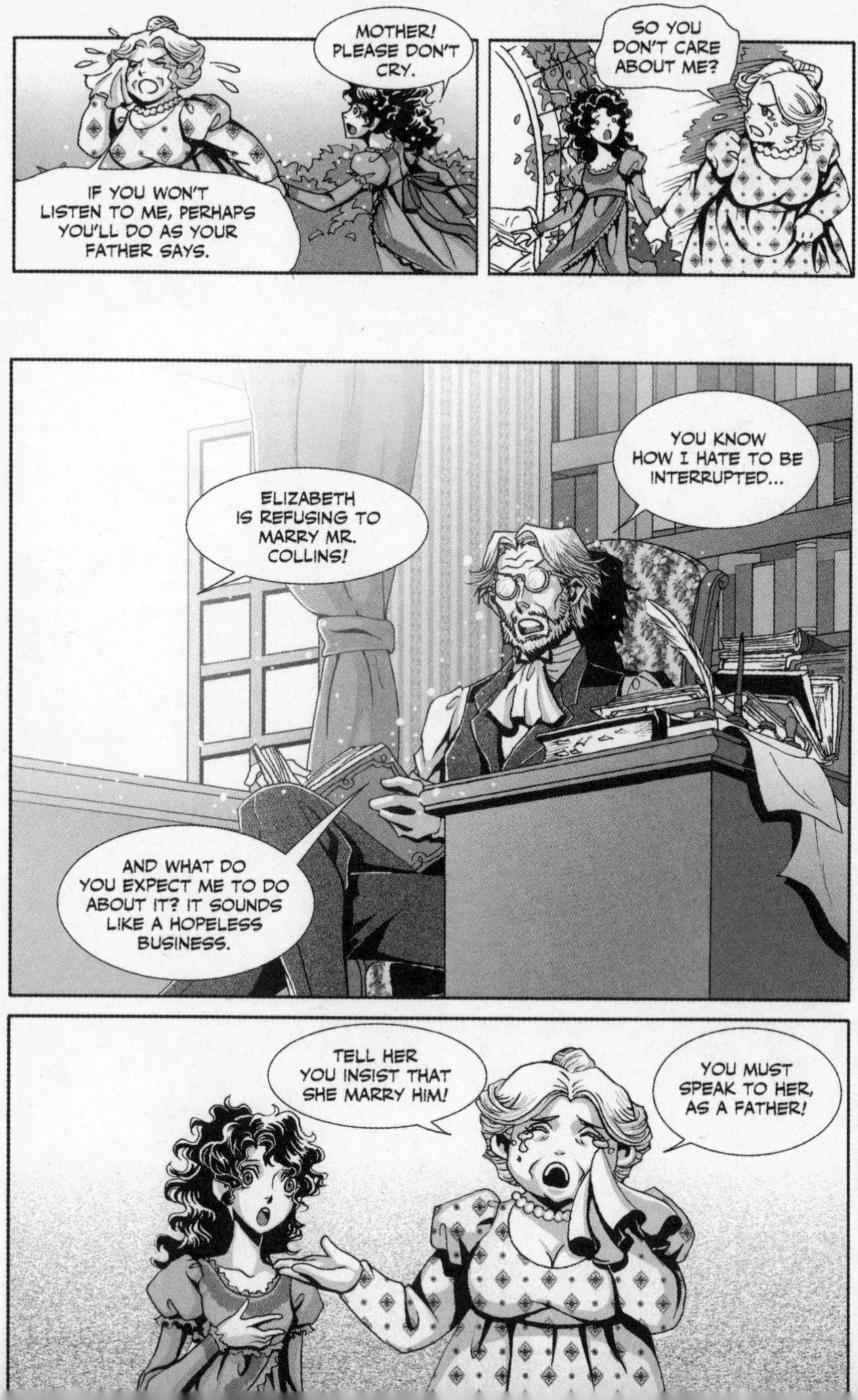
SO YOU DON'T CARE ABOUT ME?
MOTHER! PLEASE DON'T CRY.
IF YOU WON'T LISTEN TO ME, PERHAPS YOU'LL DO AS YOUR FATHER SAYS.
YOU KNOW HOW I HATE TO BE INTERRUPTED...
ELIZABETH IS REFUSING TO MARRY MR. COLLINS!
AND WHAT DO YOU EXPECT ME TO DO ABOUT IT? IT SOUNDS LIKE A HOPELESS BUSINESS.
YOU MUST SPEAK TO HER, AS A FATHER!
TELL HER YOU INSIST THAT SHE MARRY HIM!

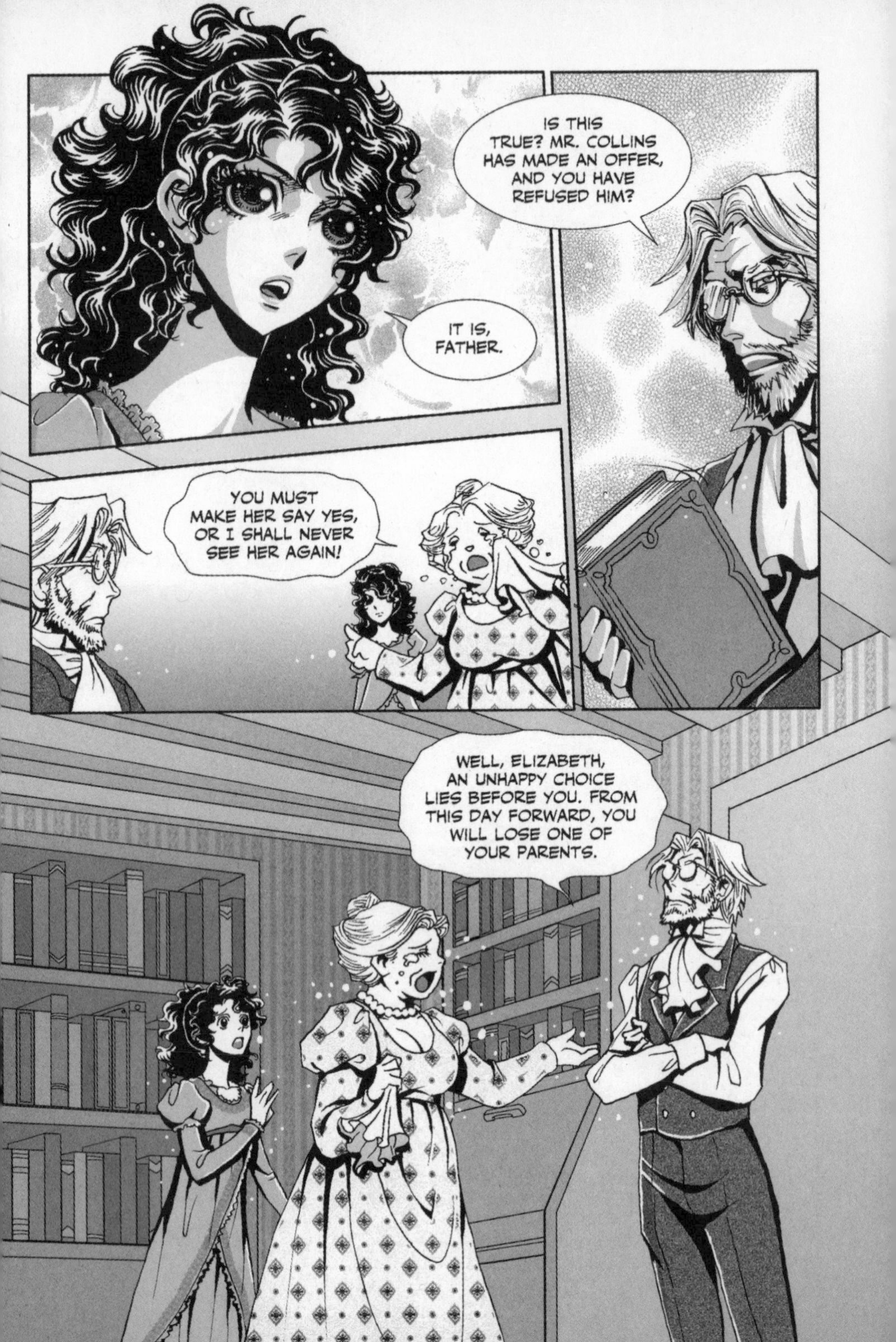
IS THIS TRUE? MR. COLLINS HAS MADE AN OFFER, AND YOU HAVE REFUSED HIM?
IT IS, FATHER.
YOU MUST MAKE HER SAY YES, OR I SHALL NEVER SEE HER AGAIN!
WELL, ELIZABETH, AN UNHAPPY CHOICE LIES BEFORE YOU. FROM THIS DAY FORWARD, YOU WILL LOSE ONE OF YOUR PARENTS.

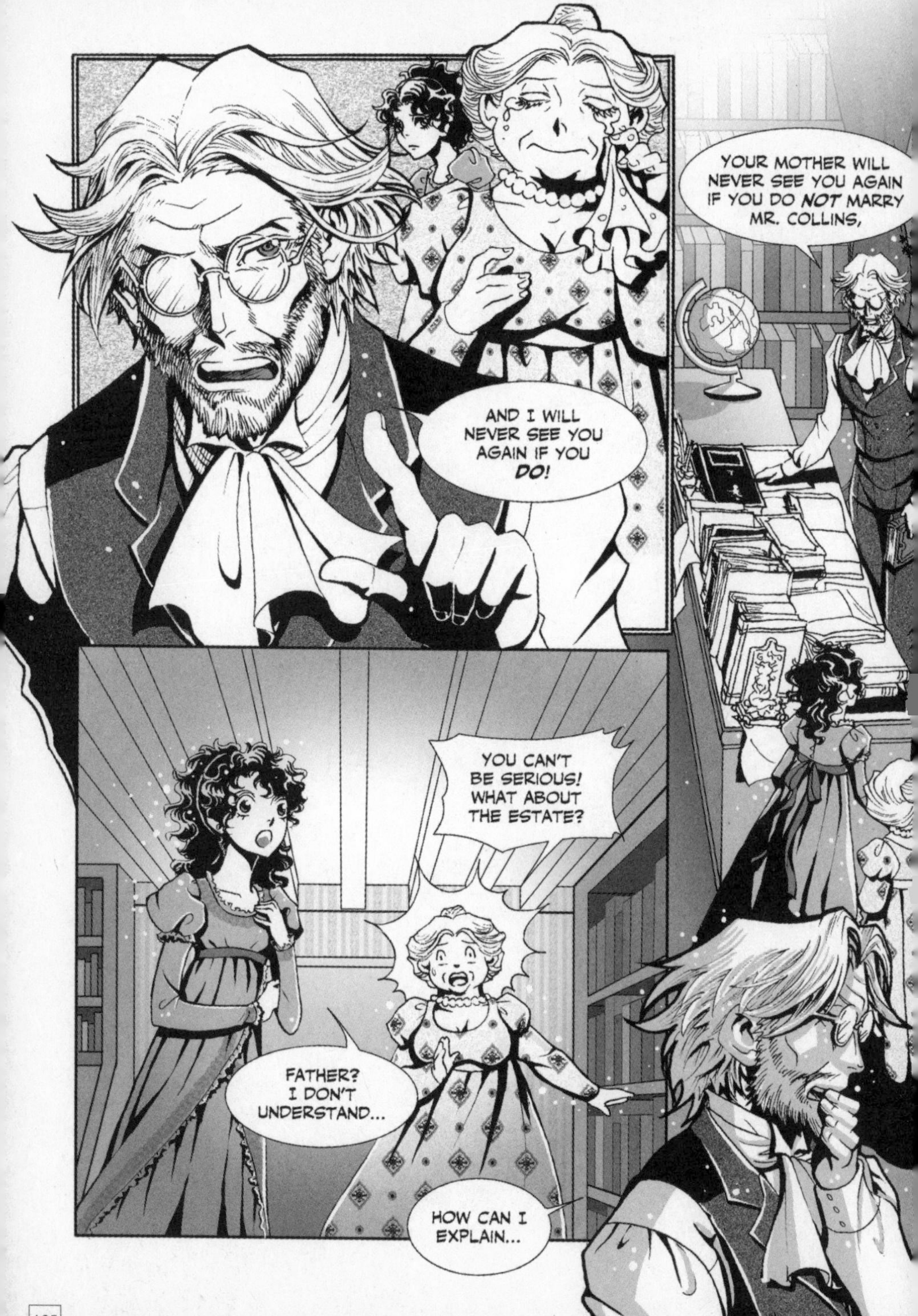
YOUR MOTHER WILL NEVER SEE YOU AGAIN IF YOU DO ***NOT*** MARRY MR. COLLINS,
AND I WILL NEVER SEE YOU AGAIN IF YOU ***DO!***
YOU CAN'T BE SERIOUS! WHAT ABOUT THE ESTATE?
FATHER? I DON'T UNDERSTAND...
HOW CAN I EXPLAIN...

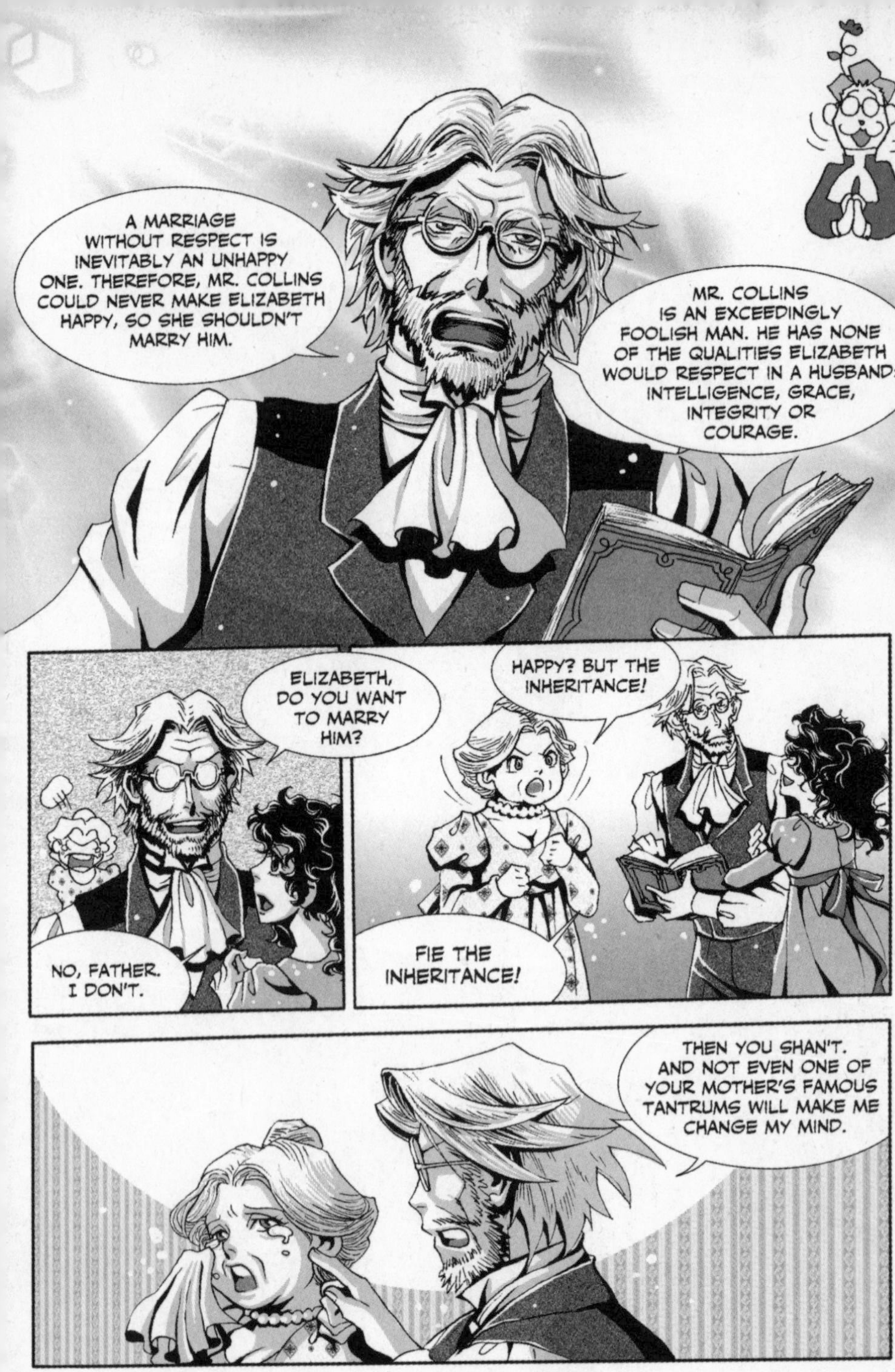
MR. COLLINS IS AN EXCEEDINGLY FOOLISH MAN. HE HAS NONE OF THE QUALITIES ELIZABETH WOULD RESPECT IN A HUSBAND: INTELLIGENCE, GRACE, INTEGRITY OR COURAGE.
A MARRIAGE WITHOUT RESPECT IS INEVITABLY AN UNHAPPY ONE. THEREFORE, MR. COLLINS COULD NEVER MAKE ELIZABETH HAPPY, SO SHE SHOULDN'T MARRY HIM.
HAPPY? BUT THE INHERITANCE!
FIE THE INHERITANCE!
ELIZABETH, DO YOU WANT TO MARRY HIM?
NO, FATHER. I DON'T.
THEN YOU SHAN'T. AND NOT EVEN ONE OF YOUR MOTHER'S FAMOUS TANTRUMS WILL MAKE ME CHANGE MY MIND.

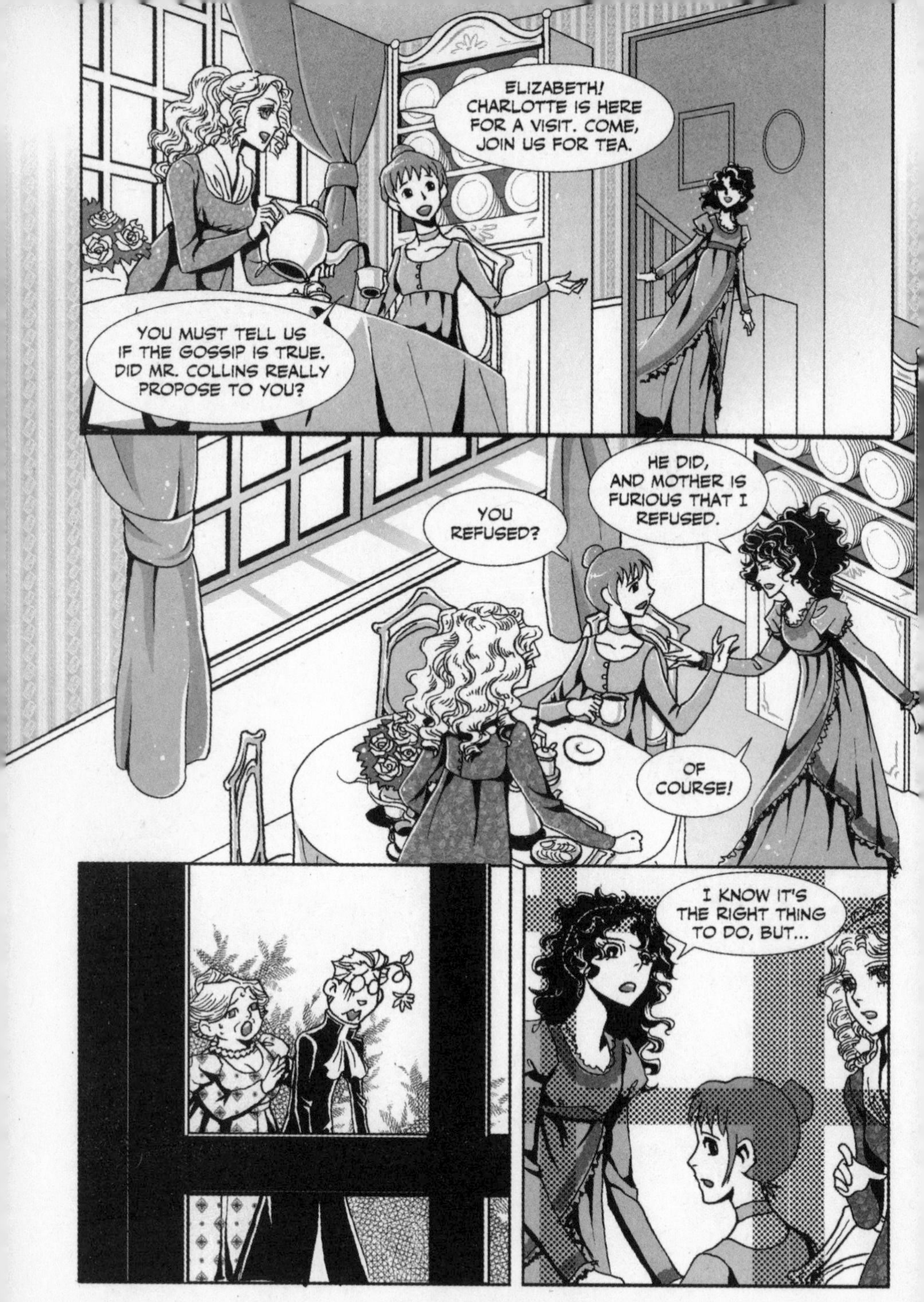
ELIZABETH! CHARLOTTE IS HERE FOR A VISIT. COME, JOIN US FOR TEA.
YOU MUST TELL US IF THE GOSSIP IS TRUE. DID MR. COLLINS REALLY PROPOSE TO YOU?
HE DID, AND MOTHER IS FURIOUS THAT I REFUSED.
YOU REFUSED?
OF COURSE!
I KNOW IT'S THE RIGHT THING TO DO, BUT...

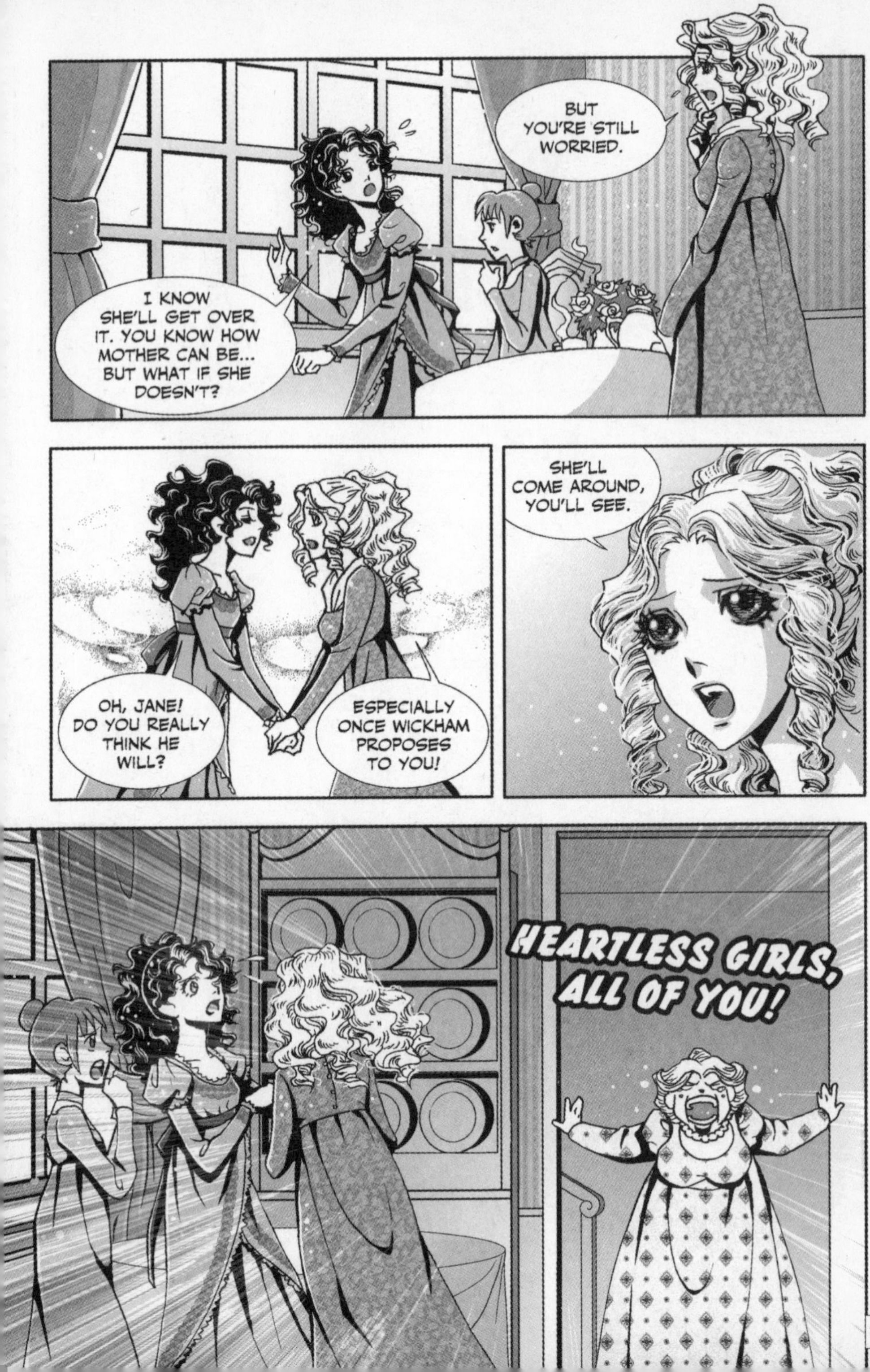
BUT YOU'RE STILL WORRIED.
I KNOW SHE'LL GET OVER IT. YOU KNOW HOW MOTHER CAN BE... BUT WHAT IF SHE DOESN'T?
SHE'LL COME AROUND, YOU'LL SEE.
ESPECIALLY ONCE WICKHAM PROPOSES TO YOU!
OH, JANE! DO YOU REALLY THINK HE WILL?
HEARTLESS GIRLS, ALL OF YOU!

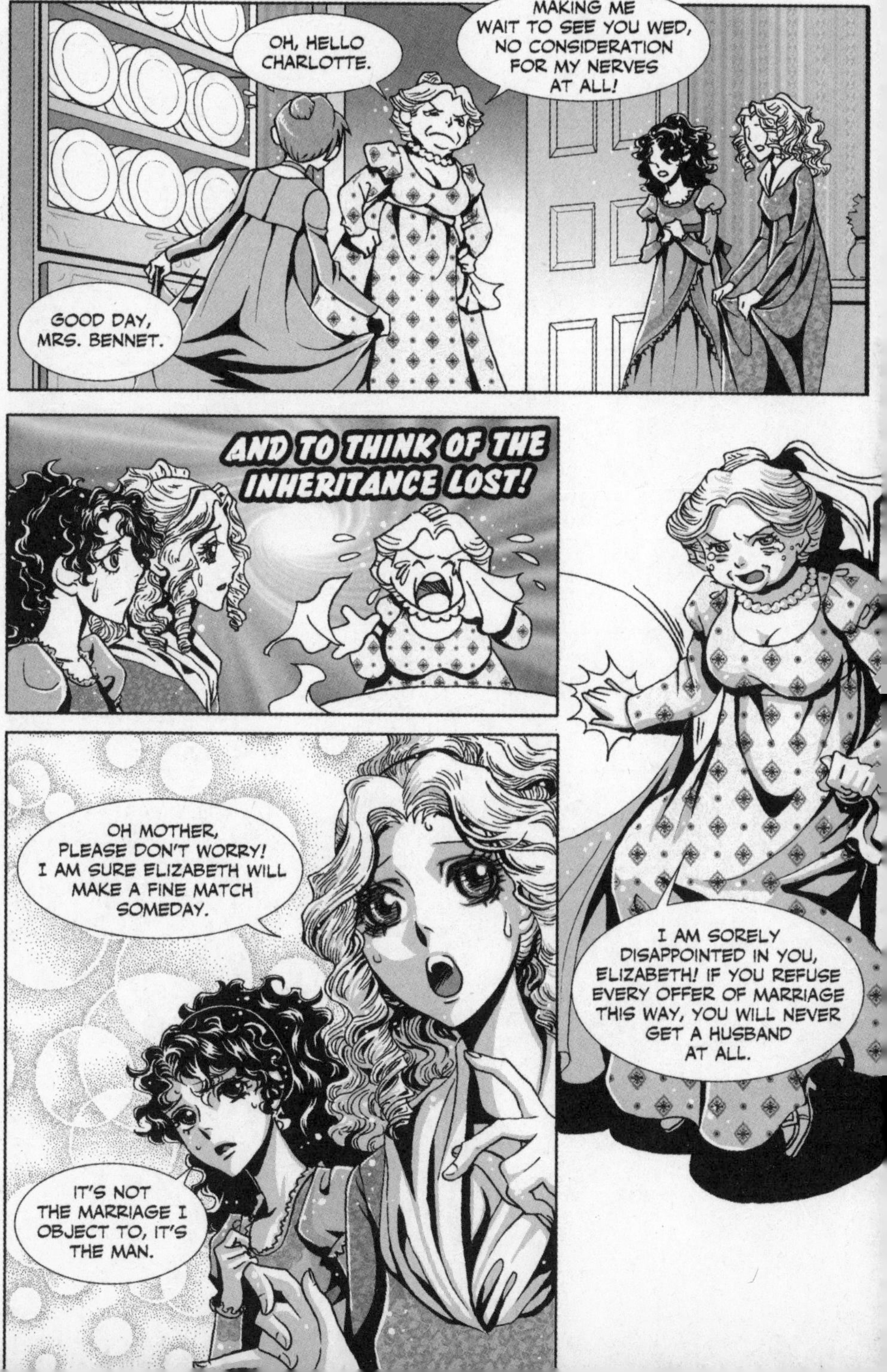
MAKING ME WAIT TO SEE YOU WED, NO CONSIDERATION FOR MY NERVES AT ALL!
OH, HELLO CHARLOTTE.
GOOD DAY, MRS. BENNET.
I AM SORELY DISAPPOINTED IN YOU, ELIZABETH! IF YOU REFUSE EVERY OFFER OF MARRIAGE THIS WAY, YOU WILL NEVER GET A HUSBAND AT ALL.
AND TO THINK OF THE INHERITANCE LOST!
OH MOTHER, PLEASE DON'T WORRY! I AM SURE ELIZABETH WILL MAKE A FINE MATCH SOMEDAY.
IT'S NOT THE MARRIAGE I OBJECT TO, IT'S THE MAN.

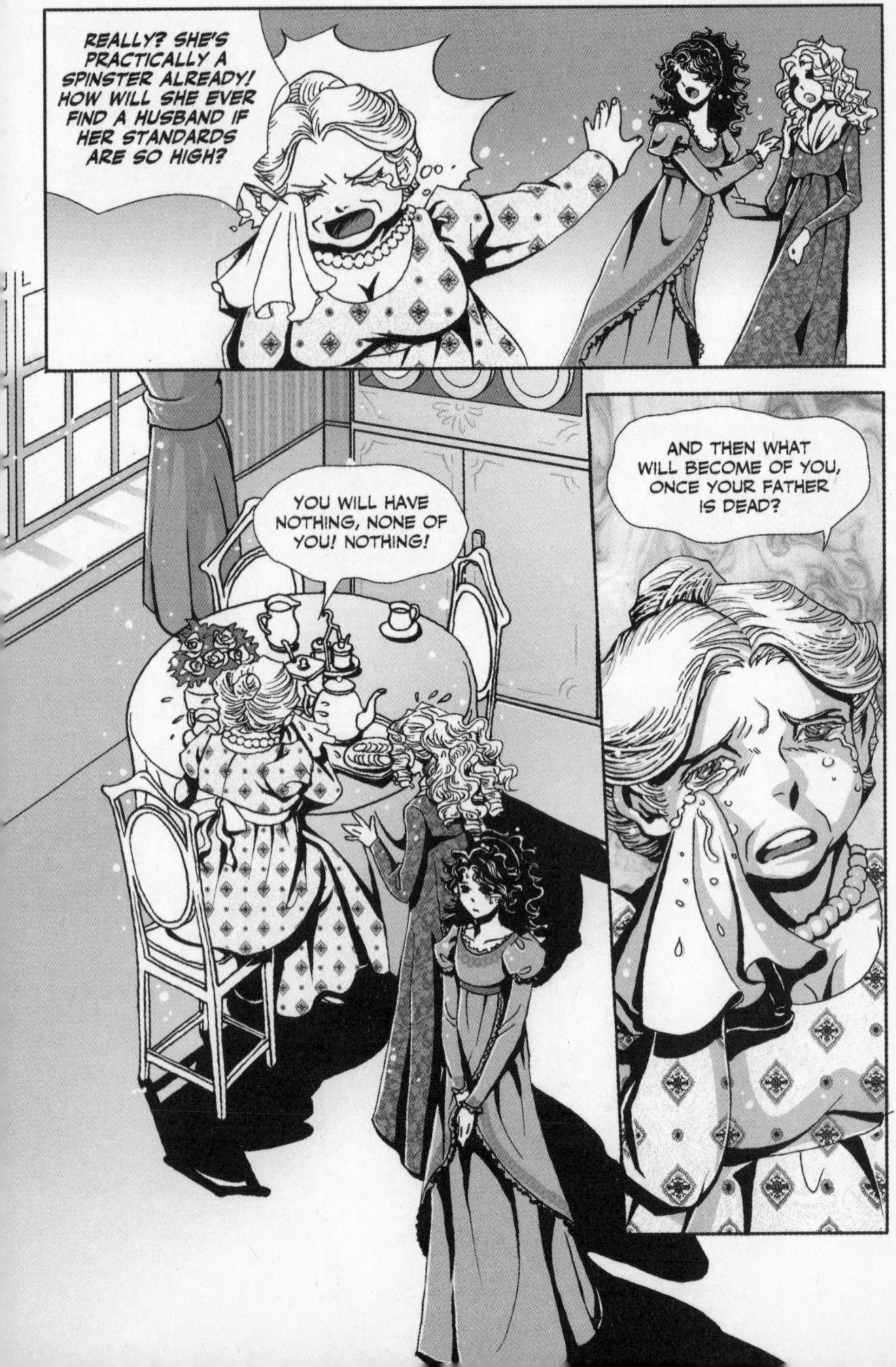
REALLY? SHE'S PRACTICALLY A SPINSTER ALREADY! HOW WILL SHE EVER FIND A HUSBAND IF HER STANDARDS ARE SO HIGH?
AND THEN WHAT WILL BECOME OF YOU, ONCE YOUR FATHER IS DEAD?
YOU WILL HAVE NOTHING, NONE OF YOU! NOTHING!

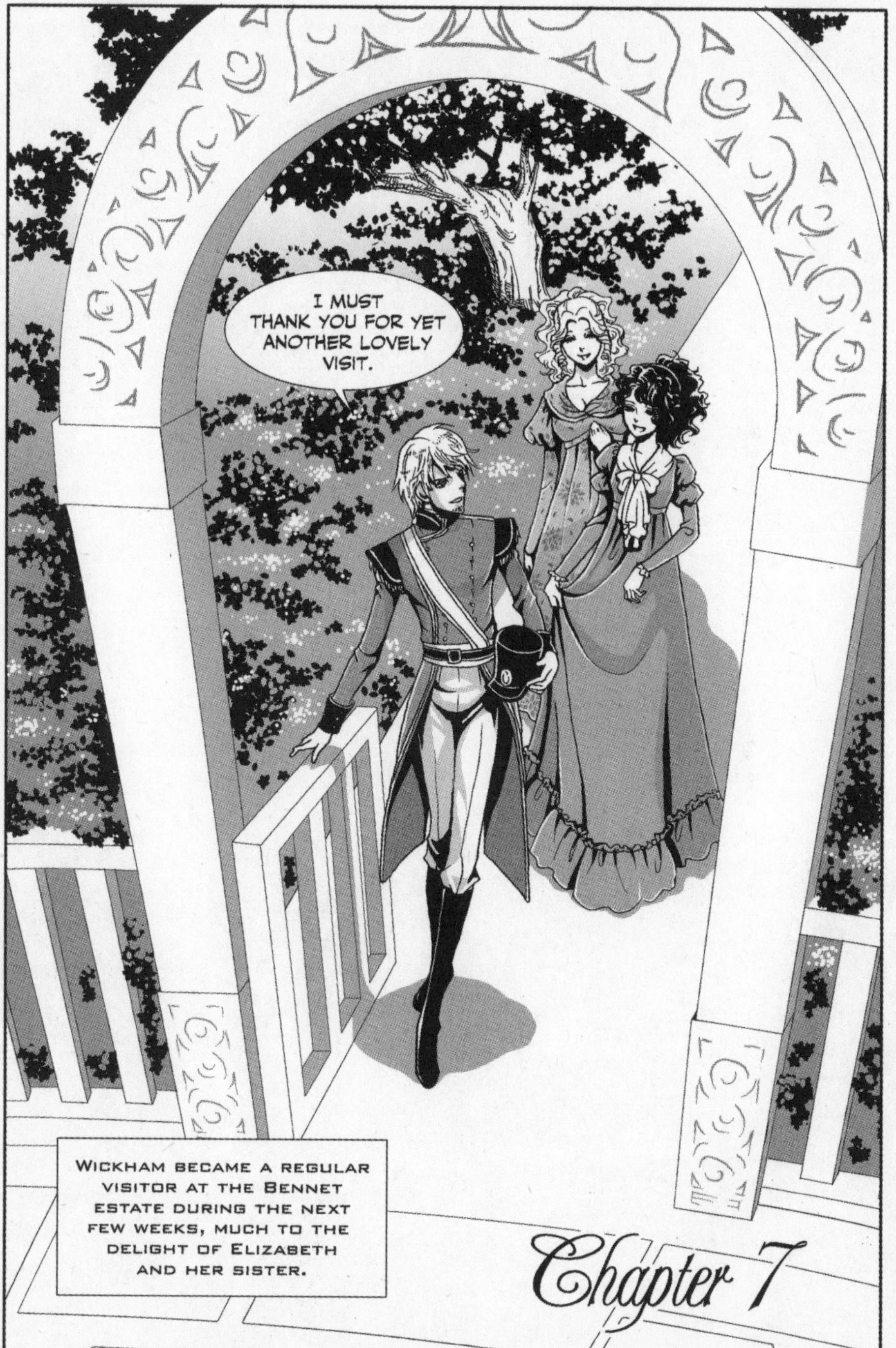
I MUST THANK YOU FOR YET ANOTHER LOVELY VISIT.
WICKHAM BECAME A REGULAR VISITOR AT THE BENNET ESTATE DURING THE NEXT FEW WEEKS, MUCH TO THE DELIGHT OF ELIZABETH AND HER SISTER.
Chapter 7

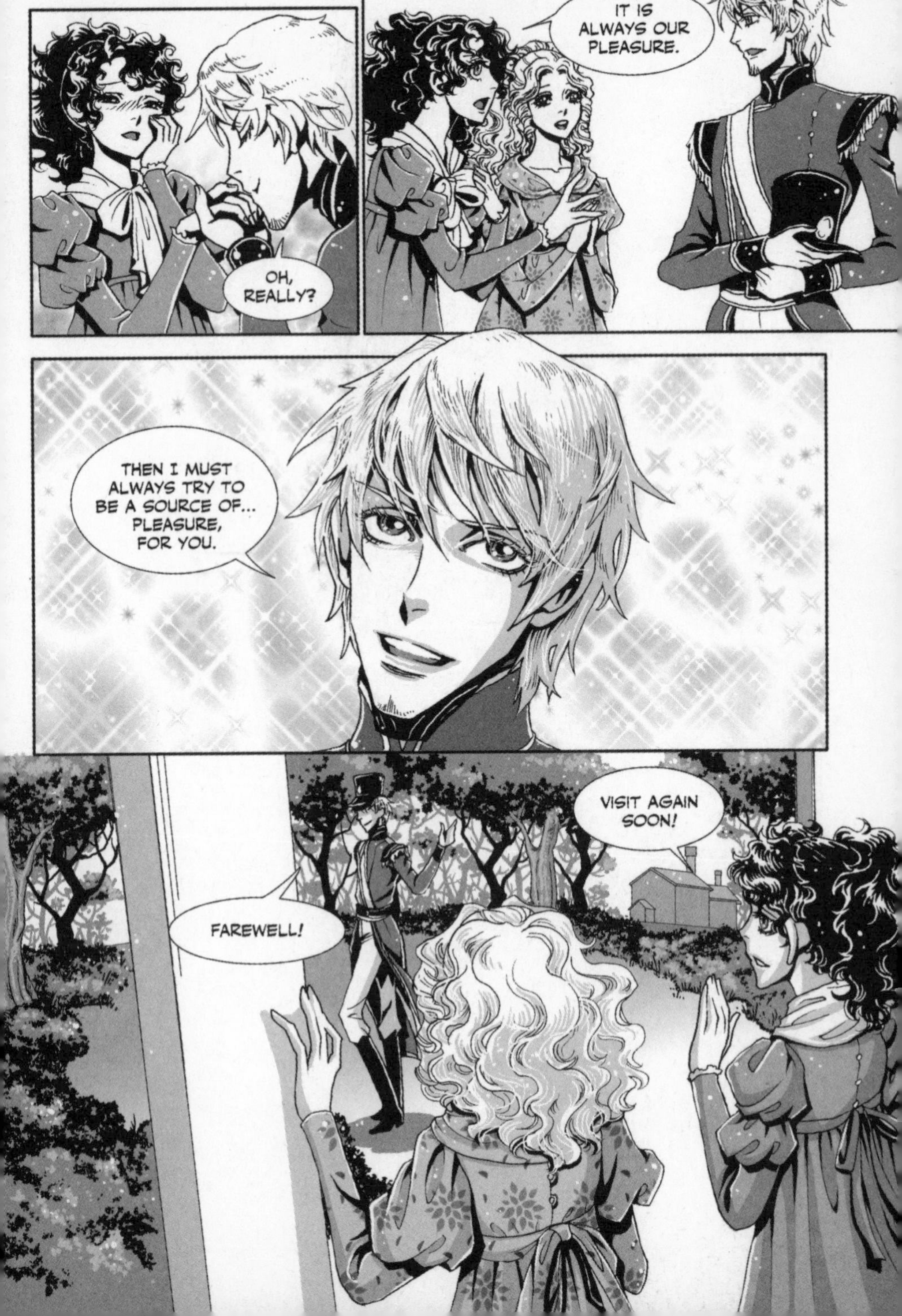
IT IS ALWAYS OUR PLEASURE.
OH, REALLY?
THEN I MUST ALWAYS TRY TO BE A SOURCE OF... PLEASURE, FOR YOU.
VISIT AGAIN SOON!
FAREWELL!

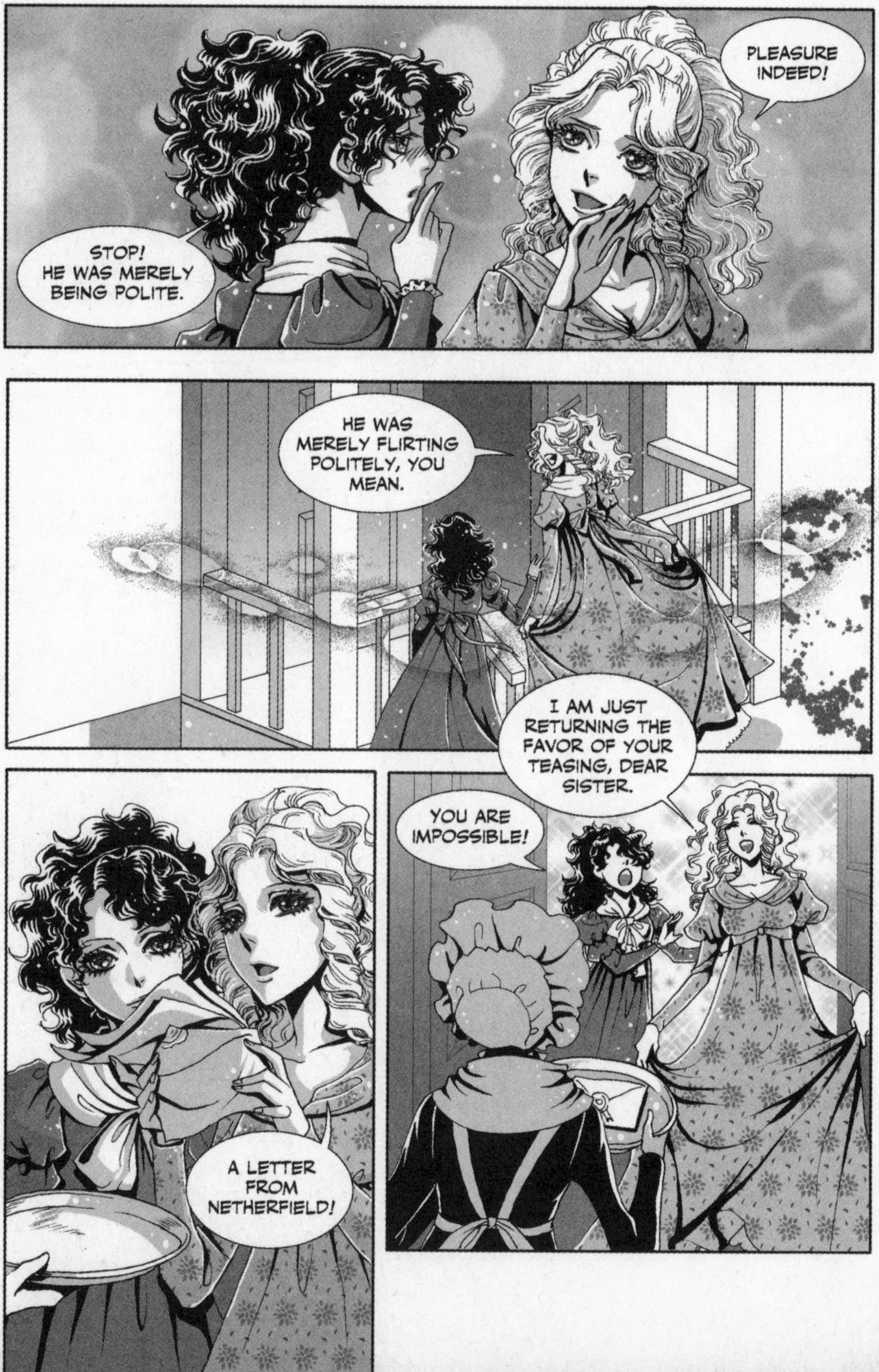
PLEASURE INDEED!
STOP! HE WAS MERELY BEING POLITE.
HE WAS MERELY FLIRTING POLITELY, YOU MEAN.
I AM JUST RETURNING THE FAVOR OF YOUR TEASING, DEAR SISTER.
YOU ARE IMPOSSIBLE!
A LETTER FROM NETHERFIELD!

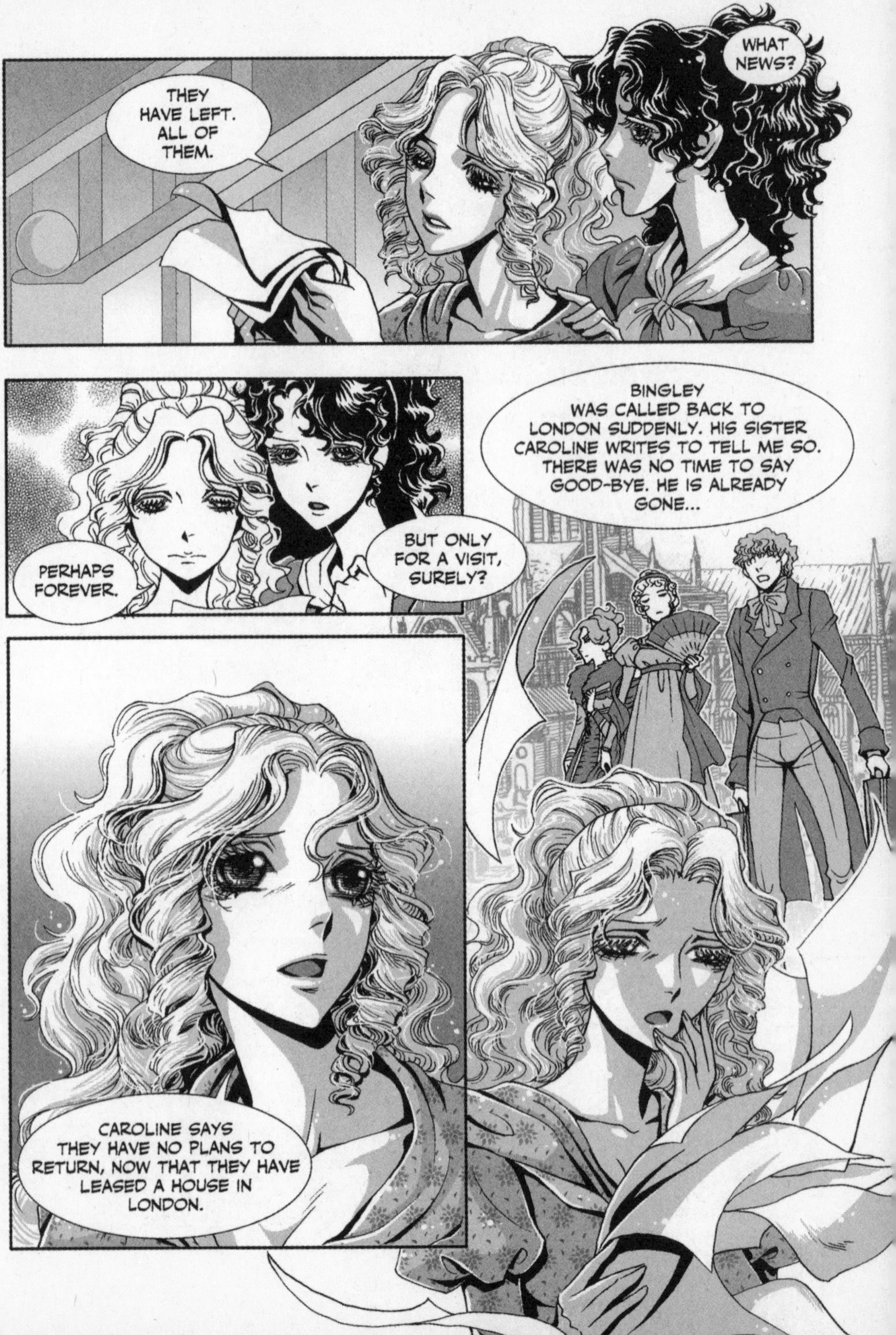
WHAT NEWS?
THEY HAVE LEFT. ALL OF THEM.
BINGLEY WAS CALLED BACK TO LONDON SUDDENLY. HIS SISTER CAROLINE WRITES TO TELL ME SO. THERE WAS NO TIME TO SAY GOOD-BYE. HE IS ALREADY GONE...
BUT ONLY FOR A VISIT, SURELY?
PERHAPS FOREVER.
CAROLINE SAYS THEY HAVE NO PLANS TO RETURN, NOW THAT THEY HAVE LEASED A HOUSE IN LONDON.

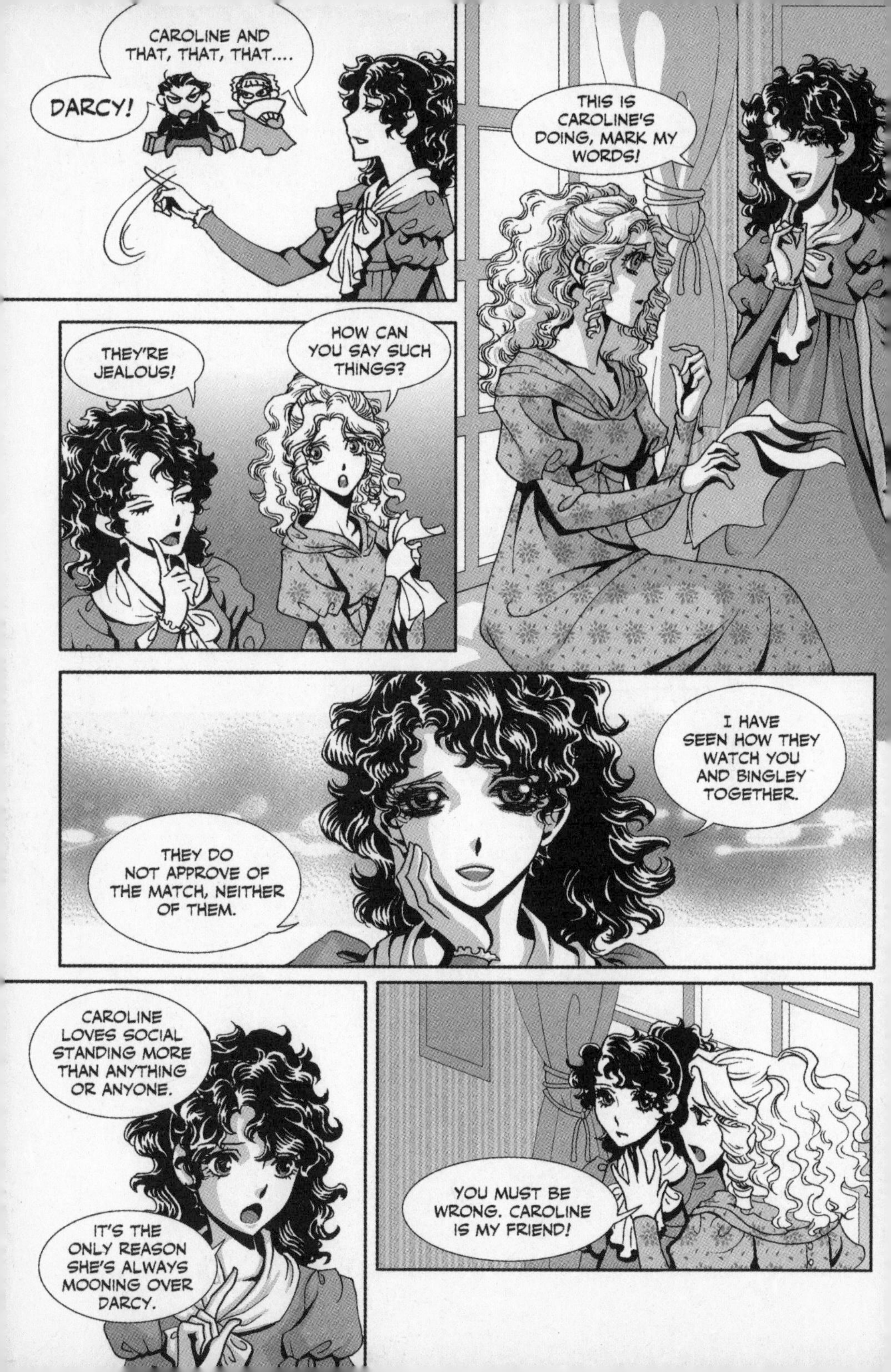
THIS IS CAROLINE'S DOING, MARK MY WORDS!
CAROLINE AND THAT, THAT, THAT....
DARCY!
HOW CAN YOU SAY SUCH THINGS?
THEY'RE JEALOUS!
I HAVE SEEN HOW THEY WATCH YOU AND BINGLEY TOGETHER.
THEY DO NOT APPROVE OF THE MATCH, NEITHER OF THEM.
YOU MUST BE WRONG. CAROLINE IS MY FRIEND!
CAROLINE LOVES SOCIAL STANDING MORE THAN ANYTHING OR ANYONE.
IT'S THE ONLY REASON SHE'S ALWAYS MOONING OVER DARCY.

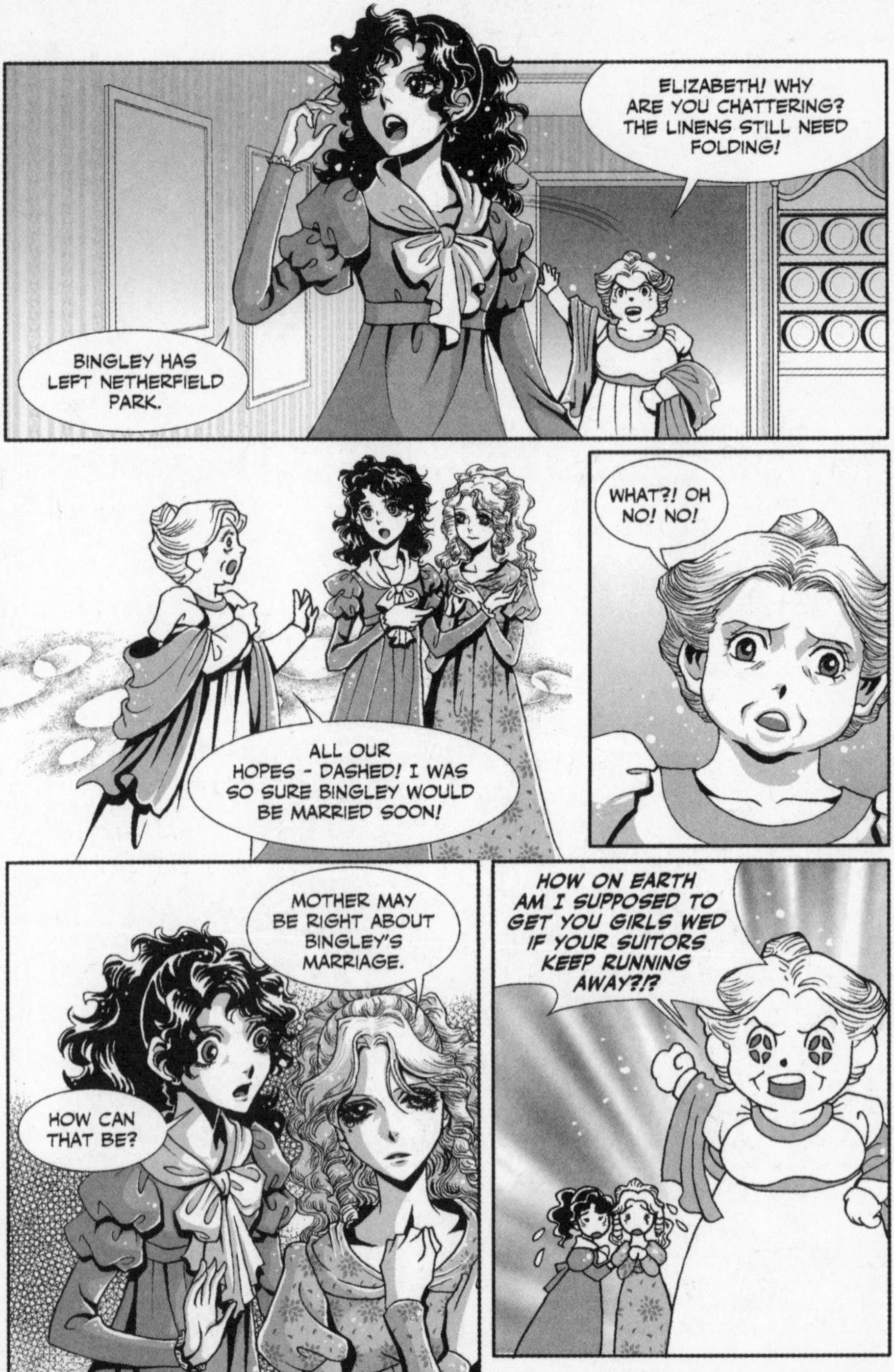
ELIZABETH! WHY ARE YOU CHATTERING? THE LINENS STILL NEED FOLDING!
BINGLEY HAS LEFT NETHERFIELD PARK.
WHAT?! OH NO! NO!
ALL OUR HOPES - DASHED! I WAS SO SURE BINGLEY WOULD BE MARRIED SOON!
HOW ON EARTH AM I SUPPOSED TO GET YOU GIRLS WED IF YOUR SUITORS KEEP RUNNING AWAY?!?
MOTHER MAY BE RIGHT ABOUT BINGLEY'S MARRIAGE.
HOW CAN THAT BE?

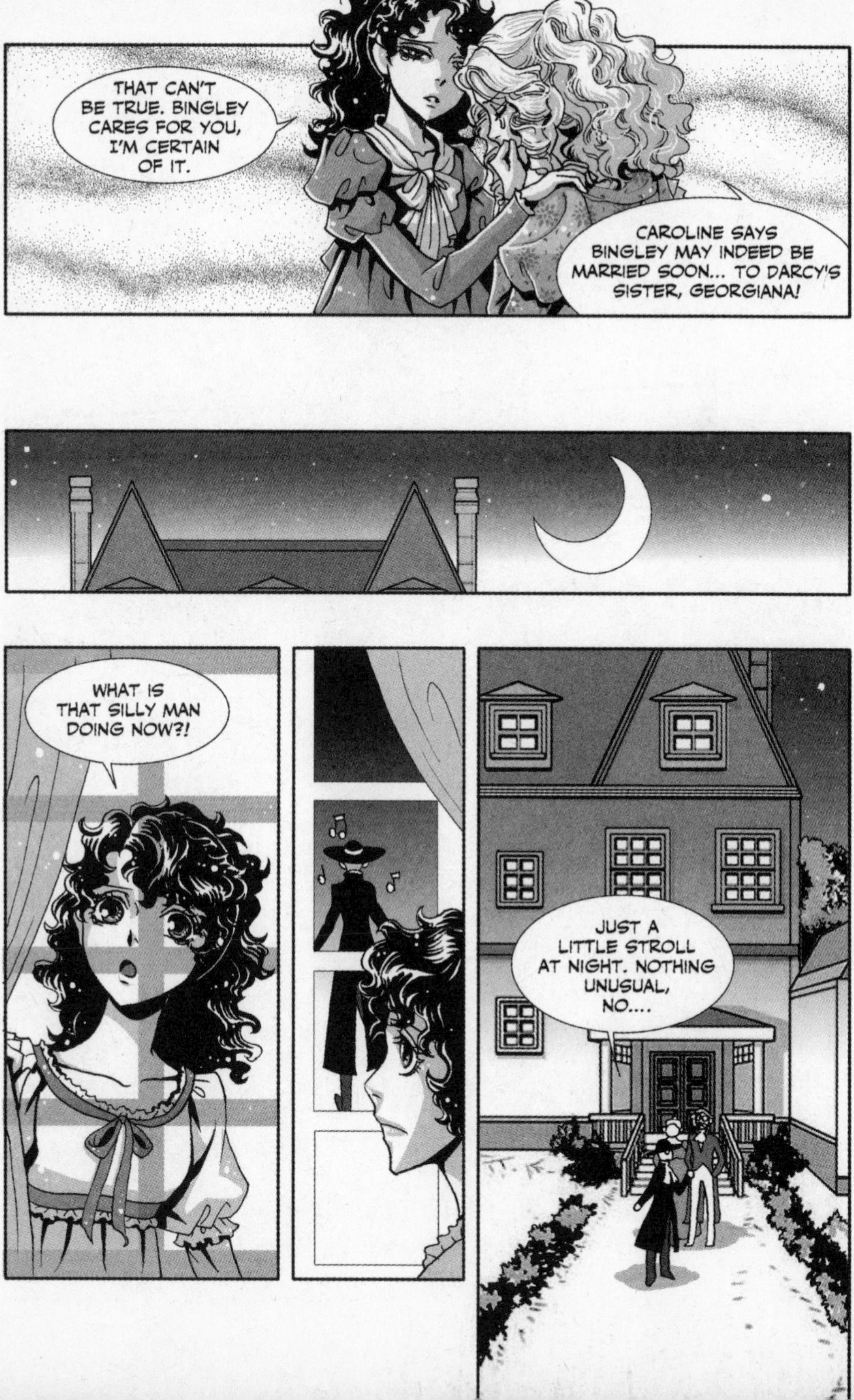
CAROLINE SAYS BINGLEY MAY INDEED BE MARRIED SOON... TO DARCY'S SISTER, GEORGIANA!
THAT CAN'T BE TRUE. BINGLEY CARES FOR YOU, I'M CERTAIN OF IT.
JUST A LITTLE STROLL AT NIGHT. NOTHING UNUSUAL, NO....
WHAT IS THAT SILLY MAN DOING NOW?!

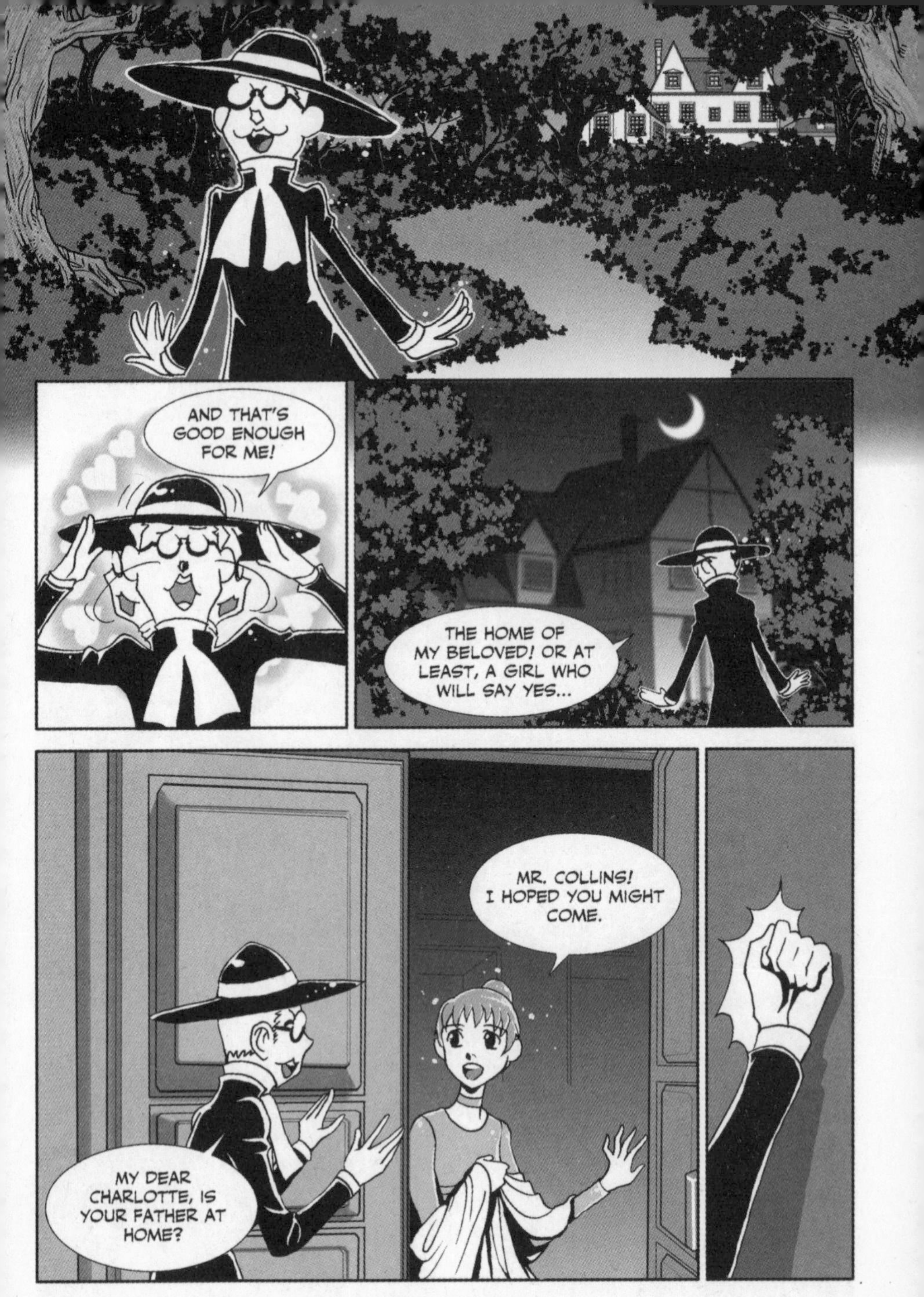
THE HOME OF MY BELOVED! OR AT LEAST, A GIRL WHO WILL SAY YES...
AND THAT'S GOOD ENOUGH FOR ME!
MR. COLLINS! I HOPED YOU MIGHT COME.
MY DEAR CHARLOTTE, IS YOUR FATHER AT HOME?

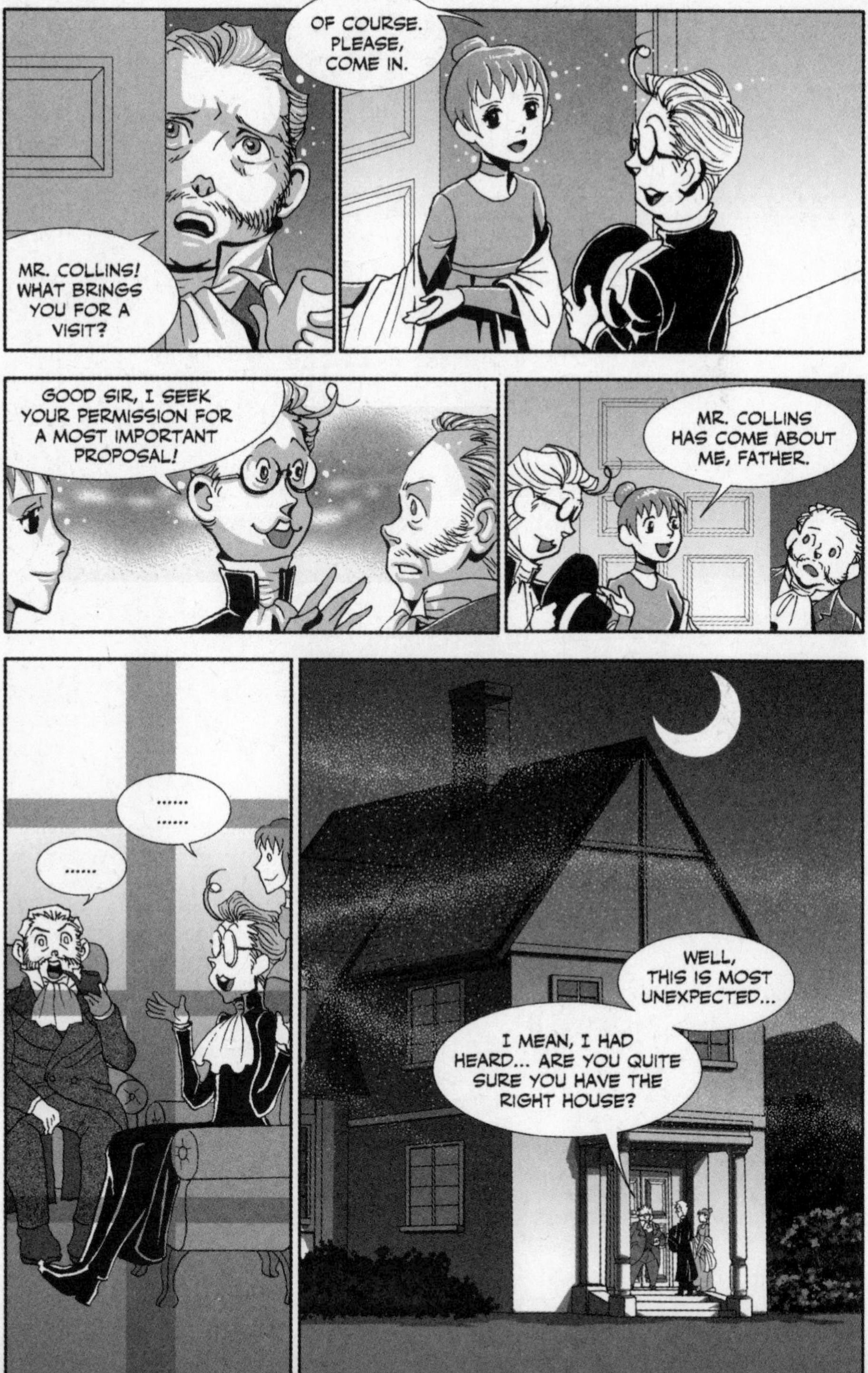
OF COURSE. PLEASE, COME IN.
MR. COLLINS! WHAT BRINGS YOU FOR A VISIT?
MR. COLLINS HAS COME ABOUT ME, FATHER.
GOOD SIR, I SEEK YOUR PERMISSION FOR A MOST IMPORTANT PROPOSAL!
WELL, THIS IS MOST UNEXPECTED...
I MEAN, I HAD HEARD... ARE YOU QUITE SURE YOU HAVE THE RIGHT HOUSE?
....
......

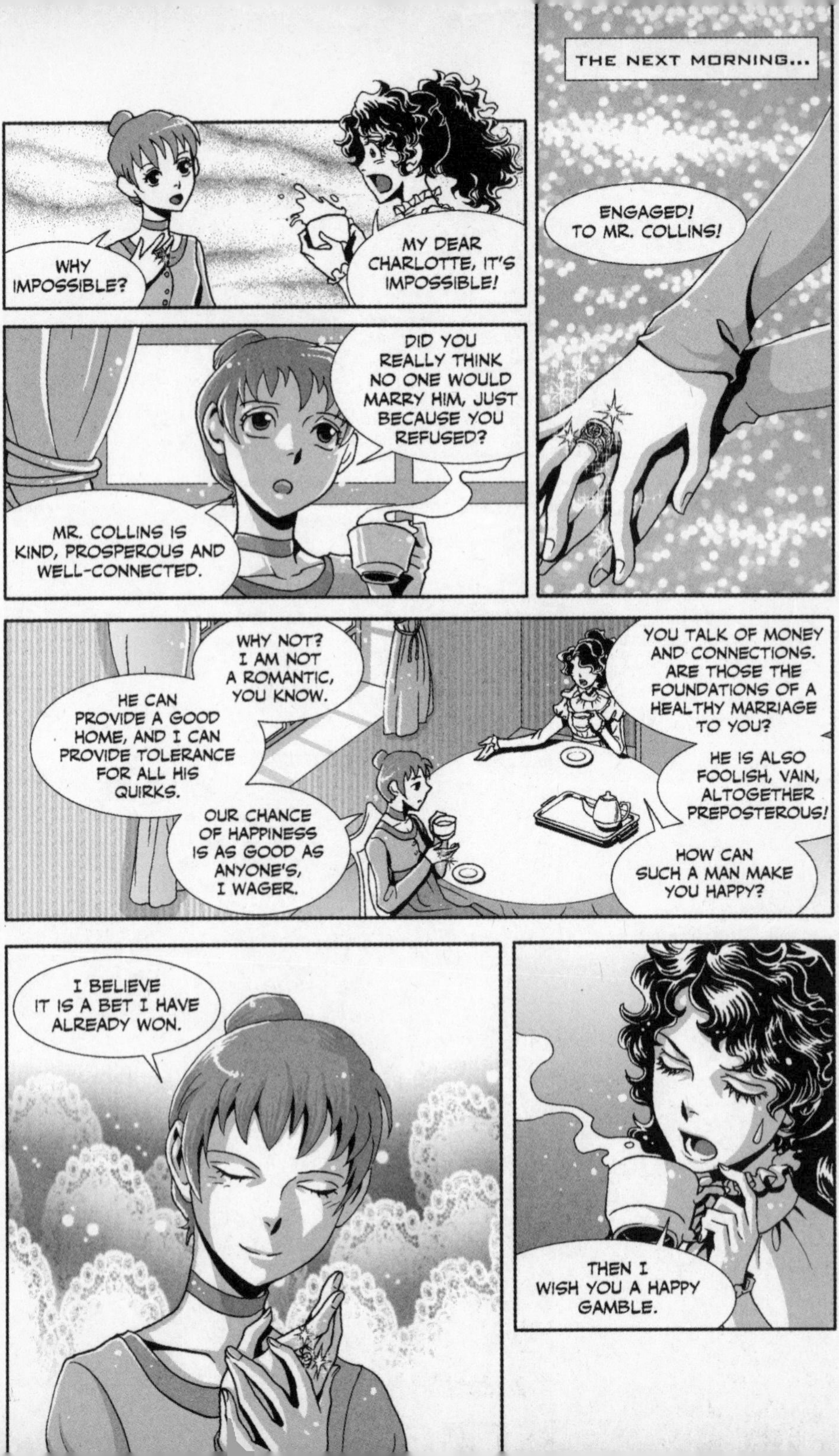
THE NEXT MORNING...
ENGAGED! TO MR. COLLINS!
MY DEAR CHARLOTTE, IT'S IMPOSSIBLE!
WHY IMPOSSIBLE?
DID YOU REALLY THINK NO ONE WOULD MARRY HIM, JUST BECAUSE YOU REFUSED?
MR. COLLINS IS KIND, PROSPEROUS AND WELL-CONNECTED.
YOU TALK OF MONEY AND CONNECTIONS. ARE THOSE THE FOUNDATIONS OF A HEALTHY MARRIAGE TO YOU?
HE IS ALSO FOOLISH, VAIN, ALTOGETHER PREPOSTEROUS!
HOW CAN SUCH A MAN MAKE YOU HAPPY?
WHY NOT? I AM NOT A ROMANTIC, YOU KNOW.
HE CAN PROVIDE A GOOD HOME, AND I CAN PROVIDE TOLERANCE FOR ALL HIS QUIRKS.
OUR CHANCE OF HAPPINESS IS AS GOOD AS ANYONE'S, I WAGER.
THEN I WISH YOU A HAPPY GAMBLE.
I BELIEVE IT IS A BET I HAVE ALREADY WON.

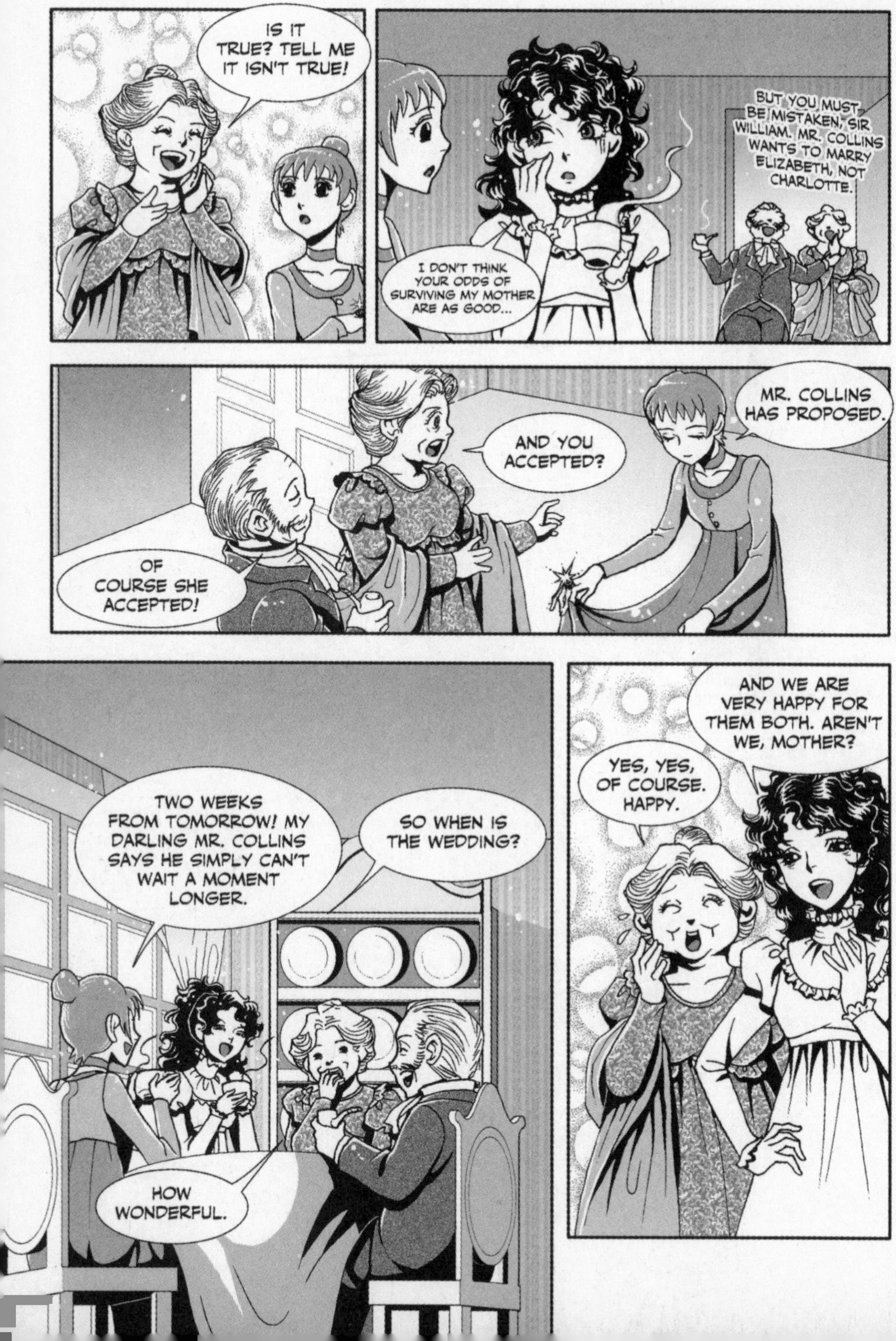
BUT YOU MUST BE MISTAKEN, SIR WILLIAM. MR. COLLINS WANTS TO MARRY ELIZABETH, NOT CHARLOTTE.
I DON'T THINK YOUR ODDS OF SURVIVING MY MOTHER ARE AS GOOD...
IS IT TRUE? TELL ME IT ISN'T TRUE!
MR. COLLINS HAS PROPOSED.
AND YOU ACCEPTED?
OF COURSE SHE ACCEPTED!
AND WE ARE VERY HAPPY FOR THEM BOTH. AREN'T WE, MOTHER?
YES, YES, OF COURSE. HAPPY.
SO WHEN IS THE WEDDING?
TWO WEEKS FROM TOMORROW! MY DARLING MR. COLLINS SAYS HE SIMPLY CAN'T WAIT A MOMENT LONGER.
HOW WONDERFUL.

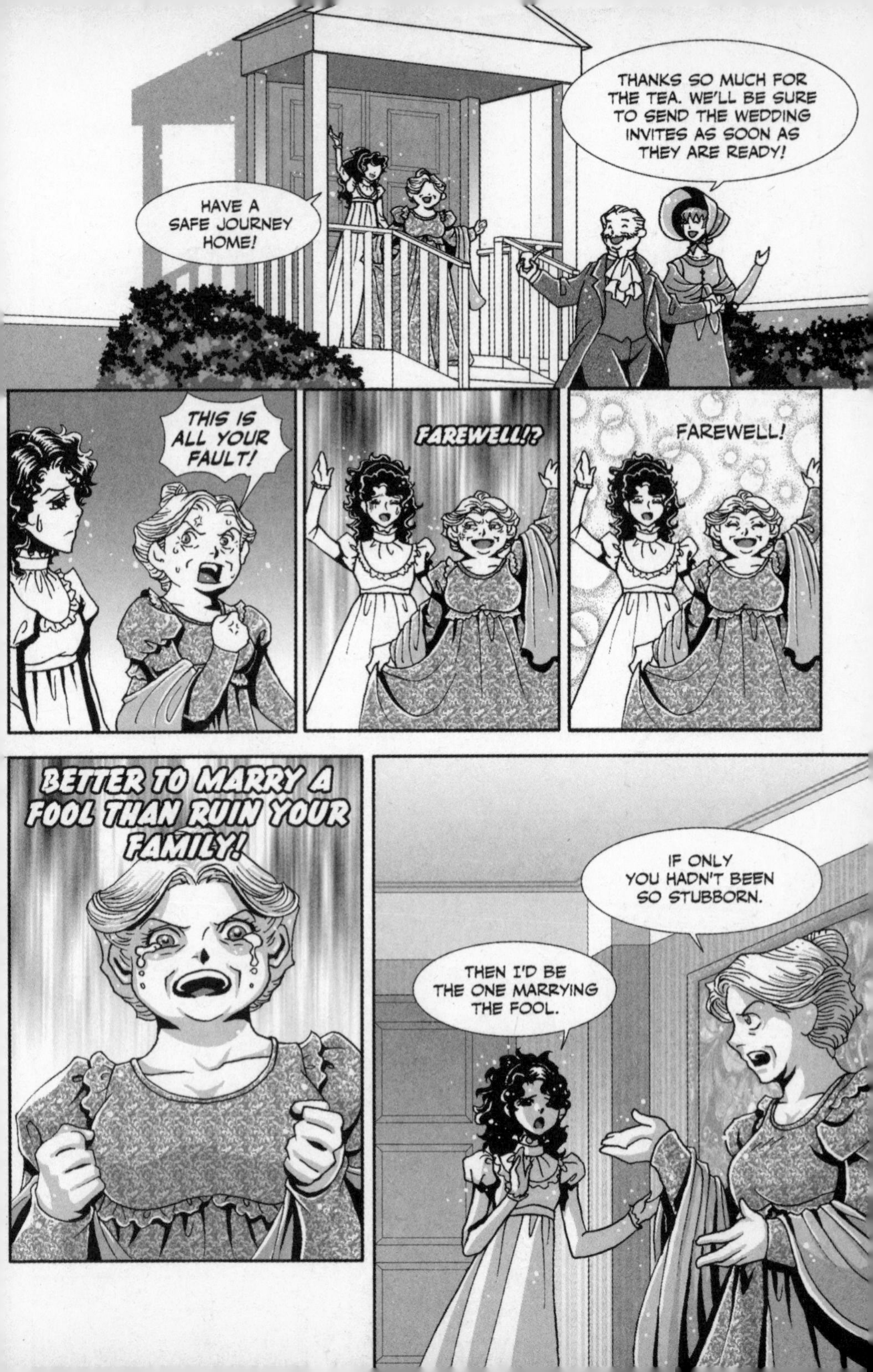
THANKS SO MUCH FOR THE TEA. WE'LL BE SURE TO SEND THE WEDDING INVITES AS SOON AS THEY ARE READY!
HAVE A SAFE JOURNEY HOME!
FAREWELL!
FAREWELL!?
THIS IS ALL YOUR FAULT!
IF ONLY YOU HADN'T BEEN SO STUBBORN.
THEN I'D BE THE ONE MARRYING THE FOOL.
BETTER TO MARRY A FOOL THAN RUIN YOUR FAMILY!

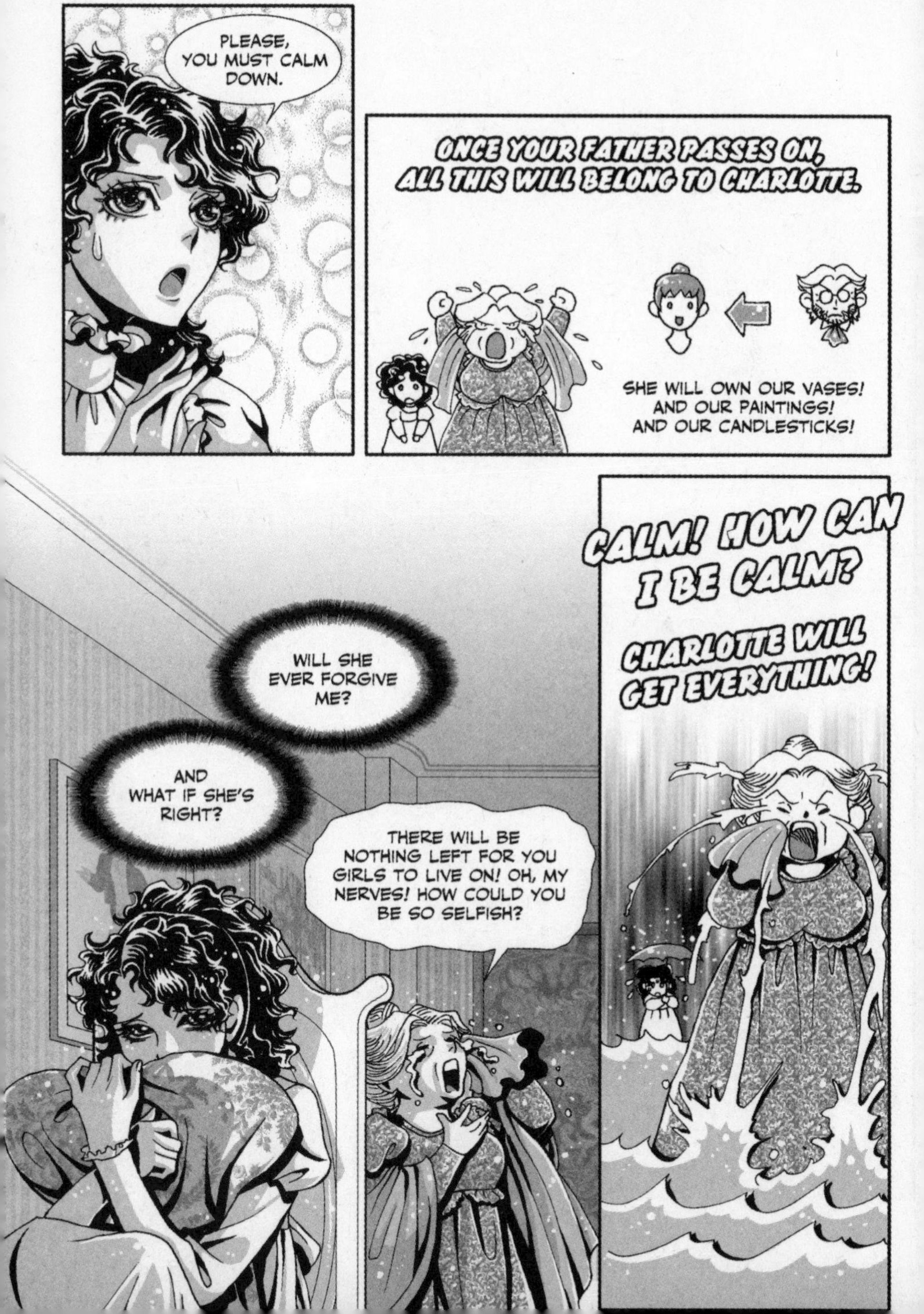
ONCE YOUR FATHER PASSES ON, ALL THIS WILL BELONG TO CHARLOTTE.
SHE WILL OWN OUR VASES! AND OUR PAINTINGS! AND OUR CANDLESTICKS!
PLEASE, YOU MUST CALM DOWN.
CALM! HOW CAN I BE CALM?
CHARLOTTE WILL GET EVERYTHING!
THERE WILL BE NOTHING LEFT FOR YOU GIRLS TO LIVE ON! OH, MY NERVES! HOW COULD YOU BE SO SELFISH?
WILL SHE EVER FORGIVE ME?
AND WHAT IF SHE'S RIGHT?

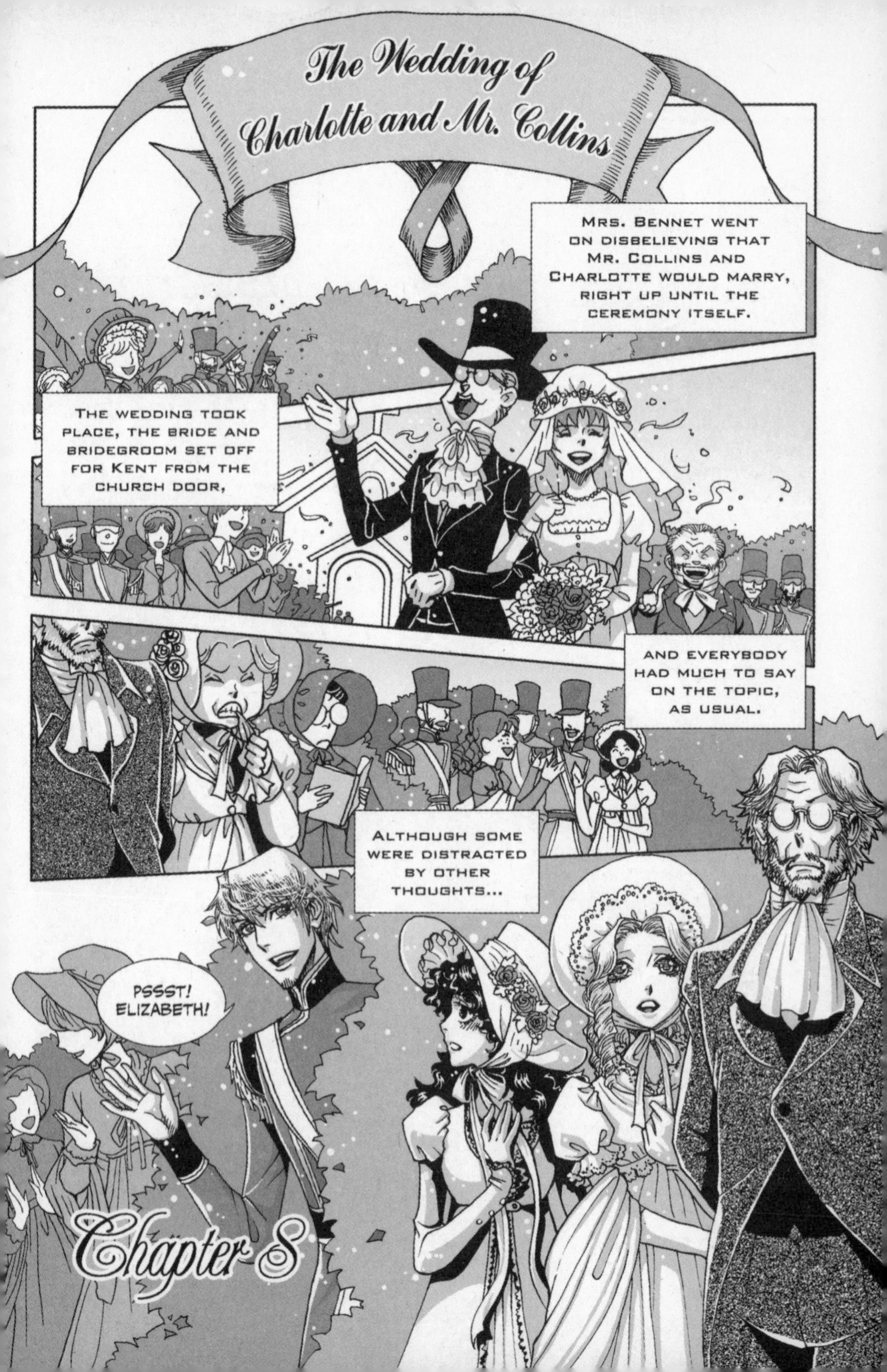
The Wedding of Charlotte and Mr. Collins
MRS. BENNET WENT ON DISBELIEVING THAT MR. COLLINS AND CHARLOTTE WOULD MARRY, RIGHT UP UNTIL THE CEREMONY ITSELF.
THE WEDDING TOOK PLACE, THE BRIDE AND BRIDEGROOM SET OFF FOR KENT FROM THE CHURCH DOOR,
AND EVERYBODY HAD MUCH TO SAY ON THE TOPIC, AS USUAL.
ALTHOUGH SOME WERE DISTRACTED BY OTHER THOUGHTS...
PSSST! ELIZABETH!
Chapter 8

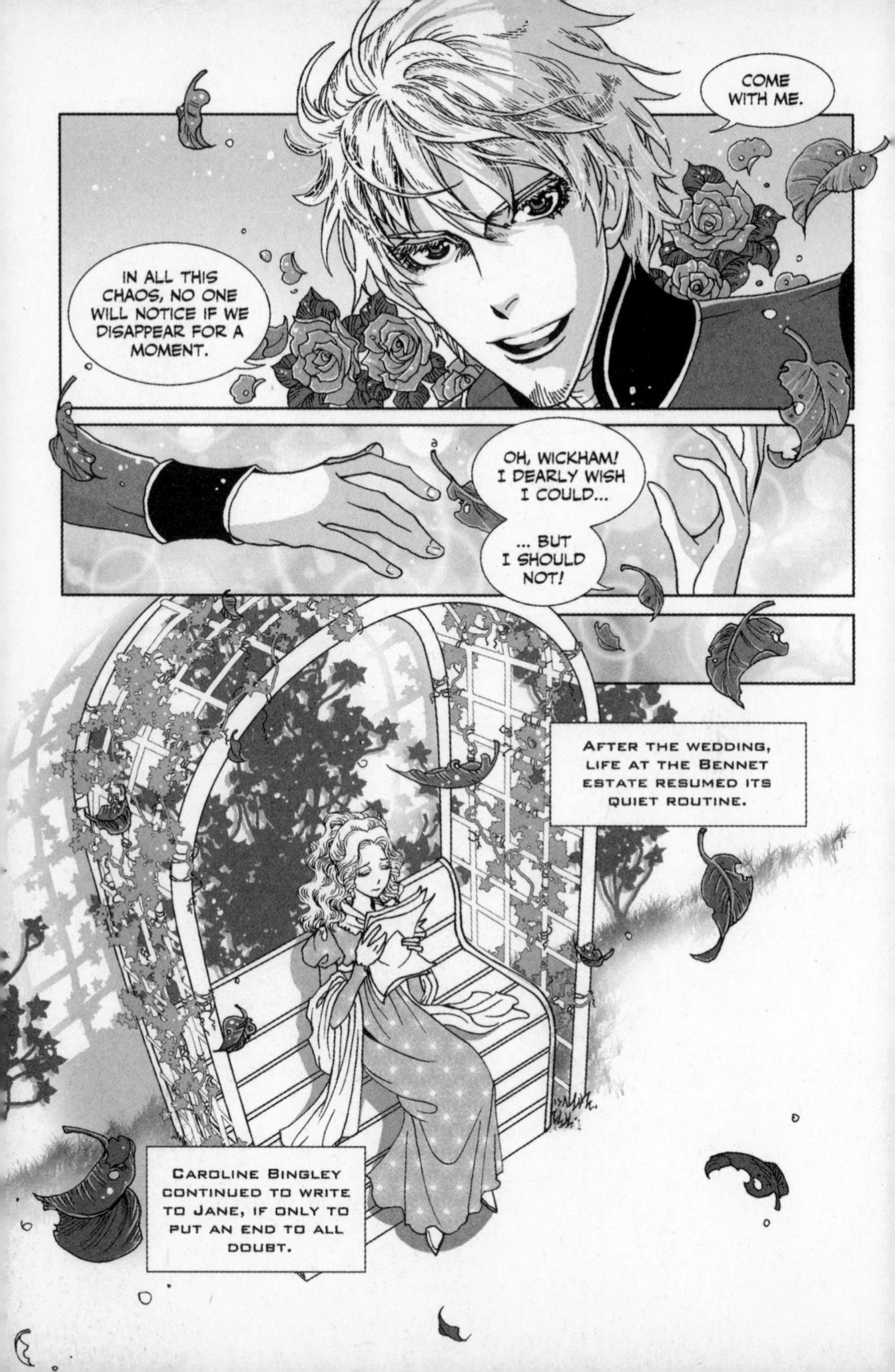
COME WITH ME.
IN ALL THIS CHAOS, NO ONE WILL NOTICE IF WE DISAPPEAR FOR A MOMENT.
OH, WICKHAM! I DEARLY WISH I COULD...
... BUT I SHOULD NOT!
AFTER THE WEDDING, LIFE AT THE BENNET ESTATE RESUMED ITS QUIET ROUTINE.
CAROLINE BINGLEY CONTINUED TO WRITE TO JANE, IF ONLY TO PUT AN END TO ALL DOUBT.

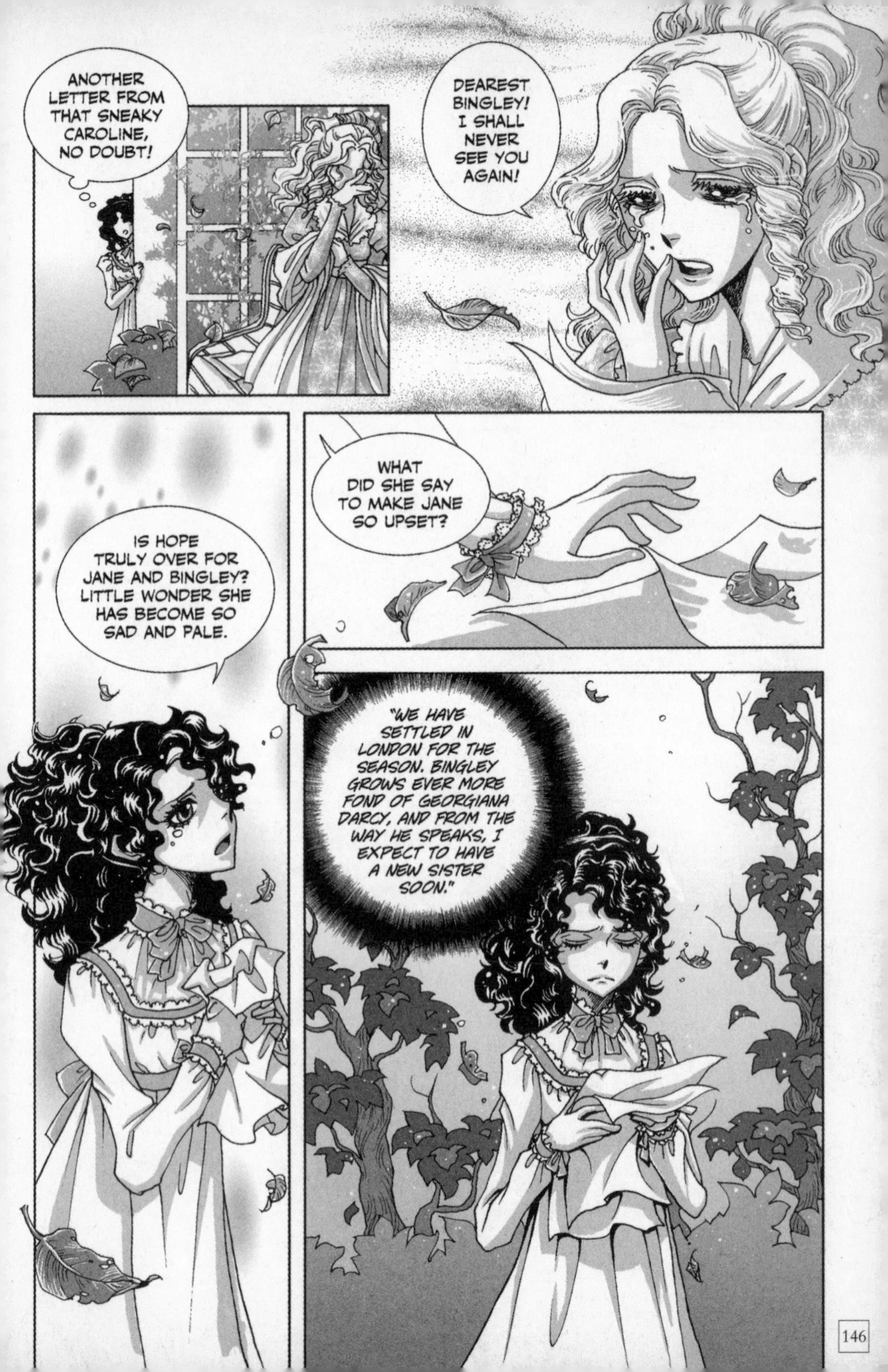
DEAREST BINGLEY! I SHALL NEVER SEE YOU AGAIN!
ANOTHER LETTER FROM THAT SNEAKY CAROLINE, NO DOUBT!
WHAT DID SHE SAY TO MAKE JANE SO UPSET?
"WE HAVE SETTLED IN LONDON FOR THE SEASON. BINGLEY GROWS EVER MORE FOND OF GEORGIANA DARCY, AND FROM THE WAY HE SPEAKS, I EXPECT TO HAVE A NEW SISTER SOON."
IS HOPE TRULY OVER FOR JANE AND BINGLEY? LITTLE WONDER SHE HAS BECOME SO SAD AND PALE.

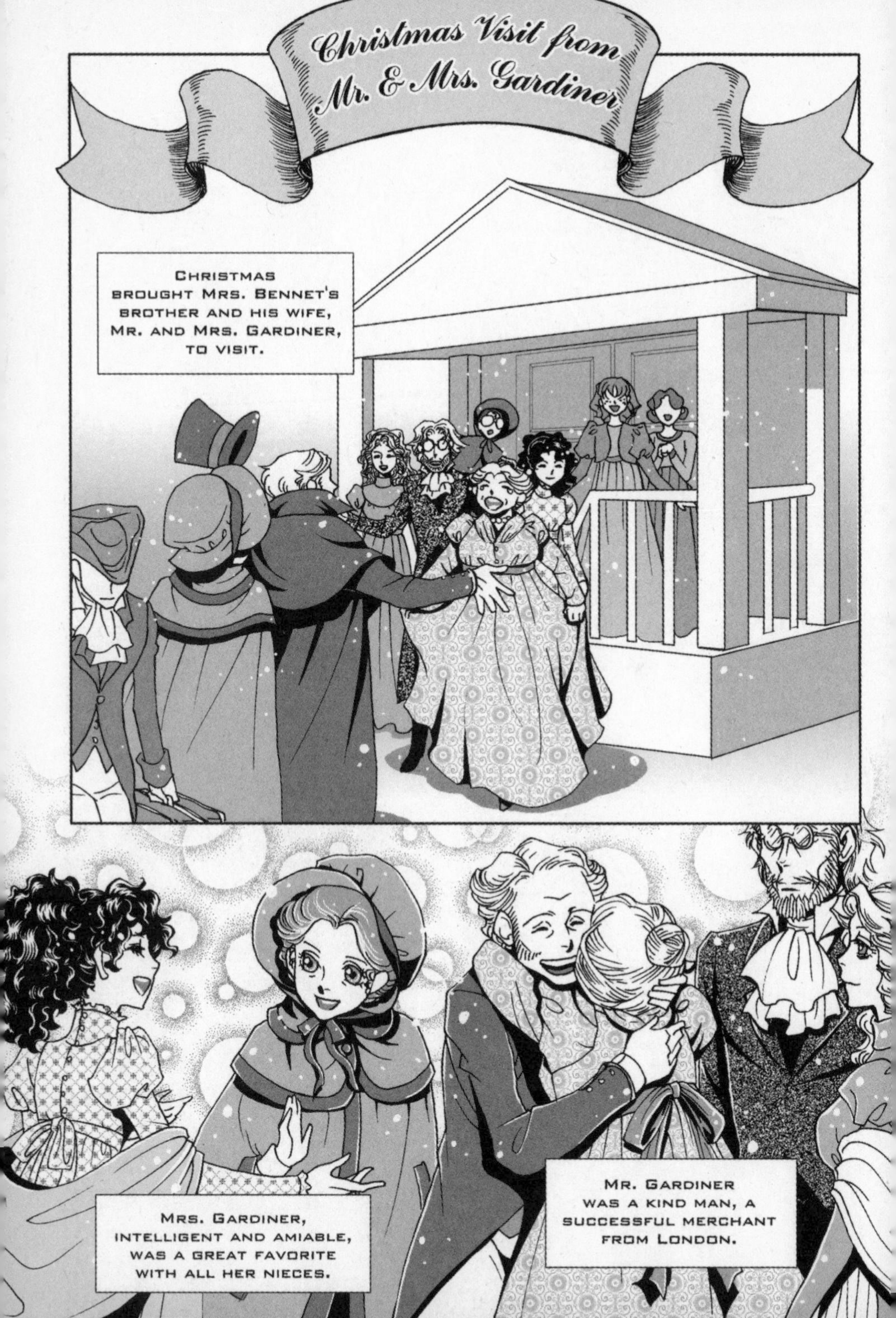
Christmas Visit from Mr. & Mrs. Gardiner
Christmas brought Mrs. Bennet's brother and his wife, Mr. and Mrs. Gardiner, to visit.
Mr. Gardiner was a kind man, a successful merchant from London.
Mrs. Gardiner, intelligent and amiable, was a great favorite with all her nieces.

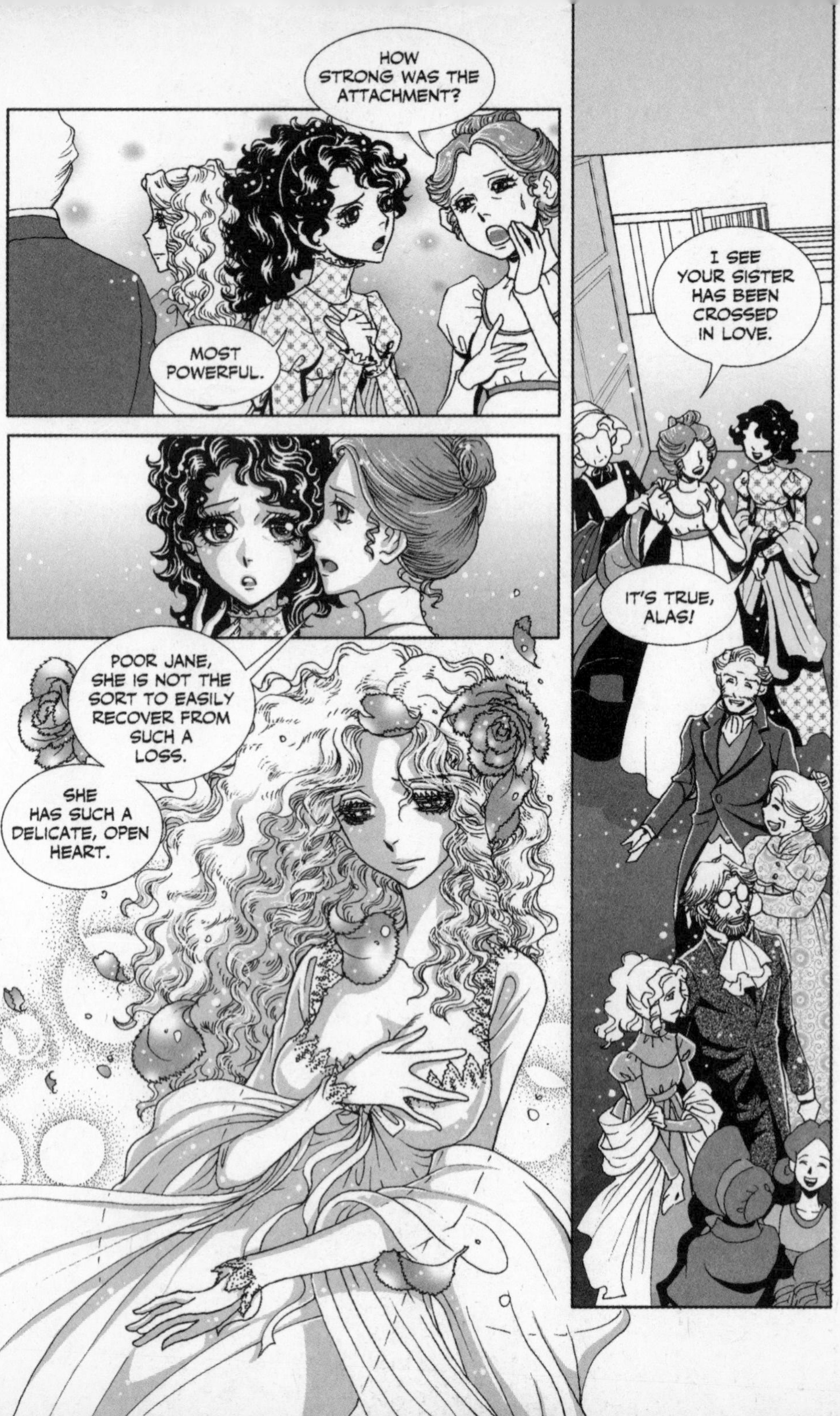
I SEE YOUR SISTER HAS BEEN CROSSED IN LOVE.
IT'S TRUE, ALAS!
HOW STRONG WAS THE ATTACHMENT?
MOST POWERFUL.
POOR JANE, SHE IS NOT THE SORT TO EASILY RECOVER FROM SUCH A LOSS.
SHE HAS SUCH A DELICATE, OPEN HEART.

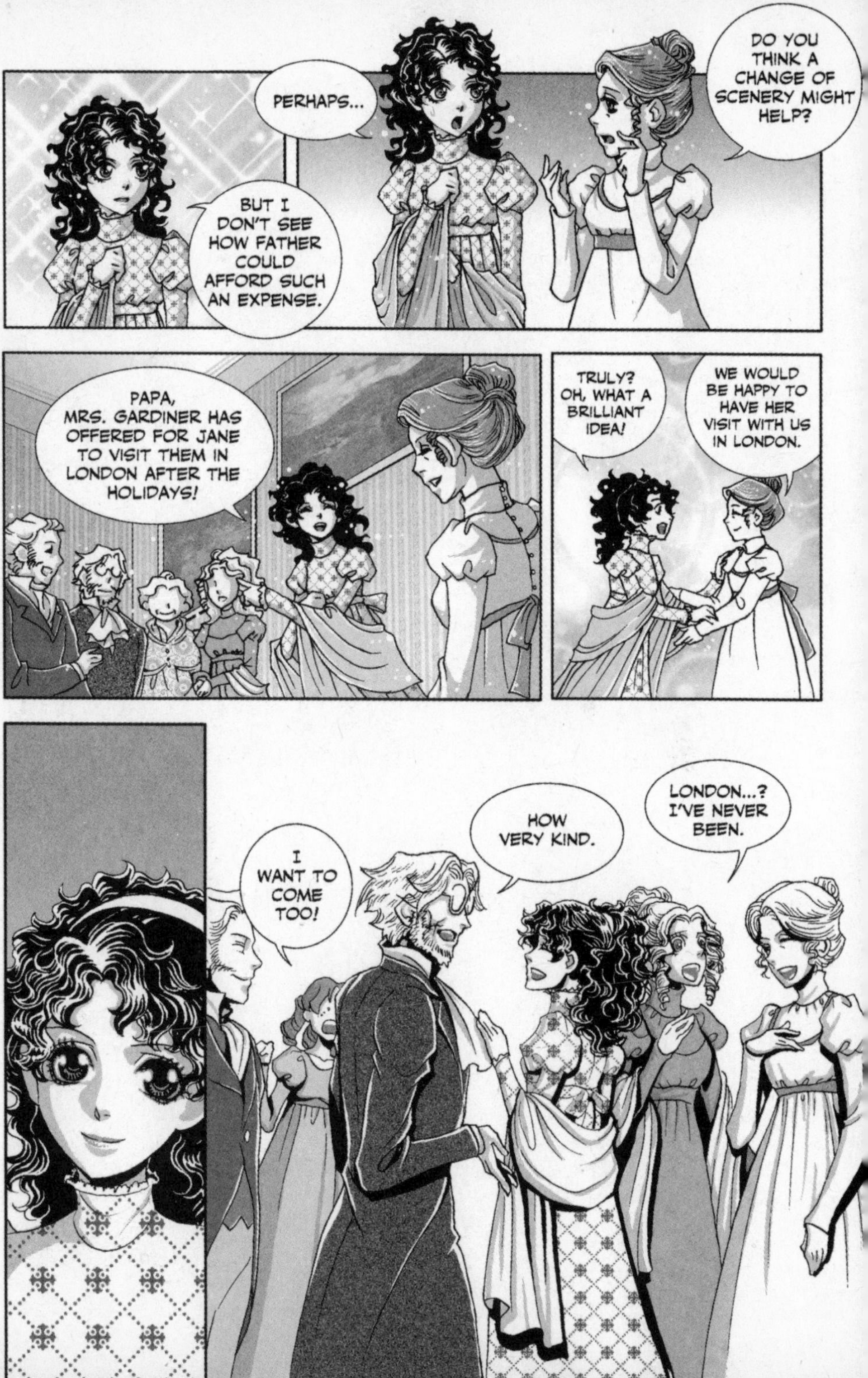
DO YOU THINK A CHANGE OF SCENERY MIGHT HELP?
PERHAPS...
BUT I DON'T SEE HOW FATHER COULD AFFORD SUCH AN EXPENSE.
WE WOULD BE HAPPY TO HAVE HER VISIT WITH US IN LONDON.
TRULY? OH, WHAT A BRILLIANT IDEA!
PAPA, MRS. GARDINER HAS OFFERED FOR JANE TO VISIT THEM IN LONDON AFTER THE HOLIDAYS!
LONDON...? I'VE NEVER BEEN.
HOW VERY KIND.
I WANT TO COME TOO!

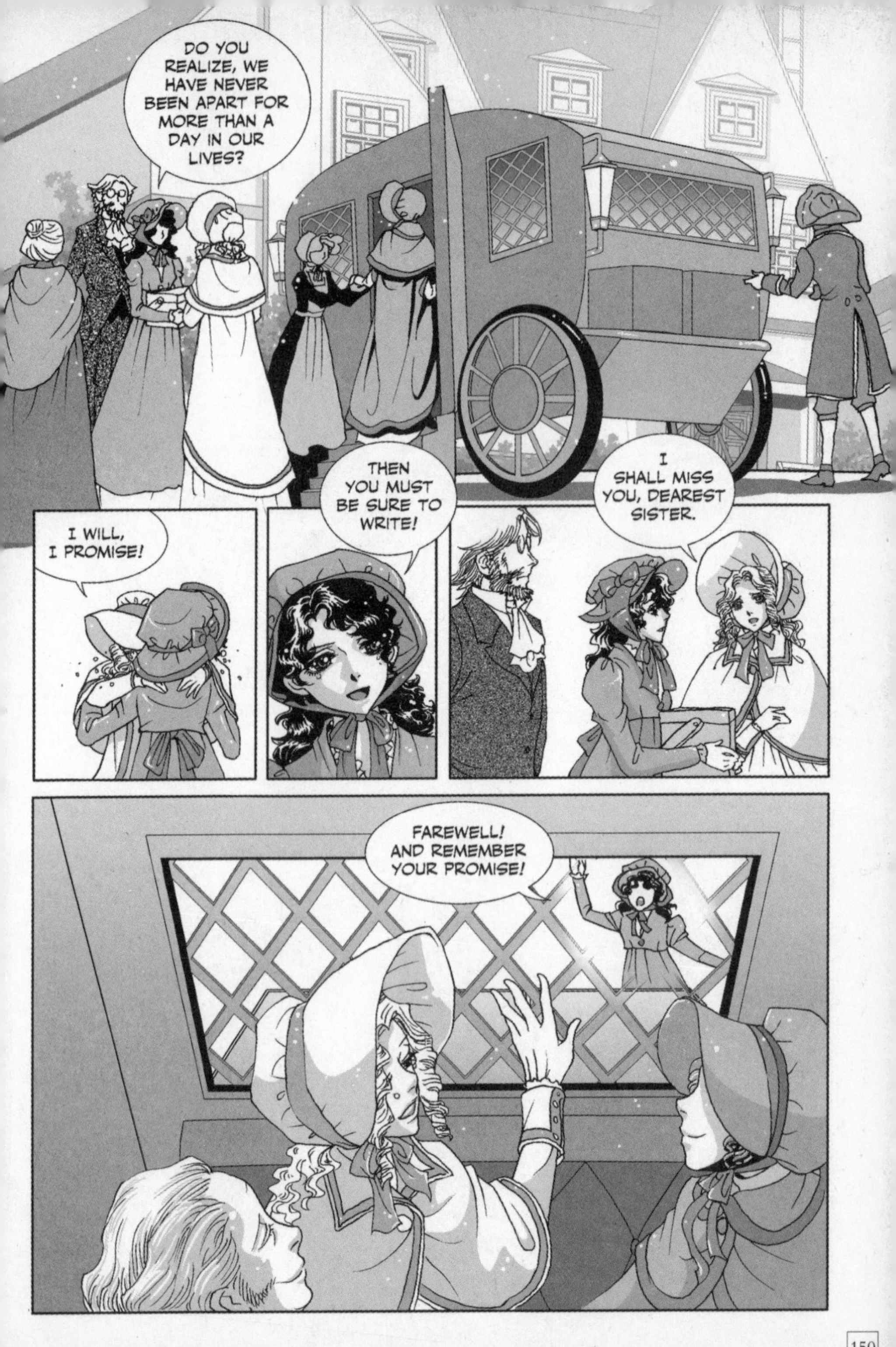
DO YOU REALIZE, WE HAVE NEVER BEEN APART FOR MORE THAN A DAY IN OUR LIVES?
I SHALL MISS YOU, DEAREST SISTER.
THEN YOU MUST BE SURE TO WRITE!
I WILL, I PROMISE!
FAREWELL! AND REMEMBER YOUR PROMISE!

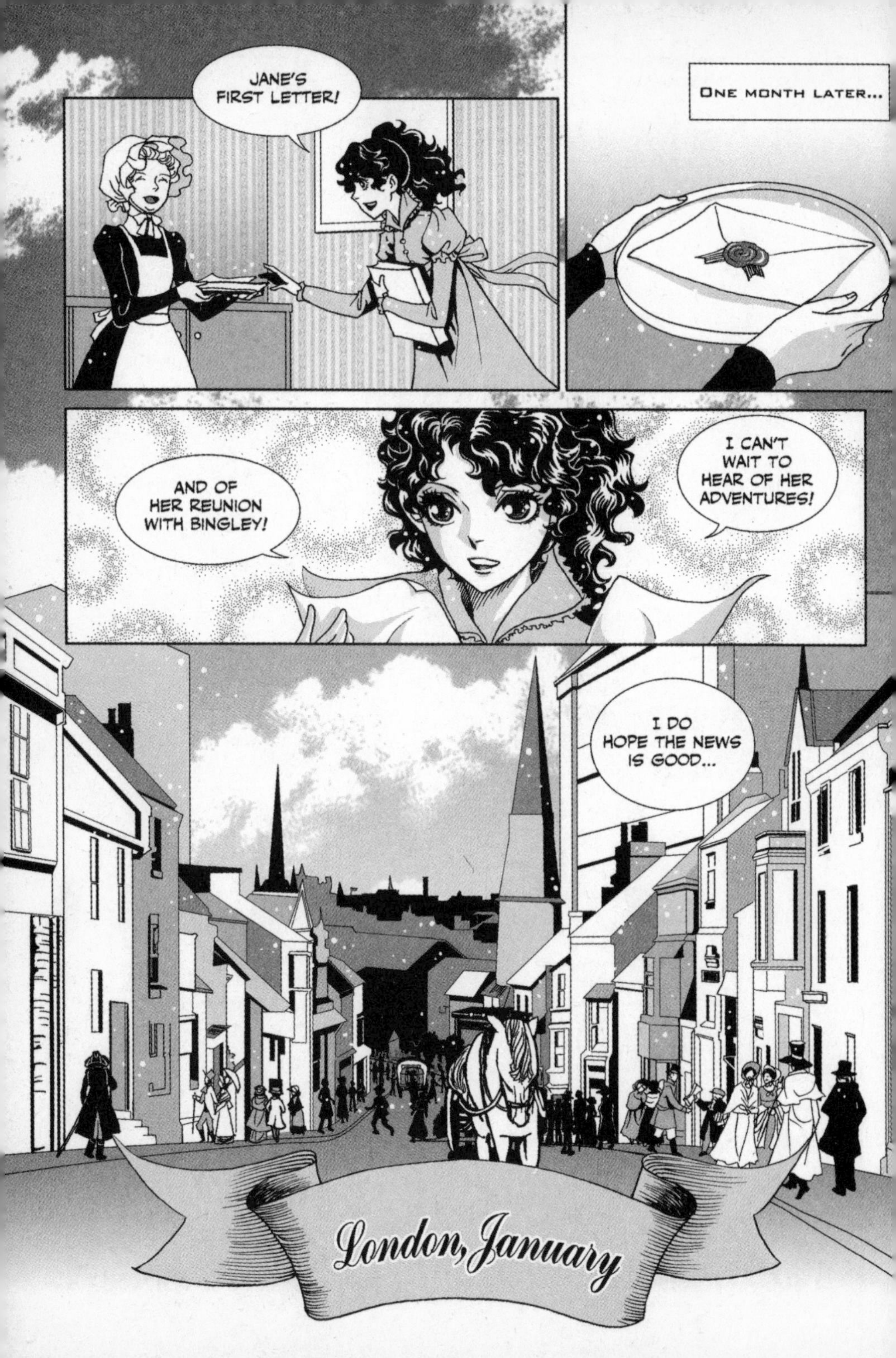
ONE MONTH LATER...
JANE'S FIRST LETTER!
I CAN'T WAIT TO HEAR OF HER ADVENTURES!
AND OF HER REUNION WITH BINGLEY!
I DO HOPE THE NEWS IS GOOD...
London, January

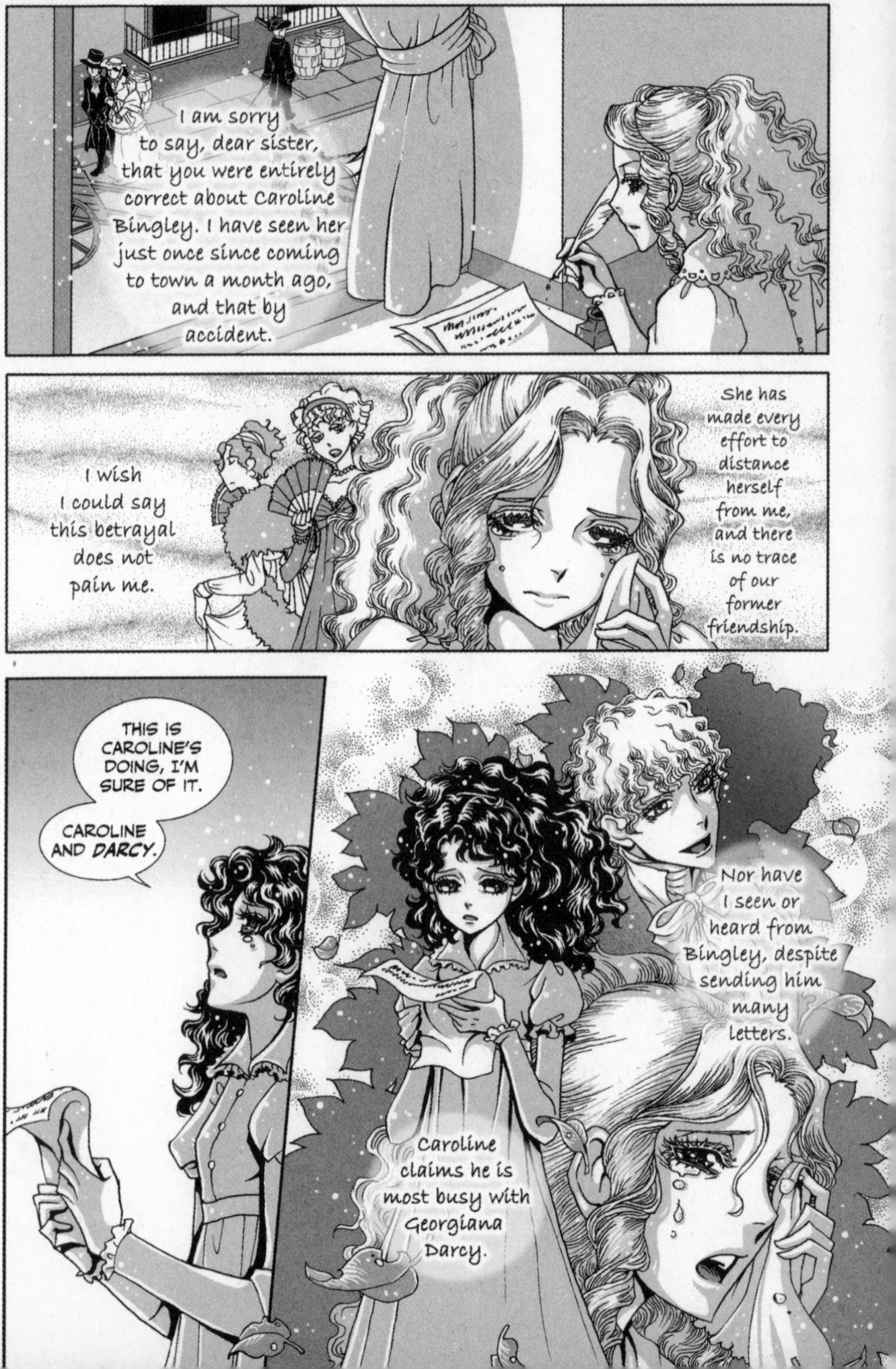
I am sorry to say, dear sister, that you were entirely correct about Caroline Bingley. I have seen her just once since coming to town a month ago, and that by accident.
She has made every effort to distance herself from me, and there is no trace of our former friendship.
I wish I could say this betrayal does not pain me.
Nor have I seen or heard from Bingley, despite sending him many letters.
Caroline claims he is most busy with Georgiana Darcy.
THIS IS CAROLINE'S DOING, I'M SURE OF IT.
CAROLINE AND *DARCY*.

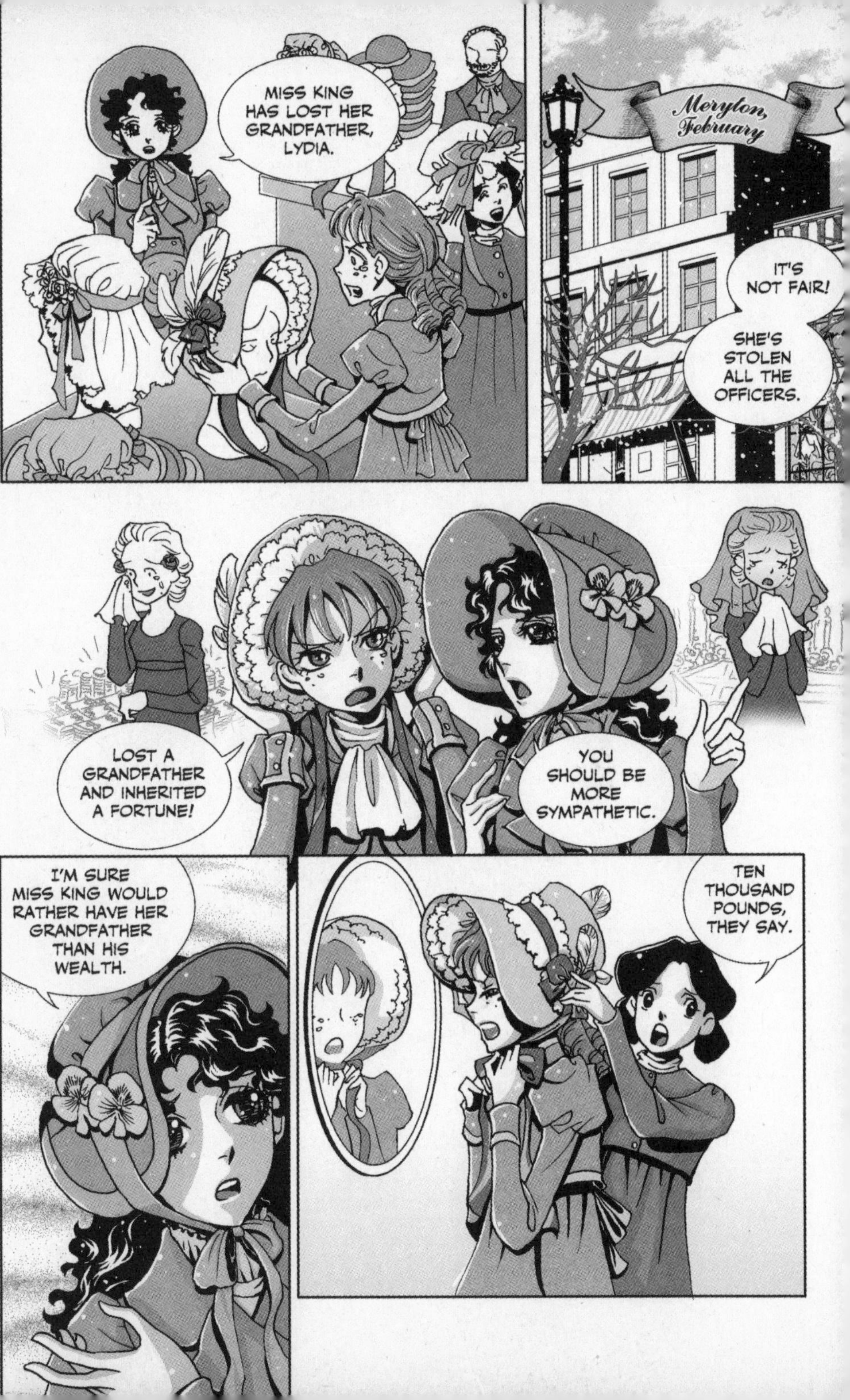
Meryton, February
IT'S NOT FAIR!
SHE'S STOLEN ALL THE OFFICERS.
MISS KING HAS LOST HER GRANDFATHER, LYDIA.
LOST A GRANDFATHER AND INHERITED A FORTUNE!
YOU SHOULD BE MORE SYMPATHETIC.
TEN THOUSAND POUNDS, THEY SAY.
I'M SURE MISS KING WOULD RATHER HAVE HER GRANDFATHER THAN HIS WEALTH.

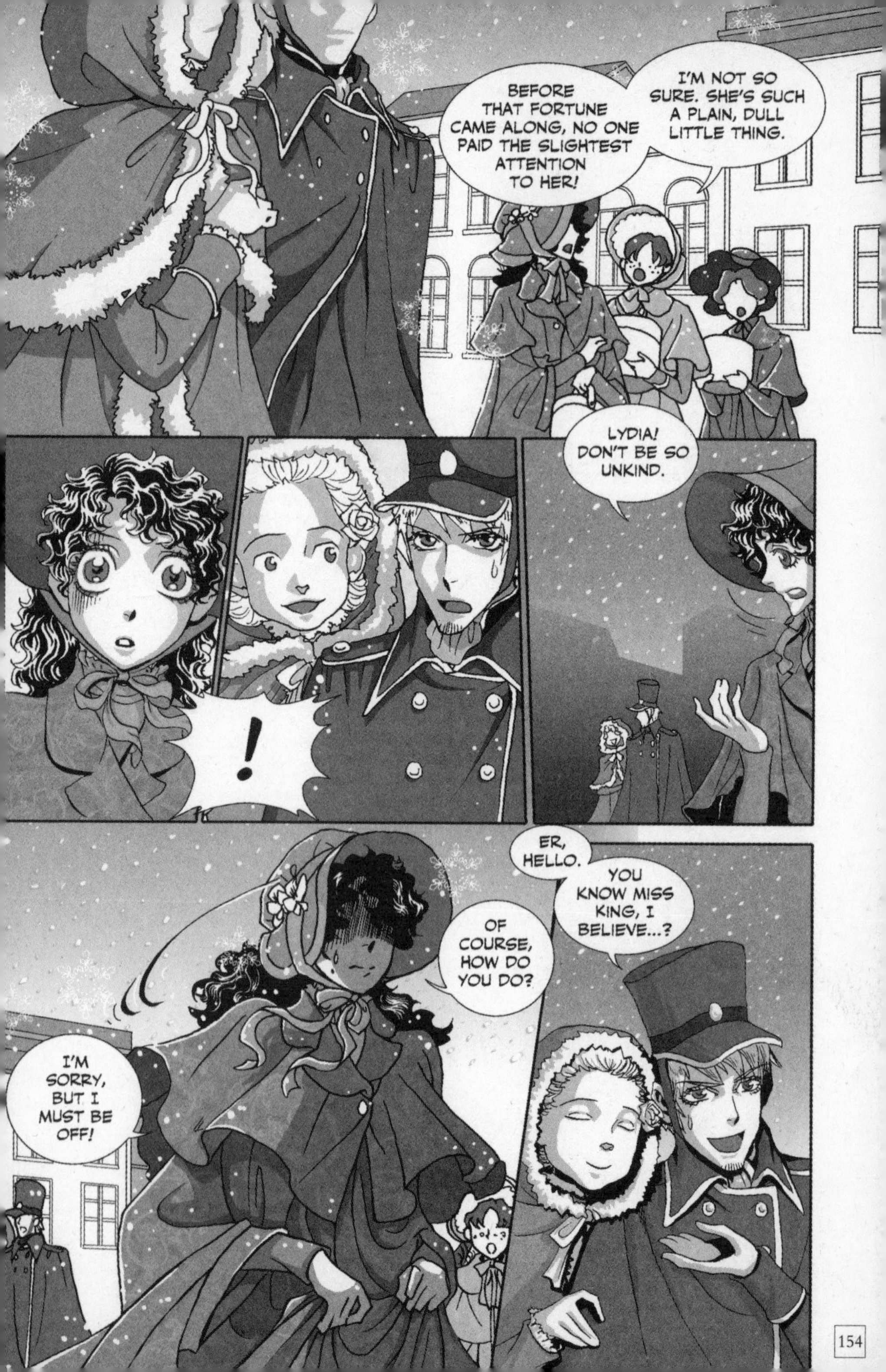
I'M NOT SO SURE. SHE'S SUCH A PLAIN, DULL LITTLE THING.
BEFORE THAT FORTUNE CAME ALONG, NO ONE PAID THE SLIGHTEST ATTENTION TO HER!
LYDIA! DON'T BE SO UNKIND.
!
ER, HELLO.
YOU KNOW MISS KING, I BELIEVE...?
OF COURSE, HOW DO YOU DO?
I'M SORRY, BUT I MUST BE OFF!

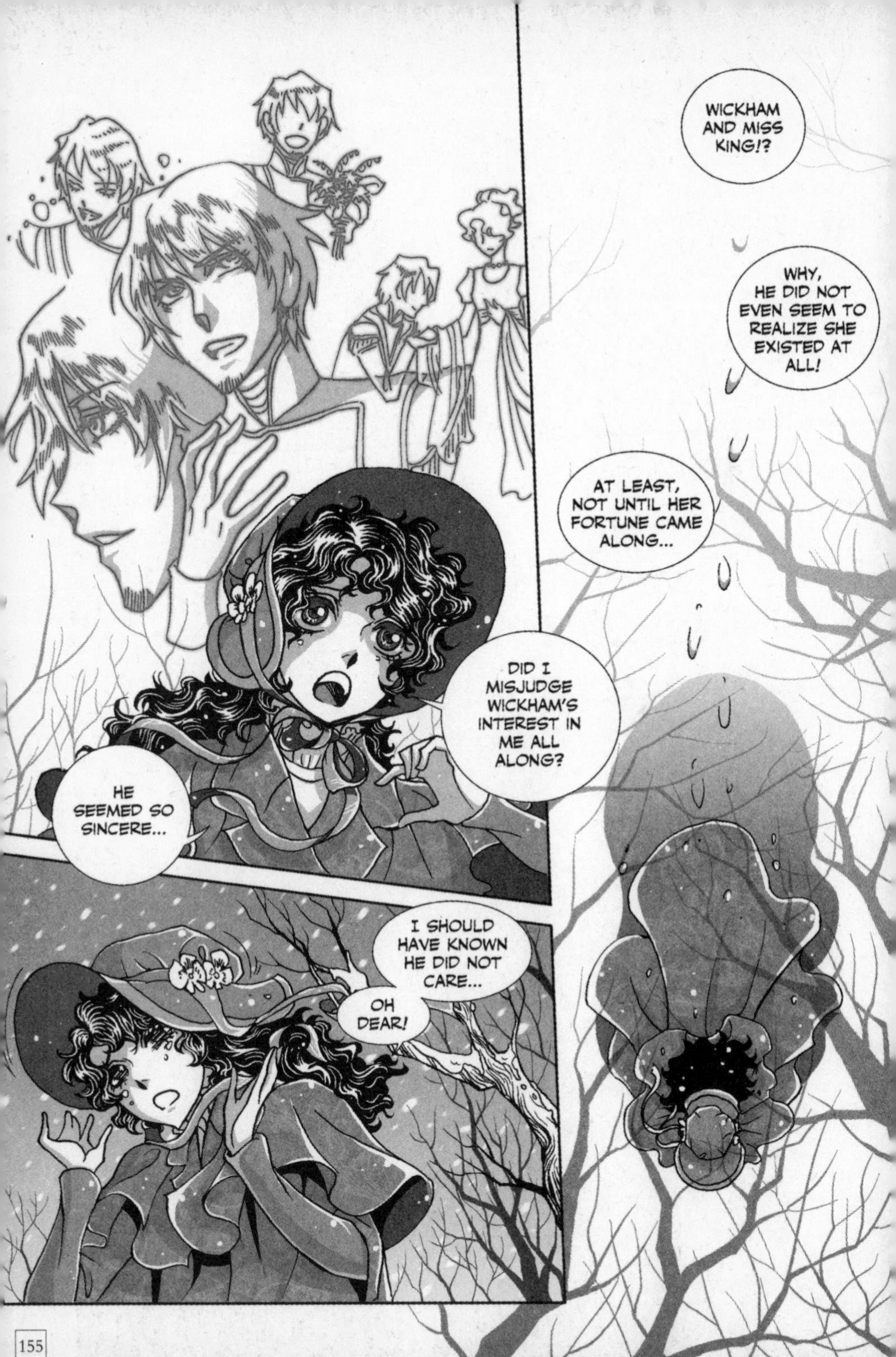
WICKHAM AND MISS KING!?
WHY, HE DID NOT EVEN SEEM TO REALIZE SHE EXISTED AT ALL!
AT LEAST, NOT UNTIL HER FORTUNE CAME ALONG...
DID I MISJUDGE WICKHAM'S INTEREST IN ME ALL ALONG?
HE SEEMED SO SINCERE...
I SHOULD HAVE KNOWN HE DID NOT CARE...
OH DEAR!

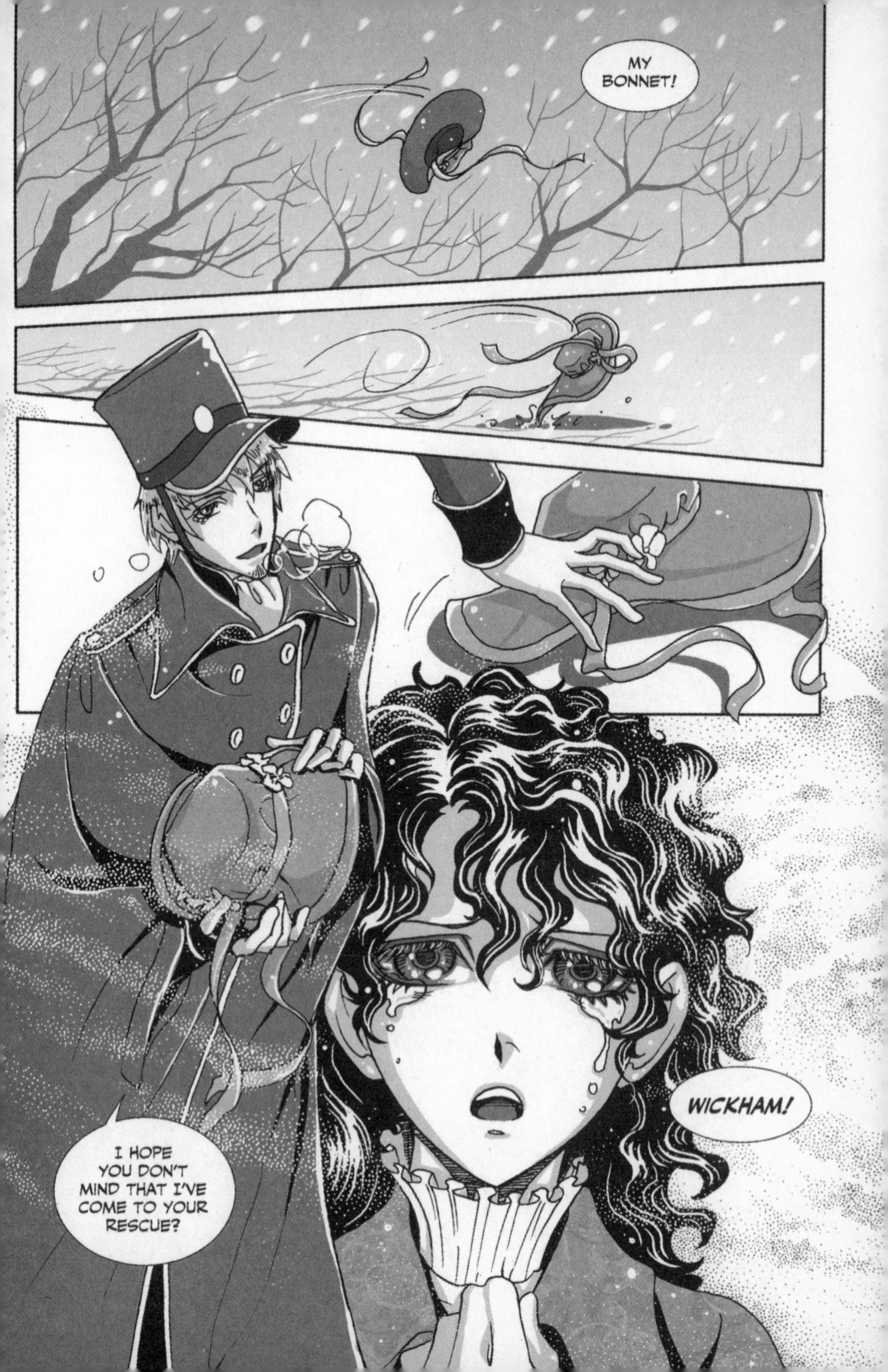
MY BONNET!
WICKHAM!
I HOPE YOU DON'T MIND THAT I'VE COME TO YOUR RESCUE?

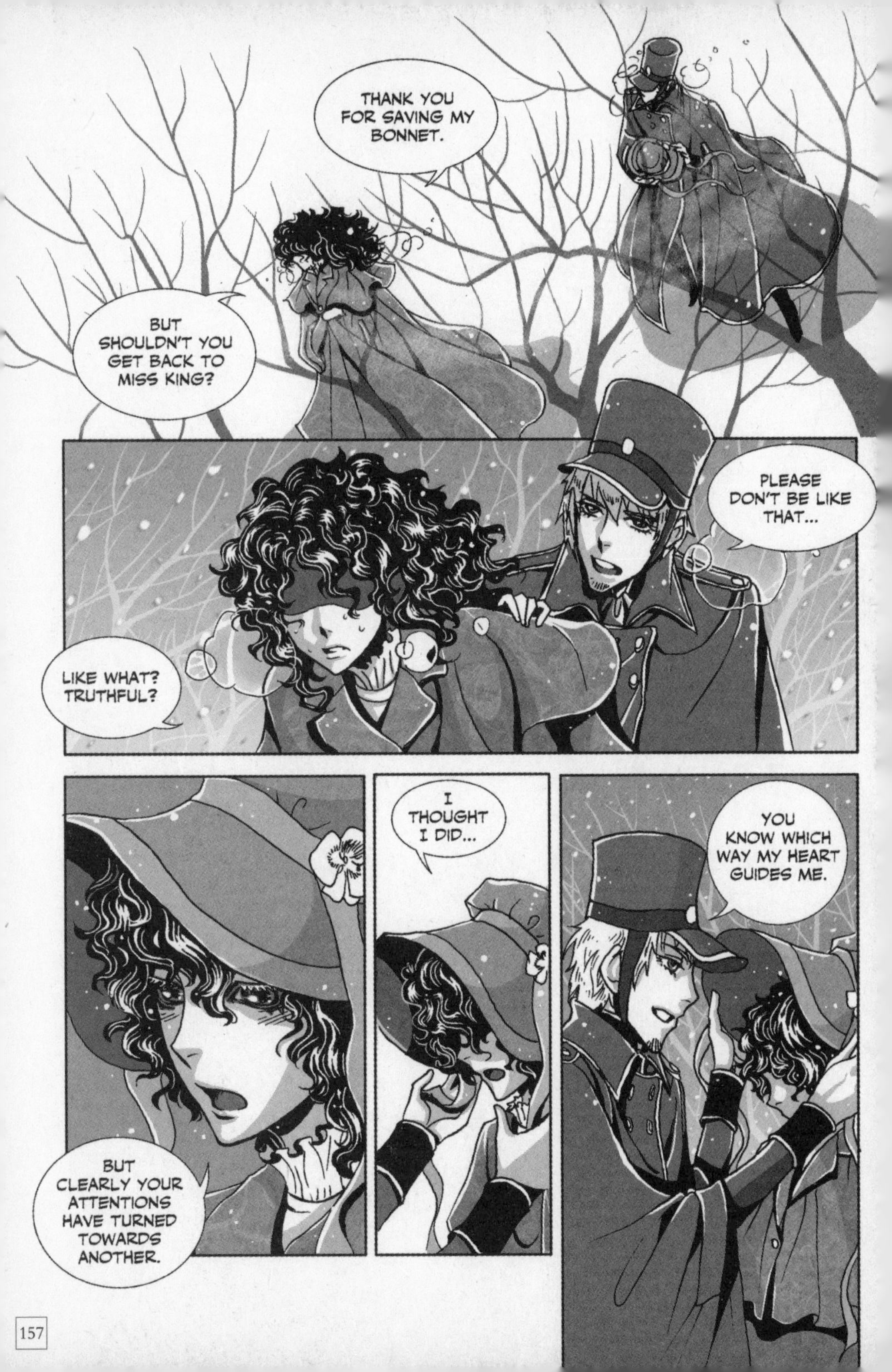
THANK YOU FOR SAVING MY BONNET.
BUT SHOULDN'T YOU GET BACK TO MISS KING?
PLEASE DON'T BE LIKE THAT...
LIKE WHAT? TRUTHFUL?
YOU KNOW WHICH WAY MY HEART GUIDES ME.
I THOUGHT I DID...
BUT CLEARLY YOUR ATTENTIONS HAVE TURNED TOWARDS ANOTHER.

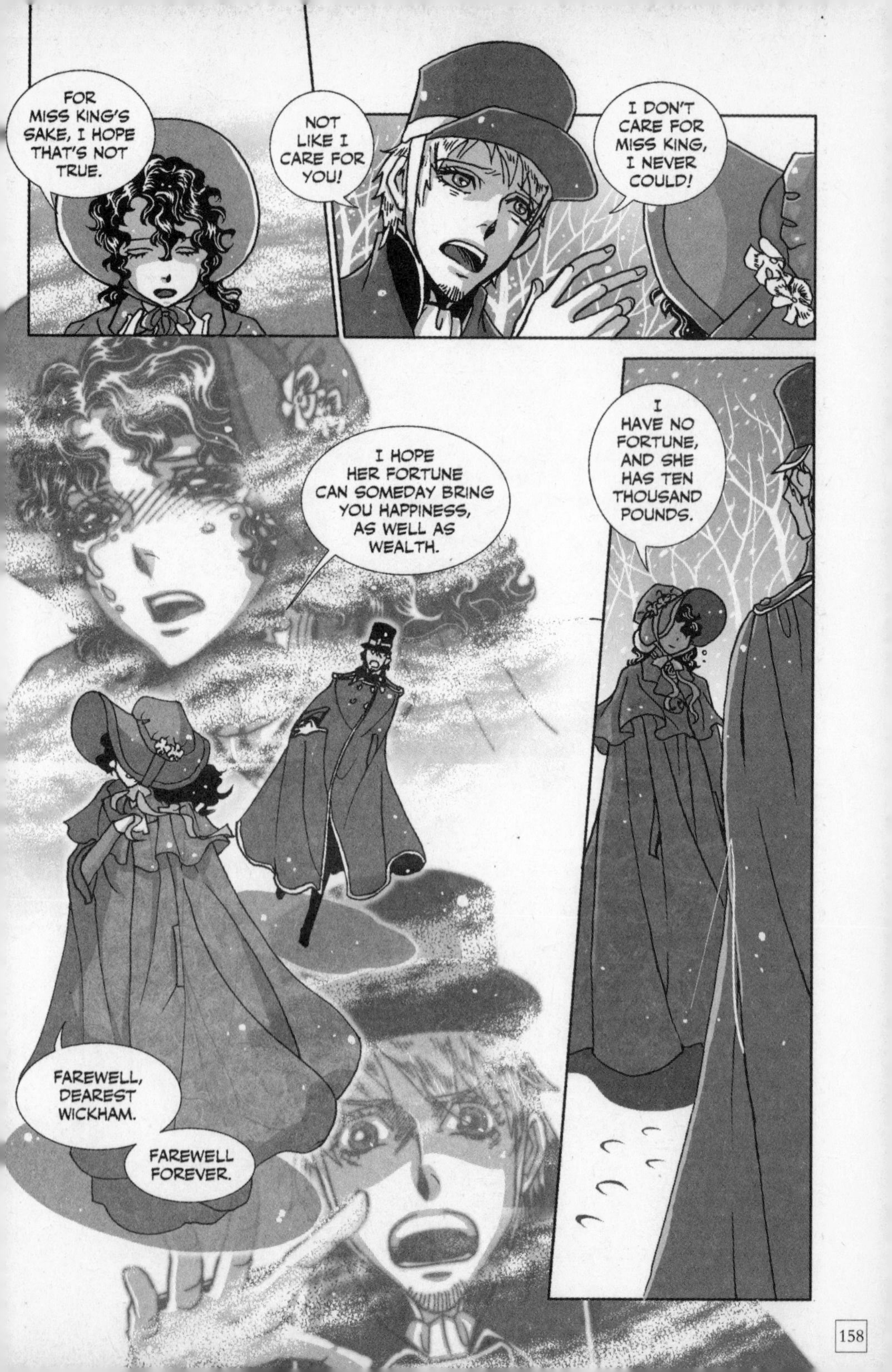
I DON'T CARE FOR MISS KING, I NEVER COULD!
NOT LIKE I CARE FOR YOU!
FOR MISS KING'S SAKE, I HOPE THAT'S NOT TRUE.
I HAVE NO FORTUNE, AND SHE HAS TEN THOUSAND POUNDS.
I HOPE HER FORTUNE CAN SOMEDAY BRING YOU HAPPINESS, AS WELL AS WEALTH.
FAREWELL, DEAREST WICKHAM.
FAREWELL FOREVER.

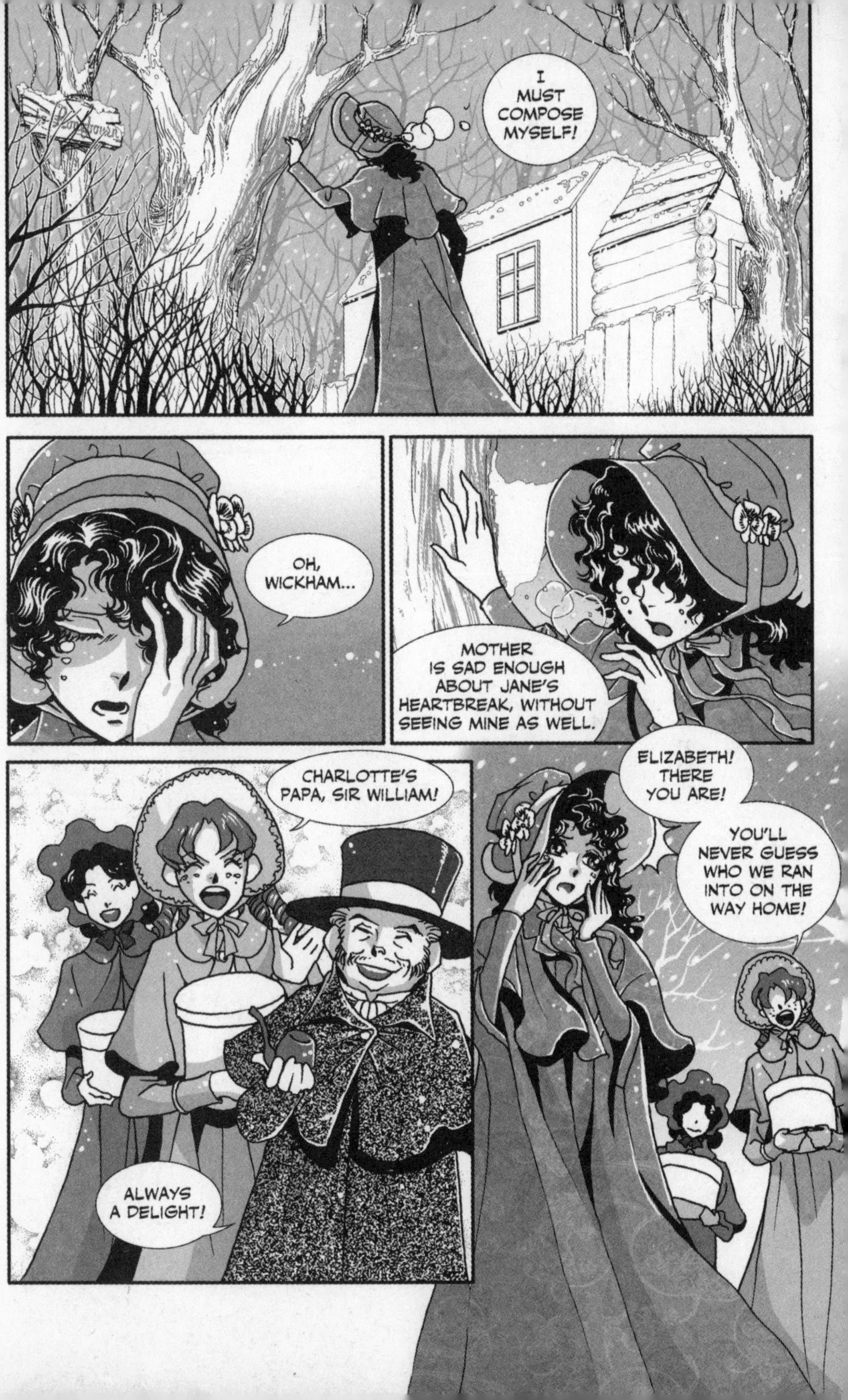

I MUST COMPOSE MYSELF!
MOTHER IS SAD ENOUGH ABOUT JANE'S HEARTBREAK, WITHOUT SEEING MINE AS WELL.
OH, WICKHAM...
ELIZABETH! THERE YOU ARE!
YOU'LL NEVER GUESS WHO WE RAN INTO ON THE WAY HOME!
CHARLOTTE'S PAPA, SIR WILLIAM!
ALWAYS A DELIGHT!

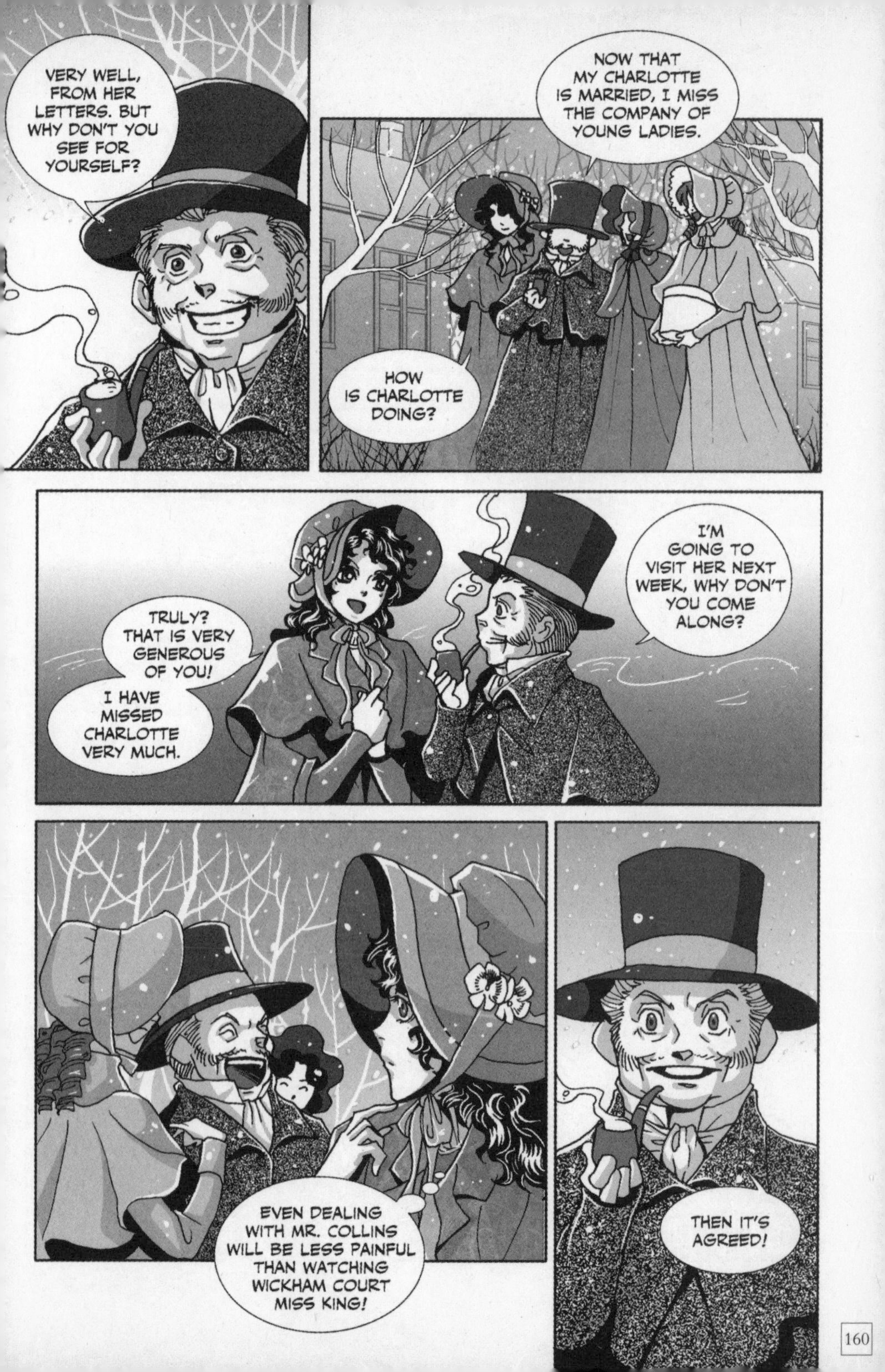
NOW THAT MY CHARLOTTE IS MARRIED, I MISS THE COMPANY OF YOUNG LADIES.
HOW IS CHARLOTTE DOING?
VERY WELL, FROM HER LETTERS. BUT WHY DON'T YOU SEE FOR YOURSELF?
I'M GOING TO VISIT HER NEXT WEEK, WHY DON'T YOU COME ALONG?
TRULY? THAT IS VERY GENEROUS OF YOU!
I HAVE MISSED CHARLOTTE VERY MUCH.
THEN IT'S AGREED!
EVEN DEALING WITH MR. COLLINS WILL BE LESS PAINFUL THAN WATCHING WICKHAM COURT MISS KING!

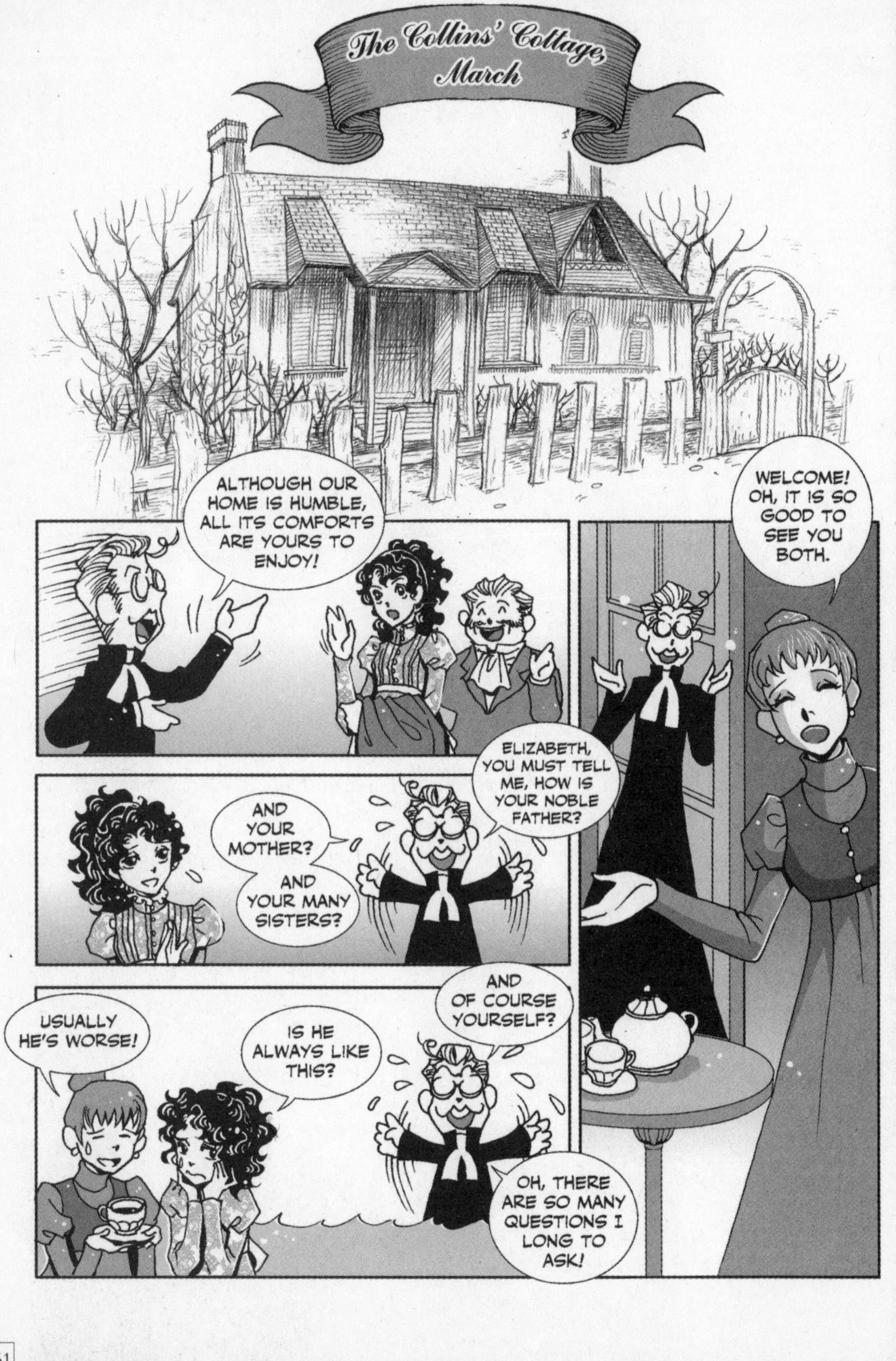
The Collins' Cottage, March
WELCOME! OH, IT IS SO GOOD TO SEE YOU BOTH.
ALTHOUGH OUR HOME IS HUMBLE, ALL ITS COMFORTS ARE YOURS TO ENJOY!
ELIZABETH, YOU MUST TELL ME, HOW IS YOUR NOBLE FATHER?
AND YOUR MOTHER?
AND YOUR MANY SISTERS?
AND OF COURSE YOURSELF?
OH, THERE ARE SO MANY QUESTIONS I LONG TO ASK!
IS HE ALWAYS LIKE THIS?
USUALLY HE'S WORSE!

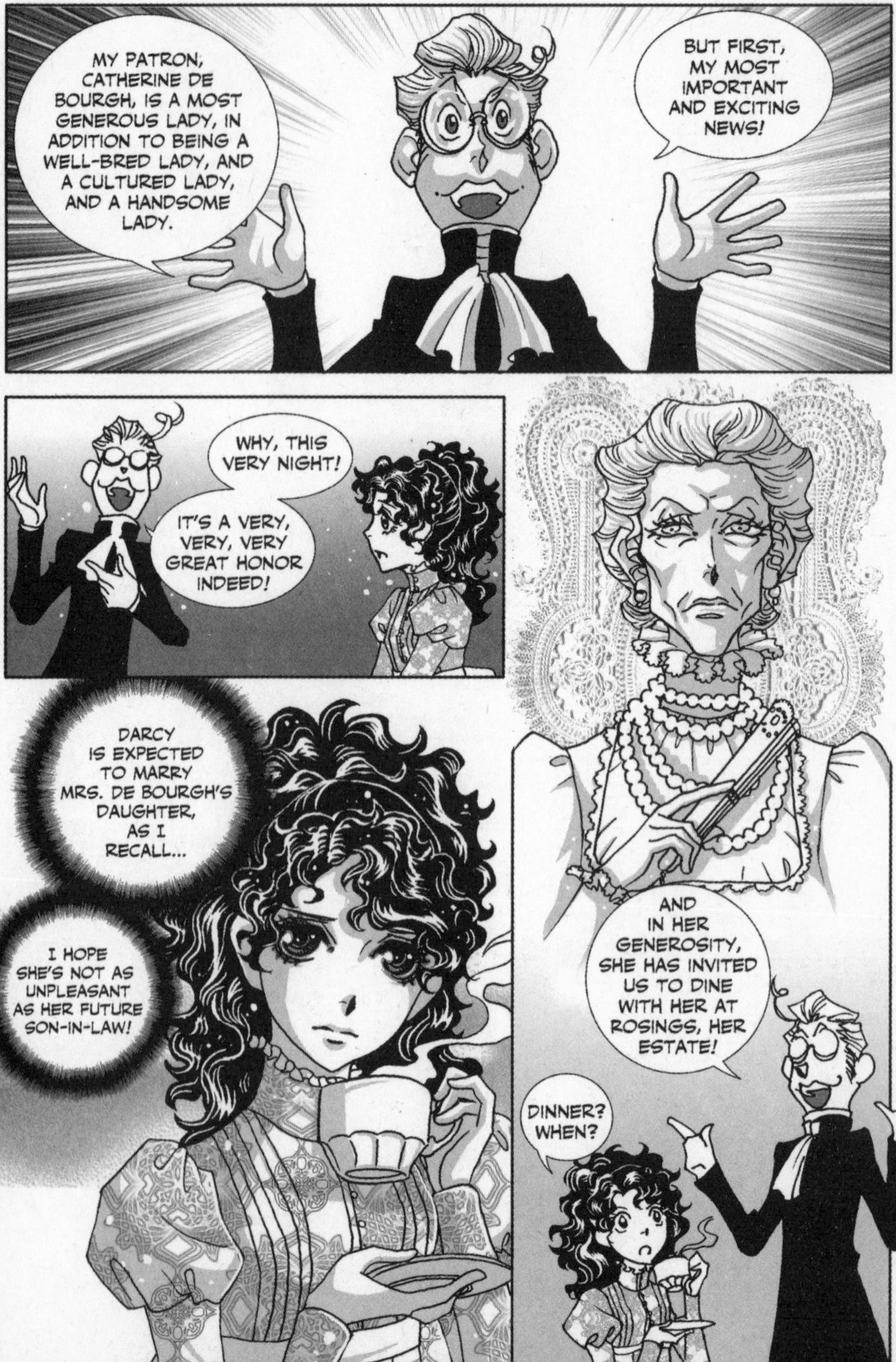
MY PATRON, CATHERINE DE BOURGH, IS A MOST GENEROUS LADY, IN ADDITION TO BEING A WELL-BRED LADY, AND A CULTURED LADY, AND A HANDSOME LADY.
BUT FIRST, MY MOST IMPORTANT AND EXCITING NEWS!
AND IN HER GENEROSITY, SHE HAS INVITED US TO DINE WITH HER AT ROSINGS, HER ESTATE!
DINNER? WHEN?
WHY, THIS VERY NIGHT!
IT'S A VERY, VERY, VERY GREAT HONOR INDEED!
DARCY IS EXPECTED TO MARRY MRS. DE BOURGH'S DAUGHTER, AS I RECALL...
I HOPE SHE'S NOT AS UNPLEASANT AS HER FUTURE SON-IN-LAW!

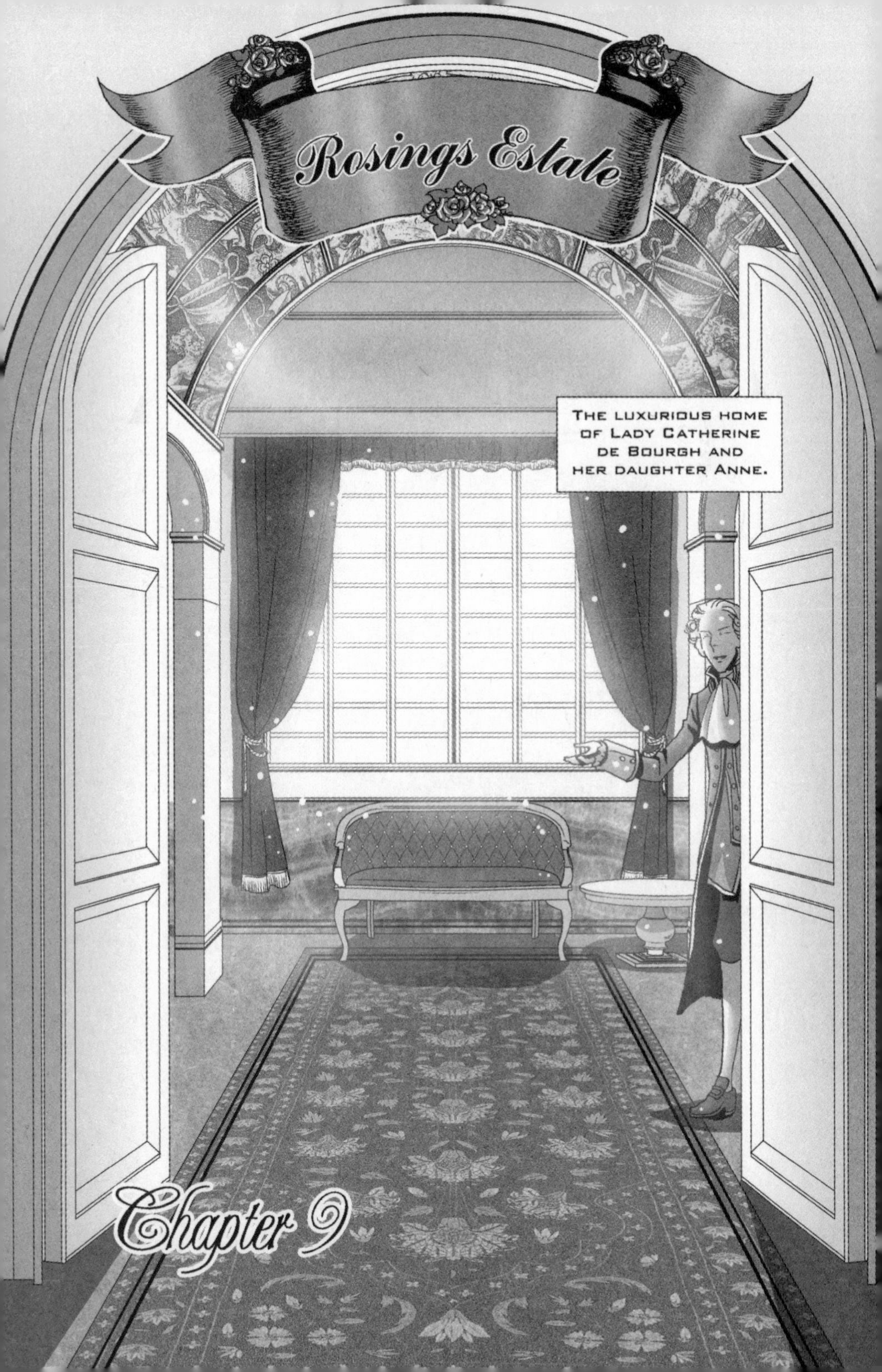
Rosings Estate
The luxurious home of Lady Catherine de Bourgh and her daughter Anne.
Chapter 9

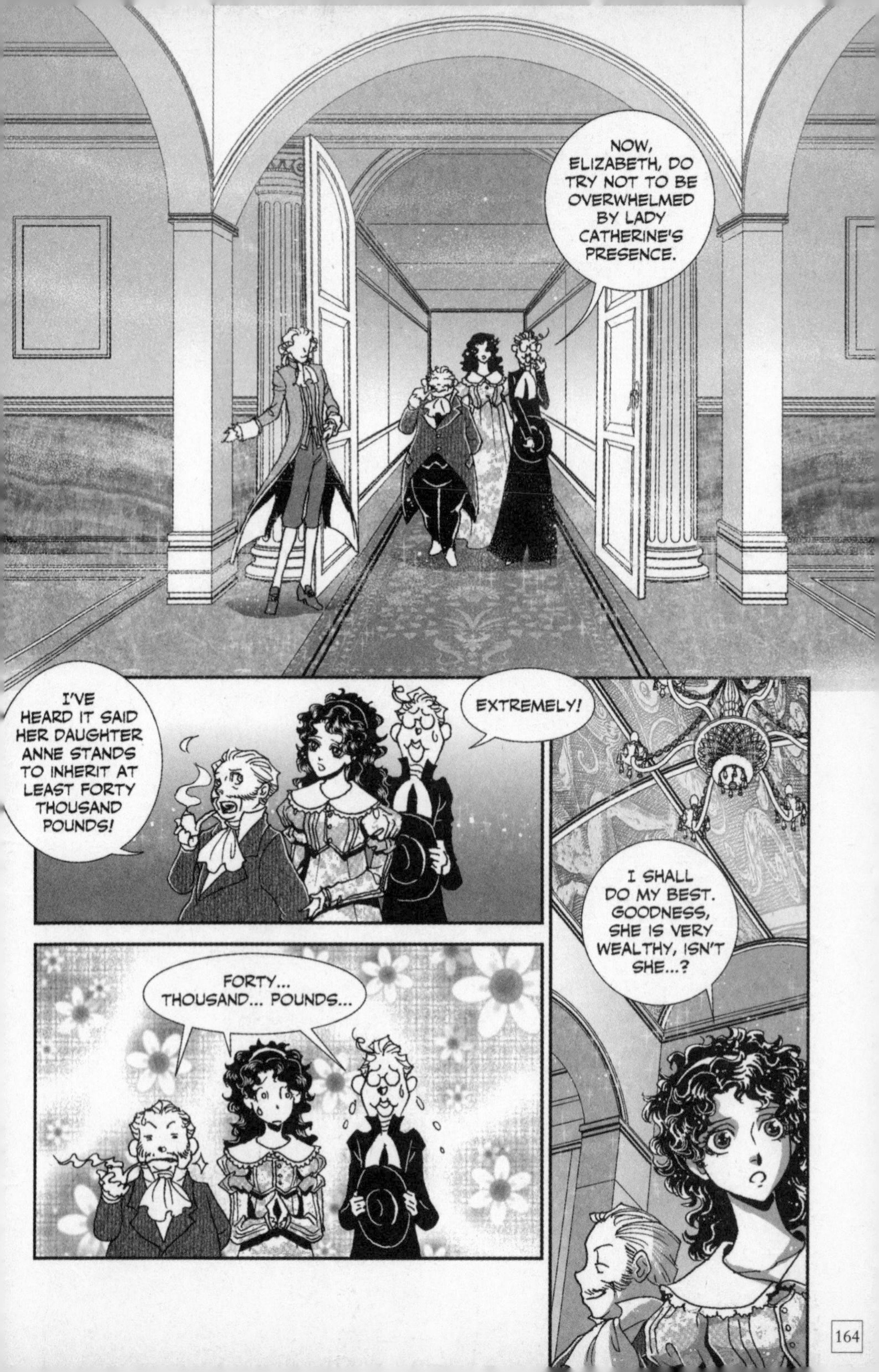
NOW, ELIZABETH, DO TRY NOT TO BE OVERWHELMED BY LADY CATHERINE'S PRESENCE.
I SHALL DO MY BEST. GOODNESS, SHE IS VERY WEALTHY, ISN'T SHE...?
EXTREMELY!
I'VE HEARD IT SAID HER DAUGHTER ANNE STANDS TO INHERIT AT LEAST FORTY THOUSAND POUNDS!
FORTY... THOUSAND... POUNDS...

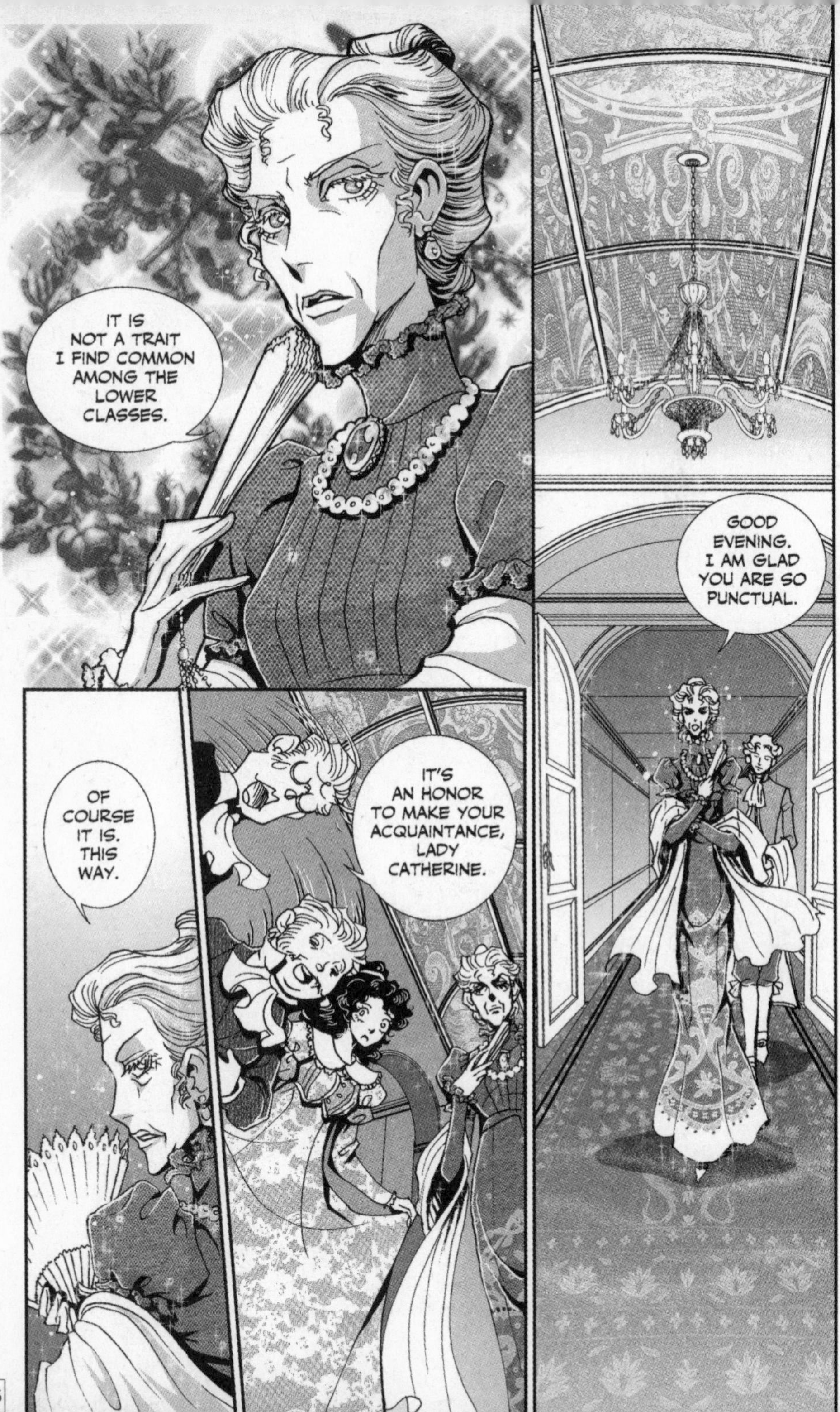
GOOD EVENING. I AM GLAD YOU ARE SO PUNCTUAL.
IT IS NOT A TRAIT I FIND COMMON AMONG THE LOWER CLASSES.
IT'S AN HONOR TO MAKE YOUR ACQUAINTANCE, LADY CATHERINE.
OF COURSE IT IS. THIS WAY.

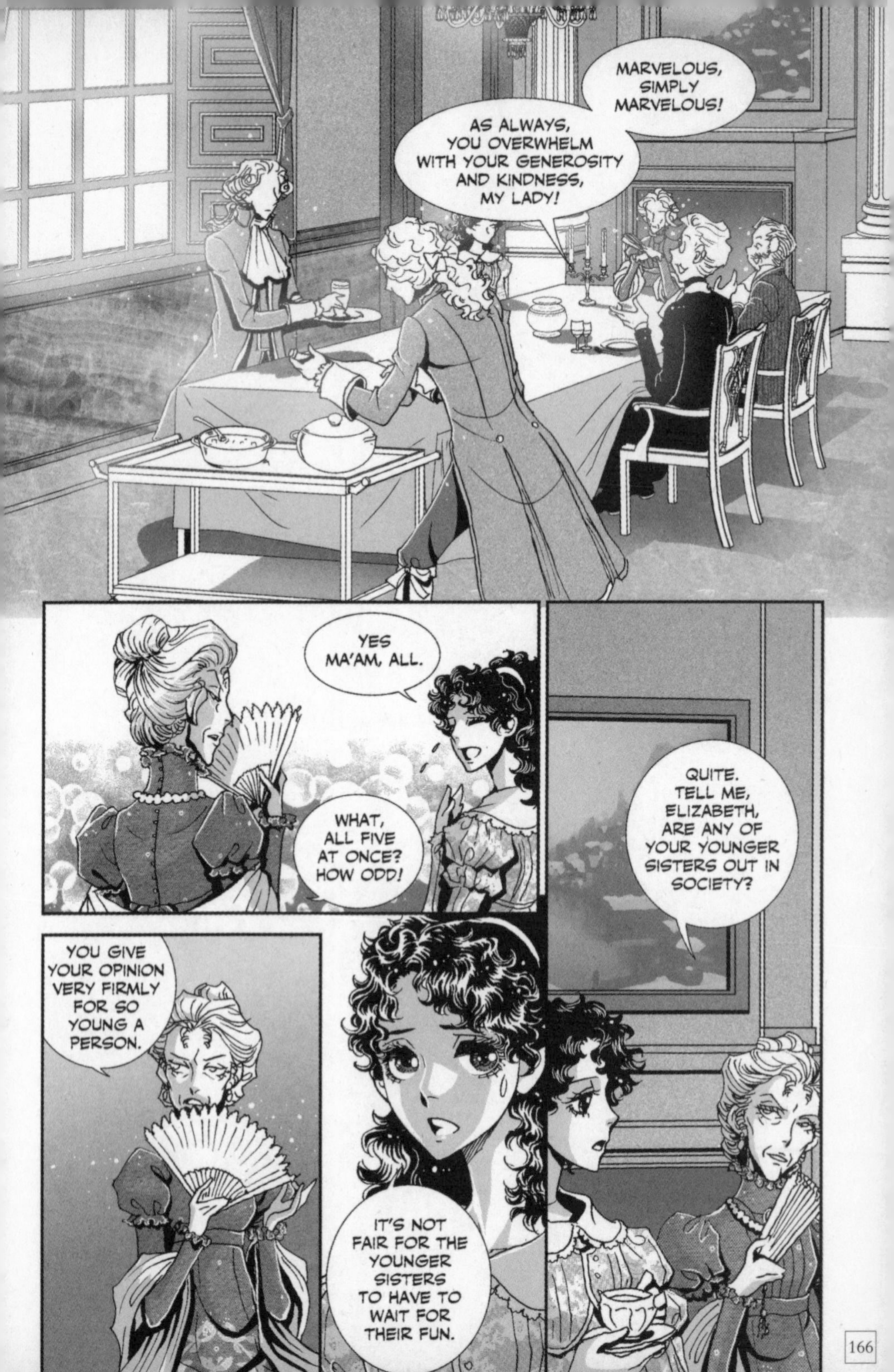
MARVELOUS, SIMPLY MARVELOUS!
AS ALWAYS, YOU OVERWHELM WITH YOUR GENEROSITY AND KINDNESS, MY LADY!
QUITE. TELL ME, ELIZABETH, ARE ANY OF YOUR YOUNGER SISTERS OUT IN SOCIETY?
YES MA'AM, ALL.
WHAT, ALL FIVE AT ONCE? HOW ODD!
IT'S NOT FAIR FOR THE YOUNGER SISTERS TO HAVE TO WAIT FOR THEIR FUN.
YOU GIVE YOUR OPINION VERY FIRMLY FOR SO YOUNG A PERSON.

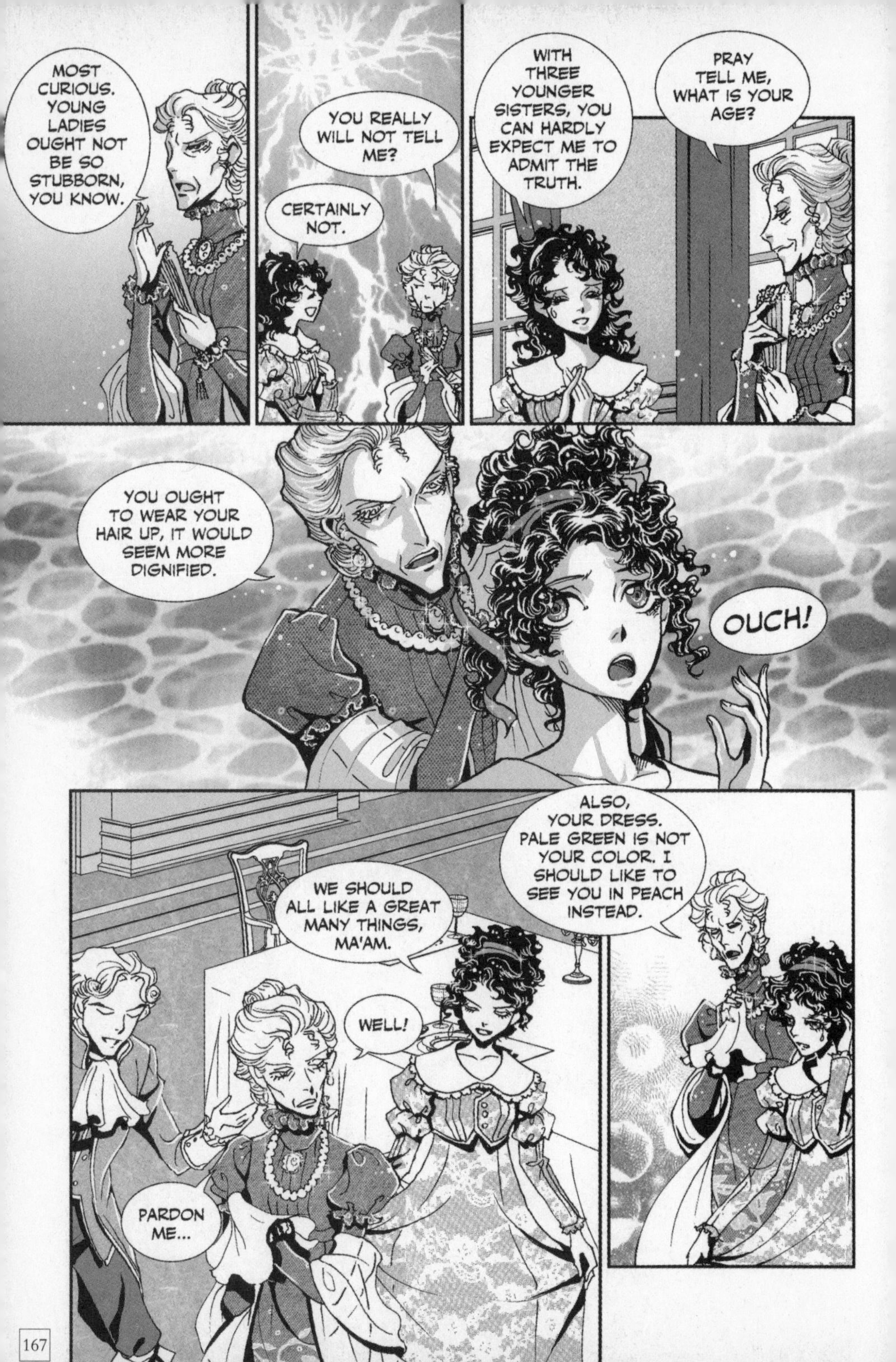
PRAY TELL ME, WHAT IS YOUR AGE?
WITH THREE YOUNGER SISTERS, YOU CAN HARDLY EXPECT ME TO ADMIT THE TRUTH.
YOU REALLY WILL NOT TELL ME?
CERTAINLY NOT.
MOST CURIOUS. YOUNG LADIES OUGHT NOT BE SO STUBBORN, YOU KNOW.
YOU OUGHT TO WEAR YOUR HAIR UP, IT WOULD SEEM MORE DIGNIFIED.
OUCH!
ALSO, YOUR DRESS. PALE GREEN IS NOT YOUR COLOR. I SHOULD LIKE TO SEE YOU IN PEACH INSTEAD.
WE SHOULD ALL LIKE A GREAT MANY THINGS, MA'AM.
WELL!
PARDON ME...

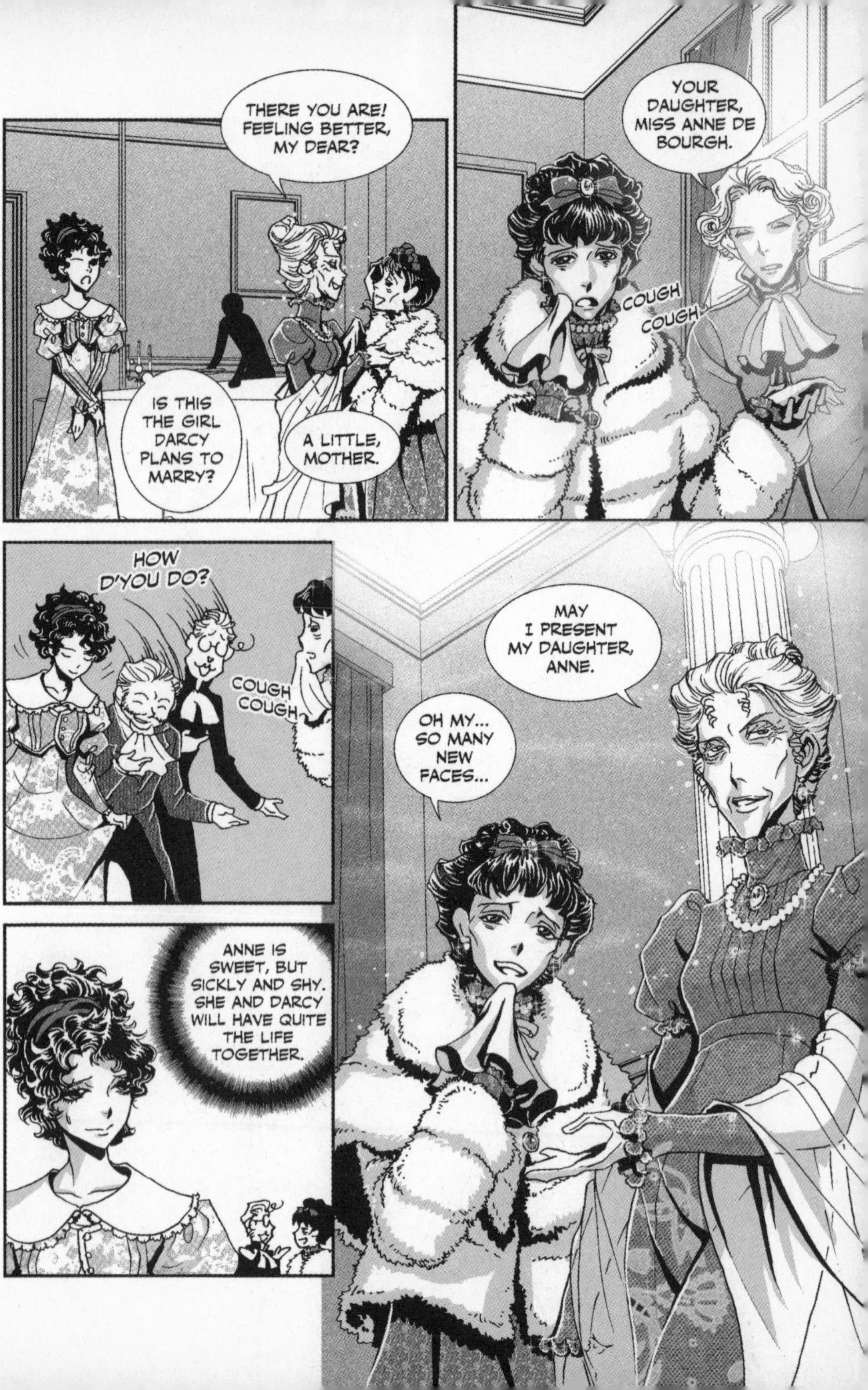
YOUR DAUGHTER, MISS ANNE DE BOURGH.
COUGH COUGH
THERE YOU ARE! FEELING BETTER, MY DEAR?
A LITTLE, MOTHER.
IS THIS THE GIRL DARCY PLANS TO MARRY?
MAY I PRESENT MY DAUGHTER, ANNE.
OH MY... SO MANY NEW FACES...
HOW D'YOU DO?
COUGH COUGH
ANNE IS SWEET, BUT SICKLY AND SHY. SHE AND DARCY WILL HAVE QUITE THE LIFE TOGETHER.

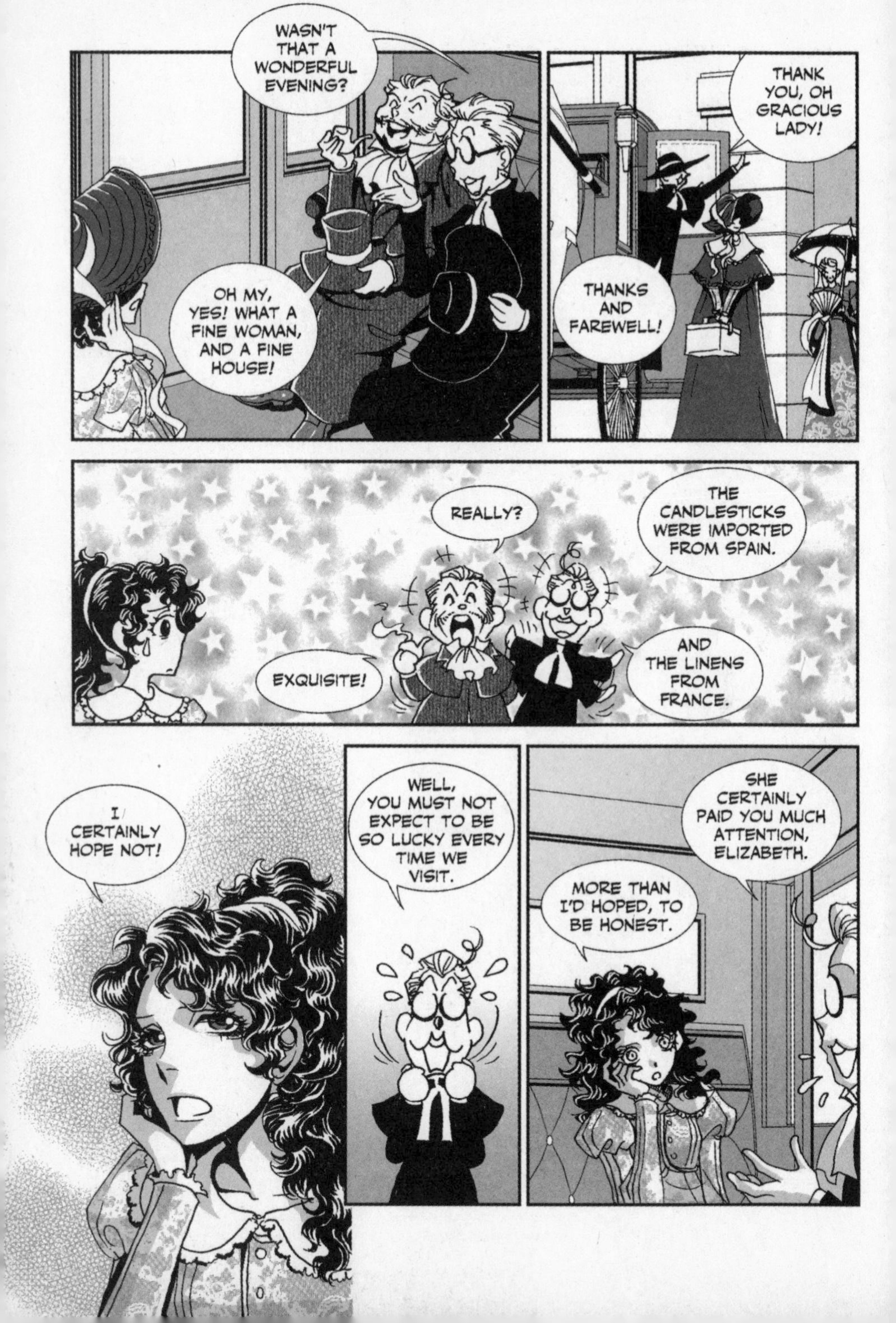
THANK YOU, OH GRACIOUS LADY!
THANKS AND FAREWELL!
WASN'T THAT A WONDERFUL EVENING?
OH MY, YES! WHAT A FINE WOMAN, AND A FINE HOUSE!
THE CANDLESTICKS WERE IMPORTED FROM SPAIN.
REALLY?
AND THE LINENS FROM FRANCE.
EXQUISITE!
SHE CERTAINLY PAID YOU MUCH ATTENTION, ELIZABETH.
MORE THAN I'D HOPED, TO BE HONEST.
WELL, YOU MUST NOT EXPECT TO BE SO LUCKY EVERY TIME WE VISIT.
I CERTAINLY HOPE NOT!

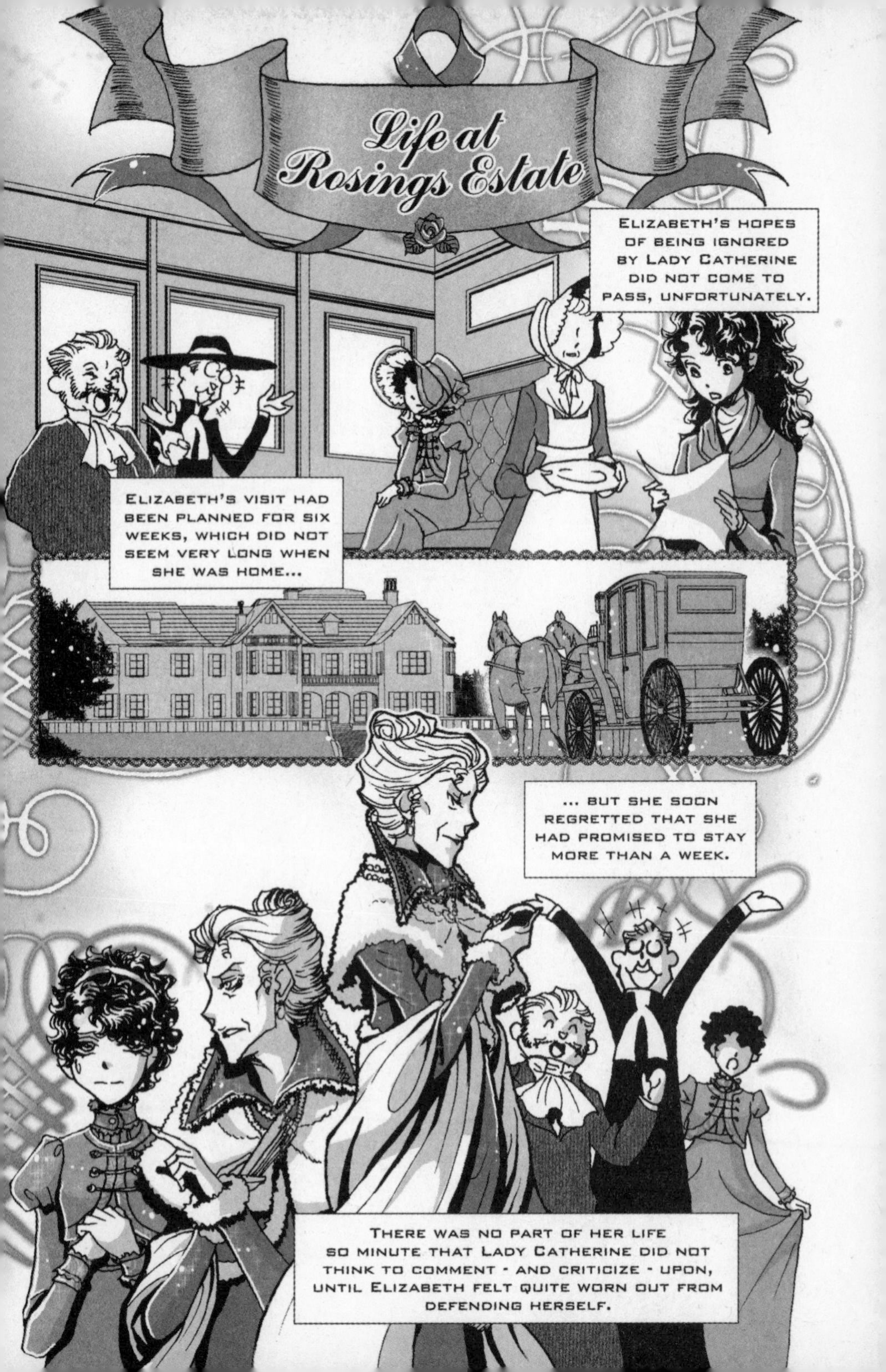
Life at Rosings Estate
Elizabeth's hopes of being ignored by Lady Catherine did not come to pass, unfortunately.
Elizabeth's visit had been planned for six weeks, which did not seem very long when she was home...
... but she soon regretted that she had promised to stay more than a week.
There was no part of her life so minute that Lady Catherine did not think to comment - and criticize - upon, until Elizabeth felt quite worn out from defending herself.

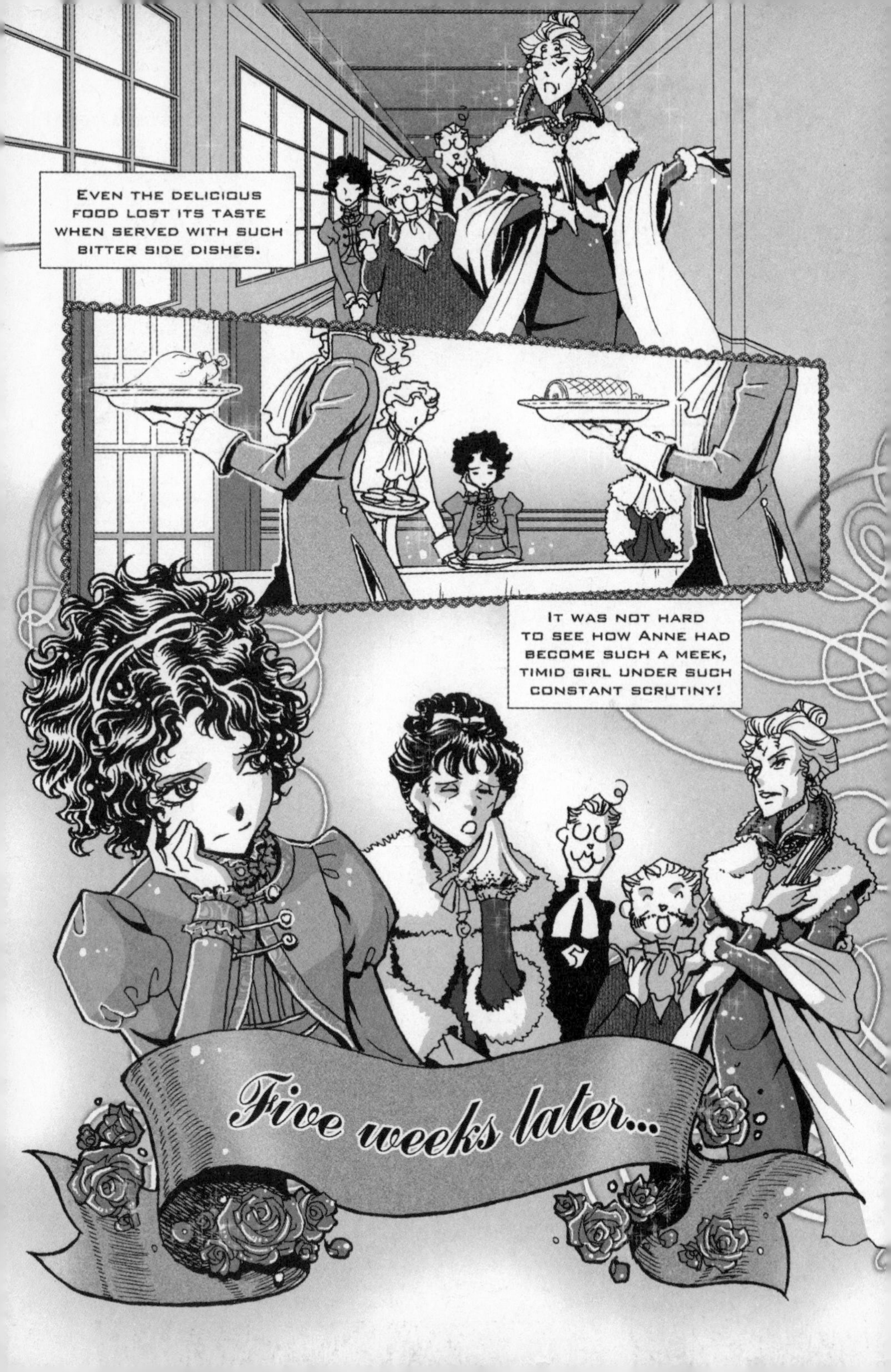
Even the delicious food lost its taste when served with such bitter side dishes.
It was not hard to see how Anne had become such a meek, timid girl under such constant scrutiny!
Five weeks later...

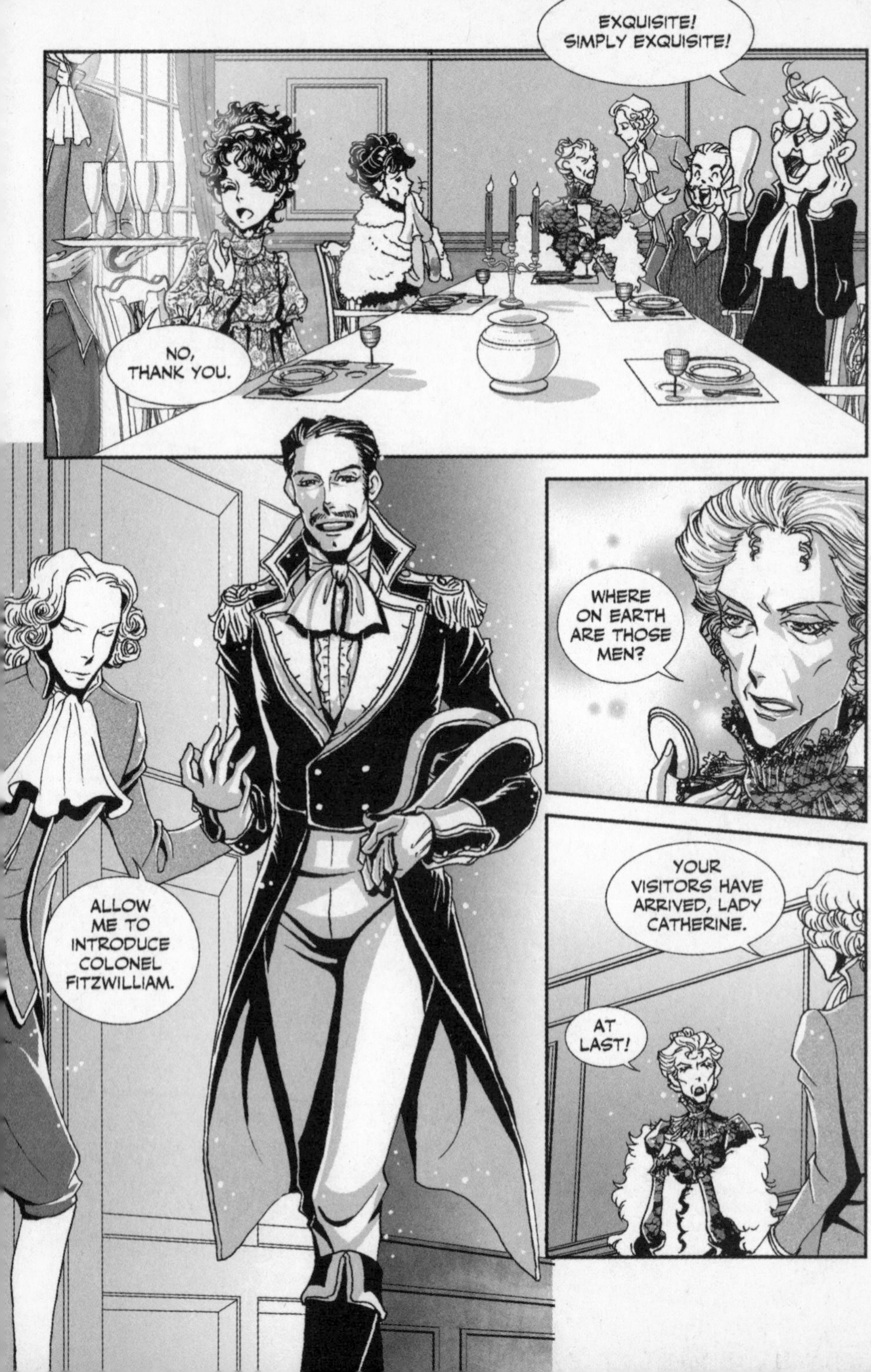
EXQUISITE! SIMPLY EXQUISITE!
NO, THANK YOU.
WHERE ON EARTH ARE THOSE MEN?
YOUR VISITORS HAVE ARRIVED, LADY CATHERINE.
AT LAST!
ALLOW ME TO INTRODUCE COLONEL FITZWILLIAM.

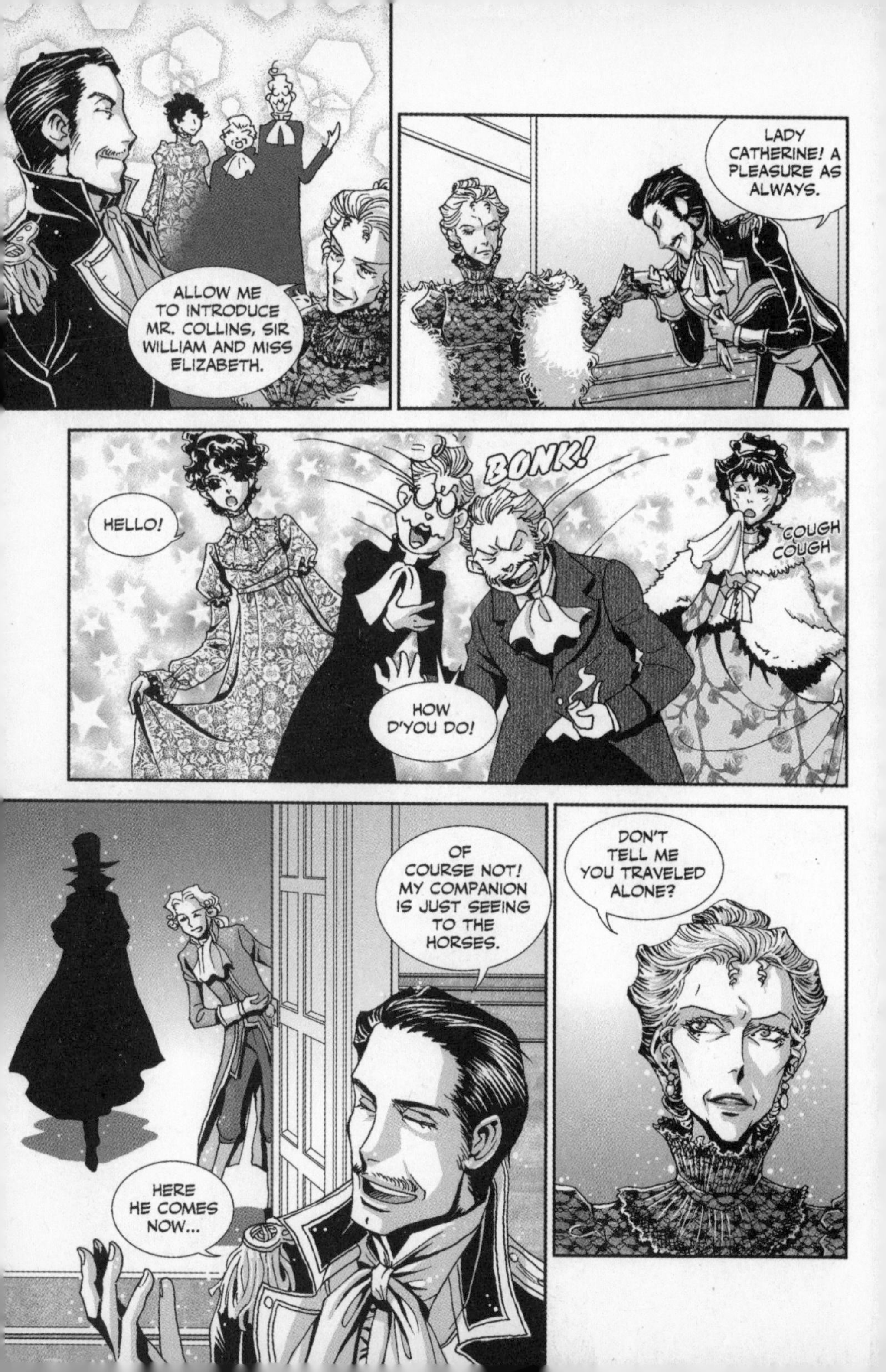
LADY CATHERINE! A PLEASURE AS ALWAYS.
ALLOW ME TO INTRODUCE MR. COLLINS, SIR WILLIAM AND MISS ELIZABETH.
BONK!
COUGH COUGH
HELLO!
HOW D'YOU DO!
DON'T TELL ME YOU TRAVELED ALONE?
OF COURSE NOT! MY COMPANION IS JUST SEEING TO THE HORSES.
HERE HE COMES NOW...

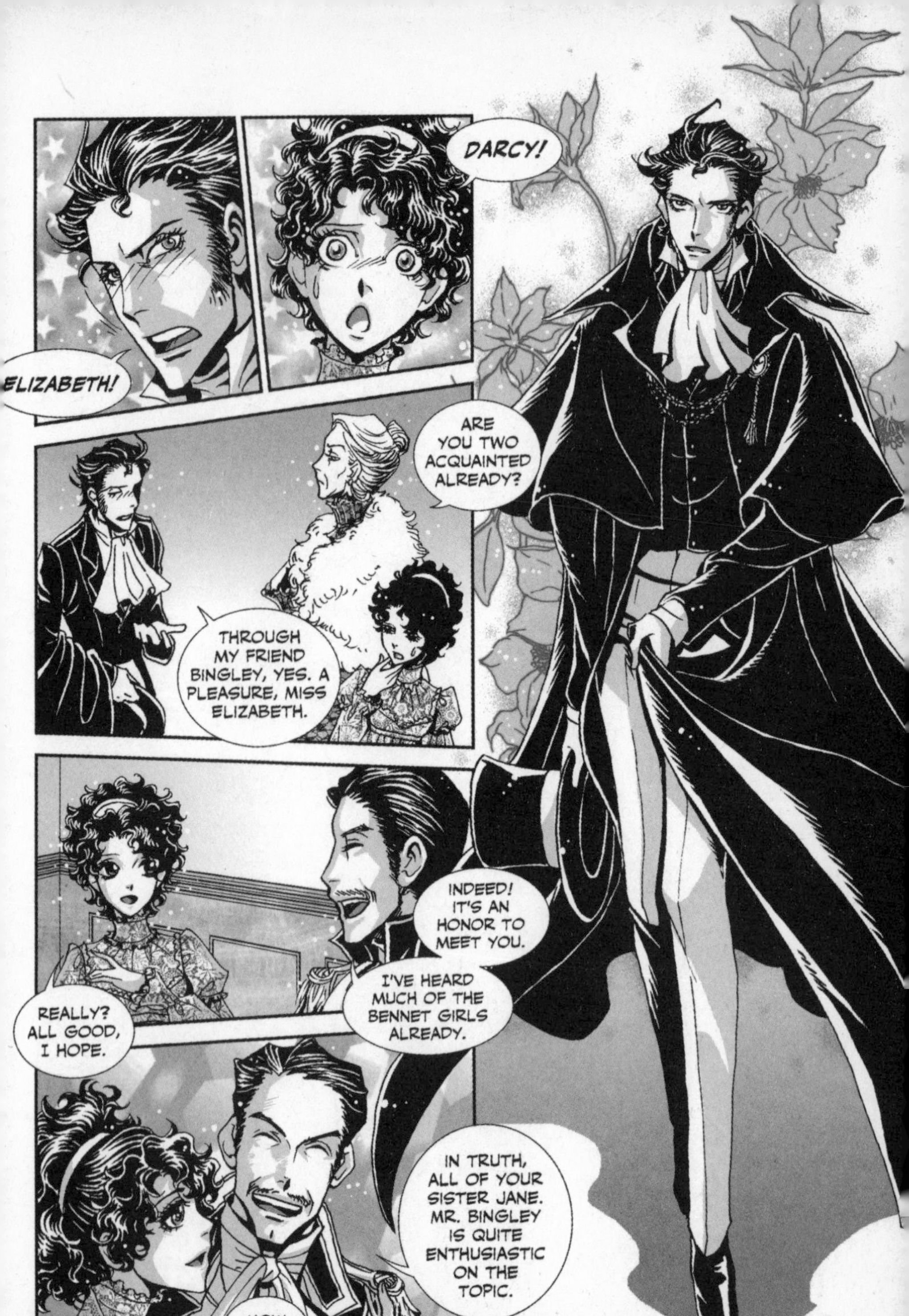
DARCY!
ELIZABETH!
ARE YOU TWO ACQUAINTED ALREADY?
THROUGH MY FRIEND BINGLEY, YES. A PLEASURE, MISS ELIZABETH.
INDEED! IT'S AN HONOR TO MEET YOU.
I'VE HEARD MUCH OF THE BENNET GIRLS ALREADY.
REALLY? ALL GOOD, I HOPE.
IN TRUTH, ALL OF YOUR SISTER JANE. MR. BINGLEY IS QUITE ENTHUSIASTIC ON THE TOPIC.
HOW KIND OF HIM!

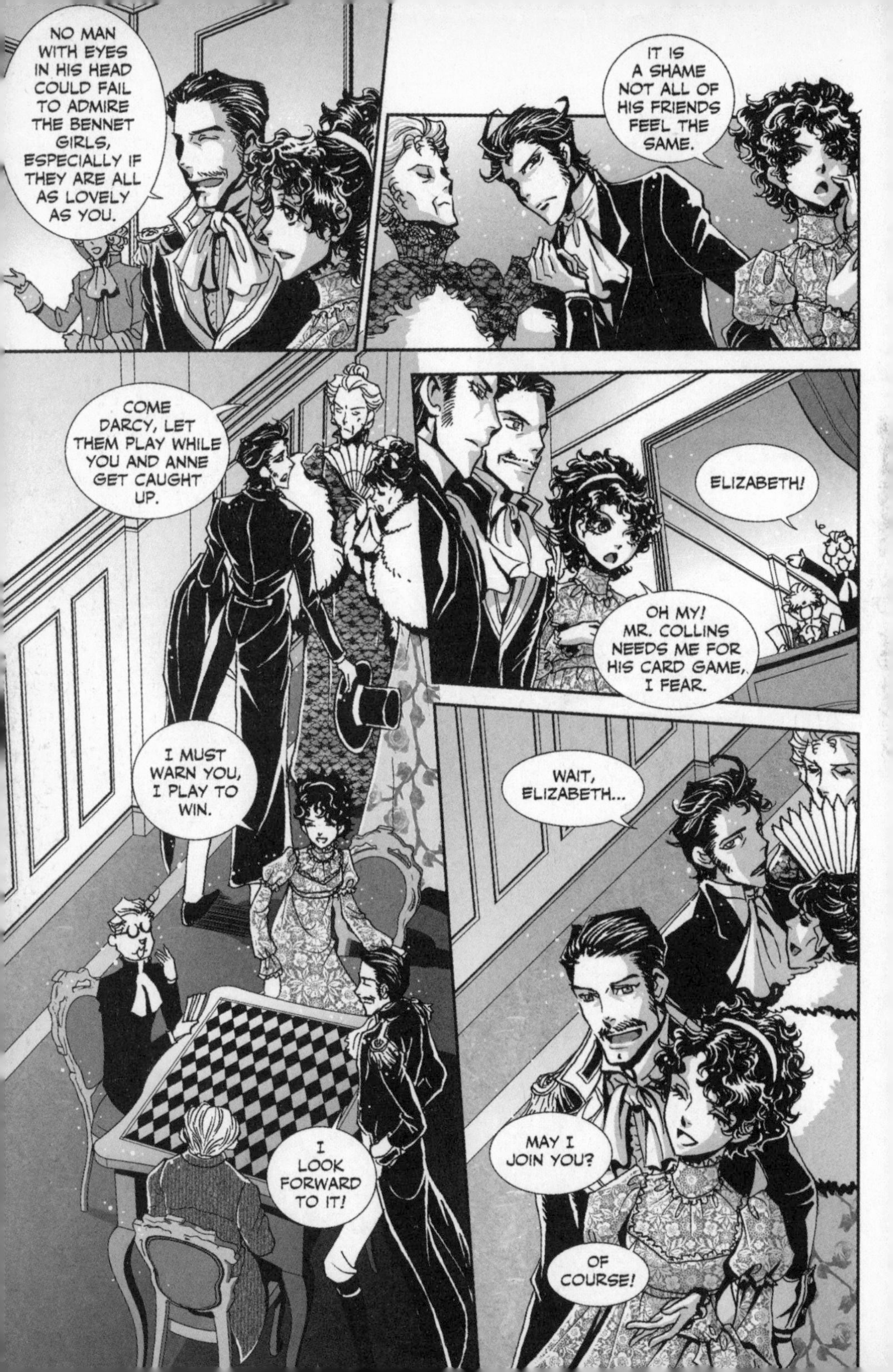
IT IS A SHAME NOT ALL OF HIS FRIENDS FEEL THE SAME.
NO MAN WITH EYES IN HIS HEAD COULD FAIL TO ADMIRE THE BENNET GIRLS, ESPECIALLY IF THEY ARE ALL AS LOVELY AS YOU.
ELIZABETH!
OH MY! MR. COLLINS NEEDS ME FOR HIS CARD GAME, I FEAR.
WAIT, ELIZABETH...
MAY I JOIN YOU?
OF COURSE!
COME DARCY, LET THEM PLAY WHILE YOU AND ANNE GET CAUGHT UP.
I MUST WARN YOU, I PLAY TO WIN.
I LOOK FORWARD TO IT!

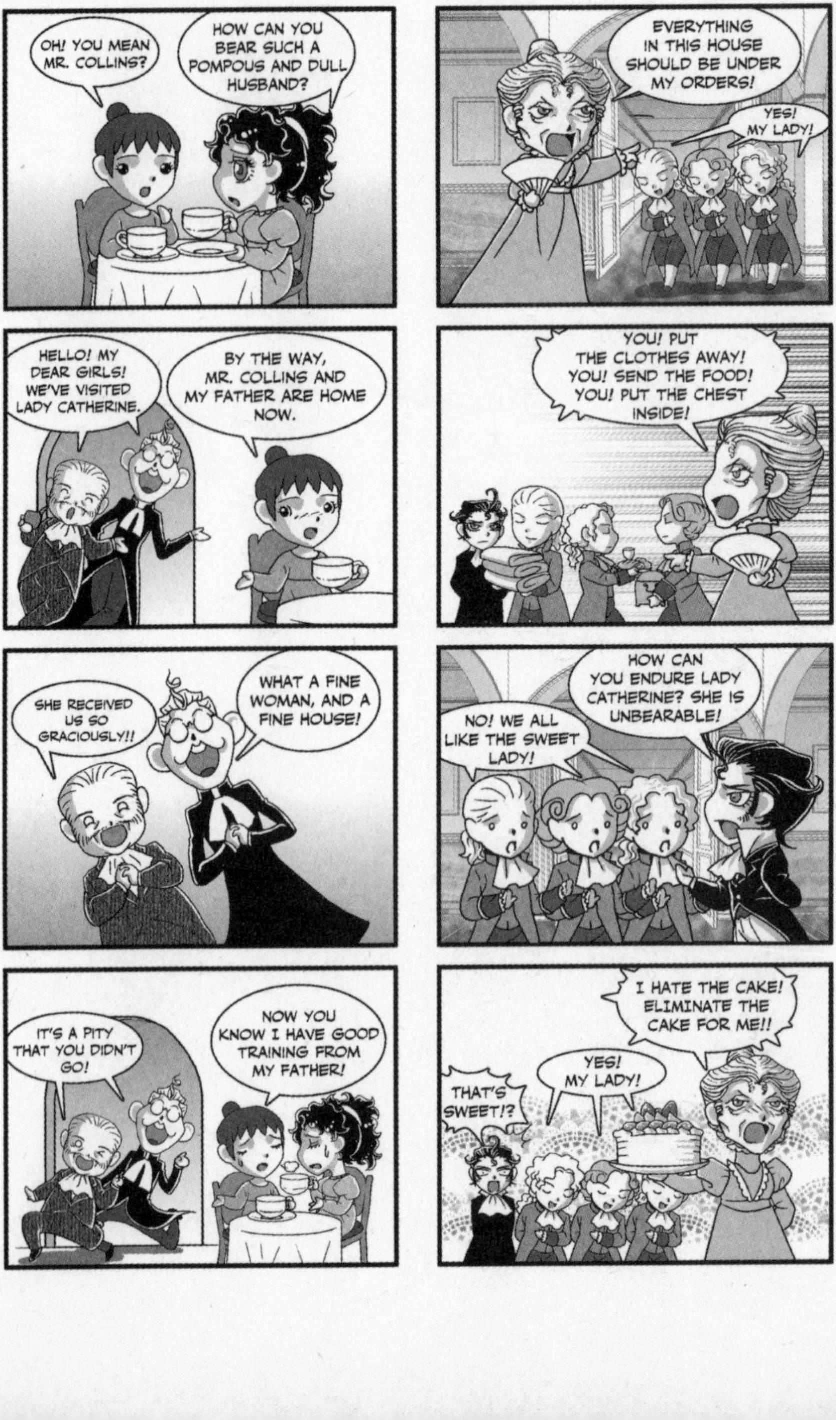
EVERYTHING IN THIS HOUSE SHOULD BE UNDER MY ORDERS!
YES! MY LADY!
YOU! PUT THE CLOTHES AWAY! YOU! SEND THE FOOD! YOU! PUT THE CHEST INSIDE!
HOW CAN YOU ENDURE LADY CATHERINE? SHE IS UNBEARABLE!
NO! WE ALL LIKE THE SWEET LADY!
I HATE THE CAKE! ELIMINATE THE CAKE FOR ME!!
YES! MY LADY!
THAT'S SWEET!?
HOW CAN YOU BEAR SUCH A POMPOUS AND DULL HUSBAND?
OH! YOU MEAN MR. COLLINS?
BY THE WAY, MR. COLLINS AND MY FATHER ARE HOME NOW.
HELLO! MY DEAR GIRLS! WE'VE VISITED LADY CATHERINE.
WHAT A FINE WOMAN, AND A FINE HOUSE!
SHE RECEIVED US SO GRACIOUSLY!!
NOW YOU KNOW I HAVE GOOD TRAINING FROM MY FATHER!
IT'S A PITY THAT YOU DIDN'T GO!

Chapter 10

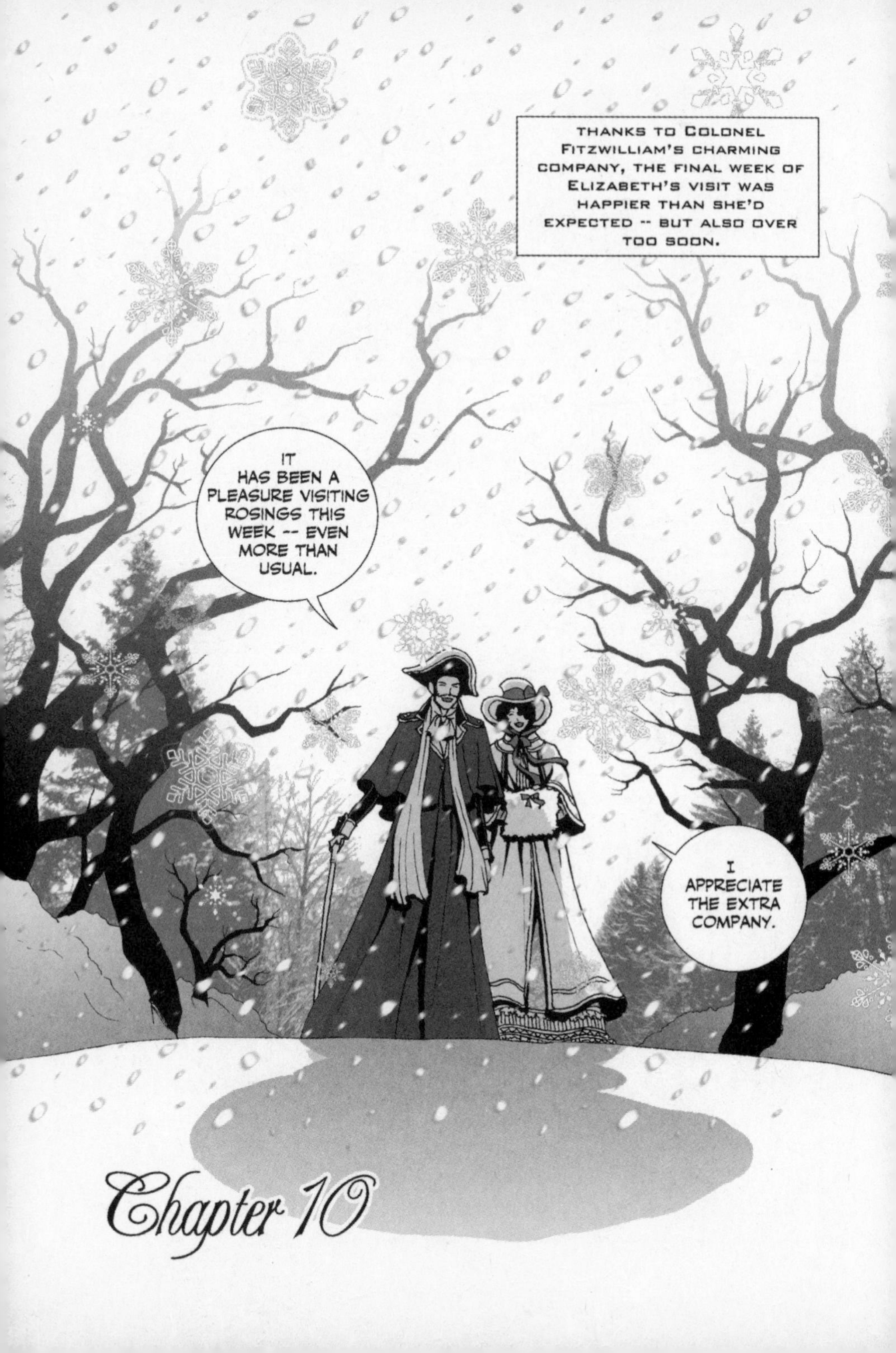
THANKS TO COLONEL FITZWILLIAM'S CHARMING COMPANY, THE FINAL WEEK OF ELIZABETH'S VISIT WAS HAPPIER THAN SHE'D EXPECTED -- BUT ALSO OVER TOO SOON.
IT HAS BEEN A PLEASURE VISITING ROSINGS THIS WEEK -- EVEN MORE THAN USUAL.
I APPRECIATE THE EXTRA COMPANY.

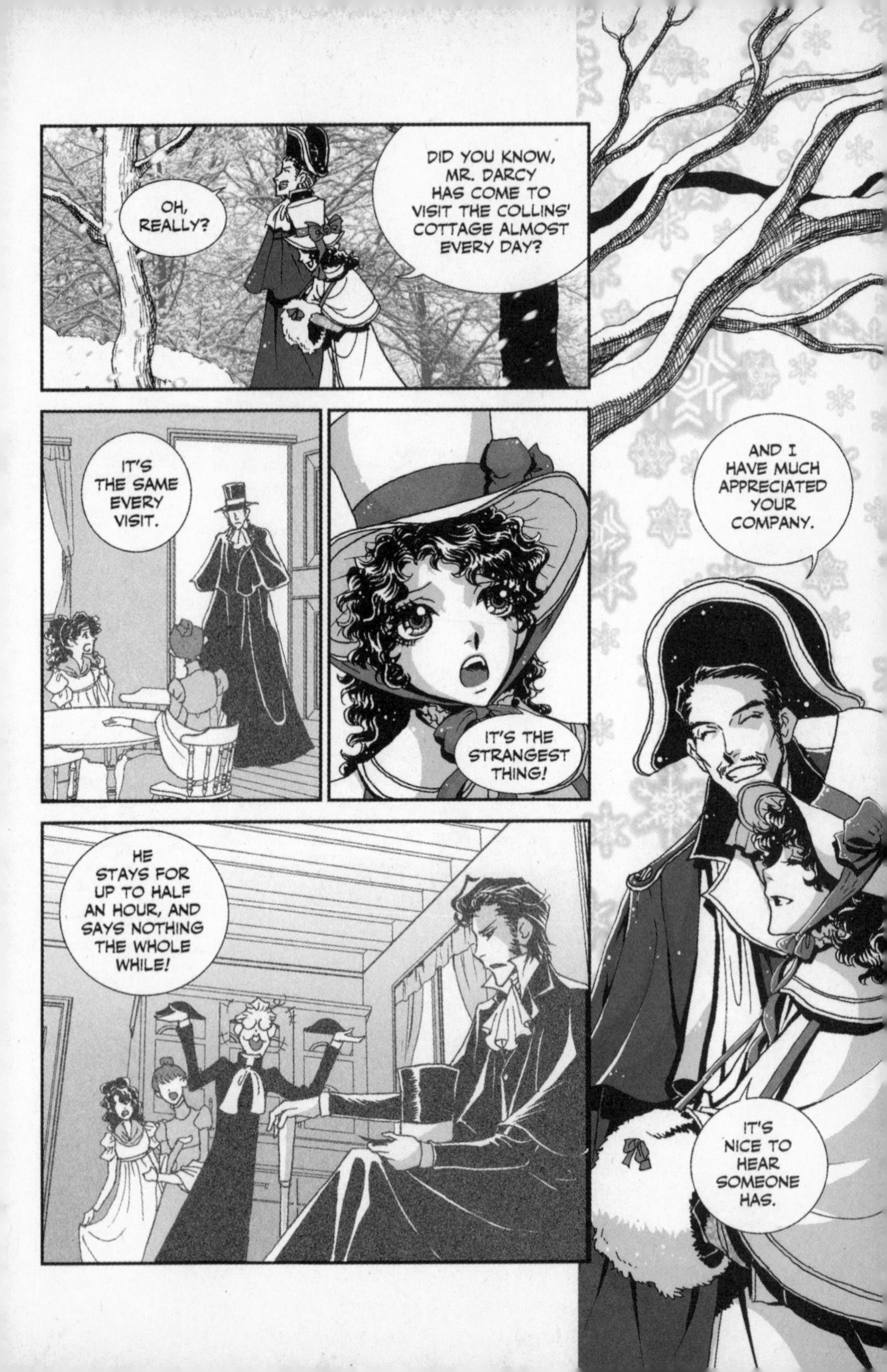
AND I HAVE MUCH APPRECIATED YOUR COMPANY.
IT'S NICE TO HEAR SOMEONE HAS.
DID YOU KNOW, MR. DARCY HAS COME TO VISIT THE COLLINS' COTTAGE ALMOST EVERY DAY?
OH, REALLY?
IT'S THE STRANGEST THING!
IT'S THE SAME EVERY VISIT.
HE STAYS FOR UP TO HALF AN HOUR, AND SAYS NOTHING THE WHOLE WHILE!

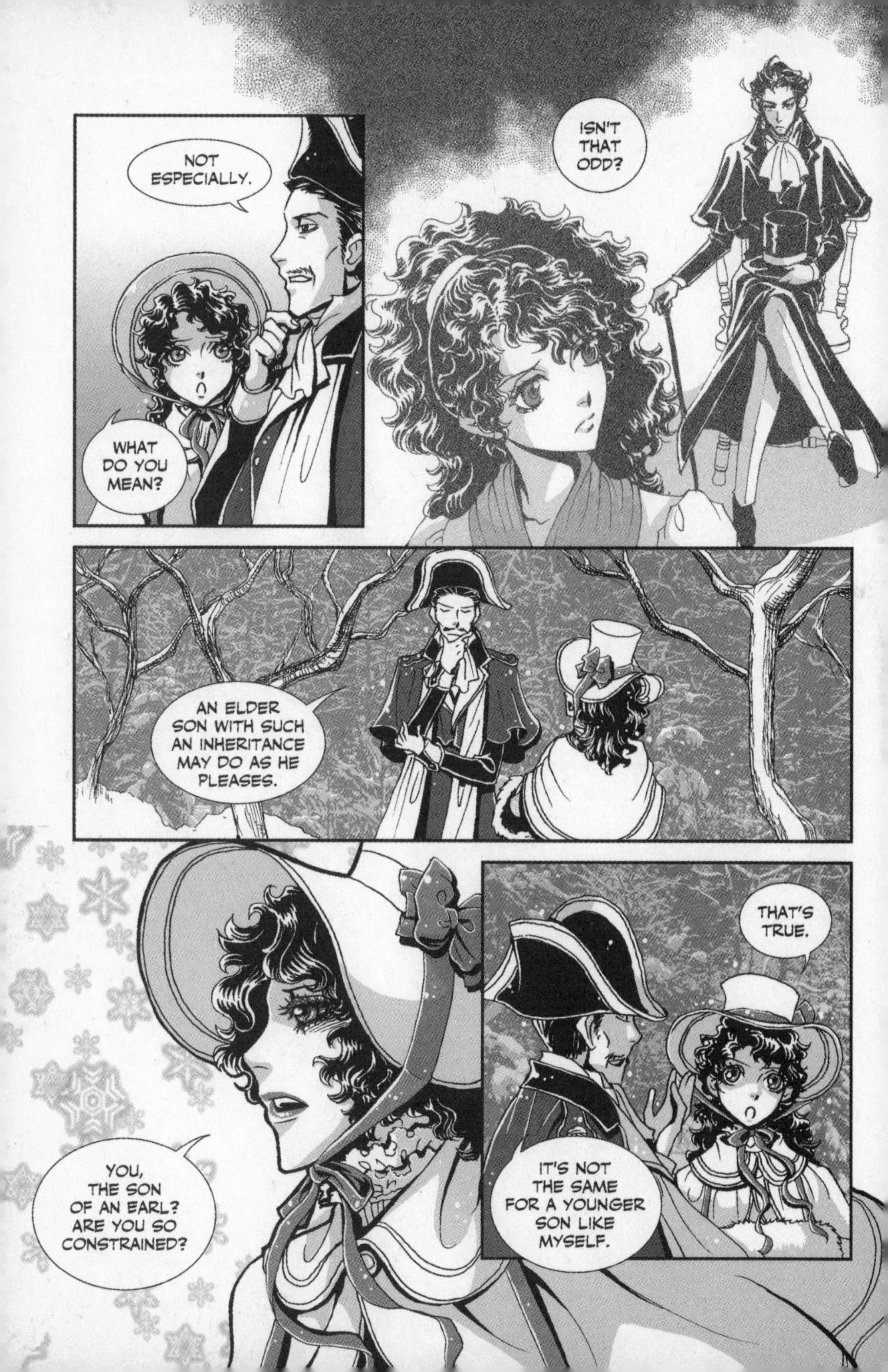
ISN'T THAT ODD?
NOT ESPECIALLY.
WHAT DO YOU MEAN?
AN ELDER SON WITH SUCH AN INHERITANCE MAY DO AS HE PLEASES.
THAT'S TRUE.
IT'S NOT THE SAME FOR A YOUNGER SON LIKE MYSELF.
YOU, THE SON OF AN EARL? ARE YOU SO CONSTRAINED?

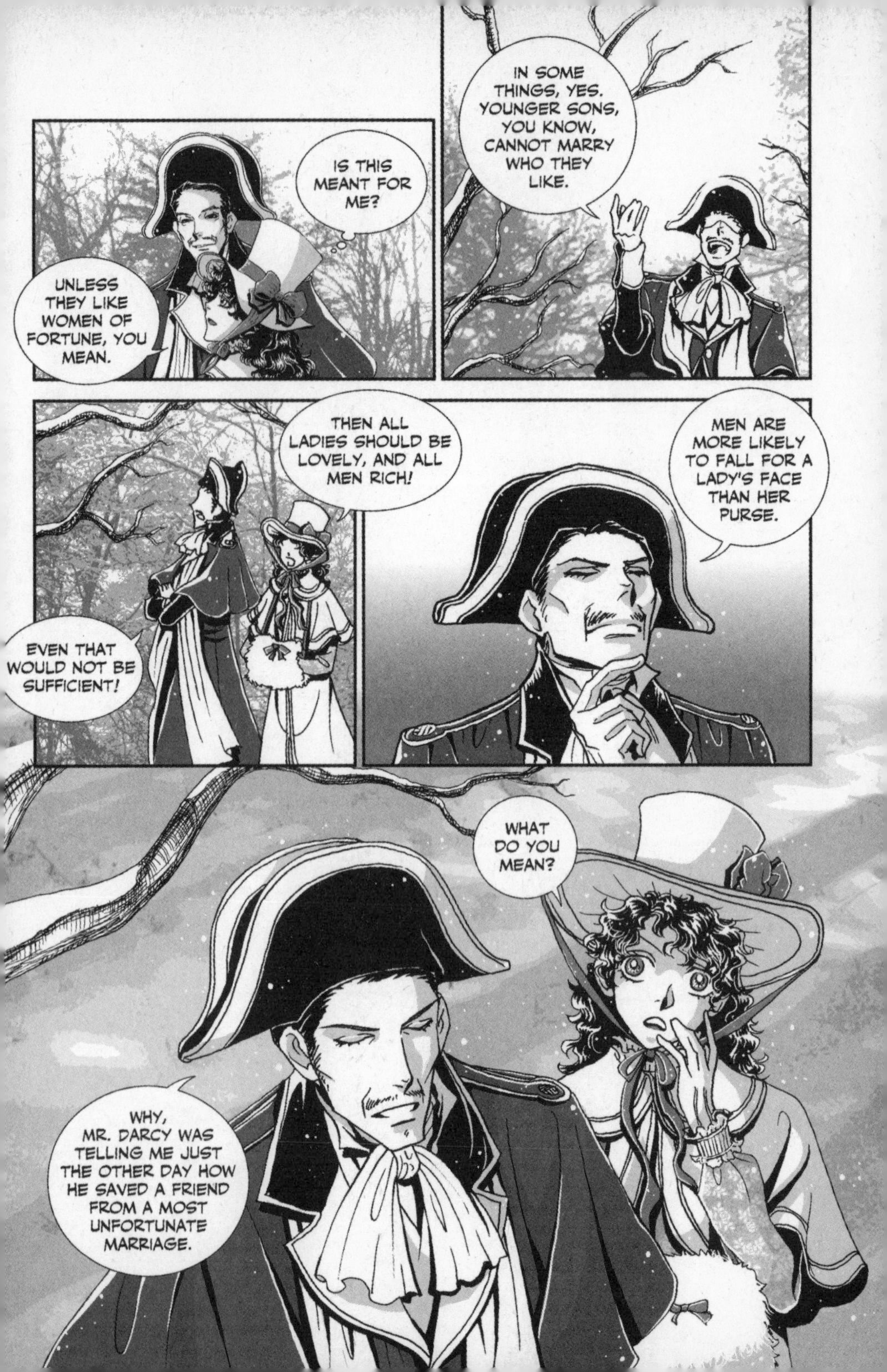
IN SOME THINGS, YES. YOUNGER SONS, YOU KNOW, CANNOT MARRY WHO THEY LIKE.
IS THIS MEANT FOR ME?
UNLESS THEY LIKE WOMEN OF FORTUNE, YOU MEAN.
MEN ARE MORE LIKELY TO FALL FOR A LADY'S FACE THAN HER PURSE.
THEN ALL LADIES SHOULD BE LOVELY, AND ALL MEN RICH!
EVEN THAT WOULD NOT BE SUFFICIENT!
WHAT DO YOU MEAN?
WHY, MR. DARCY WAS TELLING ME JUST THE OTHER DAY HOW HE SAVED A FRIEND FROM A MOST UNFORTUNATE MARRIAGE.

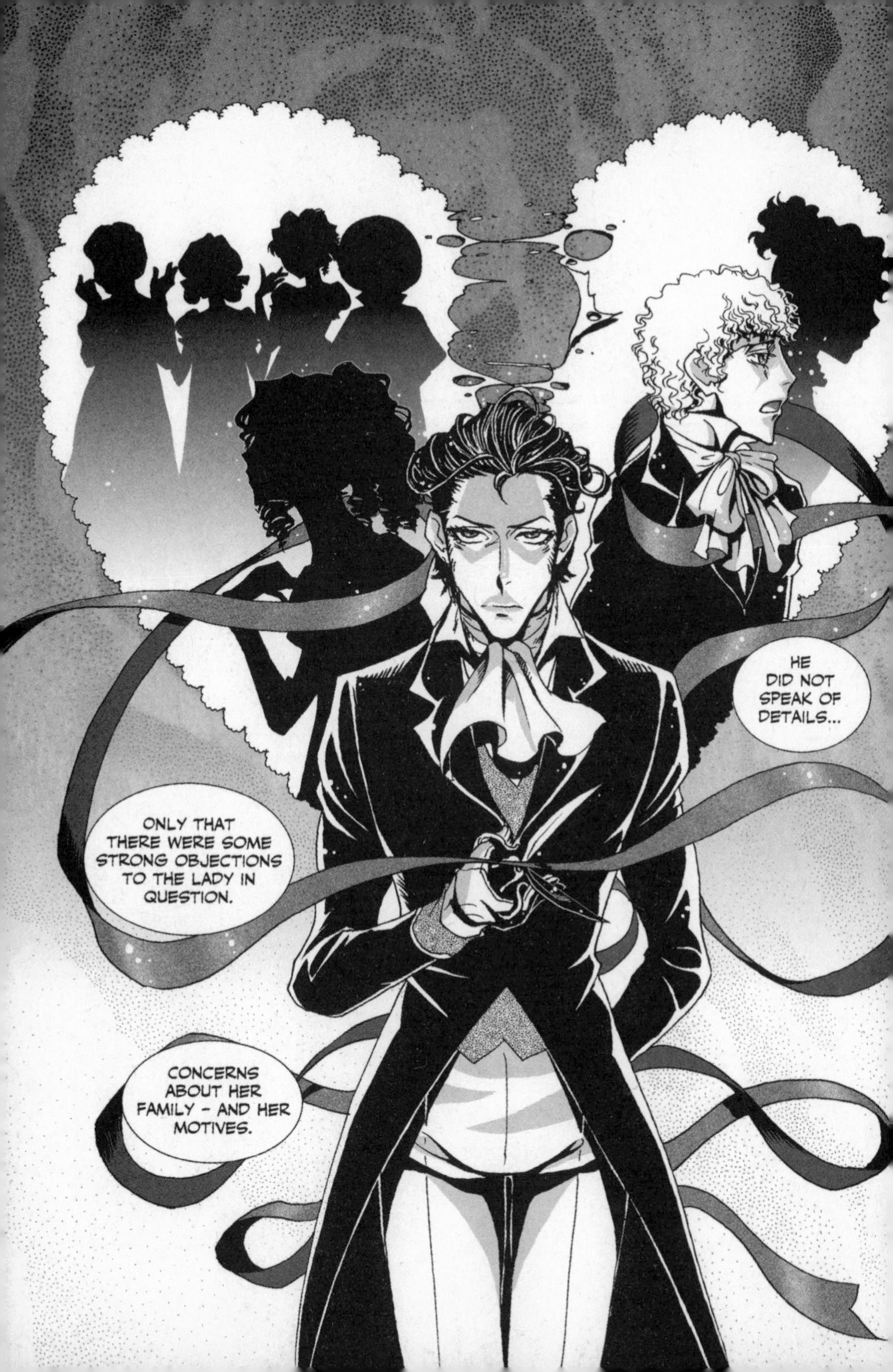
HE DID NOT SPEAK OF DETAILS...
ONLY THAT THERE WERE SOME STRONG OBJECTIONS TO THE LADY IN QUESTION.
CONCERNS ABOUT HER FAMILY - AND HER MOTIVES.

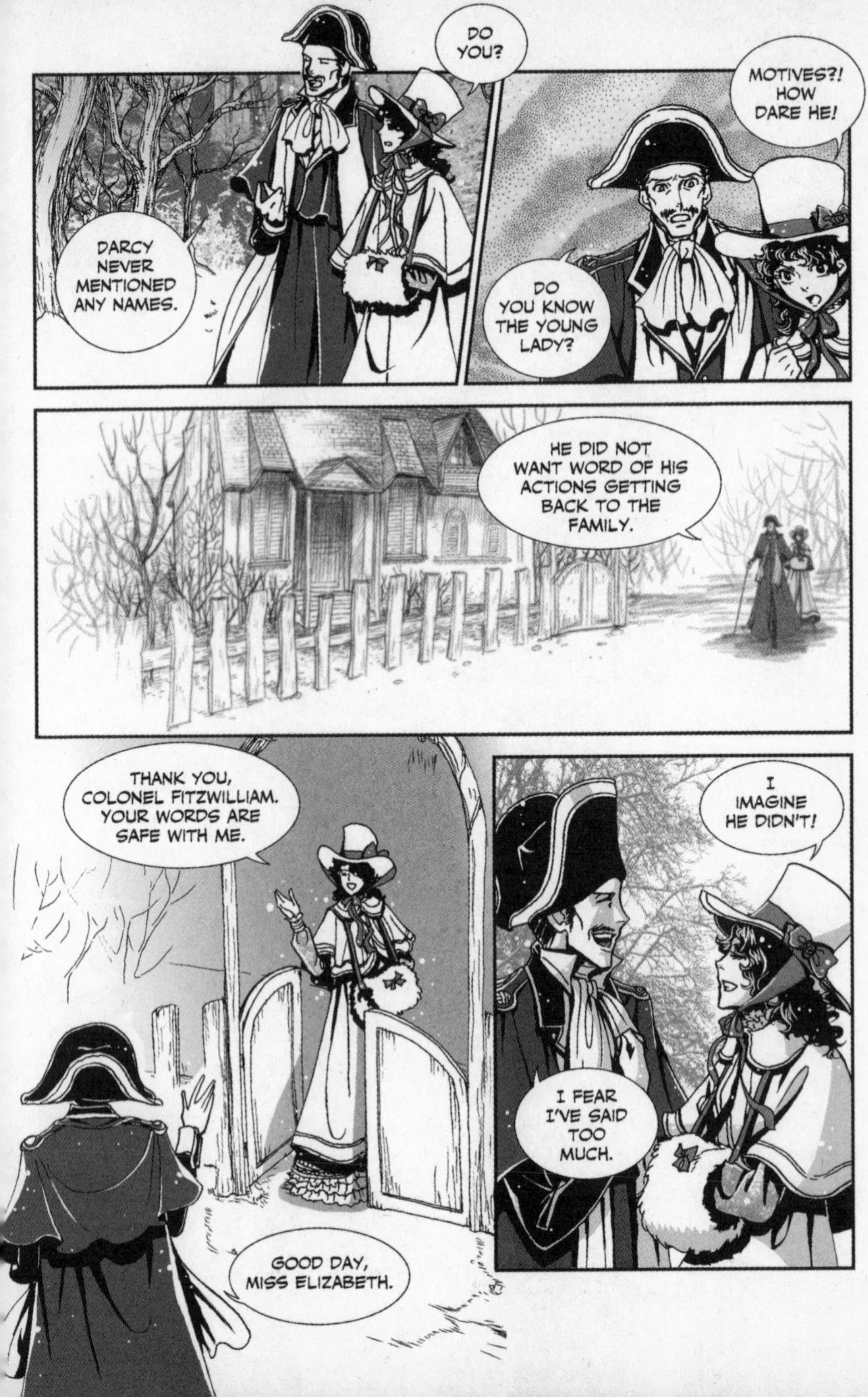
MOTIVES?! HOW DARE HE!
DO YOU KNOW THE YOUNG LADY?
DO YOU?
DARCY NEVER MENTIONED ANY NAMES.
HE DID NOT WANT WORD OF HIS ACTIONS GETTING BACK TO THE FAMILY.
I IMAGINE HE DIDN'T!
I FEAR I'VE SAID TOO MUCH.
THANK YOU, COLONEL FITZWILLIAM. YOUR WORDS ARE SAFE WITH ME.
GOOD DAY, MISS ELIZABETH.

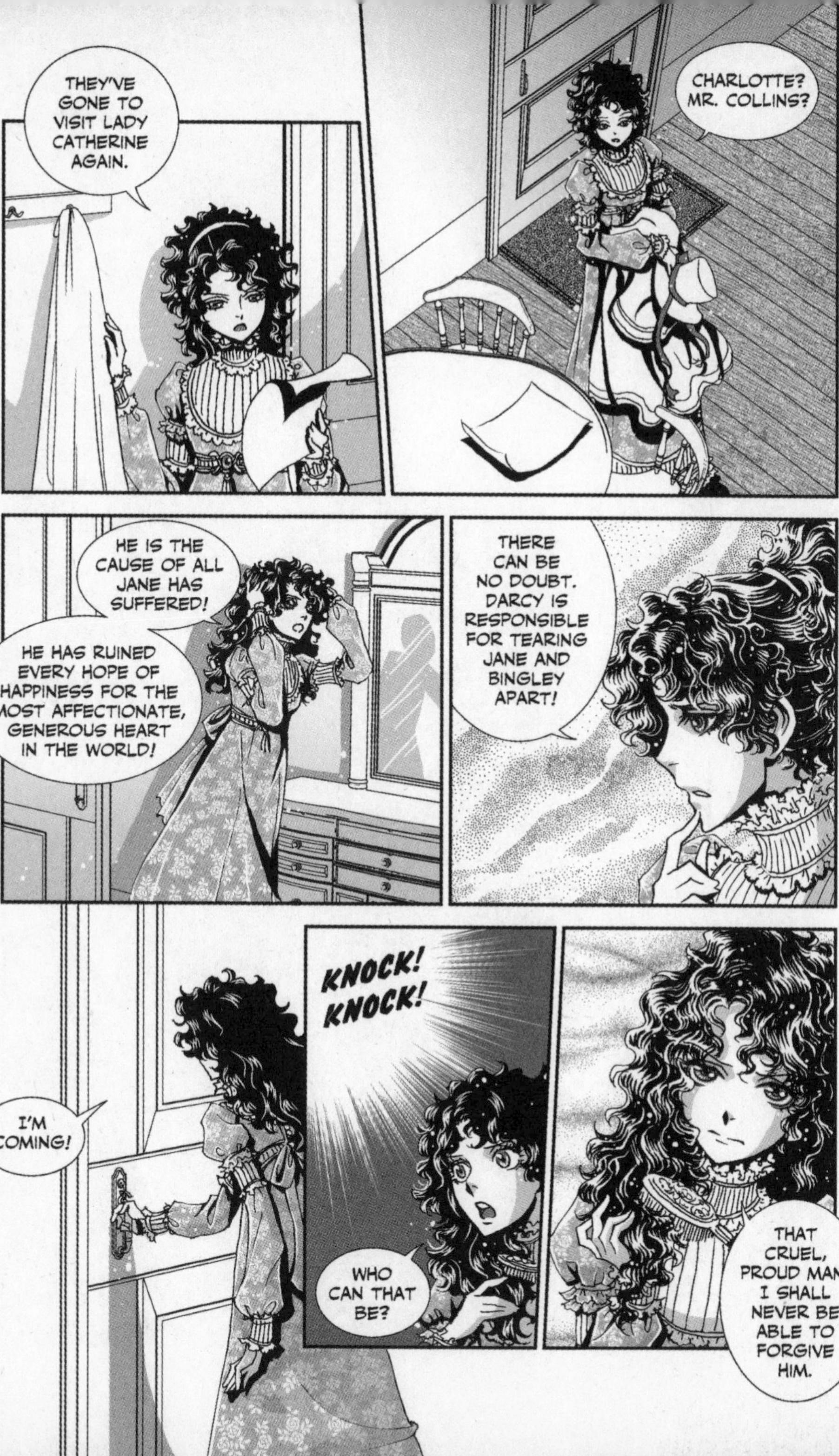
CHARLOTTE? MR. COLLINS?
THEY'VE GONE TO VISIT LADY CATHERINE AGAIN.
THERE CAN BE NO DOUBT. DARCY IS RESPONSIBLE FOR TEARING JANE AND BINGLEY APART!
HE IS THE CAUSE OF ALL JANE HAS SUFFERED!
HE HAS RUINED EVERY HOPE OF HAPPINESS FOR THE MOST AFFECTIONATE, GENEROUS HEART IN THE WORLD!
THAT CRUEL, PROUD MAN! I SHALL NEVER BE ABLE TO FORGIVE HIM.
KNOCK! KNOCK!
WHO CAN THAT BE?
I'M COMING!

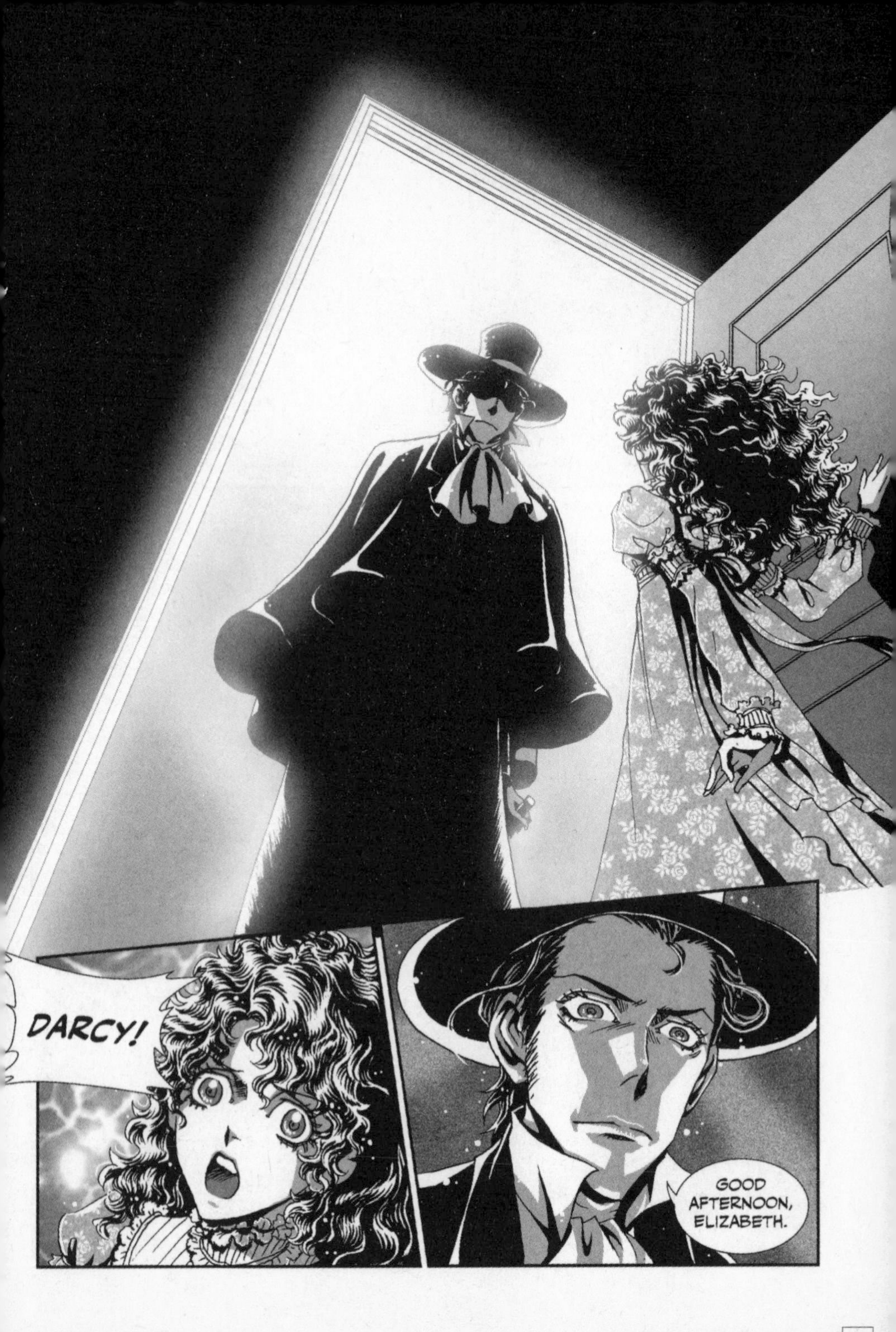
GOOD AFTERNOON, ELIZABETH.
DARCY!

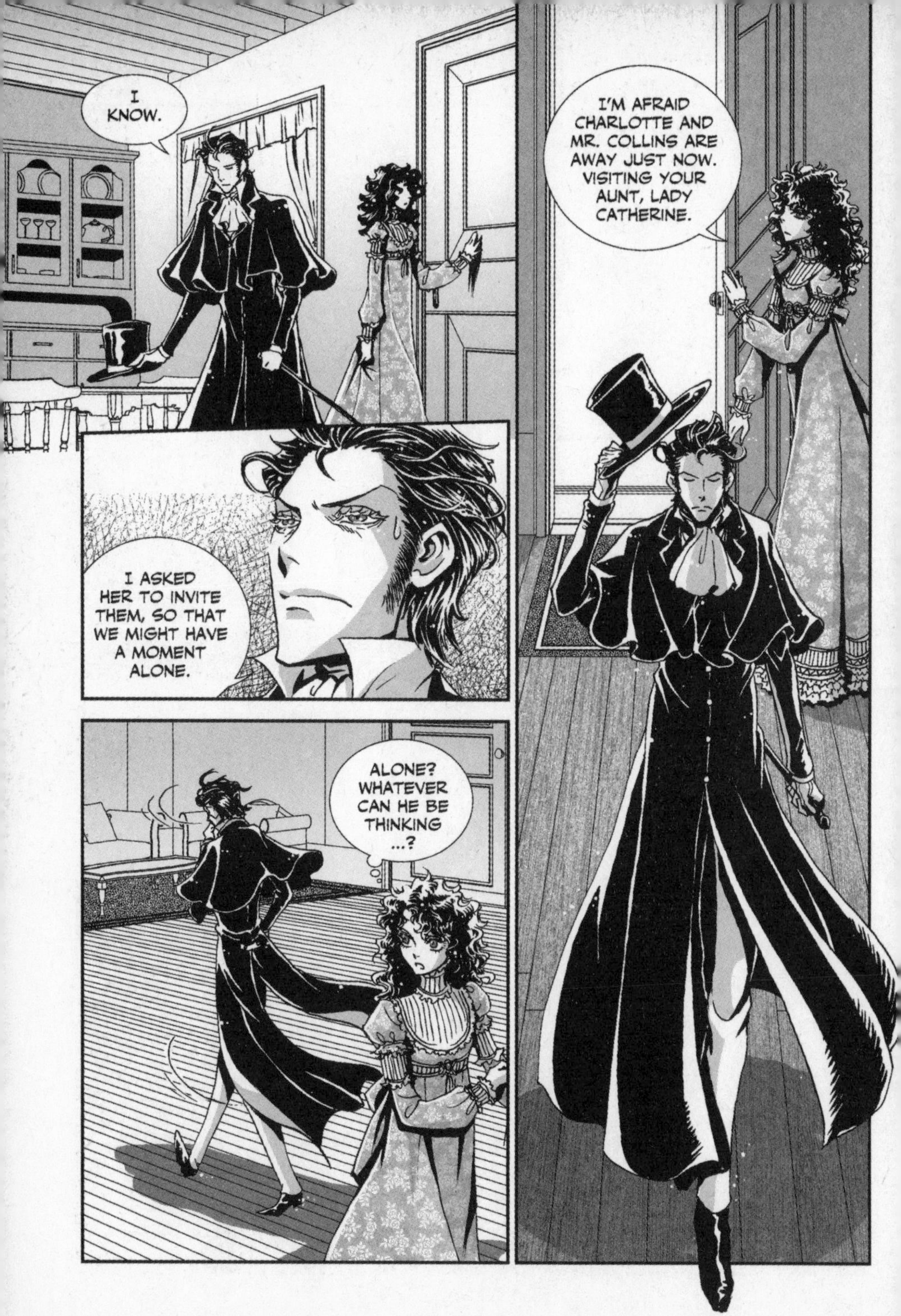
I'M AFRAID CHARLOTTE AND MR. COLLINS ARE AWAY JUST NOW. VISITING YOUR AUNT, LADY CATHERINE.
I KNOW.
I ASKED HER TO INVITE THEM, SO THAT WE MIGHT HAVE A MOMENT ALONE.
ALONE? WHATEVER CAN HE BE THINKING ...?

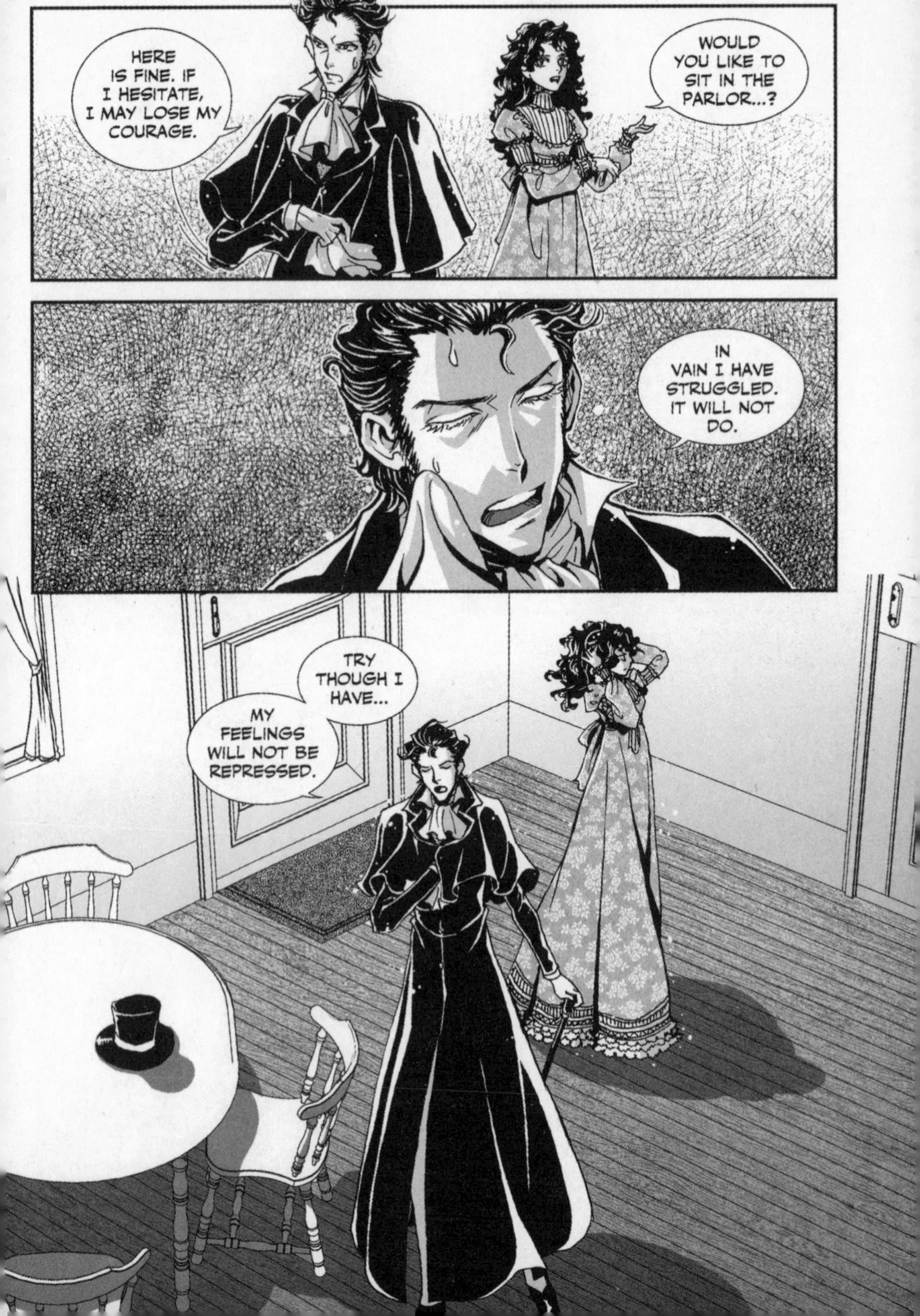
WOULD YOU LIKE TO SIT IN THE PARLOR...?
HERE IS FINE. IF I HESITATE, I MAY LOSE MY COURAGE.
IN VAIN I HAVE STRUGGLED. IT WILL NOT DO.
TRY THOUGH I HAVE...
MY FEELINGS WILL NOT BE REPRESSED.

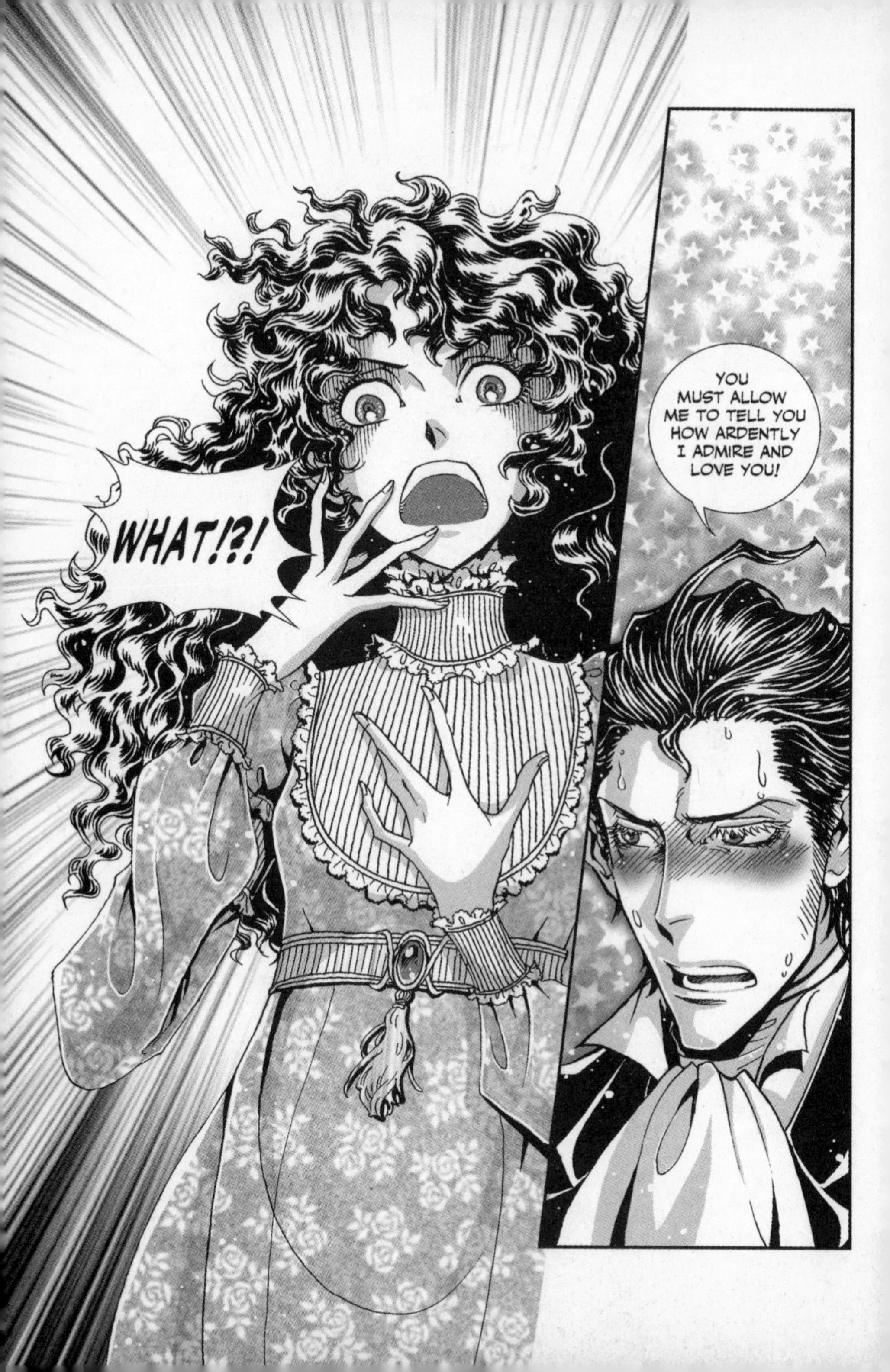
YOU MUST ALLOW ME TO TELL YOU HOW ARDENTLY I ADMIRE AND LOVE YOU!
WHAT!?!

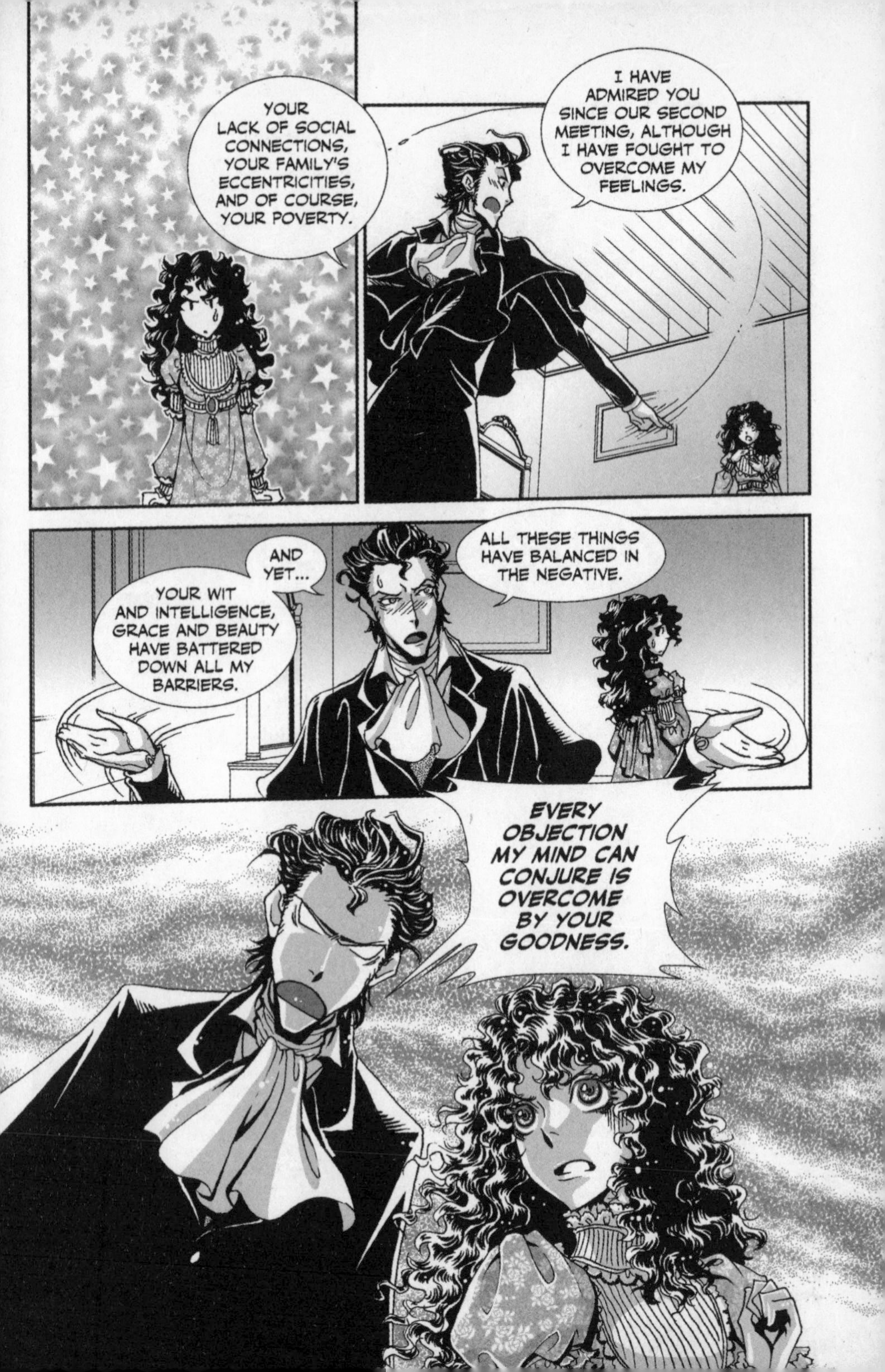
I HAVE ADMIRED YOU SINCE OUR SECOND MEETING, ALTHOUGH I HAVE FOUGHT TO OVERCOME MY FEELINGS.
YOUR LACK OF SOCIAL CONNECTIONS, YOUR FAMILY'S ECCENTRICITIES, AND OF COURSE, YOUR POVERTY.
ALL THESE THINGS HAVE BALANCED IN THE NEGATIVE.
AND YET...
YOUR WIT AND INTELLIGENCE, GRACE AND BEAUTY HAVE BATTERED DOWN ALL MY BARRIERS.
EVERY OBJECTION MY MIND CAN CONJURE IS OVERCOME BY YOUR GOODNESS.

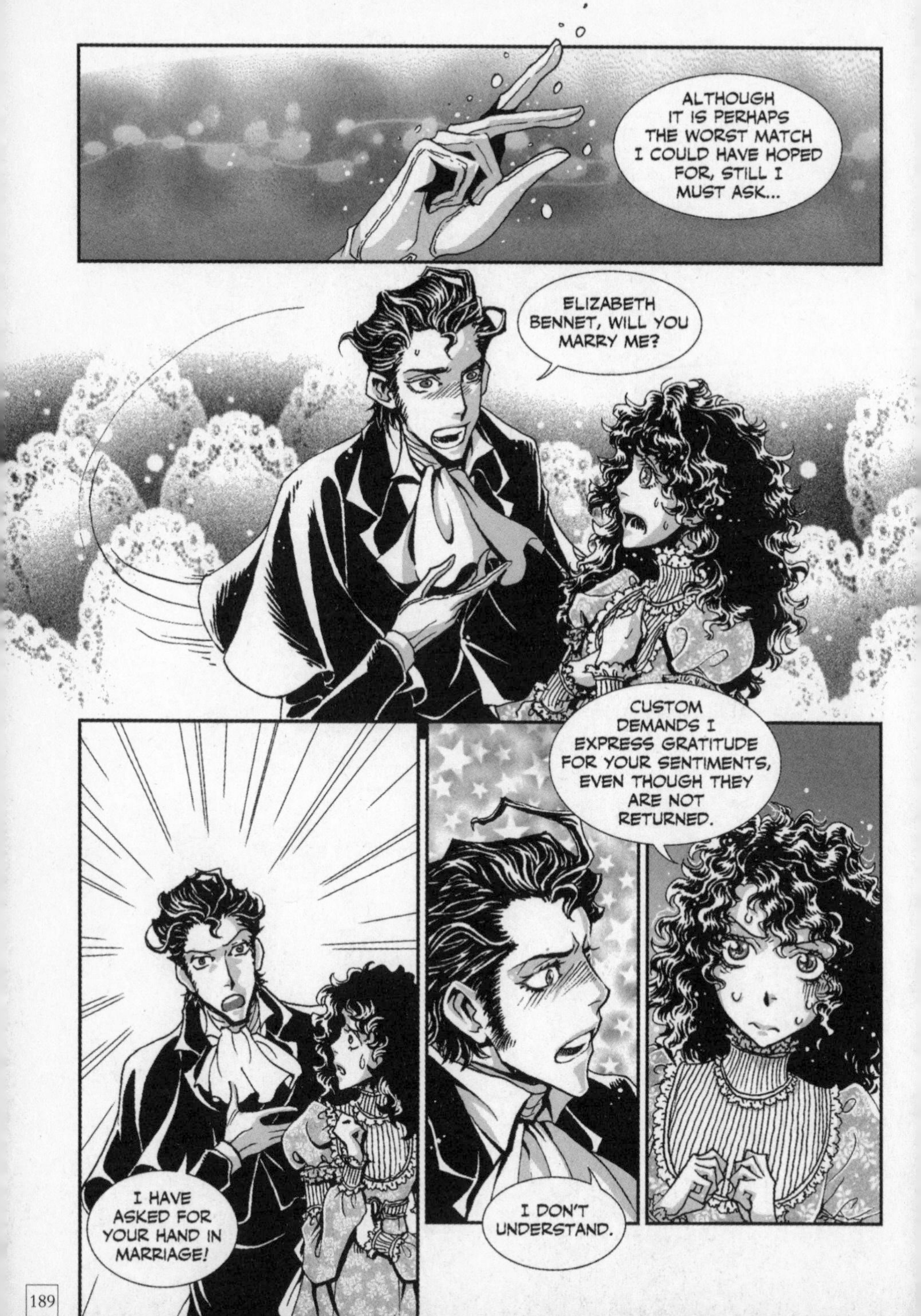
ALTHOUGH IT IS PERHAPS THE WORST MATCH I COULD HAVE HOPED FOR, STILL I MUST ASK...
ELIZABETH BENNET, WILL YOU MARRY ME?
CUSTOM DEMANDS I EXPRESS GRATITUDE FOR YOUR SENTIMENTS, EVEN THOUGH THEY ARE NOT RETURNED.
I DON'T UNDERSTAND.
I HAVE ASKED FOR YOUR HAND IN MARRIAGE!

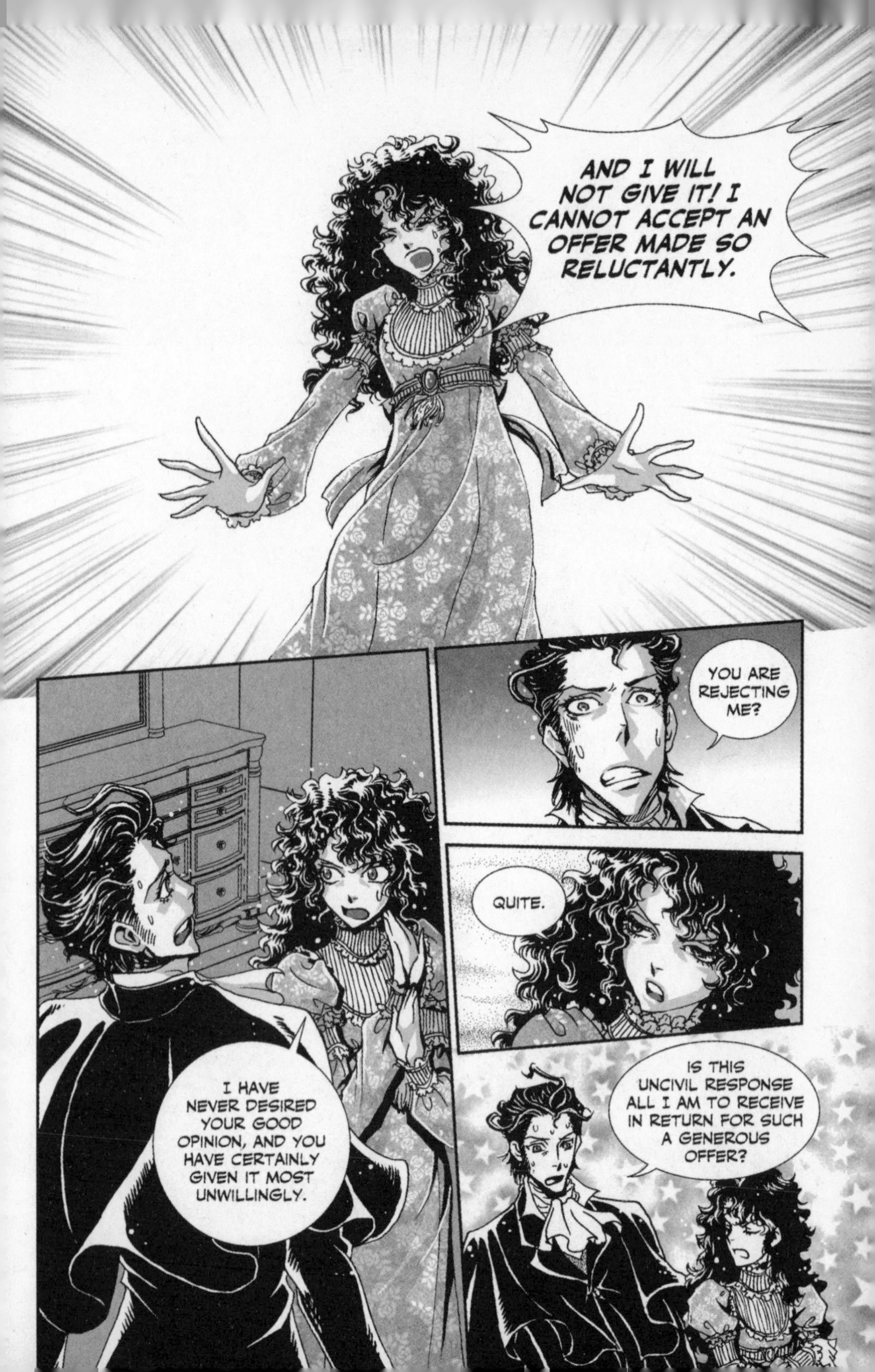
AND I WILL NOT GIVE IT! I CANNOT ACCEPT AN OFFER MADE SO RELUCTANTLY.
YOU ARE REJECTING ME?
QUITE.
IS THIS UNCIVIL RESPONSE ALL I AM TO RECEIVE IN RETURN FOR SUCH A GENEROUS OFFER?
I HAVE NEVER DESIRED YOUR GOOD OPINION, AND YOU HAVE CERTAINLY GIVEN IT MOST UNWILLINGLY.

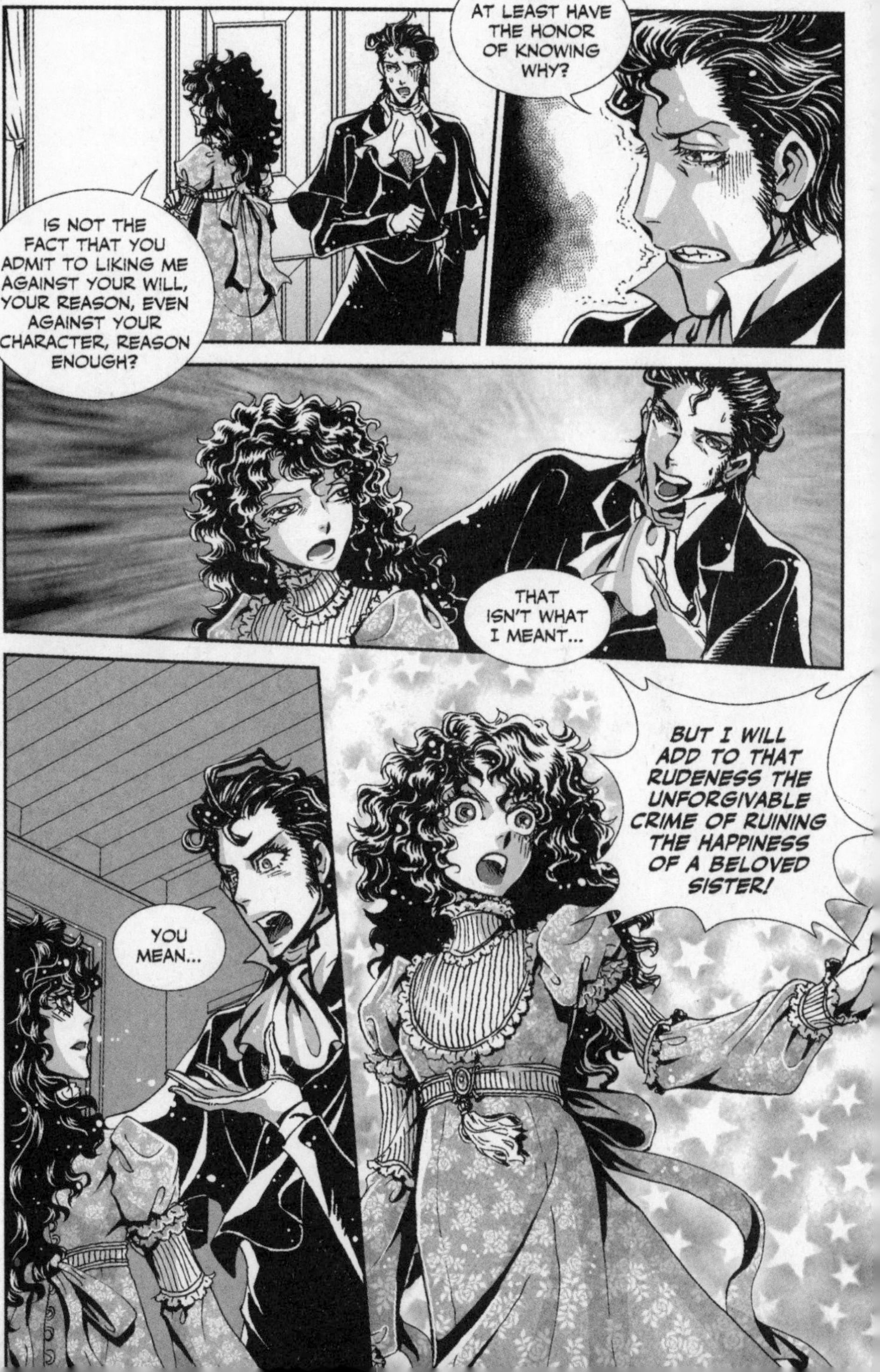
MAY I AT LEAST HAVE THE HONOR OF KNOWING WHY?
IS NOT THE FACT THAT YOU ADMIT TO LIKING ME AGAINST YOUR WILL, YOUR REASON, EVEN AGAINST YOUR CHARACTER, REASON ENOUGH?
THAT ISN'T WHAT I MEANT...
BUT I WILL ADD TO THAT RUDENESS THE UNFORGIVABLE CRIME OF RUINING THE HAPPINESS OF A BELOVED SISTER!
YOU MEAN...

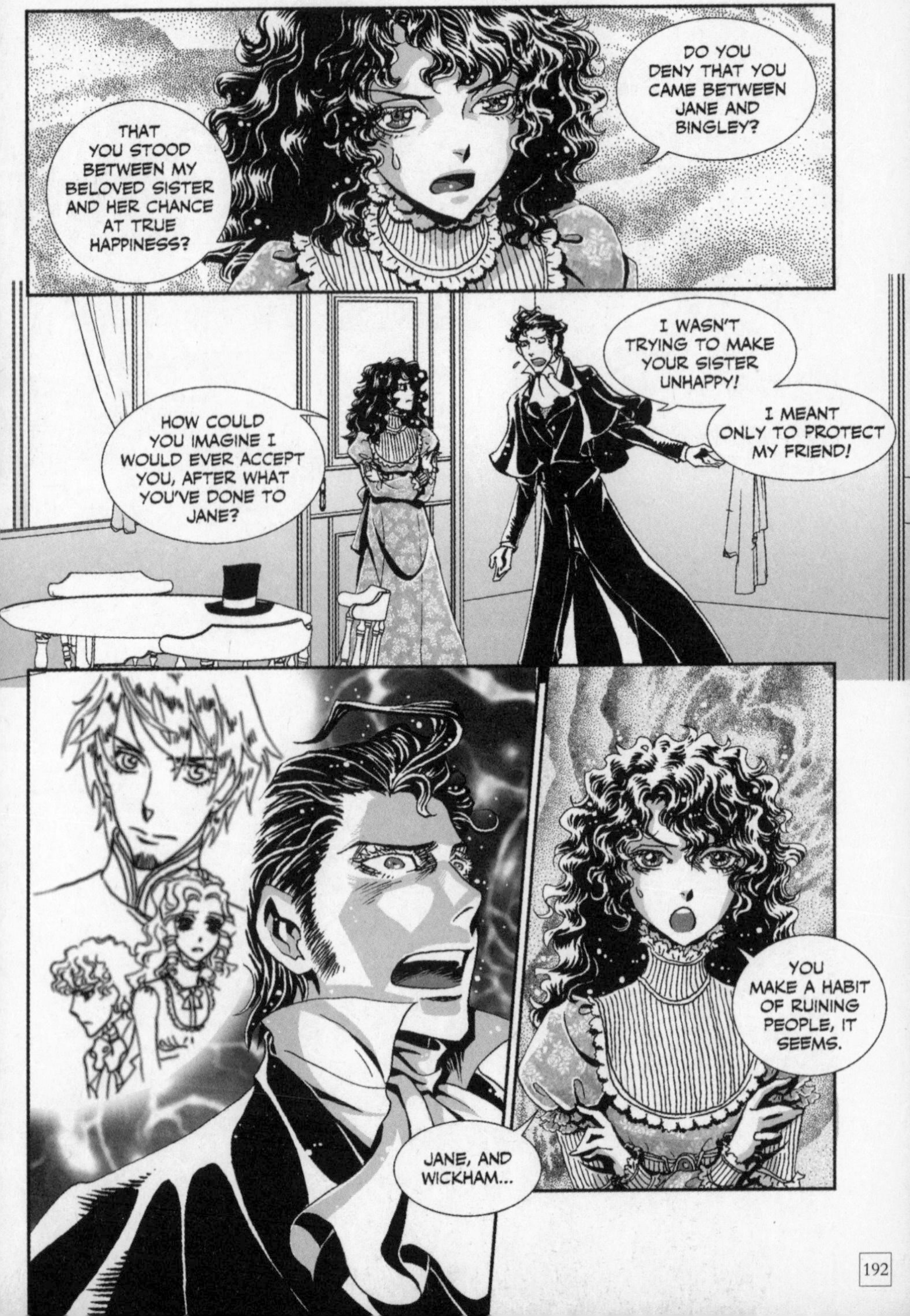
DO YOU DENY THAT YOU CAME BETWEEN JANE AND BINGLEY?
THAT YOU STOOD BETWEEN MY BELOVED SISTER AND HER CHANCE AT TRUE HAPPINESS?
I WASN'T TRYING TO MAKE YOUR SISTER UNHAPPY!
I MEANT ONLY TO PROTECT MY FRIEND!
HOW COULD YOU IMAGINE I WOULD EVER ACCEPT YOU, AFTER WHAT YOU'VE DONE TO JANE?
YOU MAKE A HABIT OF RUINING PEOPLE, IT SEEMS.
JANE, AND WICKHAM...

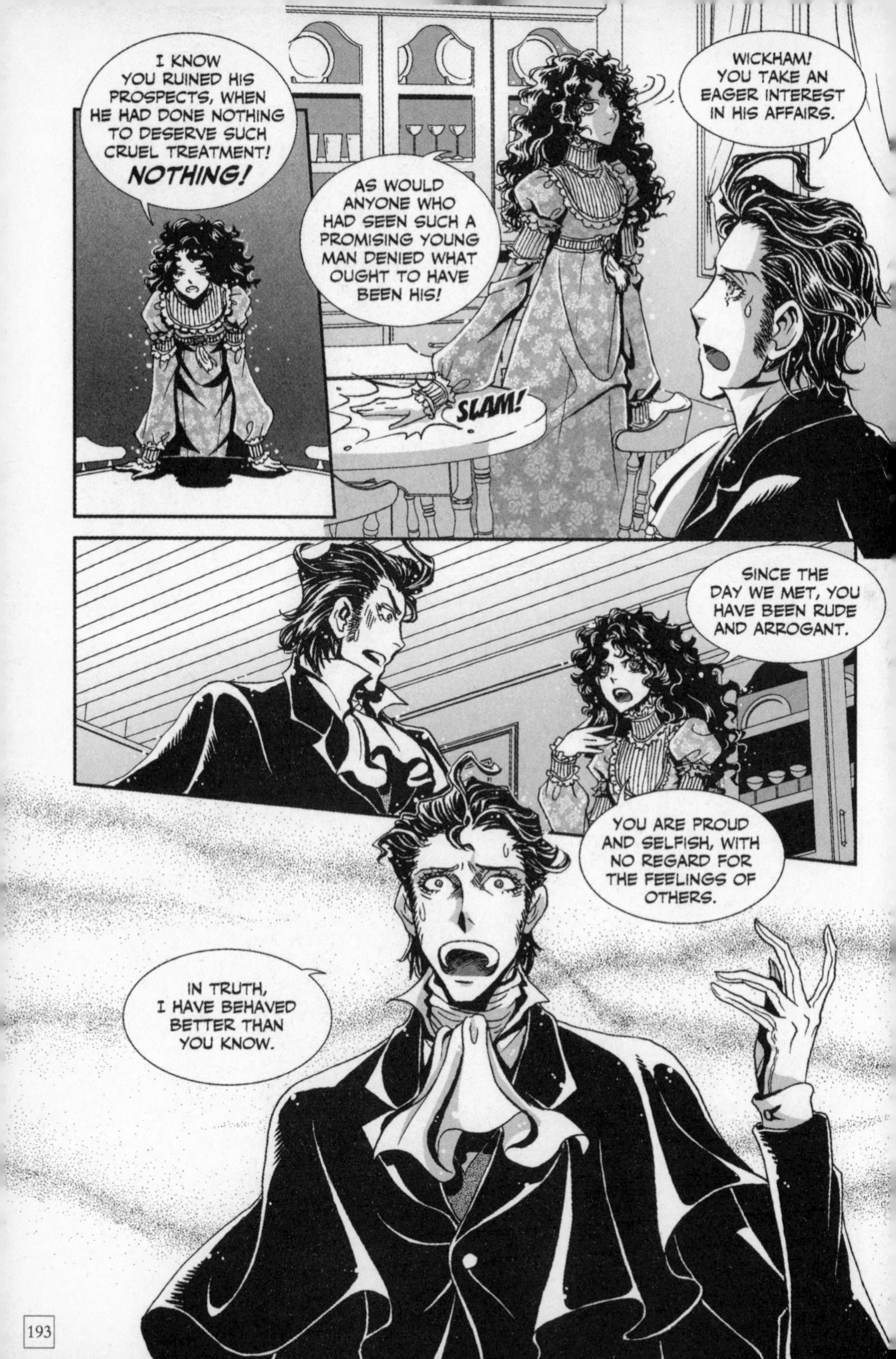
WICKHAM! YOU TAKE AN EAGER INTEREST IN HIS AFFAIRS.
AS WOULD ANYONE WHO HAD SEEN SUCH A PROMISING YOUNG MAN DENIED WHAT OUGHT TO HAVE BEEN HIS!
SLAM!
I KNOW YOU RUINED HIS PROSPECTS, WHEN HE HAD DONE NOTHING TO DESERVE SUCH CRUEL TREATMENT! ***NOTHING!***
SINCE THE DAY WE MET, YOU HAVE BEEN RUDE AND ARROGANT.
YOU ARE PROUD AND SELFISH, WITH NO REGARD FOR THE FEELINGS OF OTHERS.
IN TRUTH, I HAVE BEHAVED BETTER THAN YOU KNOW.

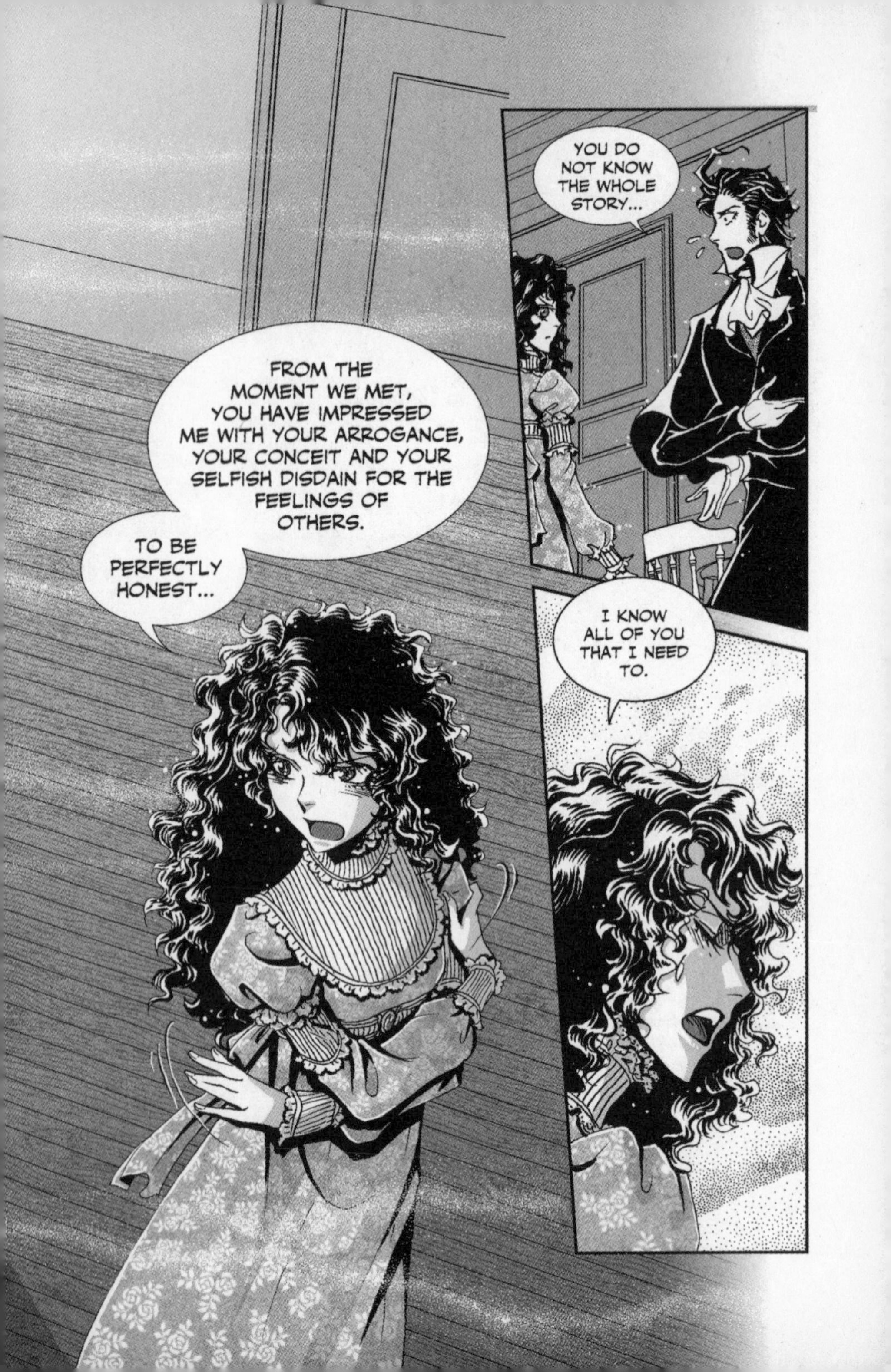
YOU DO NOT KNOW THE WHOLE STORY...
I KNOW ALL OF YOU THAT I NEED TO.
FROM THE MOMENT WE MET, YOU HAVE IMPRESSED ME WITH YOUR ARROGANCE, YOUR CONCEIT AND YOUR SELFISH DISDAIN FOR THE FEELINGS OF OTHERS.
TO BE PERFECTLY HONEST...

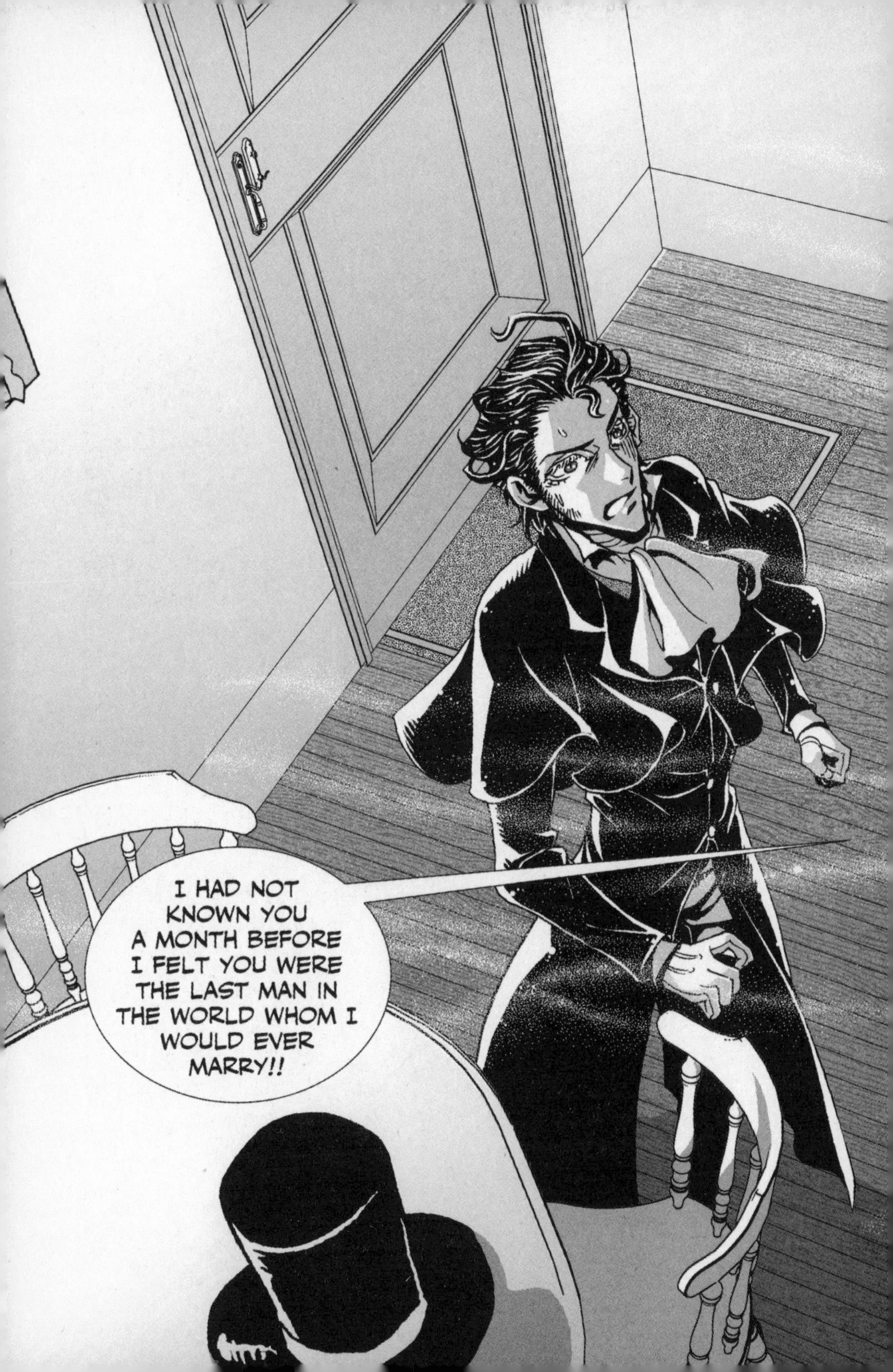
I HAD NOT KNOWN YOU A MONTH BEFORE I FELT YOU WERE THE LAST MAN IN THE WORLD WHOM I WOULD EVER MARRY!!

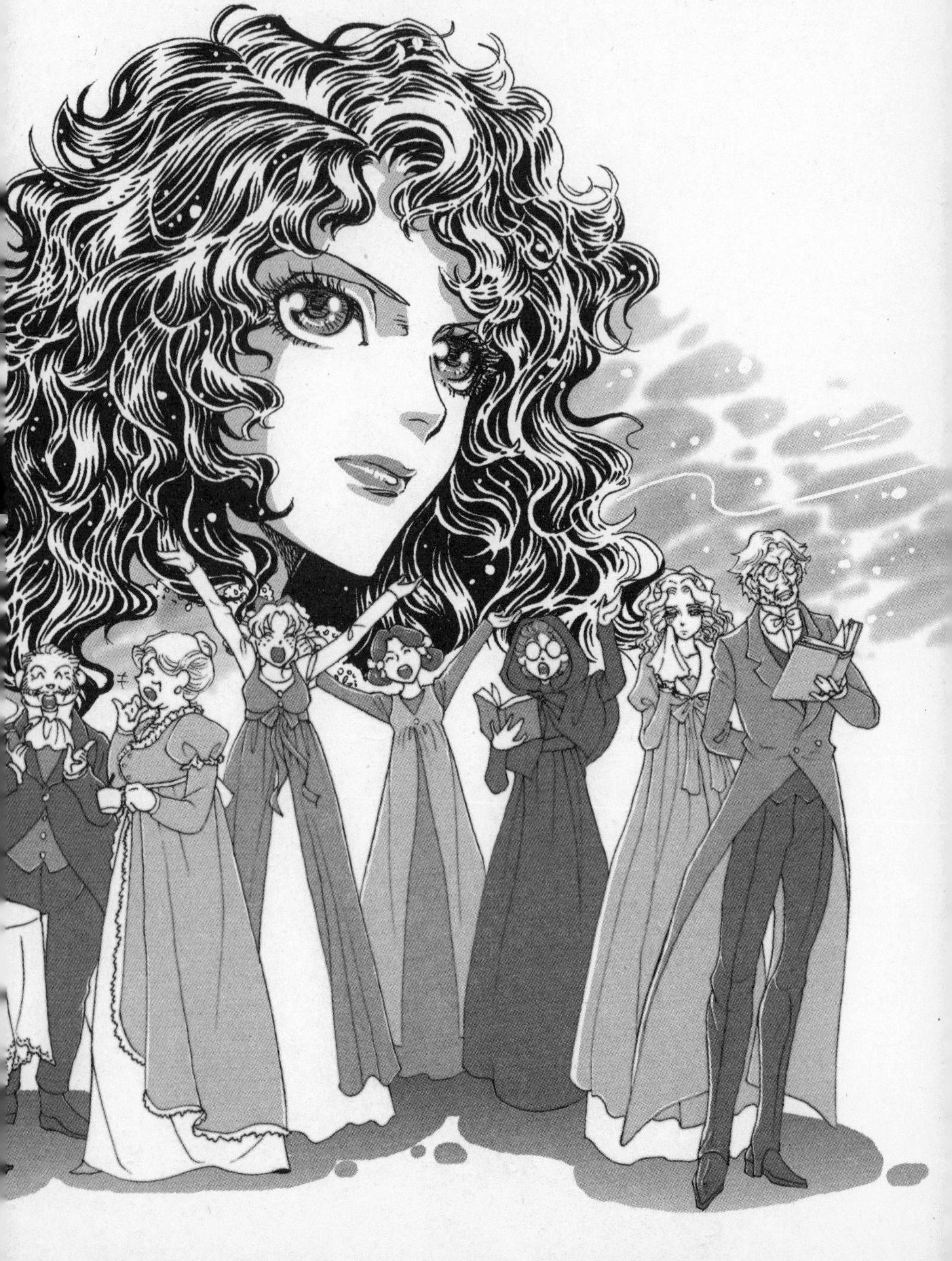

Chapter 11

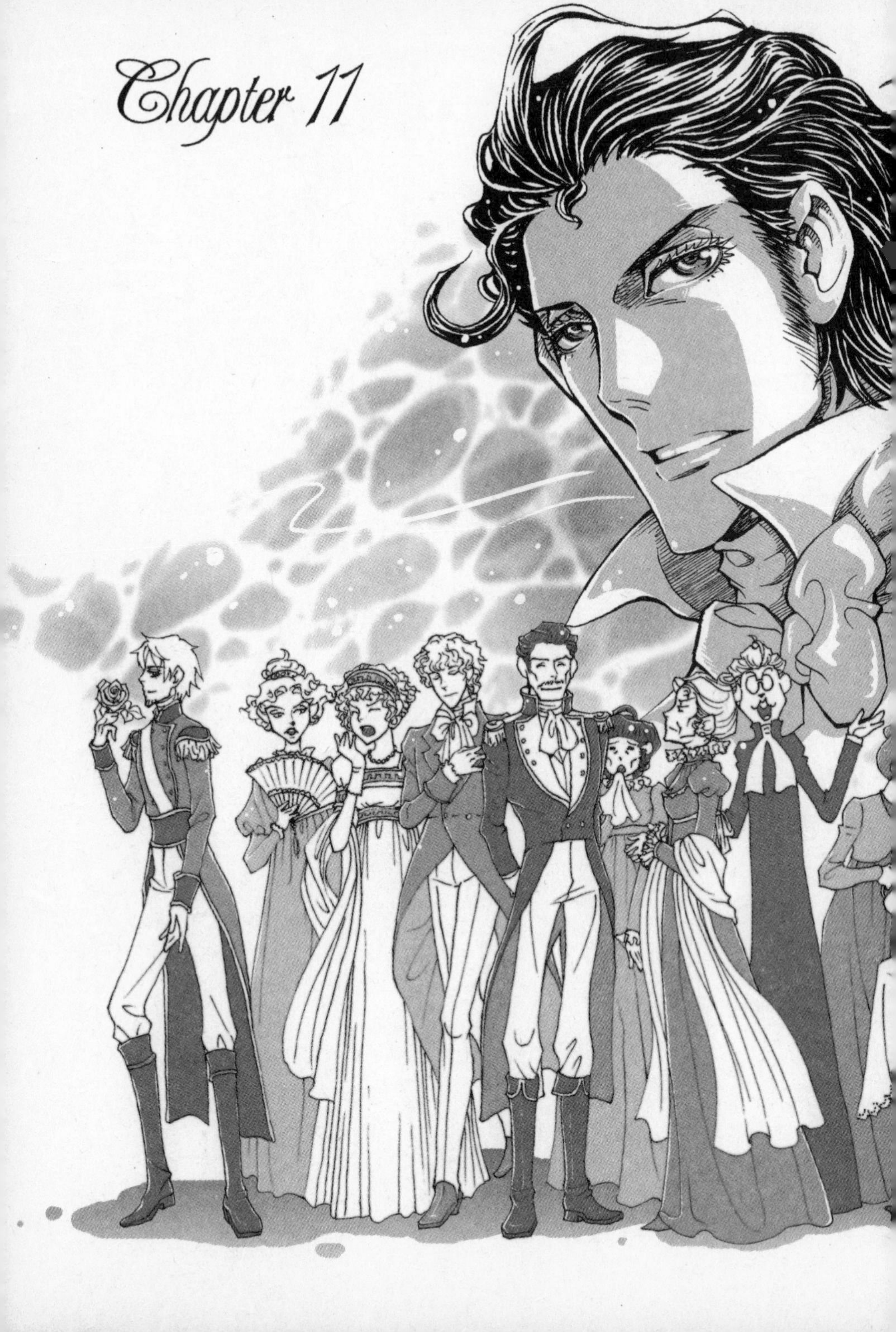

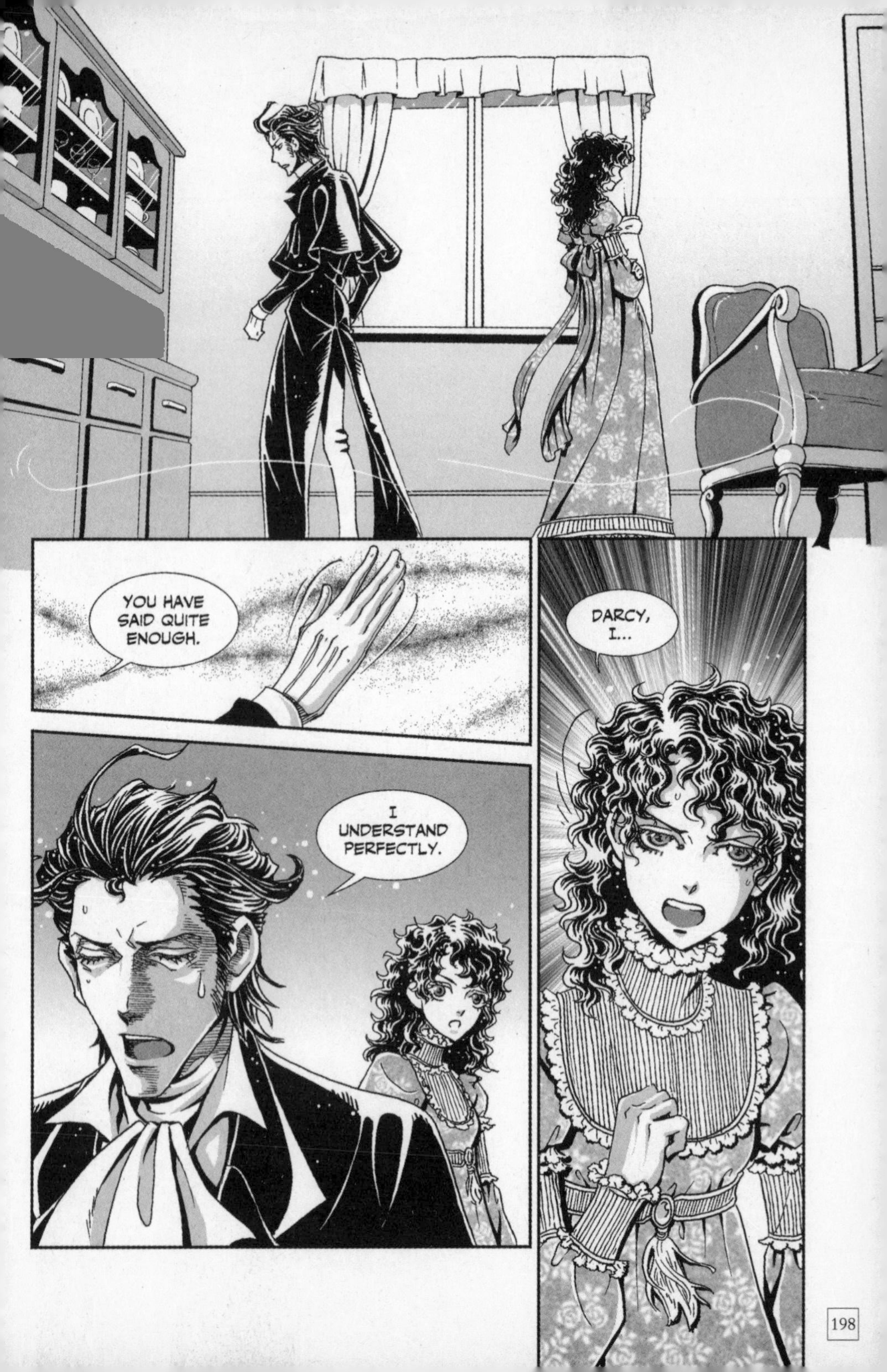
DARCY, I...
YOU HAVE SAID QUITE ENOUGH.
I UNDERSTAND PERFECTLY.

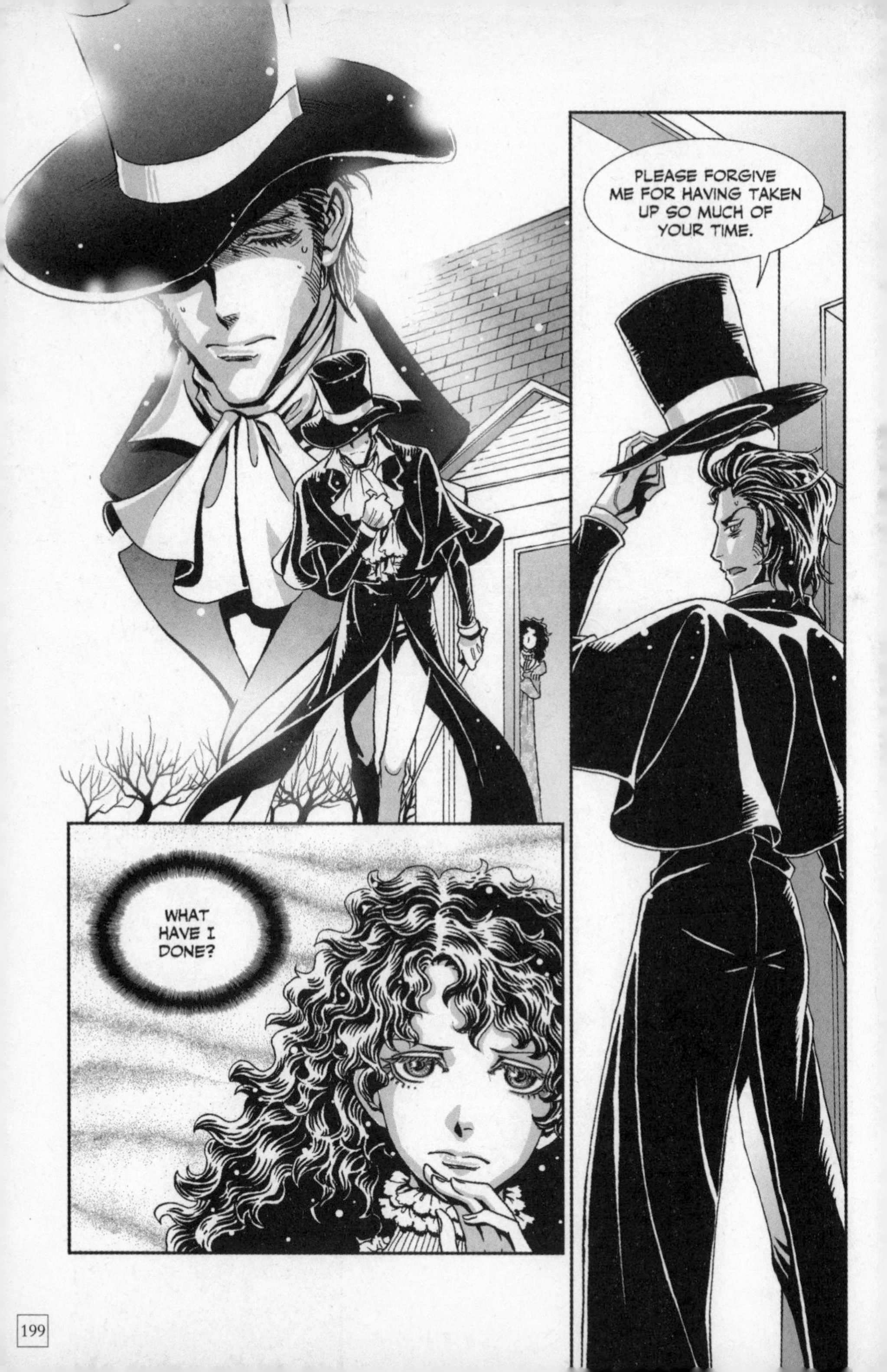
PLEASE FORGIVE ME FOR HAVING TAKEN UP SO MUCH OF YOUR TIME.
WHAT HAVE I DONE?

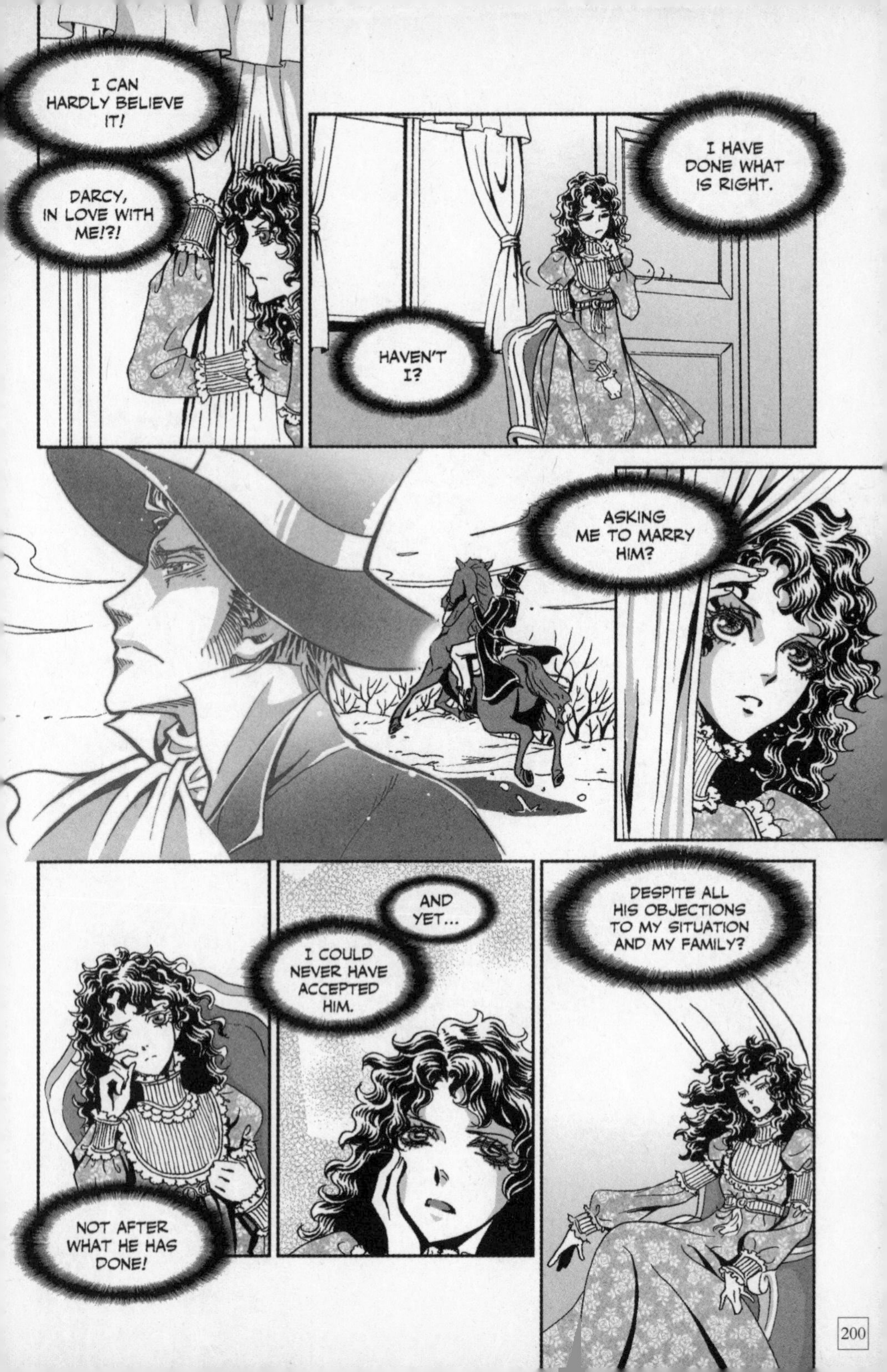
I HAVE DONE WHAT IS RIGHT.
HAVEN'T I?
I CAN HARDLY BELIEVE IT!
DARCY, IN LOVE WITH ME!?!
ASKING ME TO MARRY HIM?
DESPITE ALL HIS OBJECTIONS TO MY SITUATION AND MY FAMILY?
AND YET...
I COULD NEVER HAVE ACCEPTED HIM.
NOT AFTER WHAT HE HAS DONE!

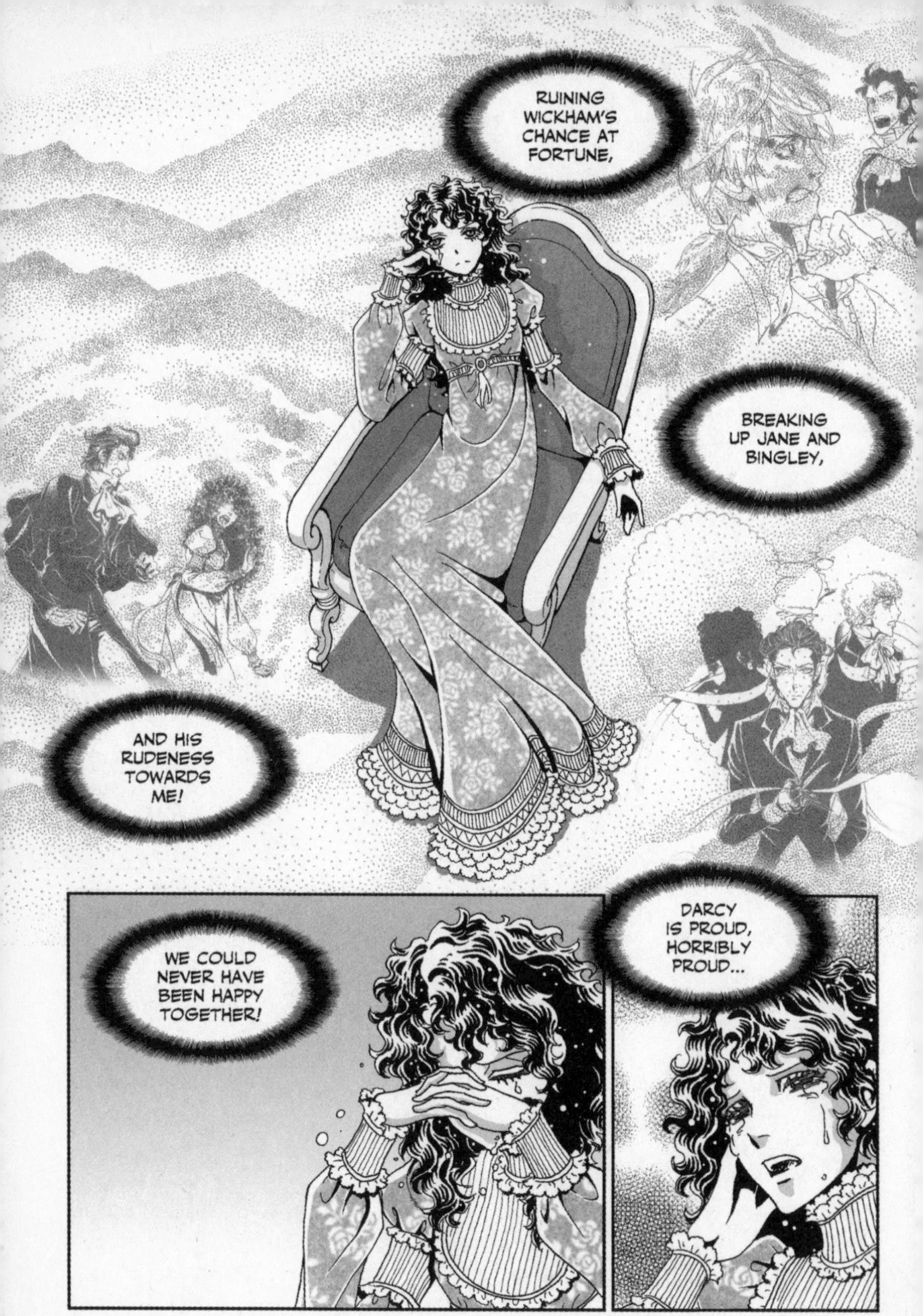
RUINING WICKHAM'S CHANCE AT FORTUNE,
BREAKING UP JANE AND BINGLEY,
AND HIS RUDENESS TOWARDS ME!
DARCY IS PROUD, HORRIBLY PROUD...
WE COULD NEVER HAVE BEEN HAPPY TOGETHER!

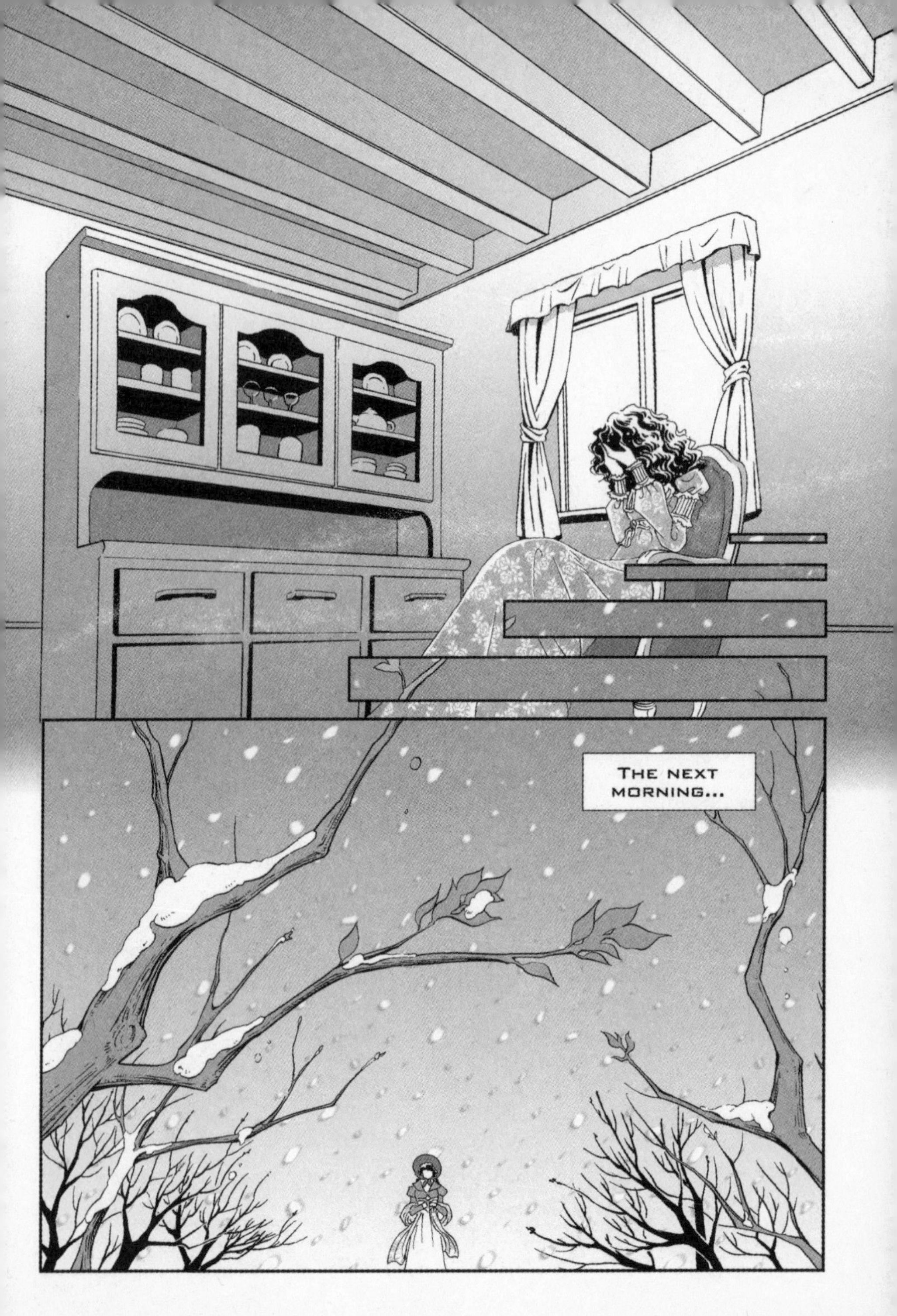
THE NEXT MORNING...

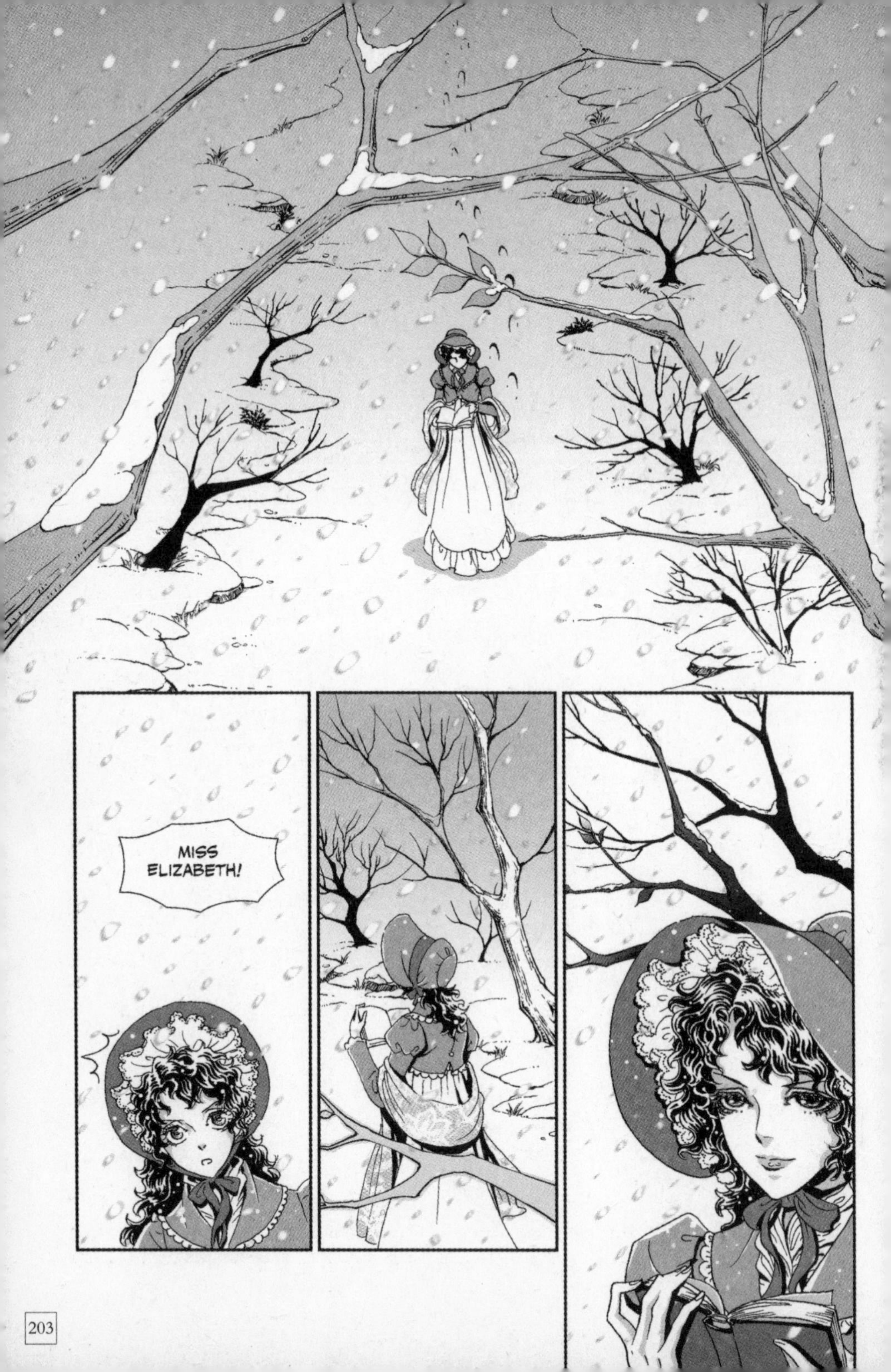
MISS ELIZABETH!

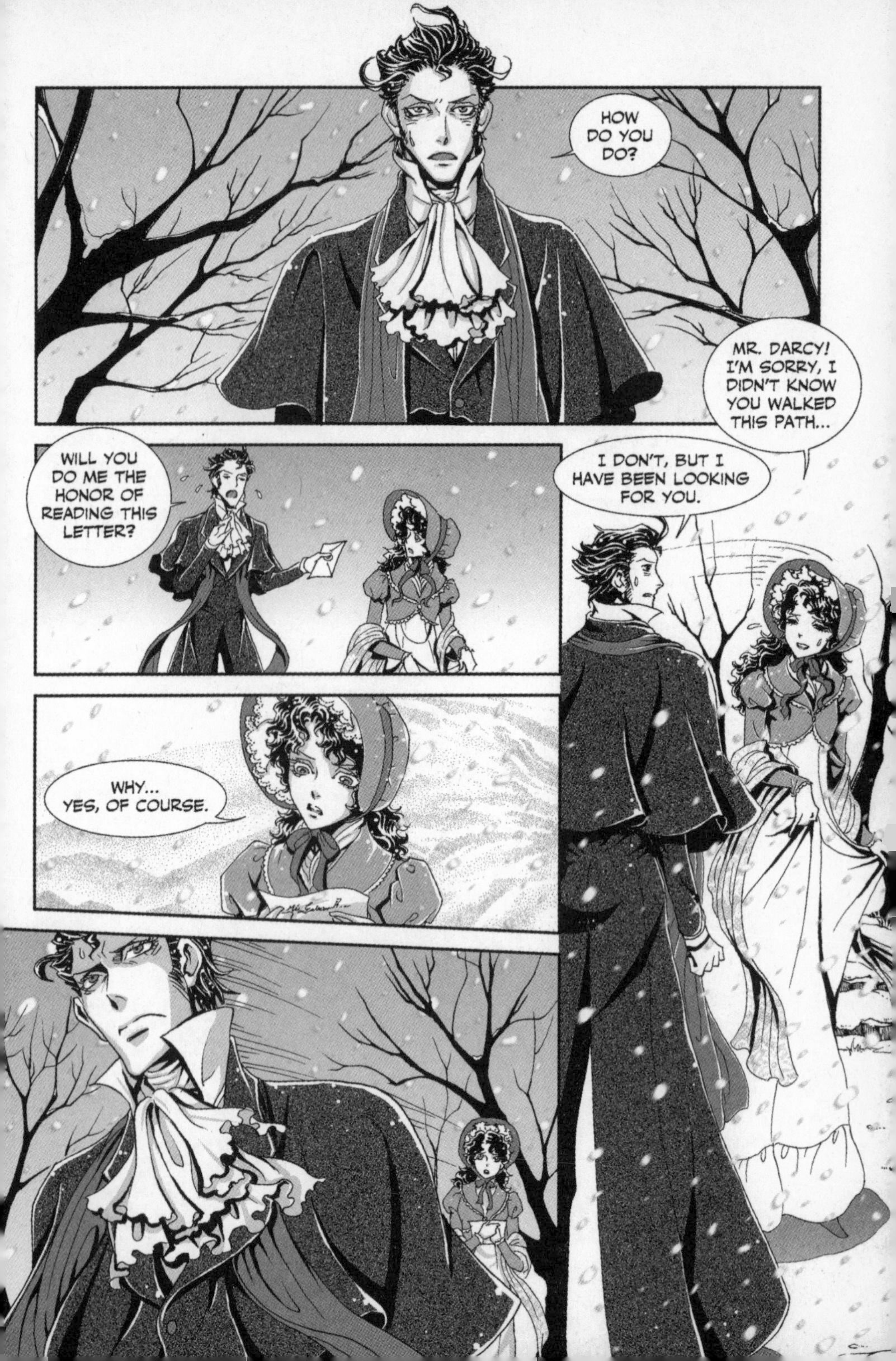
HOW DO YOU DO?
MR. DARCY! I'M SORRY, I DIDN'T KNOW YOU WALKED THIS PATH...
I DON'T, BUT I HAVE BEEN LOOKING FOR YOU.
WILL YOU DO ME THE HONOR OF READING THIS LETTER?
WHY... YES, OF COURSE.

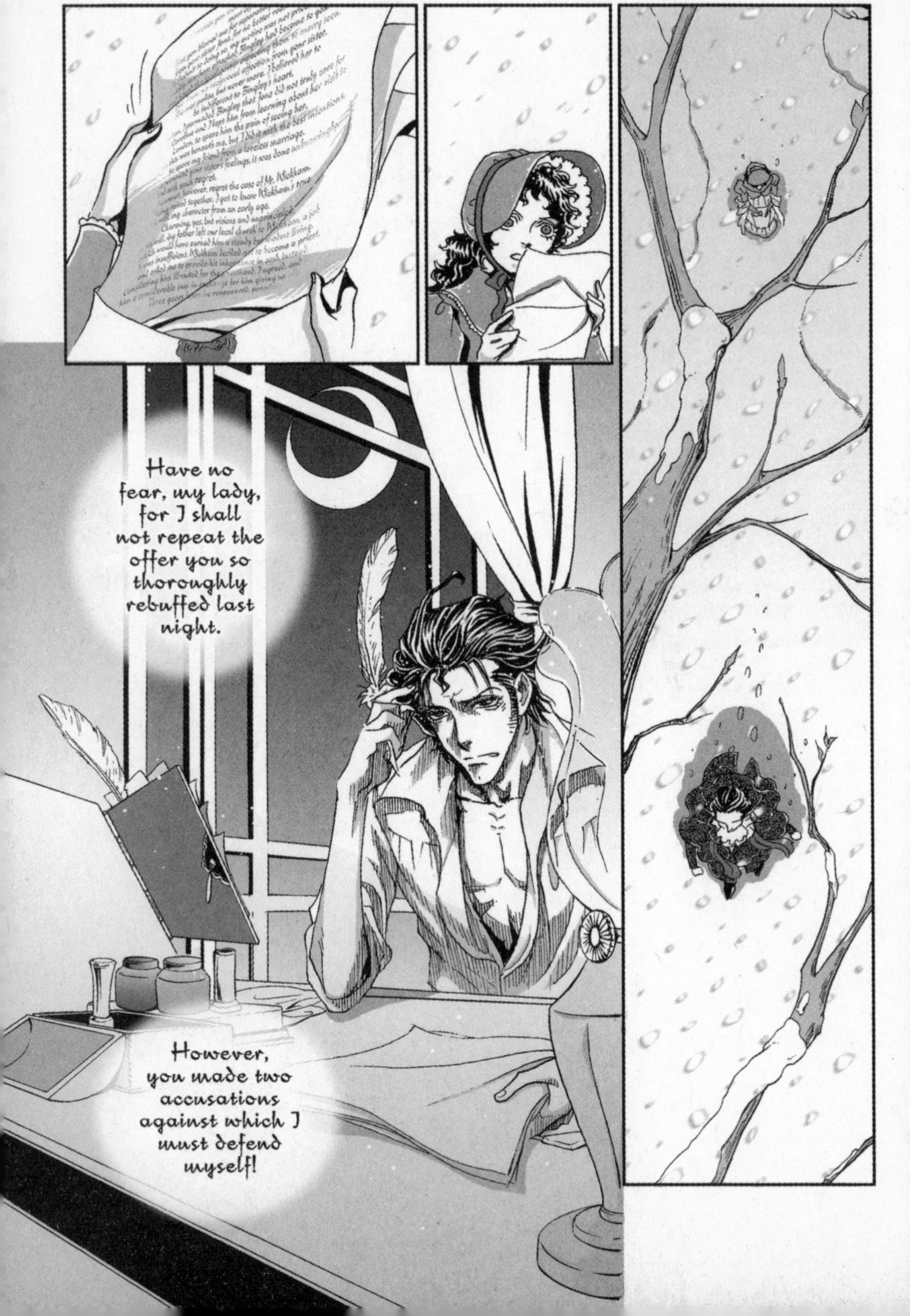

Have no fear, my lady, for I shall not repeat the offer you so thoroughly rebuffed last night.
However, you made two accusations against which I must defend myself!

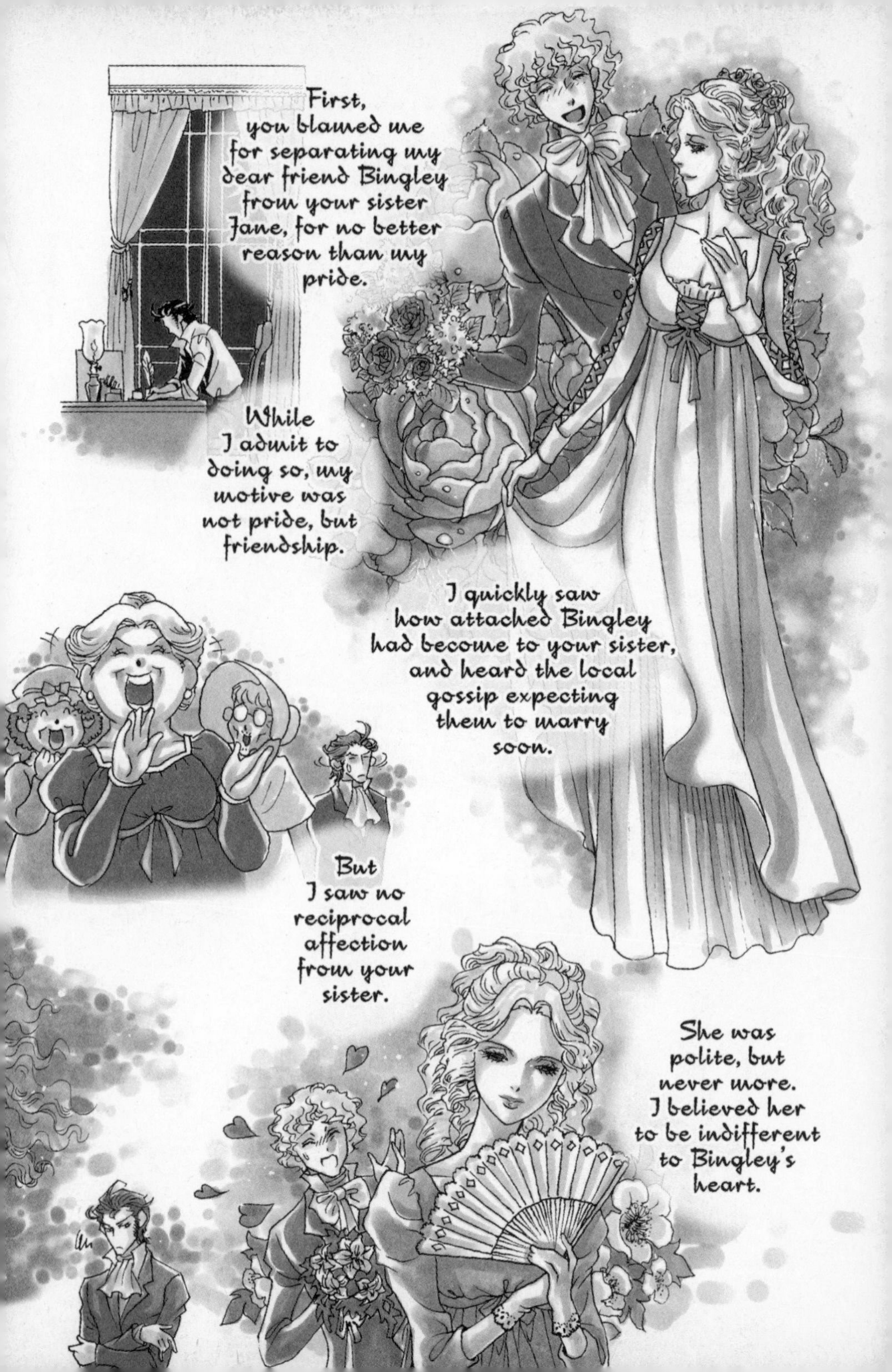
First, you blamed me for separating my dear friend Bingley from your sister Jane, for no better reason than my pride.
While I admit to doing so, my motive was not pride, but friendship.
I quickly saw how attached Bingley had become to your sister, and heard the local gossip expecting them to marry soon.
But I saw no reciprocal affection from your sister.
She was polite, but never more. I believed her to be indifferent to Bingley's heart.

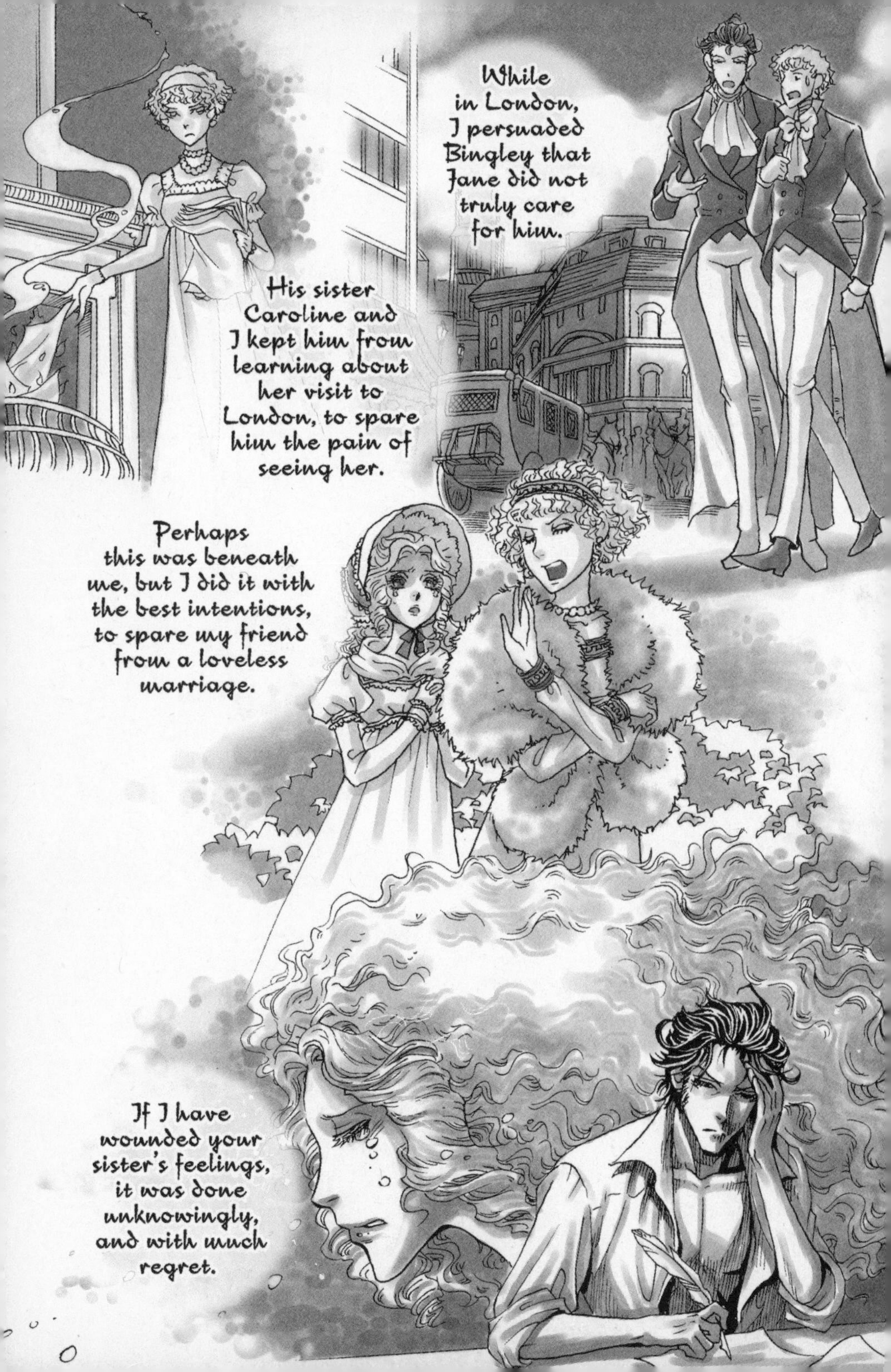
While in London, I persuaded Bingley that Jane did not truly care for him.
His sister Caroline and I kept him from learning about her visit to London, to spare him the pain of seeing her.
Perhaps this was beneath me, but I did it with the best intentions, to spare my friend from a loveless marriage.
If I have wounded your sister's feelings, it was done unknowingly, and with much regret.

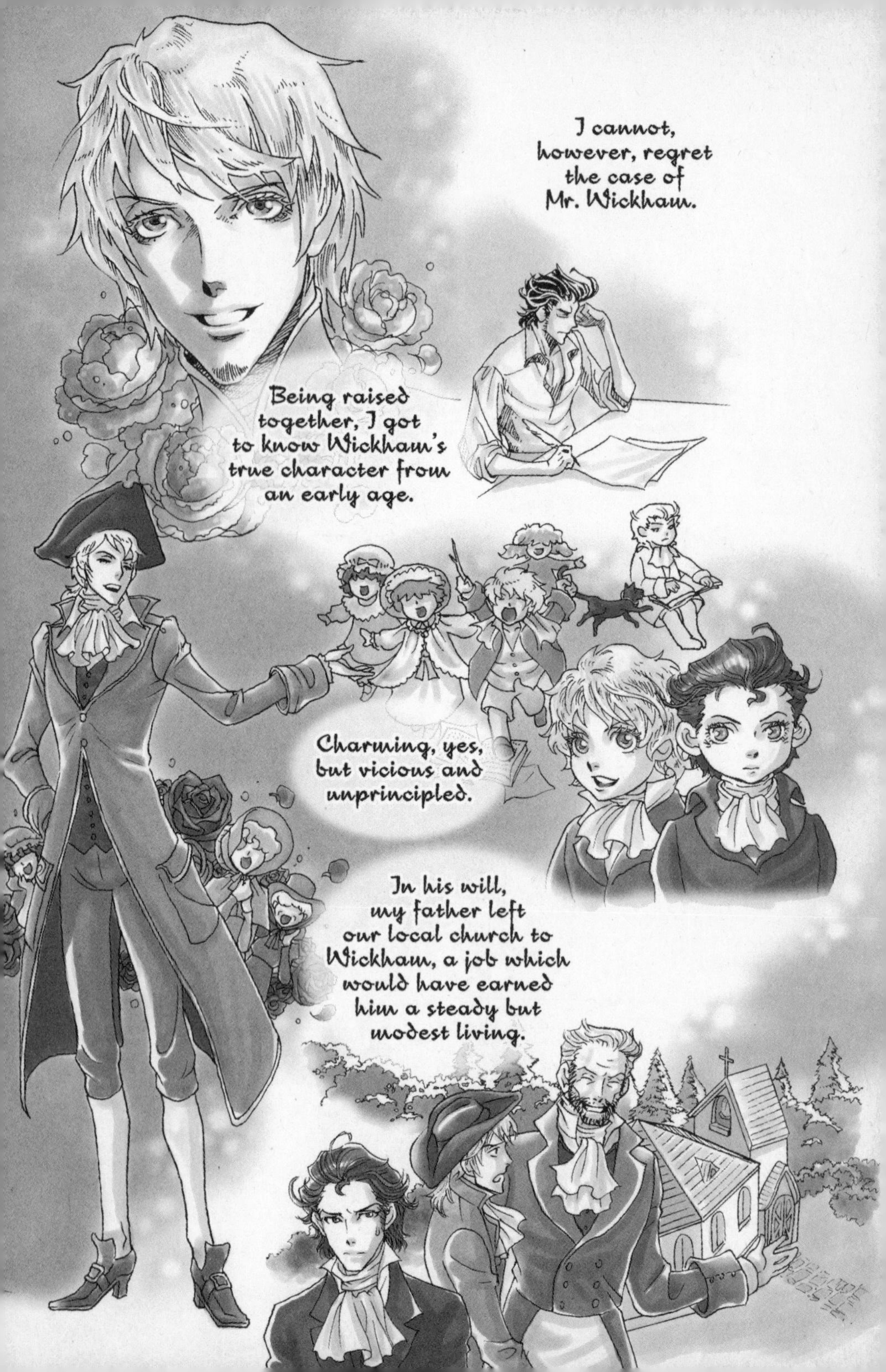
I cannot, however, regret the case of Mr. Wickham.
Being raised together, I got to know Wickham's true character from an early age.
Charming, yes, but vicious and unprincipled.
In his will, my father left our local church to Wickham, a job which would have earned him a steady but modest living.

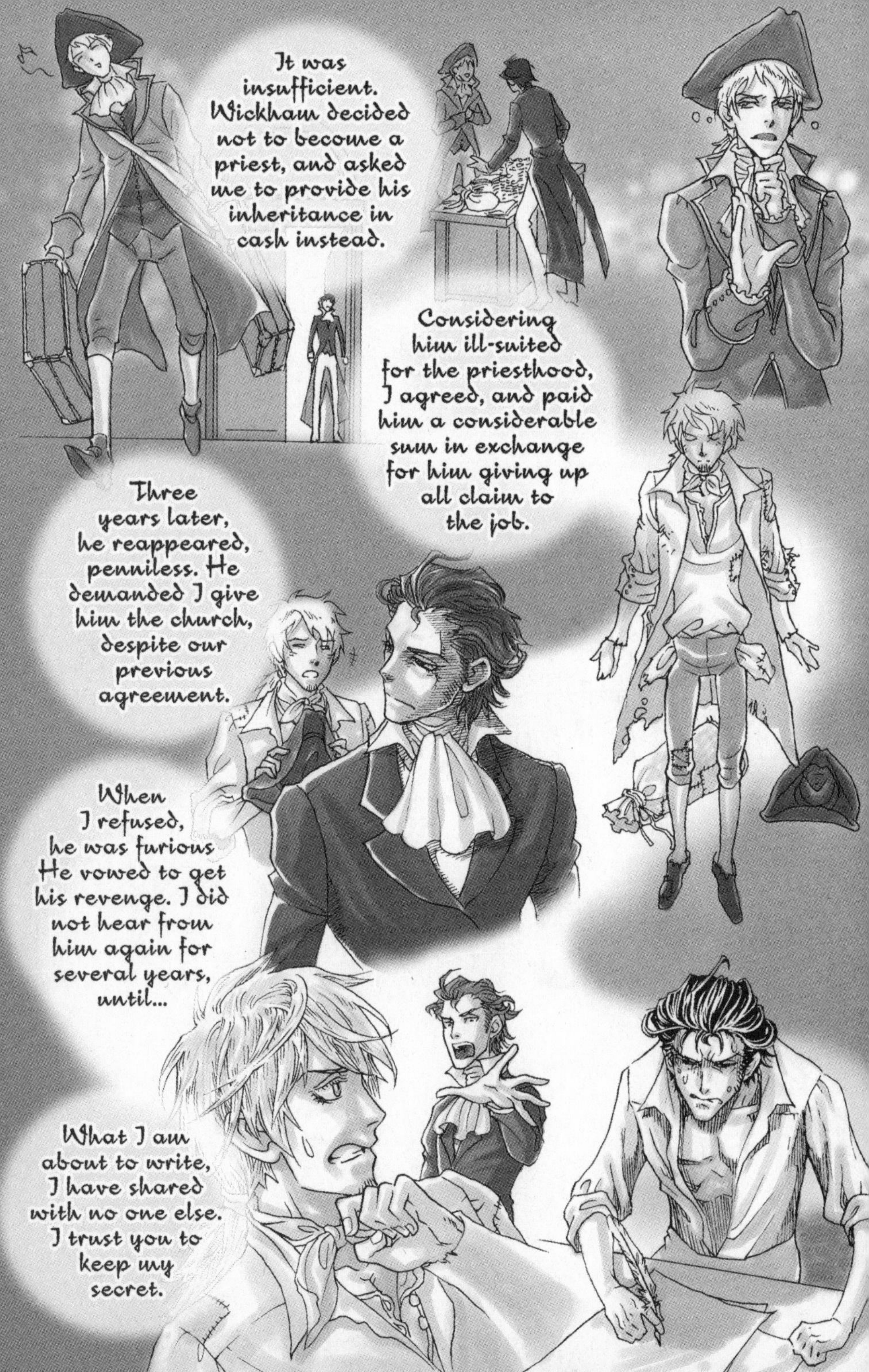
It was insufficient. Wickham decided not to become a priest, and asked me to provide his inheritance in cash instead.
Considering him ill-suited for the priesthood, I agreed, and paid him a considerable sum in exchange for him giving up all claim to the job.
Three years later, he reappeared, penniless. He demanded I give him the church, despite our previous agreement.
When I refused, he was furious He vowed to get his revenge. I did not hear from him again for several years, until...
What I am about to write, I have shared with no one else. I trust you to keep my secret.

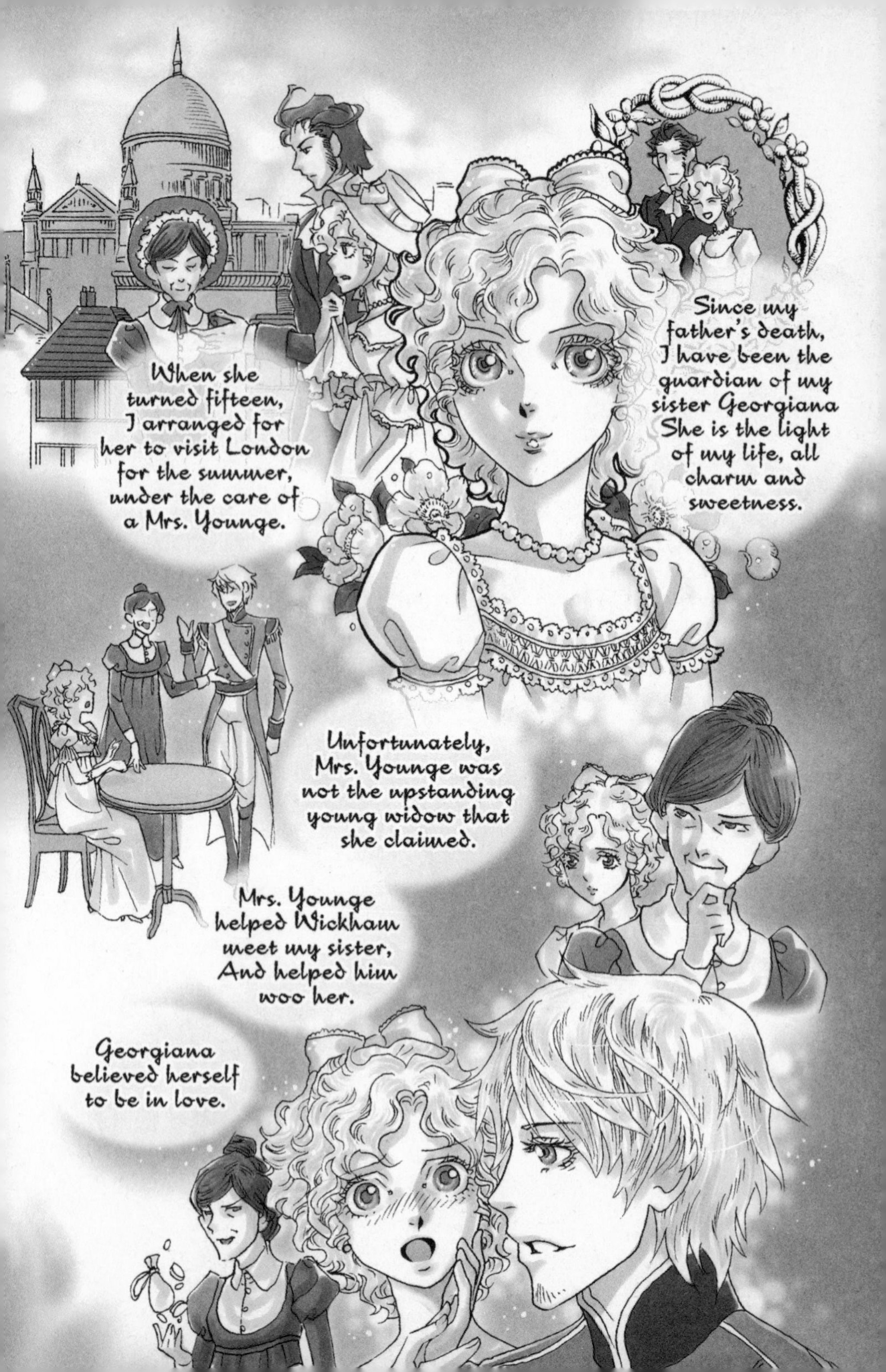
Since my father's death, I have been the guardian of my sister Georgiana She is the light of my life, all charm and sweetness.
When she turned fifteen, I arranged for her to visit London for the summer, under the care of a Mrs. Younge.
Unfortunately, Mrs. Younge was not the upstanding young widow that she claimed.
Mrs. Younge helped Wickham meet my sister, And helped him woo her.
Georgiana believed herself to be in love.

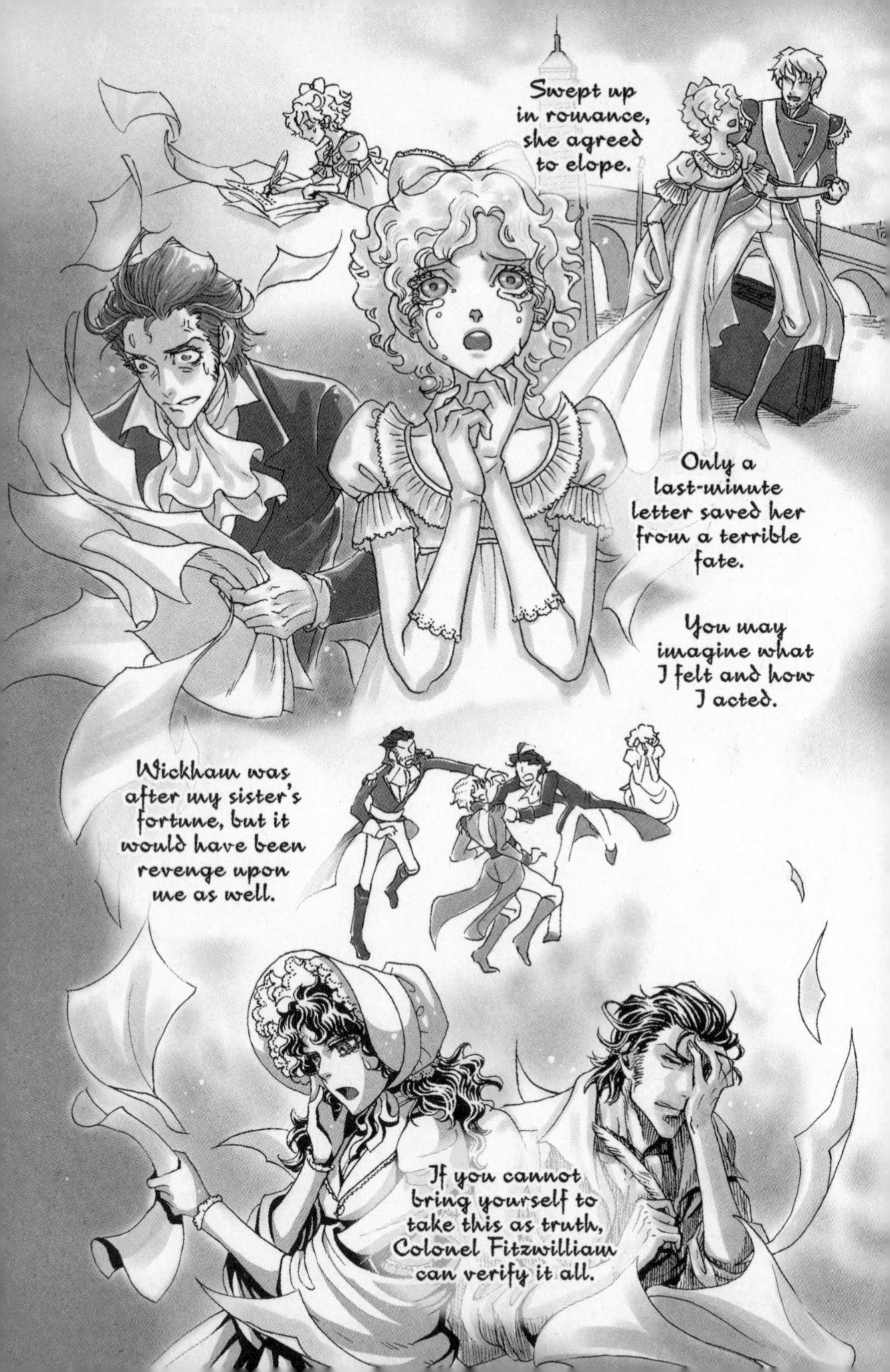
Swept up in romance, she agreed to elope.
Only a last-minute letter saved her from a terrible fate.
You may imagine what I felt and how I acted.
Wickham was after my sister's fortune, but it would have been revenge upon me as well.
If you cannot bring yourself to take this as truth, Colonel Fitzwilliam can verify it all.

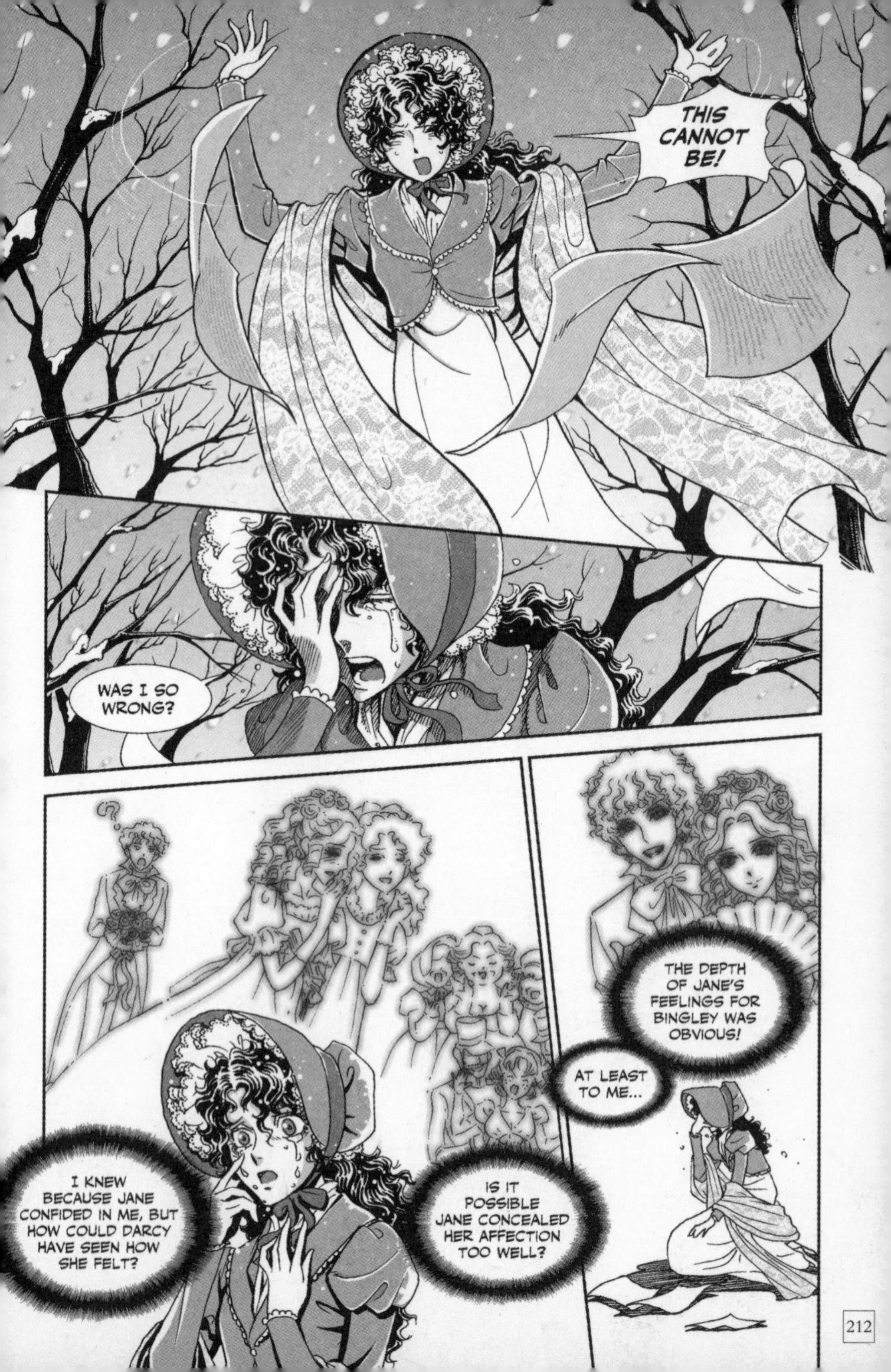
THIS CANNOT BE!
WAS I SO WRONG?
THE DEPTH OF JANE'S FEELINGS FOR BINGLEY WAS OBVIOUS!
AT LEAST TO ME...
IS IT POSSIBLE JANE CONCEALED HER AFFECTION TOO WELL?
I KNEW BECAUSE JANE CONFIDED IN ME, BUT HOW COULD DARCY HAVE SEEN HOW SHE FELT?

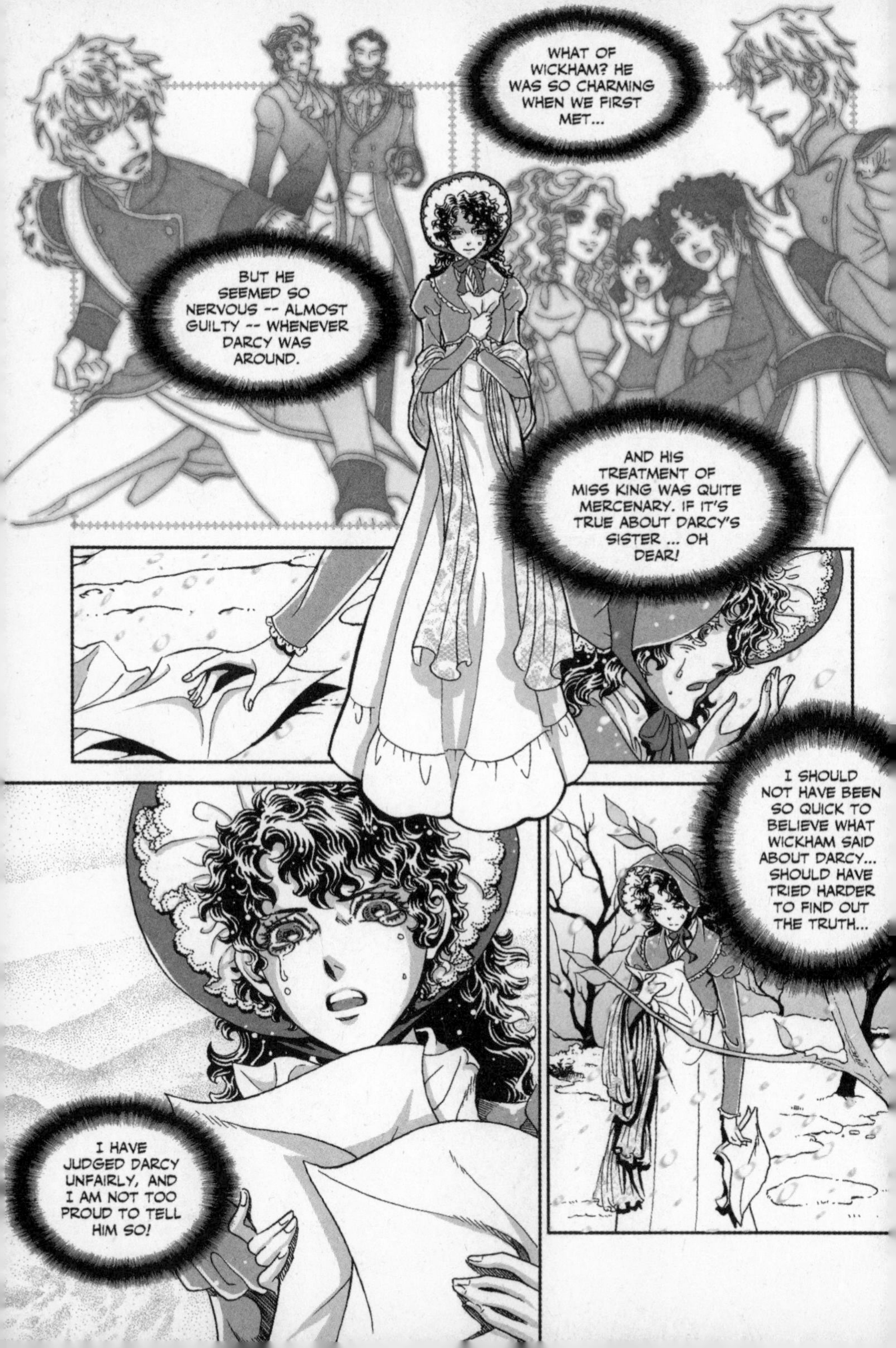
WHAT OF WICKHAM? HE WAS SO CHARMING WHEN WE FIRST MET...
BUT HE SEEMED SO NERVOUS -- ALMOST GUILTY -- WHENEVER DARCY WAS AROUND.
AND HIS TREATMENT OF MISS KING WAS QUITE MERCENARY. IF IT'S TRUE ABOUT DARCY'S SISTER ... OH DEAR!
I SHOULD NOT HAVE BEEN SO QUICK TO BELIEVE WHAT WICKHAM SAID ABOUT DARCY... SHOULD HAVE TRIED HARDER TO FIND OUT THE TRUTH...
I HAVE JUDGED DARCY UNFAIRLY, AND I AM NOT TOO PROUD TO TELL HIM SO!

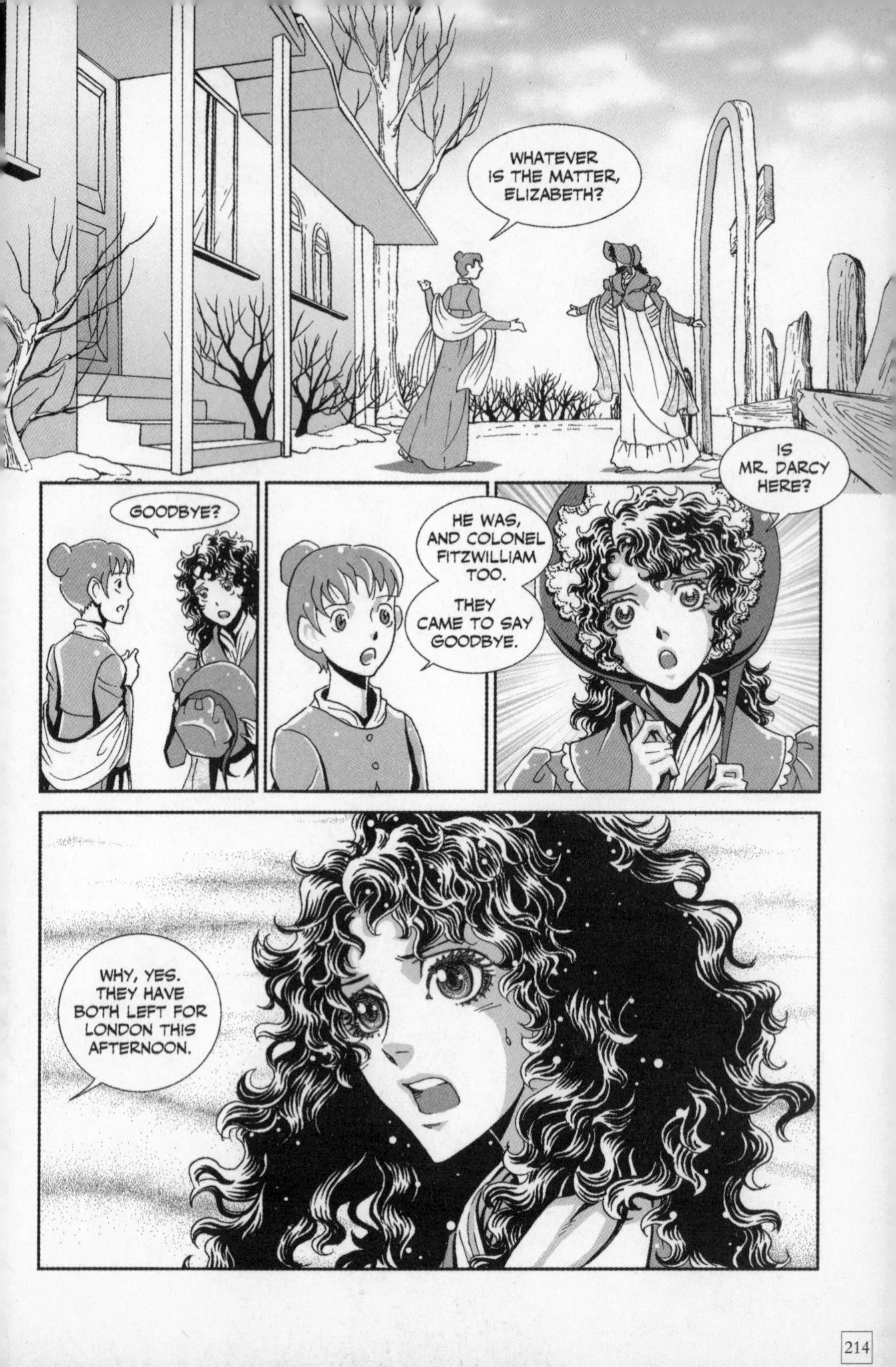
WHATEVER IS THE MATTER, ELIZABETH?
IS MR. DARCY HERE?
HE WAS, AND COLONEL FITZWILLIAM TOO.
THEY CAME TO SAY GOODBYE.
GOODBYE?
WHY, YES. THEY HAVE BOTH LEFT FOR LONDON THIS AFTERNOON.

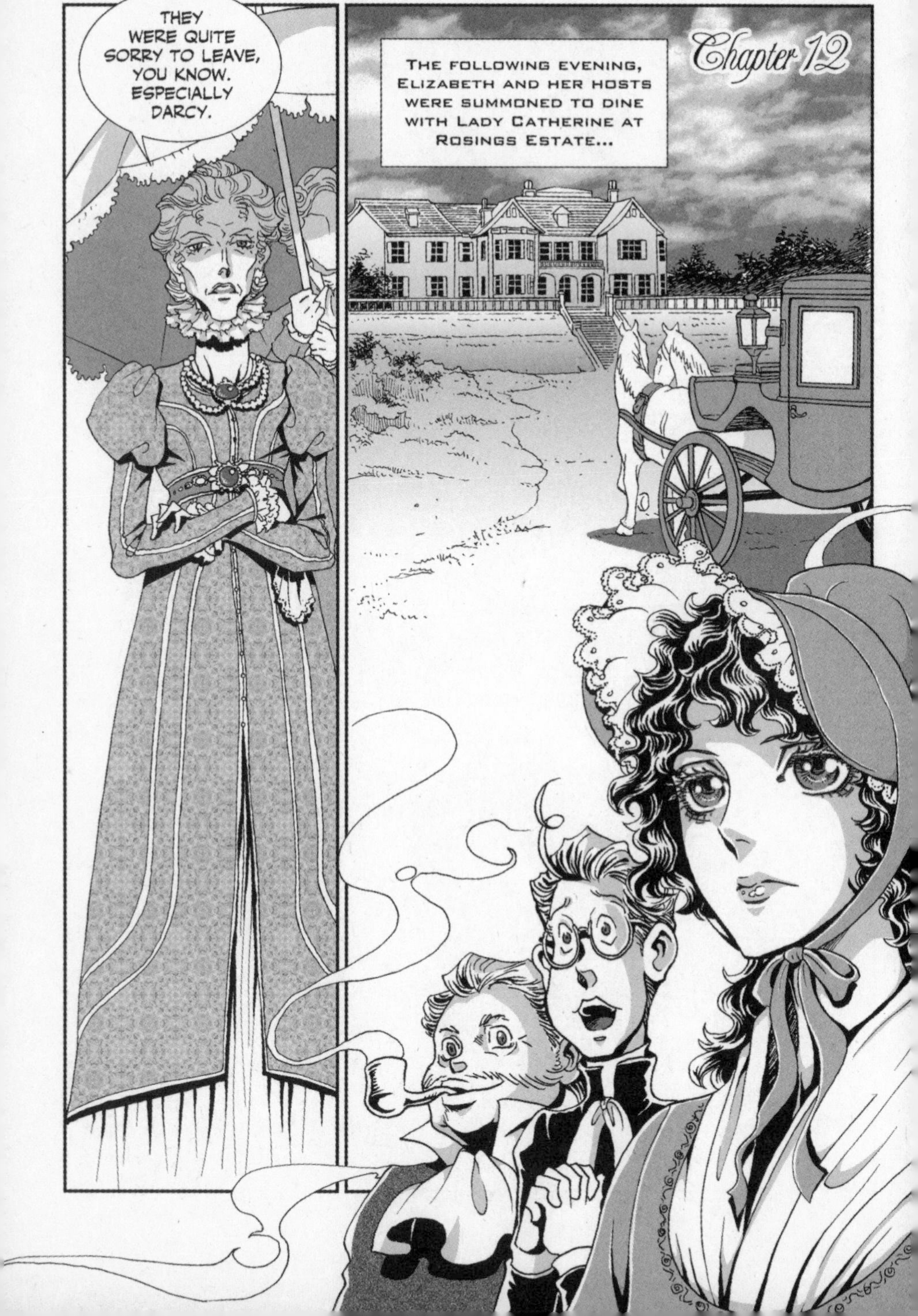
Chapter 12
THE FOLLOWING EVENING, ELIZABETH AND HER HOSTS WERE SUMMONED TO DINE WITH LADY CATHERINE AT ROSINGS ESTATE...
THEY WERE QUITE SORRY TO LEAVE, YOU KNOW. ESPECIALLY DARCY.

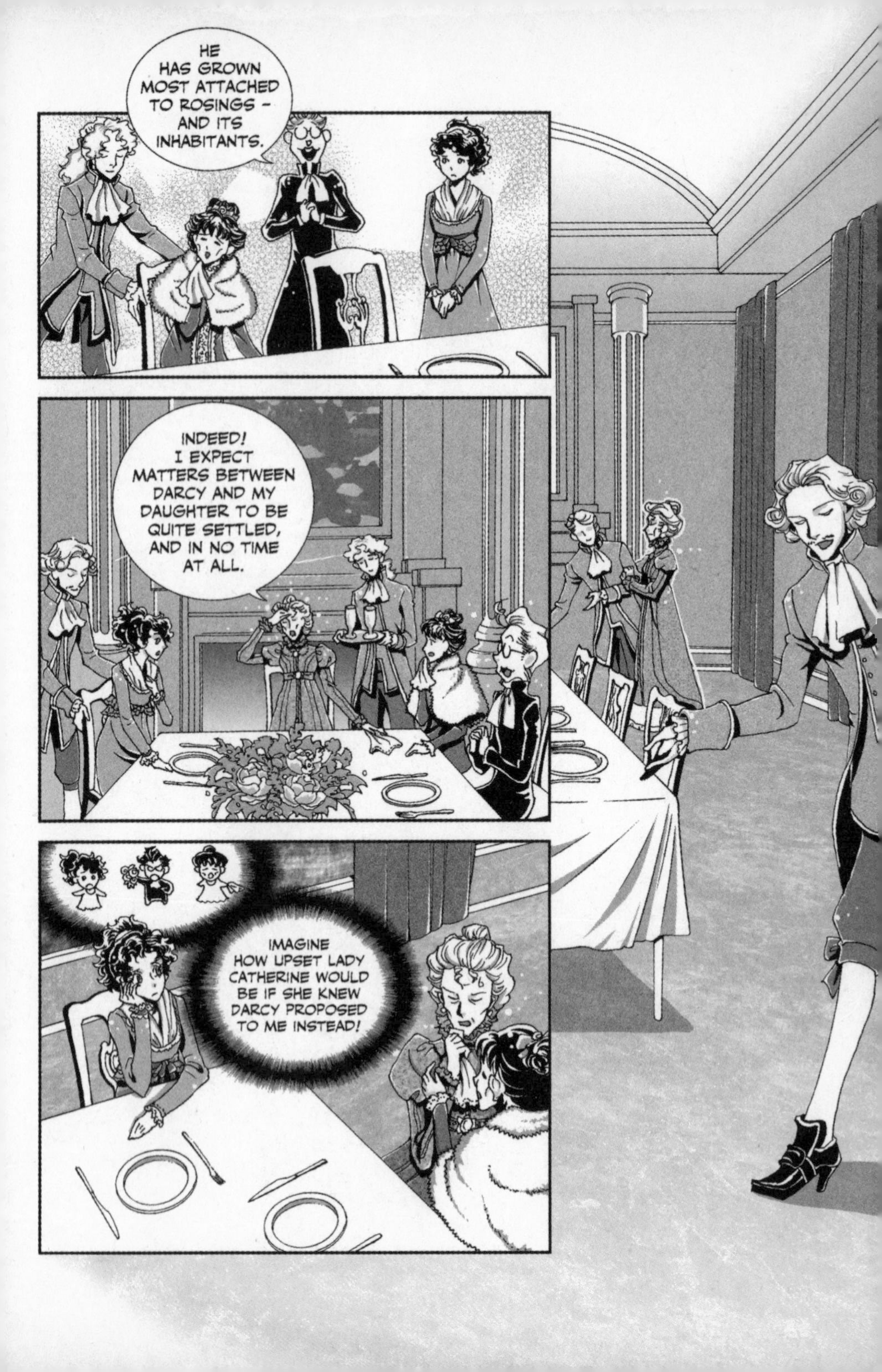
HE HAS GROWN MOST ATTACHED TO ROSINGS – AND ITS INHABITANTS.
INDEED! I EXPECT MATTERS BETWEEN DARCY AND MY DAUGHTER TO BE QUITE SETTLED, AND IN NO TIME AT ALL.
IMAGINE HOW UPSET LADY CATHERINE WOULD BE IF SHE KNEW DARCY PROPOSED TO ME INSTEAD!

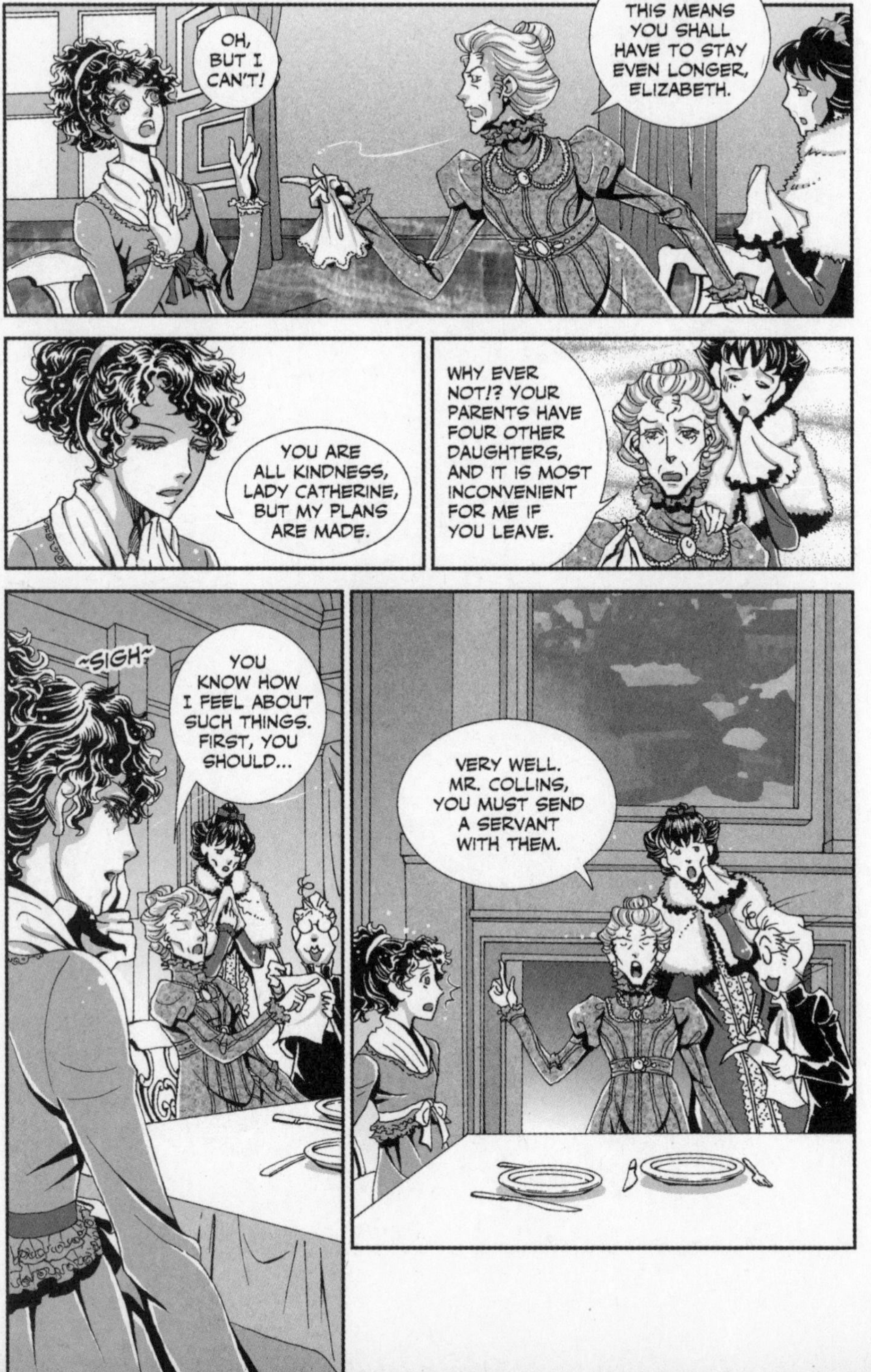

OF COURSE, THIS MEANS YOU SHALL HAVE TO STAY EVEN LONGER, ELIZABETH.
OH, BUT I CAN'T!
WHY EVER NOT!? YOUR PARENTS HAVE FOUR OTHER DAUGHTERS, AND IT IS MOST INCONVENIENT FOR ME IF YOU LEAVE.
YOU ARE ALL KINDNESS, LADY CATHERINE, BUT MY PLANS ARE MADE.
VERY WELL. MR. COLLINS, YOU MUST SEND A SERVANT WITH THEM.
YOU KNOW HOW I FEEL ABOUT SUCH THINGS. FIRST, YOU SHOULD...
~SIGH~

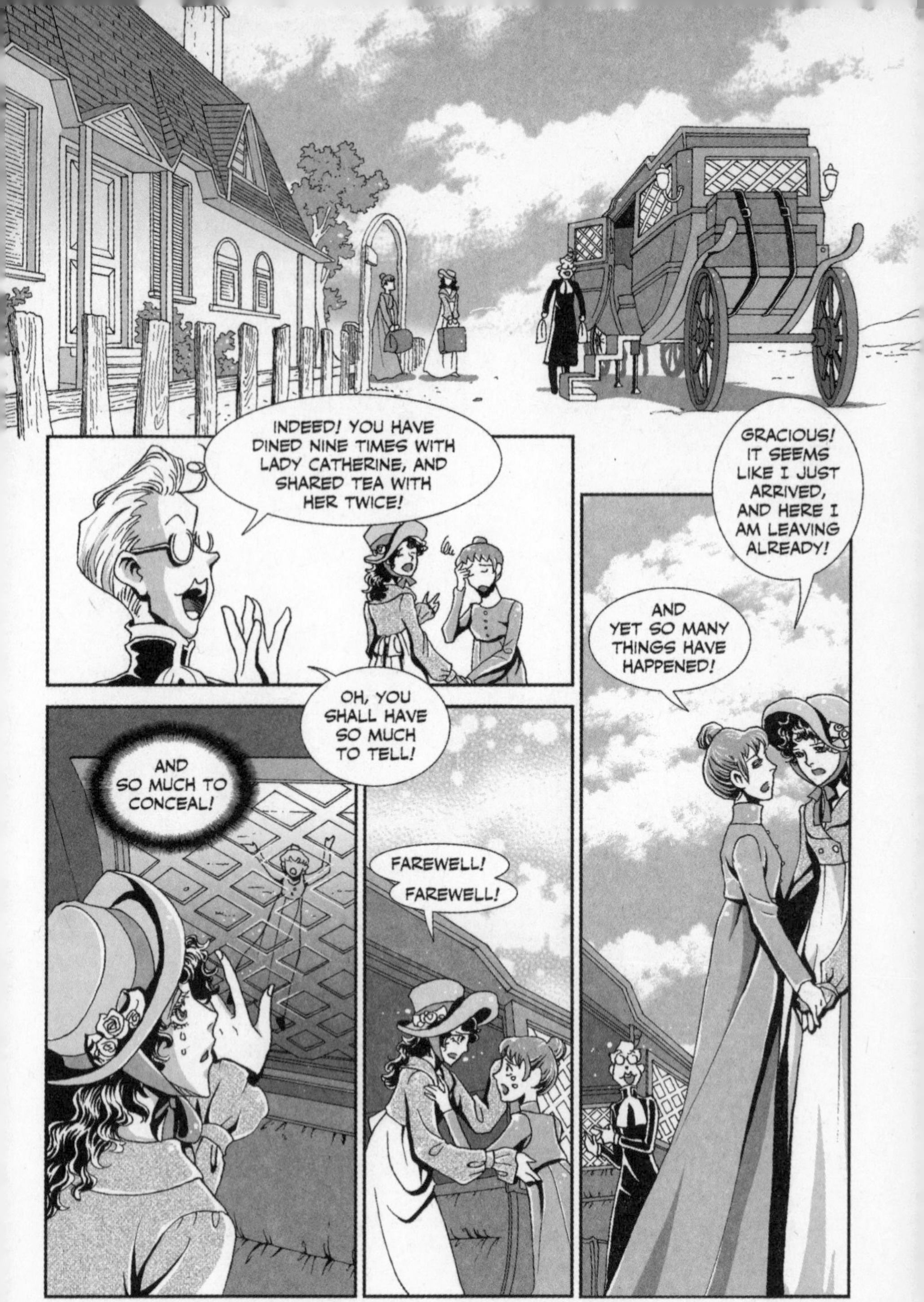
GRACIOUS! IT SEEMS LIKE I JUST ARRIVED, AND HERE I AM LEAVING ALREADY!
AND YET SO MANY THINGS HAVE HAPPENED!
INDEED! YOU HAVE DINED NINE TIMES WITH LADY CATHERINE, AND SHARED TEA WITH HER TWICE!
OH, YOU SHALL HAVE SO MUCH TO TELL!
FAREWELL!
FAREWELL!
AND SO MUCH TO CONCEAL!

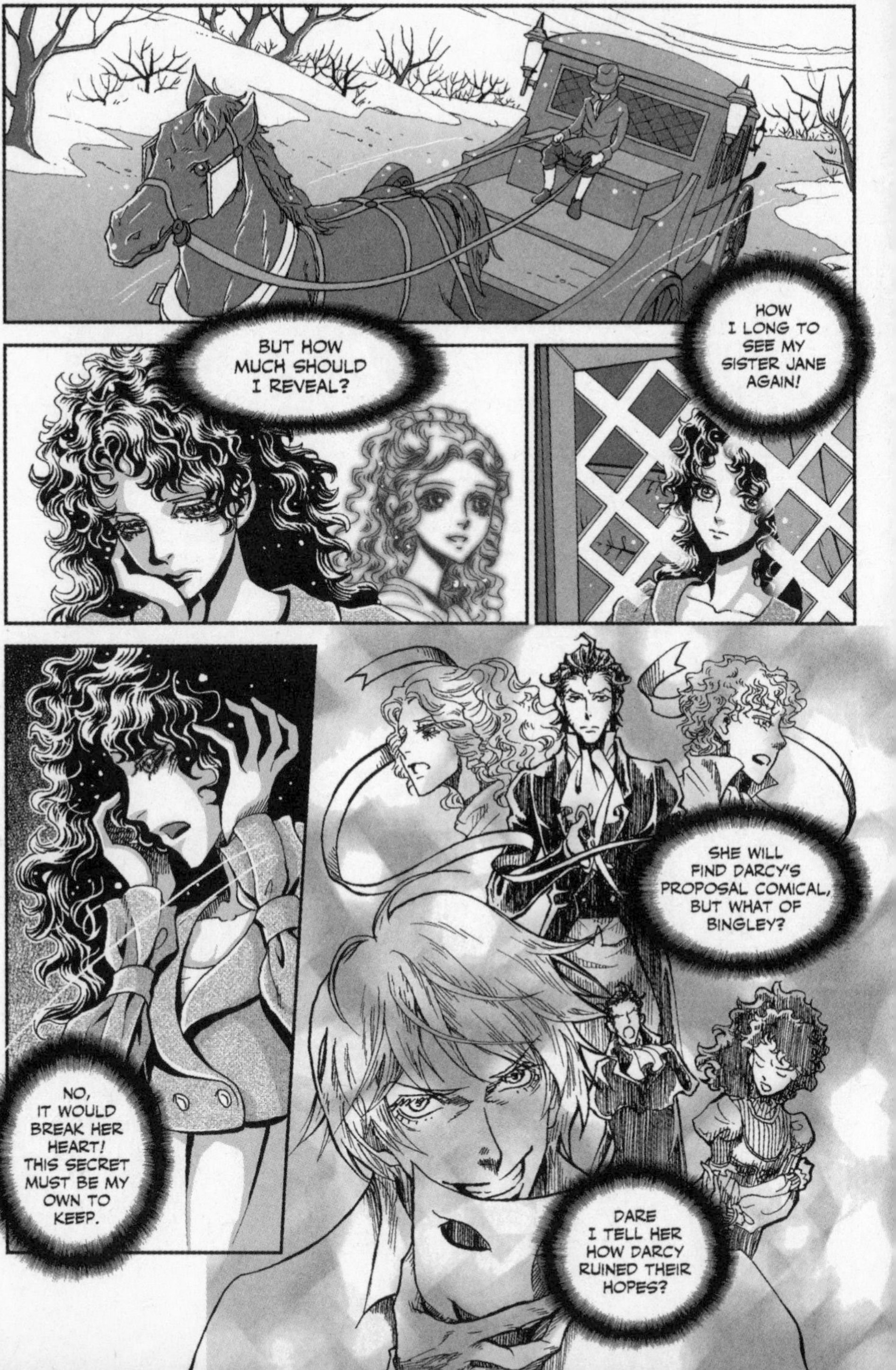
HOW I LONG TO SEE MY SISTER JANE AGAIN!
BUT HOW MUCH SHOULD I REVEAL?
SHE WILL FIND DARCY'S PROPOSAL COMICAL, BUT WHAT OF BINGLEY?
DARE I TELL HER HOW DARCY RUINED THEIR HOPES?
NO, IT WOULD BREAK HER HEART! THIS SECRET MUST BE MY OWN TO KEEP.

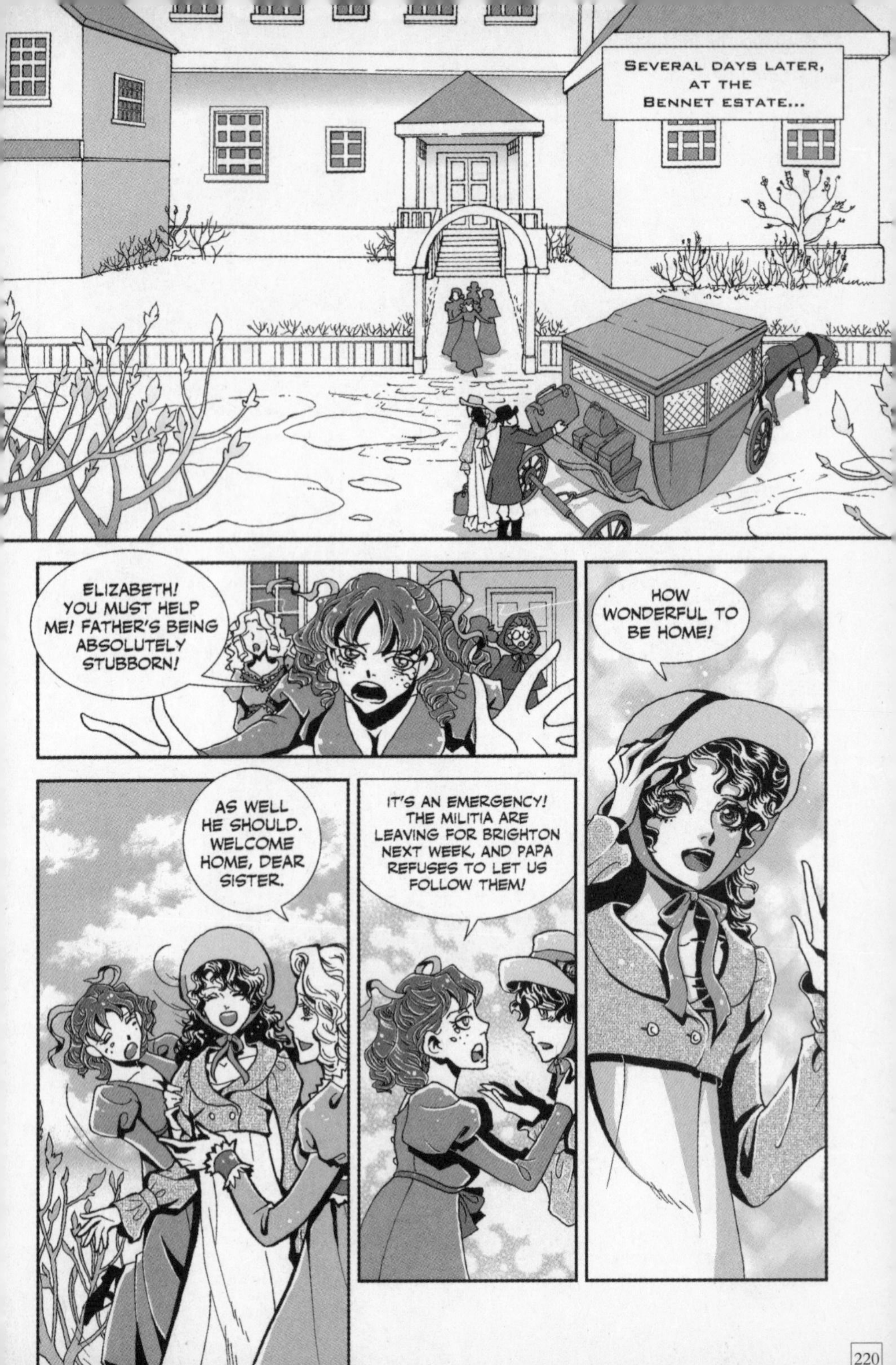
SEVERAL DAYS LATER, AT THE BENNET ESTATE...
HOW WONDERFUL TO BE HOME!
ELIZABETH! YOU MUST HELP ME! FATHER'S BEING ABSOLUTELY STUBBORN!
IT'S AN EMERGENCY! THE MILITIA ARE LEAVING FOR BRIGHTON NEXT WEEK, AND PAPA REFUSES TO LET US FOLLOW THEM!
AS WELL HE SHOULD. WELCOME HOME, DEAR SISTER.

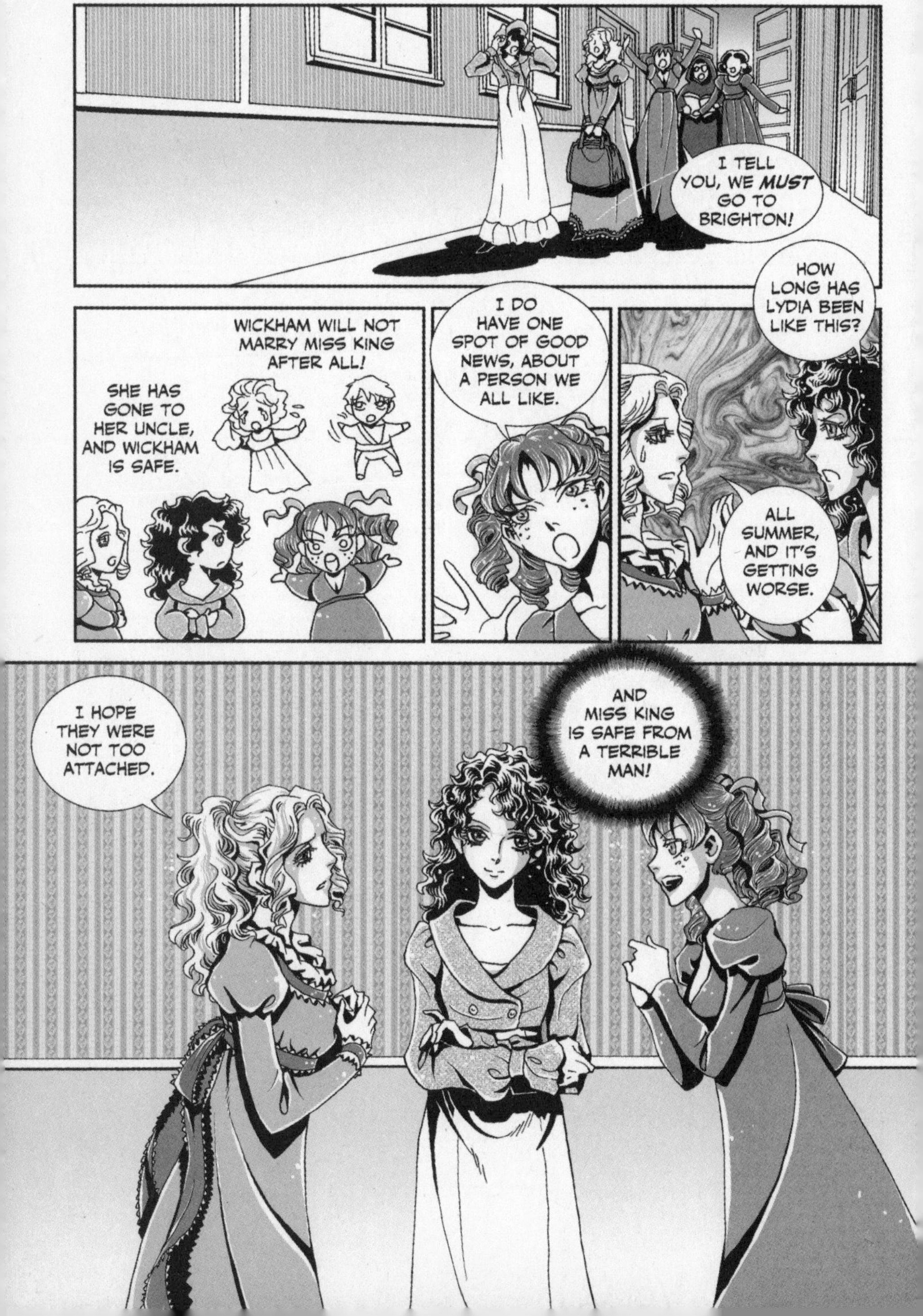
I TELL YOU, WE *MUST* GO TO BRIGHTON!
HOW LONG HAS LYDIA BEEN LIKE THIS?
ALL SUMMER, AND IT'S GETTING WORSE.
I DO HAVE ONE SPOT OF GOOD NEWS, ABOUT A PERSON WE ALL LIKE.
WICKHAM WILL NOT MARRY MISS KING AFTER ALL!
SHE HAS GONE TO HER UNCLE, AND WICKHAM IS SAFE.
I HOPE THEY WERE NOT TOO ATTACHED.
AND MISS KING IS SAFE FROM A TERRIBLE MAN!

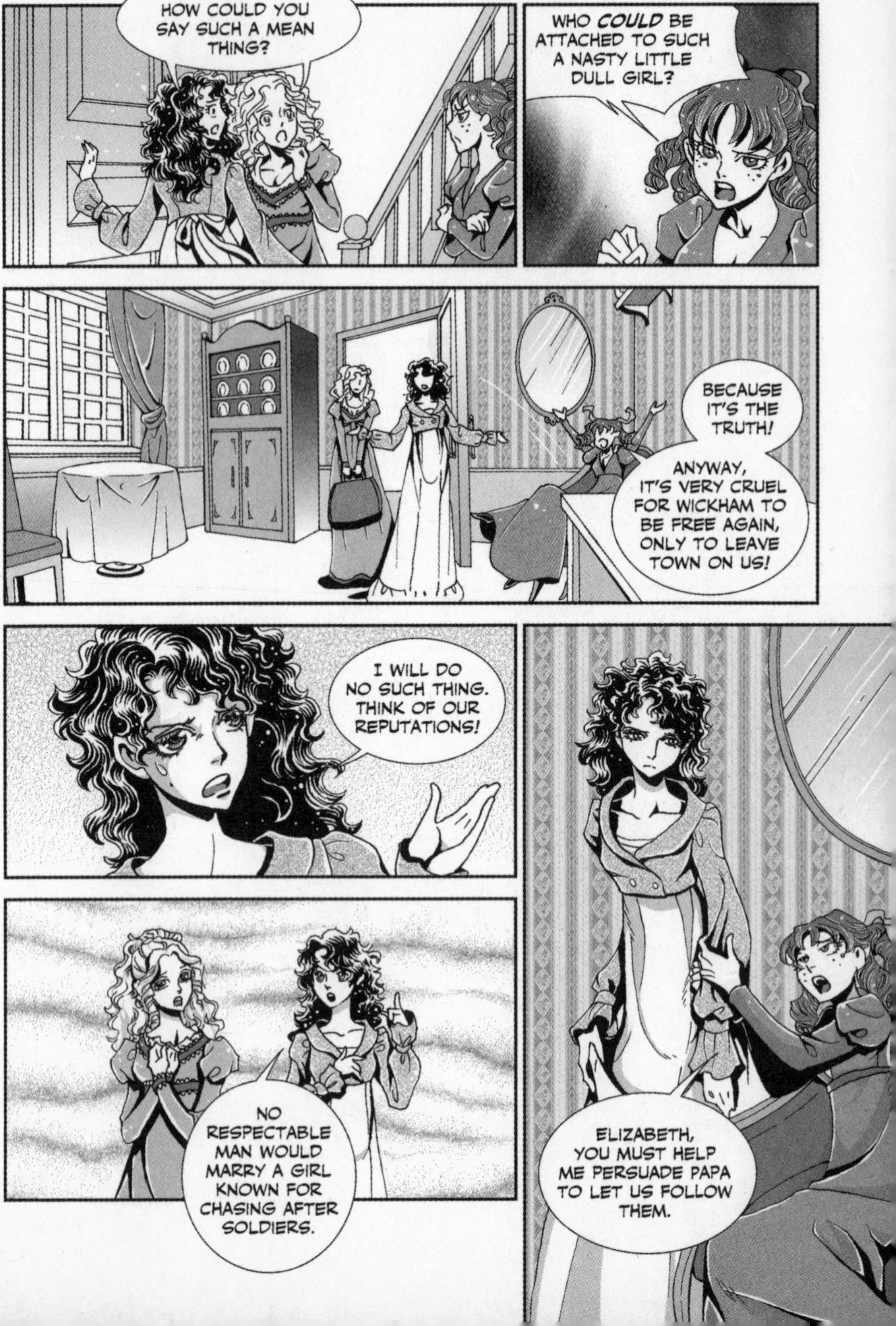
WHO COULD BE ATTACHED TO SUCH A NASTY LITTLE DULL GIRL?
LYDIA! HOW COULD YOU SAY SUCH A MEAN THING?
BECAUSE IT'S THE TRUTH!
ANYWAY, IT'S VERY CRUEL FOR WICKHAM TO BE FREE AGAIN, ONLY TO LEAVE TOWN ON US!
ELIZABETH, YOU MUST HELP ME PERSUADE PAPA TO LET US FOLLOW THEM.
I WILL DO NO SUCH THING. THINK OF OUR REPUTATIONS!
NO RESPECTABLE MAN WOULD MARRY A GIRL KNOWN FOR CHASING AFTER SOLDIERS.

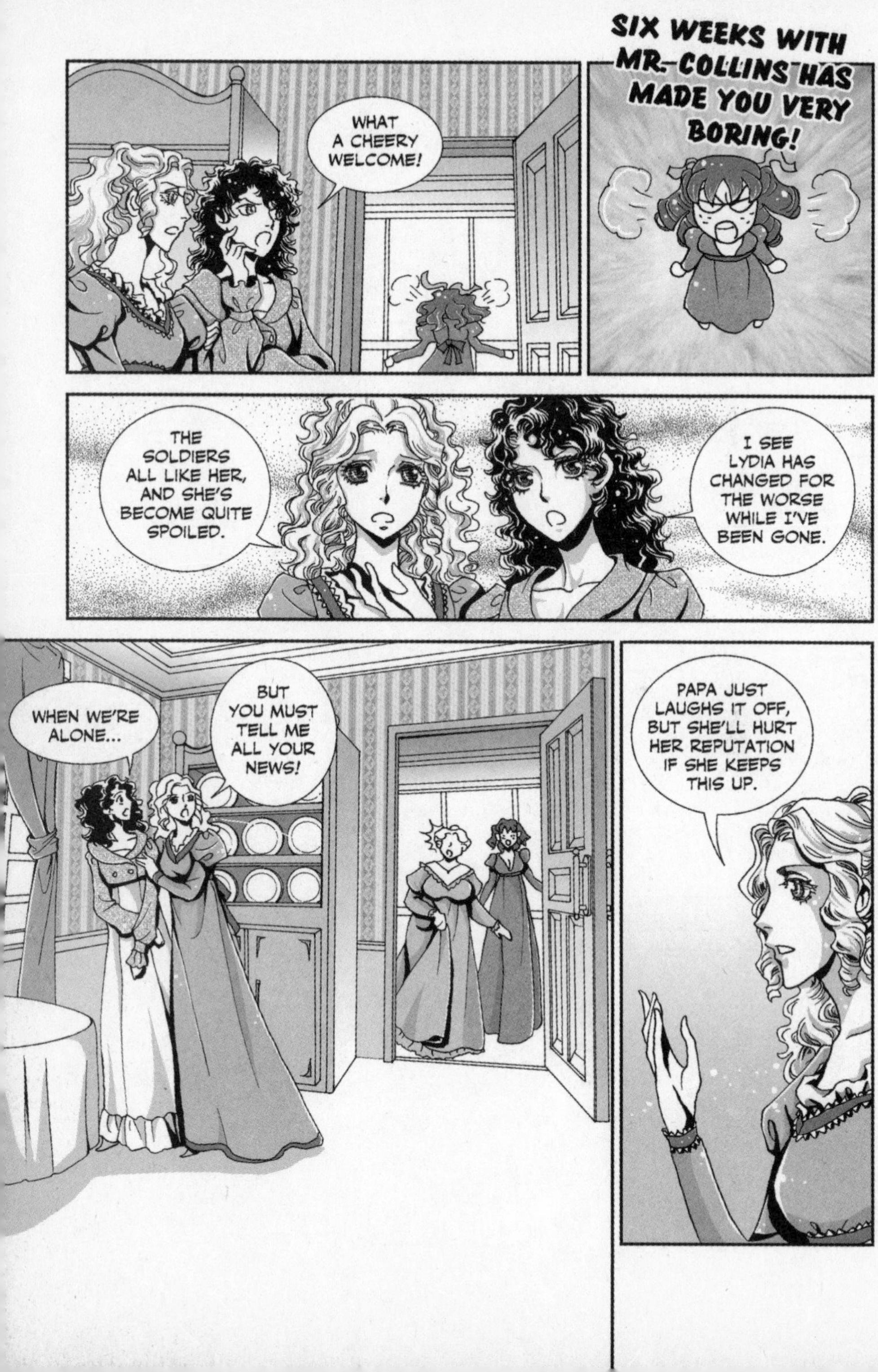
SIX WEEKS WITH MR. COLLINS HAS MADE YOU VERY BORING!
WHAT A CHEERY WELCOME!
I SEE LYDIA HAS CHANGED FOR THE WORSE WHILE I'VE BEEN GONE.
THE SOLDIERS ALL LIKE HER, AND SHE'S BECOME QUITE SPOILED.
PAPA JUST LAUGHS IT OFF, BUT SHE'LL HURT HER REPUTATION IF SHE KEEPS THIS UP.
BUT YOU MUST TELL ME ALL YOUR NEWS!
WHEN WE'RE ALONE...

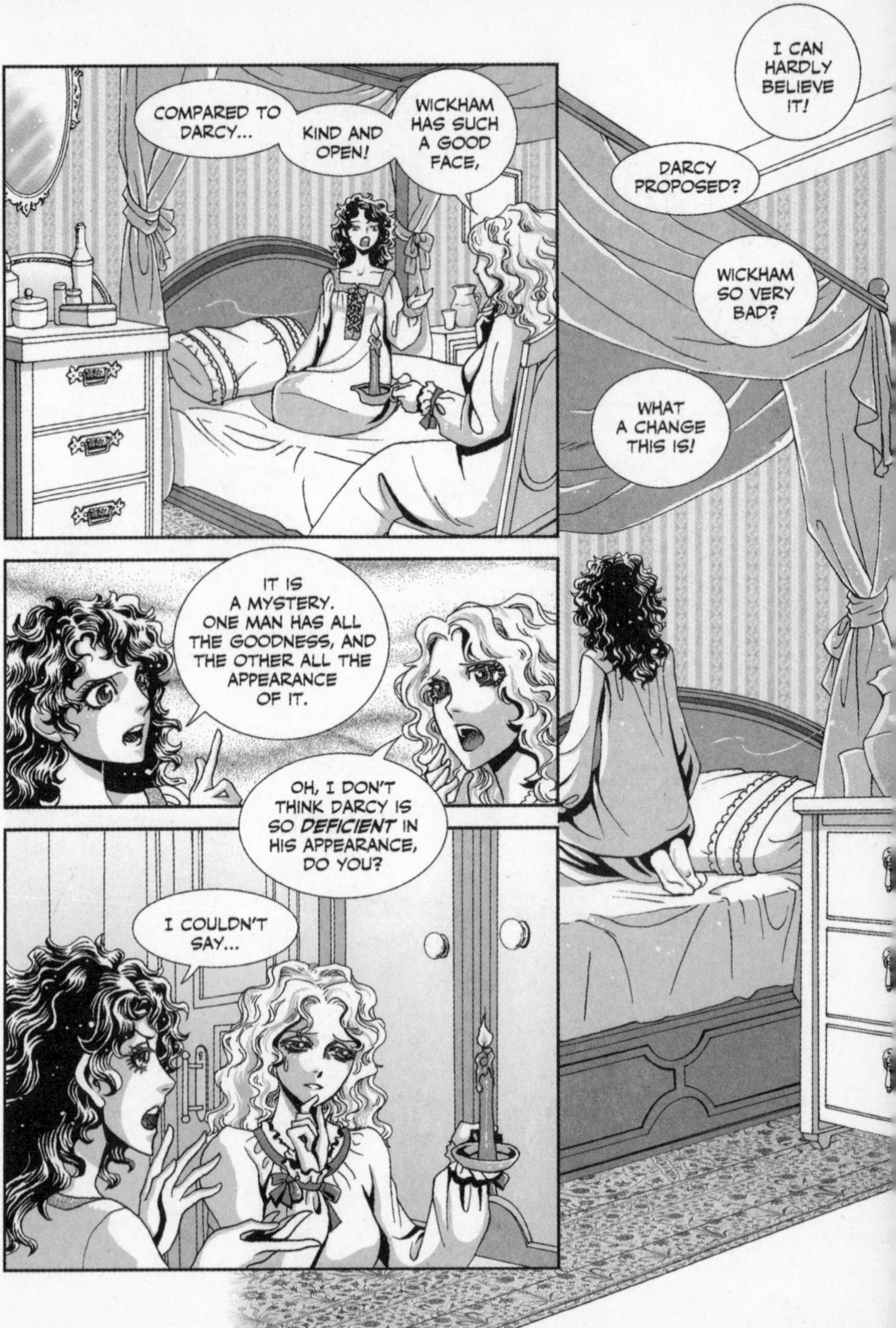
I CAN HARDLY BELIEVE IT!
DARCY PROPOSED?
WICKHAM SO VERY BAD?
WHAT A CHANGE THIS IS!
WICKHAM HAS SUCH A GOOD FACE,
KIND AND OPEN!
COMPARED TO DARCY...
IT IS A MYSTERY. ONE MAN HAS ALL THE GOODNESS, AND THE OTHER ALL THE APPEARANCE OF IT.
OH, I DON'T THINK DARCY IS SO *DEFICIENT* IN HIS APPEARANCE, DO YOU?
I COULDN'T SAY...

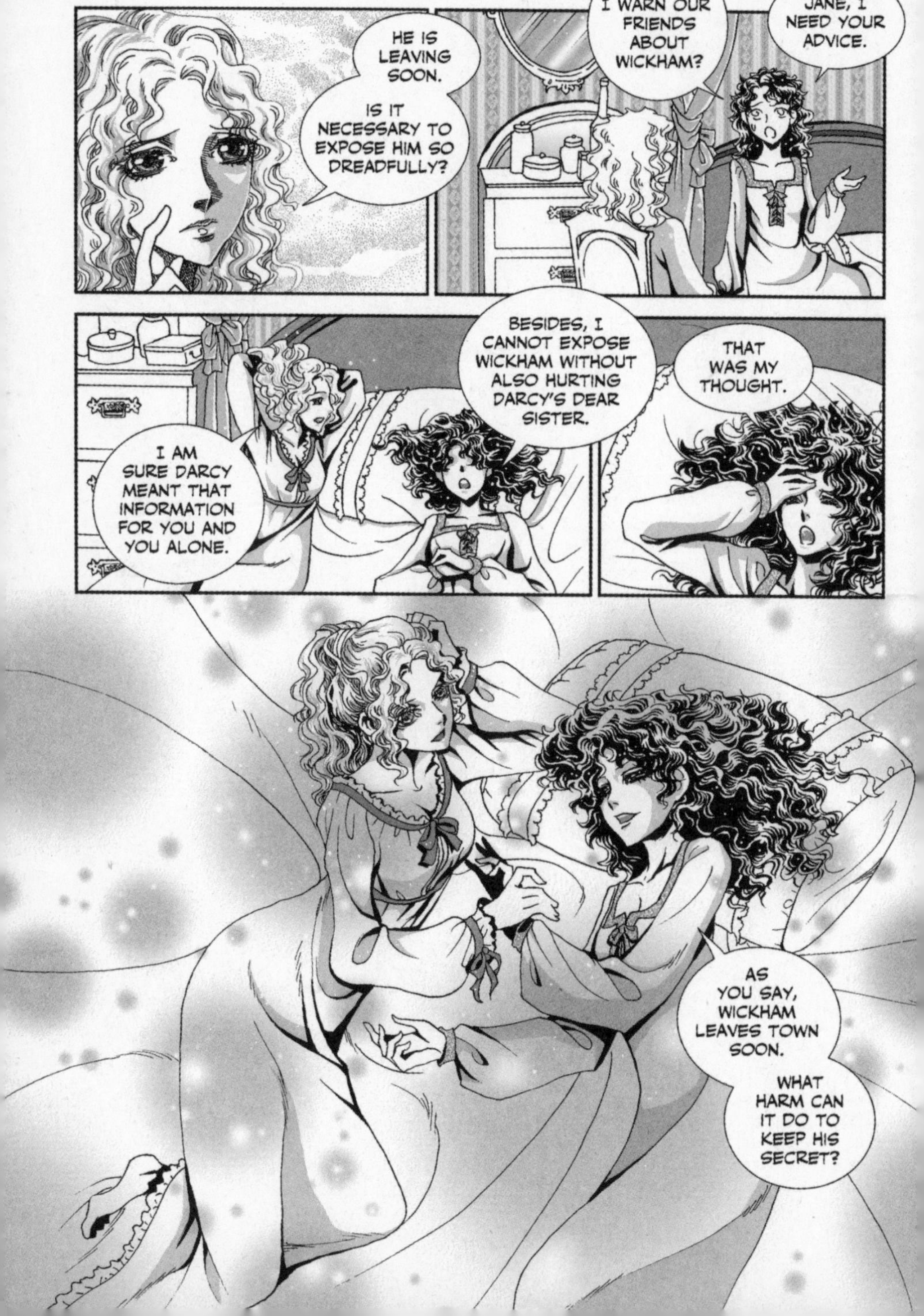
JANE, I NEED YOUR ADVICE.
SHOULD I WARN OUR FRIENDS ABOUT WICKHAM?
HE IS LEAVING SOON.
IS IT NECESSARY TO EXPOSE HIM SO DREADFULLY?
THAT WAS MY THOUGHT.
BESIDES, I CANNOT EXPOSE WICKHAM WITHOUT ALSO HURTING DARCY'S DEAR SISTER.
I AM SURE DARCY MEANT THAT INFORMATION FOR YOU AND YOU ALONE.
AS YOU SAY, WICKHAM LEAVES TOWN SOON.
WHAT HARM CAN IT DO TO KEEP HIS SECRET?

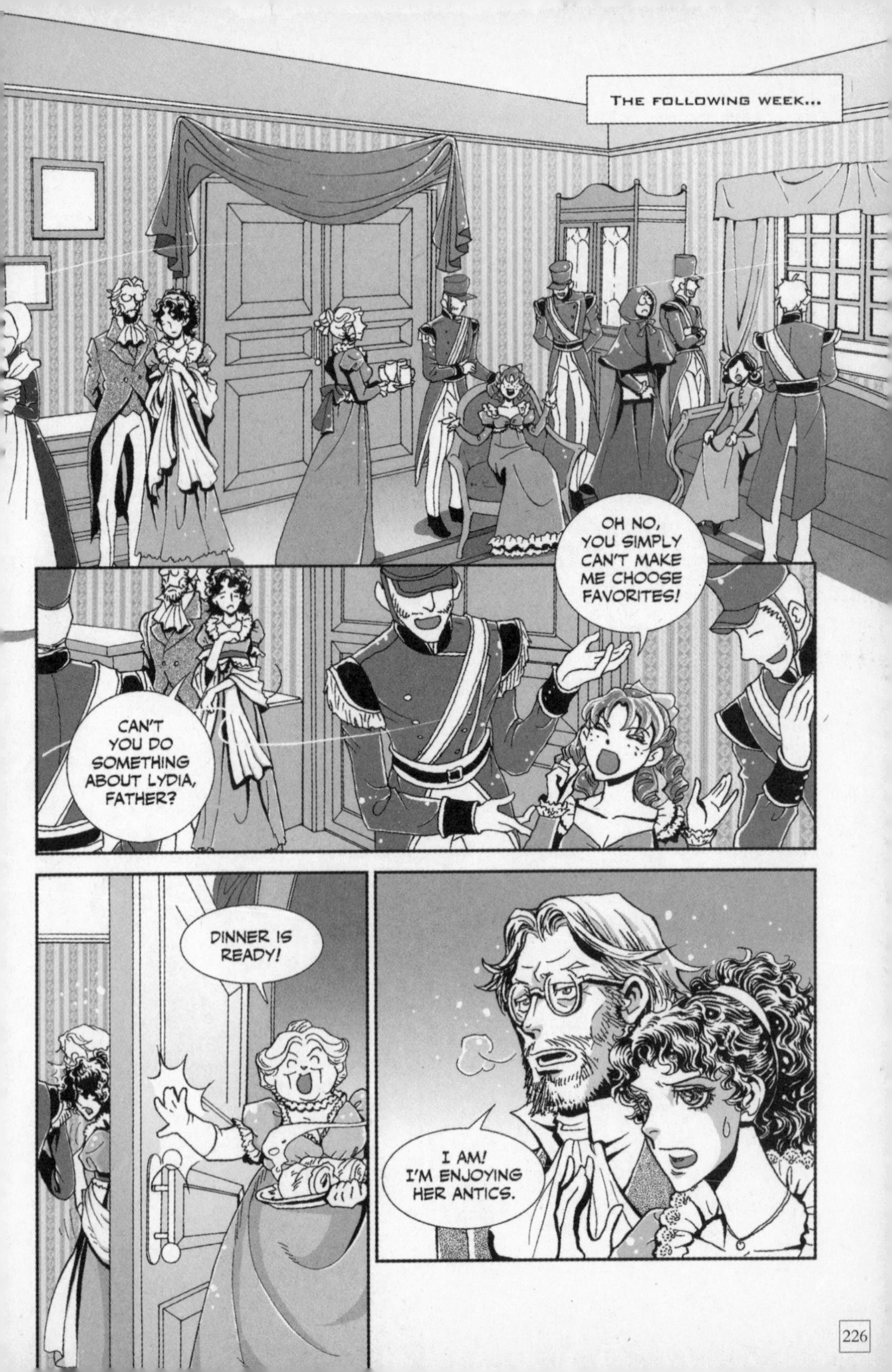
THE FOLLOWING WEEK...
OH NO, YOU SIMPLY CAN'T MAKE ME CHOOSE FAVORITES!
CAN'T YOU DO SOMETHING ABOUT LYDIA, FATHER?
I AM! I'M ENJOYING HER ANTICS.
DINNER IS READY!

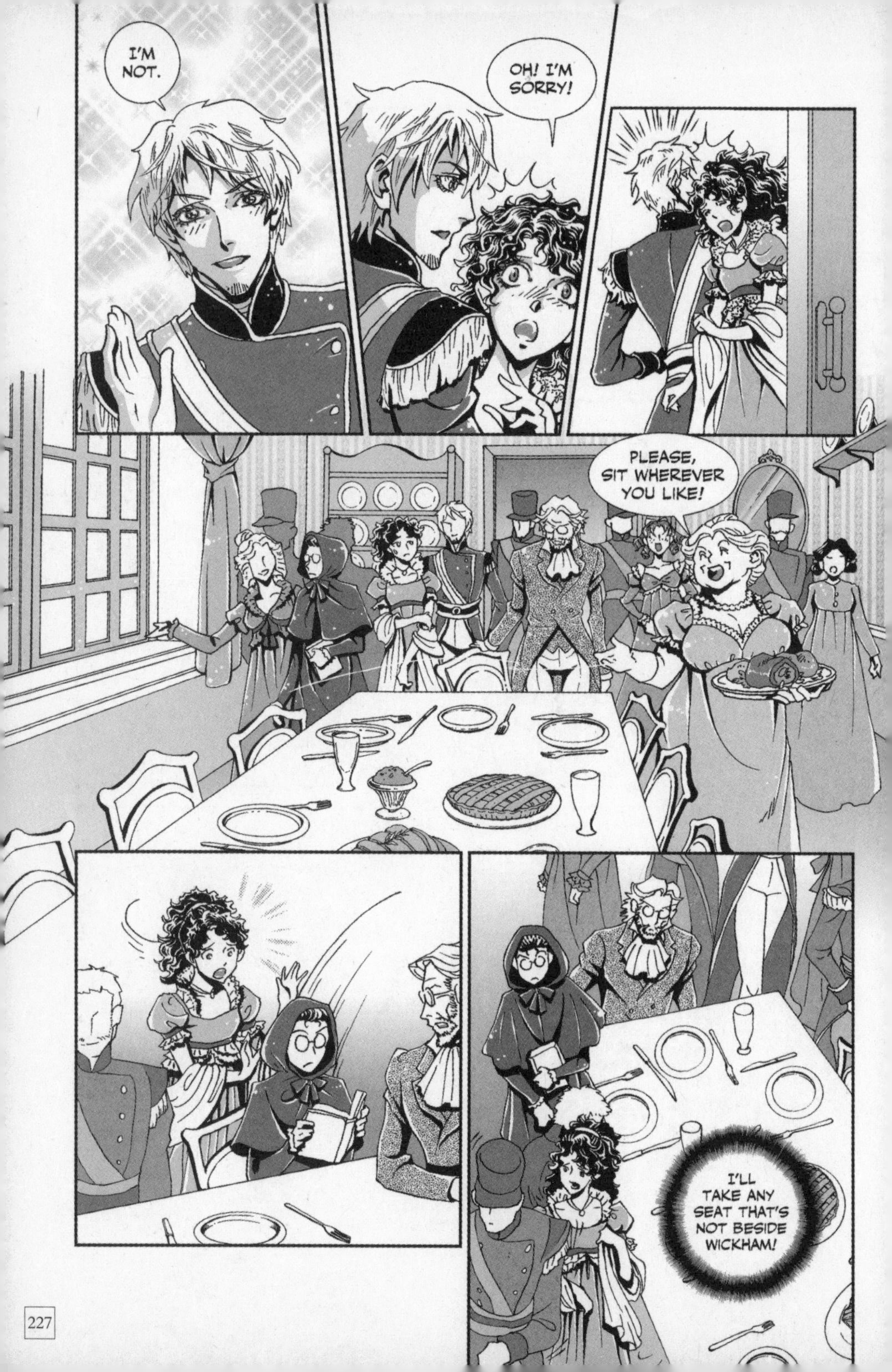
OH! I'M SORRY!
I'M NOT.
PLEASE, SIT WHEREVER YOU LIKE!
I'LL TAKE ANY SEAT THAT'S NOT BESIDE WICKHAM!

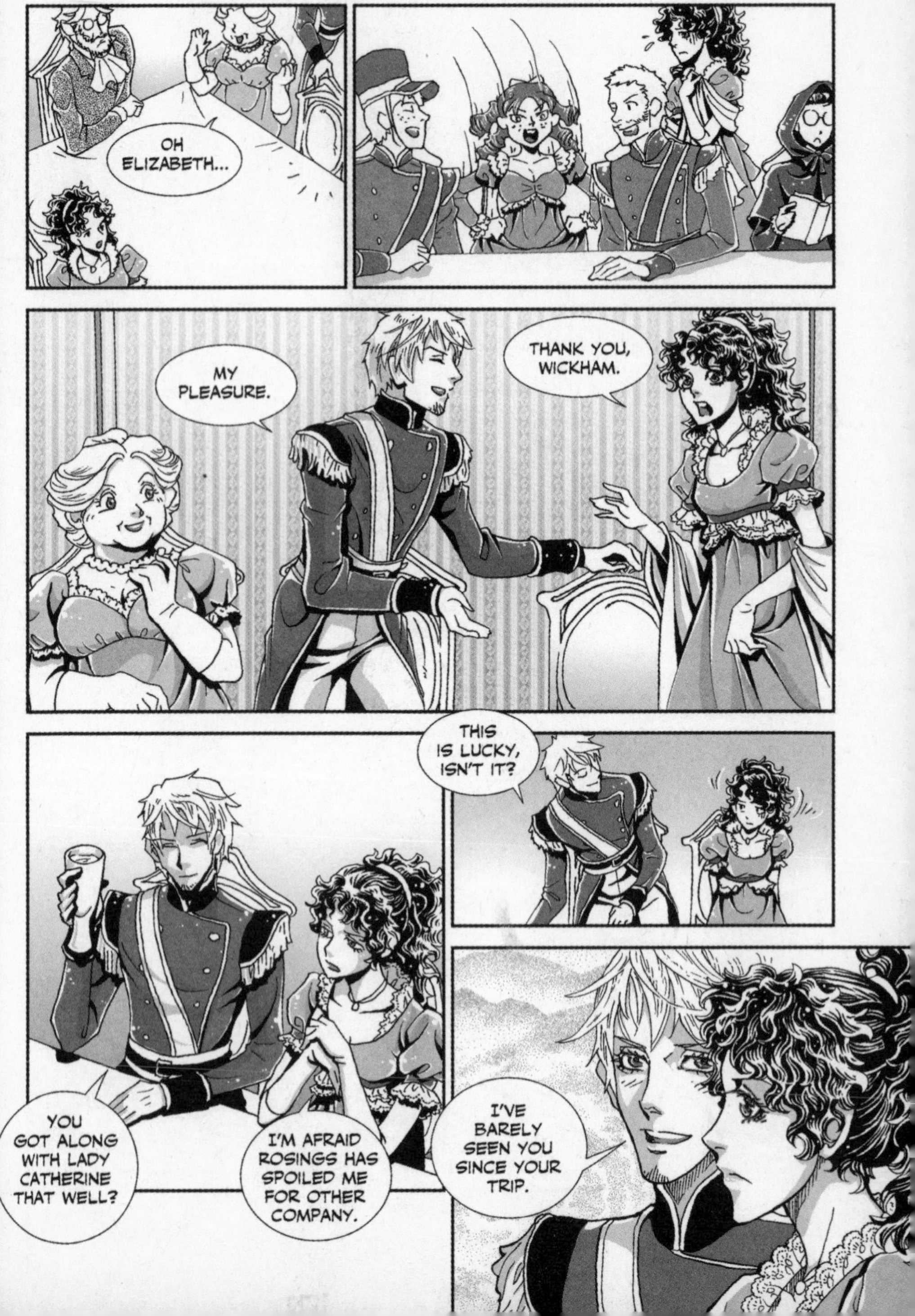
OH ELIZABETH...
THANK YOU, WICKHAM.
MY PLEASURE.
THIS IS LUCKY, ISN'T IT?
I'VE BARELY SEEN YOU SINCE YOUR TRIP.
I'M AFRAID ROSINGS HAS SPOILED ME FOR OTHER COMPANY.
YOU GOT ALONG WITH LADY CATHERINE THAT WELL?

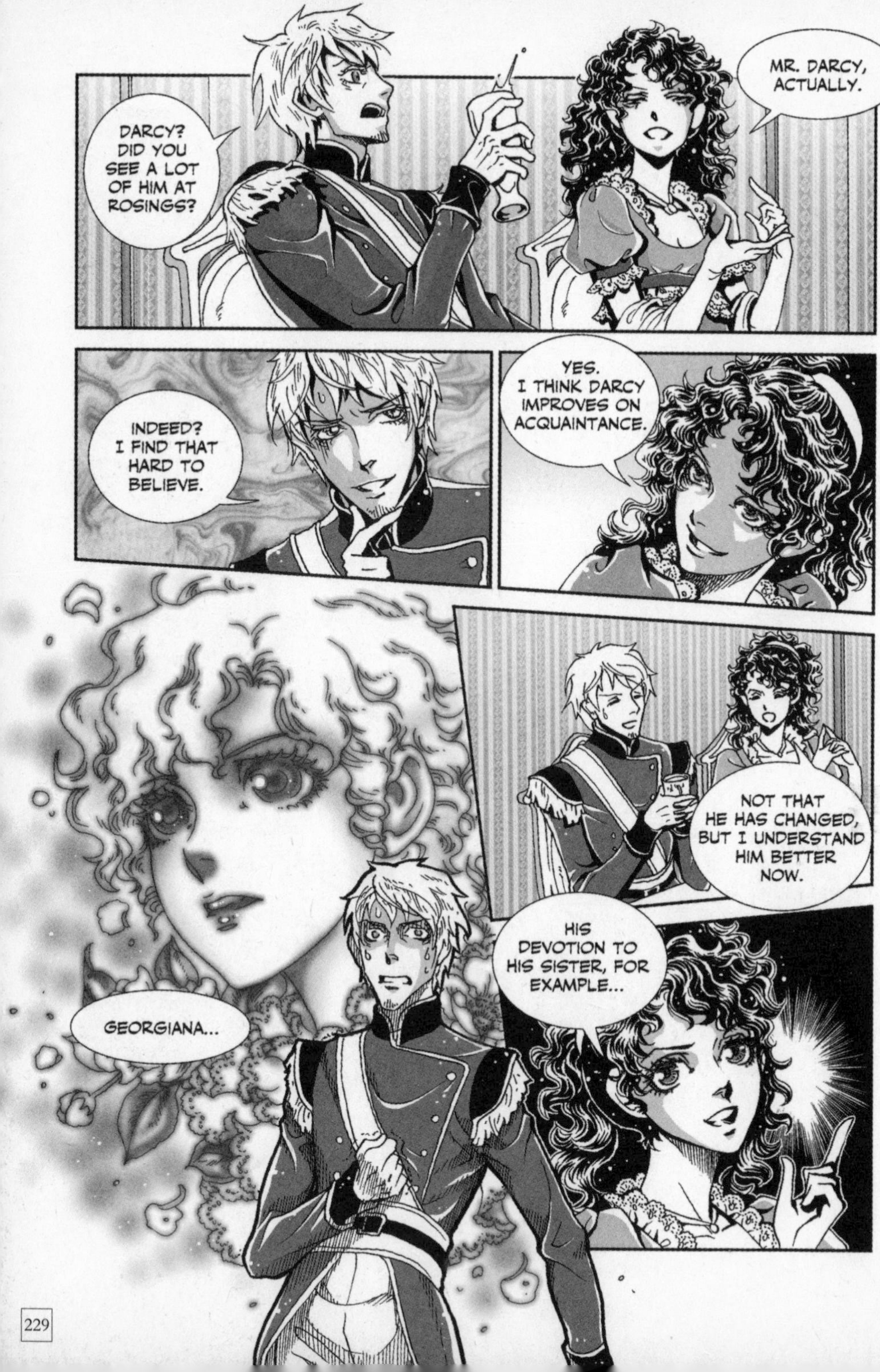

MR. DARCY, ACTUALLY.
DARCY? DID YOU SEE A LOT OF HIM AT ROSINGS?
YES. I THINK DARCY IMPROVES ON ACQUAINTANCE.
INDEED? I FIND THAT HARD TO BELIEVE.
NOT THAT HE HAS CHANGED, BUT I UNDERSTAND HIM BETTER NOW.
HIS DEVOTION TO HIS SISTER, FOR EXAMPLE...
GEORGIANA...

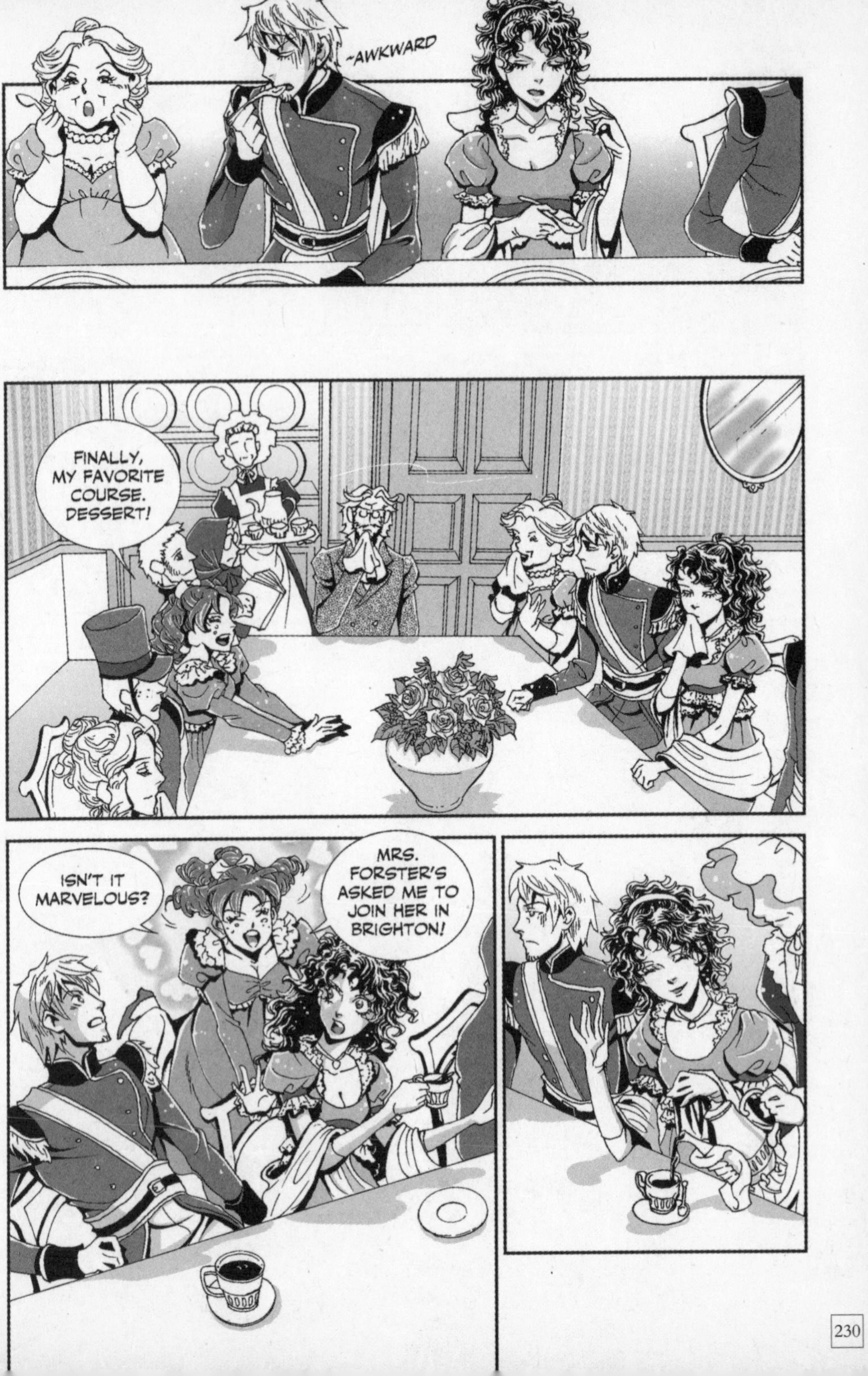
~AWKWARD
FINALLY, MY FAVORITE COURSE. DESSERT!
MRS. FORSTER'S ASKED ME TO JOIN HER IN BRIGHTON!
ISN'T IT MARVELOUS?

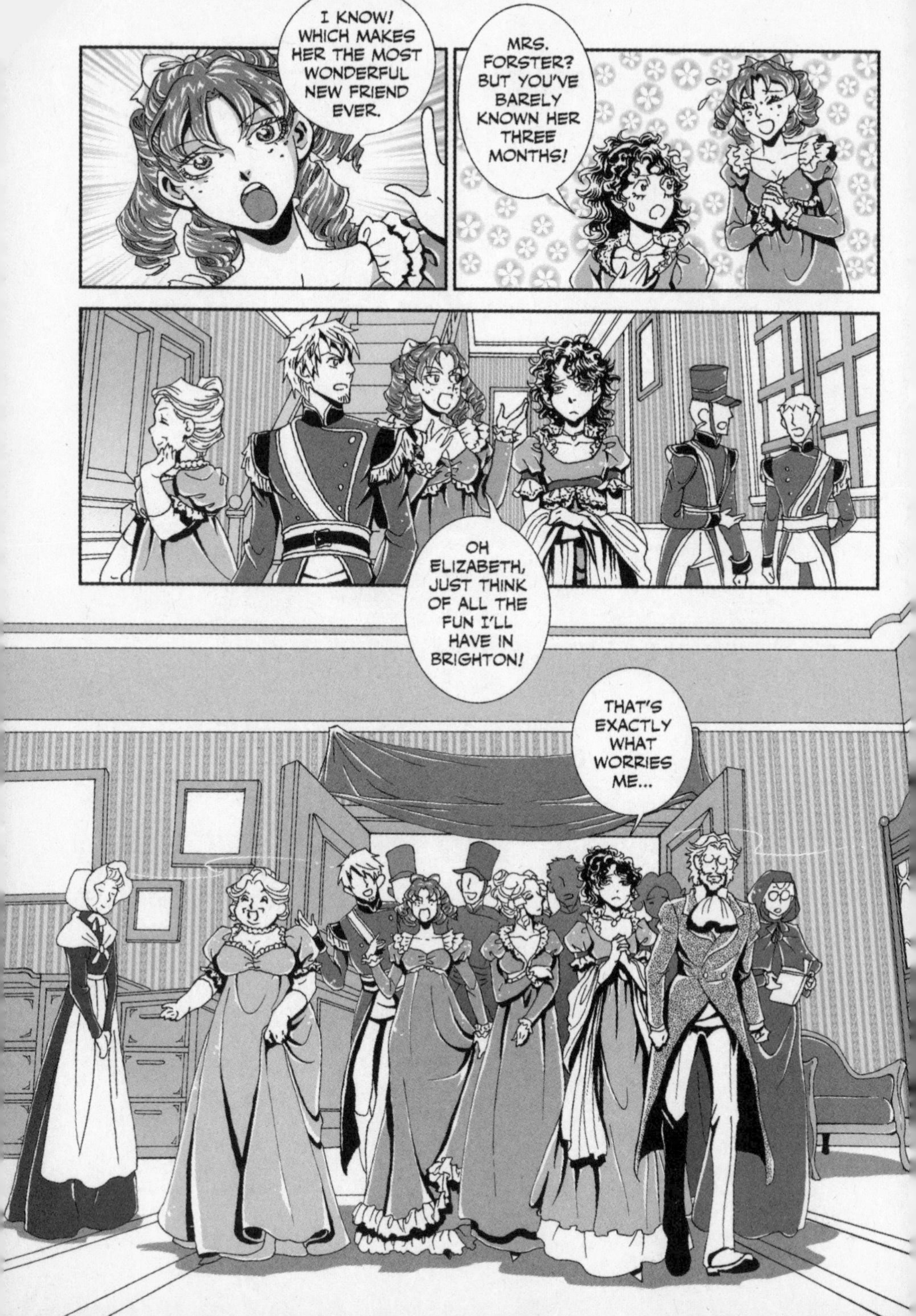
MRS. FORSTER? BUT YOU'VE BARELY KNOWN HER THREE MONTHS!
I KNOW! WHICH MAKES HER THE MOST WONDERFUL NEW FRIEND EVER.
OH ELIZABETH, JUST THINK OF ALL THE FUN I'LL HAVE IN BRIGHTON!
THAT'S EXACTLY WHAT WORRIES ME...

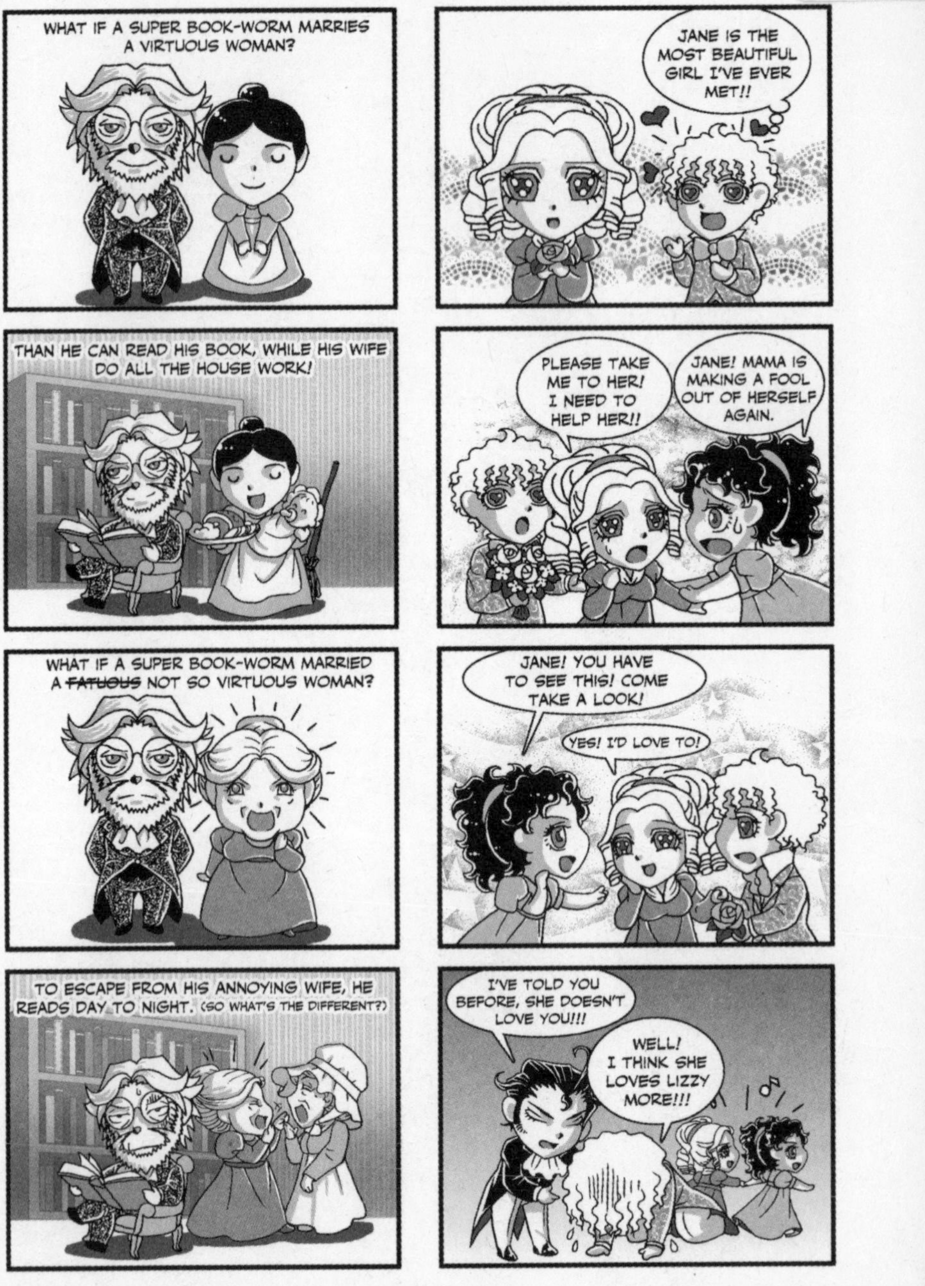

JANE IS THE MOST BEAUTIFUL GIRL I'VE EVER MET!!
JANE! MAMA IS MAKING A FOOL OUT OF HERSELF AGAIN.
PLEASE TAKE ME TO HER! I NEED TO HELP HER!!
JANE! YOU HAVE TO SEE THIS! COME TAKE A LOOK!
YES! I'D LOVE TO!
I'VE TOLD YOU BEFORE, SHE DOESN'T LOVE YOU!!!
WELL! I THINK SHE LOVES LIZZY MORE!!!
WHAT IF A SUPER BOOK-WORM MARRIES A VIRTUOUS WOMAN?
THAN HE CAN READ HIS BOOK, WHILE HIS WIFE DO ALL THE HOUSE WORK!
WHAT IF A SUPER BOOK-WORM MARRIED A ~~FATUOUS~~ NOT SO VIRTUOUS WOMAN?
TO ESCAPE FROM HIS ANNOYING WIFE, HE READS DAY TO NIGHT. (SO WHAT'S THE DIFFERENT?)

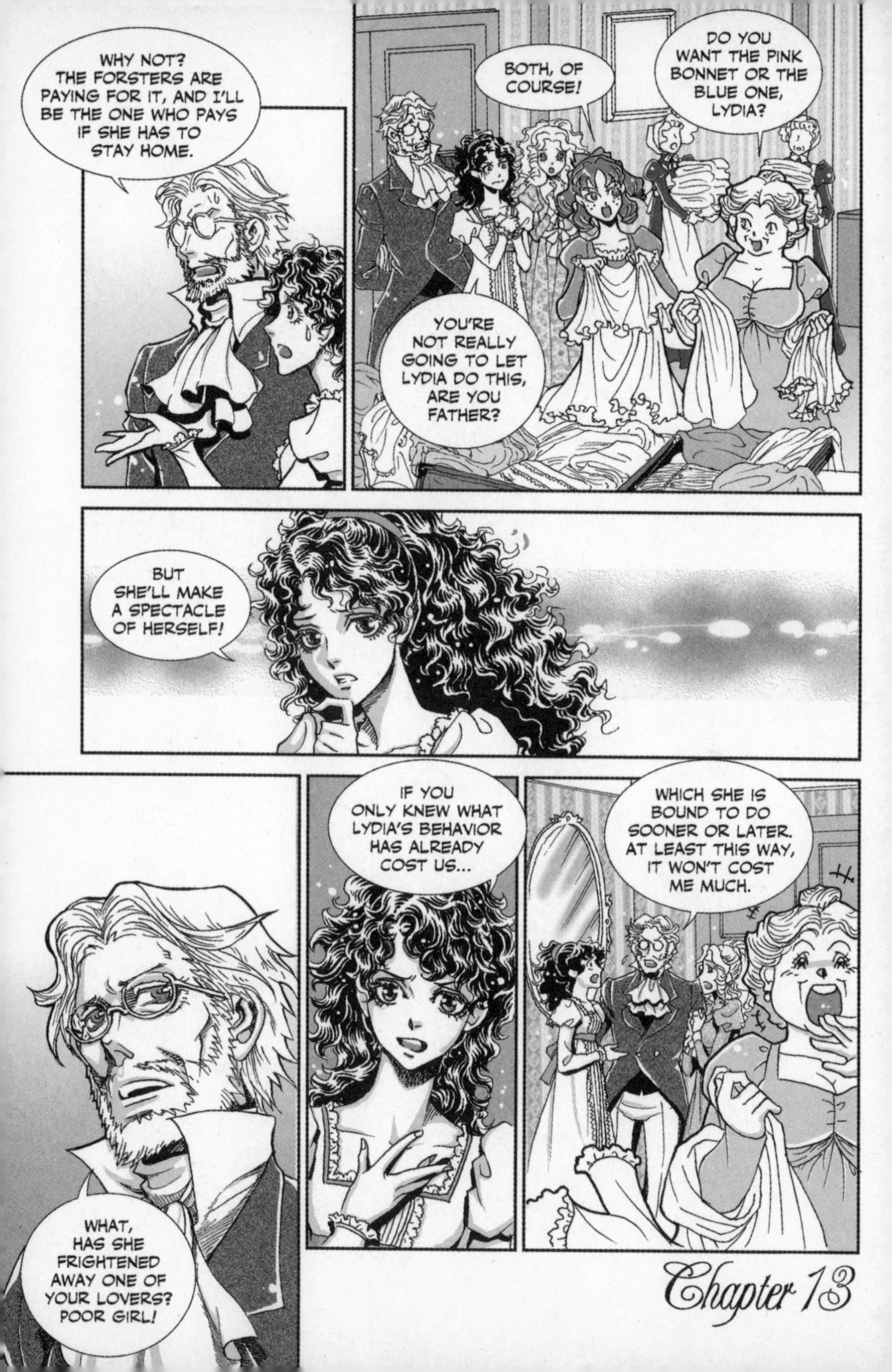
DO YOU WANT THE PINK BONNET OR THE BLUE ONE, LYDIA?
BOTH, OF COURSE!
YOU'RE NOT REALLY GOING TO LET LYDIA DO THIS, ARE YOU FATHER?
WHY NOT? THE FORSTERS ARE PAYING FOR IT, AND I'LL BE THE ONE WHO PAYS IF SHE HAS TO STAY HOME.
BUT SHE'LL MAKE A SPECTACLE OF HERSELF!
WHICH SHE IS BOUND TO DO SOONER OR LATER. AT LEAST THIS WAY, IT WON'T COST ME MUCH.
IF YOU ONLY KNEW WHAT LYDIA'S BEHAVIOR HAS ALREADY COST US...
WHAT, HAS SHE FRIGHTENED AWAY ONE OF YOUR LOVERS? POOR GIRL!

Chapter 13

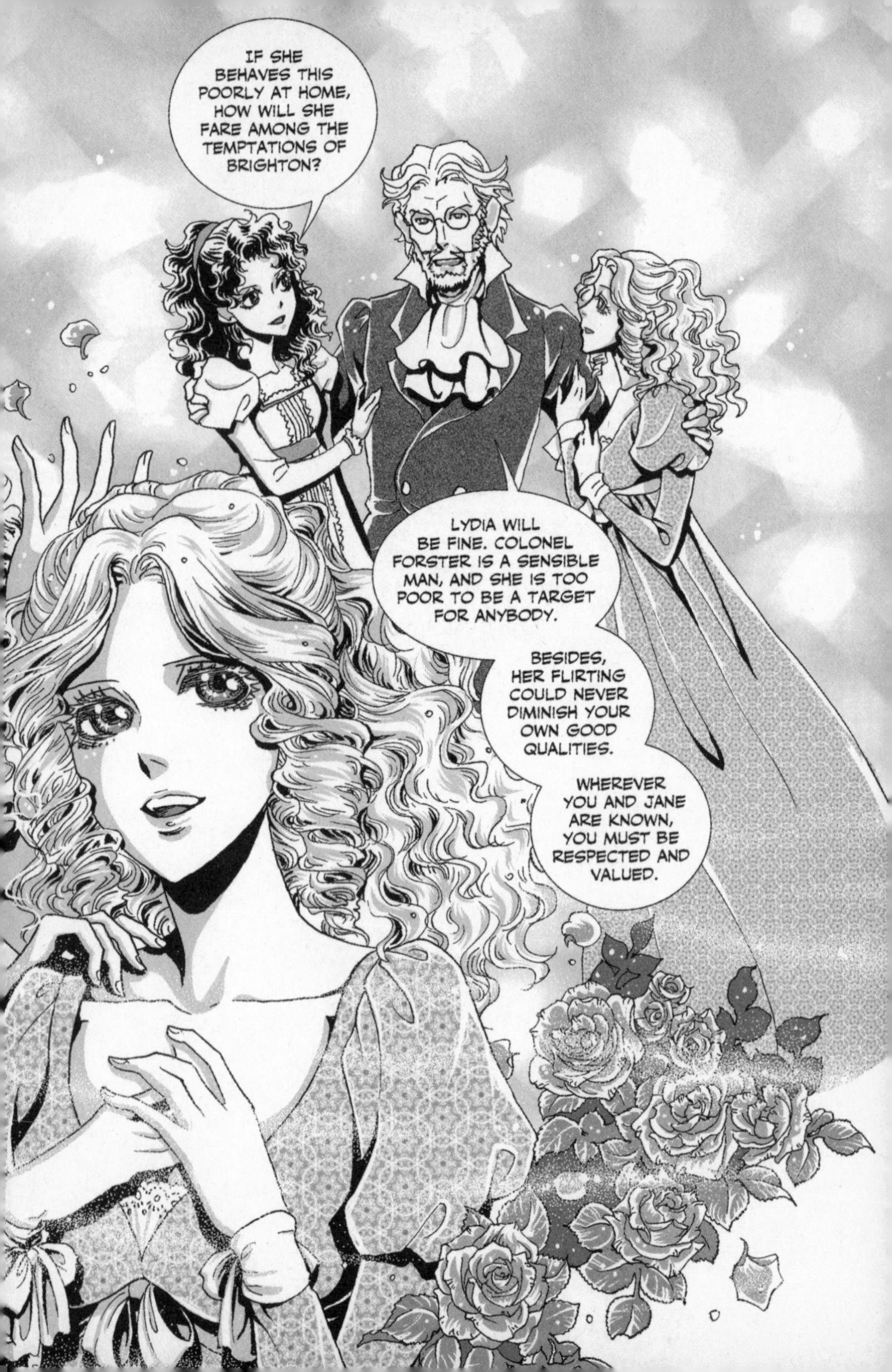
IF SHE BEHAVES THIS POORLY AT HOME, HOW WILL SHE FARE AMONG THE TEMPTATIONS OF BRIGHTON?
LYDIA WILL BE FINE. COLONEL FORSTER IS A SENSIBLE MAN, AND SHE IS TOO POOR TO BE A TARGET FOR ANYBODY.
BESIDES, HER FLIRTING COULD NEVER DIMINISH YOUR OWN GOOD QUALITIES.
WHEREVER YOU AND JANE ARE KNOWN, YOU MUST BE RESPECTED AND VALUED.

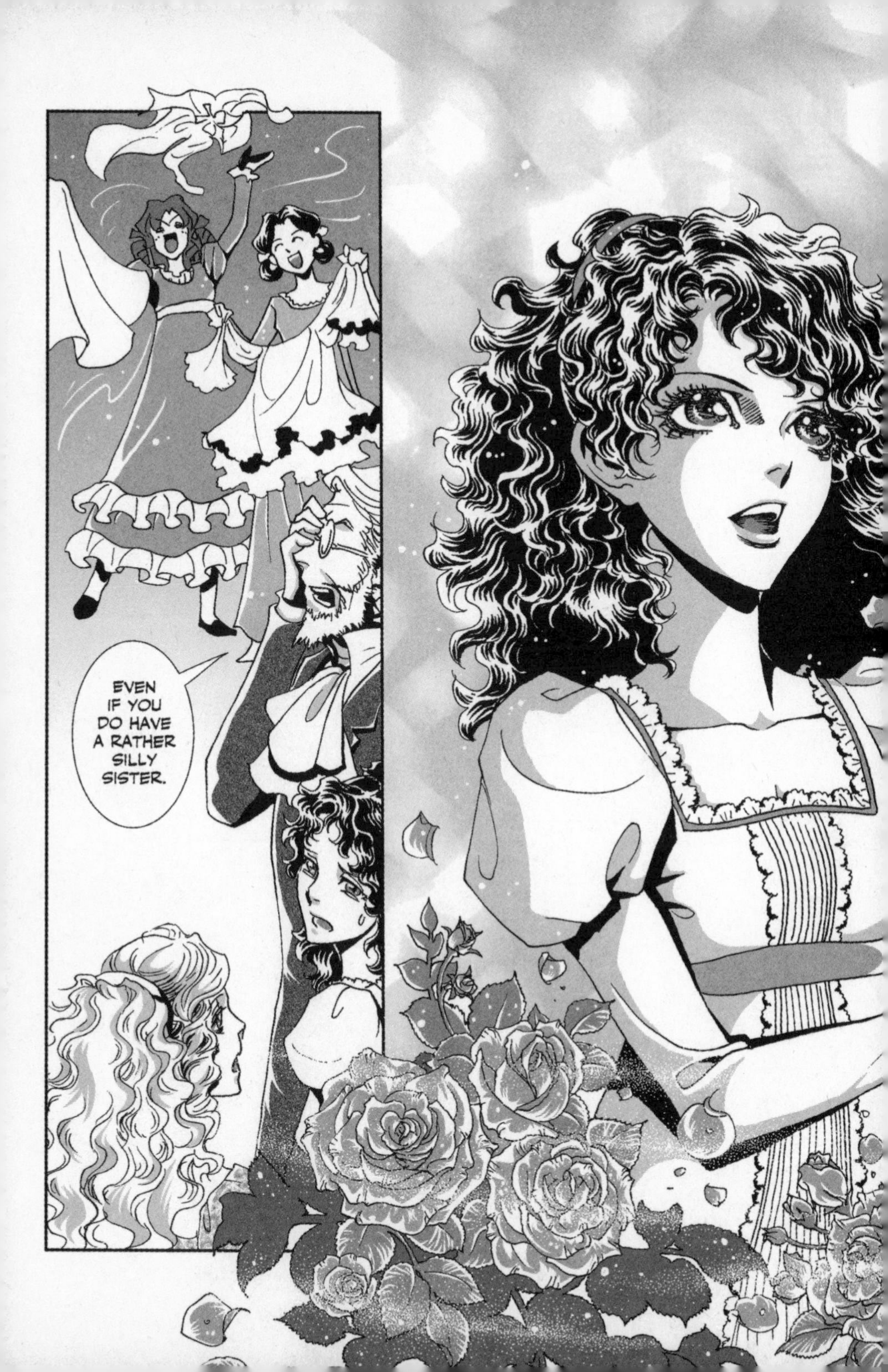
EVEN IF YOU DO HAVE A RATHER SILLY SISTER.

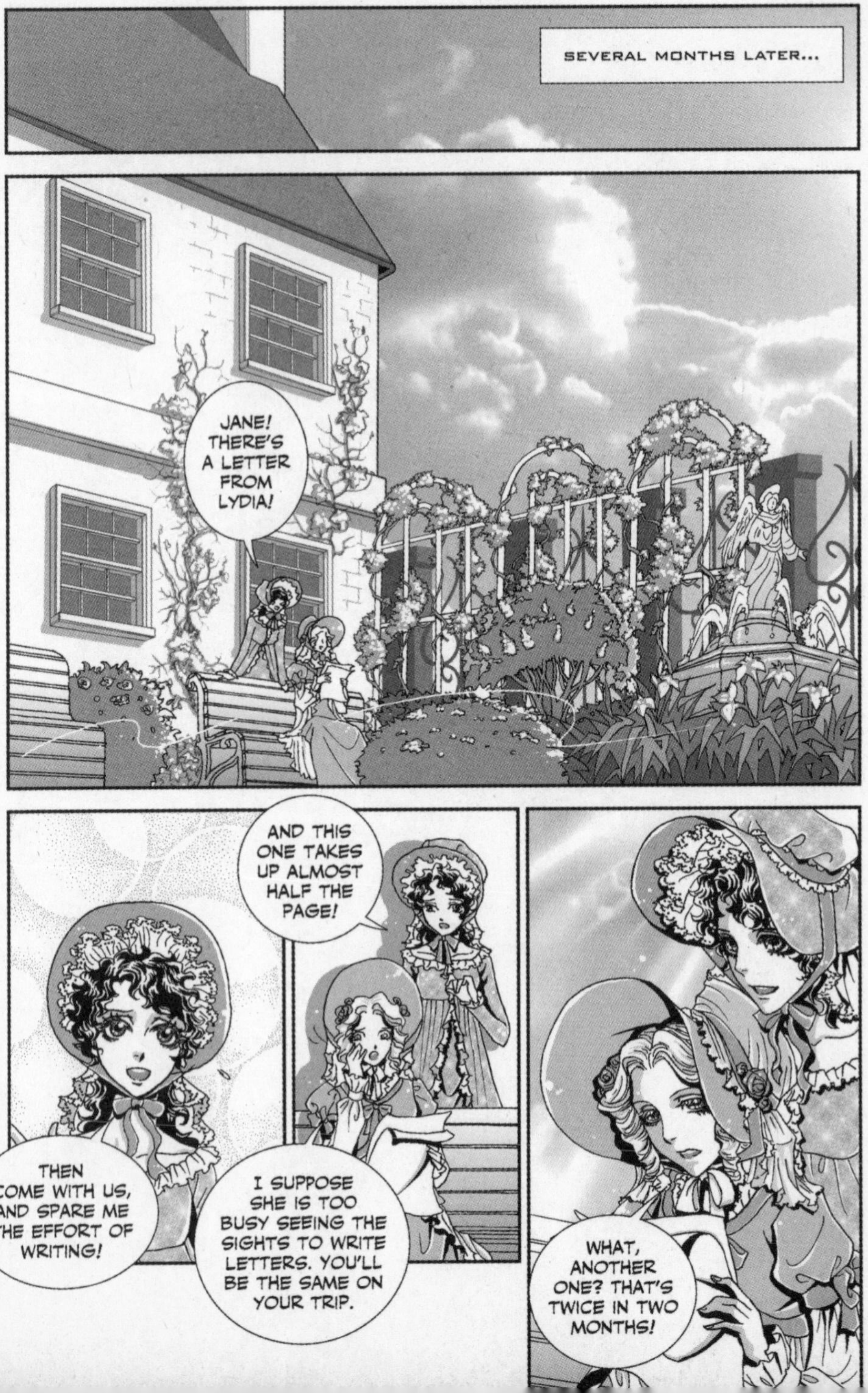
SEVERAL MONTHS LATER...
JANE! THERE'S A LETTER FROM LYDIA!
WHAT, ANOTHER ONE? THAT'S TWICE IN TWO MONTHS!
AND THIS ONE TAKES UP ALMOST HALF THE PAGE!
I SUPPOSE SHE IS TOO BUSY SEEING THE SIGHTS TO WRITE LETTERS. YOU'LL BE THE SAME ON YOUR TRIP.
THEN COME WITH US, AND SPARE ME THE EFFORT OF WRITING!

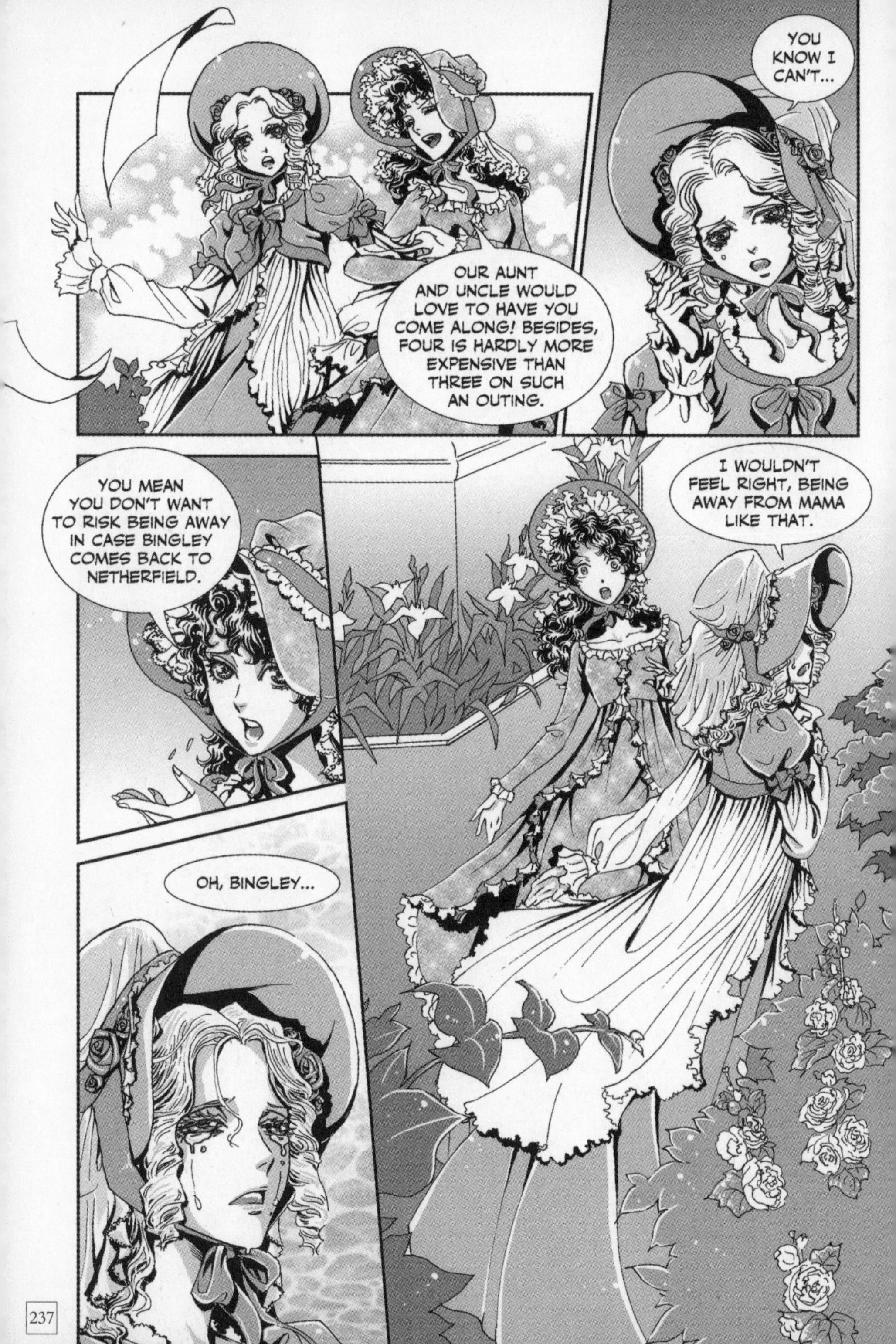
YOU KNOW I CAN'T...
OUR AUNT AND UNCLE WOULD LOVE TO HAVE YOU COME ALONG! BESIDES, FOUR IS HARDLY MORE EXPENSIVE THAN THREE ON SUCH AN OUTING.
I WOULDN'T FEEL RIGHT, BEING AWAY FROM MAMA LIKE THAT.
YOU MEAN YOU DON'T WANT TO RISK BEING AWAY IN CASE BINGLEY COMES BACK TO NETHERFIELD.
OH, BINGLEY...

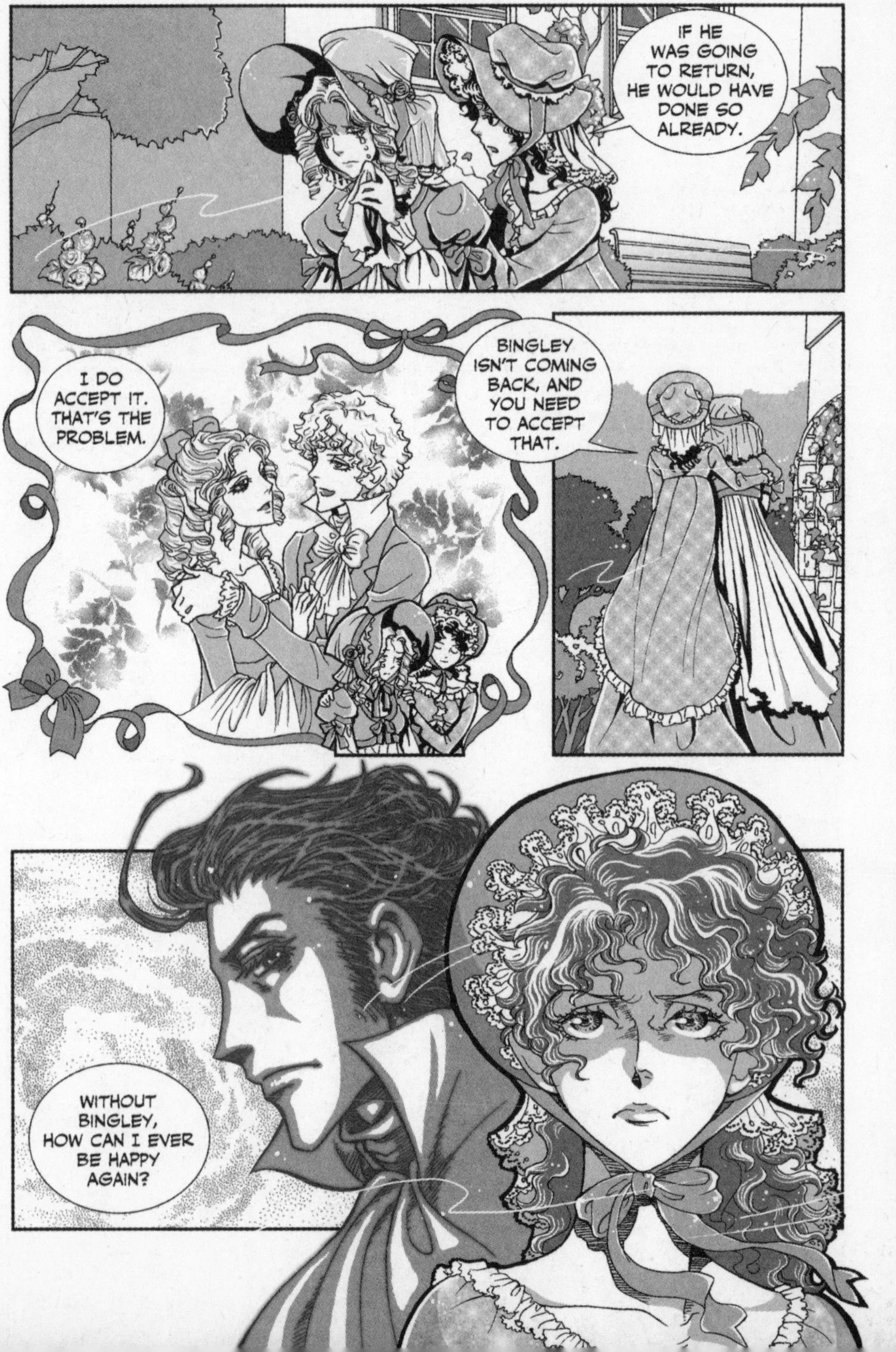
IF HE WAS GOING TO RETURN, HE WOULD HAVE DONE SO ALREADY.
BINGLEY ISN'T COMING BACK, AND YOU NEED TO ACCEPT THAT.
I DO ACCEPT IT. THAT'S THE PROBLEM.
WITHOUT BINGLEY, HOW CAN I EVER BE HAPPY AGAIN?

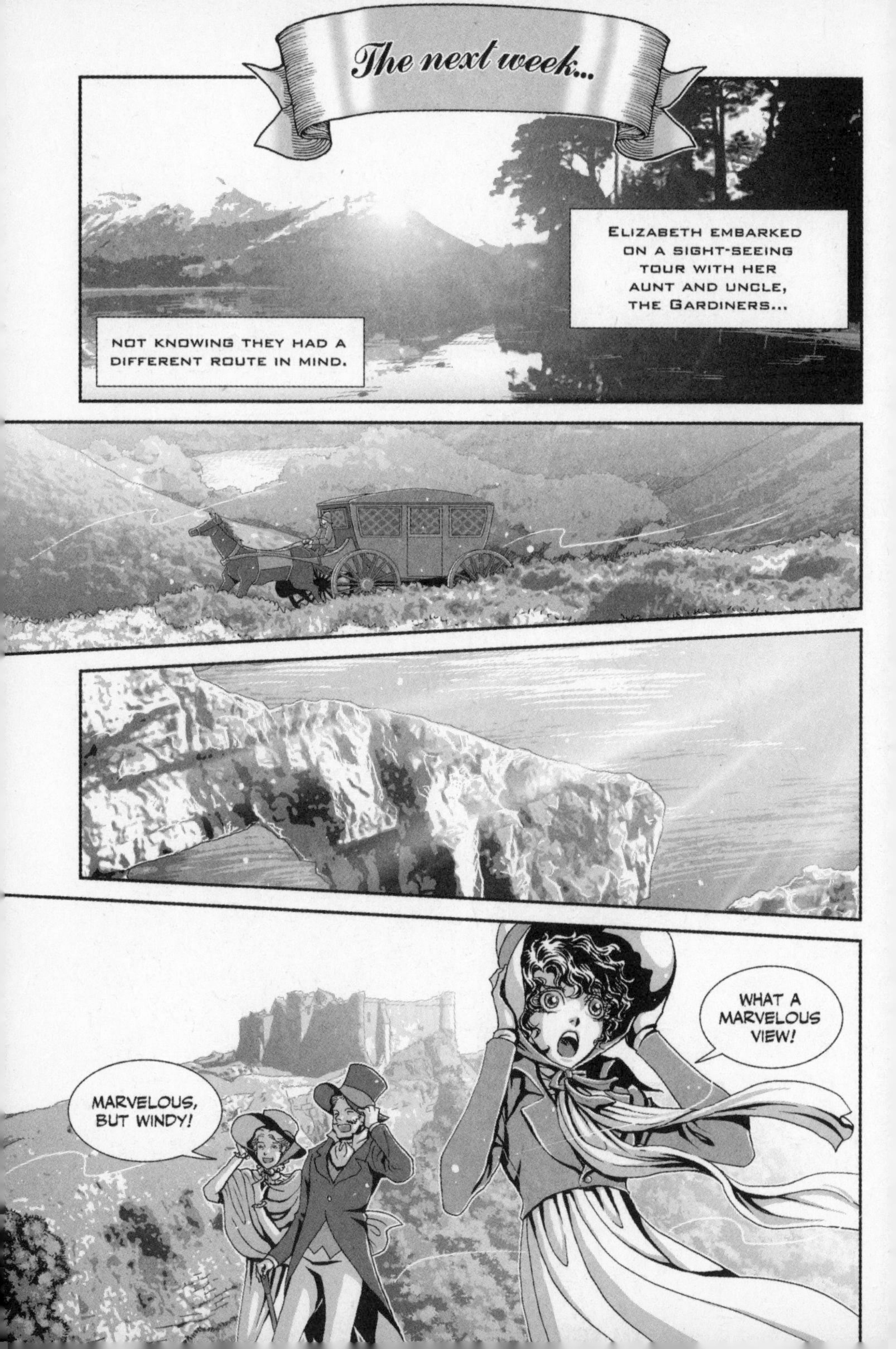
The next week...
ELIZABETH EMBARKED ON A SIGHT-SEEING TOUR WITH HER AUNT AND UNCLE, THE GARDINERS...
NOT KNOWING THEY HAD A DIFFERENT ROUTE IN MIND.
WHAT A MARVELOUS VIEW!
MARVELOUS, BUT WINDY!

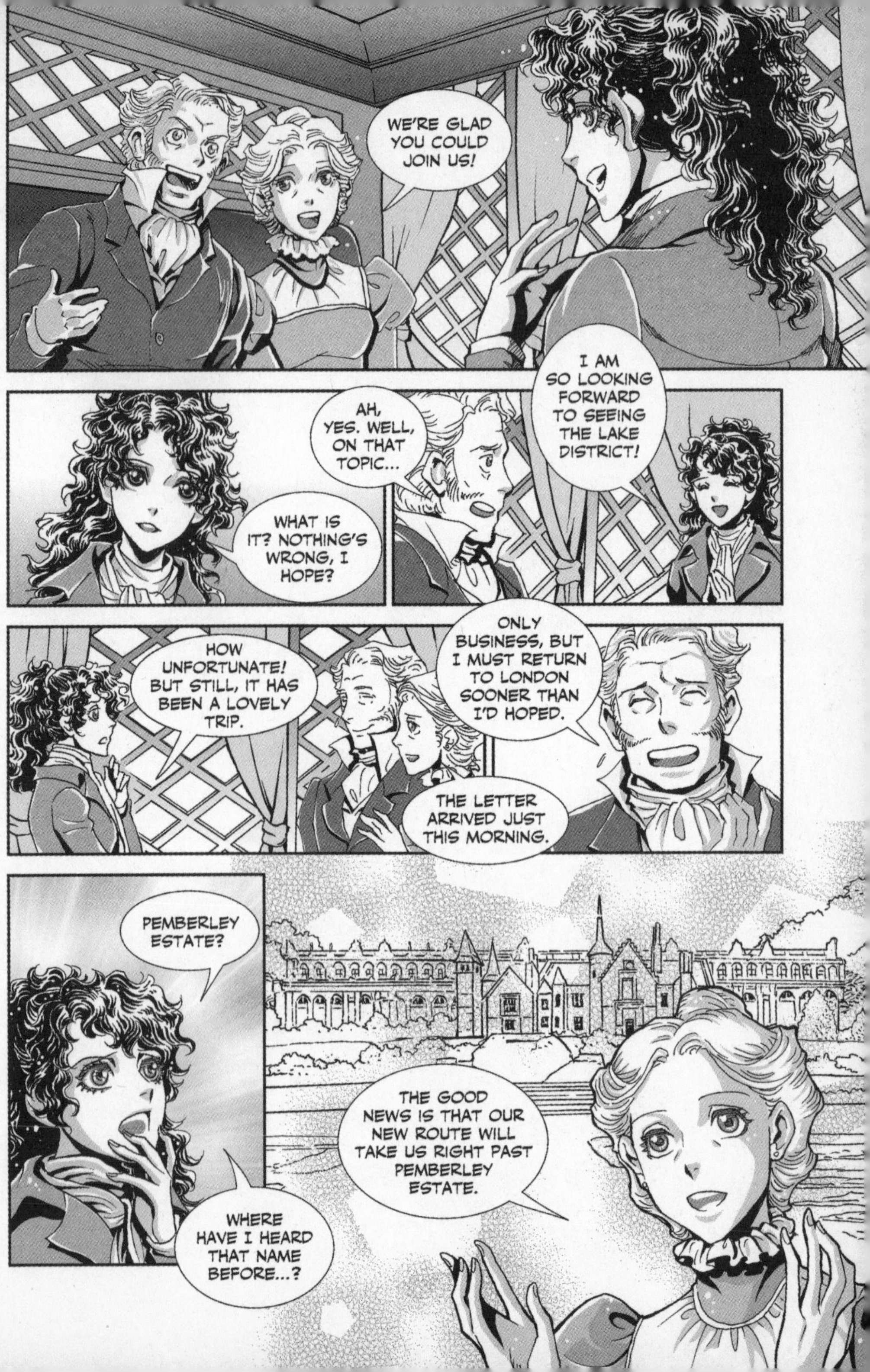
WE'RE GLAD YOU COULD JOIN US!
I AM SO LOOKING FORWARD TO SEEING THE LAKE DISTRICT!
AH, YES. WELL, ON THAT TOPIC...
WHAT IS IT? NOTHING'S WRONG, I HOPE?
ONLY BUSINESS, BUT I MUST RETURN TO LONDON SOONER THAN I'D HOPED.
THE LETTER ARRIVED JUST THIS MORNING.
HOW UNFORTUNATE! BUT STILL, IT HAS BEEN A LOVELY TRIP.
THE GOOD NEWS IS THAT OUR NEW ROUTE WILL TAKE US RIGHT PAST PEMBERLEY ESTATE.
PEMBERLEY ESTATE?
WHERE HAVE I HEARD THAT NAME BEFORE...?

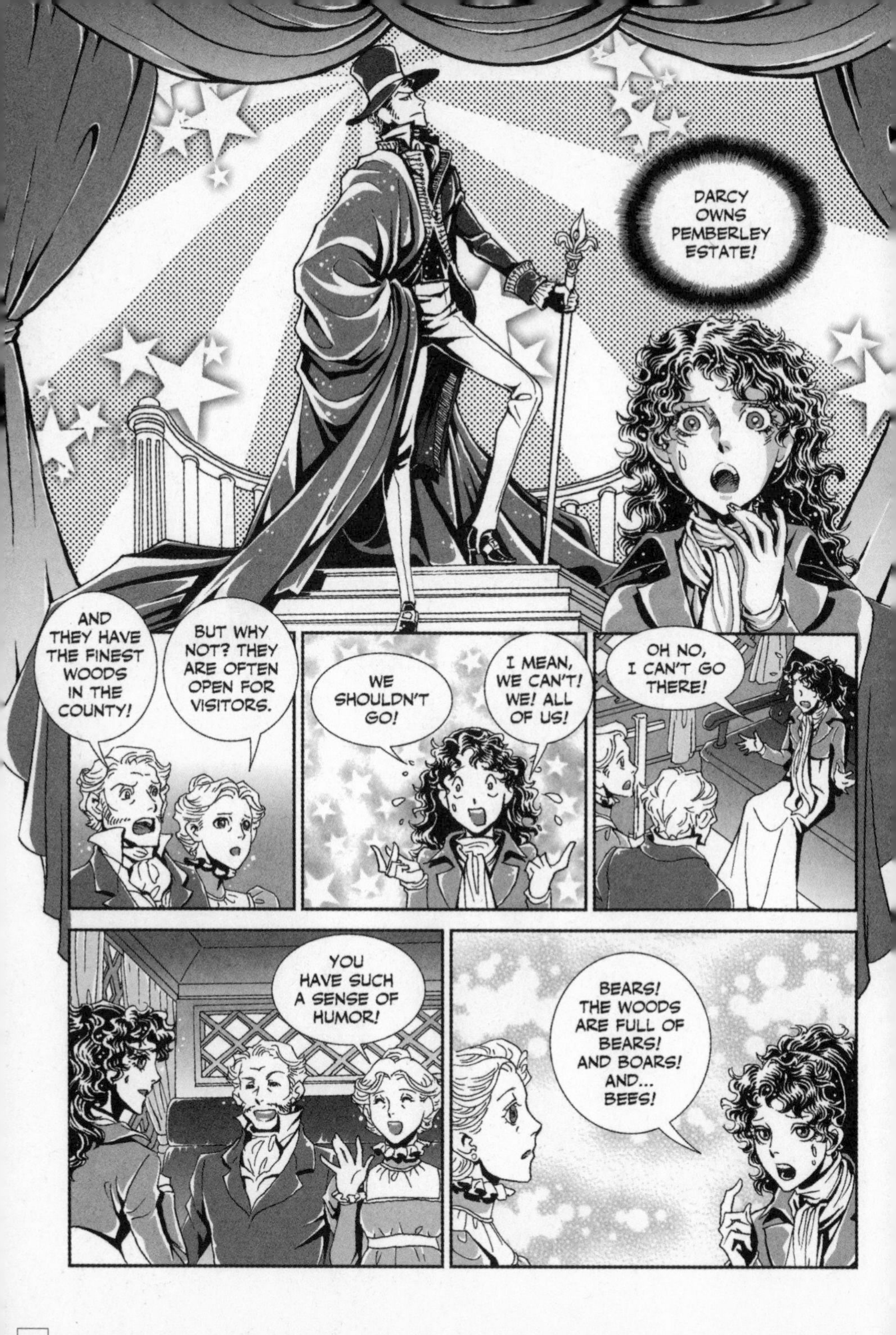
DARCY OWNS PEMBERLEY ESTATE!
OH NO, I CAN'T GO THERE!
I MEAN, WE CAN'T! WE! ALL OF US!
WE SHOULDN'T GO!
BUT WHY NOT? THEY ARE OFTEN OPEN FOR VISITORS.
AND THEY HAVE THE FINEST WOODS IN THE COUNTY!
BEARS! THE WOODS ARE FULL OF BEARS! AND BOARS! AND... BEES!
YOU HAVE SUCH A SENSE OF HUMOR!

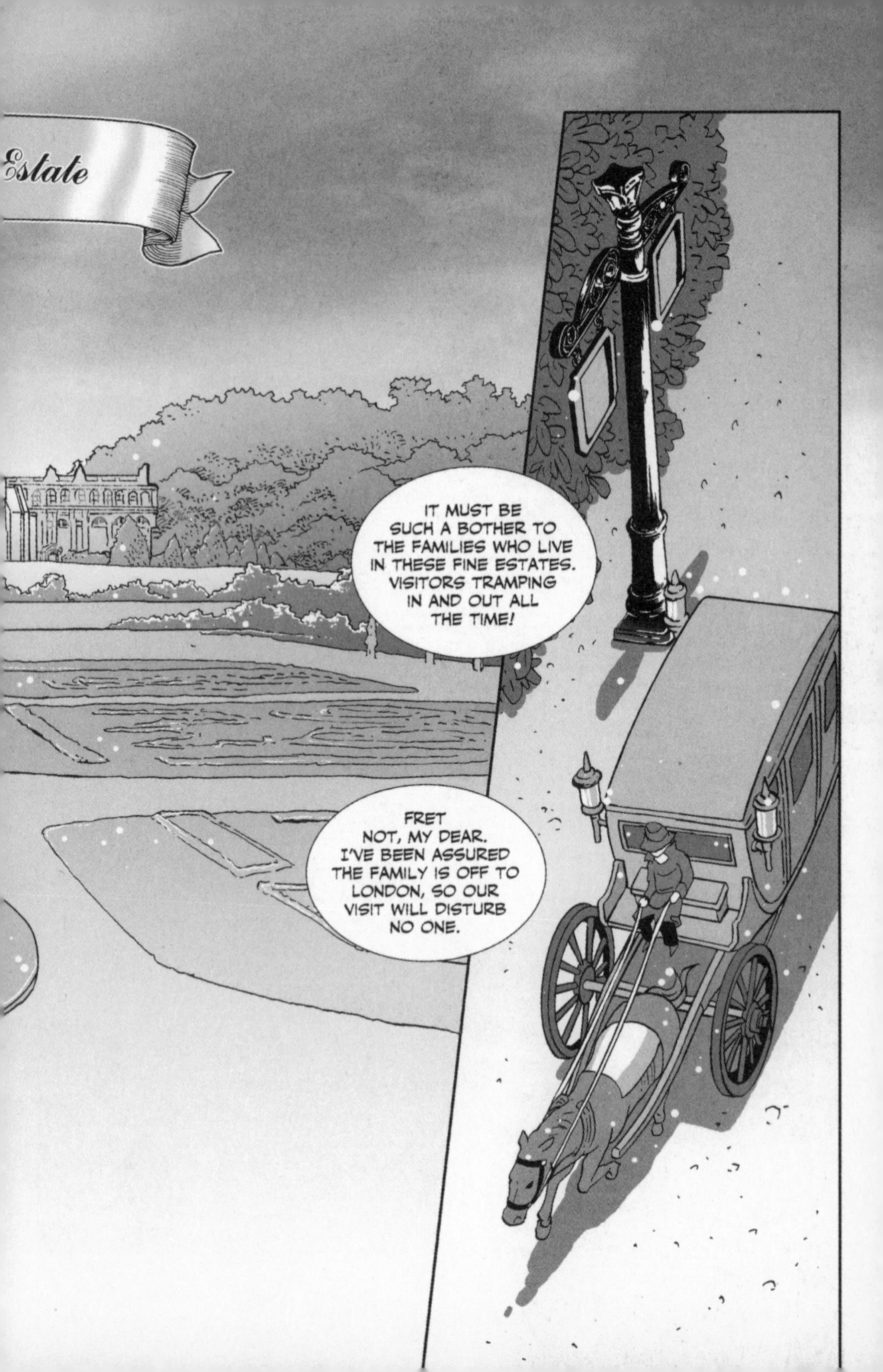
Estate
IT MUST BE SUCH A BOTHER TO THE FAMILIES WHO LIVE IN THESE FINE ESTATES. VISITORS TRAMPING IN AND OUT ALL THE TIME!
FRET NOT, MY DEAR. I'VE BEEN ASSURED THE FAMILY IS OFF TO LONDON, SO OUR VISIT WILL DISTURB NO ONE.

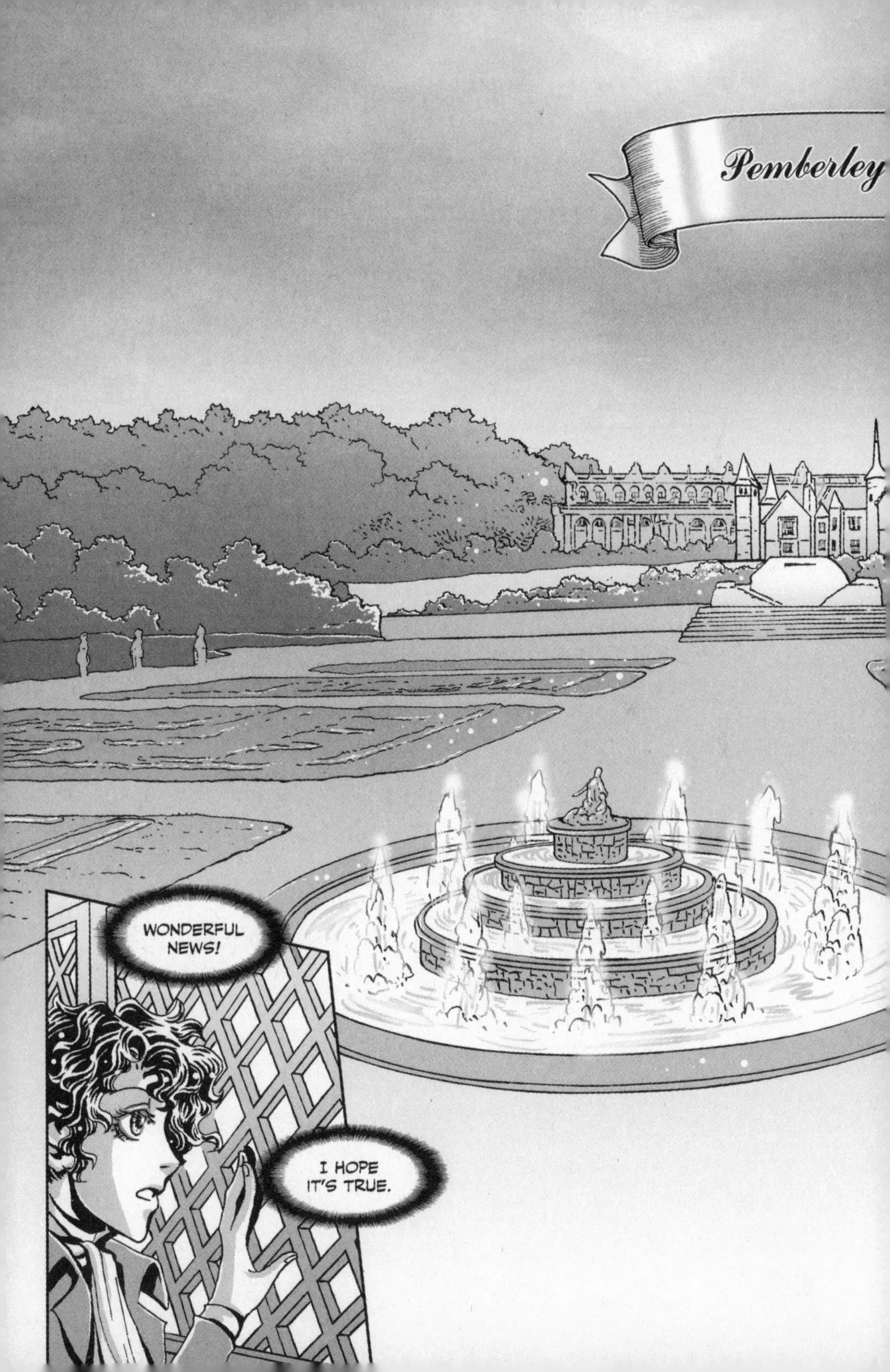
Pemberley
WONDERFUL NEWS!
I HOPE IT'S TRUE.

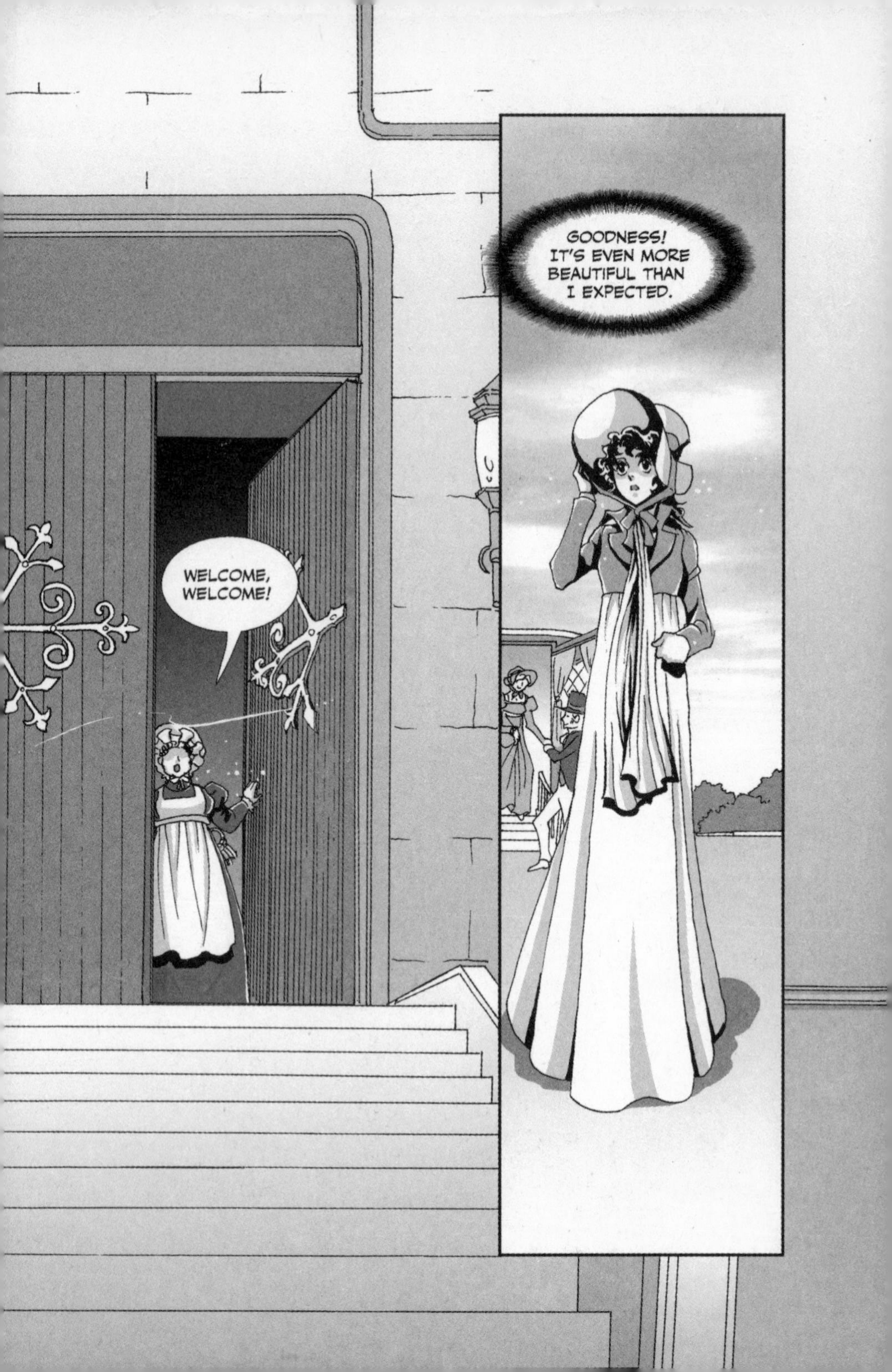
GOODNESS! IT'S EVEN MORE BEAUTIFUL THAN I EXPECTED.
WELCOME, WELCOME!

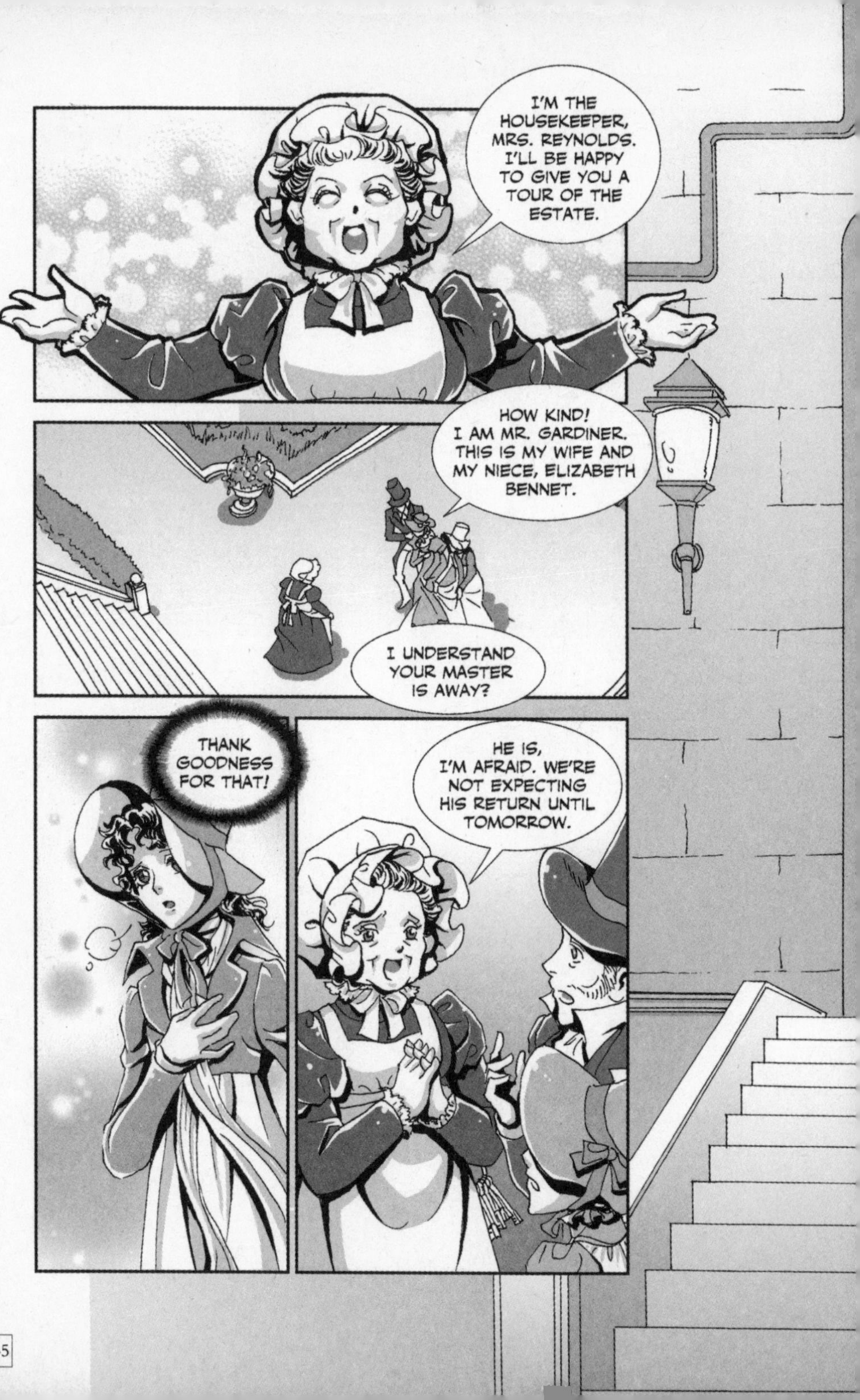
I'M THE HOUSEKEEPER, MRS. REYNOLDS. I'LL BE HAPPY TO GIVE YOU A TOUR OF THE ESTATE.
HOW KIND! I AM MR. GARDINER. THIS IS MY WIFE AND MY NIECE, ELIZABETH BENNET.
I UNDERSTAND YOUR MASTER IS AWAY?
HE IS, I'M AFRAID. WE'RE NOT EXPECTING HIS RETURN UNTIL TOMORROW.
THANK GOODNESS FOR THAT!

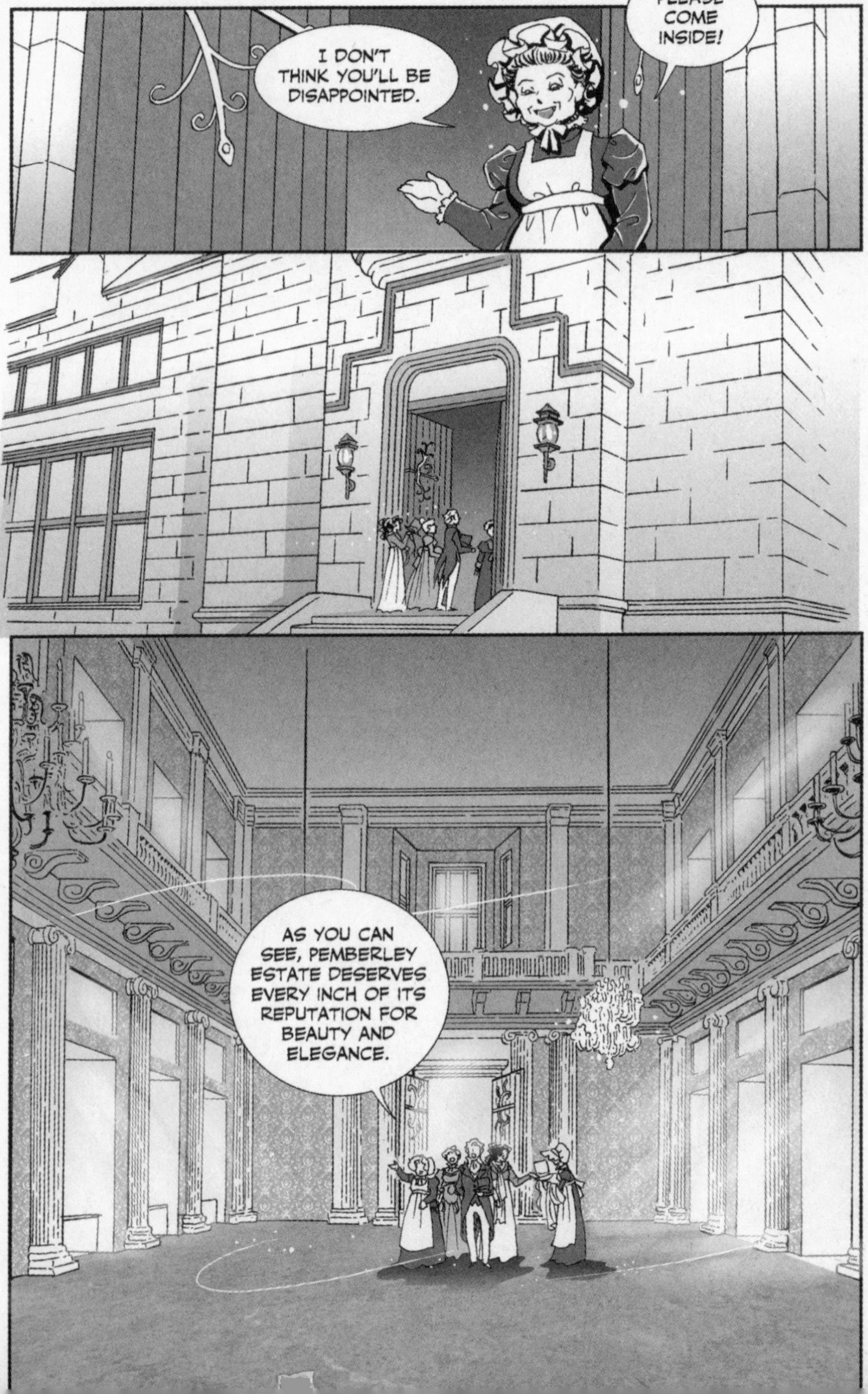
PLEASE COME INSIDE!
I DON'T THINK YOU'LL BE DISAPPOINTED.
AS YOU CAN SEE, PEMBERLEY ESTATE DESERVES EVERY INCH OF ITS REPUTATION FOR BEAUTY AND ELEGANCE.

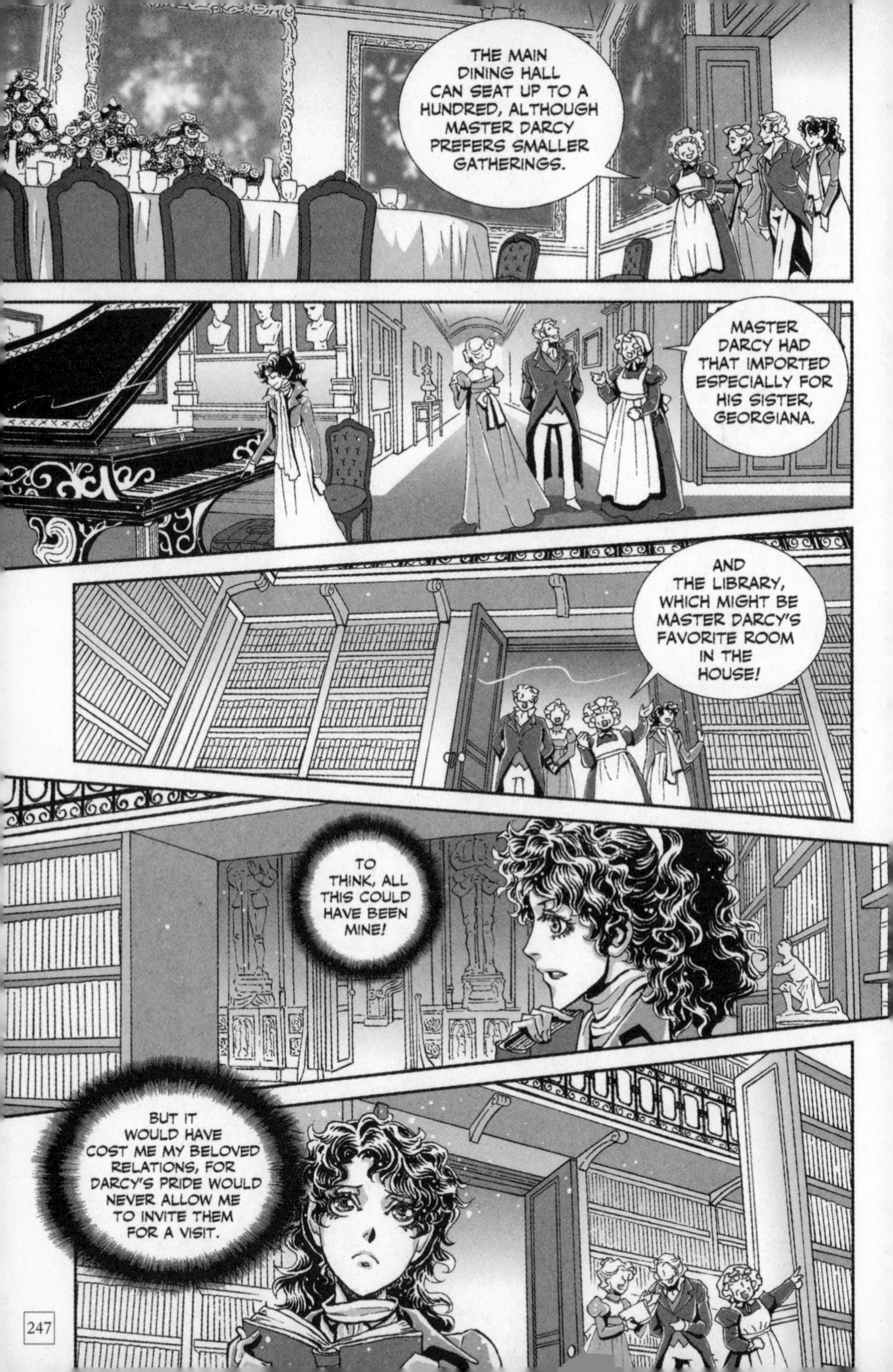
THE MAIN DINING HALL CAN SEAT UP TO A HUNDRED, ALTHOUGH MASTER DARCY PREFERS SMALLER GATHERINGS.
MASTER DARCY HAD THAT IMPORTED ESPECIALLY FOR HIS SISTER, GEORGIANA.
AND THE LIBRARY, WHICH MIGHT BE MASTER DARCY'S FAVORITE ROOM IN THE HOUSE!
TO THINK, ALL THIS COULD HAVE BEEN MINE!
BUT IT WOULD HAVE COST ME MY BELOVED RELATIONS, FOR DARCY'S PRIDE WOULD NEVER ALLOW ME TO INVITE THEM FOR A VISIT.

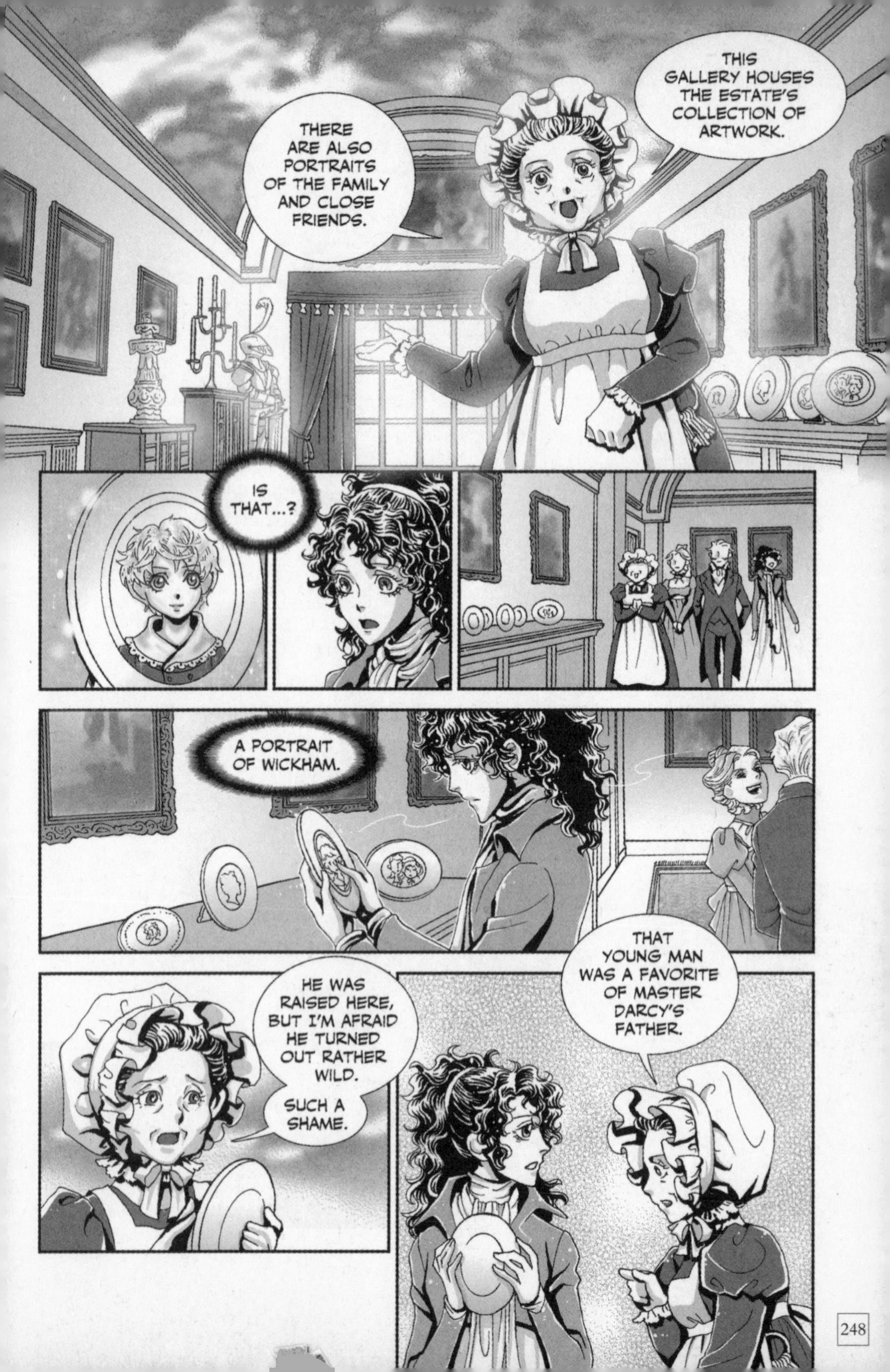
THIS GALLERY HOUSES THE ESTATE'S COLLECTION OF ARTWORK.
THERE ARE ALSO PORTRAITS OF THE FAMILY AND CLOSE FRIENDS.
IS THAT...?
A PORTRAIT OF WICKHAM.
THAT YOUNG MAN WAS A FAVORITE OF MASTER DARCY'S FATHER.
HE WAS RAISED HERE, BUT I'M AFRAID HE TURNED OUT RATHER WILD.
SUCH A SHAME.

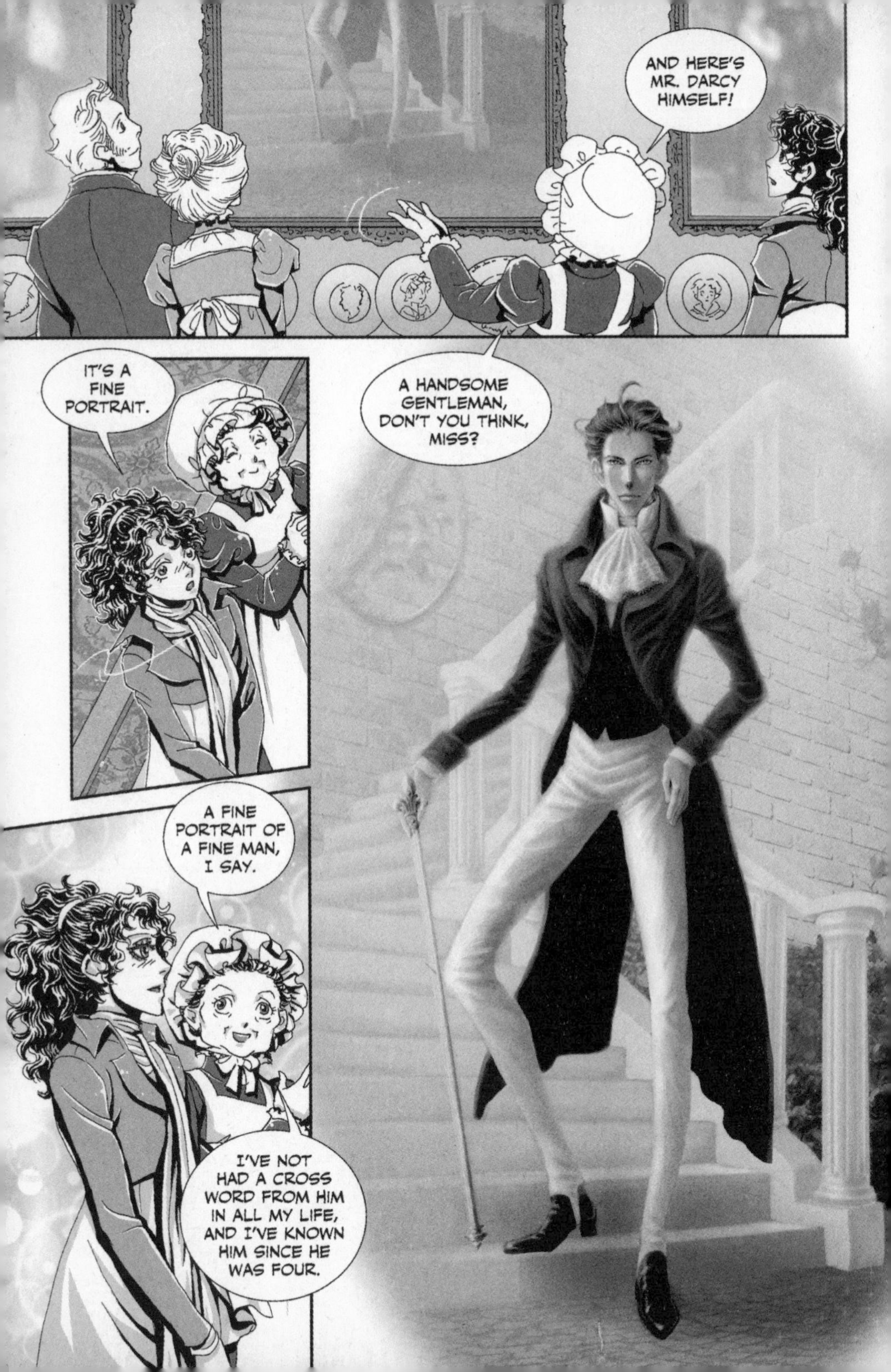
AND HERE'S MR. DARCY HIMSELF!
A HANDSOME GENTLEMAN, DON'T YOU THINK, MISS?
IT'S A FINE PORTRAIT.
A FINE PORTRAIT OF A FINE MAN, I SAY.
I'VE NOT HAD A CROSS WORD FROM HIM IN ALL MY LIFE, AND I'VE KNOWN HIM SINCE HE WAS FOUR.

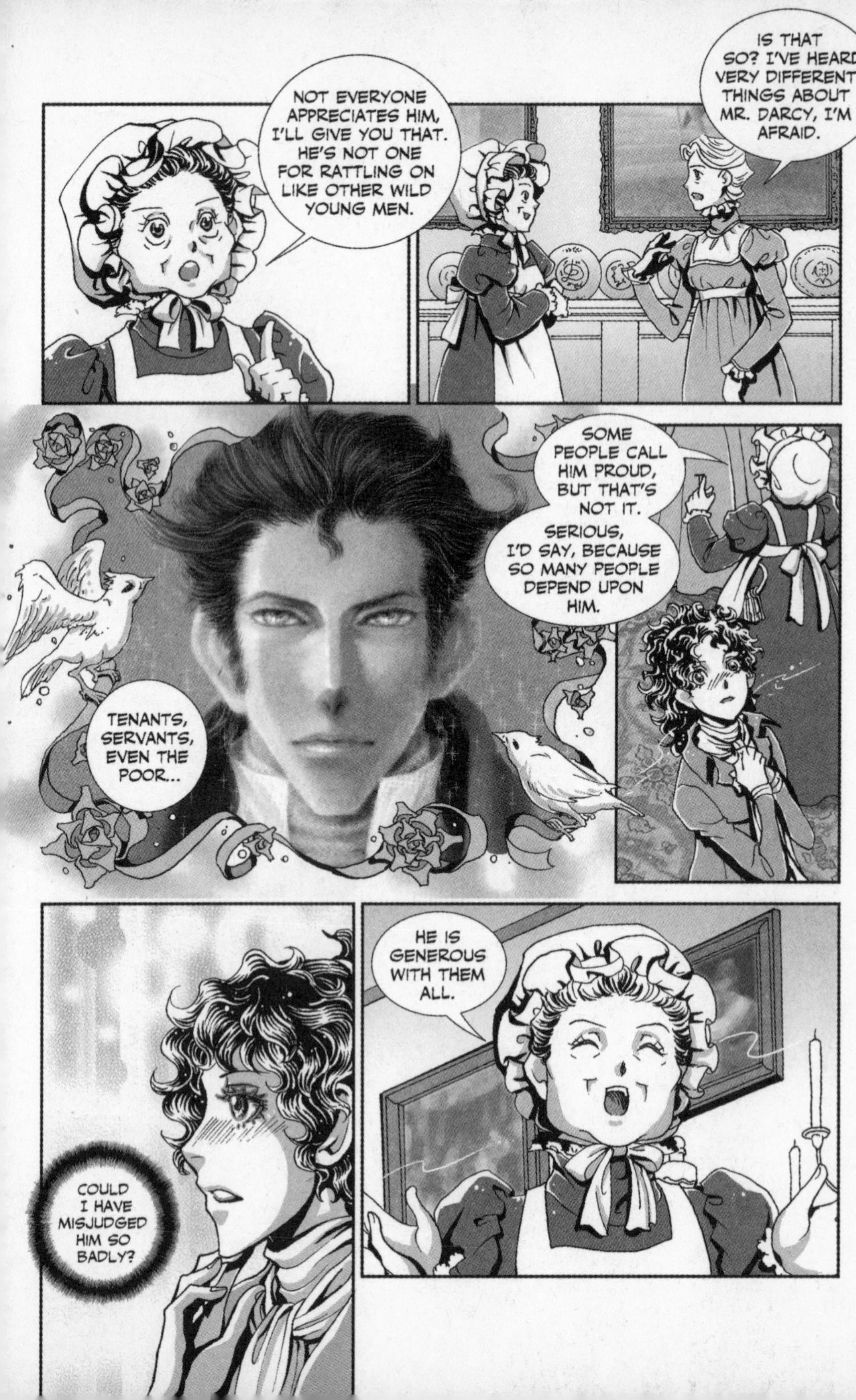
IS THAT SO? I'VE HEARD VERY DIFFERENT THINGS ABOUT MR. DARCY, I'M AFRAID.
NOT EVERYONE APPRECIATES HIM, I'LL GIVE YOU THAT. HE'S NOT ONE FOR RATTLING ON LIKE OTHER WILD YOUNG MEN.
SOME PEOPLE CALL HIM PROUD, BUT THAT'S NOT IT.
SERIOUS, I'D SAY, BECAUSE SO MANY PEOPLE DEPEND UPON HIM.
TENANTS, SERVANTS, EVEN THE POOR...
HE IS GENEROUS WITH THEM ALL.
COULD I HAVE MISJUDGED HIM SO BADLY?

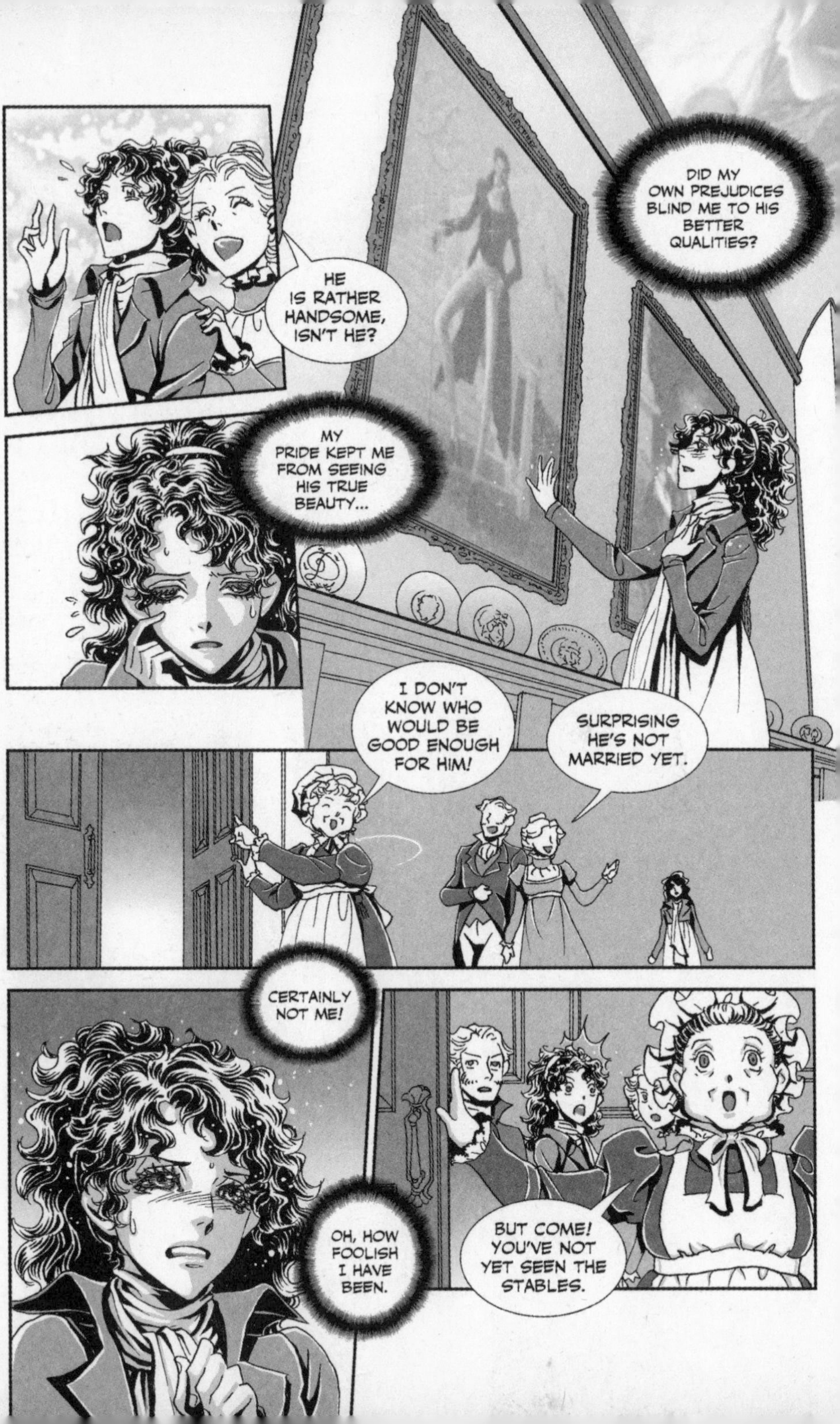
DID MY OWN PREJUDICES BLIND ME TO HIS BETTER QUALITIES?
HE IS RATHER HANDSOME, ISN'T HE?
MY PRIDE KEPT ME FROM SEEING HIS TRUE BEAUTY...
SURPRISING HE'S NOT MARRIED YET.
I DON'T KNOW WHO WOULD BE GOOD ENOUGH FOR HIM!
BUT COME! YOU'VE NOT YET SEEN THE STABLES.
CERTAINLY NOT ME!
OH, HOW FOOLISH I HAVE BEEN.

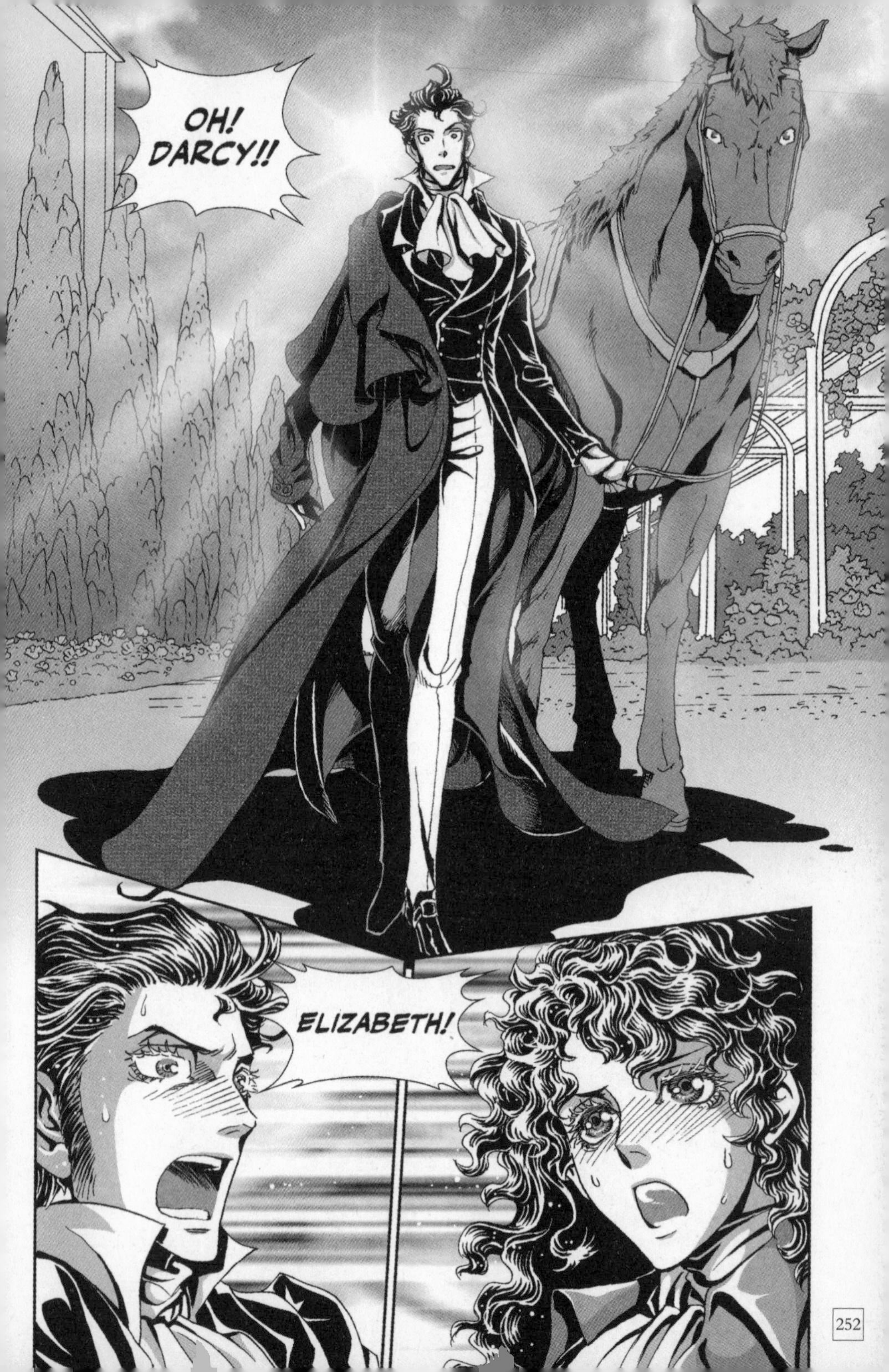
OH! DARCY!!
ELIZABETH!

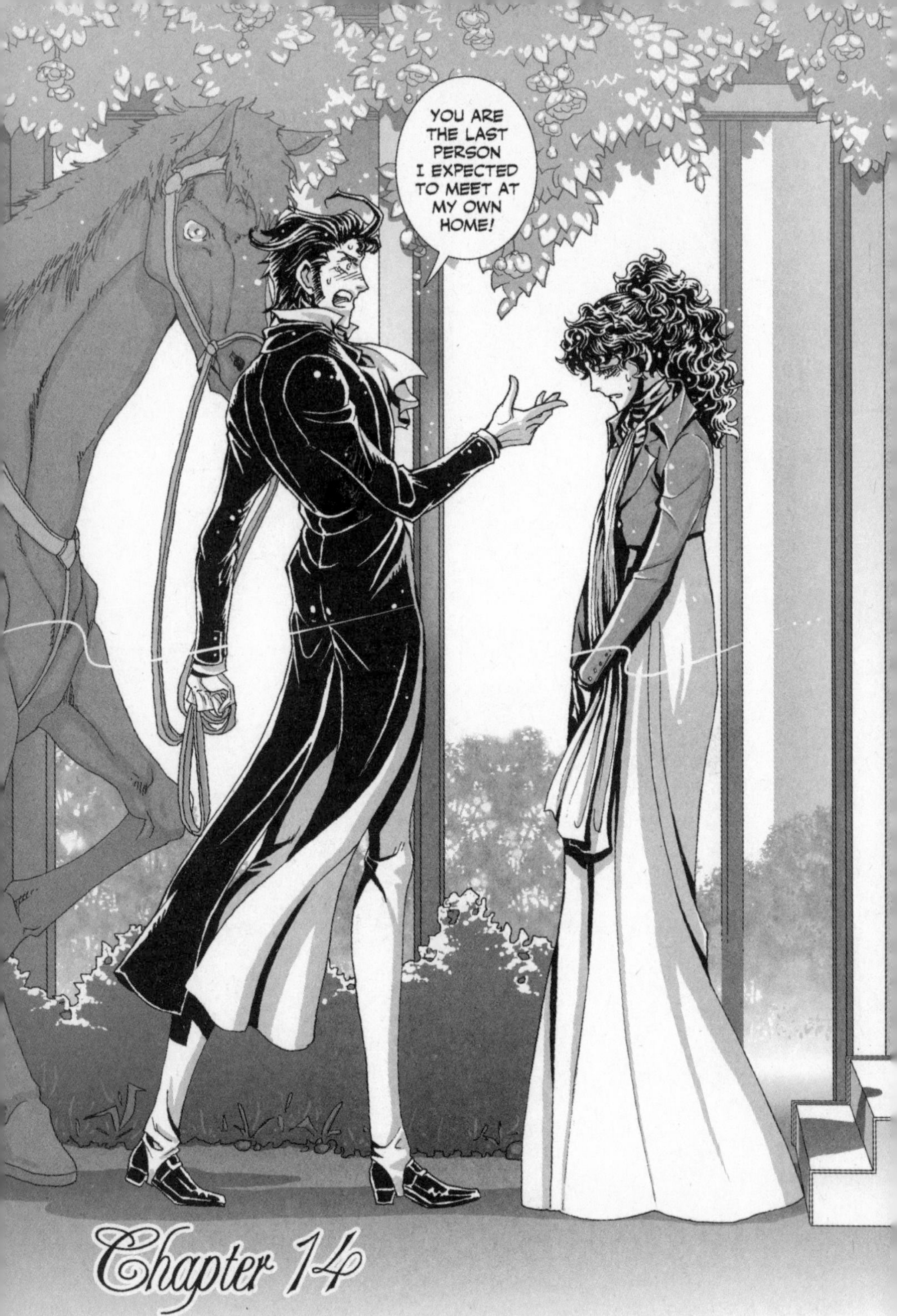
YOU ARE THE LAST PERSON I EXPECTED TO MEET AT MY OWN HOME!

Chapter 14

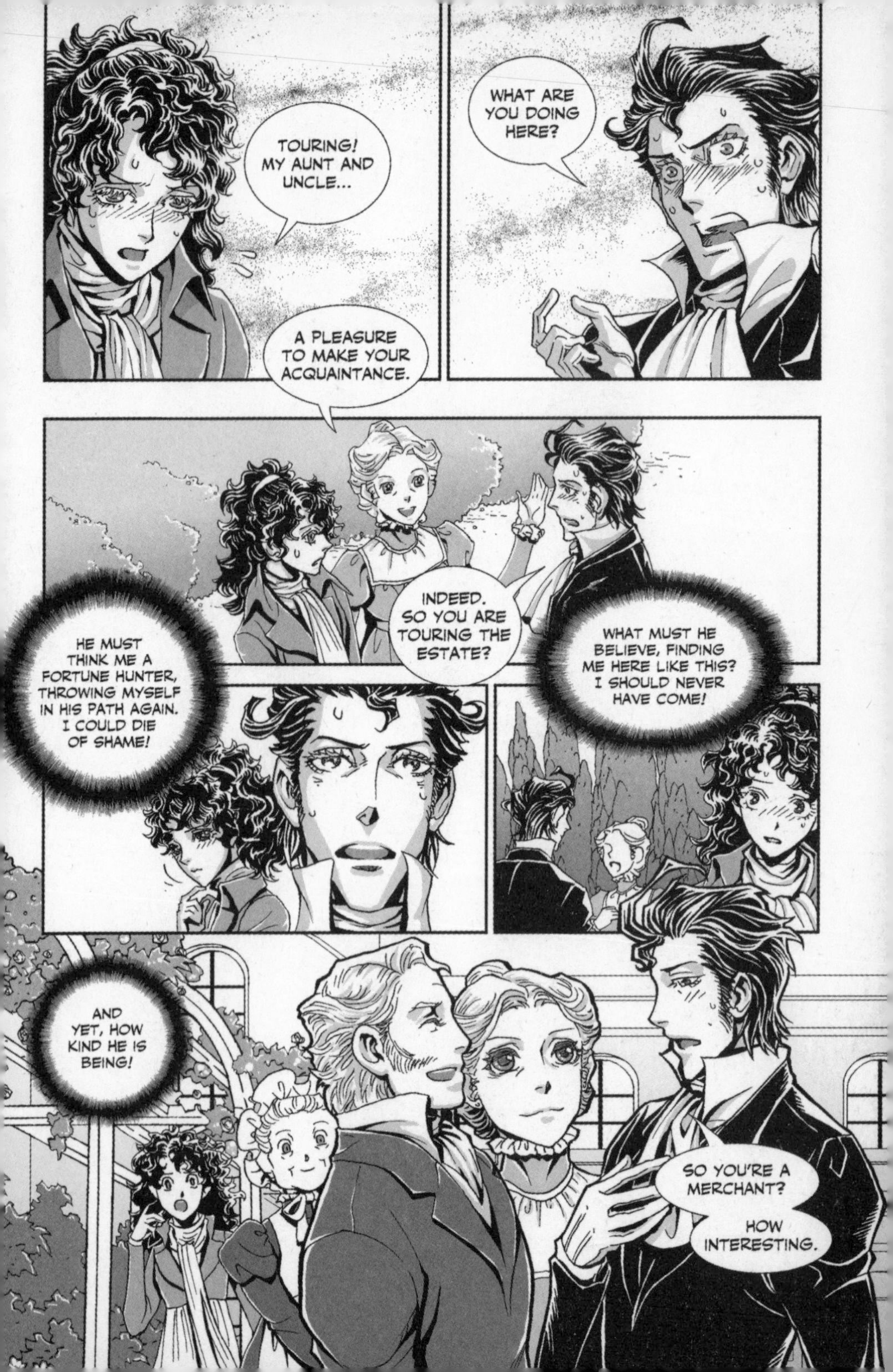
WHAT ARE YOU DOING HERE?
TOURING! MY AUNT AND UNCLE...
A PLEASURE TO MAKE YOUR ACQUAINTANCE.
INDEED. SO YOU ARE TOURING THE ESTATE?
WHAT MUST HE BELIEVE, FINDING ME HERE LIKE THIS? I SHOULD NEVER HAVE COME!
HE MUST THINK ME A FORTUNE HUNTER, THROWING MYSELF IN HIS PATH AGAIN. I COULD DIE OF SHAME!
AND YET, HOW KIND HE IS BEING!
SO YOU'RE A MERCHANT?
HOW INTERESTING.

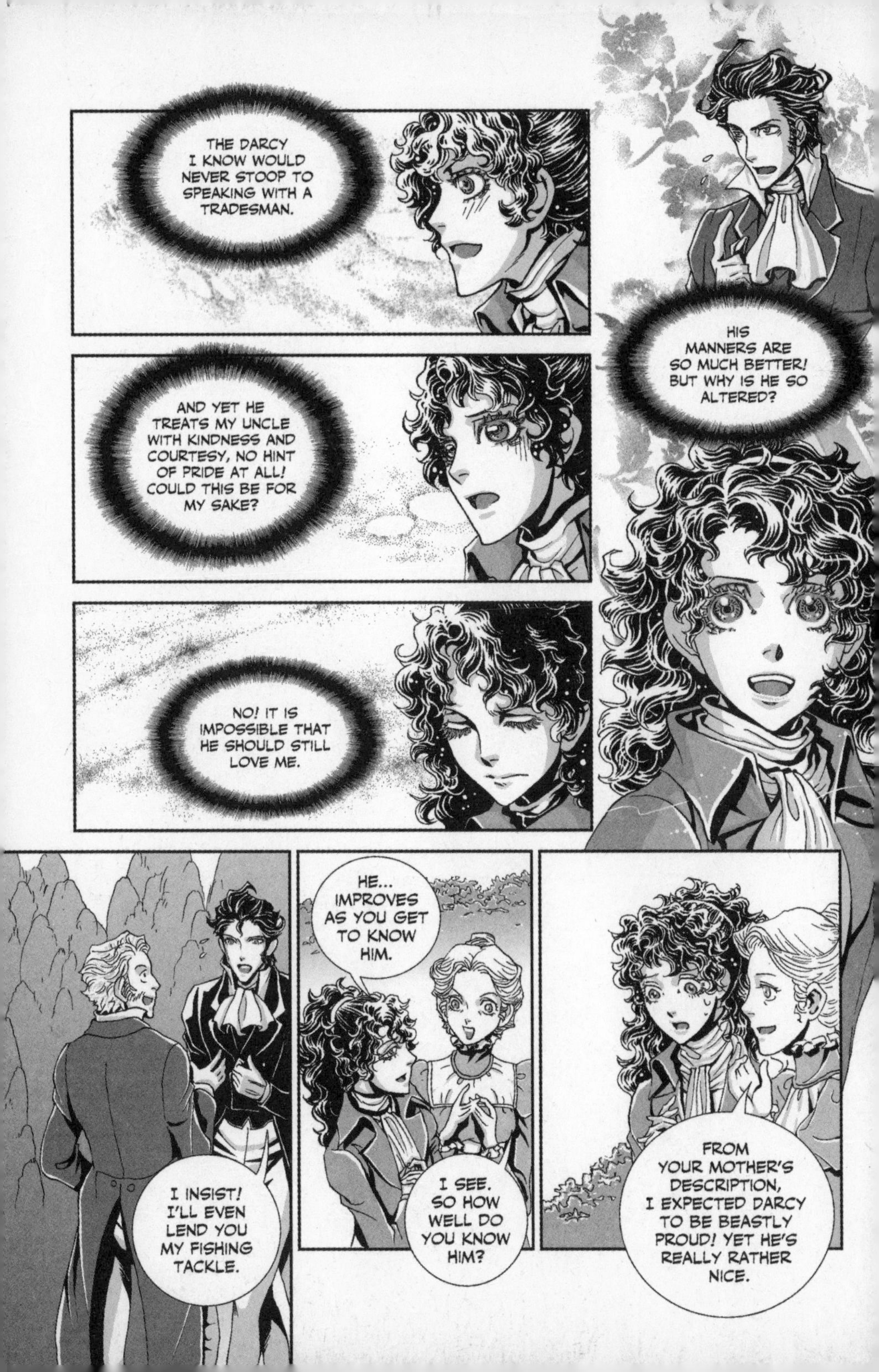
HIS MANNERS ARE SO MUCH BETTER! BUT WHY IS HE SO ALTERED?
THE DARCY I KNOW WOULD NEVER STOOP TO SPEAKING WITH A TRADESMAN.
AND YET HE TREATS MY UNCLE WITH KINDNESS AND COURTESY, NO HINT OF PRIDE AT ALL! COULD THIS BE FOR MY SAKE?
NO! IT IS IMPOSSIBLE THAT HE SHOULD STILL LOVE ME.
FROM YOUR MOTHER'S DESCRIPTION, I EXPECTED DARCY TO BE BEASTLY PROUD! YET HE'S REALLY RATHER NICE.
I SEE. SO HOW WELL DO YOU KNOW HIM?
HE... IMPROVES AS YOU GET TO KNOW HIM.
I INSIST! I'LL EVEN LEND YOU MY FISHING TACKLE.

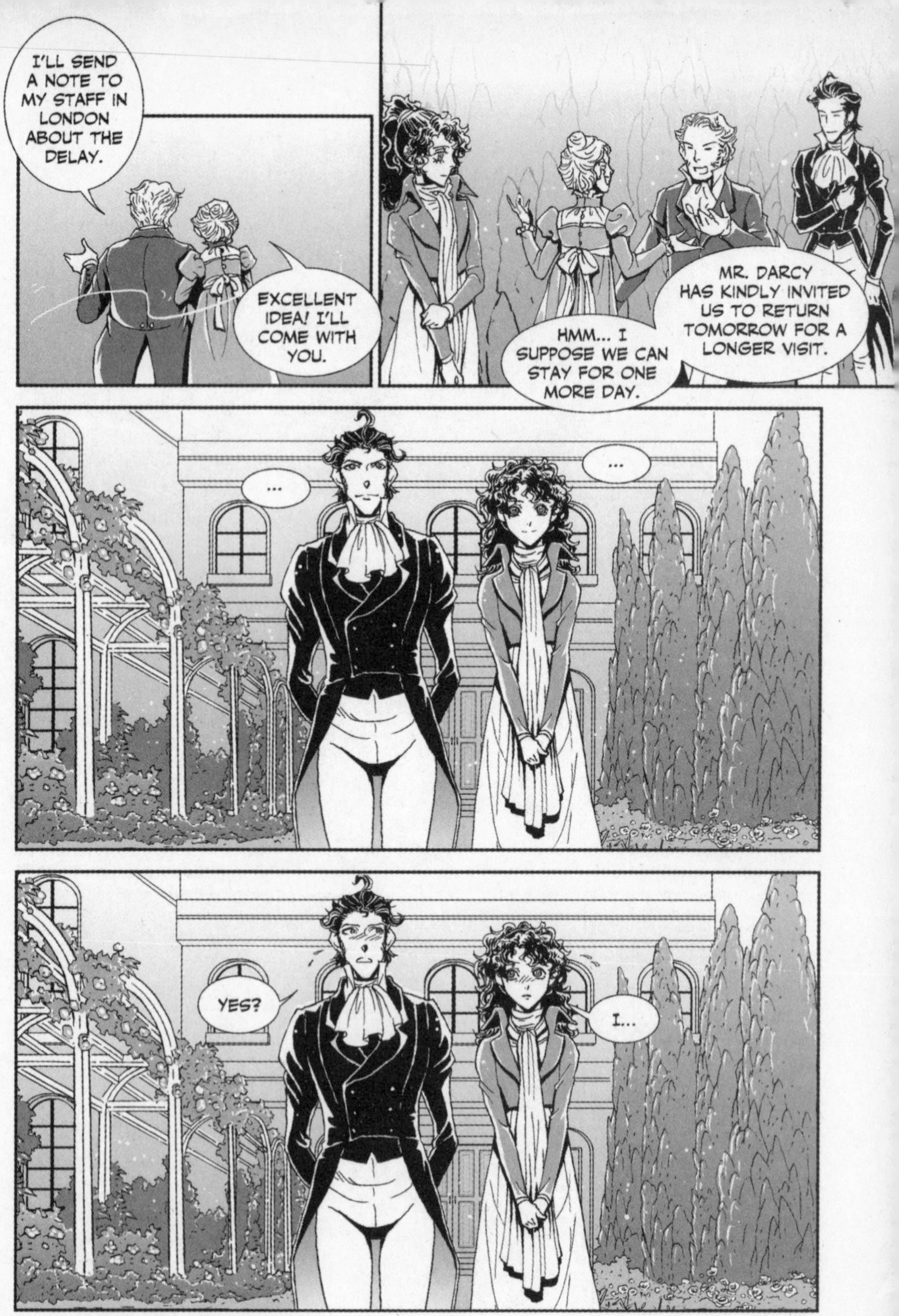
MR. DARCY HAS KINDLY INVITED US TO RETURN TOMORROW FOR A LONGER VISIT.
HMM... I SUPPOSE WE CAN STAY FOR ONE MORE DAY.
I'LL SEND A NOTE TO MY STAFF IN LONDON ABOUT THE DELAY.
EXCELLENT IDEA! I'LL COME WITH YOU.
...
...
I...
YES?

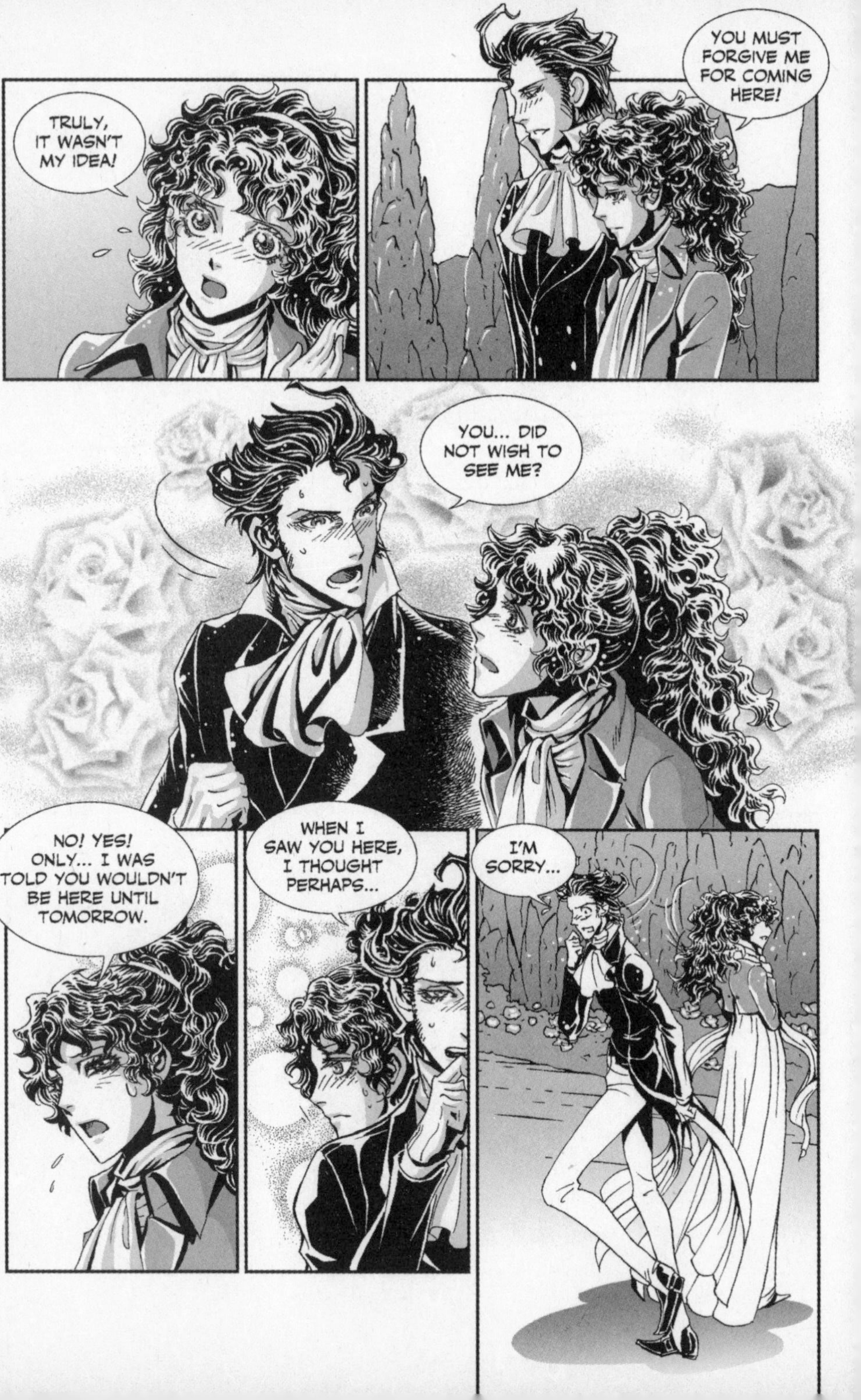
YOU MUST FORGIVE ME FOR COMING HERE!
TRULY, IT WASN'T MY IDEA!
YOU... DID NOT WISH TO SEE ME?
I'M SORRY...
WHEN I SAW YOU HERE, I THOUGHT PERHAPS...
NO! YES! ONLY... I WAS TOLD YOU WOULDN'T BE HERE UNTIL TOMORROW.

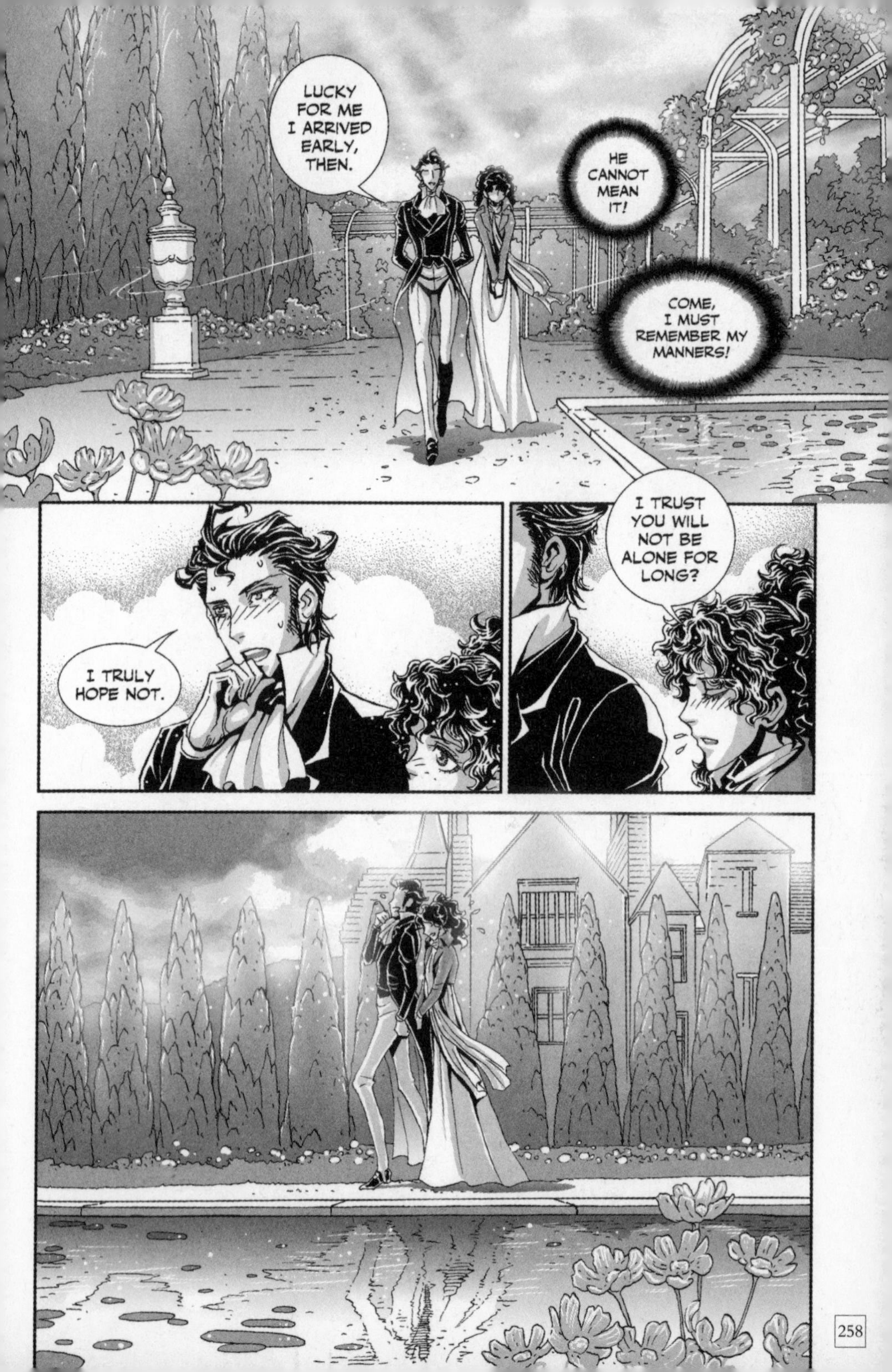
LUCKY FOR ME I ARRIVED EARLY, THEN.
HE CANNOT MEAN IT!
COME, I MUST REMEMBER MY MANNERS!
I TRUST YOU WILL NOT BE ALONE FOR LONG?
I TRULY HOPE NOT.

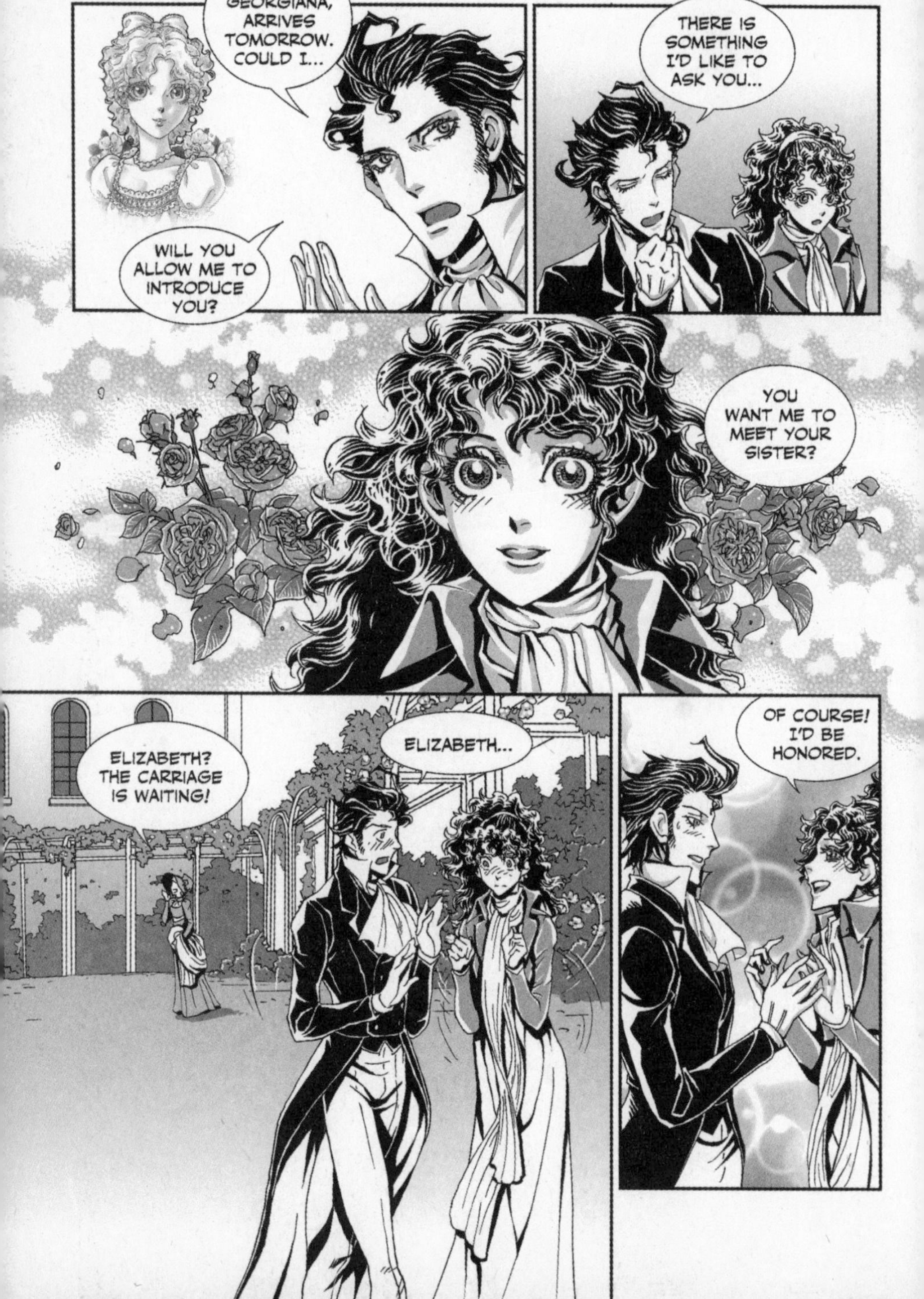
THERE IS SOMETHING I'D LIKE TO ASK YOU...
MY SISTER, GEORGIANA, ARRIVES TOMORROW. COULD I...
WILL YOU ALLOW ME TO INTRODUCE YOU?
YOU WANT ME TO MEET YOUR SISTER?
OF COURSE! I'D BE HONORED.
ELIZABETH...
ELIZABETH? THE CARRIAGE IS WAITING!

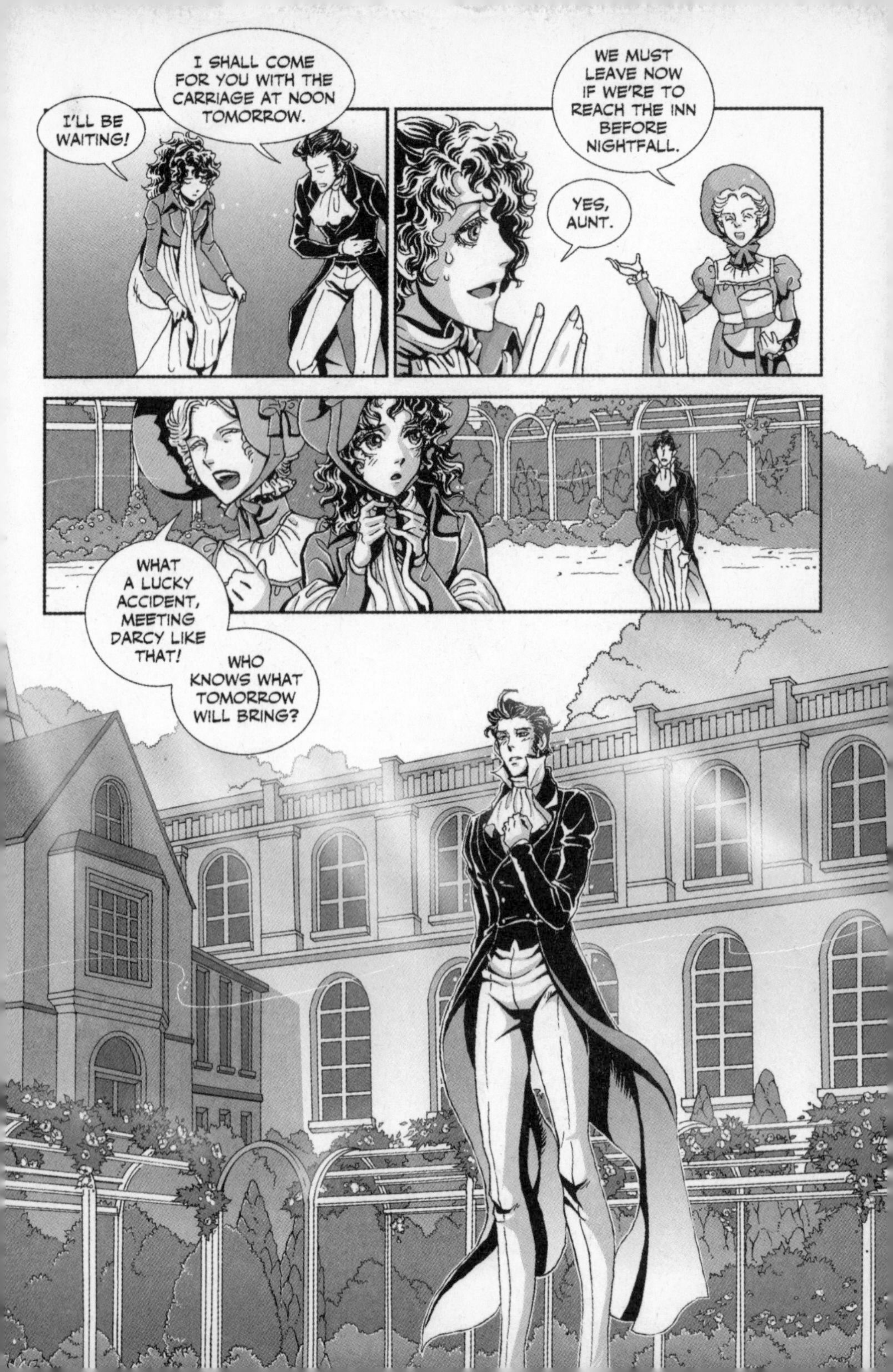
WE MUST LEAVE NOW IF WE'RE TO REACH THE INN BEFORE NIGHTFALL.
YES, AUNT.
I SHALL COME FOR YOU WITH THE CARRIAGE AT NOON TOMORROW.
I'LL BE WAITING!
WHAT A LUCKY ACCIDENT, MEETING DARCY LIKE THAT!
WHO KNOWS WHAT TOMORROW WILL BRING?

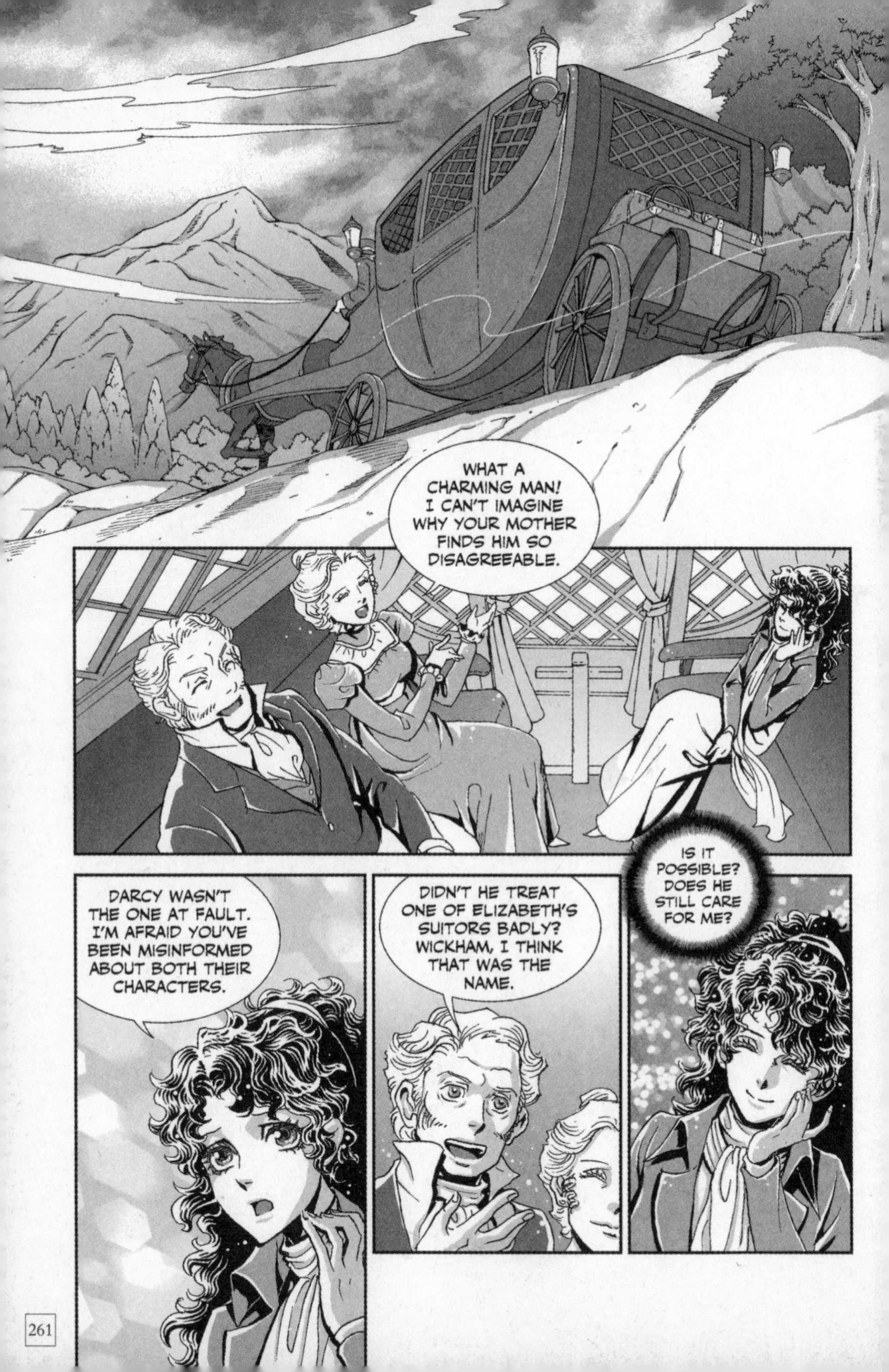
WHAT A CHARMING MAN! I CAN'T IMAGINE WHY YOUR MOTHER FINDS HIM SO DISAGREEABLE.
IS IT POSSIBLE? DOES HE STILL CARE FOR ME?
DIDN'T HE TREAT ONE OF ELIZABETH'S SUITORS BADLY? WICKHAM, I THINK THAT WAS THE NAME.
DARCY WASN'T THE ONE AT FAULT. I'M AFRAID YOU'VE BEEN MISINFORMED ABOUT BOTH THEIR CHARACTERS.

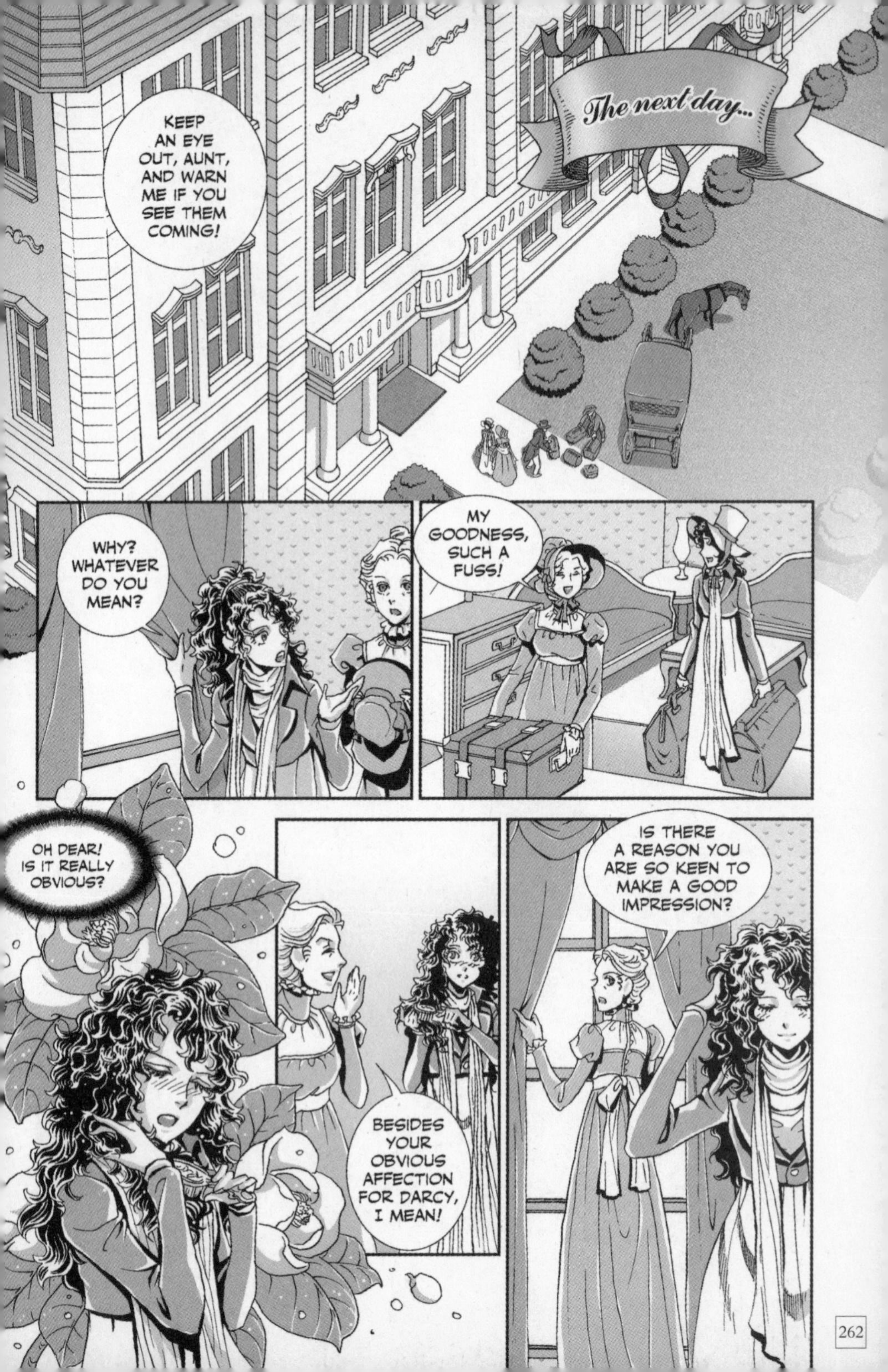
The next day...
KEEP AN EYE OUT, AUNT, AND WARN ME IF YOU SEE THEM COMING!
MY GOODNESS, SUCH A FUSS!
WHY? WHATEVER DO YOU MEAN?
IS THERE A REASON YOU ARE SO KEEN TO MAKE A GOOD IMPRESSION?
BESIDES YOUR OBVIOUS AFFECTION FOR DARCY, I MEAN!
OH DEAR! IS IT REALLY OBVIOUS?

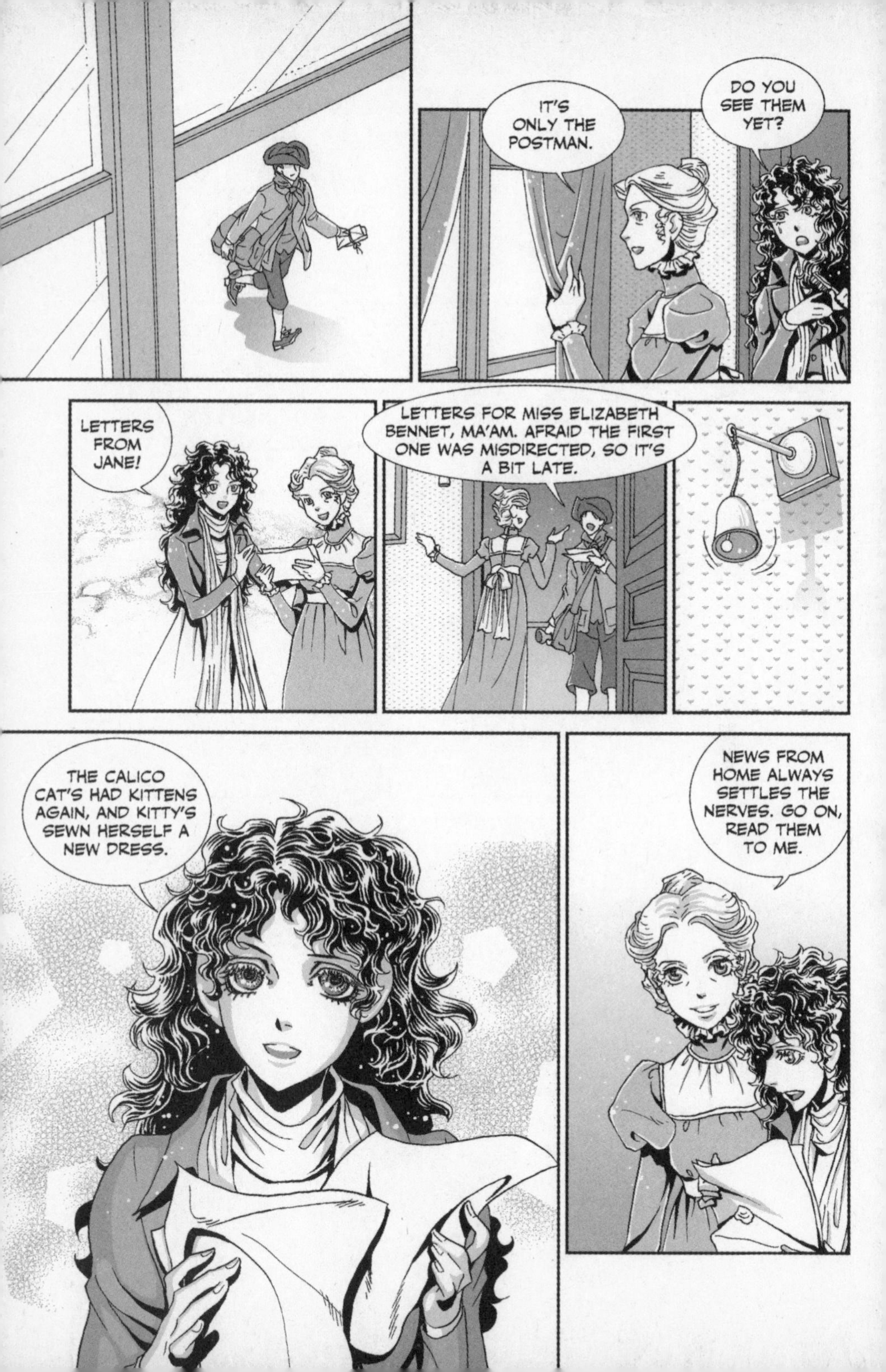
DO YOU SEE THEM YET?
IT'S ONLY THE POSTMAN.
LETTERS FOR MISS ELIZABETH BENNET, MA'AM. AFRAID THE FIRST ONE WAS MISDIRECTED, SO IT'S A BIT LATE.
LETTERS FROM JANE!
NEWS FROM HOME ALWAYS SETTLES THE NERVES. GO ON, READ THEM TO ME.
THE CALICO CAT'S HAD KITTENS AGAIN, AND KITTY'S SEWN HERSELF A NEW DRESS.

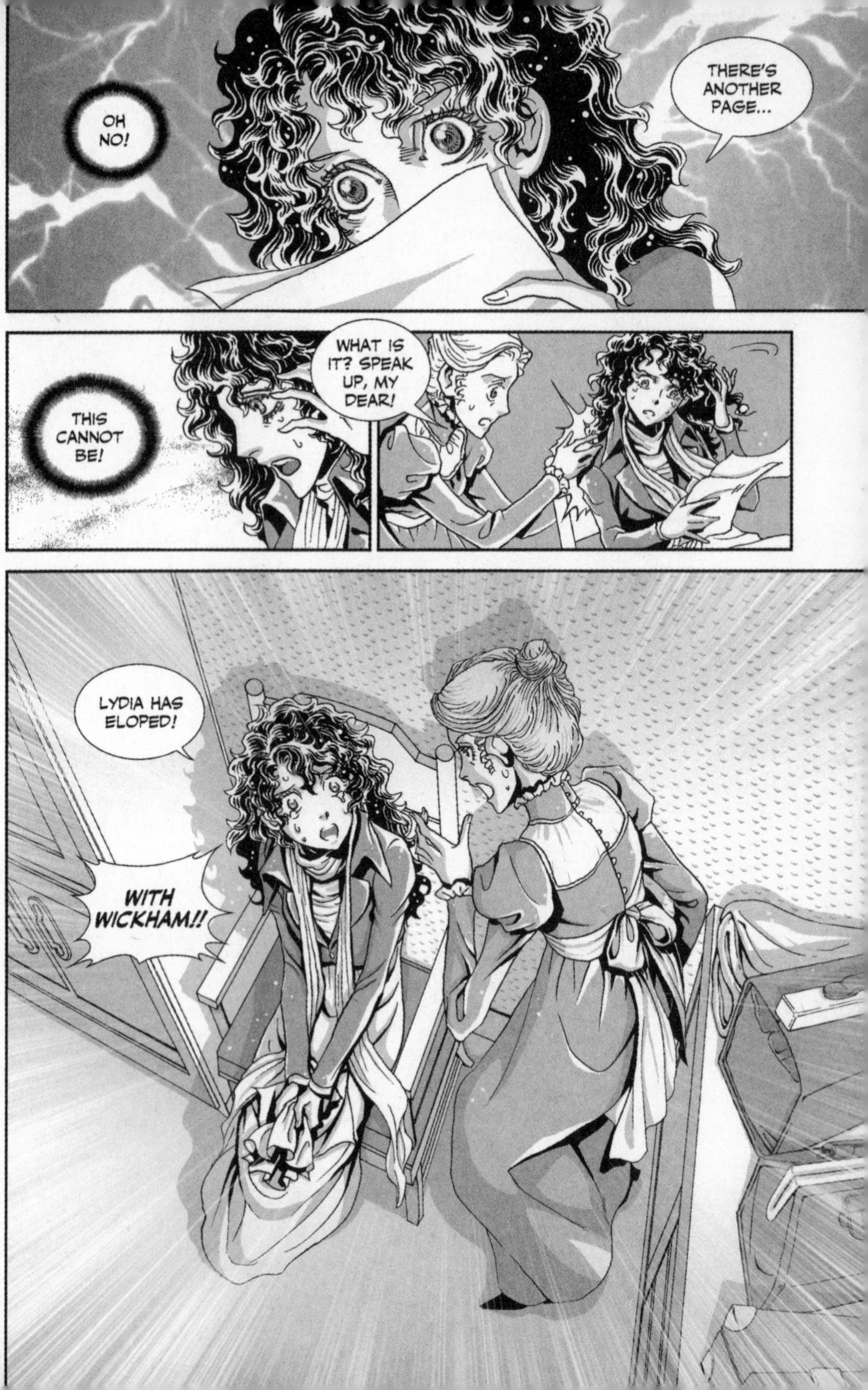
THERE'S ANOTHER PAGE...
OH NO!
WHAT IS IT? SPEAK UP, MY DEAR!
THIS CANNOT BE!
LYDIA HAS ELOPED!
WITH WICKHAM!!

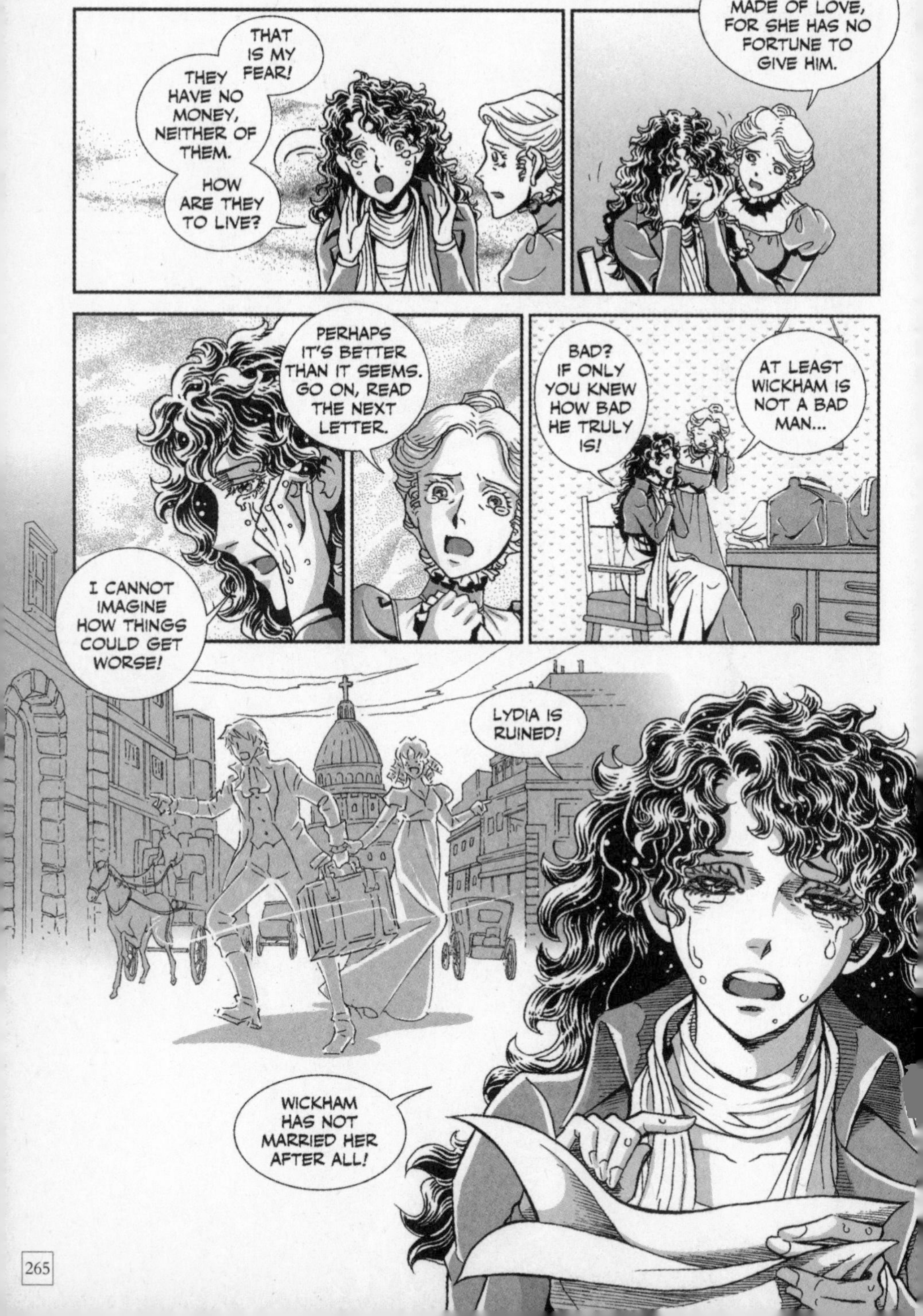
AT LEAST IT IS A CHOICE MADE OF LOVE, FOR SHE HAS NO FORTUNE TO GIVE HIM.
THAT IS MY FEAR!
THEY HAVE NO MONEY, NEITHER OF THEM.
HOW ARE THEY TO LIVE?
AT LEAST WICKHAM IS NOT A BAD MAN...
BAD? IF ONLY YOU KNEW HOW BAD HE TRULY IS!
PERHAPS IT'S BETTER THAN IT SEEMS. GO ON, READ THE NEXT LETTER.
I CANNOT IMAGINE HOW THINGS COULD GET WORSE!
LYDIA IS RUINED!
WICKHAM HAS NOT MARRIED HER AFTER ALL!

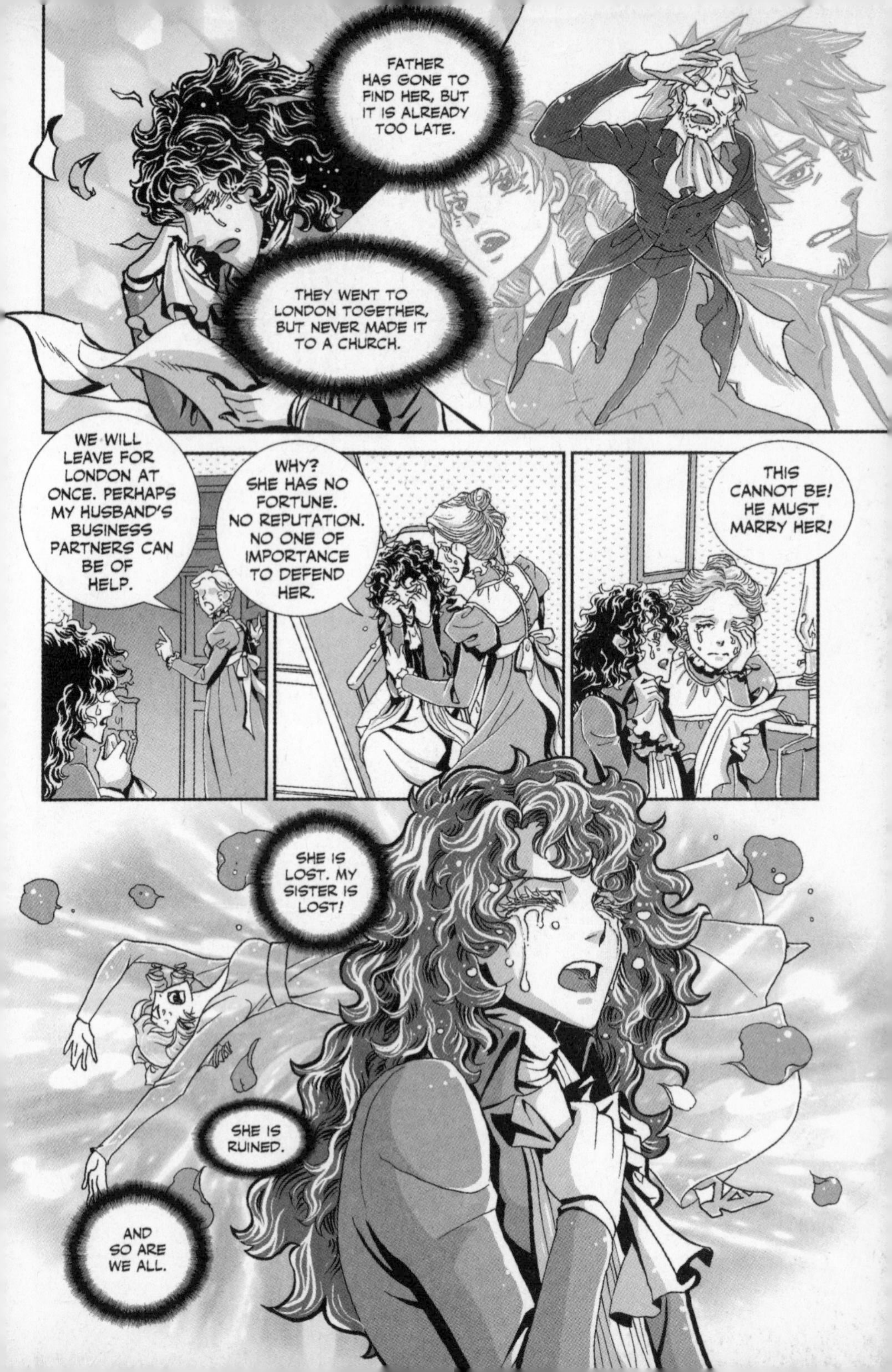
FATHER HAS GONE TO FIND HER, BUT IT IS ALREADY TOO LATE.
THEY WENT TO LONDON TOGETHER, BUT NEVER MADE IT TO A CHURCH.
THIS CANNOT BE! HE MUST MARRY HER!
WHY? SHE HAS NO FORTUNE. NO REPUTATION. NO ONE OF IMPORTANCE TO DEFEND HER.
WE WILL LEAVE FOR LONDON AT ONCE. PERHAPS MY HUSBAND'S BUSINESS PARTNERS CAN BE OF HELP.
SHE IS LOST. MY SISTER IS LOST!
SHE IS RUINED.
AND SO ARE WE ALL.

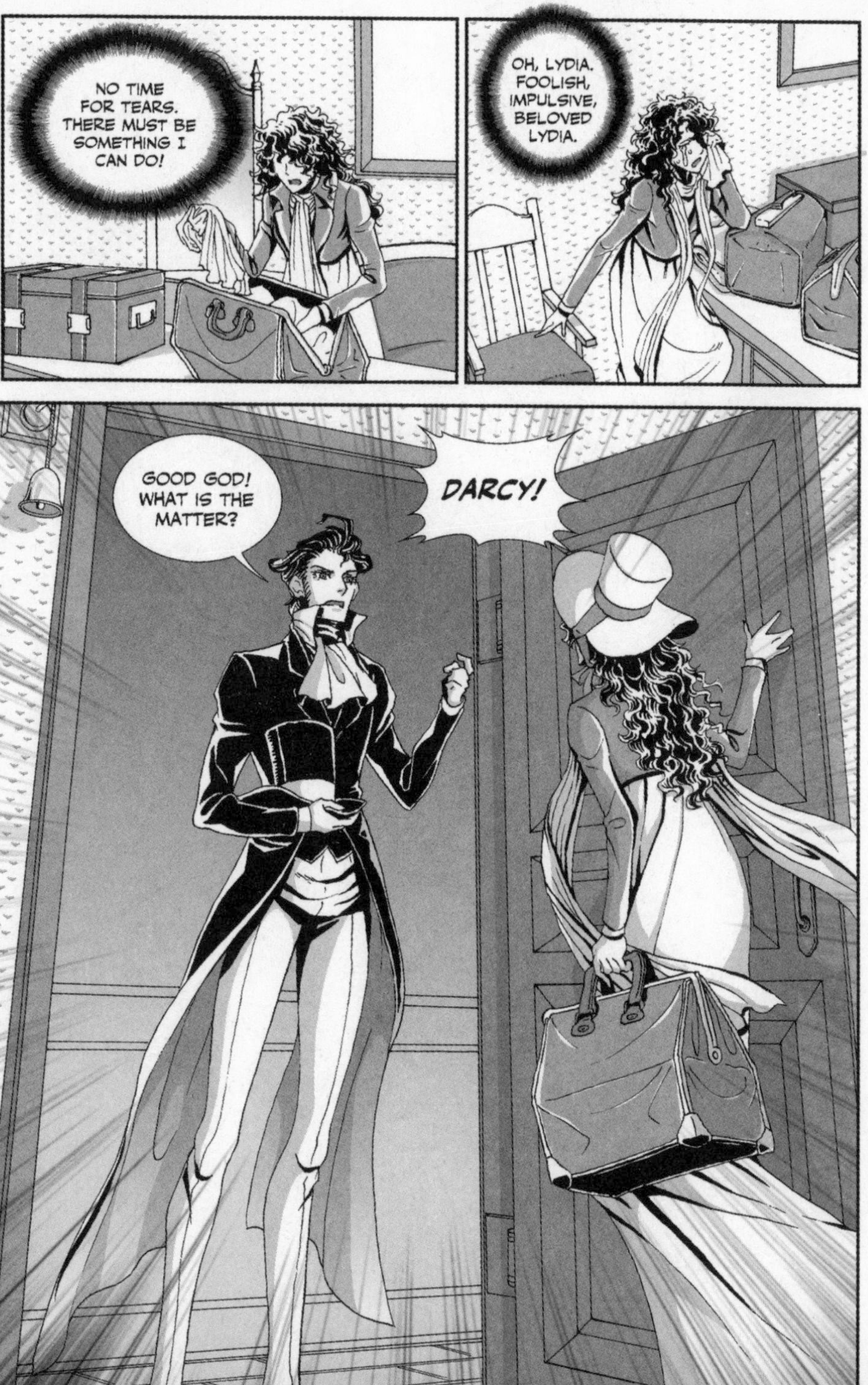
OH, LYDIA. FOOLISH, IMPULSIVE, BELOVED LYDIA.
NO TIME FOR TEARS. THERE MUST BE SOMETHING I CAN DO!
DARCY!
GOOD GOD! WHAT IS THE MATTER?

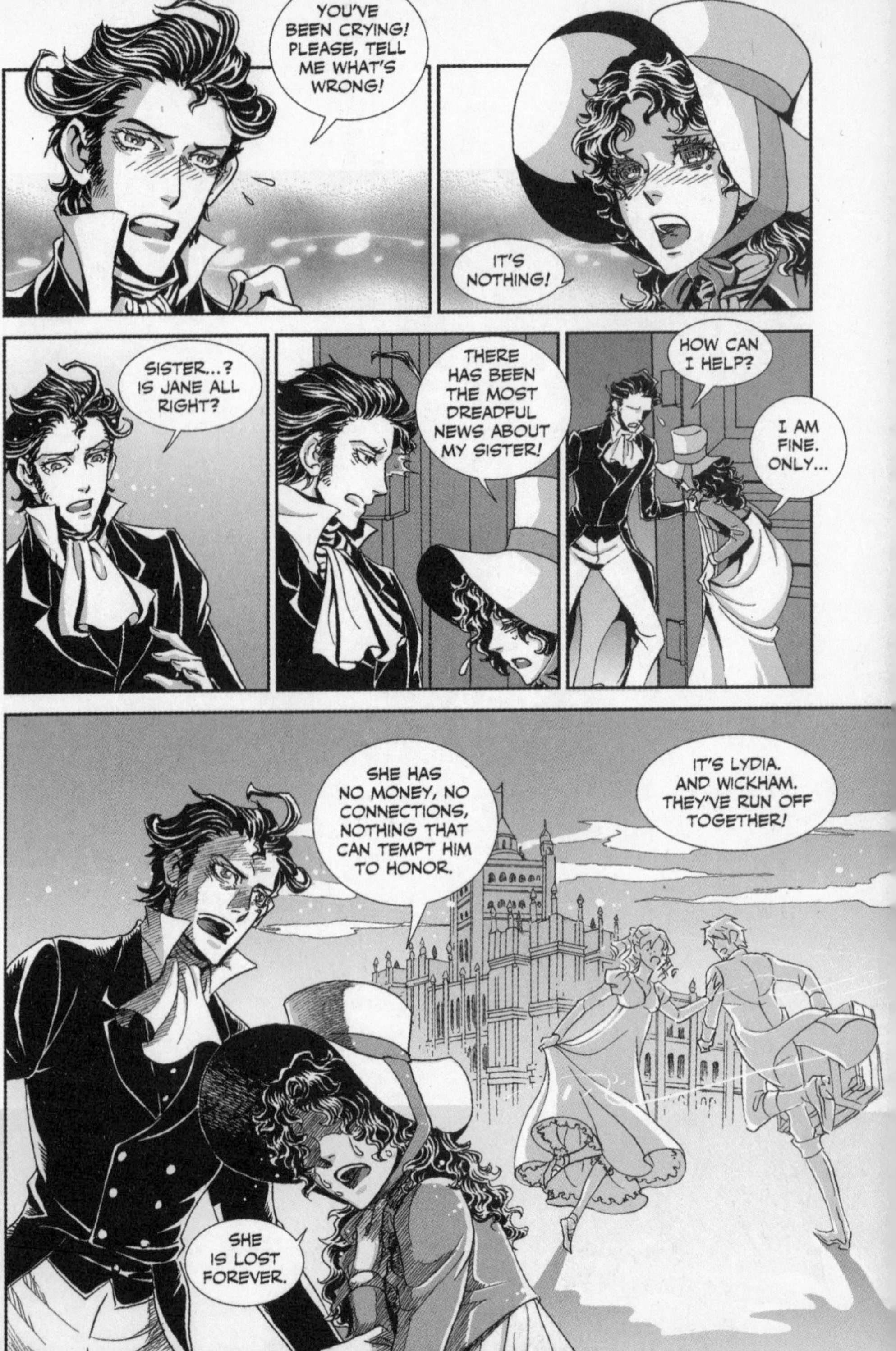
IT'S NOTHING!
YOU'VE BEEN CRYING! PLEASE, TELL ME WHAT'S WRONG!
HOW CAN I HELP?
I AM FINE. ONLY...
THERE HAS BEEN THE MOST DREADFUL NEWS ABOUT MY SISTER!
SISTER...? IS JANE ALL RIGHT?
IT'S LYDIA. AND WICKHAM. THEY'VE RUN OFF TOGETHER!
SHE HAS NO MONEY, NO CONNECTIONS, NOTHING THAT CAN TEMPT HIM TO HONOR.
SHE IS LOST FOREVER.

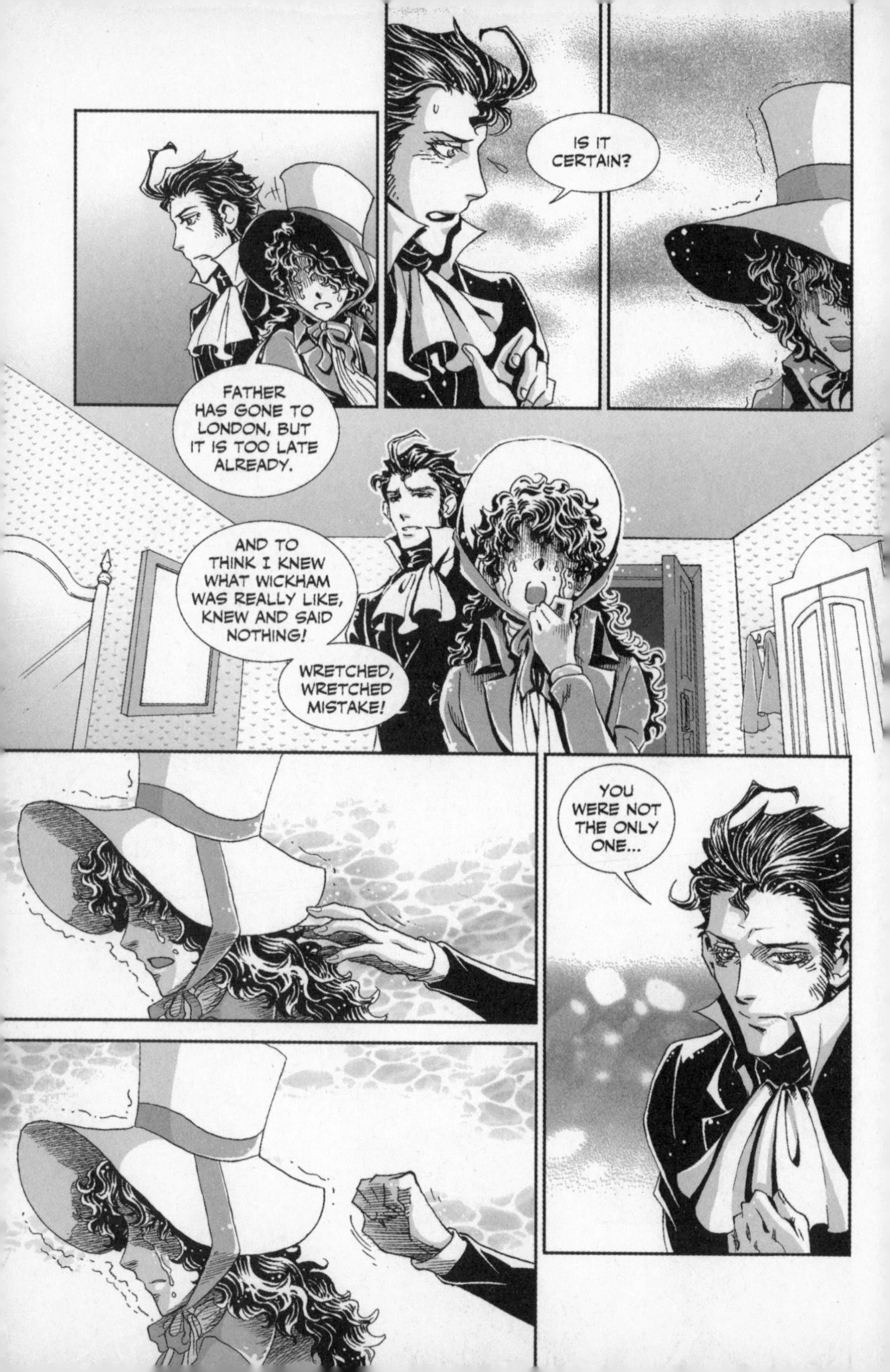
IS IT CERTAIN?
FATHER HAS GONE TO LONDON, BUT IT IS TOO LATE ALREADY.
AND TO THINK I KNEW WHAT WICKHAM WAS REALLY LIKE, KNEW AND SAID NOTHING!
WRETCHED, WRETCHED MISTAKE!
YOU WERE NOT THE ONLY ONE...

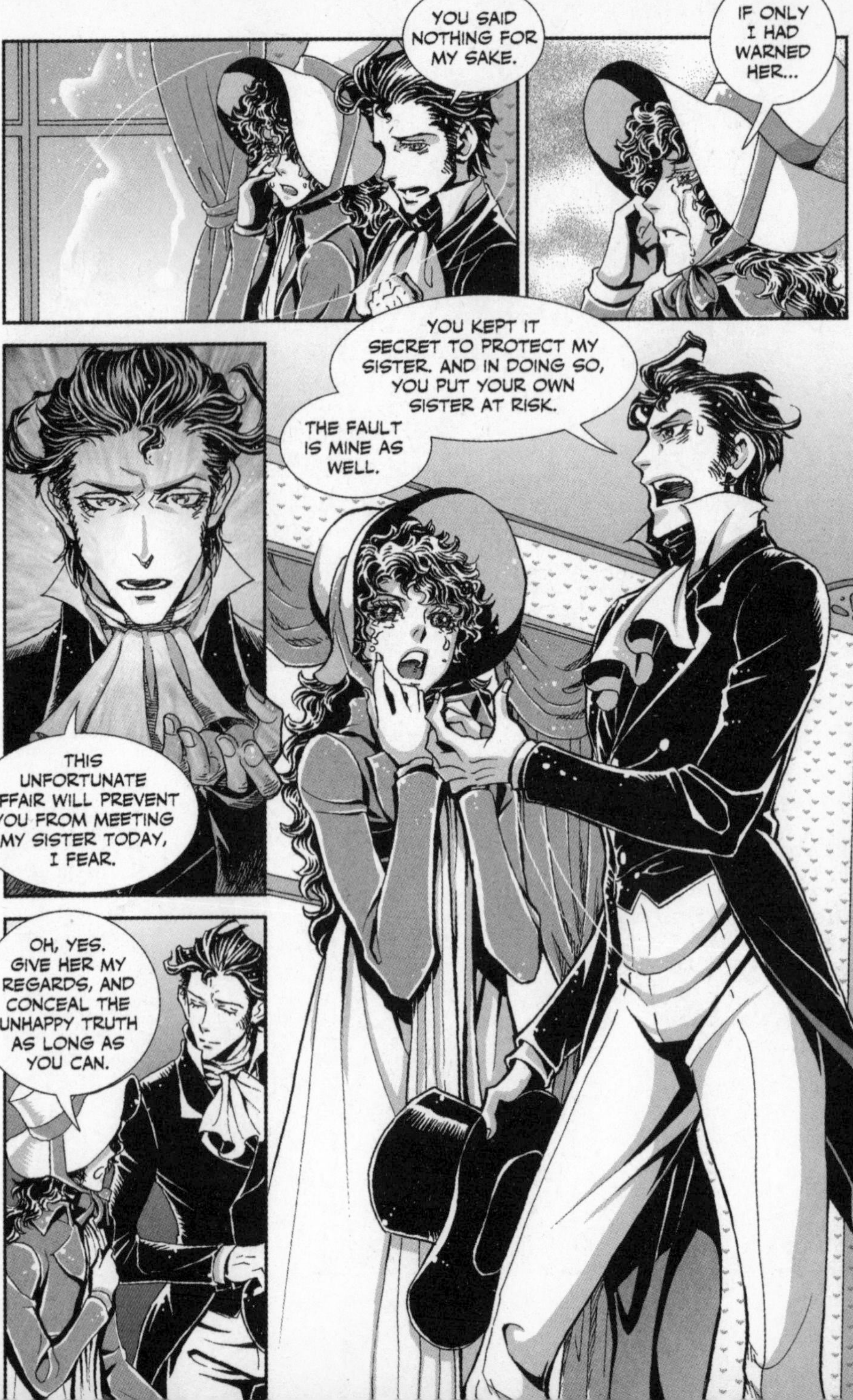
IF ONLY I HAD WARNED HER...
YOU SAID NOTHING FOR MY SAKE.
YOU KEPT IT SECRET TO PROTECT MY SISTER. AND IN DOING SO, YOU PUT YOUR OWN SISTER AT RISK.
THE FAULT IS MINE AS WELL.
THIS UNFORTUNATE AFFAIR WILL PREVENT YOU FROM MEETING MY SISTER TODAY, I FEAR.
OH, YES. GIVE HER MY REGARDS, AND CONCEAL THE UNHAPPY TRUTH AS LONG AS YOU CAN.

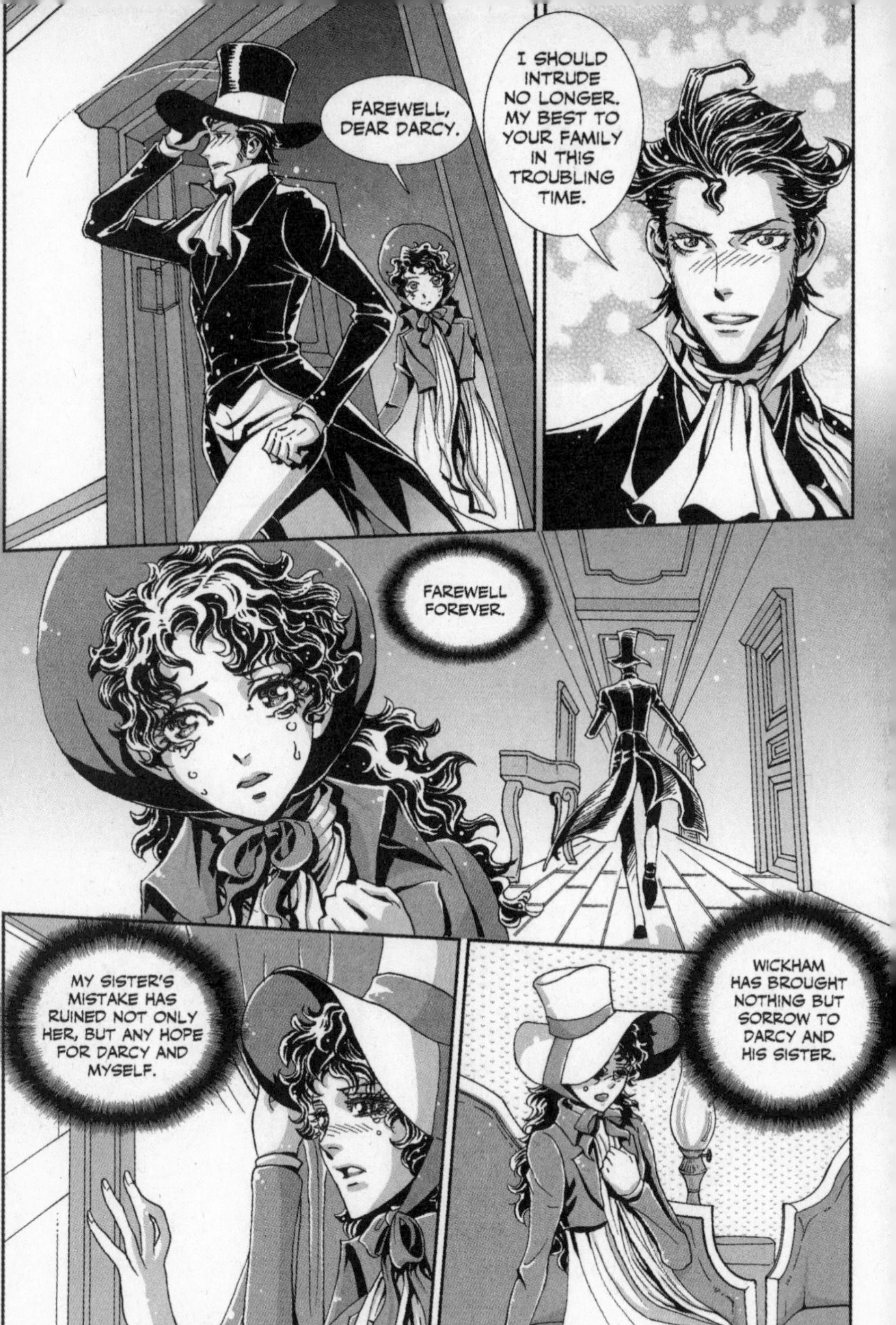
I SHOULD INTRUDE NO LONGER. MY BEST TO YOUR FAMILY IN THIS TROUBLING TIME.
FAREWELL, DEAR DARCY.
FAREWELL FOREVER.
WICKHAM HAS BROUGHT NOTHING BUT SORROW TO DARCY AND HIS SISTER.
MY SISTER'S MISTAKE HAS RUINED NOT ONLY HER, BUT ANY HOPE FOR DARCY AND MYSELF.

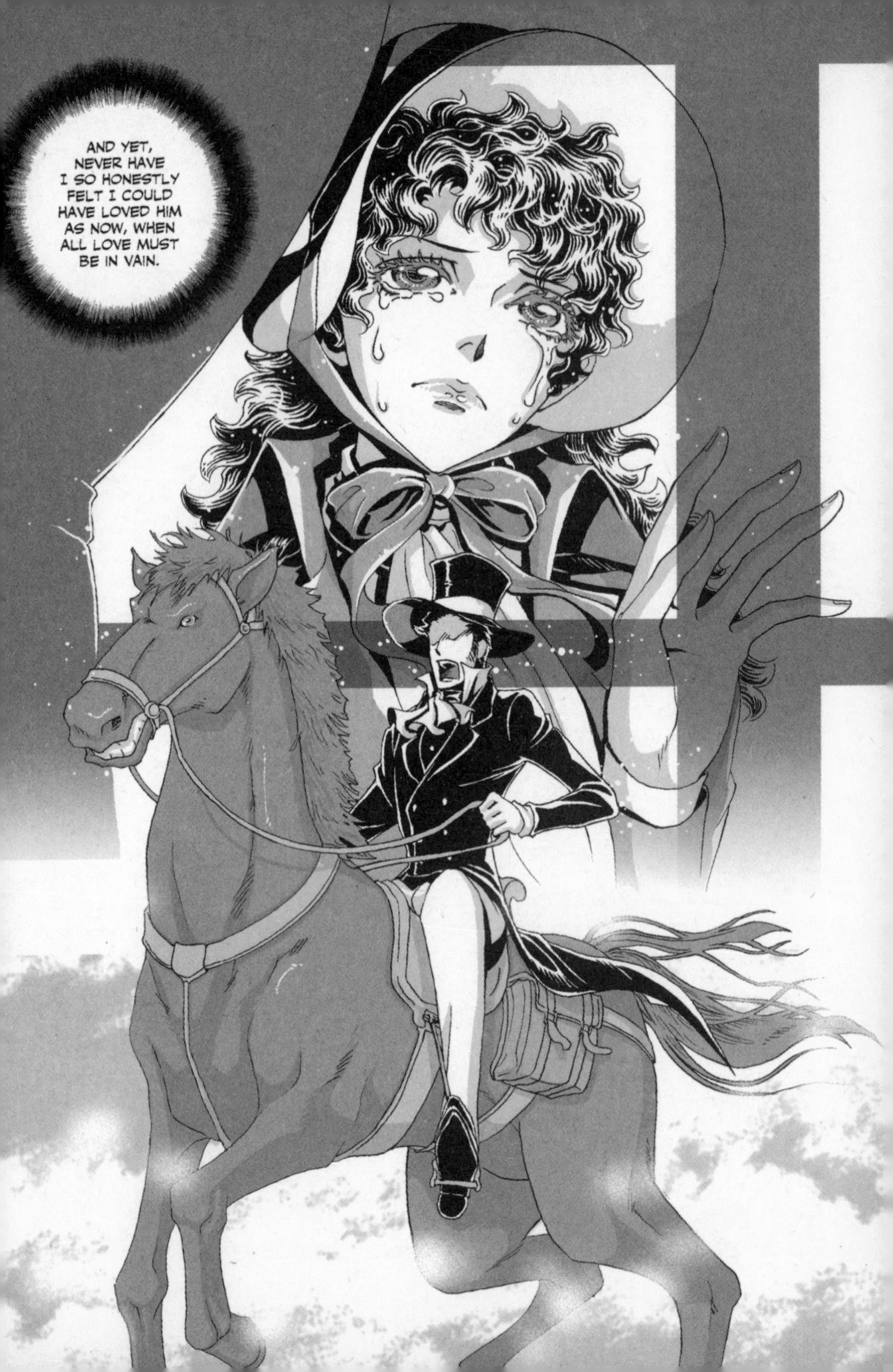
AND YET, NEVER HAVE I SO HONESTLY FELT I COULD HAVE LOVED HIM AS NOW, WHEN ALL LOVE MUST BE IN VAIN.

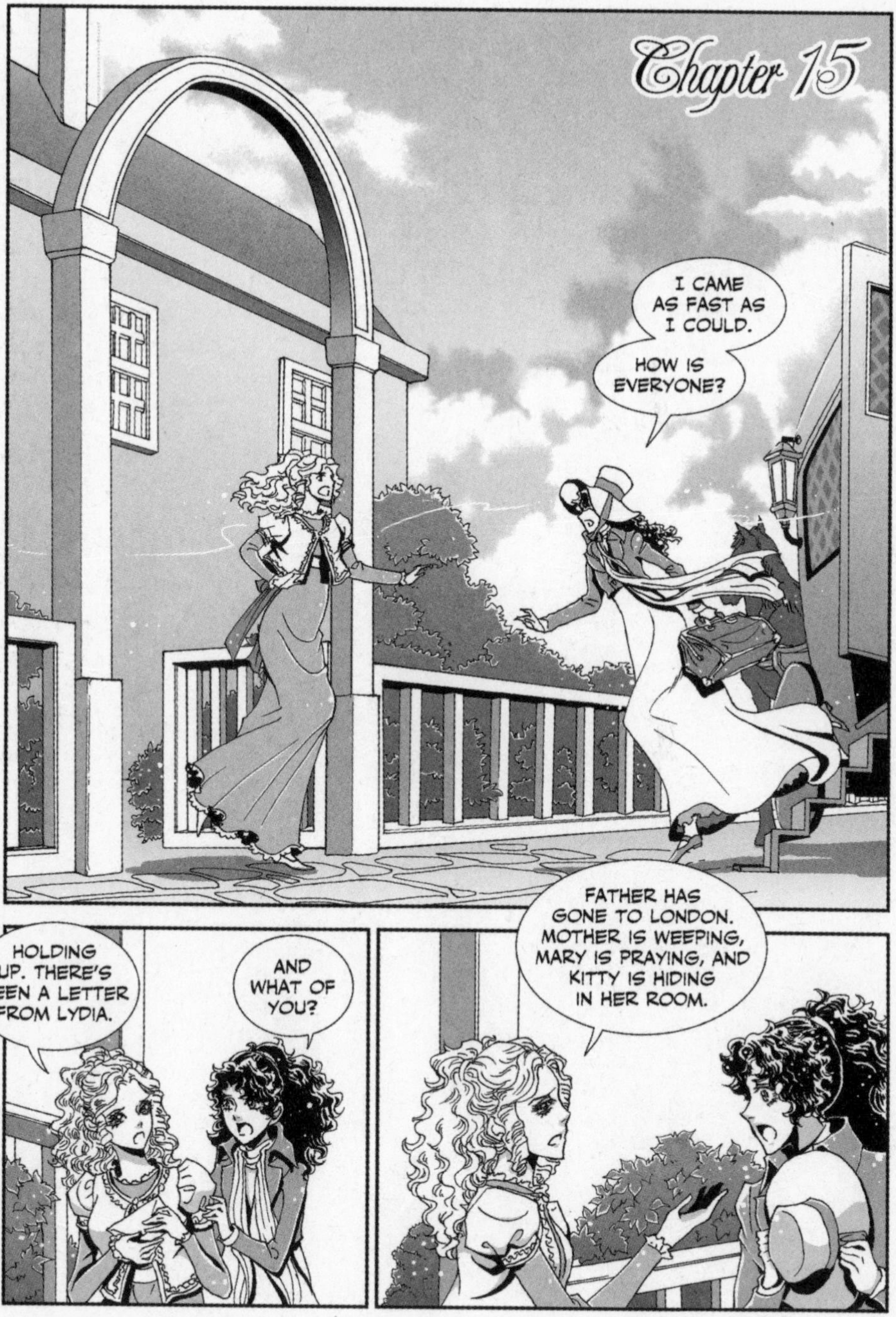
Chapter 15
I CAME AS FAST AS I COULD.
HOW IS EVERYONE?
FATHER HAS GONE TO LONDON. MOTHER IS WEEPING, MARY IS PRAYING, AND KITTY IS HIDING IN HER ROOM.
AND WHAT OF YOU?
HOLDING UP. THERE'S BEEN A LETTER FROM LYDIA.

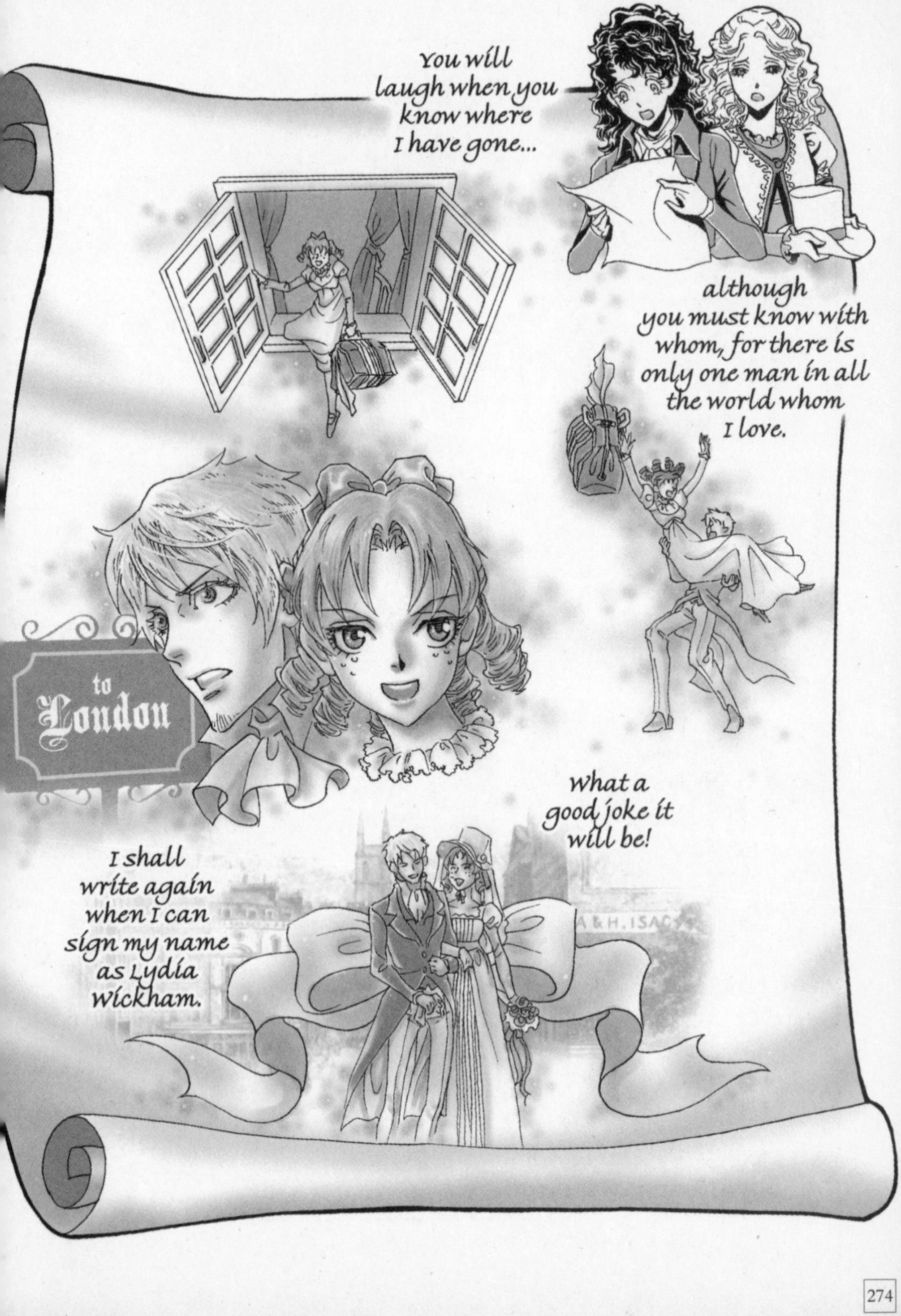
You will laugh when you know where I have gone...
although you must know with whom, for there is only one man in all the world whom I love.
to London
What a good joke it will be!
I shall write again when I can sign my name as Lydia Wickham.
A & H. ISAC

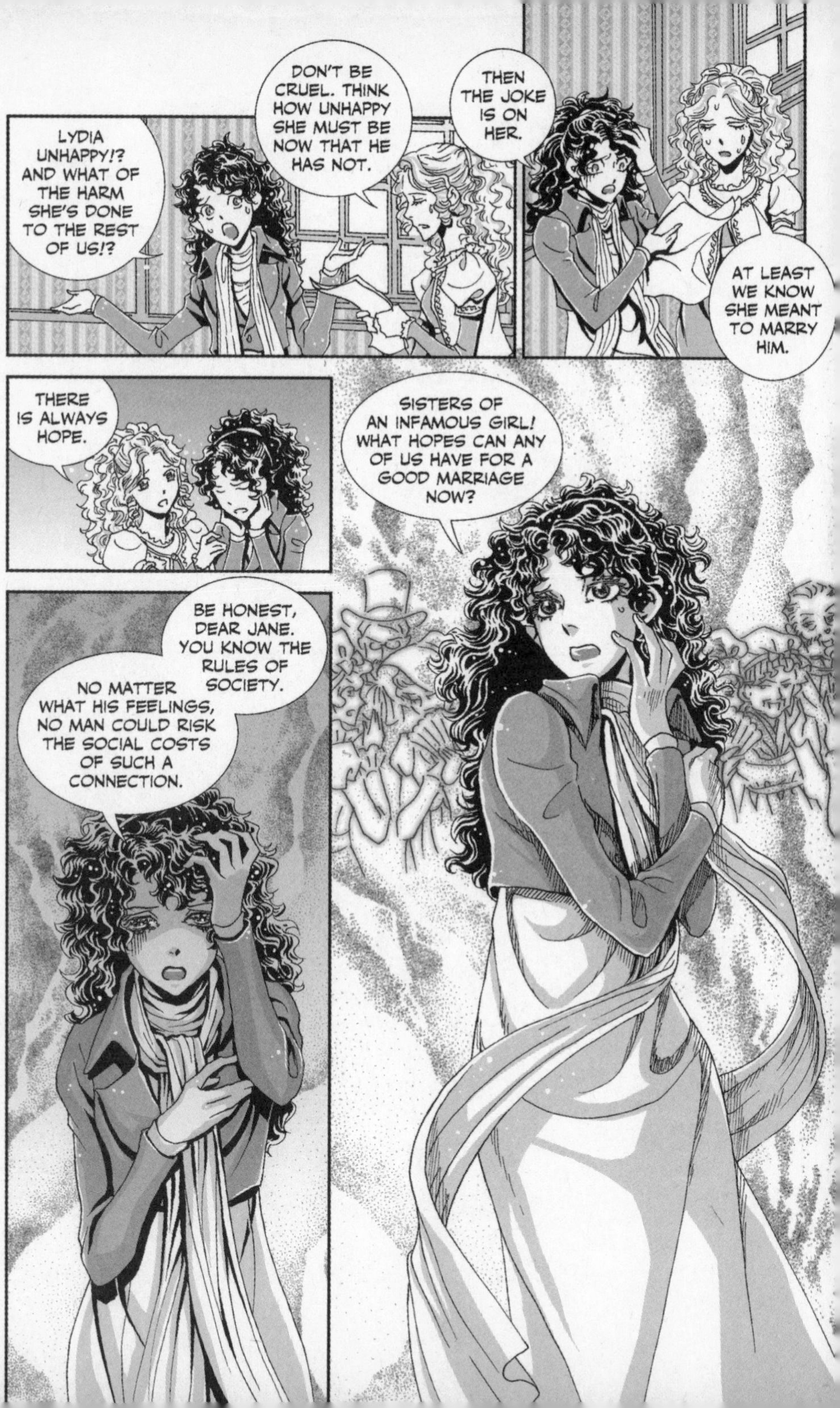

THEN THE JOKE IS ON HER.
AT LEAST WE KNOW SHE MEANT TO MARRY HIM.
DON'T BE CRUEL. THINK HOW UNHAPPY SHE MUST BE NOW THAT HE HAS NOT.
LYDIA UNHAPPY!? AND WHAT OF THE HARM SHE'S DONE TO THE REST OF US!?
SISTERS OF AN INFAMOUS GIRL! WHAT HOPES CAN ANY OF US HAVE FOR A GOOD MARRIAGE NOW?
THERE IS ALWAYS HOPE.
BE HONEST, DEAR JANE. YOU KNOW THE RULES OF SOCIETY.
NO MATTER WHAT HIS FEELINGS, NO MAN COULD RISK THE SOCIAL COSTS OF SUCH A CONNECTION.

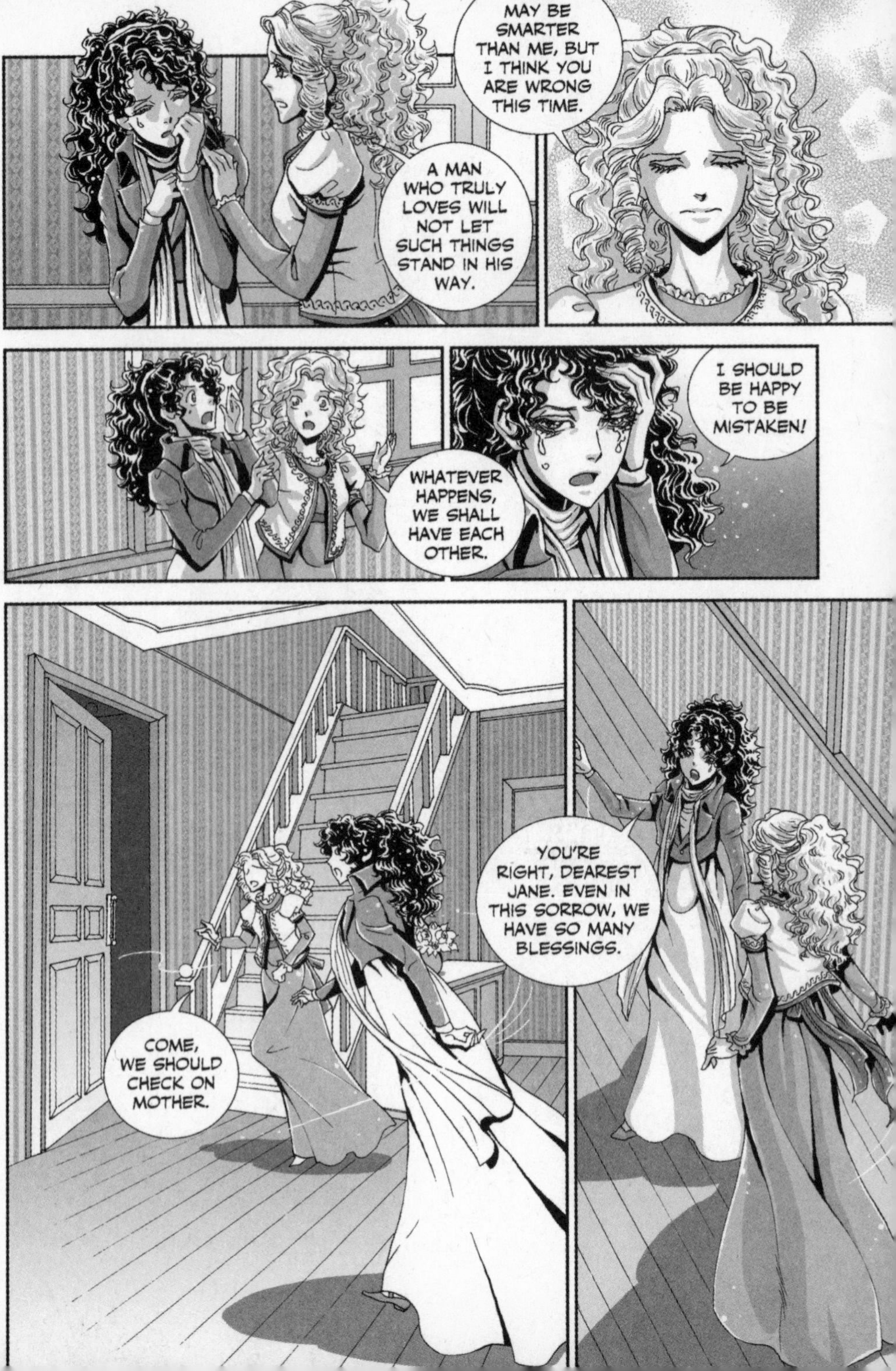
YOU MAY BE SMARTER THAN ME, BUT I THINK YOU ARE WRONG THIS TIME.
A MAN WHO TRULY LOVES WILL NOT LET SUCH THINGS STAND IN HIS WAY.
I SHOULD BE HAPPY TO BE MISTAKEN!
WHATEVER HAPPENS, WE SHALL HAVE EACH OTHER.
YOU'RE RIGHT, DEAREST JANE. EVEN IN THIS SORROW, WE HAVE SO MANY BLESSINGS.
COME, WE SHOULD CHECK ON MOTHER.

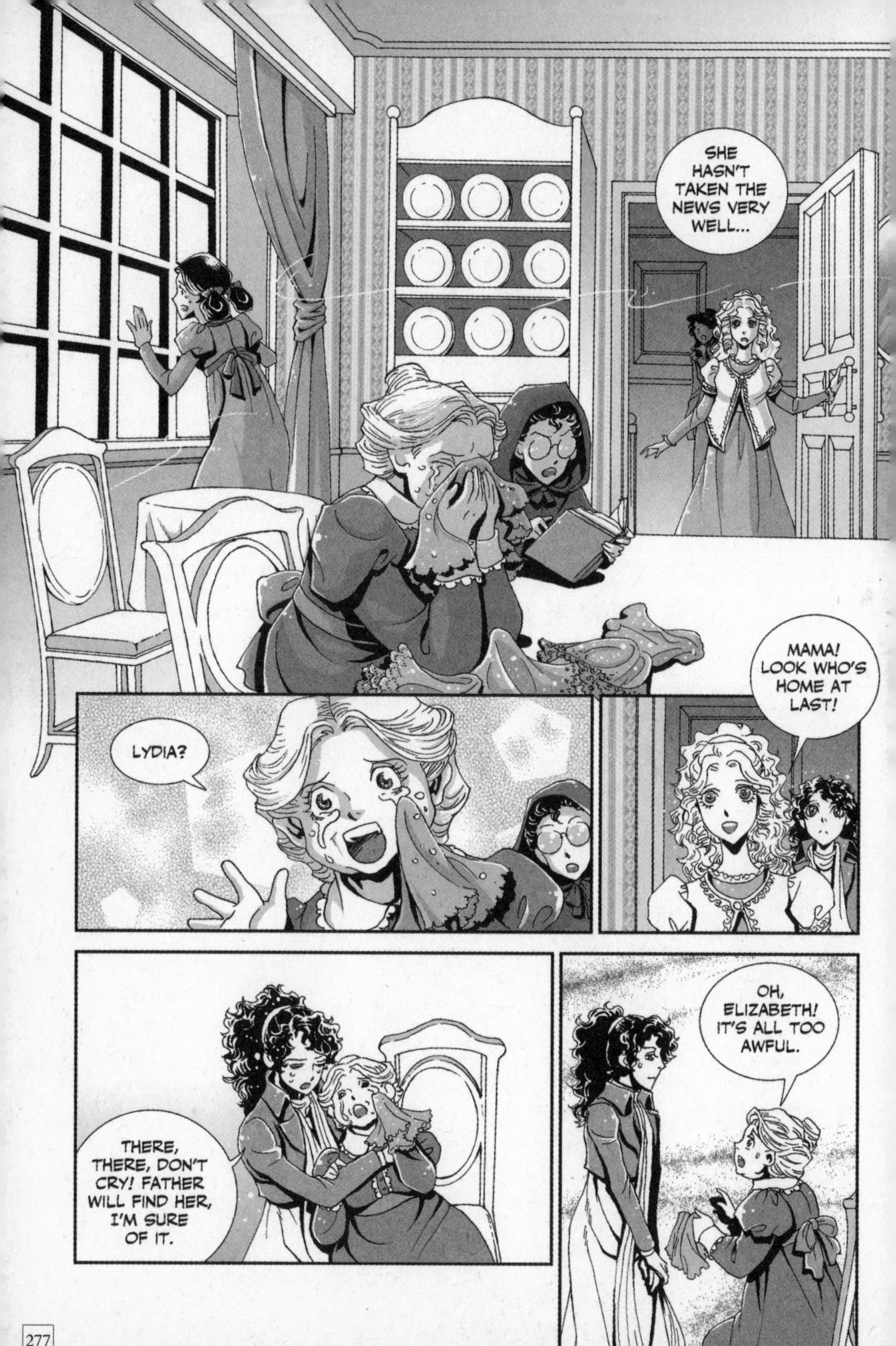
SHE HASN'T TAKEN THE NEWS VERY WELL...
MAMA! LOOK WHO'S HOME AT LAST!
LYDIA?
OH, ELIZABETH! IT'S ALL TOO AWFUL.
THERE, THERE, DON'T CRY! FATHER WILL FIND HER, I'M SURE OF IT.

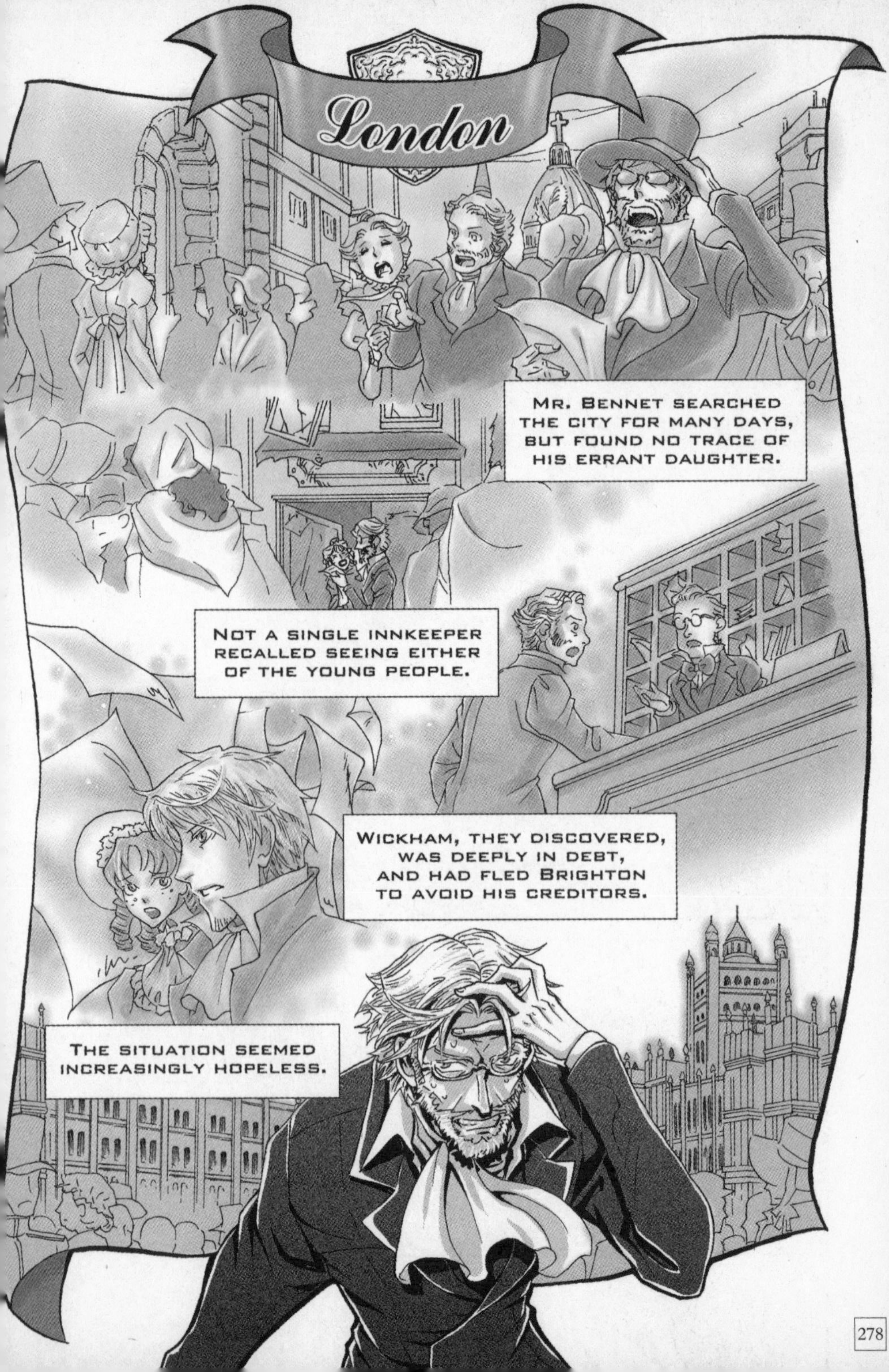
London
Mr. Bennet searched the city for many days, but found no trace of his errant daughter.
Not a single innkeeper recalled seeing either of the young people.
Wickham, they discovered, was deeply in debt, and had fled Brighton to avoid his creditors.
The situation seemed increasingly hopeless.

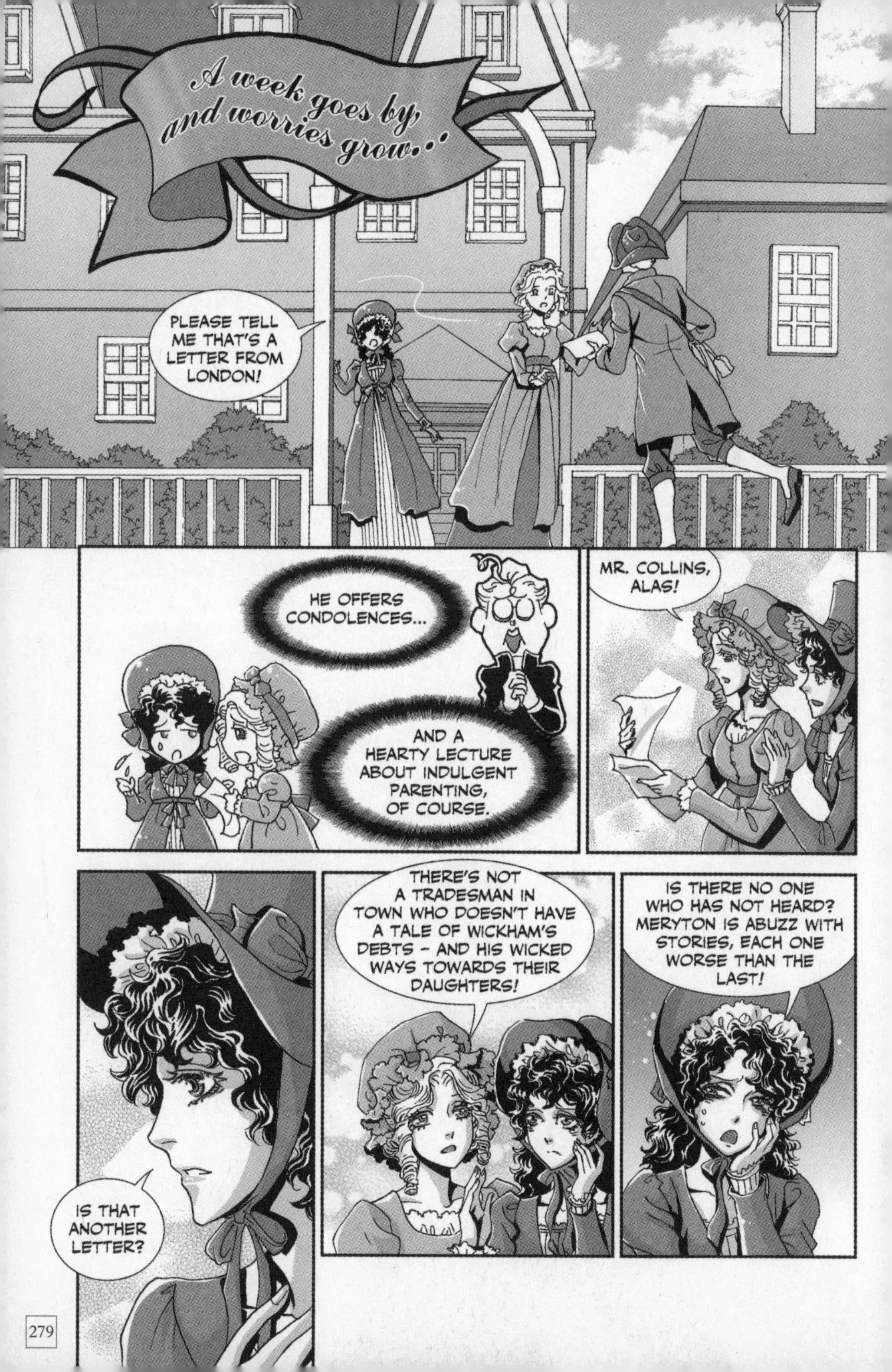
A week goes by, and worries grow...
PLEASE TELL ME THAT'S A LETTER FROM LONDON!
MR. COLLINS, ALAS!
HE OFFERS CONDOLENCES...
AND A HEARTY LECTURE ABOUT INDULGENT PARENTING, OF COURSE.
IS THERE NO ONE WHO HAS NOT HEARD? MERYTON IS ABUZZ WITH STORIES, EACH ONE WORSE THAN THE LAST!
THERE'S NOT A TRADESMAN IN TOWN WHO DOESN'T HAVE A TALE OF WICKHAM'S DEBTS – AND HIS WICKED WAYS TOWARDS THEIR DAUGHTERS!
IS THAT ANOTHER LETTER?

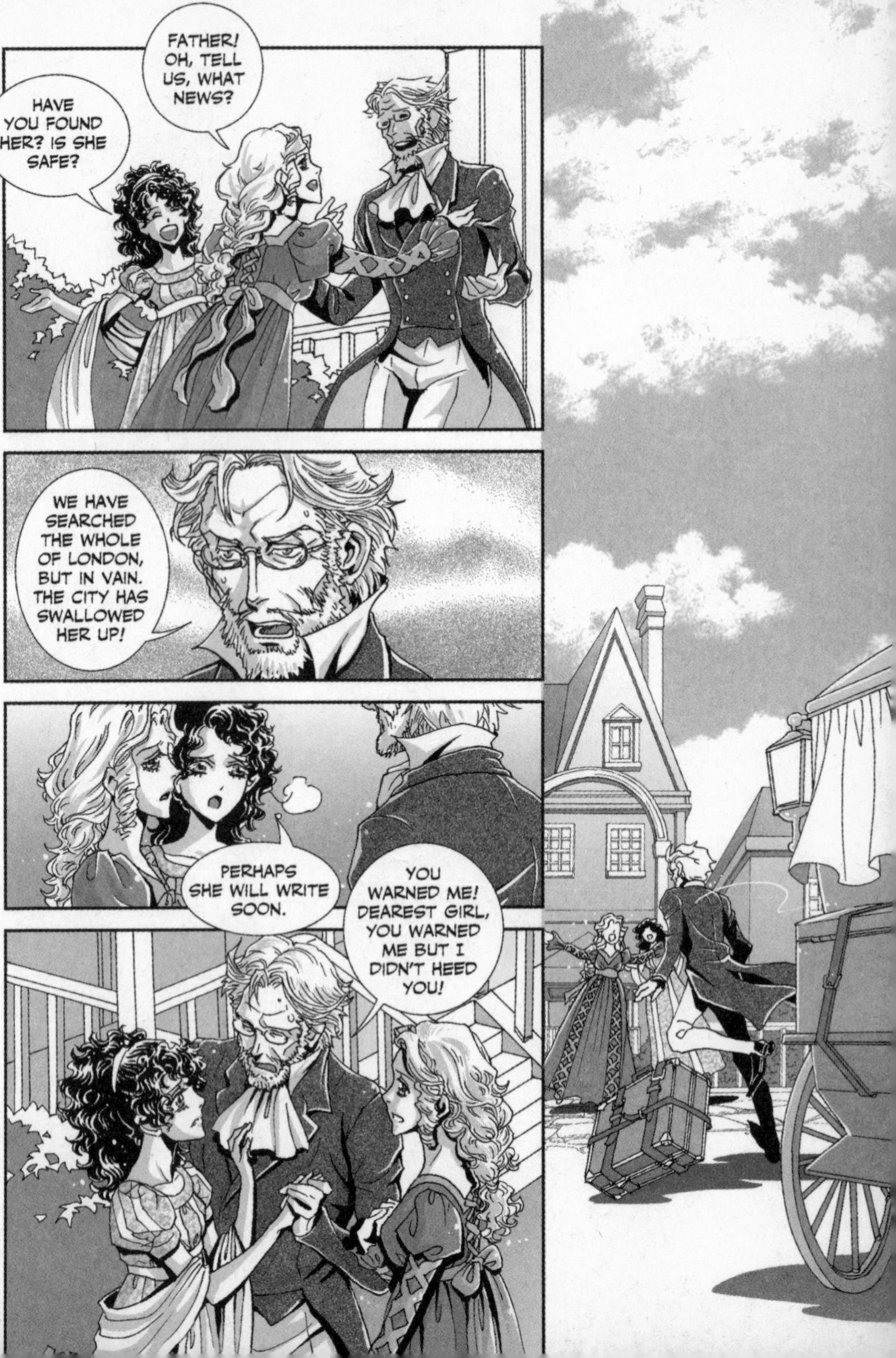
FATHER! OH, TELL US, WHAT NEWS?
HAVE YOU FOUND HER? IS SHE SAFE?
WE HAVE SEARCHED THE WHOLE OF LONDON, BUT IN VAIN. THE CITY HAS SWALLOWED HER UP!
PERHAPS SHE WILL WRITE SOON.
YOU WARNED ME! DEAREST GIRL, YOU WARNED ME BUT I DIDN'T HEED YOU!

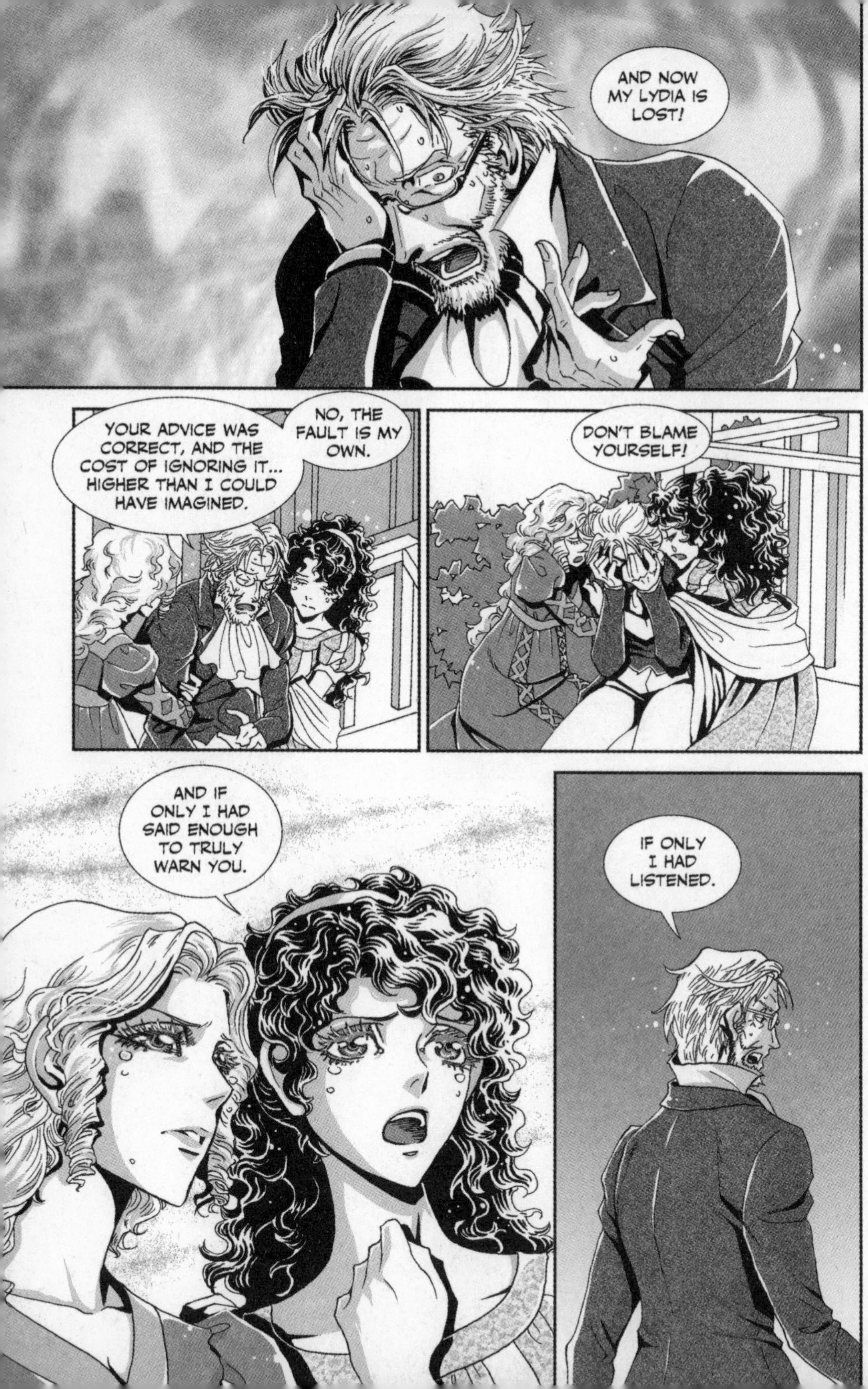
AND NOW MY LYDIA IS LOST!
DON'T BLAME YOURSELF!
NO, THE FAULT IS MY OWN.
YOUR ADVICE WAS CORRECT, AND THE COST OF IGNORING IT... HIGHER THAN I COULD HAVE IMAGINED.
IF ONLY I HAD LISTENED.
AND IF ONLY I HAD SAID ENOUGH TO TRULY WARN YOU.

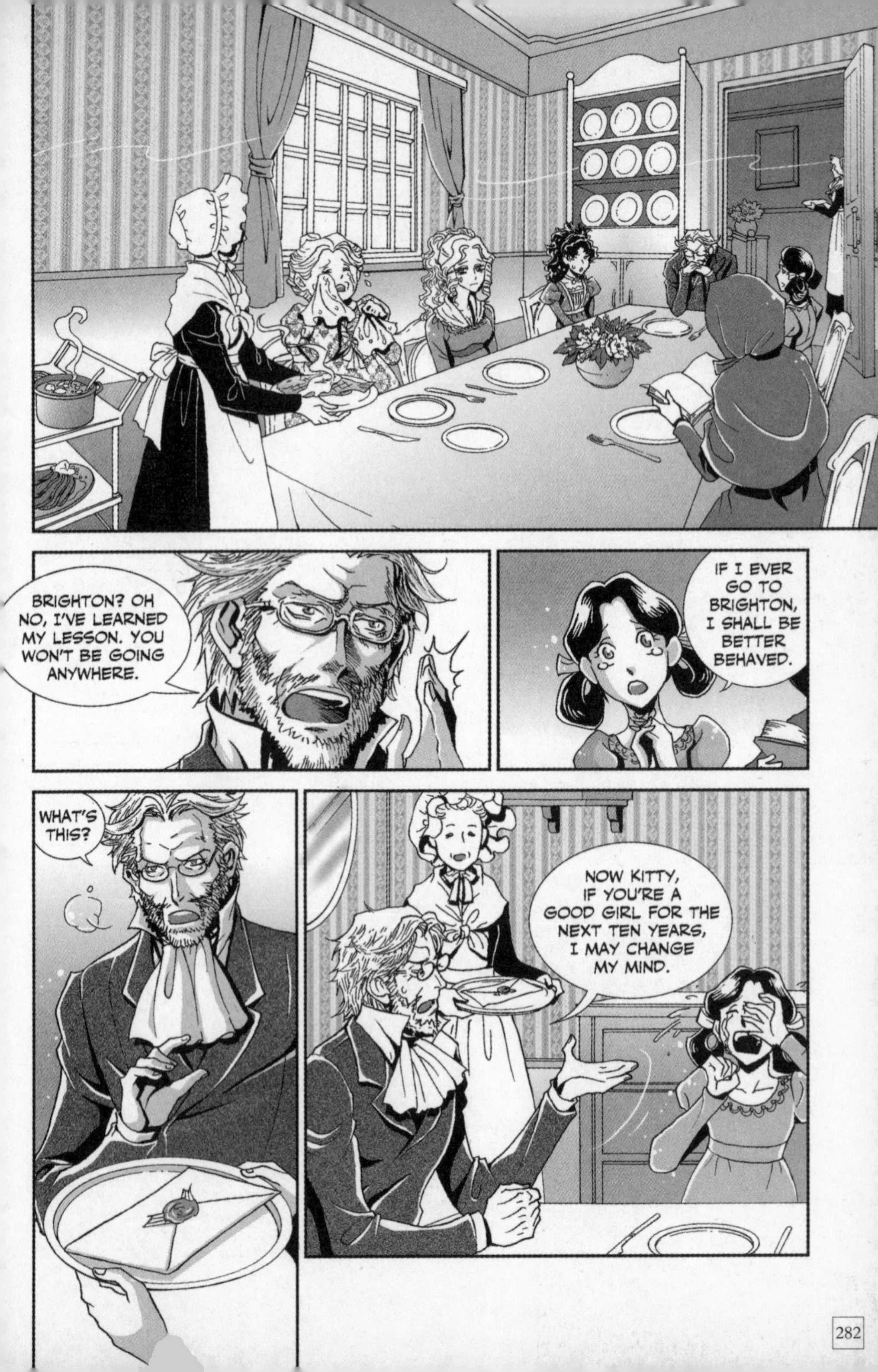
IF I EVER GO TO BRIGHTON, I SHALL BE BETTER BEHAVED.
BRIGHTON? OH NO, I'VE LEARNED MY LESSON. YOU WON'T BE GOING ANYWHERE.
NOW KITTY, IF YOU'RE A GOOD GIRL FOR THE NEXT TEN YEARS, I MAY CHANGE MY MIND.
WHAT'S THIS?

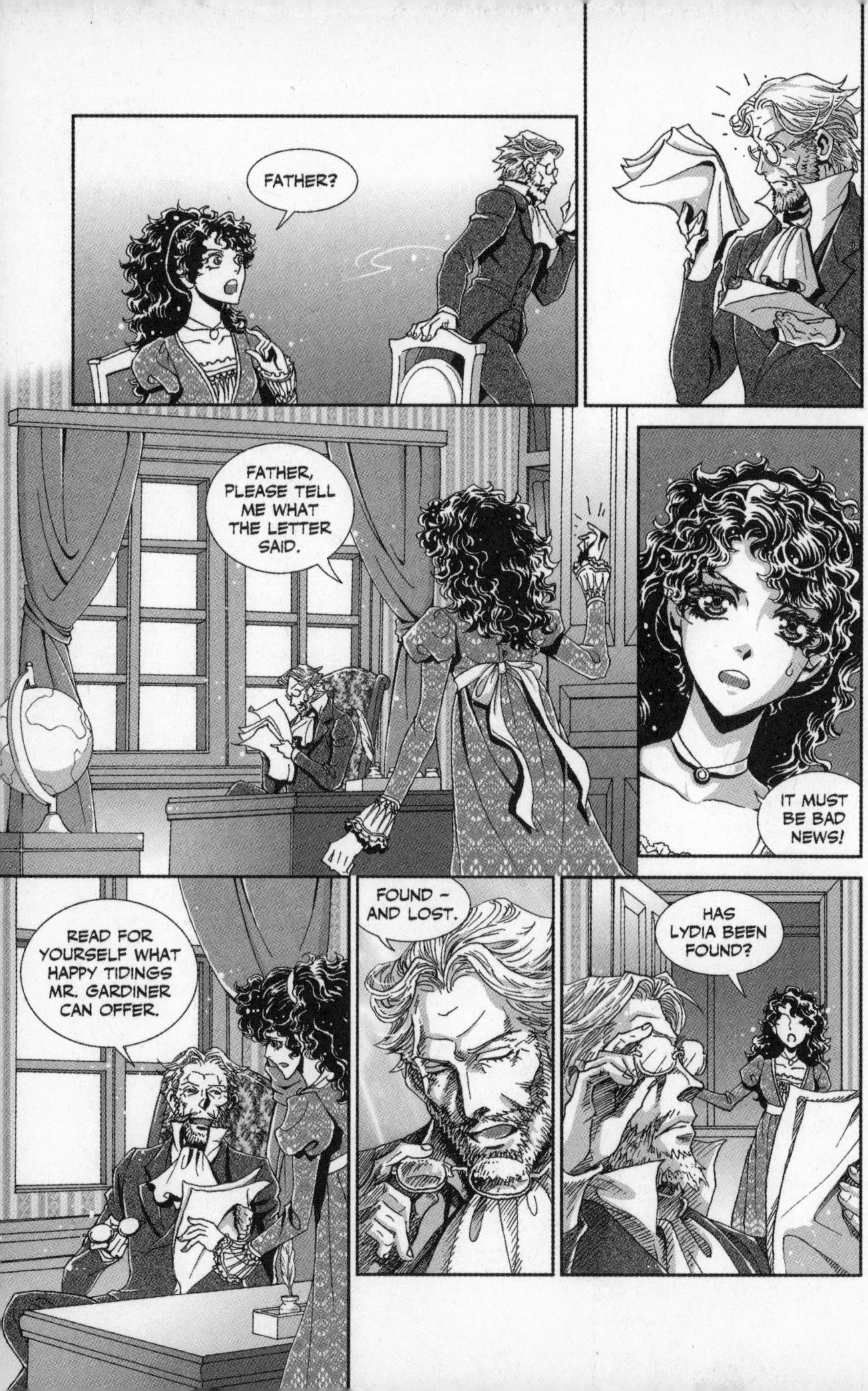
FATHER?
IT MUST BE BAD NEWS!
FATHER, PLEASE TELL ME WHAT THE LETTER SAID.
HAS LYDIA BEEN FOUND?
FOUND – AND LOST.
READ FOR YOURSELF WHAT HAPPY TIDINGS MR. GARDINER CAN OFFER.

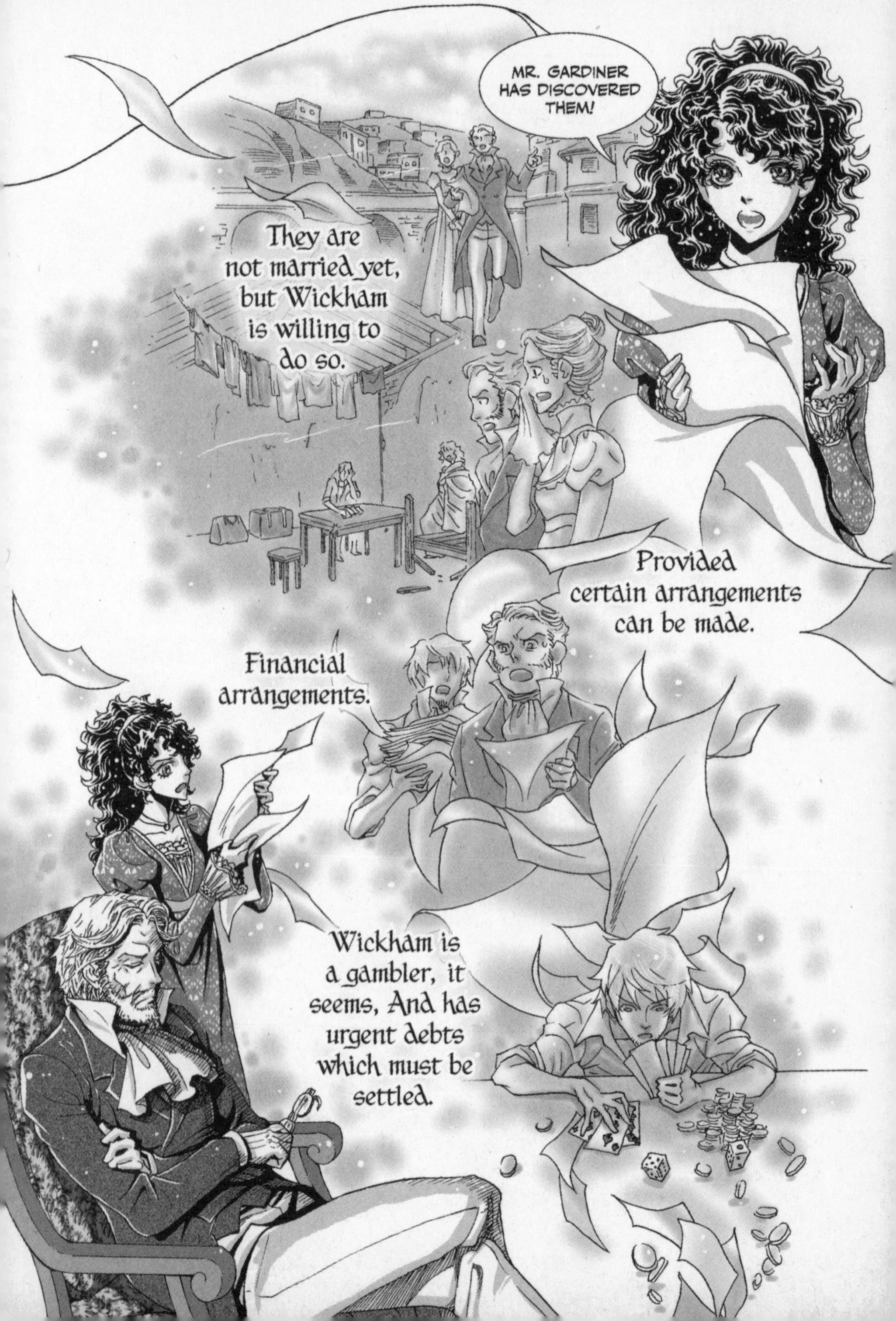
MR. GARDINER HAS DISCOVERED THEM!
They are not married yet, but Wickham is willing to do so.
Provided certain arrangements can be made.
Financial arrangements.
Wickham is a gambler, it seems, And has urgent debts which must be settled.

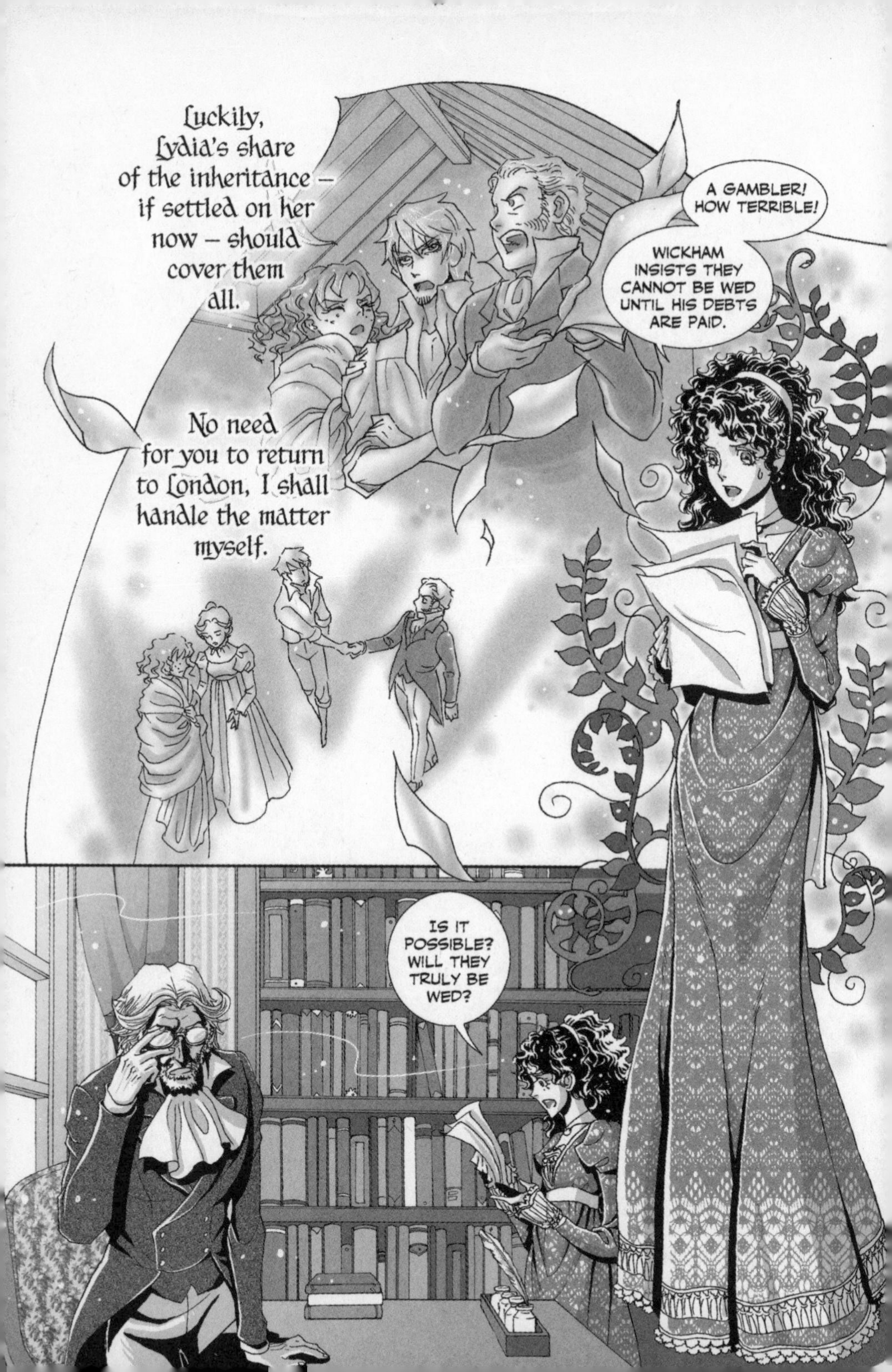
A GAMBLER! HOW TERRIBLE!
WICKHAM INSISTS THEY CANNOT BE WED UNTIL HIS DEBTS ARE PAID.
Luckily, Lydia's share of the inheritance – if settled on her now – should cover them all.
No need for you to return to London, I shall handle the matter myself.
IS IT POSSIBLE? WILL THEY TRULY BE WED?

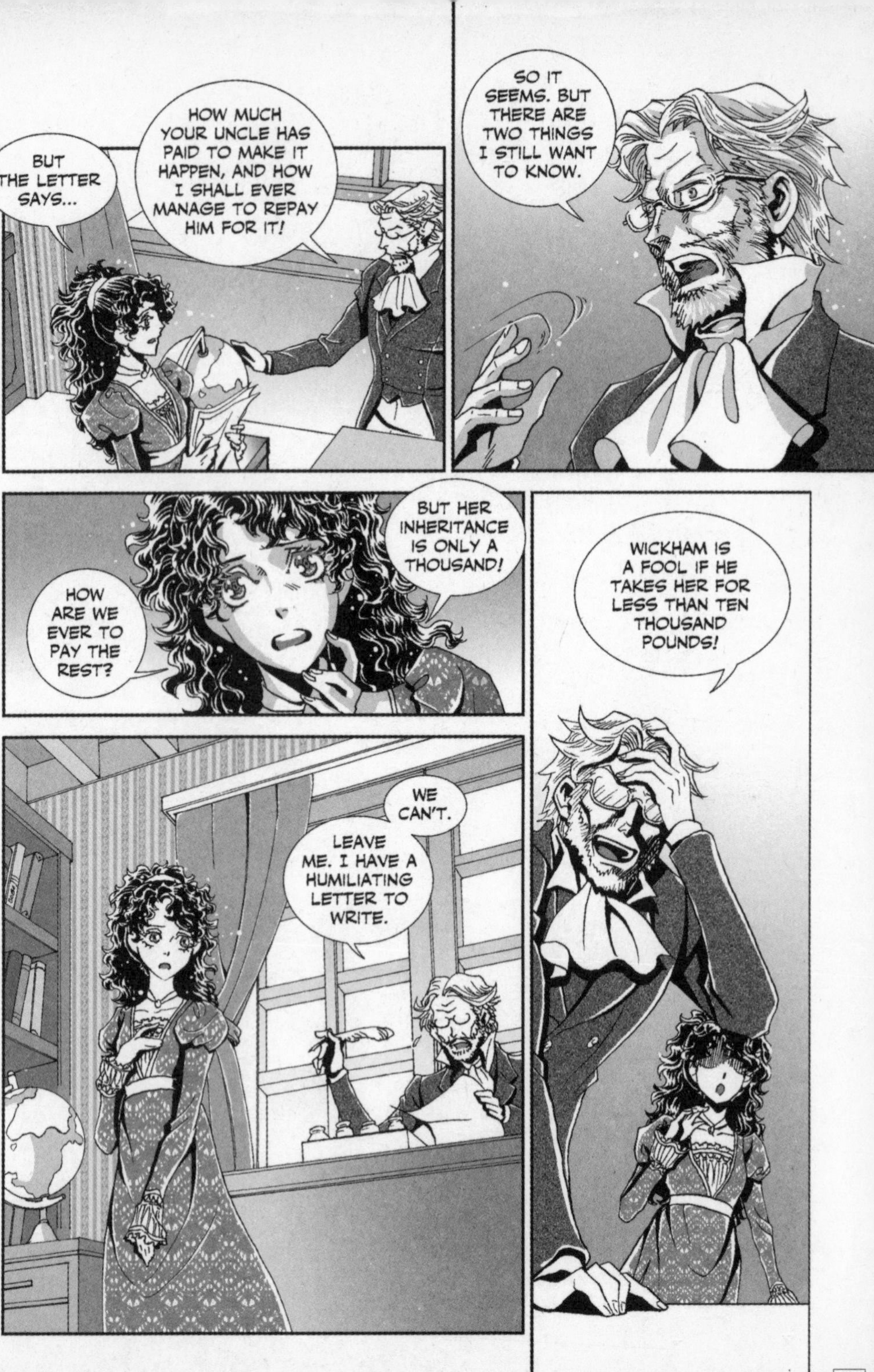
SO IT SEEMS. BUT THERE ARE TWO THINGS I STILL WANT TO KNOW.
BUT THE LETTER SAYS...
HOW MUCH YOUR UNCLE HAS PAID TO MAKE IT HAPPEN, AND HOW I SHALL EVER MANAGE TO REPAY HIM FOR IT!
WICKHAM IS A FOOL IF HE TAKES HER FOR LESS THAN TEN THOUSAND POUNDS!
BUT HER INHERITANCE IS ONLY A THOUSAND!
HOW ARE WE EVER TO PAY THE REST?
WE CAN'T.
LEAVE ME. I HAVE A HUMILIATING LETTER TO WRITE.

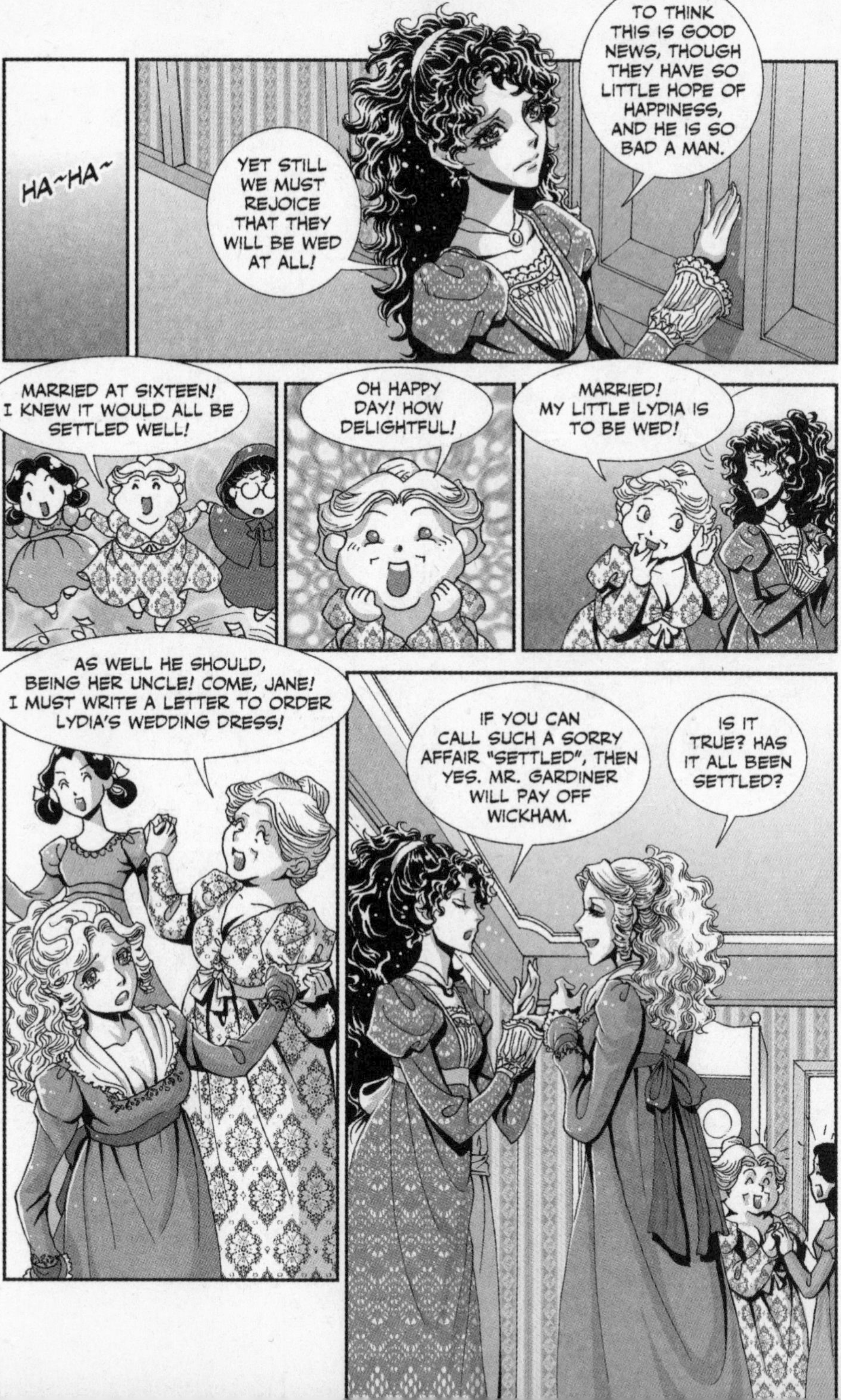
TO THINK THIS IS GOOD NEWS, THOUGH THEY HAVE SO LITTLE HOPE OF HAPPINESS, AND HE IS SO BAD A MAN.
YET STILL WE MUST REJOICE THAT THEY WILL BE WED AT ALL!
HA~HA~
MARRIED! MY LITTLE LYDIA IS TO BE WED!
OH HAPPY DAY! HOW DELIGHTFUL!
MARRIED AT SIXTEEN! I KNEW IT WOULD ALL BE SETTLED WELL!
IS IT TRUE? HAS IT ALL BEEN SETTLED?
IF YOU CAN CALL SUCH A SORRY AFFAIR "SETTLED", THEN YES. MR. GARDINER WILL PAY OFF WICKHAM.
AS WELL HE SHOULD, BEING HER UNCLE! COME, JANE! I MUST WRITE A LETTER TO ORDER LYDIA'S WEDDING DRESS!

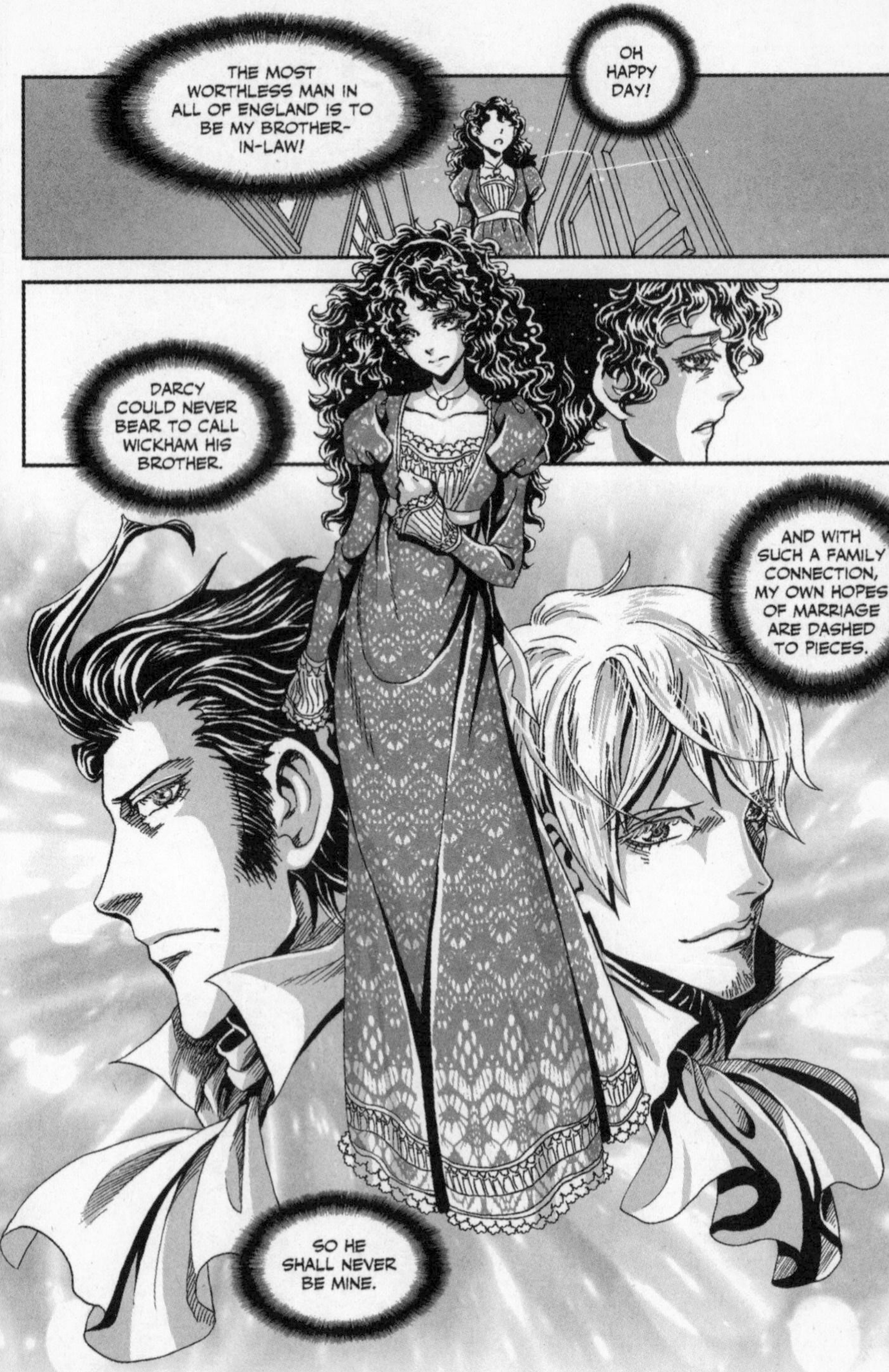
OH HAPPY DAY!
THE MOST WORTHLESS MAN IN ALL OF ENGLAND IS TO BE MY BROTHER-IN-LAW!
DARCY COULD NEVER BEAR TO CALL WICKHAM HIS BROTHER.
AND WITH SUCH A FAMILY CONNECTION, MY OWN HOPES OF MARRIAGE ARE DASHED TO PIECES.
SO HE SHALL NEVER BE MINE.

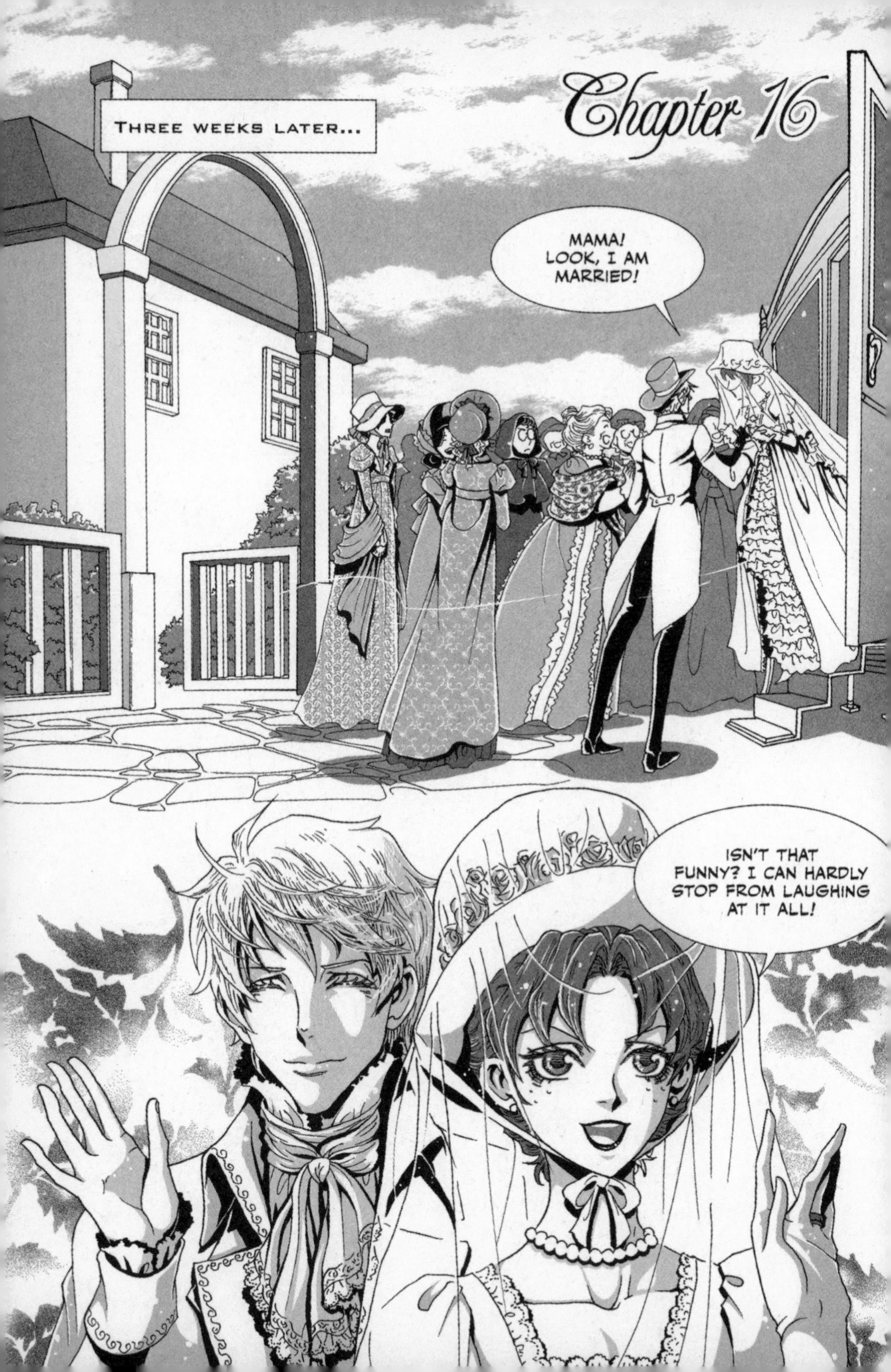
Chapter 16
THREE WEEKS LATER...
MAMA! LOOK, I AM MARRIED!
ISN'T THAT FUNNY? I CAN HARDLY STOP FROM LAUGHING AT IT ALL!

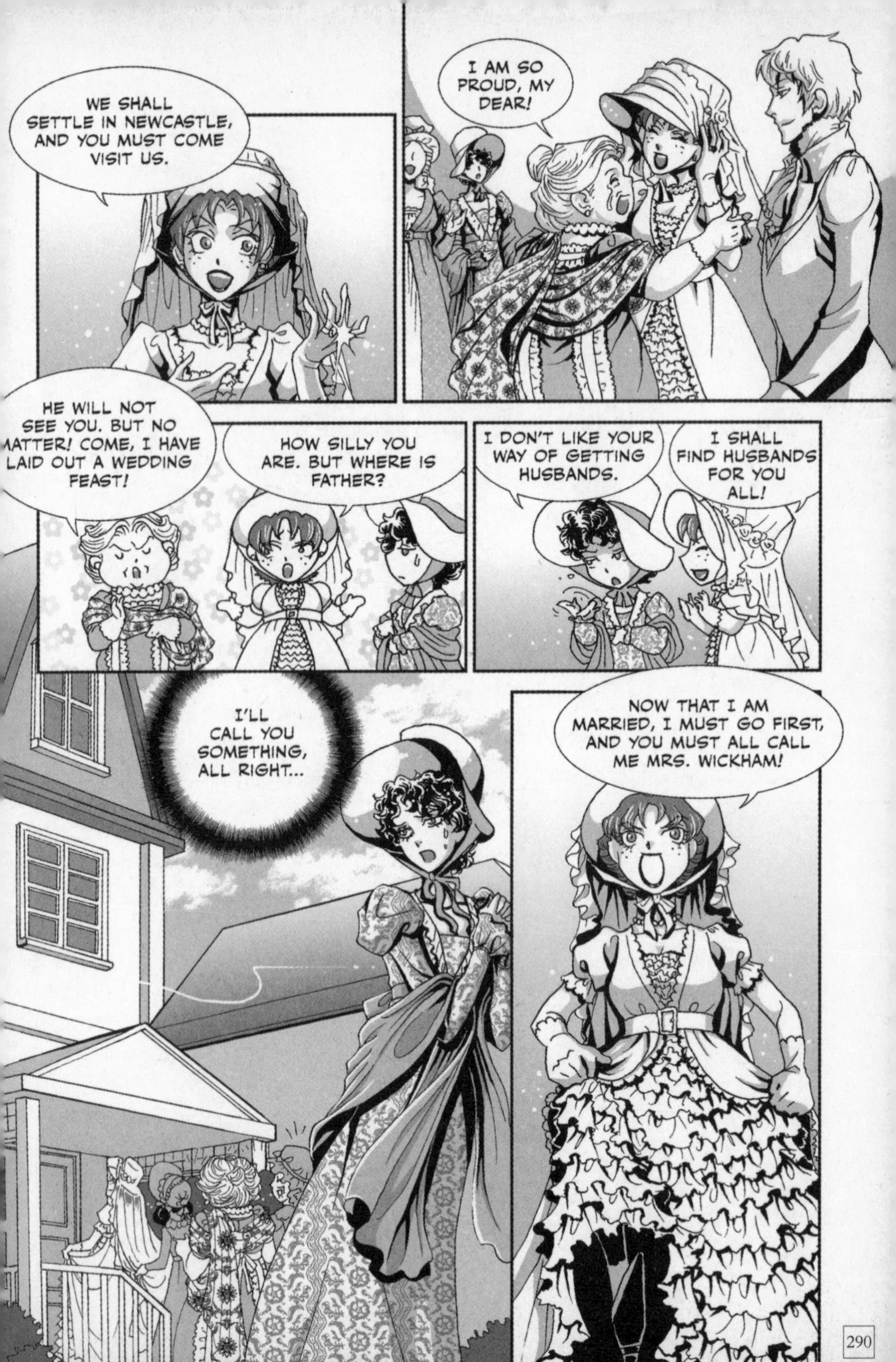
I AM SO PROUD, MY DEAR!
WE SHALL SETTLE IN NEWCASTLE, AND YOU MUST COME VISIT US.
I SHALL FIND HUSBANDS FOR YOU ALL!
I DON'T LIKE YOUR WAY OF GETTING HUSBANDS.
HOW SILLY YOU ARE. BUT WHERE IS FATHER?
HE WILL NOT SEE YOU. BUT NO MATTER! COME, I HAVE LAID OUT A WEDDING FEAST!
NOW THAT I AM MARRIED, I MUST GO FIRST, AND YOU MUST ALL CALL ME MRS. WICKHAM!
I'LL CALL YOU SOMETHING, ALL RIGHT...

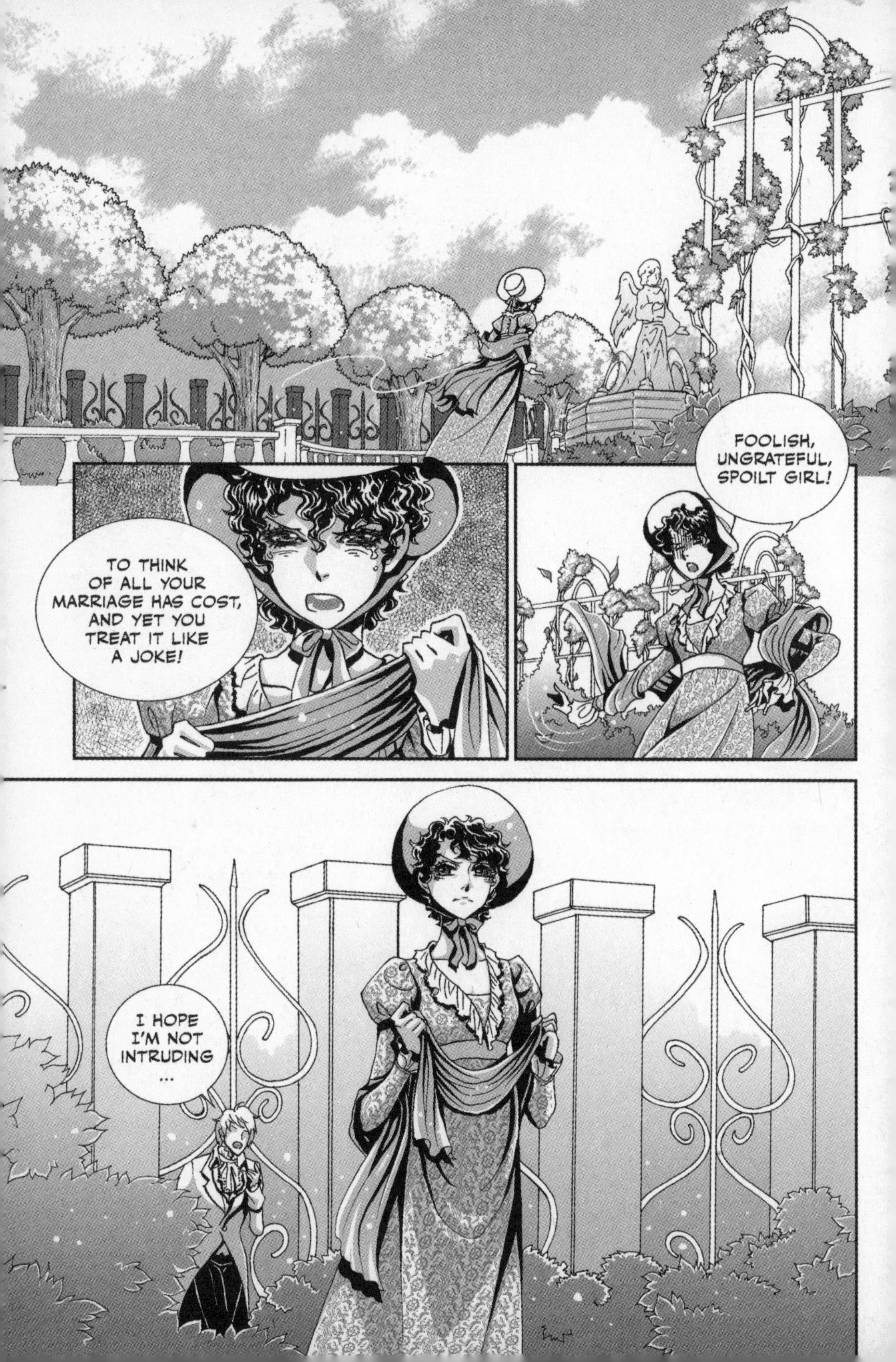
FOOLISH, UNGRATEFUL, SPOILT GIRL!
TO THINK OF ALL YOUR MARRIAGE HAS COST, AND YET YOU TREAT IT LIKE A JOKE!
I HOPE I'M NOT INTRUDING ...

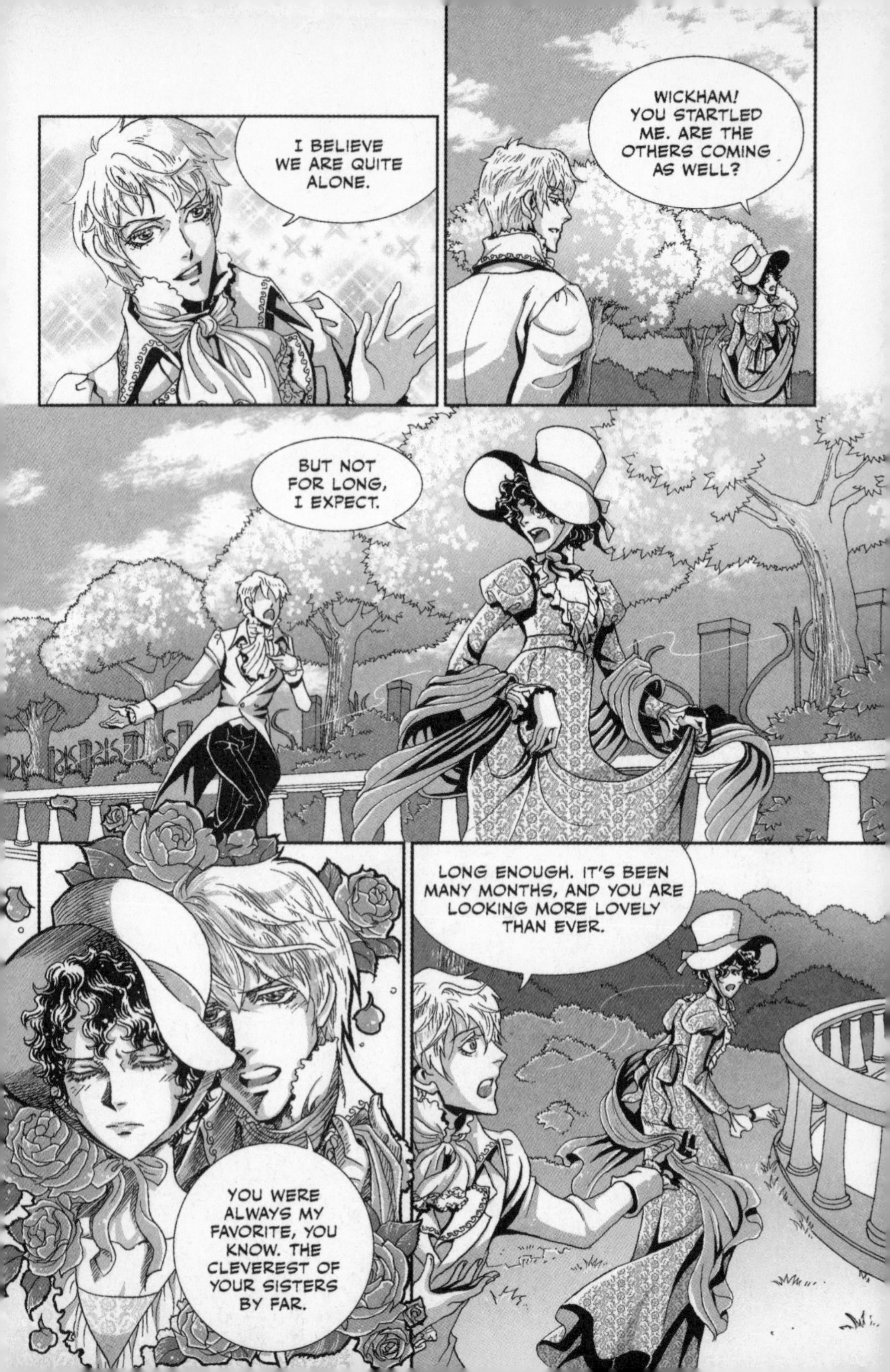
WICKHAM! YOU STARTLED ME. ARE THE OTHERS COMING AS WELL?
I BELIEVE WE ARE QUITE ALONE.
BUT NOT FOR LONG, I EXPECT.
LONG ENOUGH. IT'S BEEN MANY MONTHS, AND YOU ARE LOOKING MORE LOVELY THAN EVER.
YOU WERE ALWAYS MY FAVORITE, YOU KNOW. THE CLEVEREST OF YOUR SISTERS BY FAR.

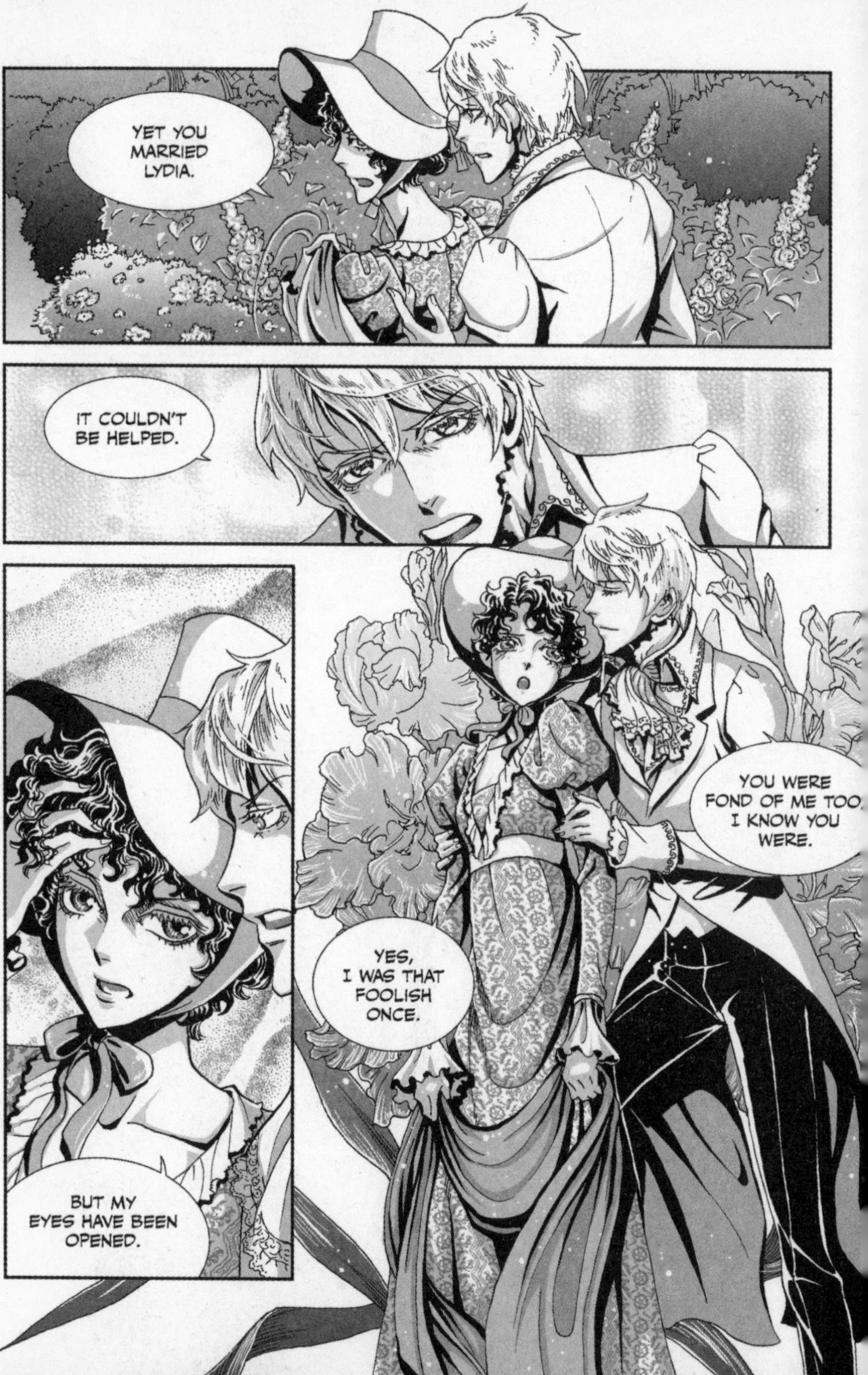
YET YOU MARRIED LYDIA.
IT COULDN'T BE HELPED.
YOU WERE FOND OF ME TOO, I KNOW YOU WERE.
YES, I WAS THAT FOOLISH ONCE.
BUT MY EYES HAVE BEEN OPENED.

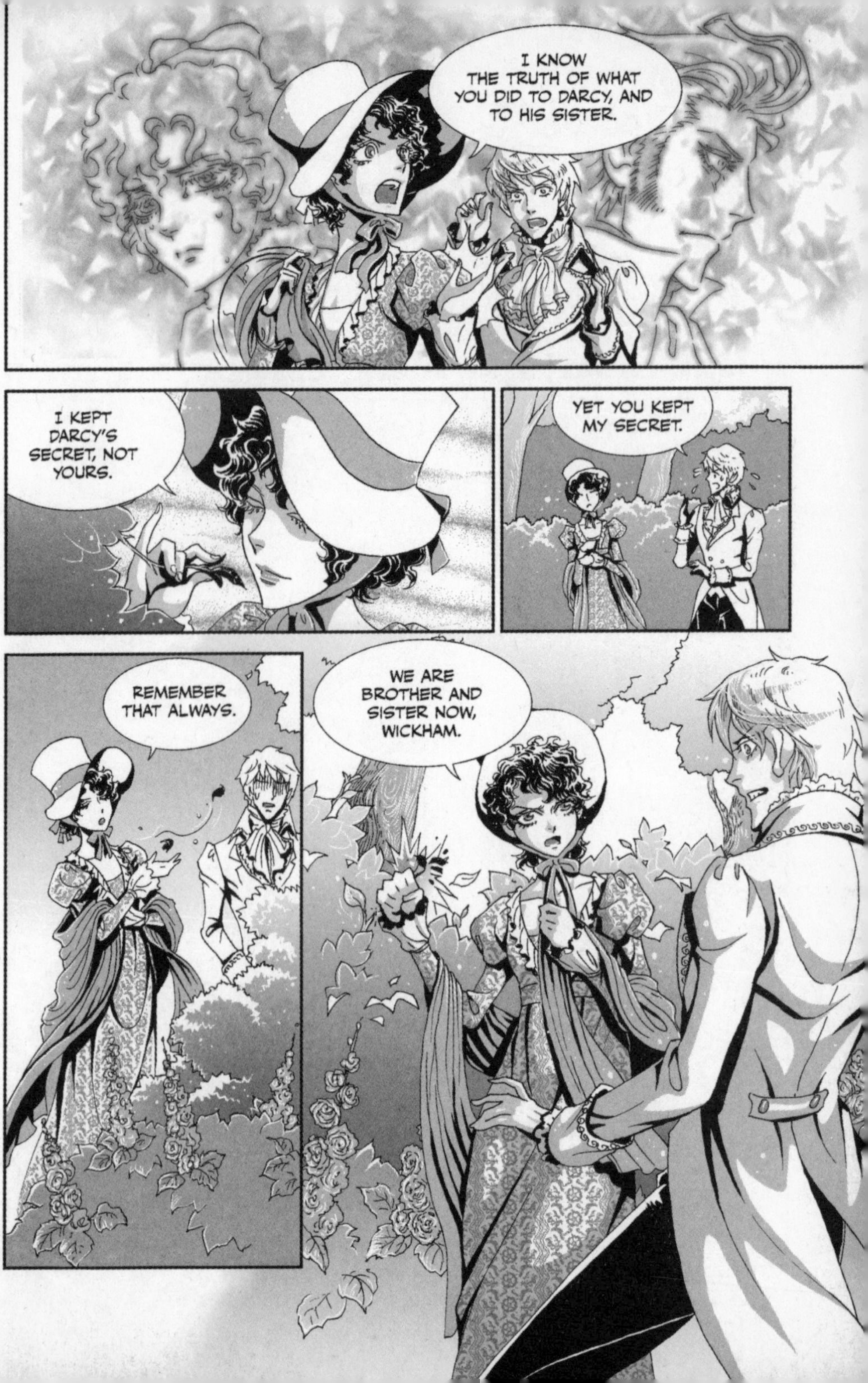
I KNOW THE TRUTH OF WHAT YOU DID TO DARCY, AND TO HIS SISTER.
YET YOU KEPT MY SECRET.
I KEPT DARCY'S SECRET, NOT YOURS.
WE ARE BROTHER AND SISTER NOW, WICKHAM.
REMEMBER THAT ALWAYS.

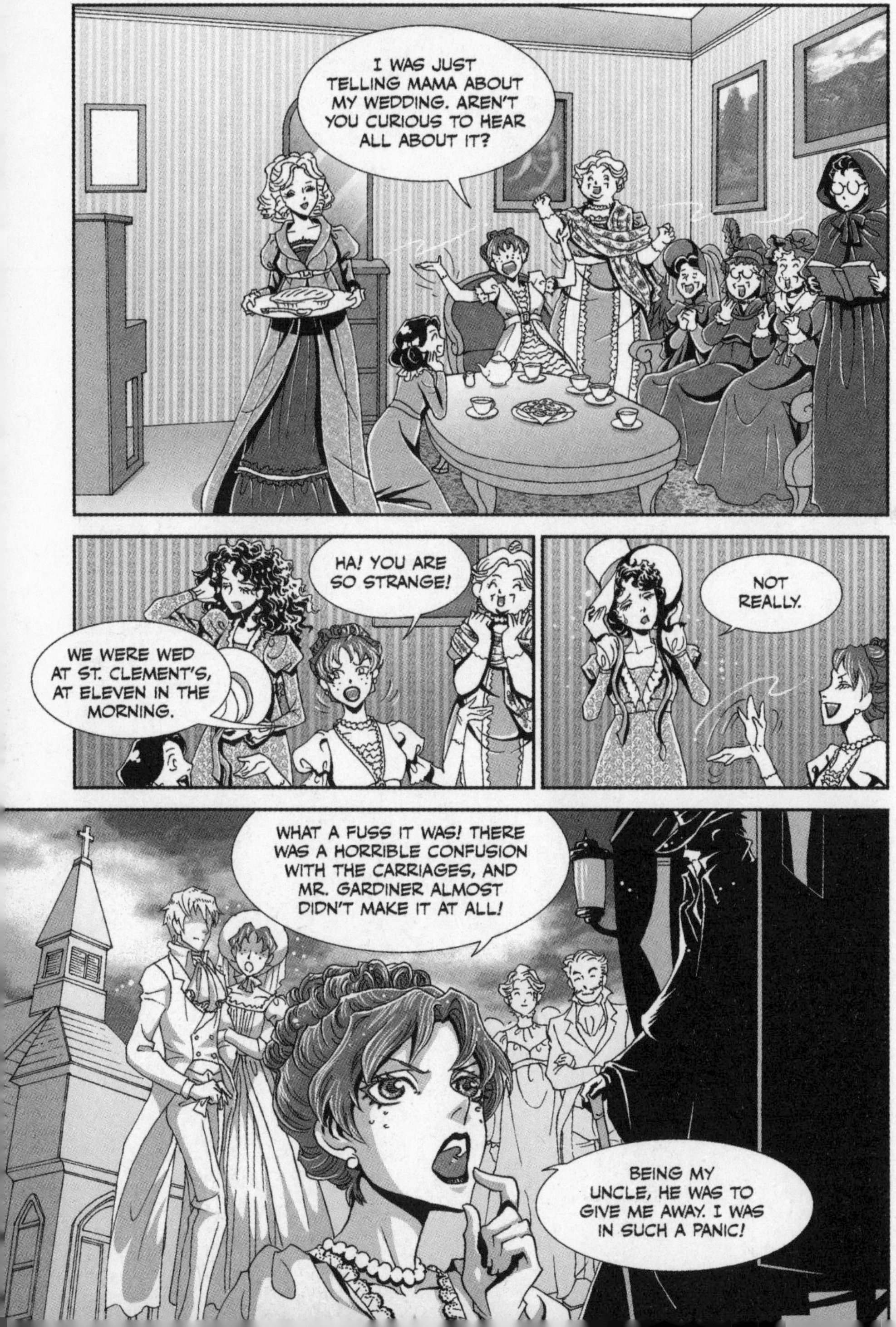
I WAS JUST TELLING MAMA ABOUT MY WEDDING. AREN'T YOU CURIOUS TO HEAR ALL ABOUT IT?
NOT REALLY.
HA! YOU ARE SO STRANGE!
WE WERE WED AT ST. CLEMENT'S, AT ELEVEN IN THE MORNING.
WHAT A FUSS IT WAS! THERE WAS A HORRIBLE CONFUSION WITH THE CARRIAGES, AND MR. GARDINER ALMOST DIDN'T MAKE IT AT ALL!
BEING MY UNCLE, HE WAS TO GIVE ME AWAY. I WAS IN SUCH A PANIC!

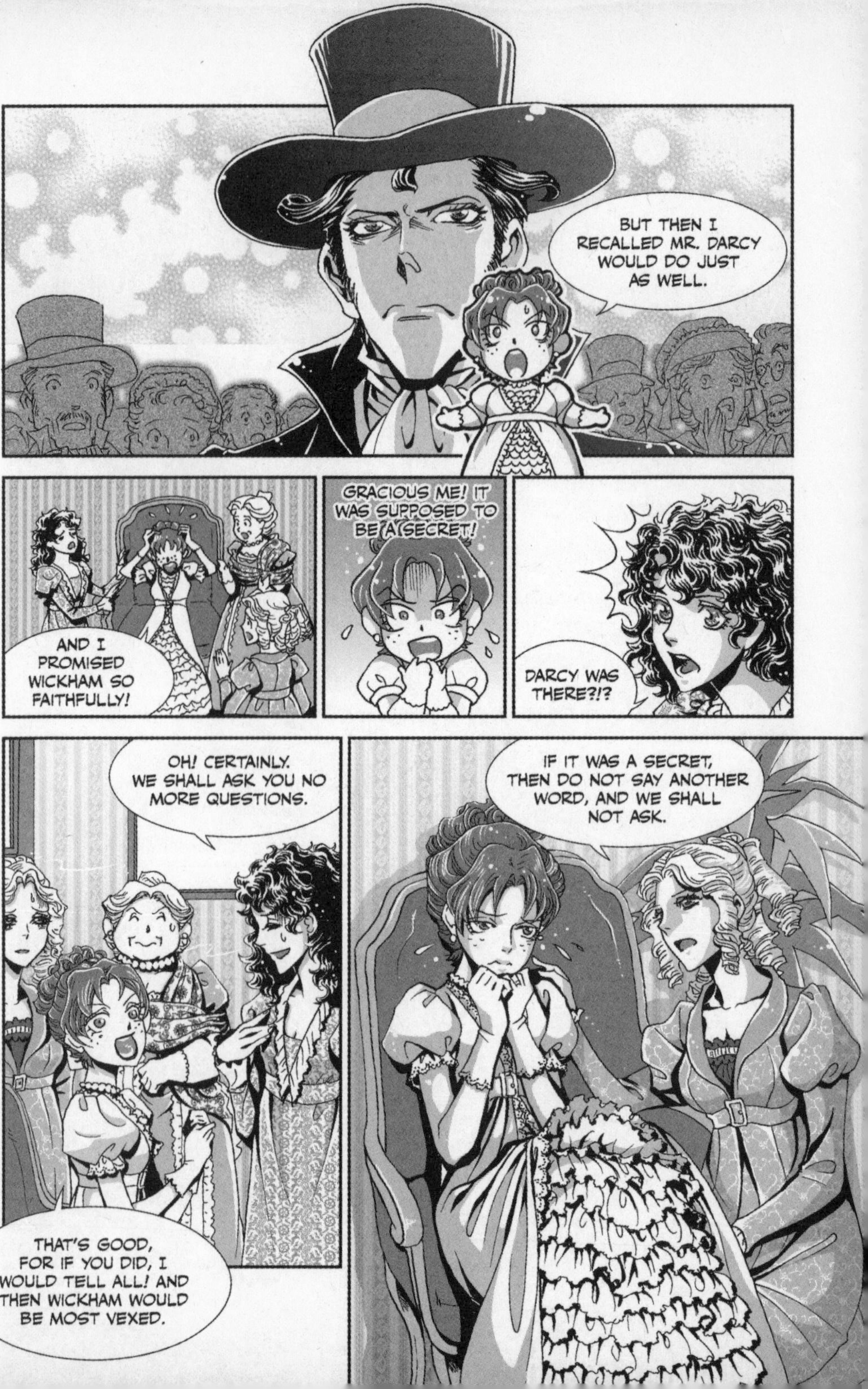
BUT THEN I RECALLED MR. DARCY WOULD DO JUST AS WELL.
DARCY WAS THERE?!?
GRACIOUS ME! IT WAS SUPPOSED TO BE A SECRET!
AND I PROMISED WICKHAM SO FAITHFULLY!
IF IT WAS A SECRET, THEN DO NOT SAY ANOTHER WORD, AND WE SHALL NOT ASK.
OH! CERTAINLY. WE SHALL ASK YOU NO MORE QUESTIONS.
THAT'S GOOD, FOR IF YOU DID, I WOULD TELL ALL! AND THEN WICKHAM WOULD BE MOST VEXED.

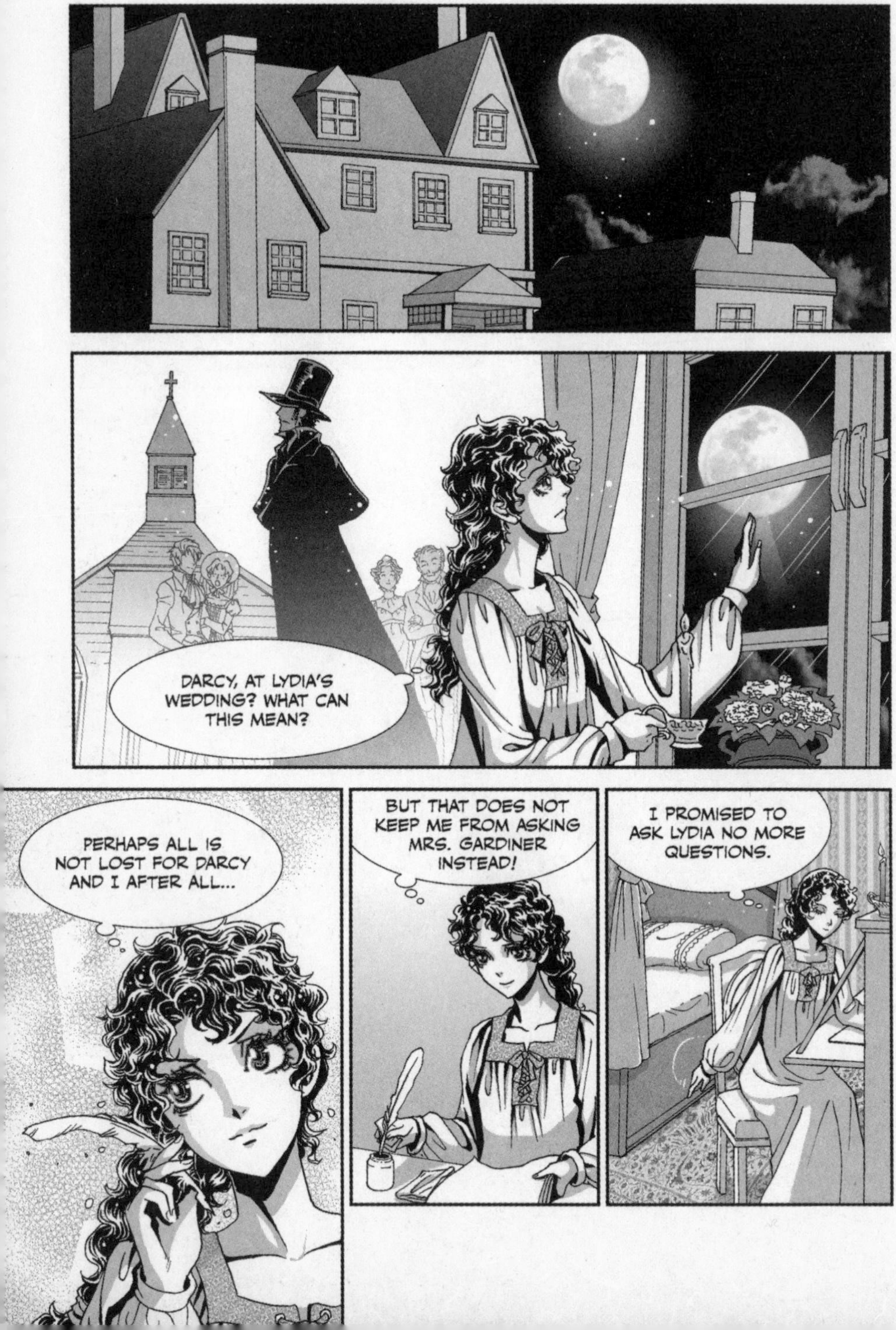
DARCY, AT LYDIA'S WEDDING? WHAT CAN THIS MEAN?
I PROMISED TO ASK LYDIA NO MORE QUESTIONS.
BUT THAT DOES NOT KEEP ME FROM ASKING MRS. GARDINER INSTEAD!
PERHAPS ALL IS NOT LOST FOR DARCY AND I AFTER ALL...

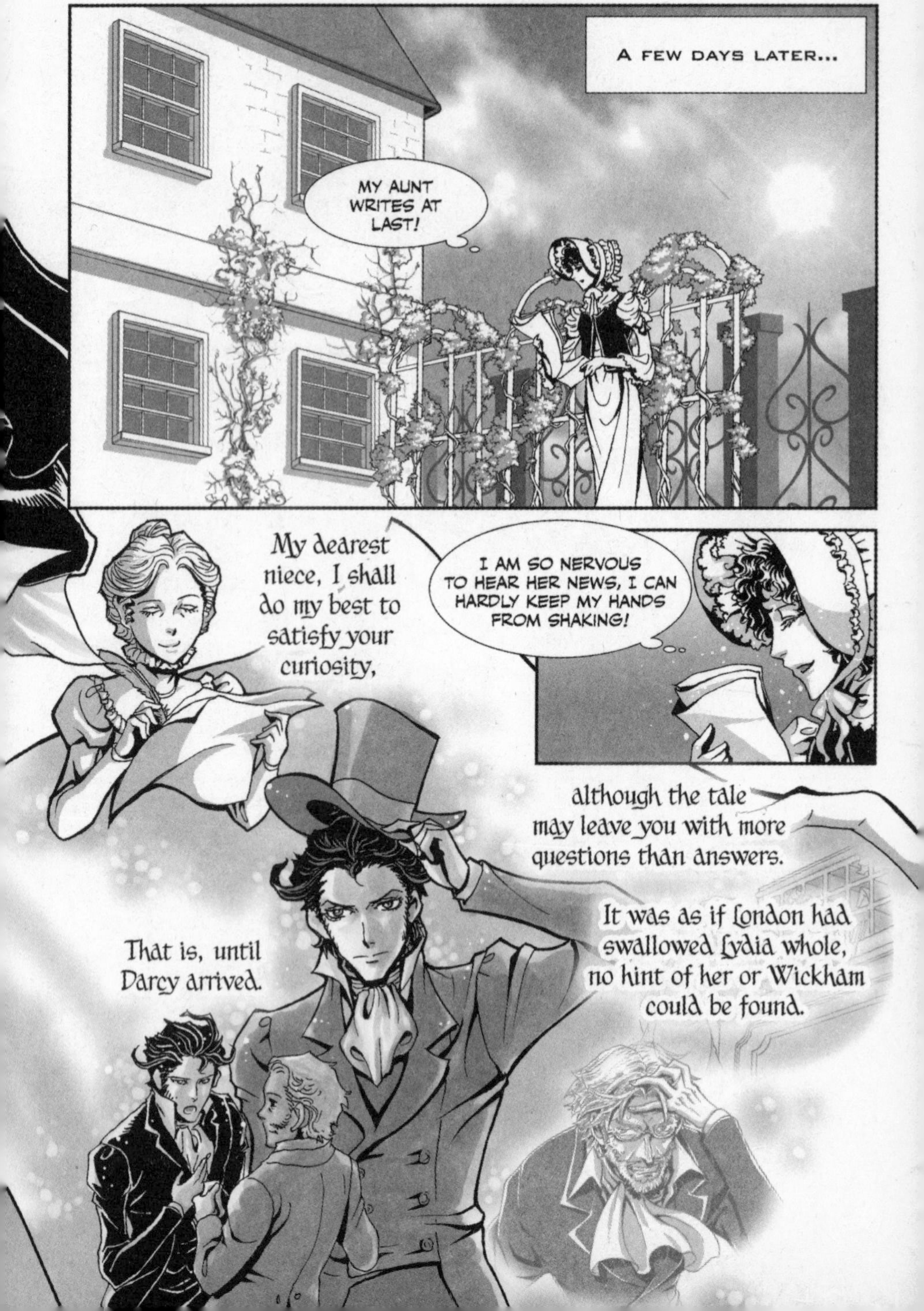
A FEW DAYS LATER...
MY AUNT WRITES AT LAST!
I AM SO NERVOUS TO HEAR HER NEWS, I CAN HARDLY KEEP MY HANDS FROM SHAKING!
My dearest niece, I shall do my best to satisfy your curiosity,
although the tale may leave you with more questions than answers.
It was as if London had swallowed Lydia whole, no hint of her or Wickham could be found.
That is, until Darcy arrived.

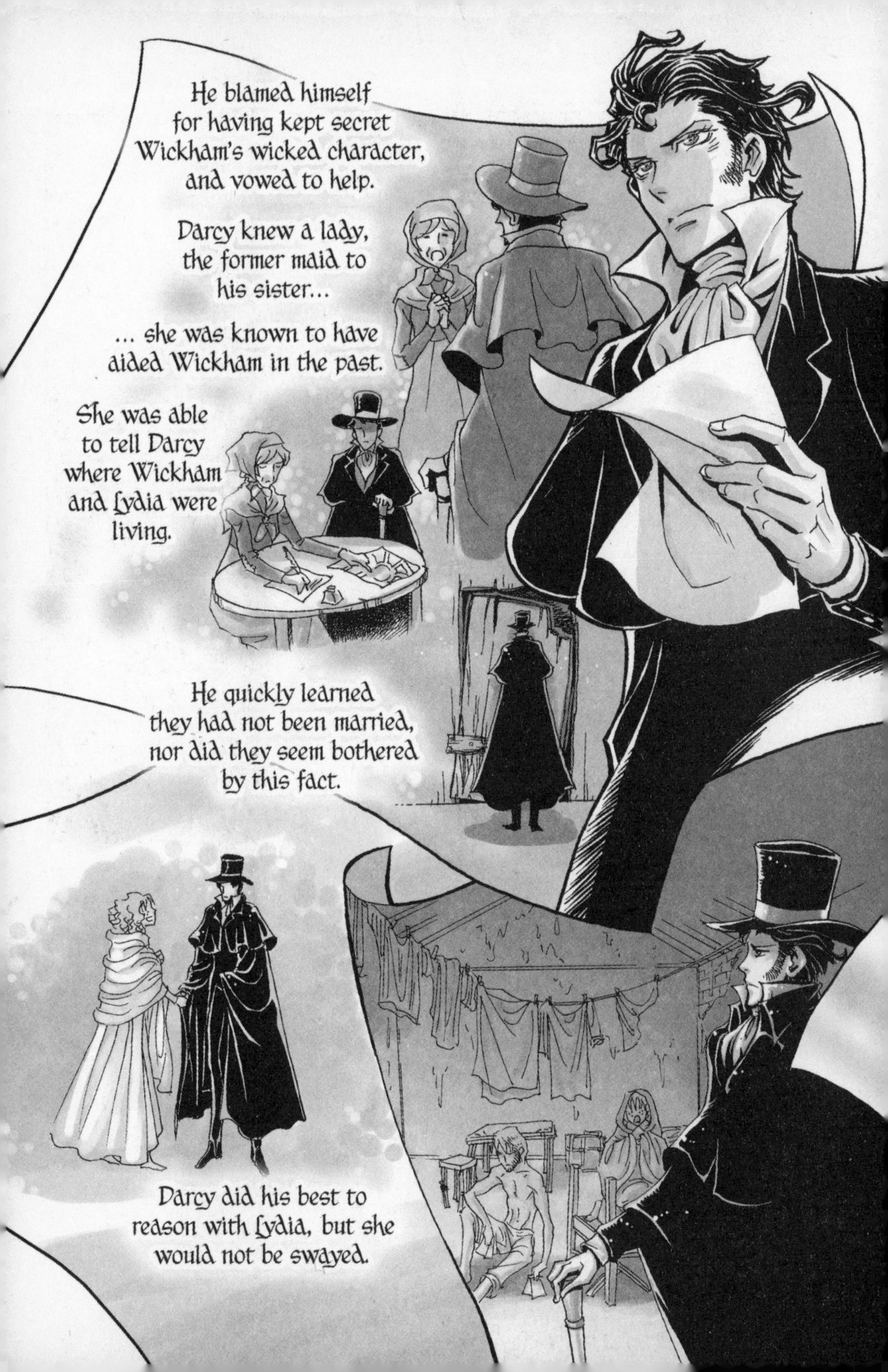
He blamed himself for having kept secret Wickham's wicked character, and vowed to help.
Darcy knew a lady, the former maid to his sister...
... she was known to have aided Wickham in the past.
She was able to tell Darcy where Wickham and Lydia were living.
He quickly learned they had not been married, nor did they seem bothered by this fact.
Darcy did his best to reason with Lydia, but she would not be swayed.

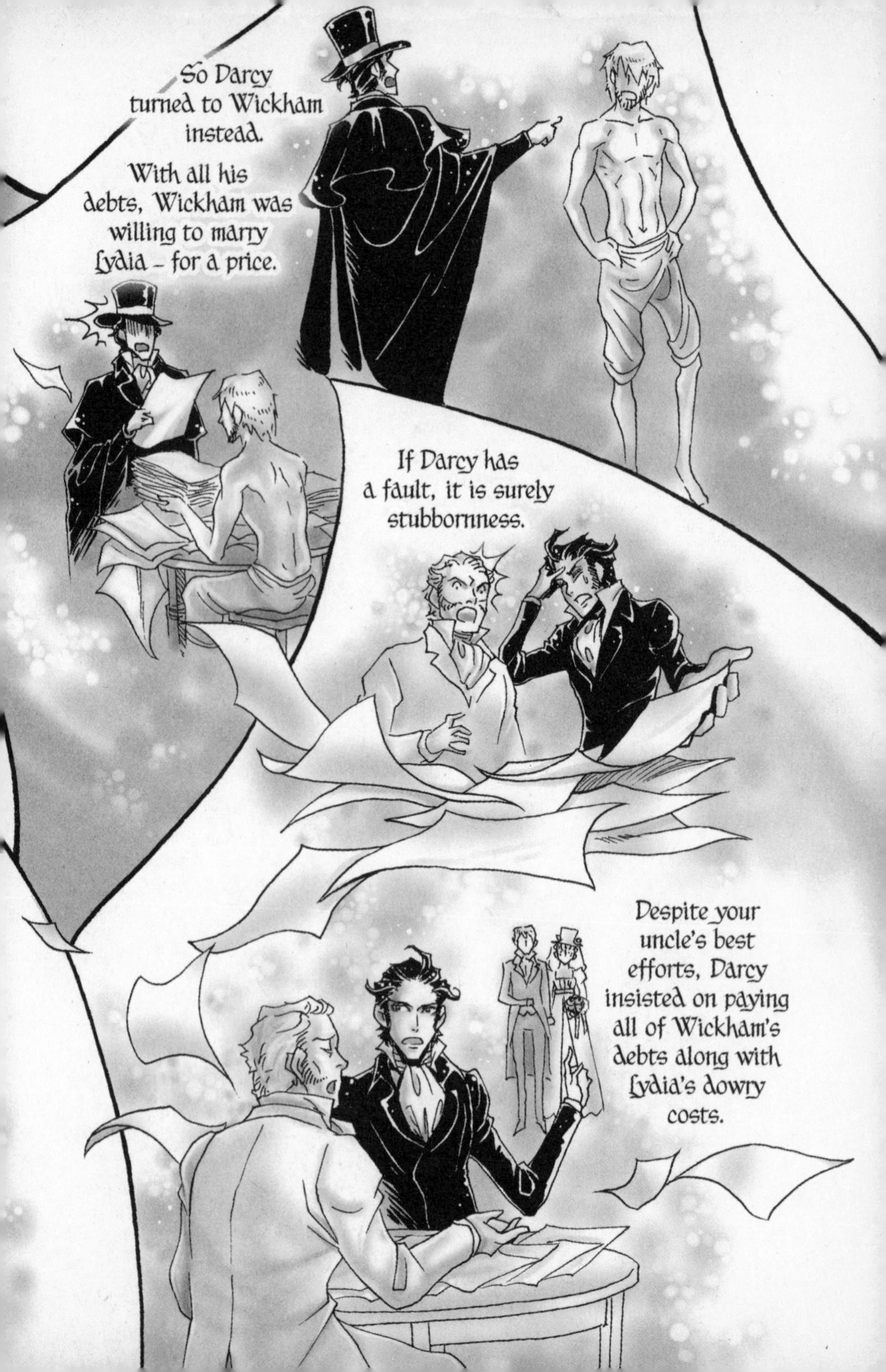
So Darcy turned to Wickham instead.
With all his debts, Wickham was willing to marry Lydia – for a price.
If Darcy has a fault, it is surely stubbornness.
Despite your uncle's best efforts, Darcy insisted on paying all of Wickham's debts along with Lydia's dowry costs.

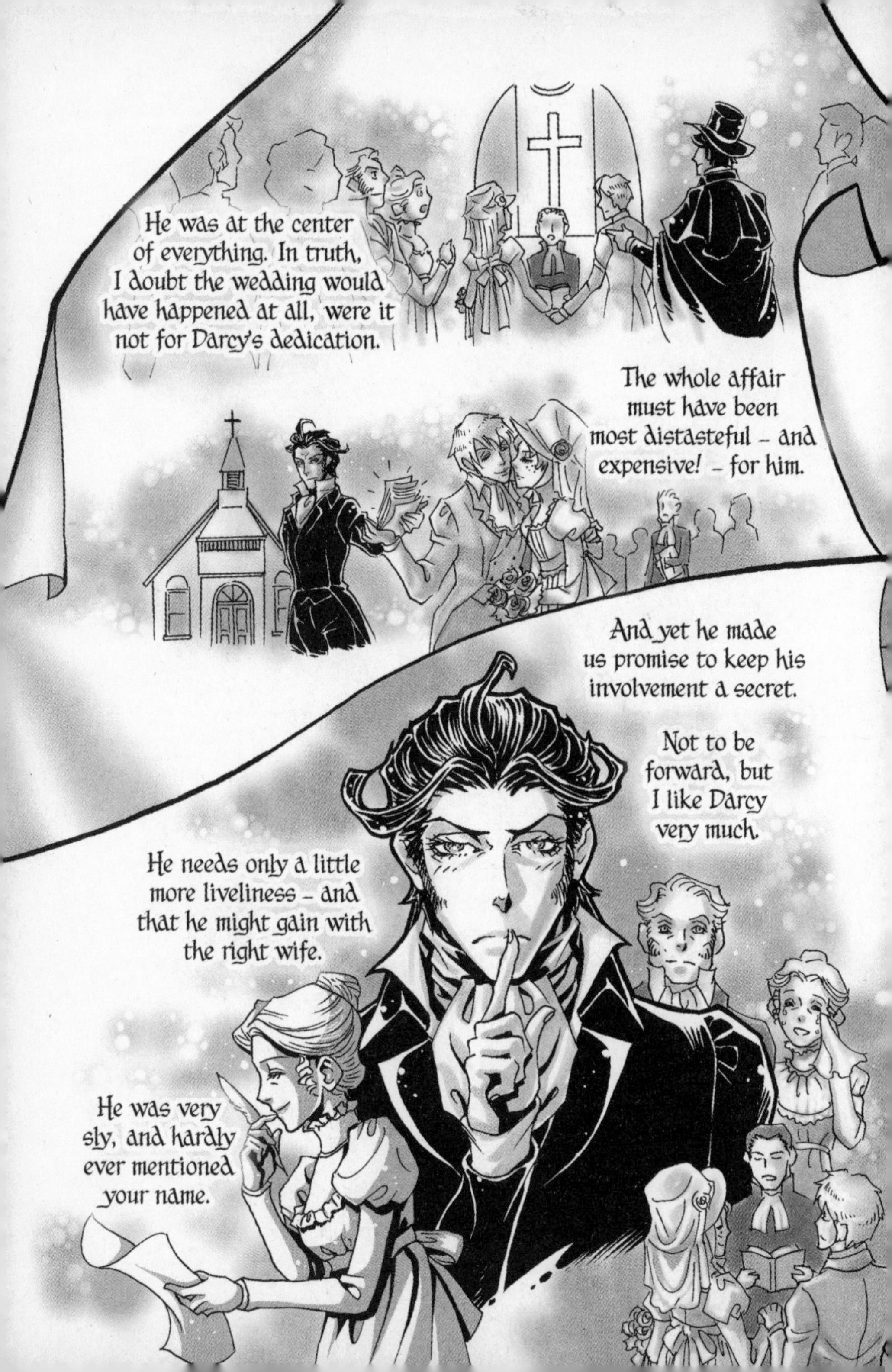
He was at the center of everything. In truth, I doubt the wedding would have happened at all, were it not for Darcy's dedication.
The whole affair must have been most distasteful – and expensive! – for him.
And yet he made us promise to keep his involvement a secret.
Not to be forward, but I like Darcy very much.
He needs only a little more liveliness – and that he might gain with the right wife.
He was very sly, and hardly ever mentioned your name.

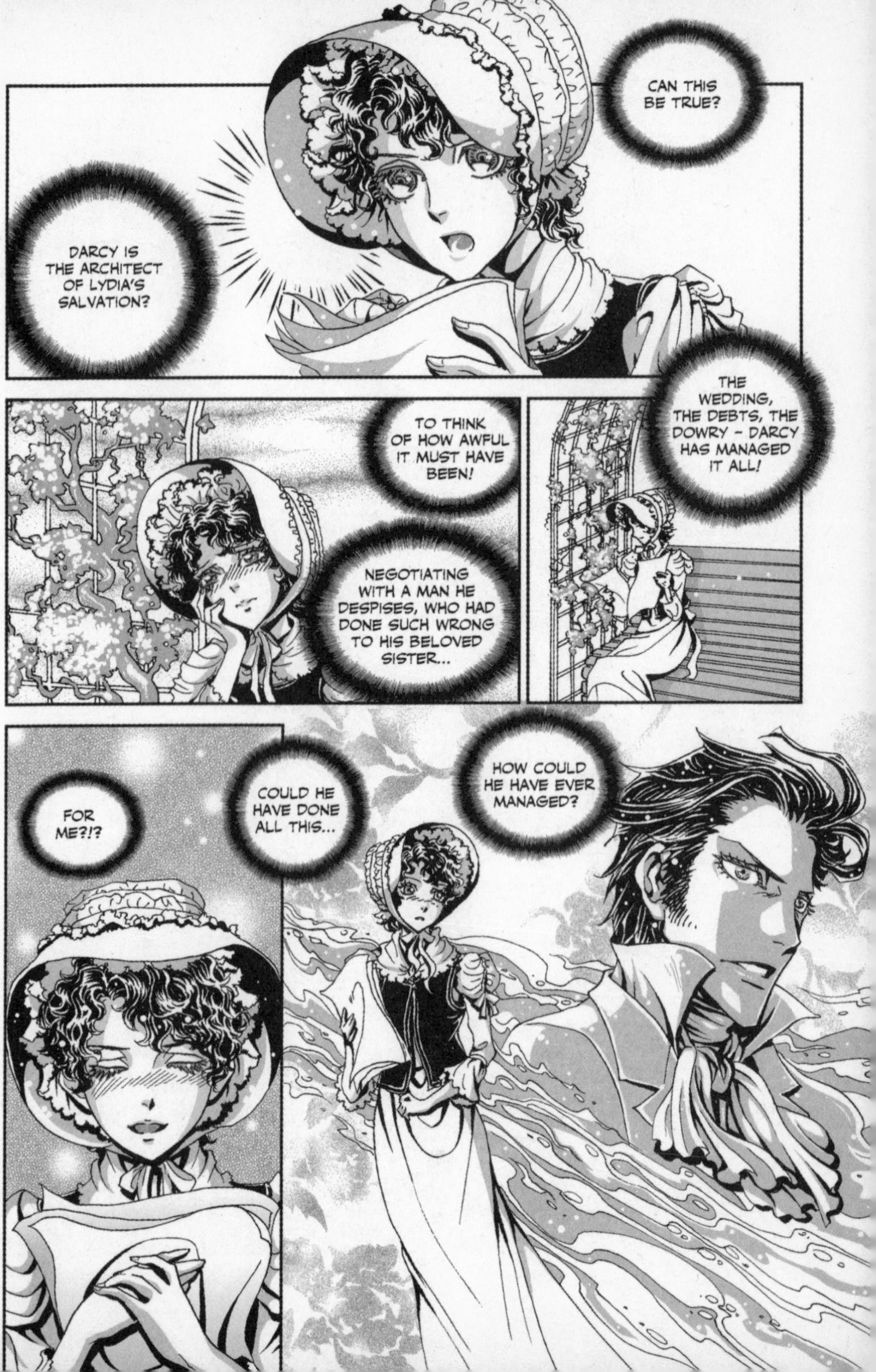
CAN THIS BE TRUE?
DARCY IS THE ARCHITECT OF LYDIA'S SALVATION?
THE WEDDING, THE DEBTS, THE DOWRY - DARCY HAS MANAGED IT ALL!
TO THINK OF HOW AWFUL IT MUST HAVE BEEN!
NEGOTIATING WITH A MAN HE DESPISES, WHO HAD DONE SUCH WRONG TO HIS BELOVED SISTER...
HOW COULD HE HAVE EVER MANAGED?
COULD HE HAVE DONE ALL THIS...
FOR ME?!?

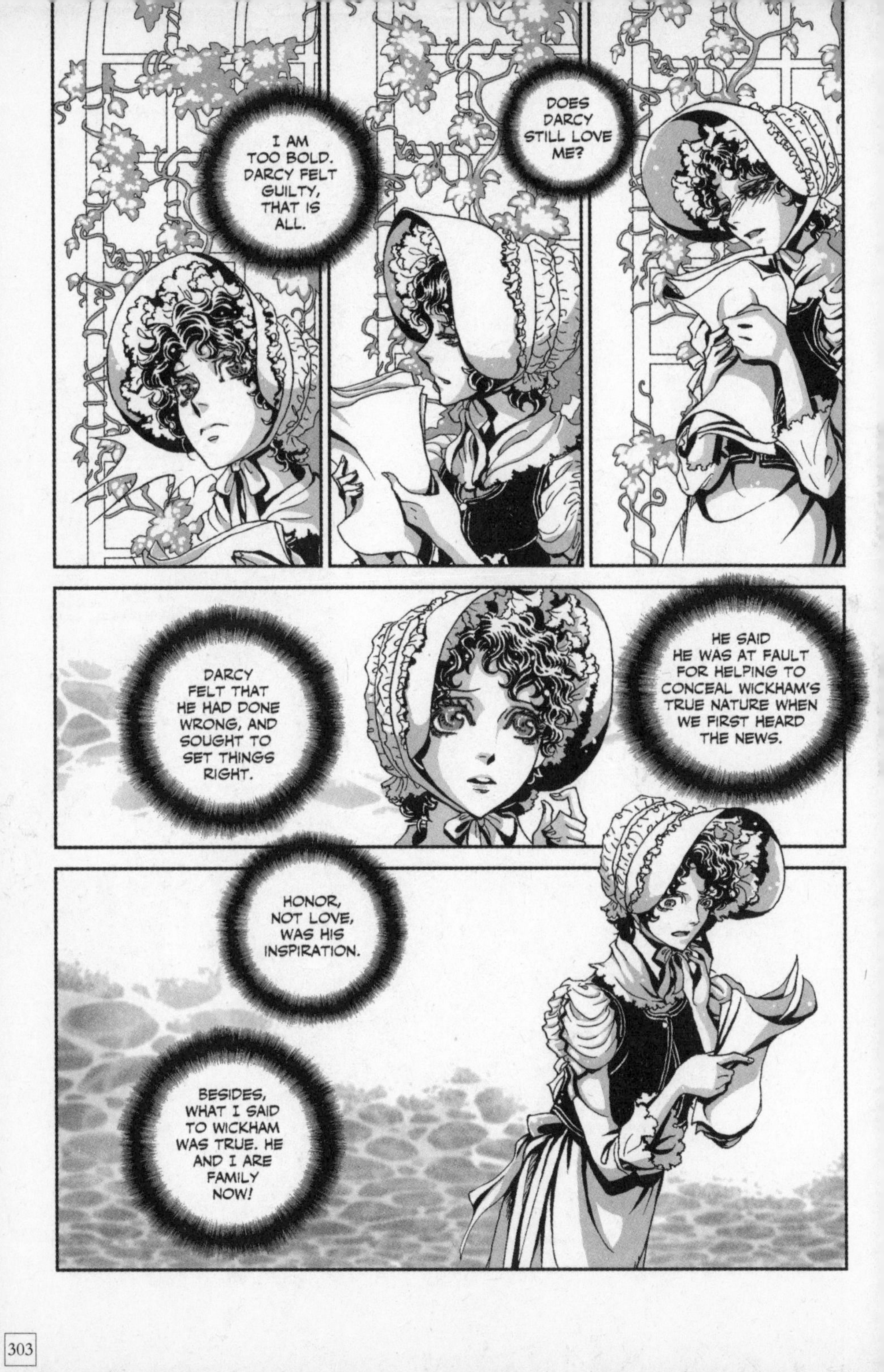
DOES DARCY STILL LOVE ME?
I AM TOO BOLD. DARCY FELT GUILTY, THAT IS ALL.
HE SAID HE WAS AT FAULT FOR HELPING TO CONCEAL WICKHAM'S TRUE NATURE WHEN WE FIRST HEARD THE NEWS.
DARCY FELT THAT HE HAD DONE WRONG, AND SOUGHT TO SET THINGS RIGHT.
HONOR, NOT LOVE, WAS HIS INSPIRATION.
BESIDES, WHAT I SAID TO WICKHAM WAS TRUE. HE AND I ARE FAMILY NOW!

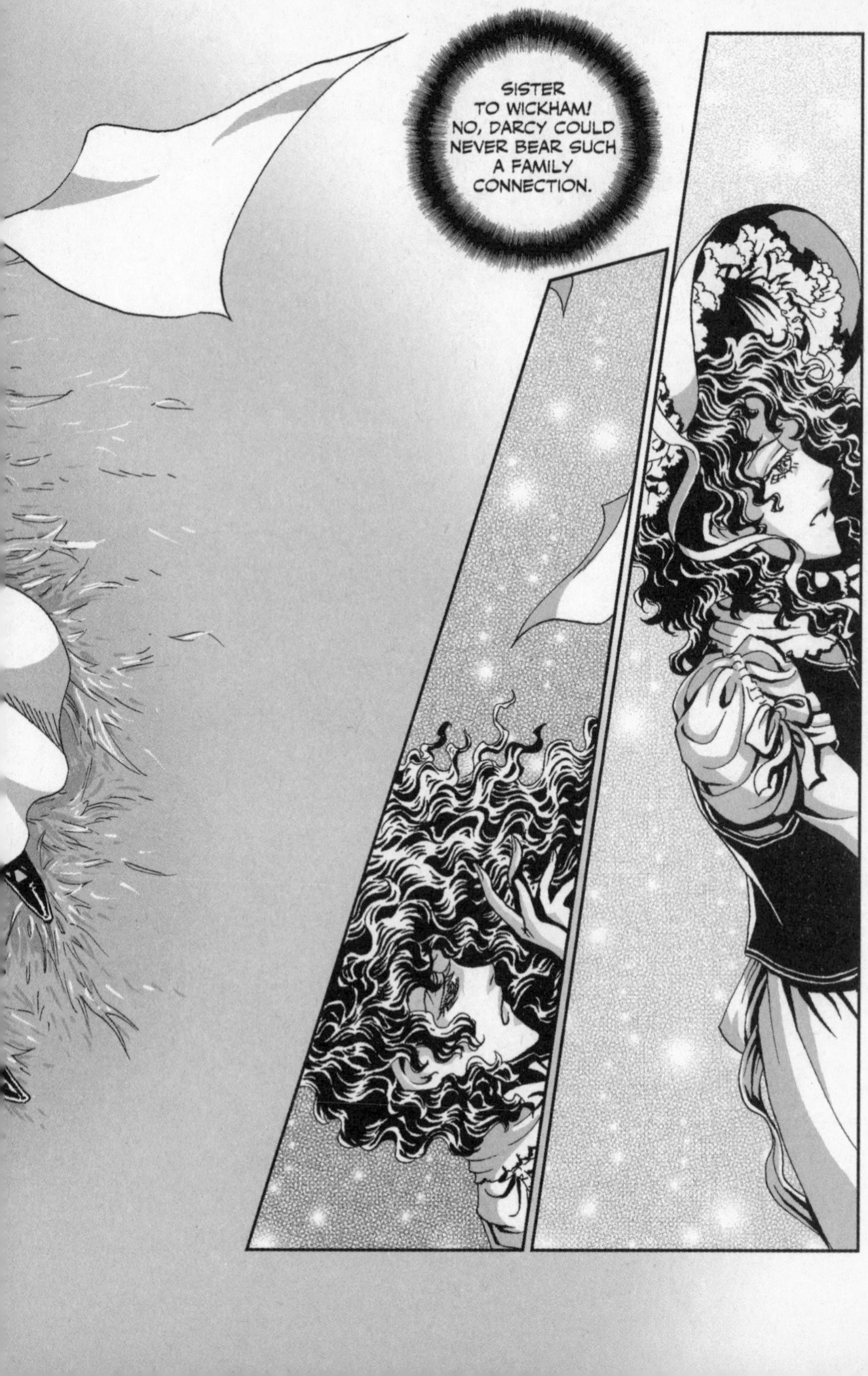
SISTER TO WICKHAM! NO, DARCY COULD NEVER BEAR SUCH A FAMILY CONNECTION.

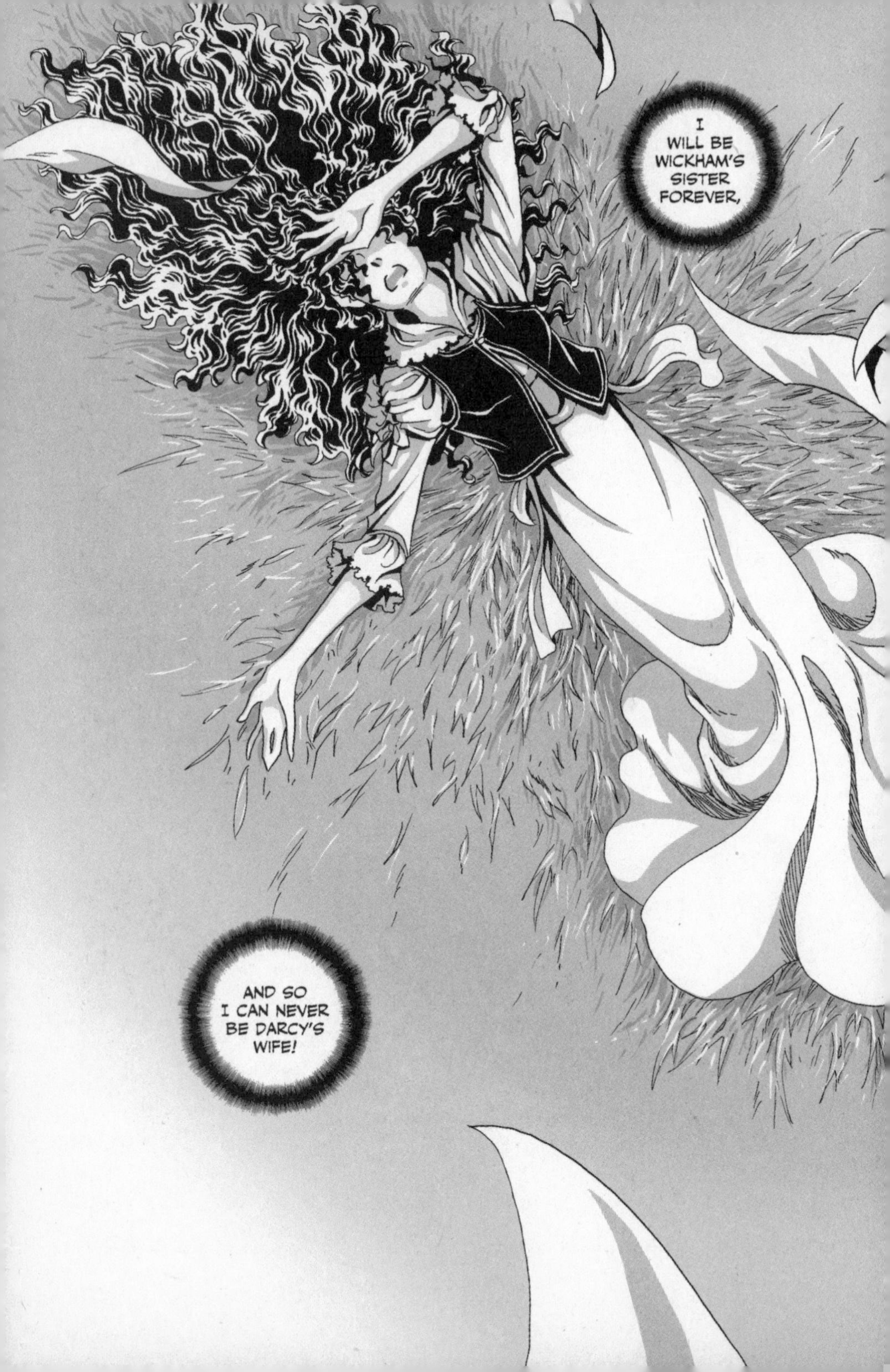
I WILL BE WICKHAM'S SISTER FOREVER,
AND SO I CAN NEVER BE DARCY'S WIFE!

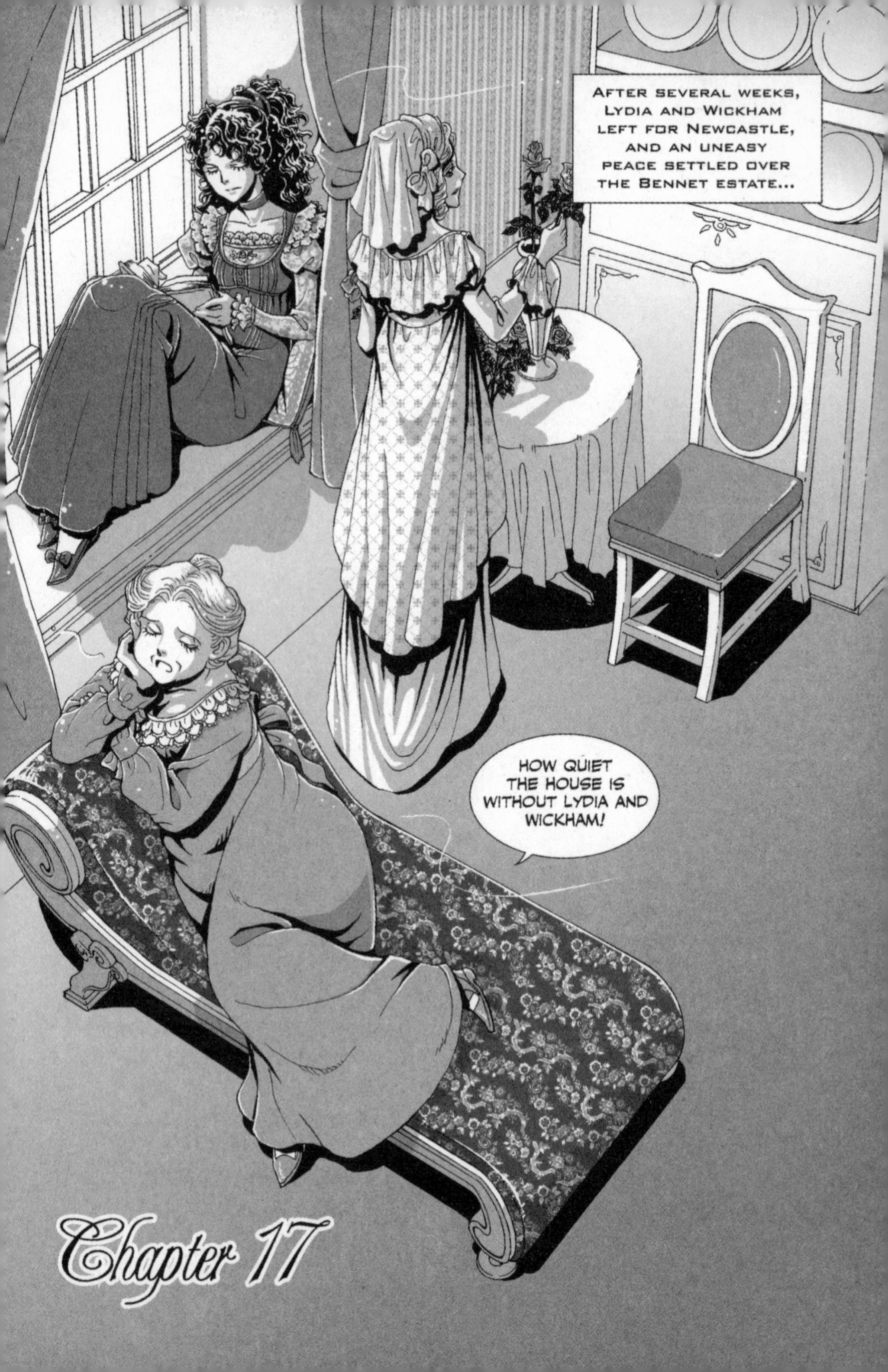
After several weeks, Lydia and Wickham left for Newcastle, and an uneasy peace settled over the Bennet estate...
How quiet the house is without Lydia and Wickham!
Chapter 17

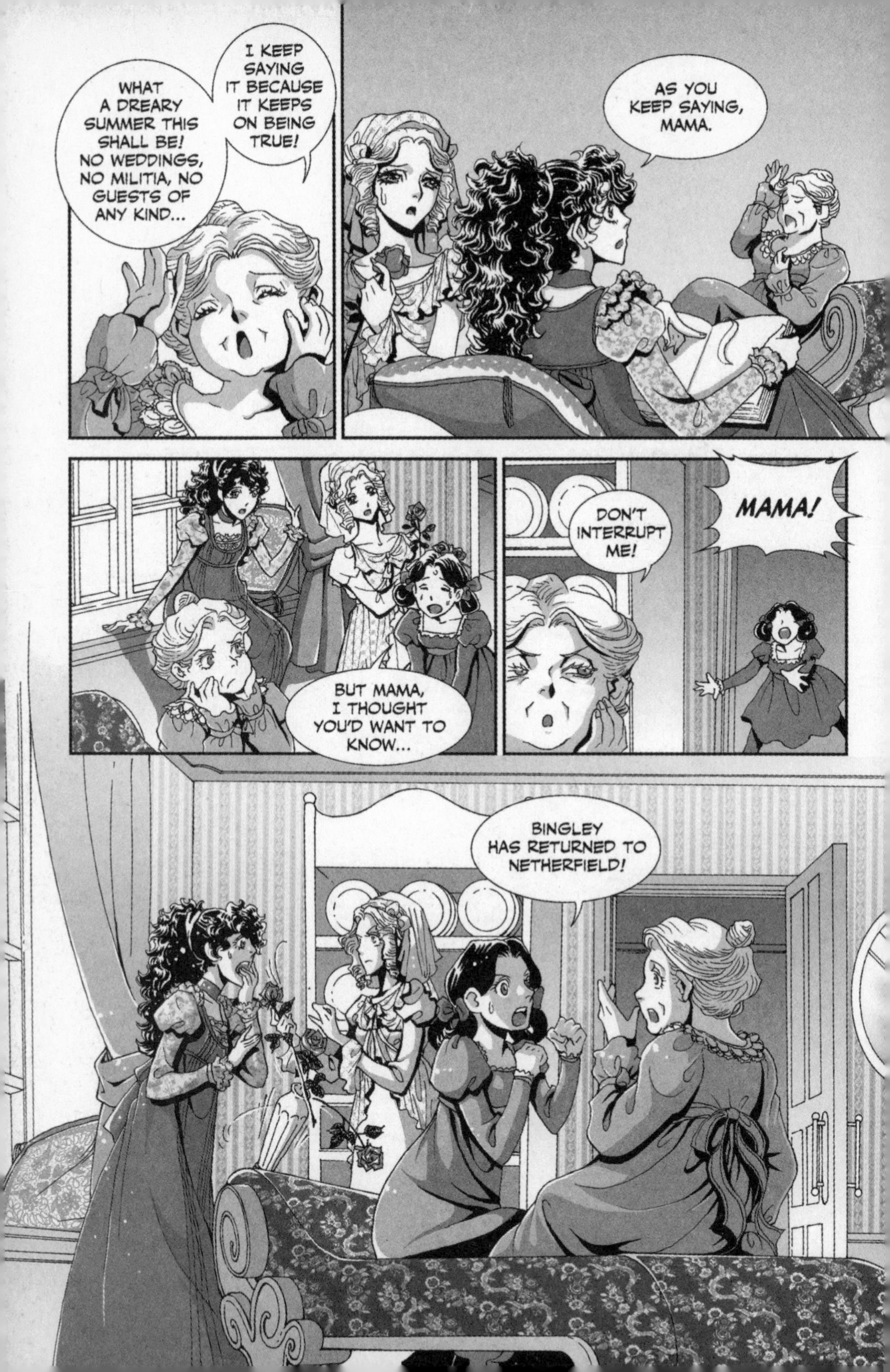
AS YOU KEEP SAYING, MAMA.
I KEEP SAYING IT BECAUSE IT KEEPS ON BEING TRUE!
WHAT A DREARY SUMMER THIS SHALL BE! NO WEDDINGS, NO MILITIA, NO GUESTS OF ANY KIND...
MAMA!
DON'T INTERRUPT ME!
BUT MAMA, I THOUGHT YOU'D WANT TO KNOW...
BINGLEY HAS RETURNED TO NETHERFIELD!

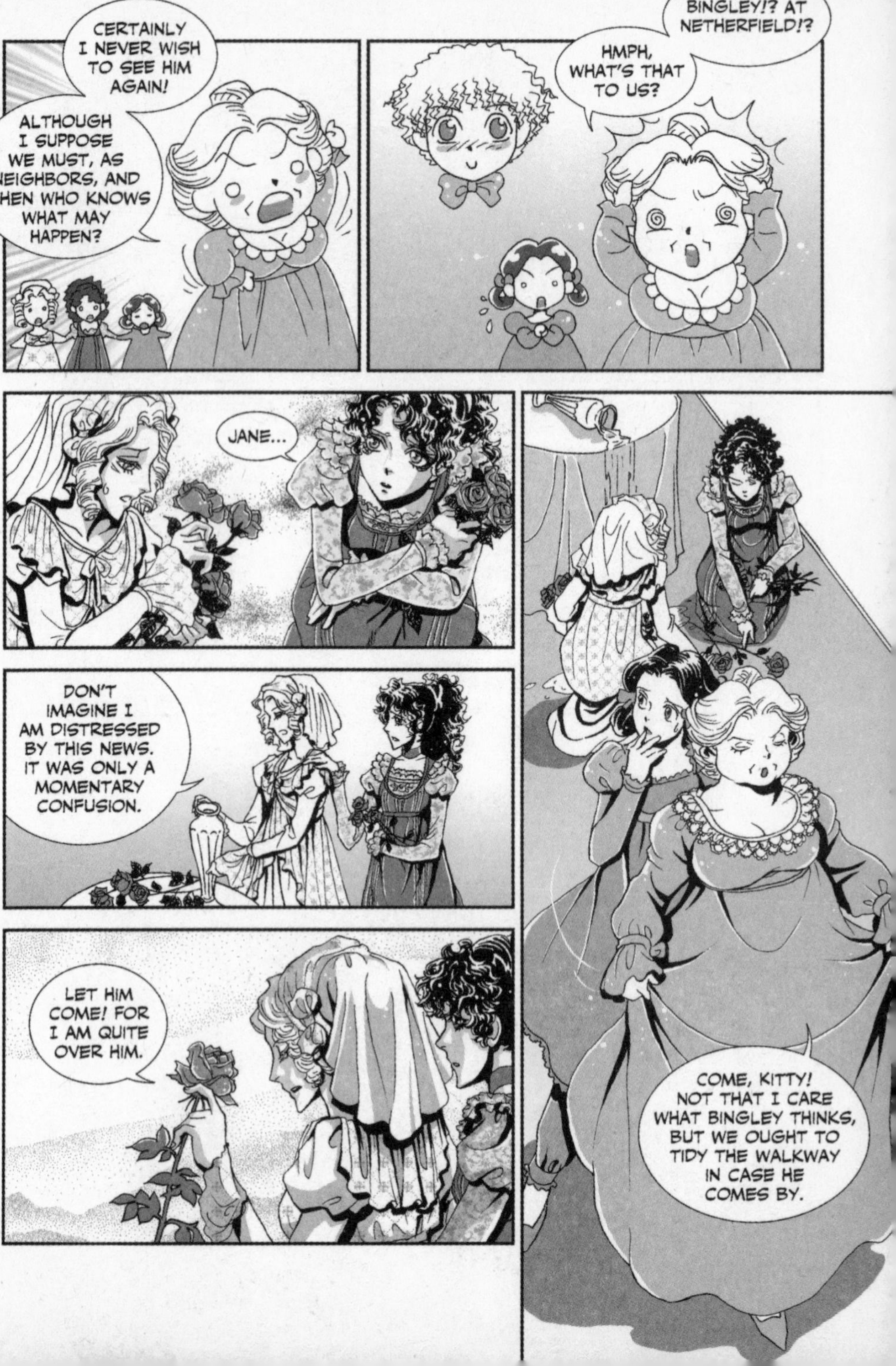
BINGLEY!? AT NETHERFIELD!?
HMPH, WHAT'S THAT TO US?
CERTAINLY I NEVER WISH TO SEE HIM AGAIN!
ALTHOUGH I SUPPOSE WE MUST, AS NEIGHBORS, AND THEN WHO KNOWS WHAT MAY HAPPEN?
COME, KITTY! NOT THAT I CARE WHAT BINGLEY THINKS, BUT WE OUGHT TO TIDY THE WALKWAY IN CASE HE COMES BY.
JANE...
DON'T IMAGINE I AM DISTRESSED BY THIS NEWS. IT WAS ONLY A MOMENTARY CONFUSION.
LET HIM COME! FOR I AM QUITE OVER HIM.

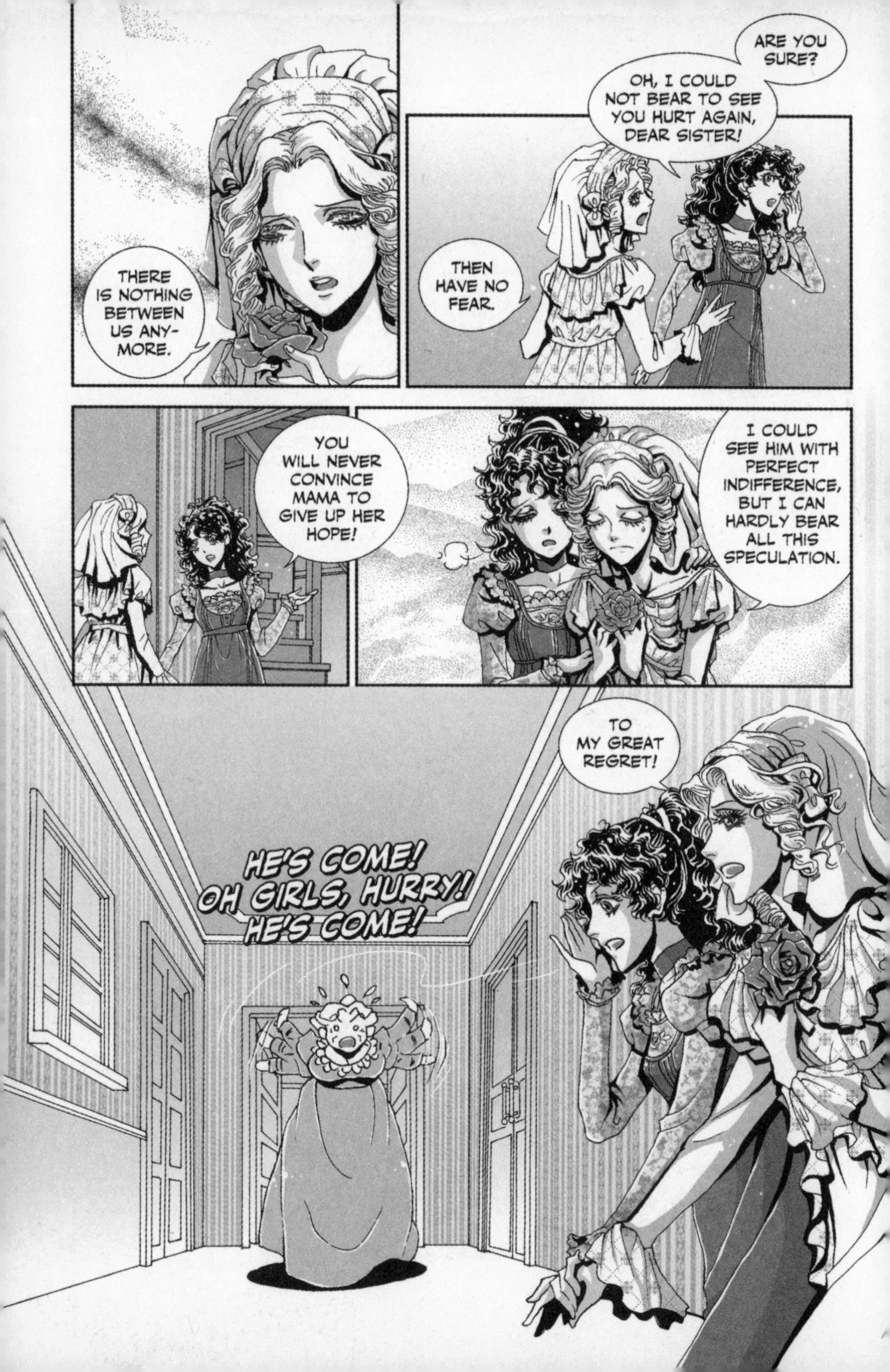
ARE YOU SURE?
OH, I COULD NOT BEAR TO SEE YOU HURT AGAIN, DEAR SISTER!
THEN HAVE NO FEAR.
THERE IS NOTHING BETWEEN US ANY-MORE.
I COULD SEE HIM WITH PERFECT INDIFFERENCE, BUT I CAN HARDLY BEAR ALL THIS SPECULATION.
YOU WILL NEVER CONVINCE MAMA TO GIVE UP HER HOPE!
TO MY GREAT REGRET!
HE'S COME! OH GIRLS, HURRY! HE'S COME!

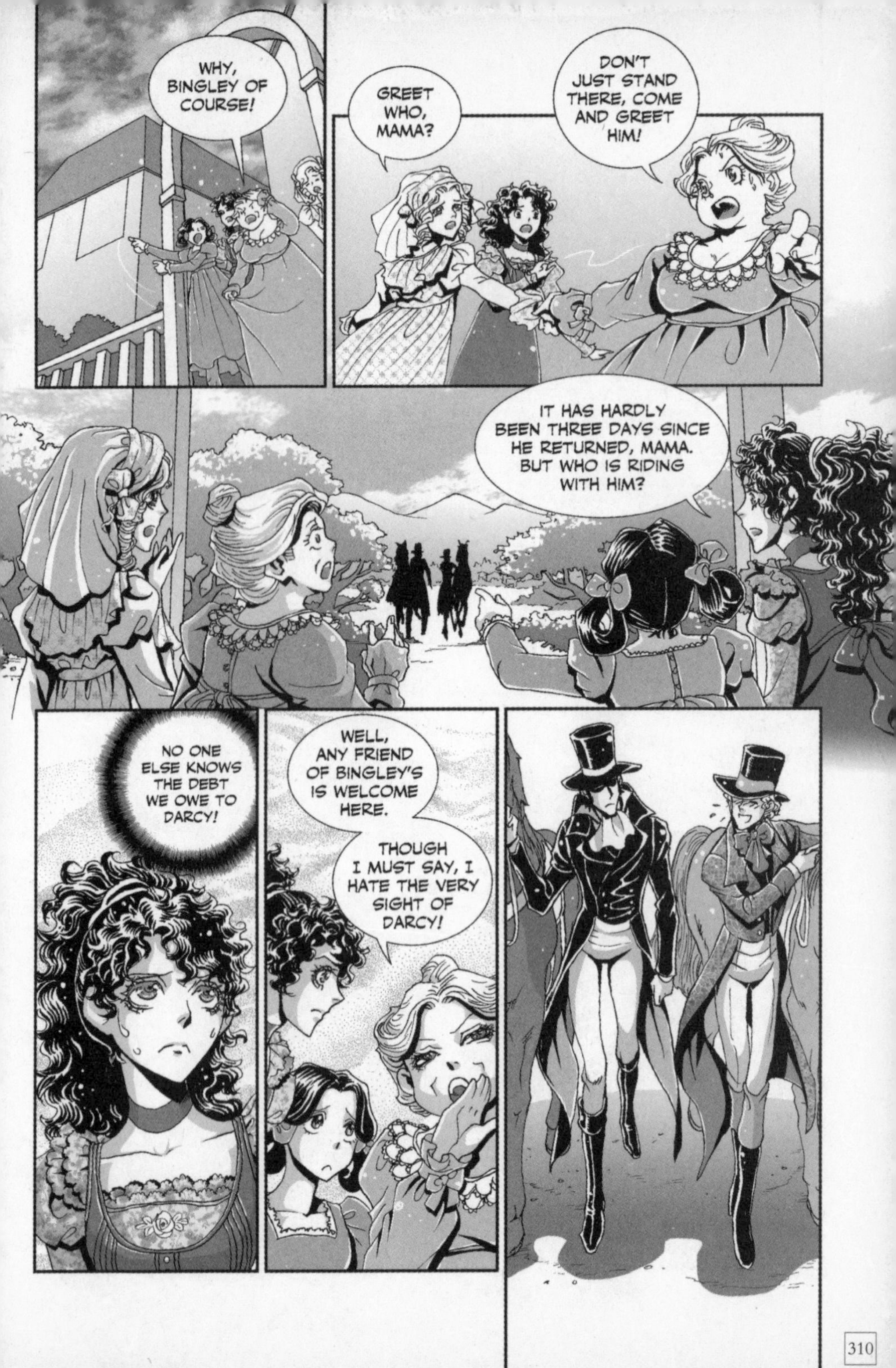
DON'T JUST STAND THERE, COME AND GREET HIM!
GREET WHO, MAMA?
WHY, BINGLEY OF COURSE!
IT HAS HARDLY BEEN THREE DAYS SINCE HE RETURNED, MAMA. BUT WHO IS RIDING WITH HIM?
WELL, ANY FRIEND OF BINGLEY'S IS WELCOME HERE.
THOUGH I MUST SAY, I HATE THE VERY SIGHT OF DARCY!
NO ONE ELSE KNOWS THE DEBT WE OWE TO DARCY!

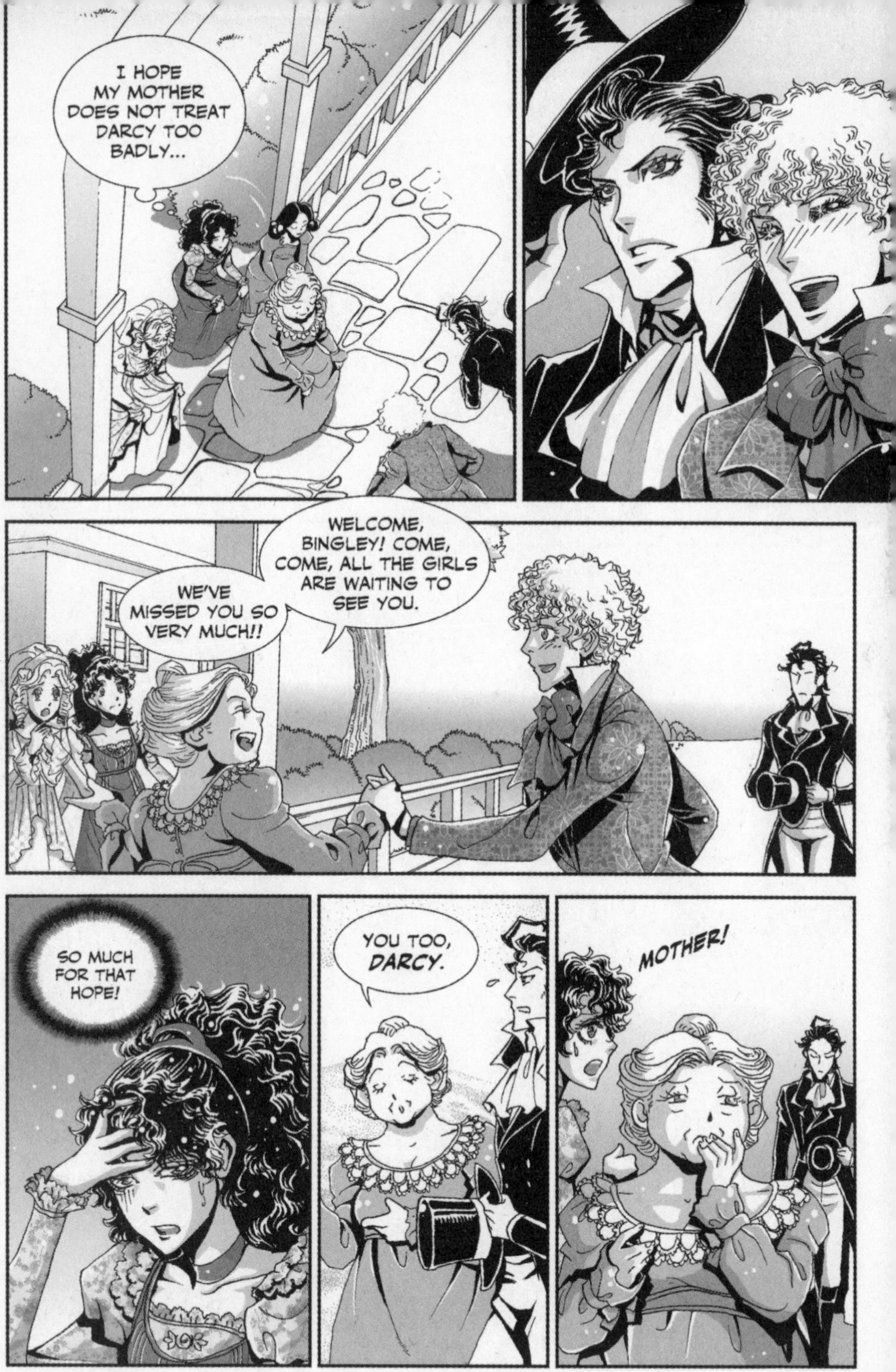
I HOPE MY MOTHER DOES NOT TREAT DARCY TOO BADLY...
WELCOME, BINGLEY! COME, COME, ALL THE GIRLS ARE WAITING TO SEE YOU.
WE'VE MISSED YOU SO VERY MUCH!!
MOTHER!
YOU TOO, DARCY.
SO MUCH FOR THAT HOPE!

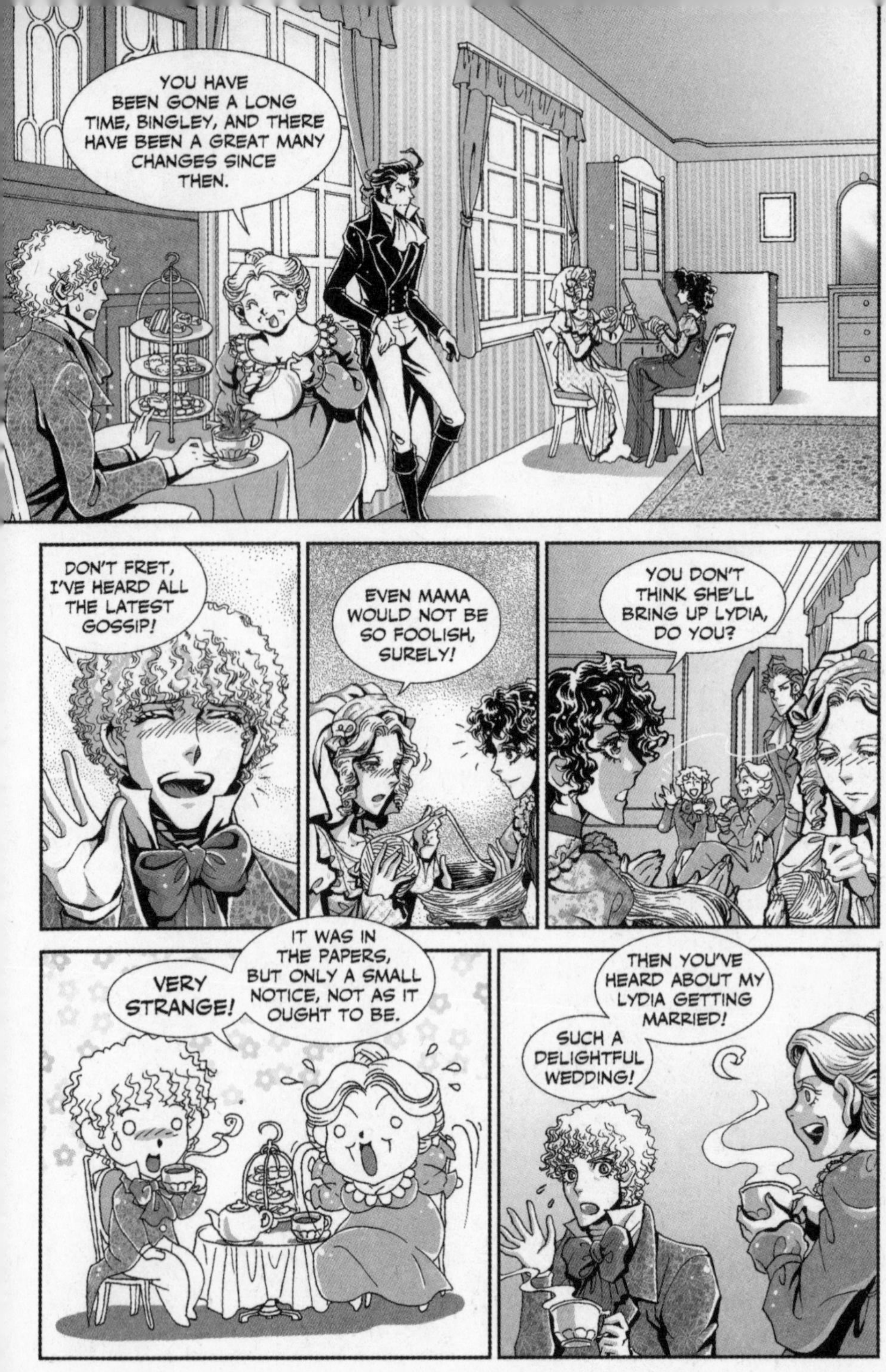
YOU HAVE BEEN GONE A LONG TIME, BINGLEY, AND THERE HAVE BEEN A GREAT MANY CHANGES SINCE THEN.
YOU DON'T THINK SHE'LL BRING UP LYDIA, DO YOU?
EVEN MAMA WOULD NOT BE SO FOOLISH, SURELY!
DON'T FRET, I'VE HEARD ALL THE LATEST GOSSIP!
THEN YOU'VE HEARD ABOUT MY LYDIA GETTING MARRIED!
SUCH A DELIGHTFUL WEDDING!
IT WAS IN THE PAPERS, BUT ONLY A SMALL NOTICE, NOT AS IT OUGHT TO BE.
VERY STRANGE!

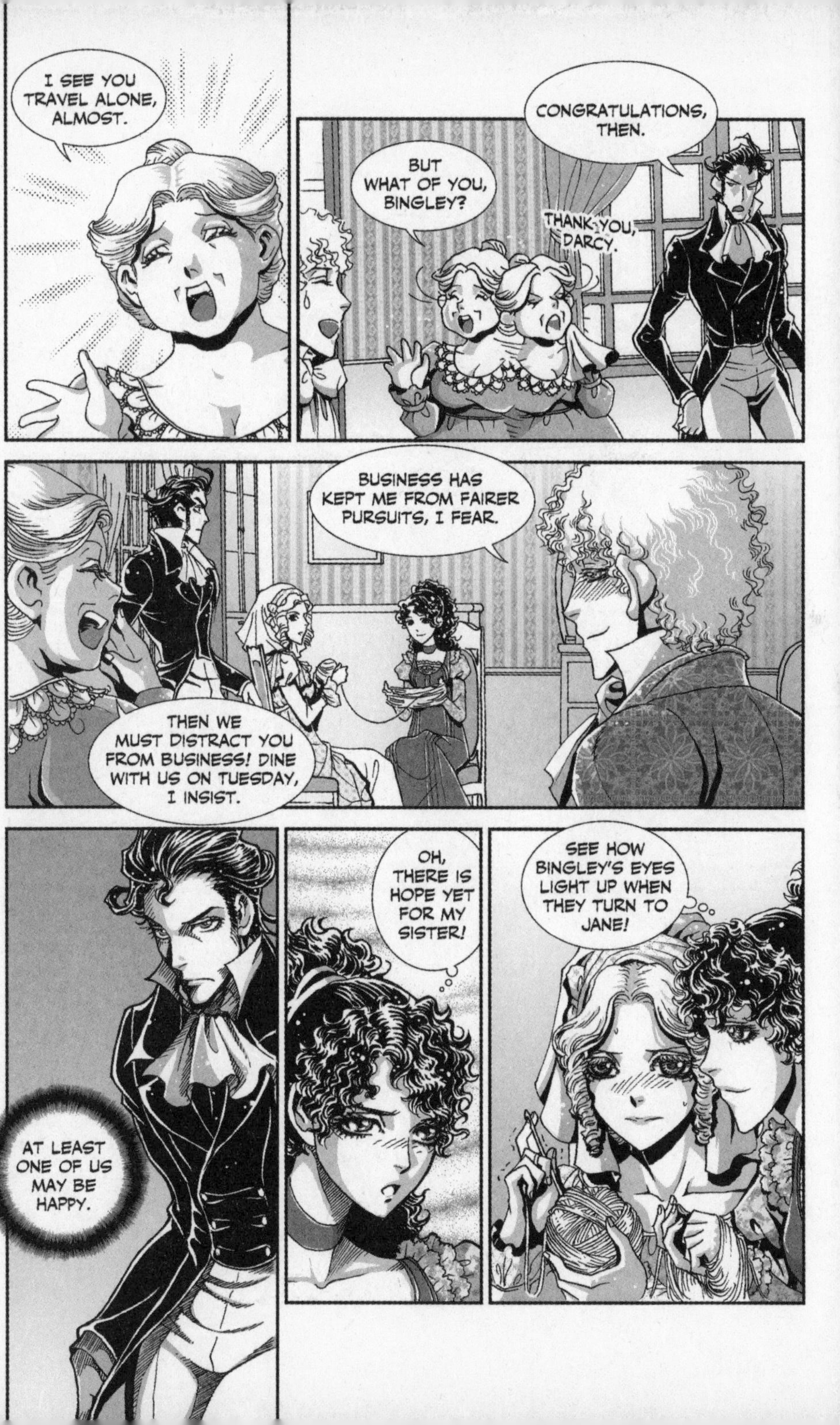
CONGRATULATIONS, THEN.
THANK YOU, DARCY.
BUT WHAT OF YOU, BINGLEY?
I SEE YOU TRAVEL ALONE, ALMOST.
BUSINESS HAS KEPT ME FROM FAIRER PURSUITS, I FEAR.
THEN WE MUST DISTRACT YOU FROM BUSINESS! DINE WITH US ON TUESDAY, I INSIST.
SEE HOW BINGLEY'S EYES LIGHT UP WHEN THEY TURN TO JANE!
OH, THERE IS HOPE YET FOR MY SISTER!
AT LEAST ONE OF US MAY BE HAPPY.

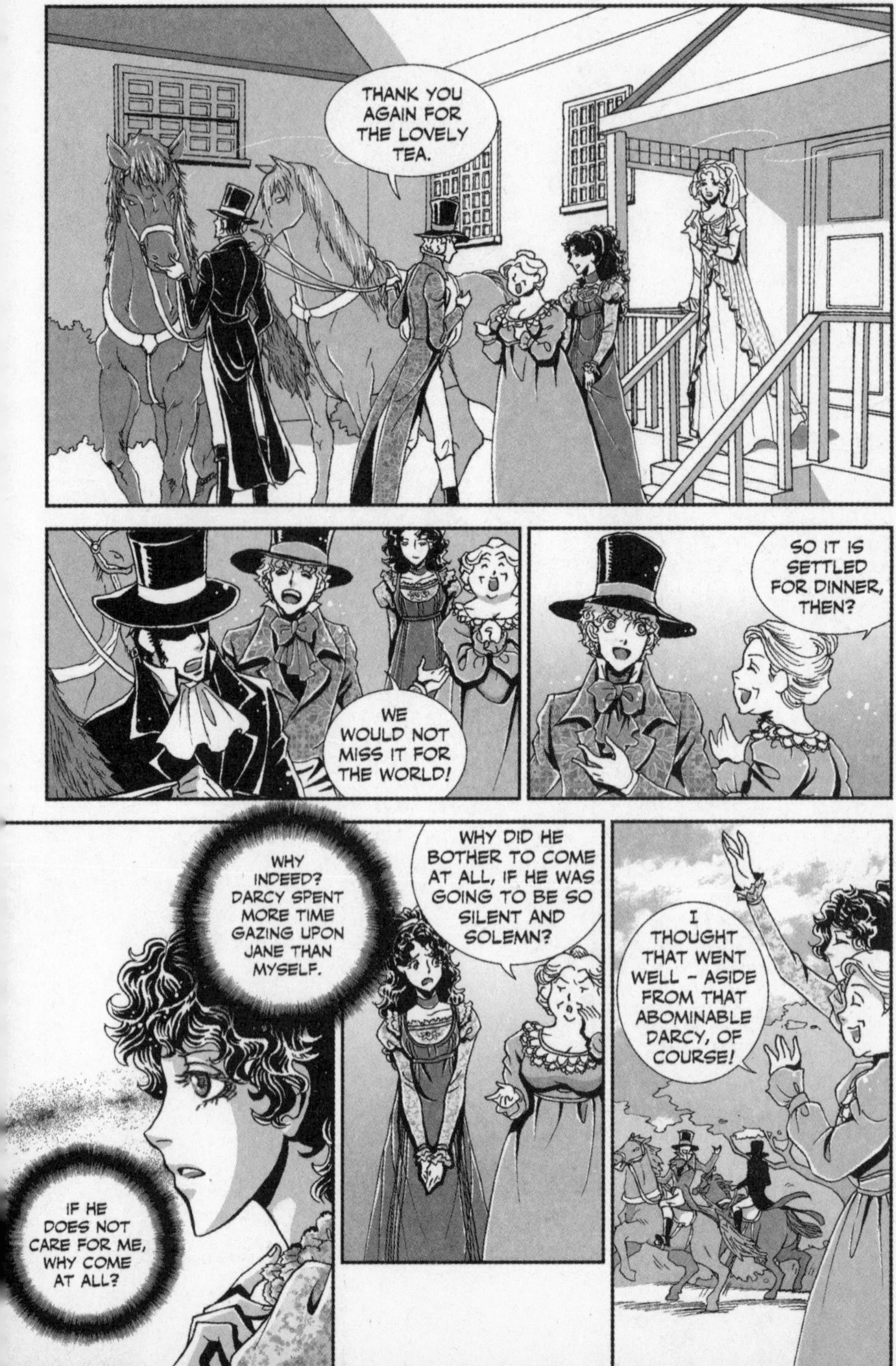
THANK YOU AGAIN FOR THE LOVELY TEA.
SO IT IS SETTLED FOR DINNER, THEN?
WE WOULD NOT MISS IT FOR THE WORLD!
I THOUGHT THAT WENT WELL - ASIDE FROM THAT ABOMINABLE DARCY, OF COURSE!
WHY DID HE BOTHER TO COME AT ALL, IF HE WAS GOING TO BE SO SILENT AND SOLEMN?
WHY INDEED? DARCY SPENT MORE TIME GAZING UPON JANE THAN MYSELF.
IF HE DOES NOT CARE FOR ME, WHY COME AT ALL?

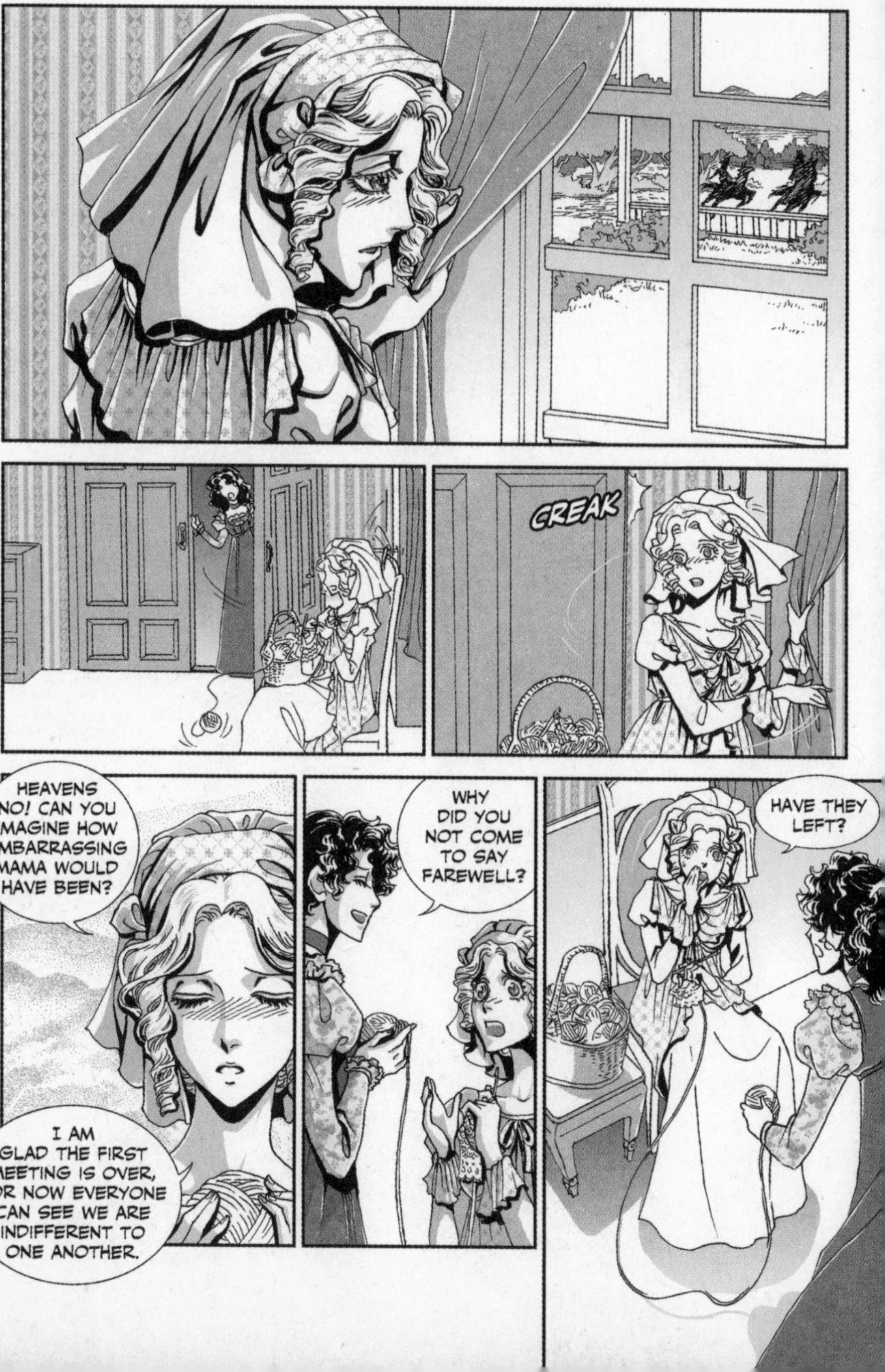
CREAK
HAVE THEY LEFT?
WHY DID YOU NOT COME TO SAY FAREWELL?
HEAVENS NO! CAN YOU IMAGINE HOW EMBARRASSING MAMA WOULD HAVE BEEN?
I AM GLAD THE FIRST MEETING IS OVER, FOR NOW EVERYONE CAN SEE WE ARE INDIFFERENT TO ONE ANOTHER.

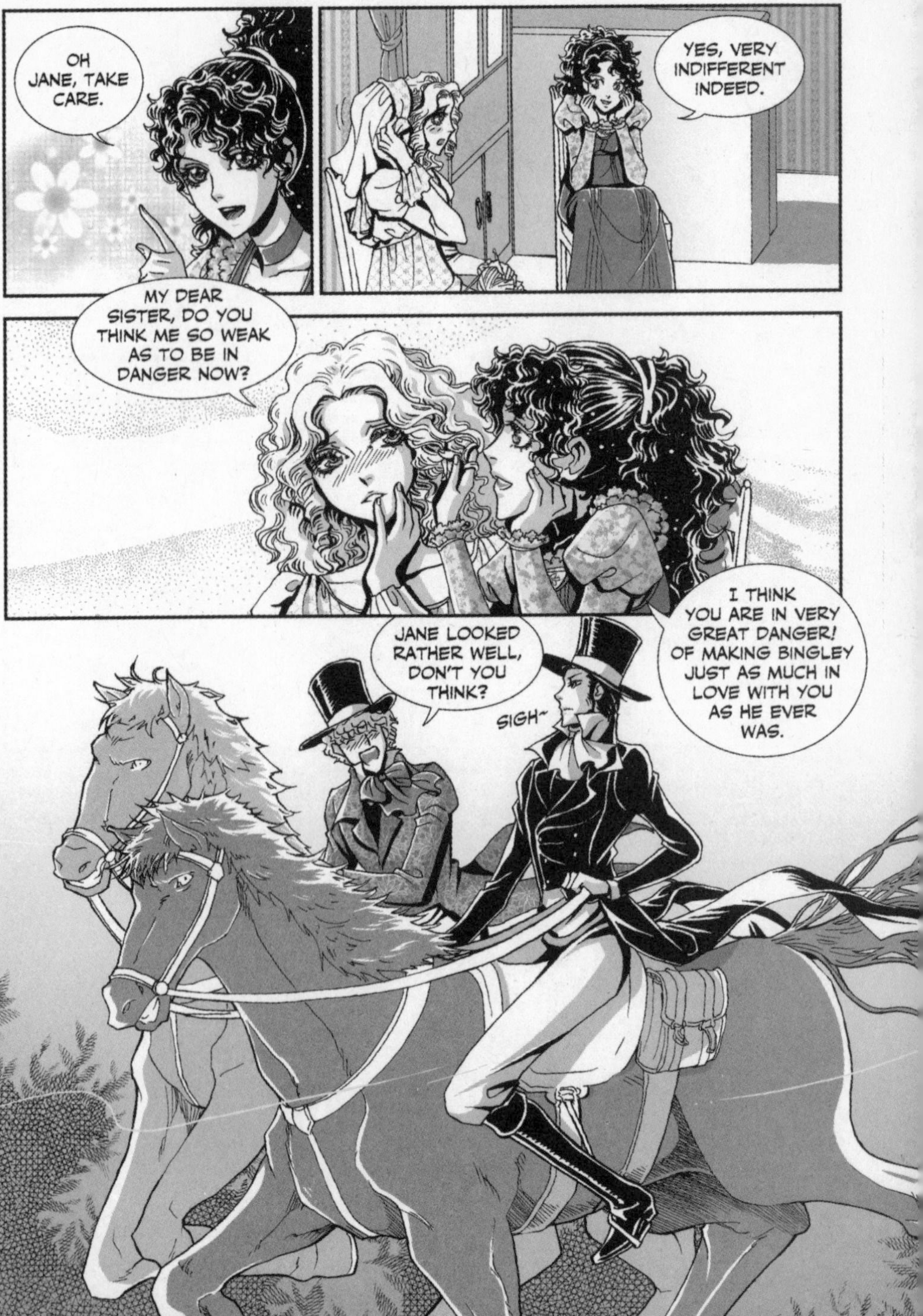
YES, VERY INDIFFERENT INDEED.
OH JANE, TAKE CARE.
MY DEAR SISTER, DO YOU THINK ME SO WEAK AS TO BE IN DANGER NOW?
I THINK YOU ARE IN VERY GREAT DANGER! OF MAKING BINGLEY JUST AS MUCH IN LOVE WITH YOU AS HE EVER WAS.
JANE LOOKED RATHER WELL, DON'T YOU THINK?
SIGH~

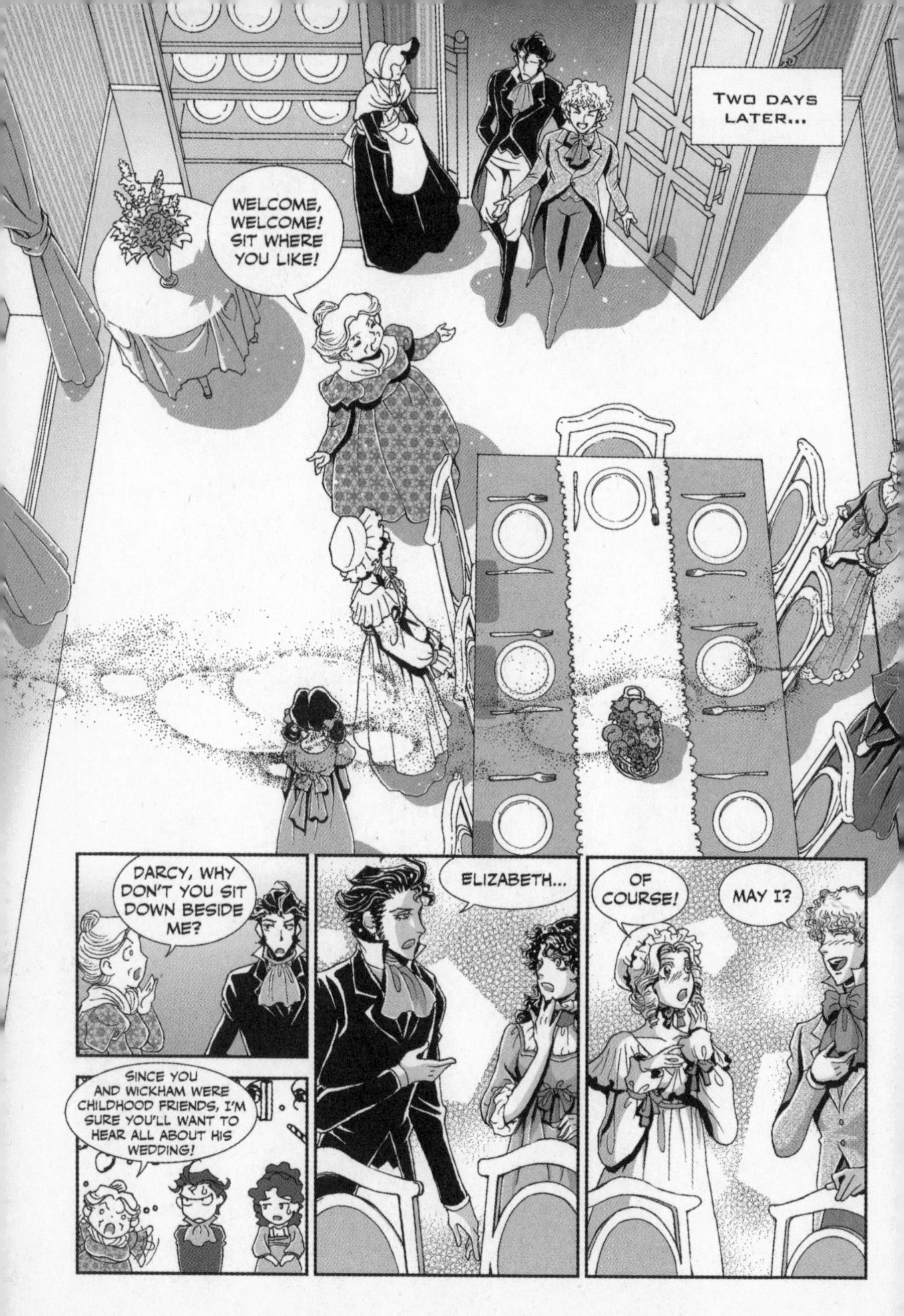
TWO DAYS LATER...
WELCOME, WELCOME! SIT WHERE YOU LIKE!
MAY I?
OF COURSE!
ELIZABETH...
DARCY, WHY DON'T YOU SIT DOWN BESIDE ME?
SINCE YOU AND WICKHAM WERE CHILDHOOD FRIENDS, I'M SURE YOU'LL WANT TO HEAR ALL ABOUT HIS WEDDING!

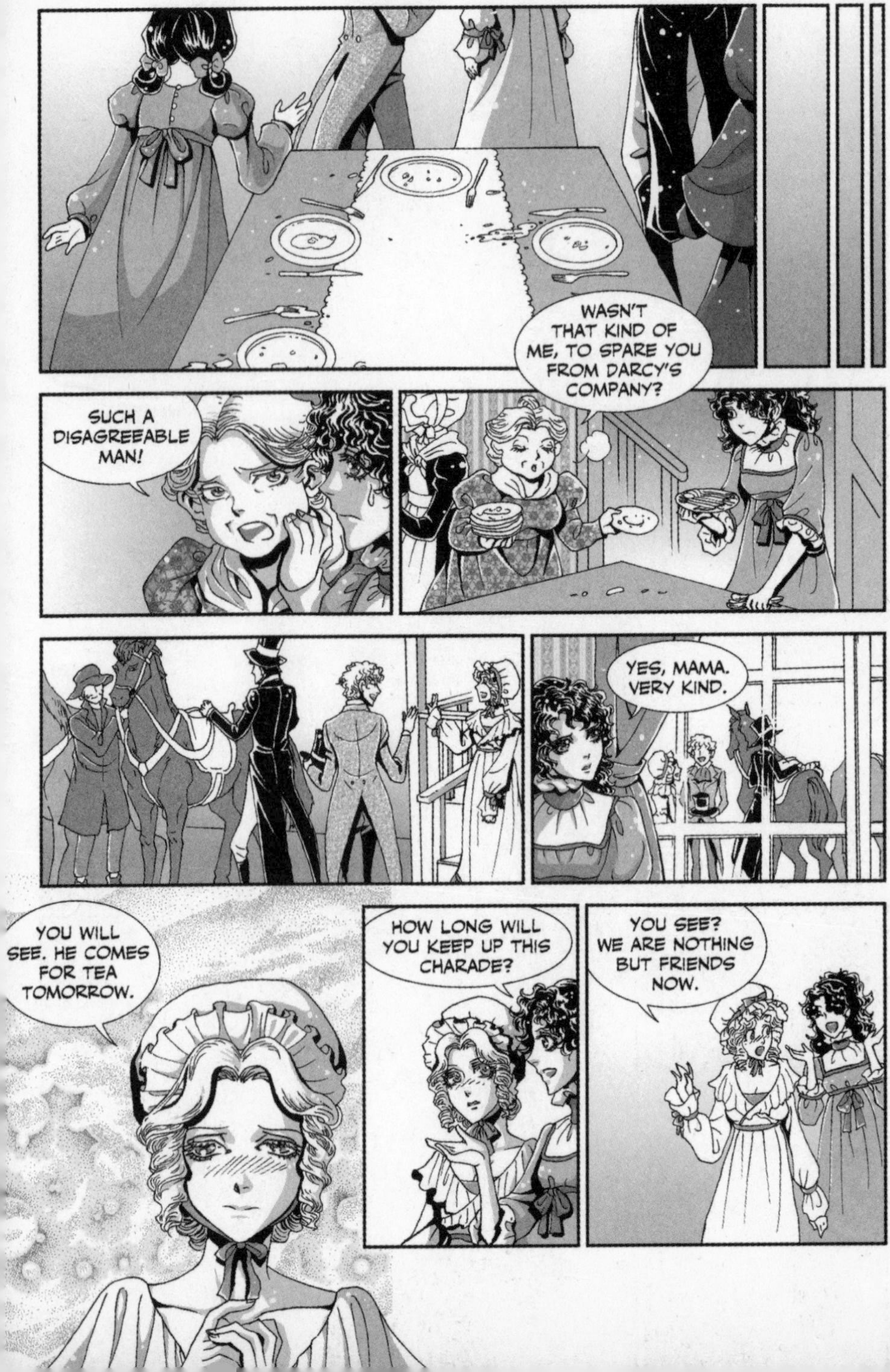
WASN'T THAT KIND OF ME, TO SPARE YOU FROM DARCY'S COMPANY?
SUCH A DISAGREEABLE MAN!
YES, MAMA. VERY KIND.
YOU SEE? WE ARE NOTHING BUT FRIENDS NOW.
HOW LONG WILL YOU KEEP UP THIS CHARADE?
YOU WILL SEE. HE COMES FOR TEA TOMORROW.

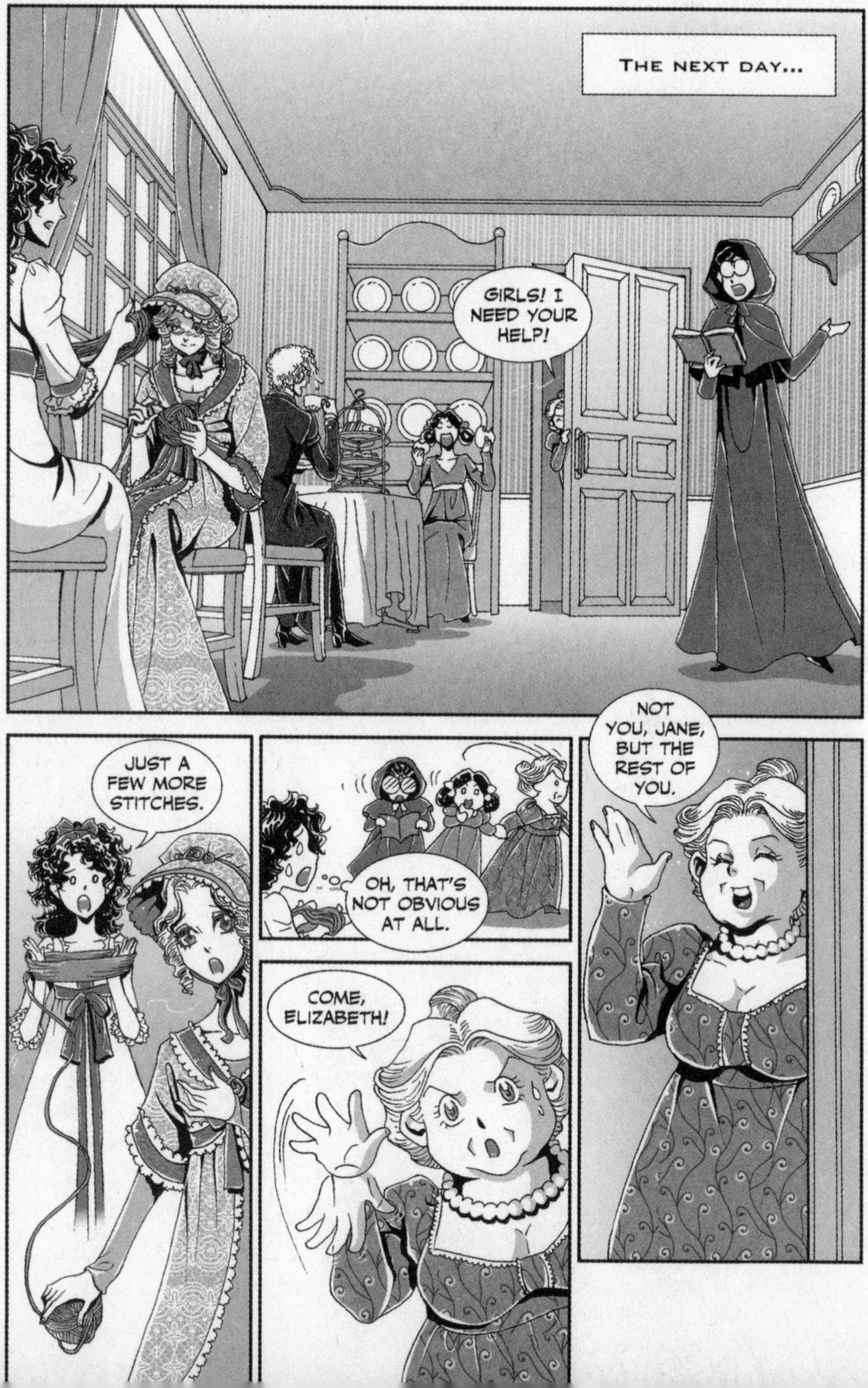
THE NEXT DAY...
GIRLS! I NEED YOUR HELP!
NOT YOU, JANE, BUT THE REST OF YOU.
OH, THAT'S NOT OBVIOUS AT ALL.
COME, ELIZABETH!
JUST A FEW MORE STITCHES.

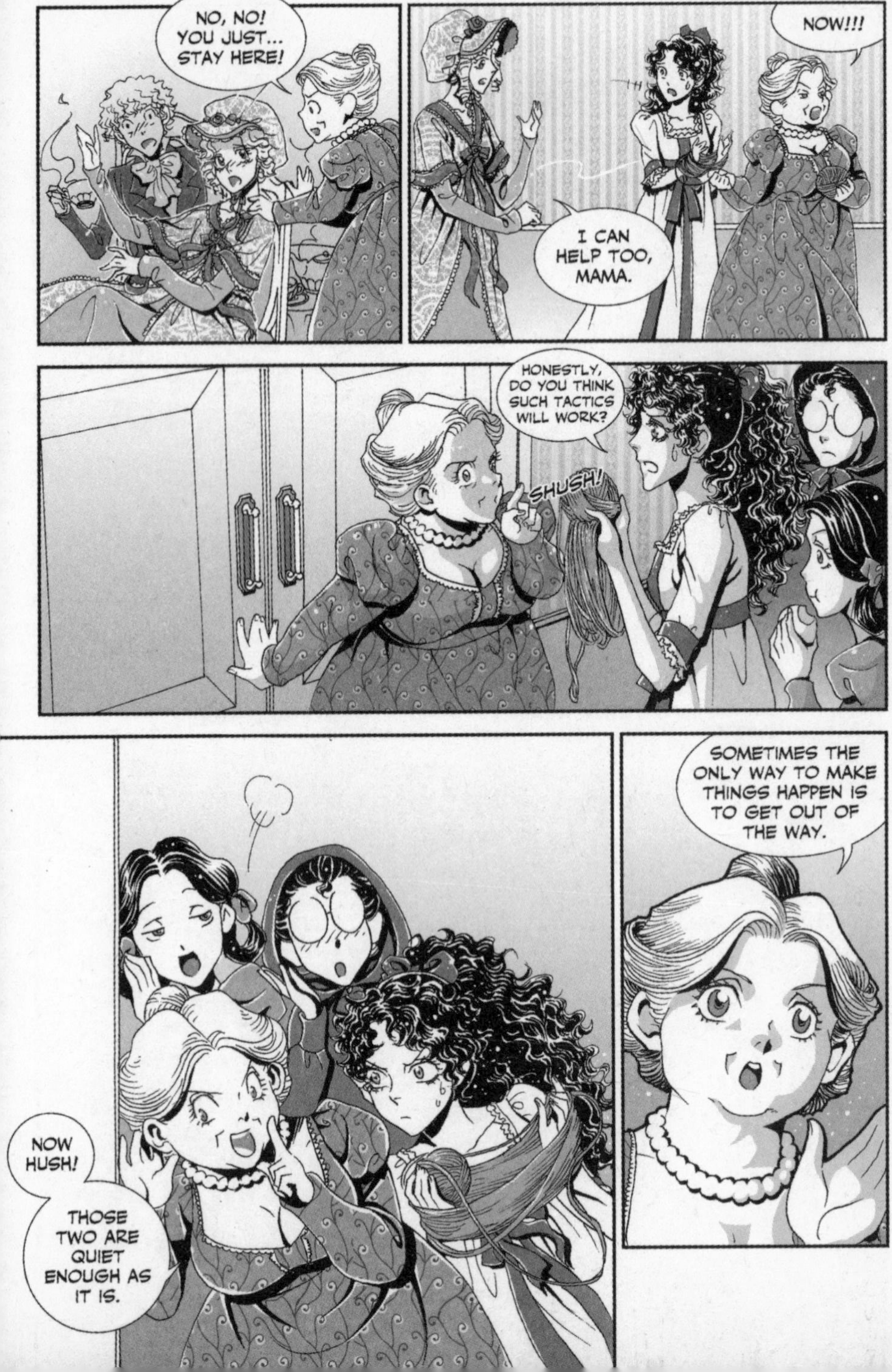
NOW!!!
I CAN HELP TOO, MAMA.
NO, NO! YOU JUST... STAY HERE!
HONESTLY, DO YOU THINK SUCH TACTICS WILL WORK?
SHUSH!
SOMETIMES THE ONLY WAY TO MAKE THINGS HAPPEN IS TO GET OUT OF THE WAY.
NOW HUSH!
THOSE TWO ARE QUIET ENOUGH AS IT IS.

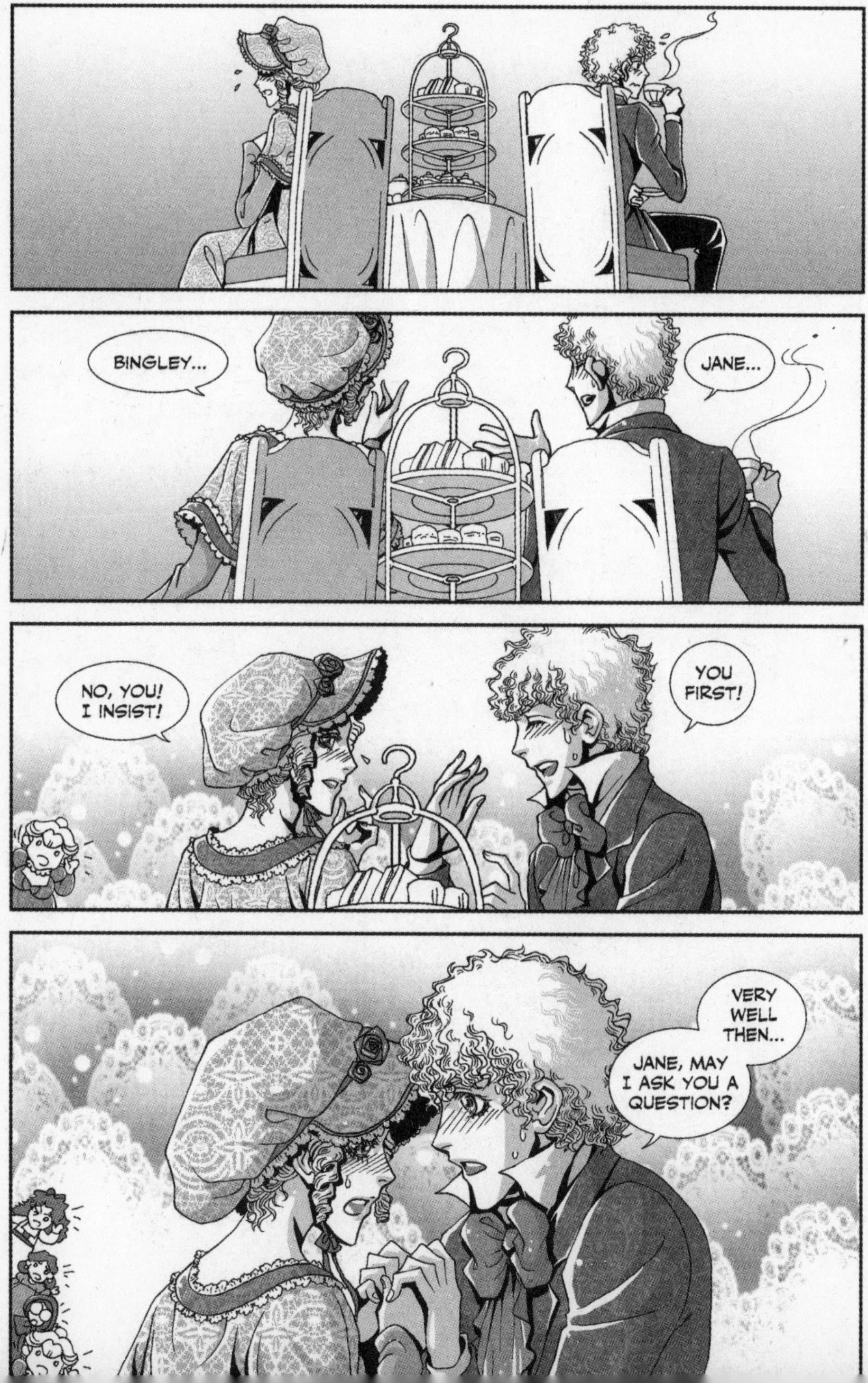
JANE...
BINGLEY...
YOU FIRST!
NO, YOU! I INSIST!
VERY WELL THEN...
JANE, MAY I ASK YOU A QUESTION?

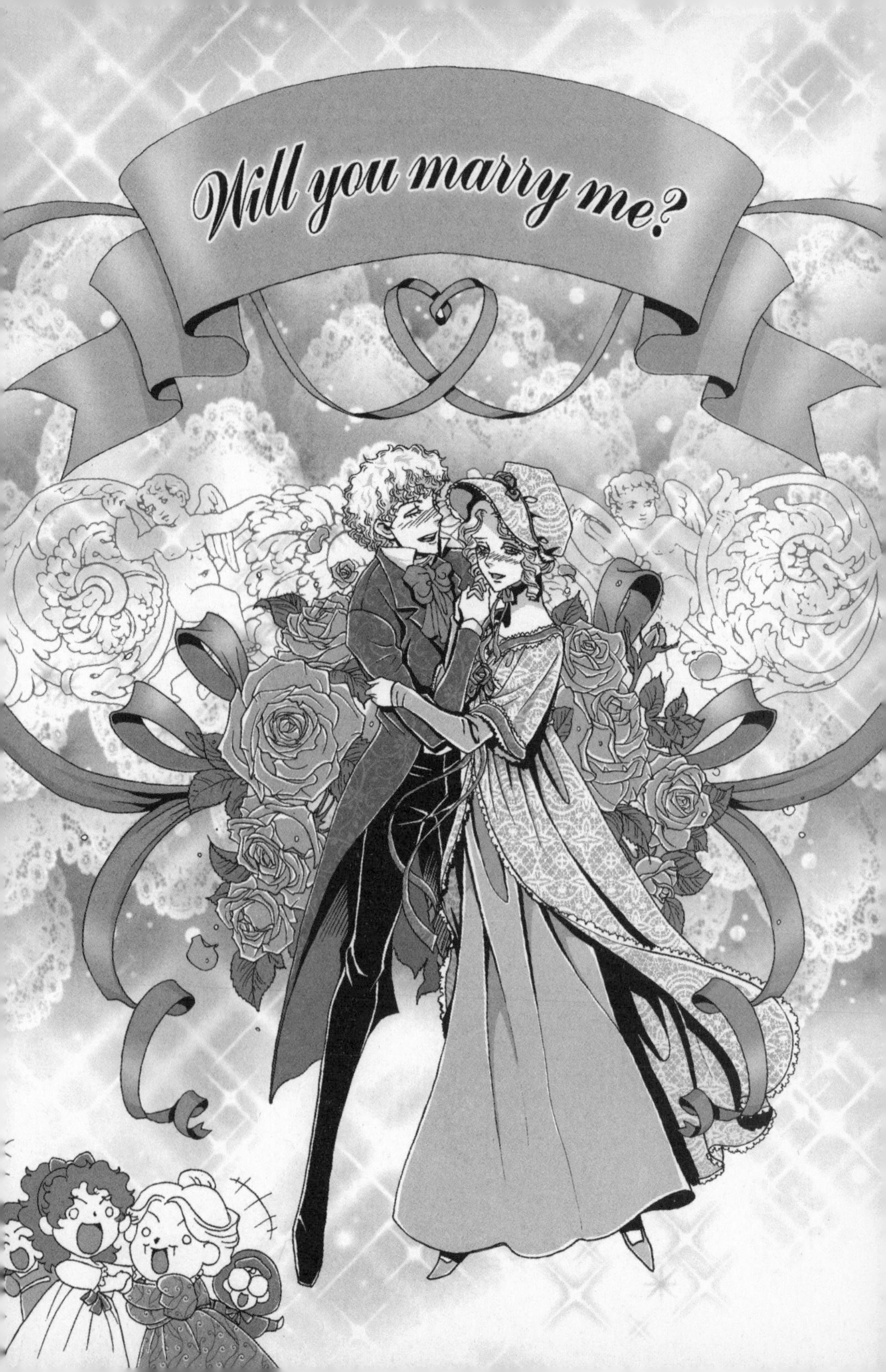
Will you marry me?

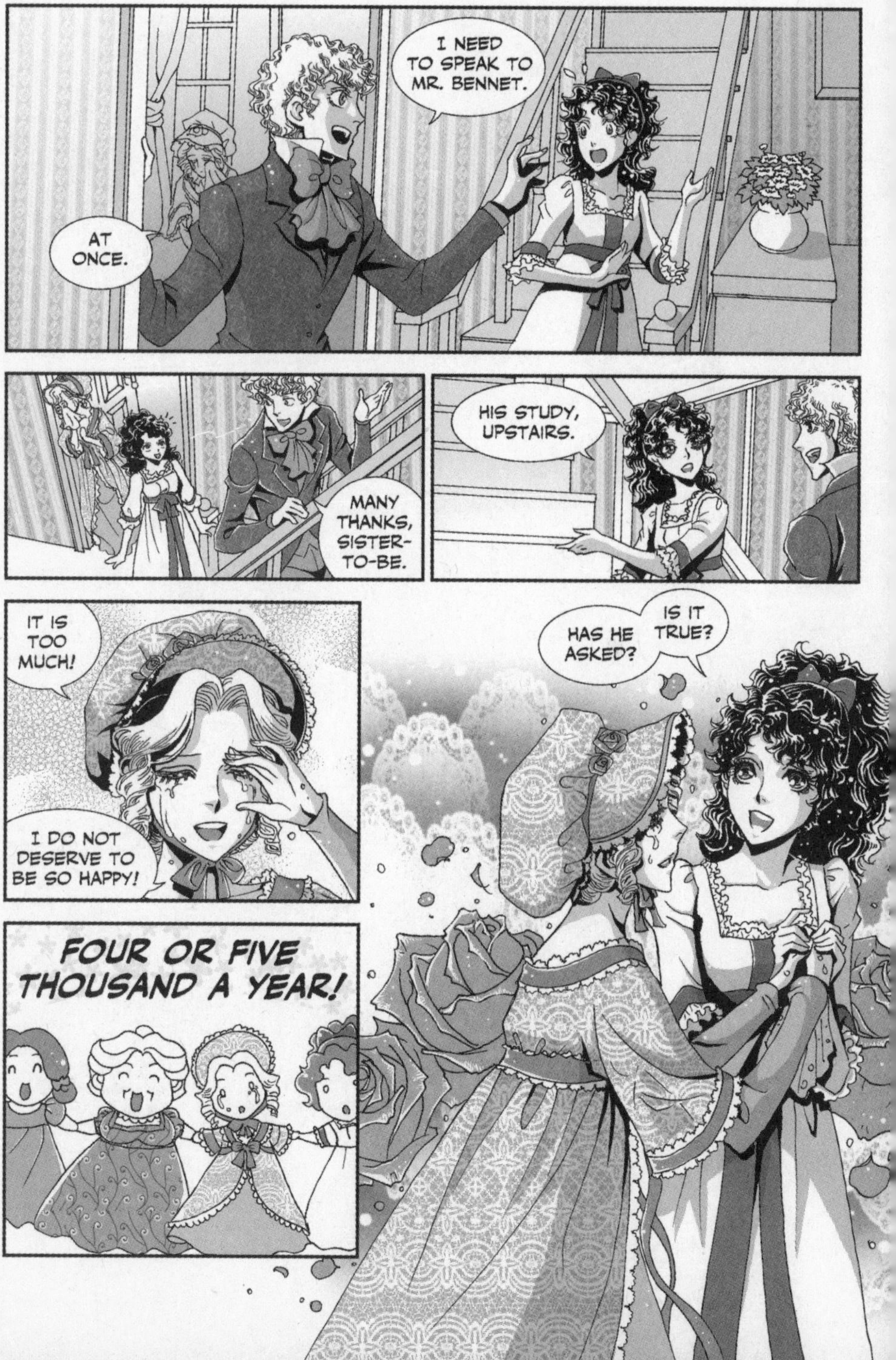
I NEED TO SPEAK TO MR. BENNET.
AT ONCE.
HIS STUDY, UPSTAIRS.
MANY THANKS, SISTER-TO-BE.
IS IT TRUE?
HAS HE ASKED?
IT IS TOO MUCH!
I DO NOT DESERVE TO BE SO HAPPY!
FOUR OR FIVE THOUSAND A YEAR!

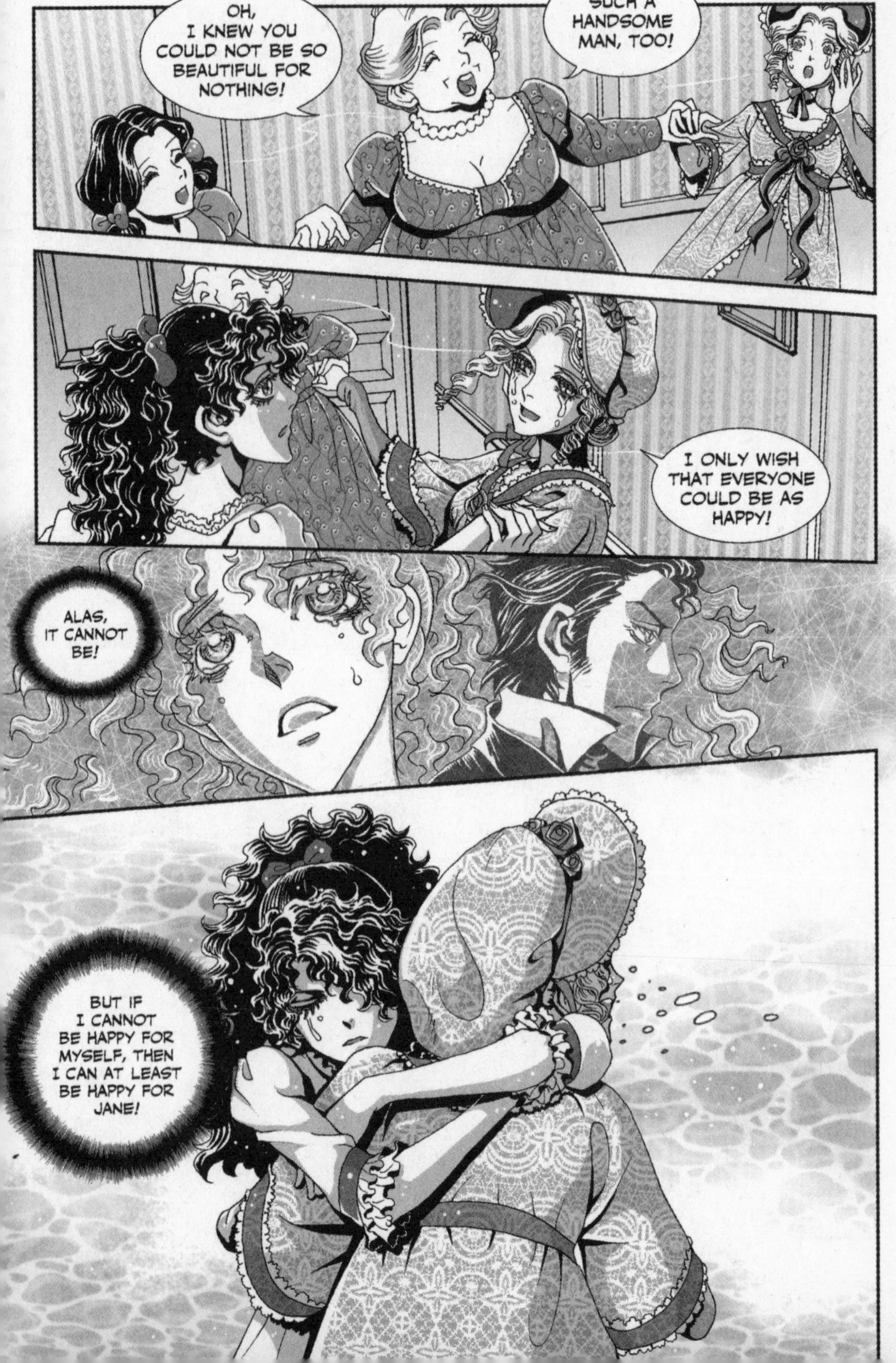
SUCH A HANDSOME MAN, TOO!
OH, I KNEW YOU COULD NOT BE SO BEAUTIFUL FOR NOTHING!
I ONLY WISH THAT EVERYONE COULD BE AS HAPPY!
ALAS, IT CANNOT BE!
BUT IF I CANNOT BE HAPPY FOR MYSELF, THEN I CAN AT LEAST BE HAPPY FOR JANE!

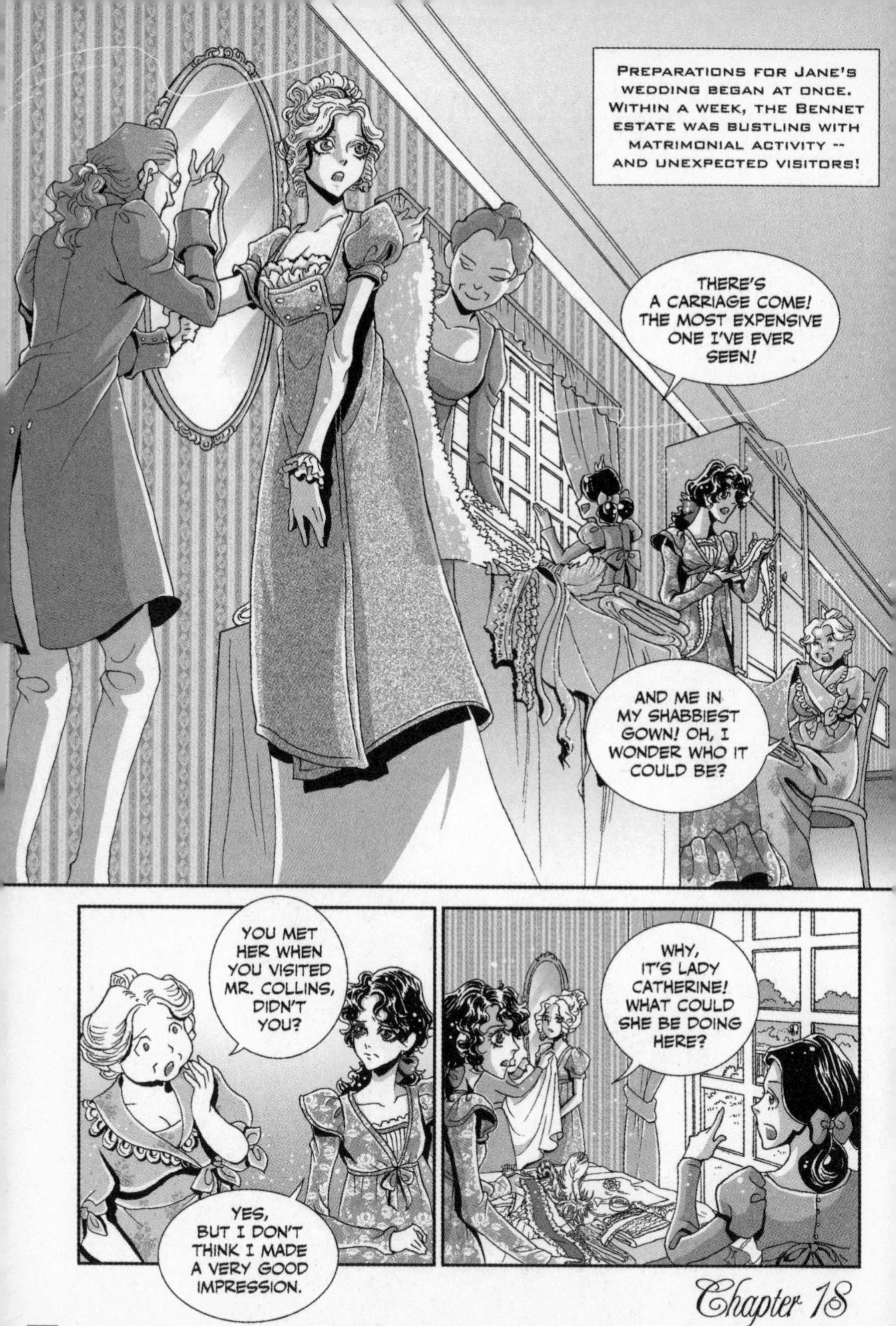
PREPARATIONS FOR JANE'S WEDDING BEGAN AT ONCE. WITHIN A WEEK, THE BENNET ESTATE WAS BUSTLING WITH MATRIMONIAL ACTIVITY -- AND UNEXPECTED VISITORS!
THERE'S A CARRIAGE COME! THE MOST EXPENSIVE ONE I'VE EVER SEEN!
AND ME IN MY SHABBIEST GOWN! OH, I WONDER WHO IT COULD BE?
WHY, IT'S LADY CATHERINE! WHAT COULD SHE BE DOING HERE?
YOU MET HER WHEN YOU VISITED MR. COLLINS, DIDN'T YOU?
YES, BUT I DON'T THINK I MADE A VERY GOOD IMPRESSION.

Chapter 18

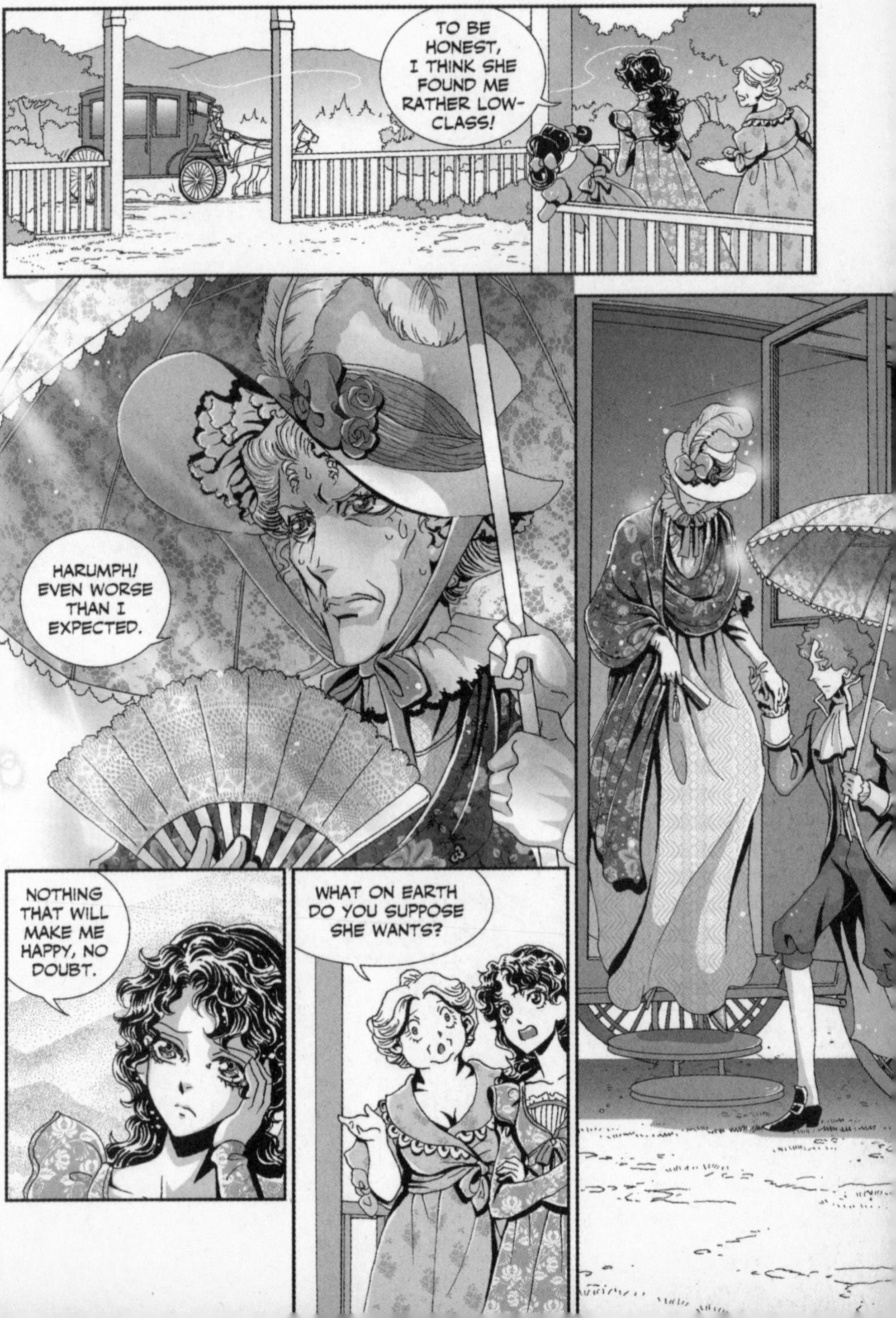
TO BE HONEST, I THINK SHE FOUND ME RATHER LOW-CLASS!
HARUMPH! EVEN WORSE THAN I EXPECTED.
WHAT ON EARTH DO YOU SUPPOSE SHE WANTS?
NOTHING THAT WILL MAKE ME HAPPY, NO DOUBT.

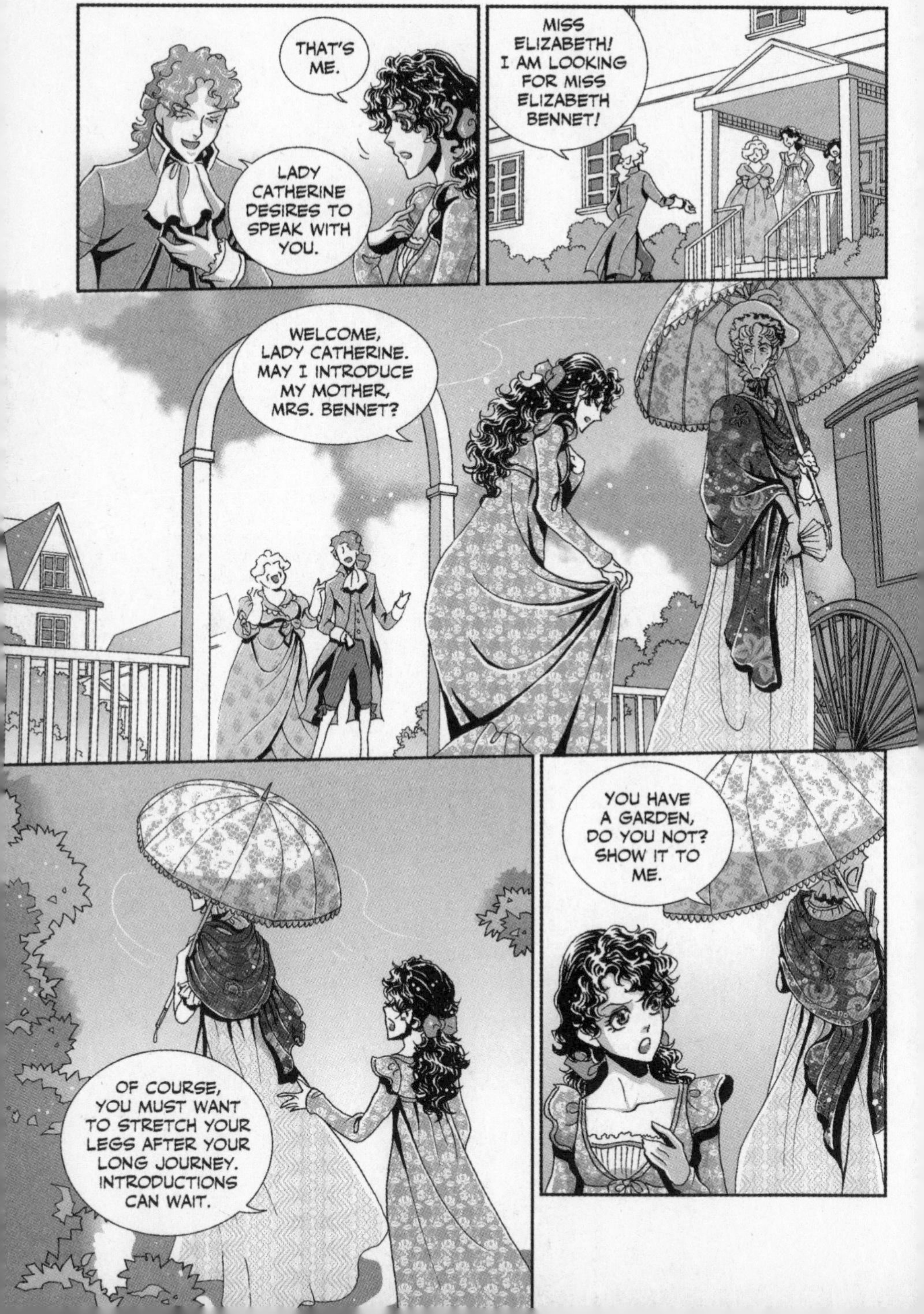
MISS ELIZABETH! I AM LOOKING FOR MISS ELIZABETH BENNET!
THAT'S ME.
LADY CATHERINE DESIRES TO SPEAK WITH YOU.
WELCOME, LADY CATHERINE. MAY I INTRODUCE MY MOTHER, MRS. BENNET?
YOU HAVE A GARDEN, DO YOU NOT? SHOW IT TO ME.
OF COURSE, YOU MUST WANT TO STRETCH YOUR LEGS AFTER YOUR LONG JOURNEY. INTRODUCTIONS CAN WAIT.

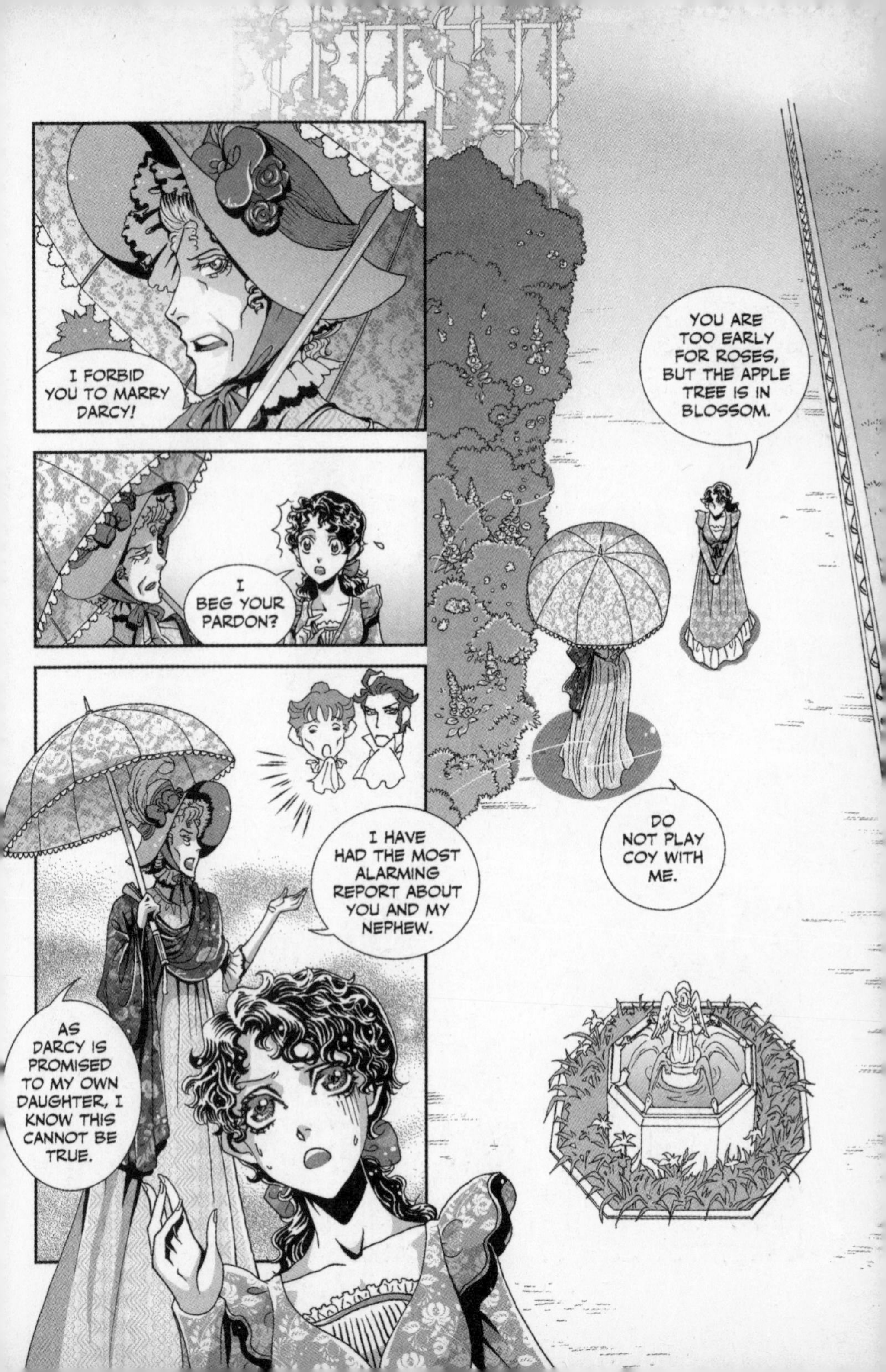
YOU ARE TOO EARLY FOR ROSES, BUT THE APPLE TREE IS IN BLOSSOM.
DO NOT PLAY COY WITH ME.
I FORBID YOU TO MARRY DARCY!
I BEG YOUR PARDON?
I HAVE HAD THE MOST ALARMING REPORT ABOUT YOU AND MY NEPHEW.
AS DARCY IS PROMISED TO MY OWN DAUGHTER, I KNOW THIS CANNOT BE TRUE.

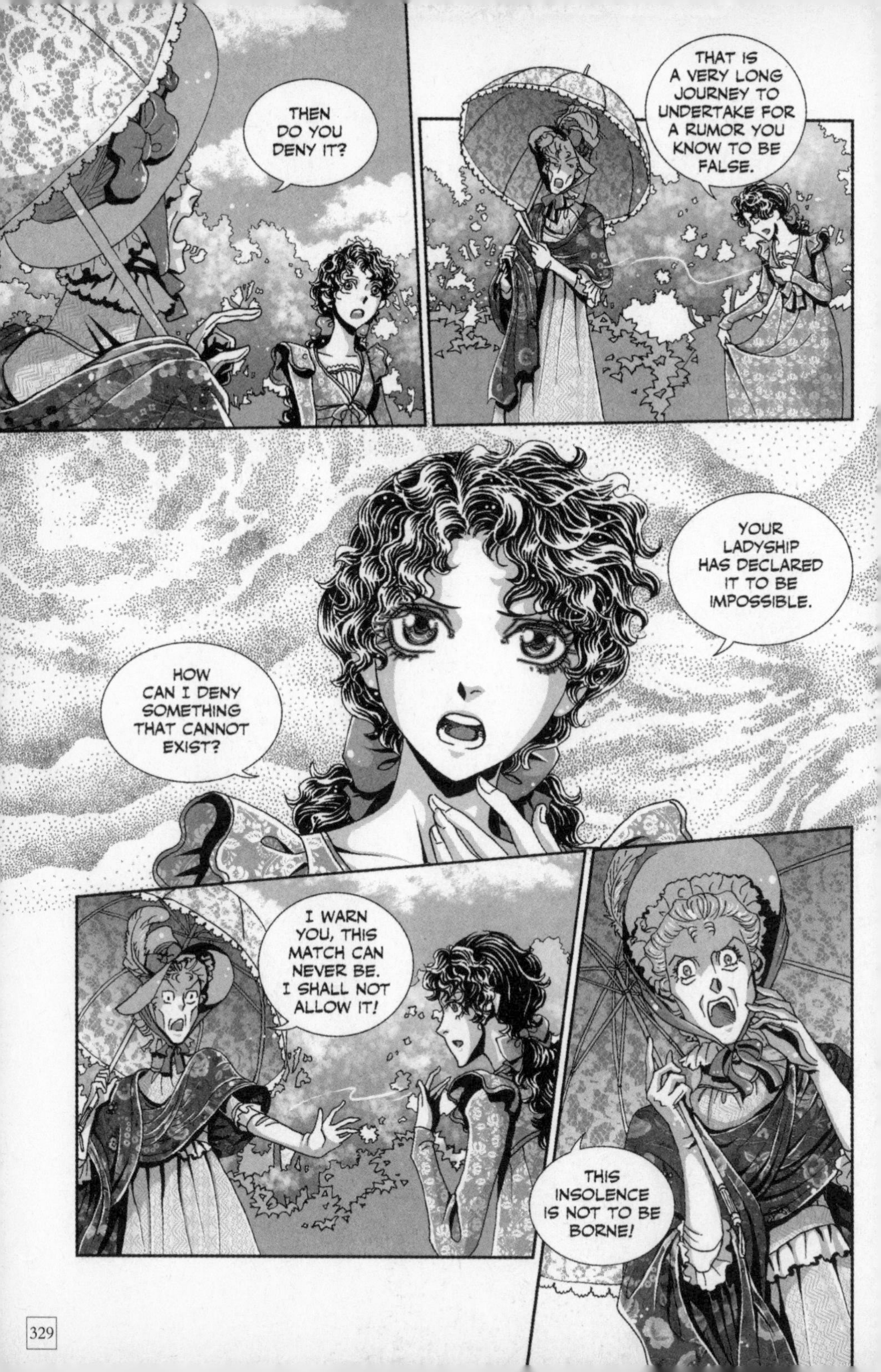
THAT IS A VERY LONG JOURNEY TO UNDERTAKE FOR A RUMOR YOU KNOW TO BE FALSE.
THEN DO YOU DENY IT?
YOUR LADYSHIP HAS DECLARED IT TO BE IMPOSSIBLE.
HOW CAN I DENY SOMETHING THAT CANNOT EXIST?
THIS INSOLENCE IS NOT TO BE BORNE!
I WARN YOU, THIS MATCH CAN NEVER BE. I SHALL NOT ALLOW IT!

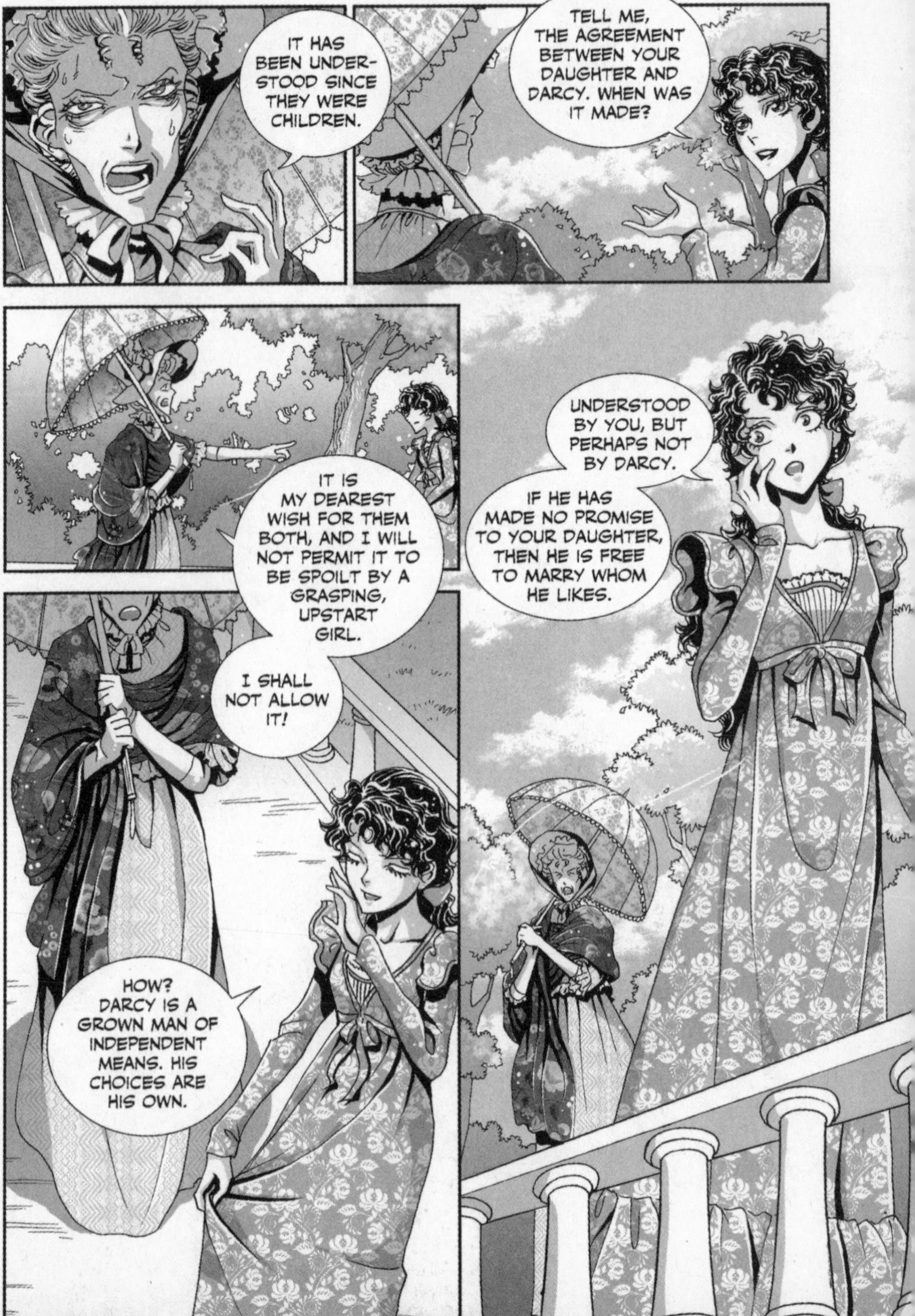
TELL ME, THE AGREEMENT BETWEEN YOUR DAUGHTER AND DARCY. WHEN WAS IT MADE?
IT HAS BEEN UNDER-STOOD SINCE THEY WERE CHILDREN.
UNDERSTOOD BY YOU, BUT PERHAPS NOT BY DARCY.
IF HE HAS MADE NO PROMISE TO YOUR DAUGHTER, THEN HE IS FREE TO MARRY WHOM HE LIKES.
IT IS MY DEAREST WISH FOR THEM BOTH, AND I WILL NOT PERMIT IT TO BE SPOILT BY A GRASPING, UPSTART GIRL.
I SHALL NOT ALLOW IT!
HOW? DARCY IS A GROWN MAN OF INDEPENDENT MEANS. HIS CHOICES ARE HIS OWN.

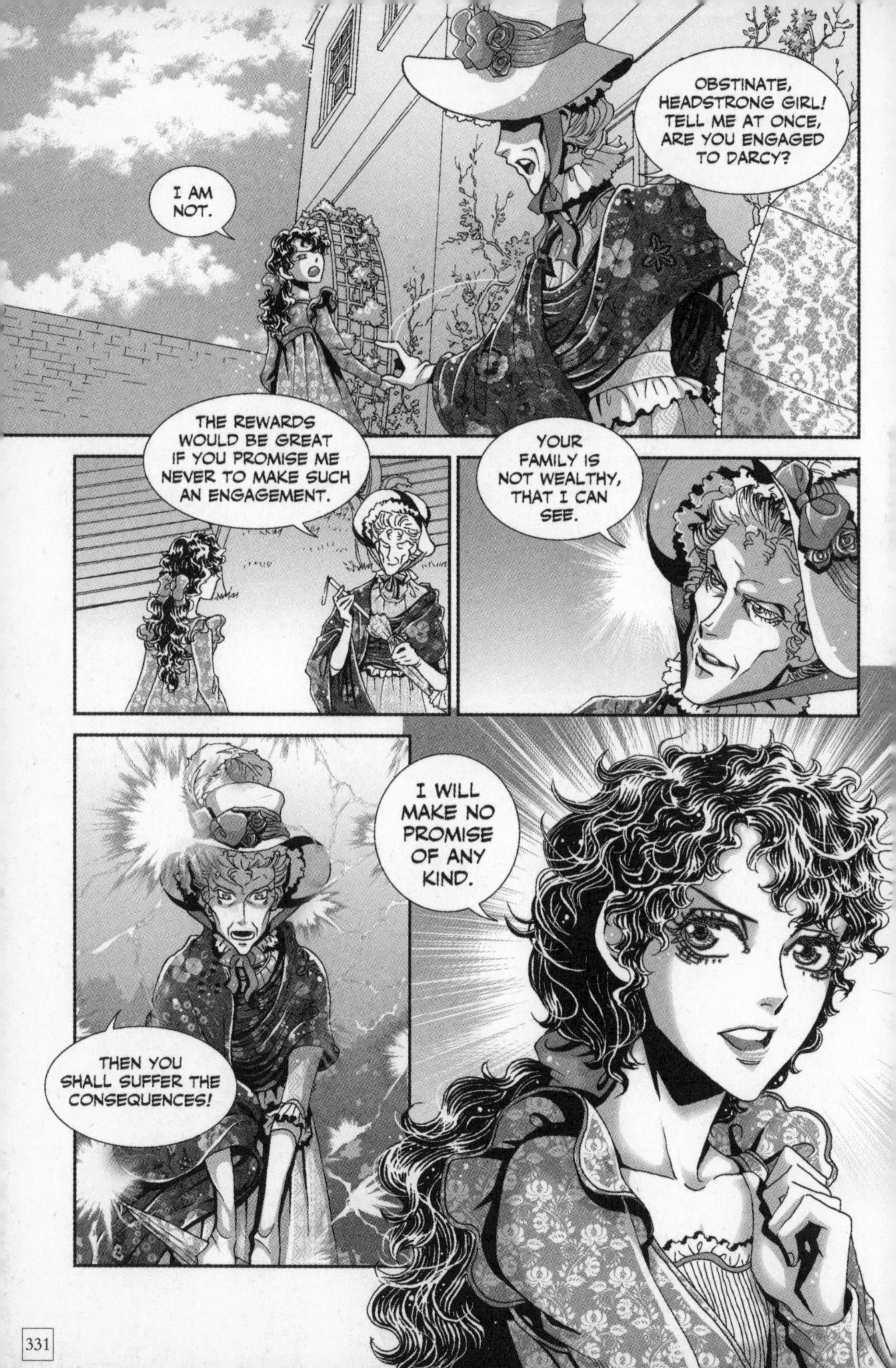
OBSTINATE, HEADSTRONG GIRL! TELL ME AT ONCE, ARE YOU ENGAGED TO DARCY?
I AM NOT.
YOUR FAMILY IS NOT WEALTHY, THAT I CAN SEE.
THE REWARDS WOULD BE GREAT IF YOU PROMISE ME NEVER TO MAKE SUCH AN ENGAGEMENT.
I WILL MAKE NO PROMISE OF ANY KIND.
THEN YOU SHALL SUFFER THE CONSEQUENCES!

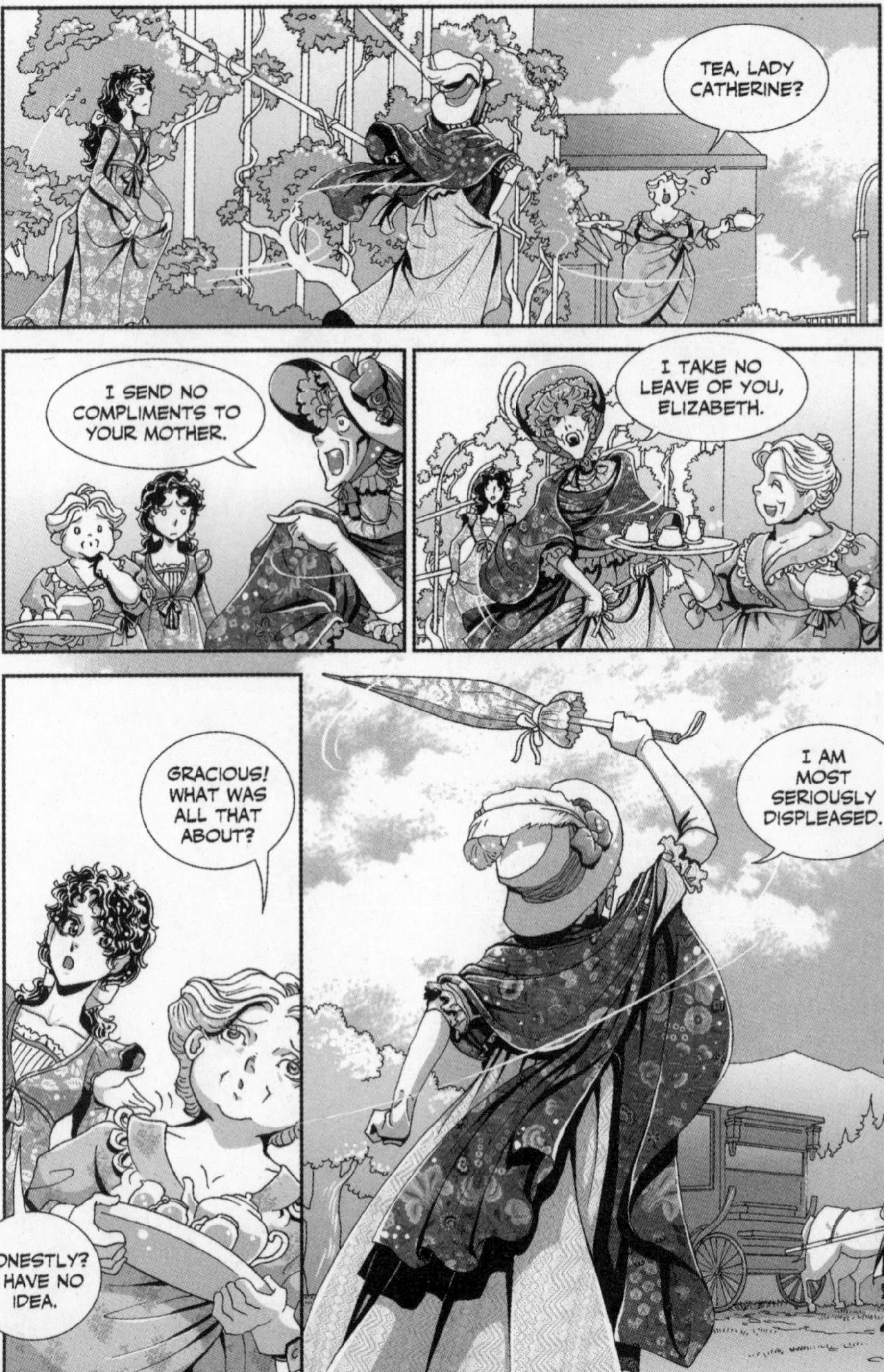
TEA, LADY CATHERINE?
I TAKE NO LEAVE OF YOU, ELIZABETH.
I SEND NO COMPLIMENTS TO YOUR MOTHER.
I AM MOST SERIOUSLY DISPLEASED.
GRACIOUS! WHAT WAS ALL THAT ABOUT?
HONESTLY? I HAVE NO IDEA.

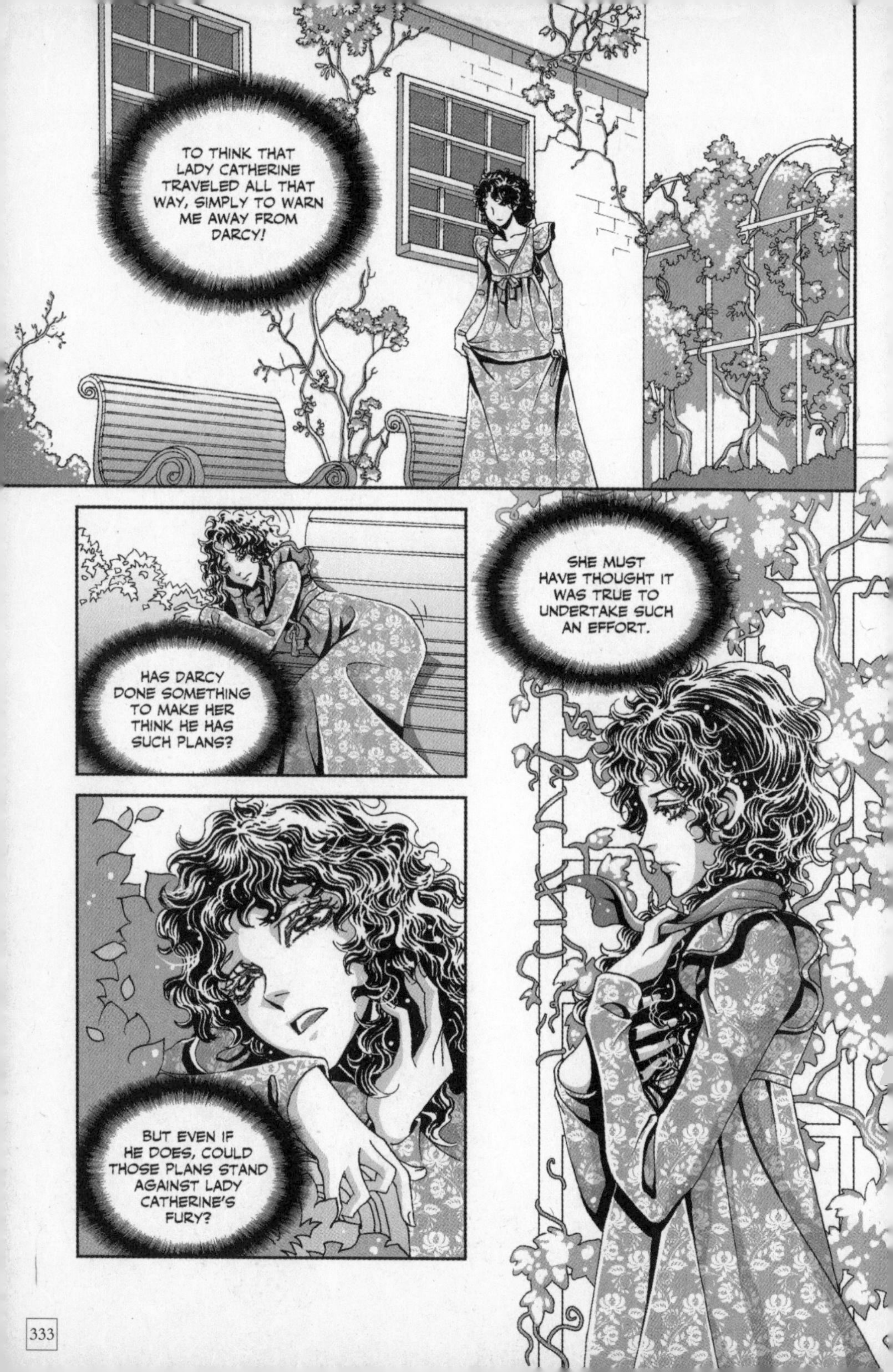
TO THINK THAT LADY CATHERINE TRAVELED ALL THAT WAY, SIMPLY TO WARN ME AWAY FROM DARCY!
SHE MUST HAVE THOUGHT IT WAS TRUE TO UNDERTAKE SUCH AN EFFORT.
HAS DARCY DONE SOMETHING TO MAKE HER THINK HE HAS SUCH PLANS?
BUT EVEN IF HE DOES, COULD THOSE PLANS STAND AGAINST LADY CATHERINE'S FURY?

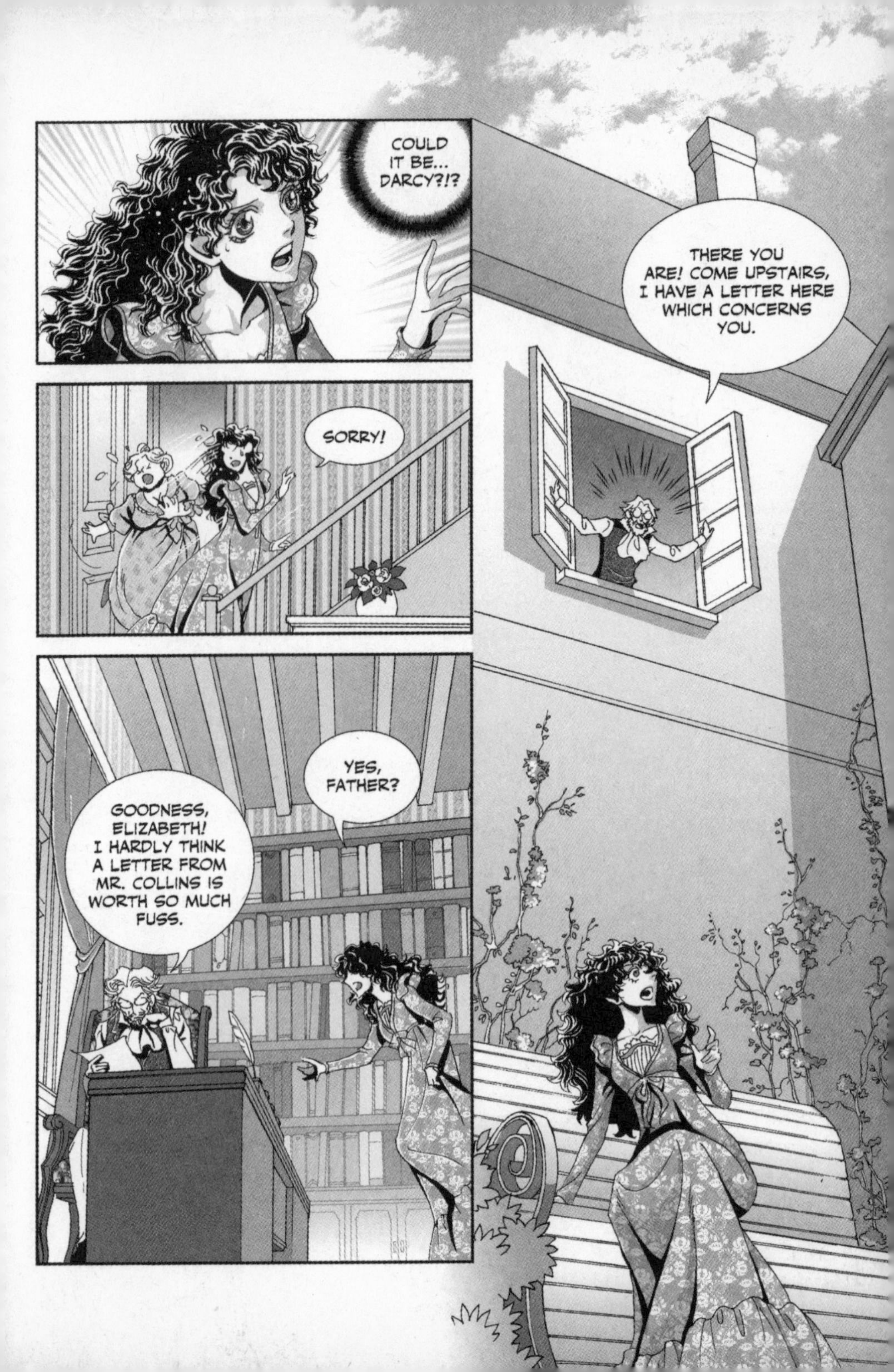
THERE YOU ARE! COME UPSTAIRS, I HAVE A LETTER HERE WHICH CONCERNS YOU.
COULD IT BE... DARCY?!?
SORRY!
YES, FATHER?
GOODNESS, ELIZABETH! I HARDLY THINK A LETTER FROM MR. COLLINS IS WORTH SO MUCH FUSS.

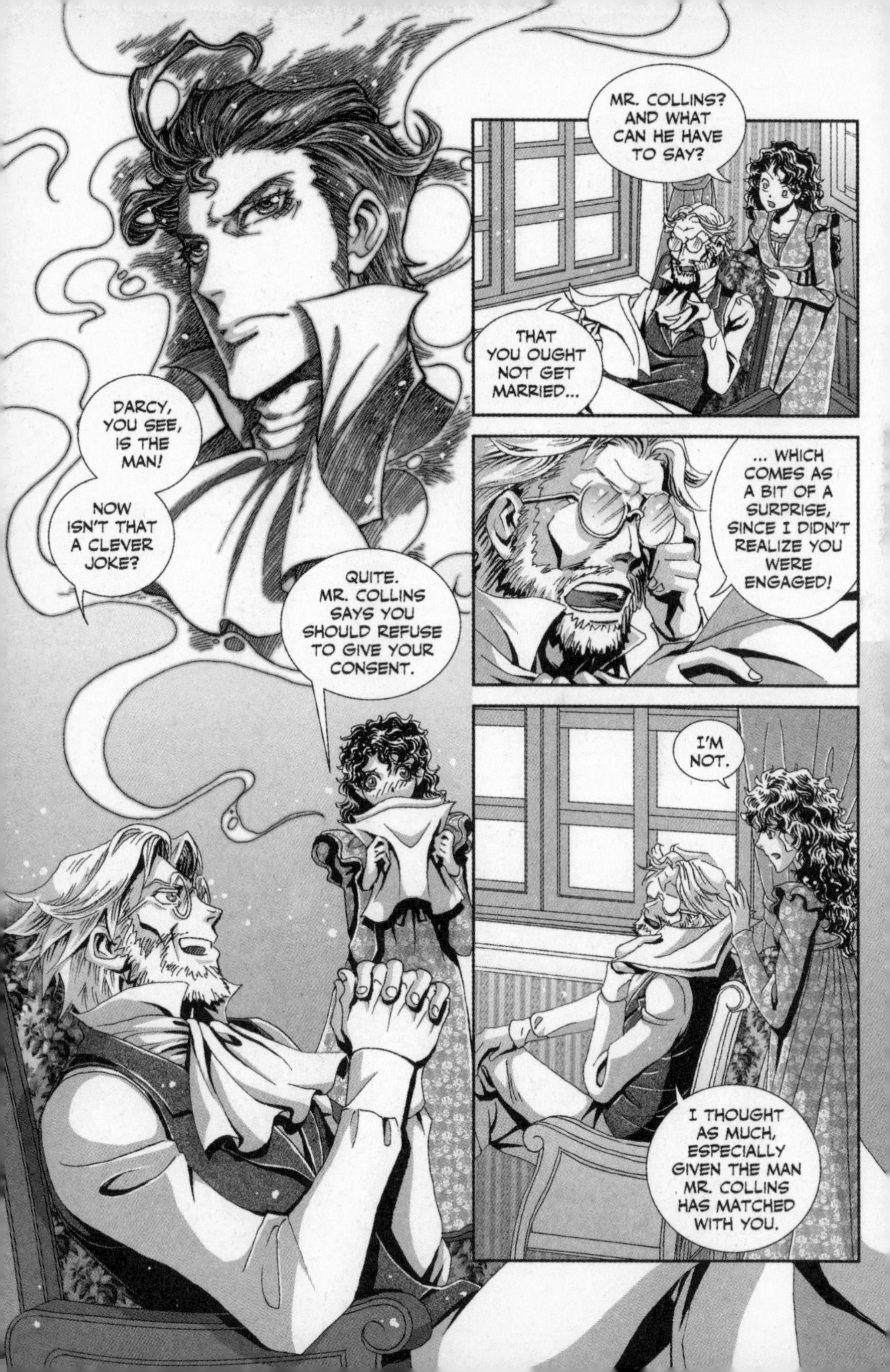
MR. COLLINS? AND WHAT CAN HE HAVE TO SAY?
THAT YOU OUGHT NOT GET MARRIED...
... WHICH COMES AS A BIT OF A SURPRISE, SINCE I DIDN'T REALIZE YOU WERE ENGAGED!
I'M NOT.
I THOUGHT AS MUCH, ESPECIALLY GIVEN THE MAN MR. COLLINS HAS MATCHED WITH YOU.
DARCY, YOU SEE, IS THE MAN!
NOW ISN'T THAT A CLEVER JOKE?
QUITE. MR. COLLINS SAYS YOU SHOULD REFUSE TO GIVE YOUR CONSENT.

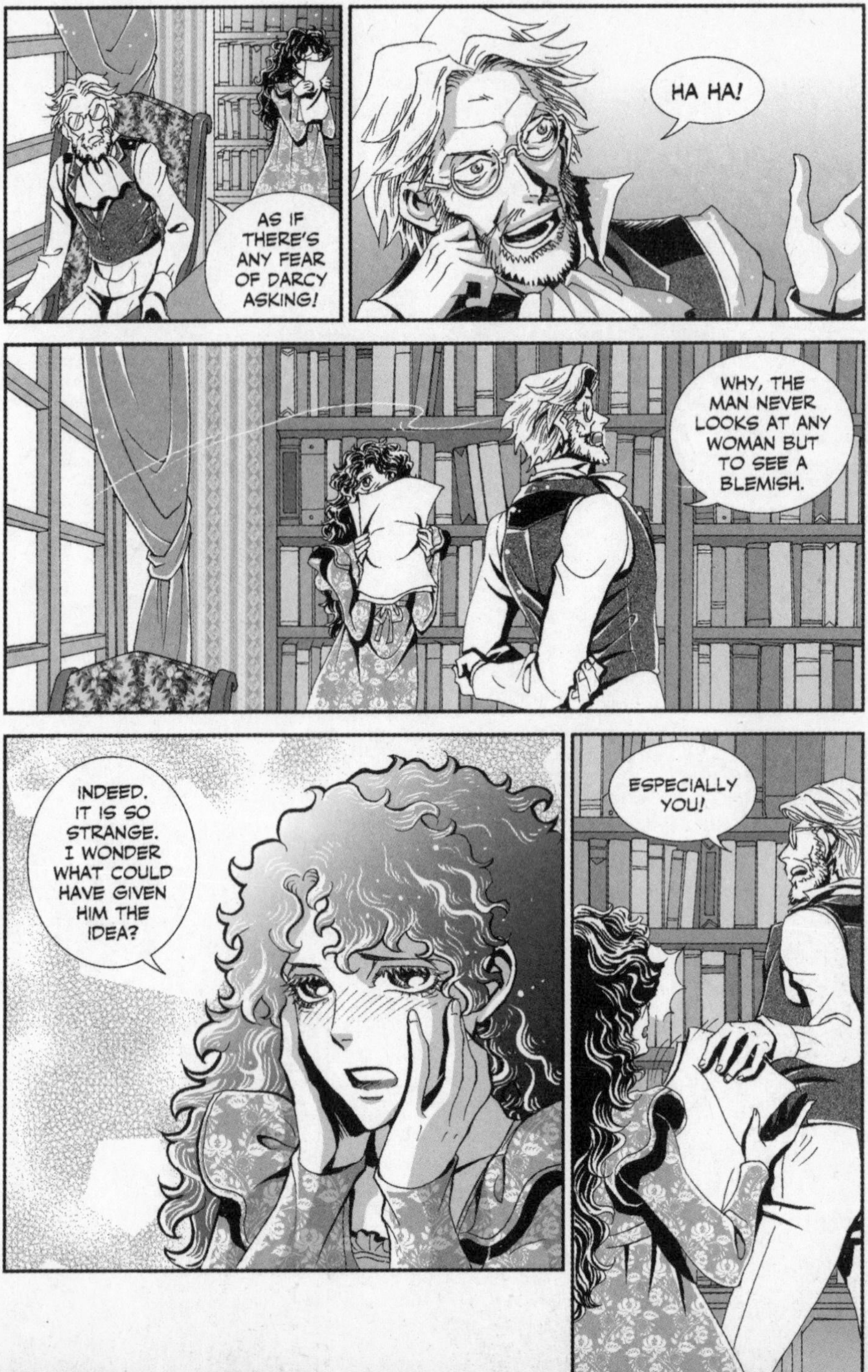
HA HA!
AS IF THERE'S ANY FEAR OF DARCY ASKING!
WHY, THE MAN NEVER LOOKS AT ANY WOMAN BUT TO SEE A BLEMISH.
ESPECIALLY YOU!
INDEED. IT IS SO STRANGE. I WONDER WHAT COULD HAVE GIVEN HIM THE IDEA?

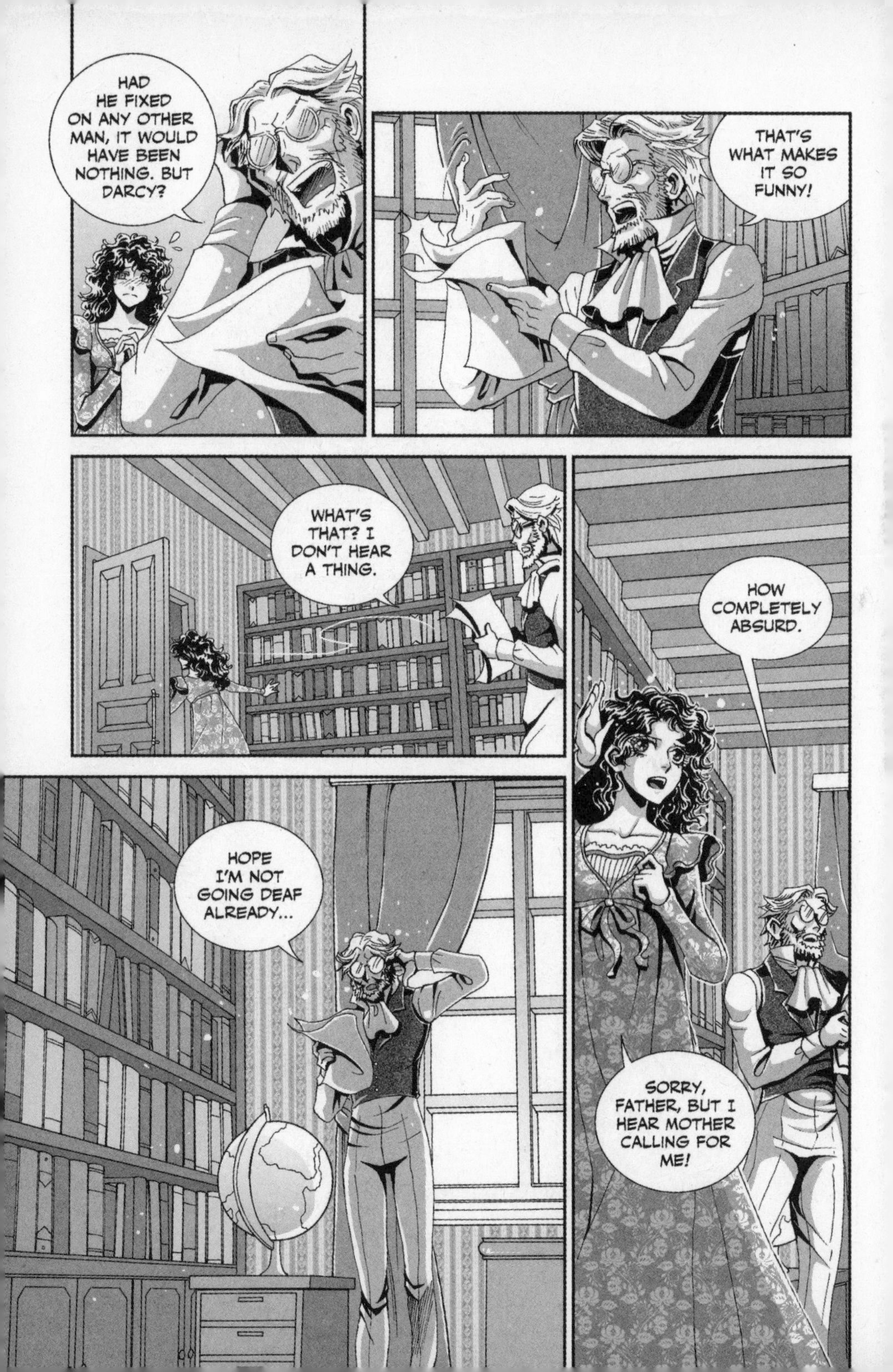
THAT'S WHAT MAKES IT SO FUNNY!
HAD HE FIXED ON ANY OTHER MAN, IT WOULD HAVE BEEN NOTHING. BUT DARCY?
HOW COMPLETELY ABSURD.
SORRY, FATHER, BUT I HEAR MOTHER CALLING FOR ME!
WHAT'S THAT? I DON'T HEAR A THING.
HOPE I'M NOT GOING DEAF ALREADY...

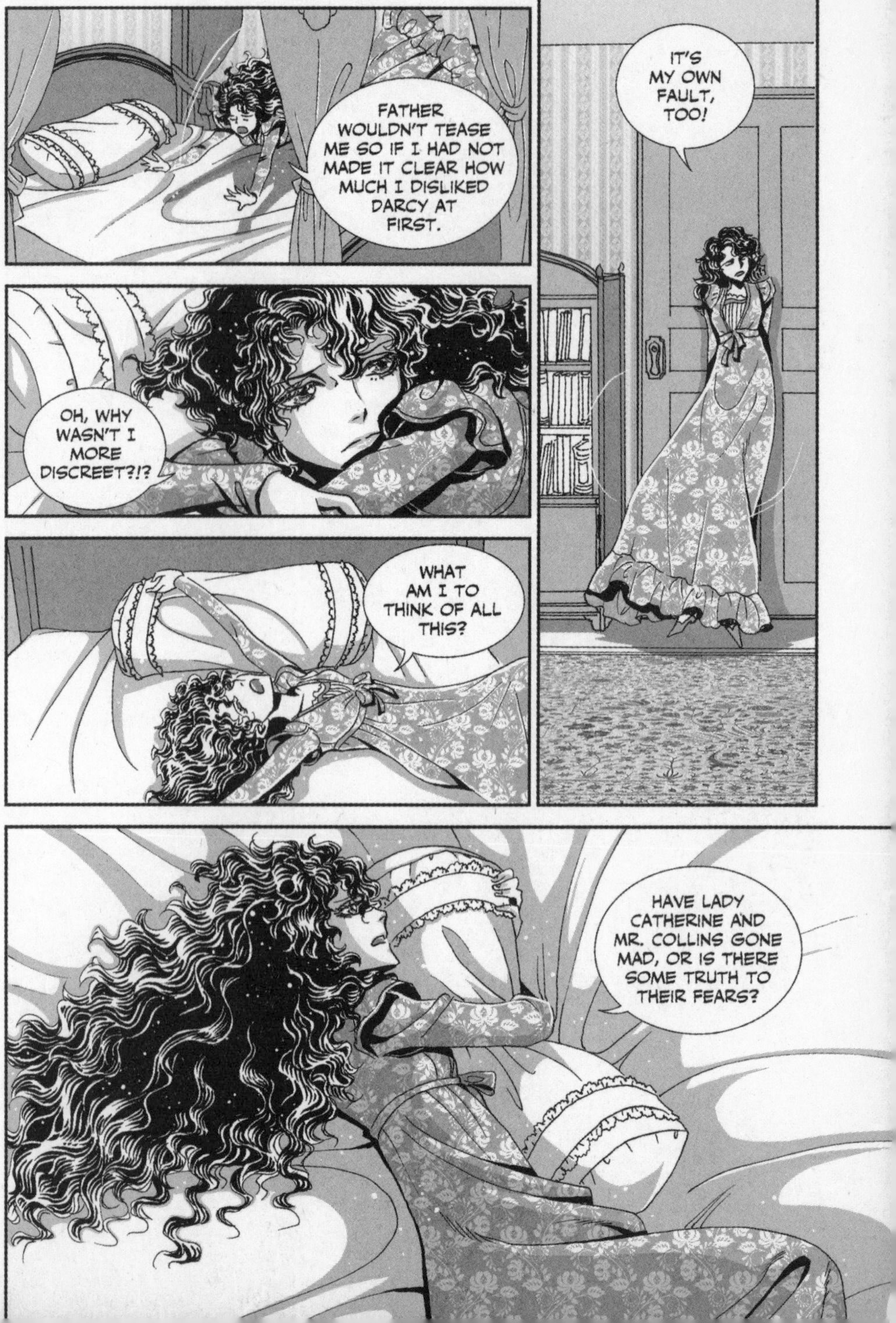
IT'S MY OWN FAULT, TOO!
FATHER WOULDN'T TEASE ME SO IF I HAD NOT MADE IT CLEAR HOW MUCH I DISLIKED DARCY AT FIRST.
OH, WHY WASN'T I MORE DISCREET?!?
WHAT AM I TO THINK OF ALL THIS?
HAVE LADY CATHERINE AND MR. COLLINS GONE MAD, OR IS THERE SOME TRUTH TO THEIR FEARS?

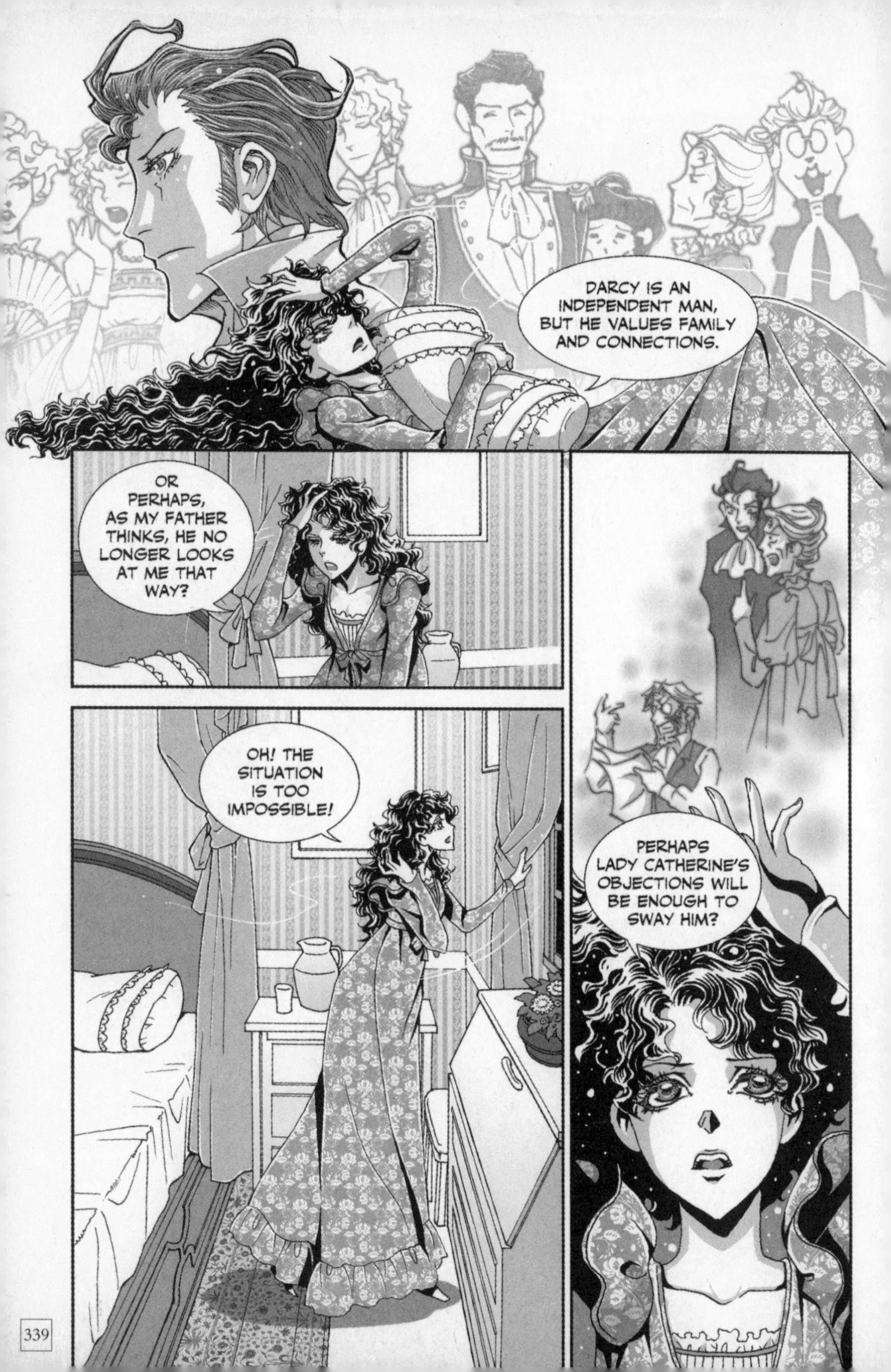
DARCY IS AN INDEPENDENT MAN, BUT HE VALUES FAMILY AND CONNECTIONS.
PERHAPS LADY CATHERINE'S OBJECTIONS WILL BE ENOUGH TO SWAY HIM?
OR PERHAPS, AS MY FATHER THINKS, HE NO LONGER LOOKS AT ME THAT WAY?
OH! THE SITUATION IS TOO IMPOSSIBLE!

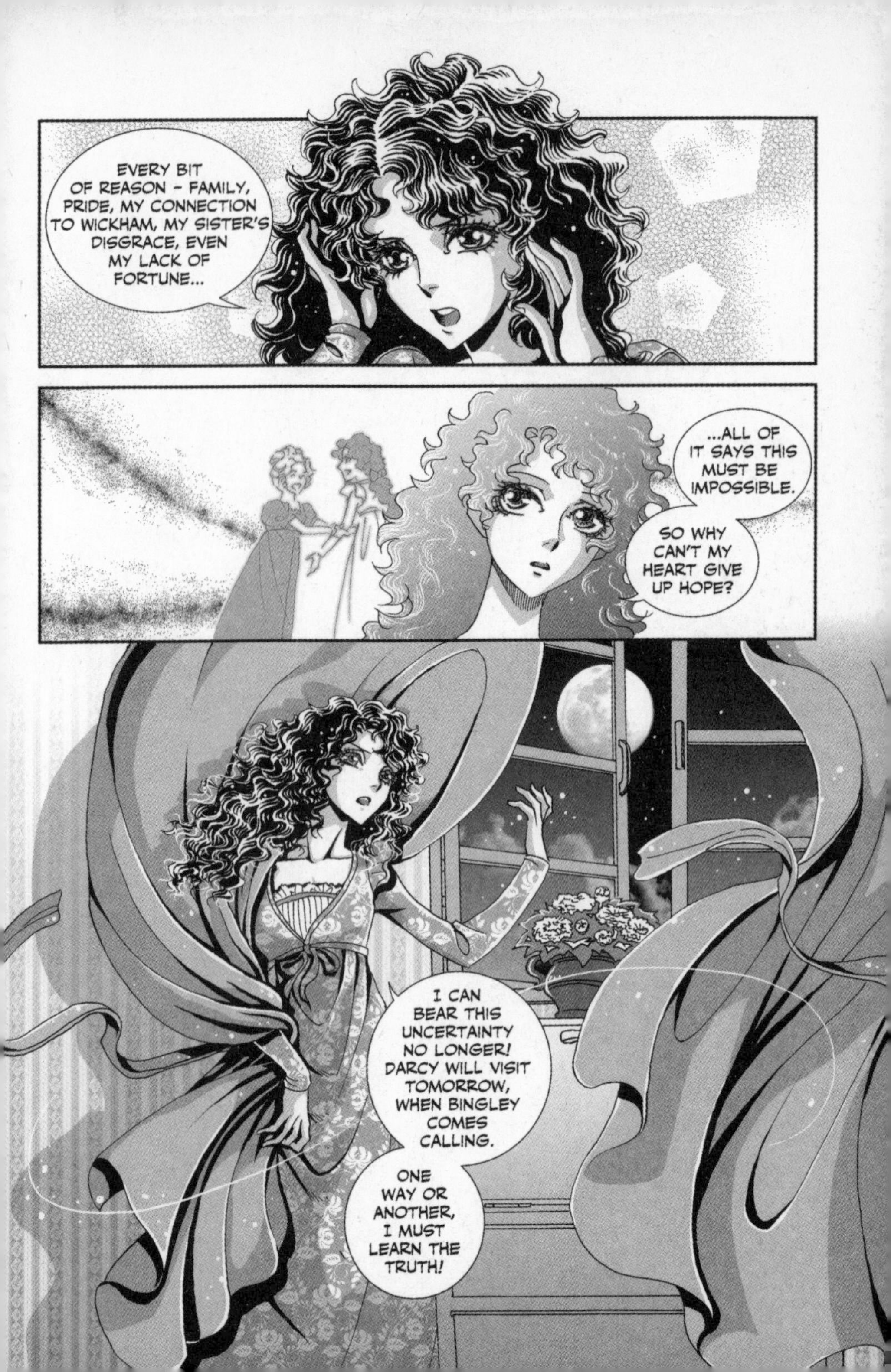
EVERY BIT OF REASON - FAMILY, PRIDE, MY CONNECTION TO WICKHAM, MY SISTER'S DISGRACE, EVEN MY LACK OF FORTUNE...
...ALL OF IT SAYS THIS MUST BE IMPOSSIBLE.
SO WHY CAN'T MY HEART GIVE UP HOPE?
I CAN BEAR THIS UNCERTAINTY NO LONGER! DARCY WILL VISIT TOMORROW, WHEN BINGLEY COMES CALLING.
ONE WAY OR ANOTHER, I MUST LEARN THE TRUTH!

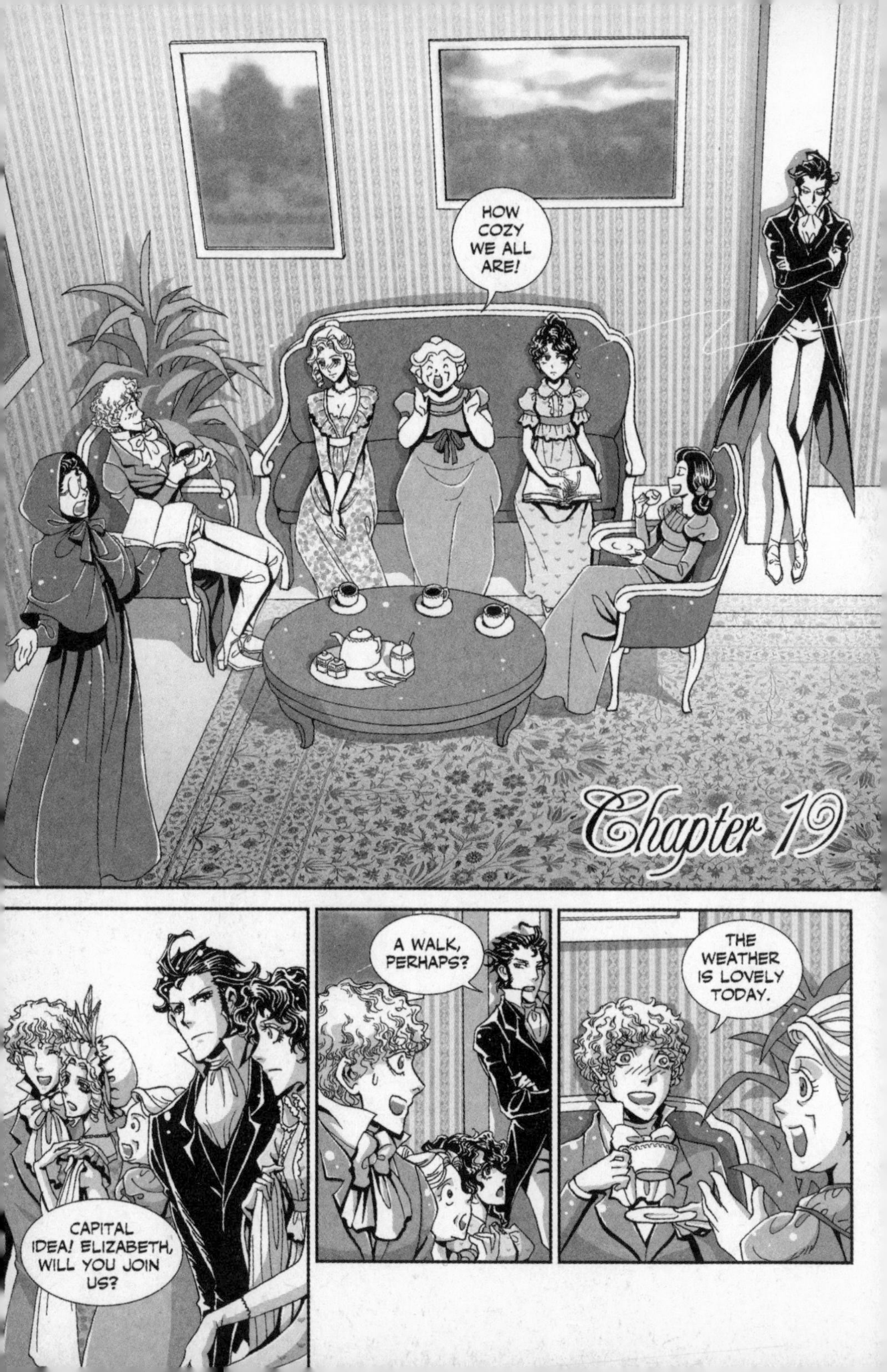
HOW COZY WE ALL ARE!
Chapter 19
THE WEATHER IS LOVELY TODAY.
A WALK, PERHAPS?
CAPITAL IDEA! ELIZABETH, WILL YOU JOIN US?

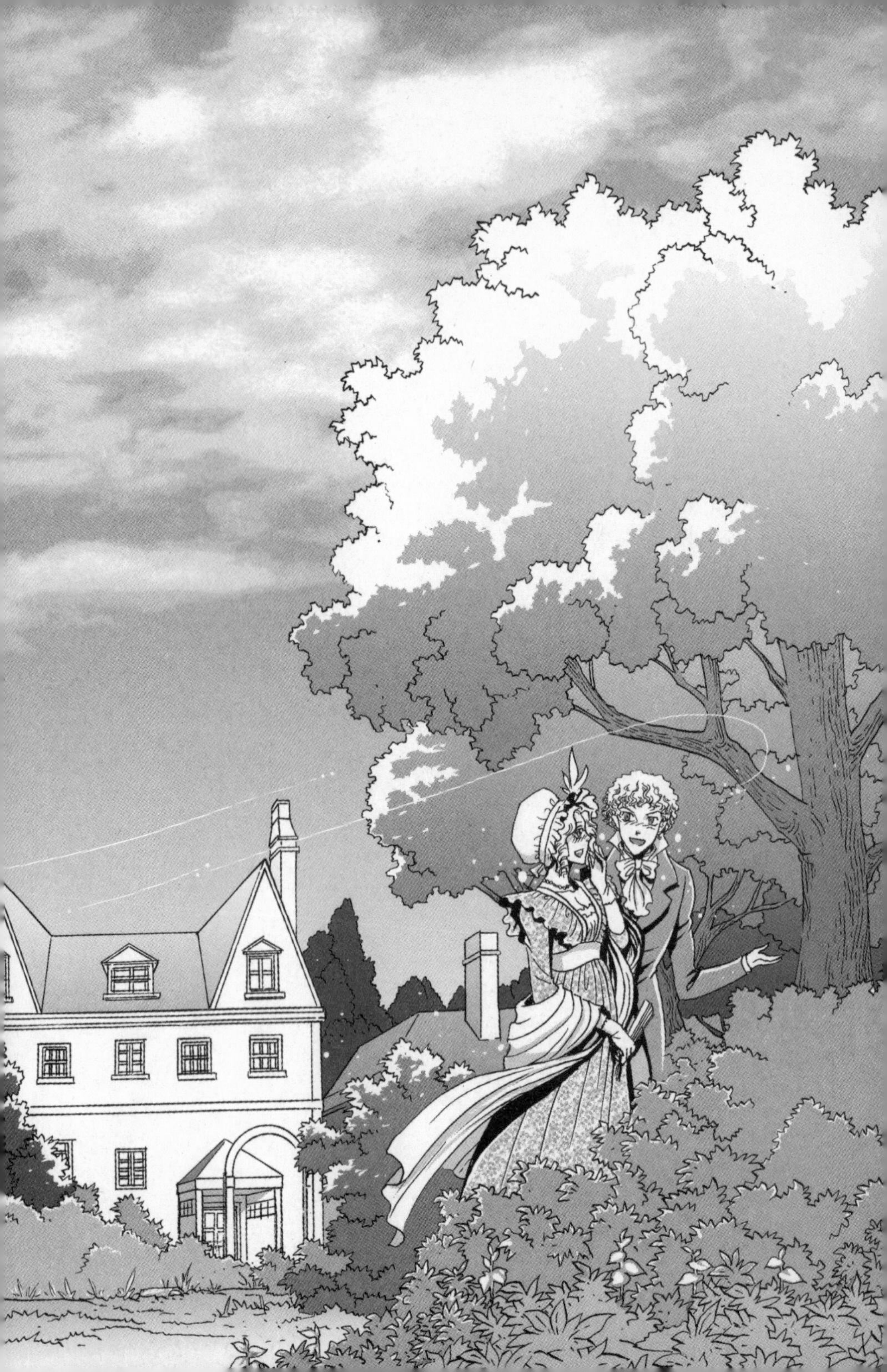

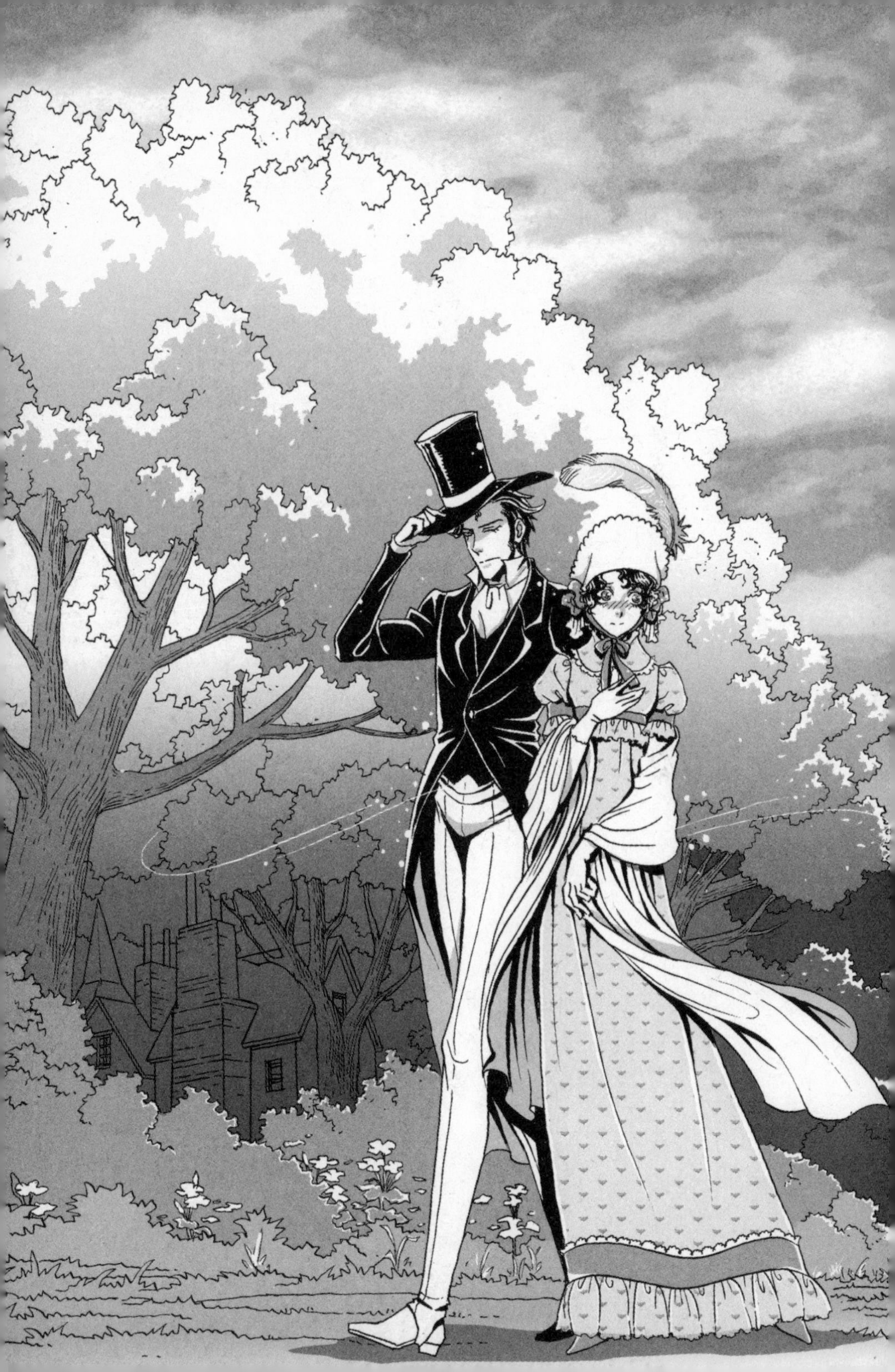

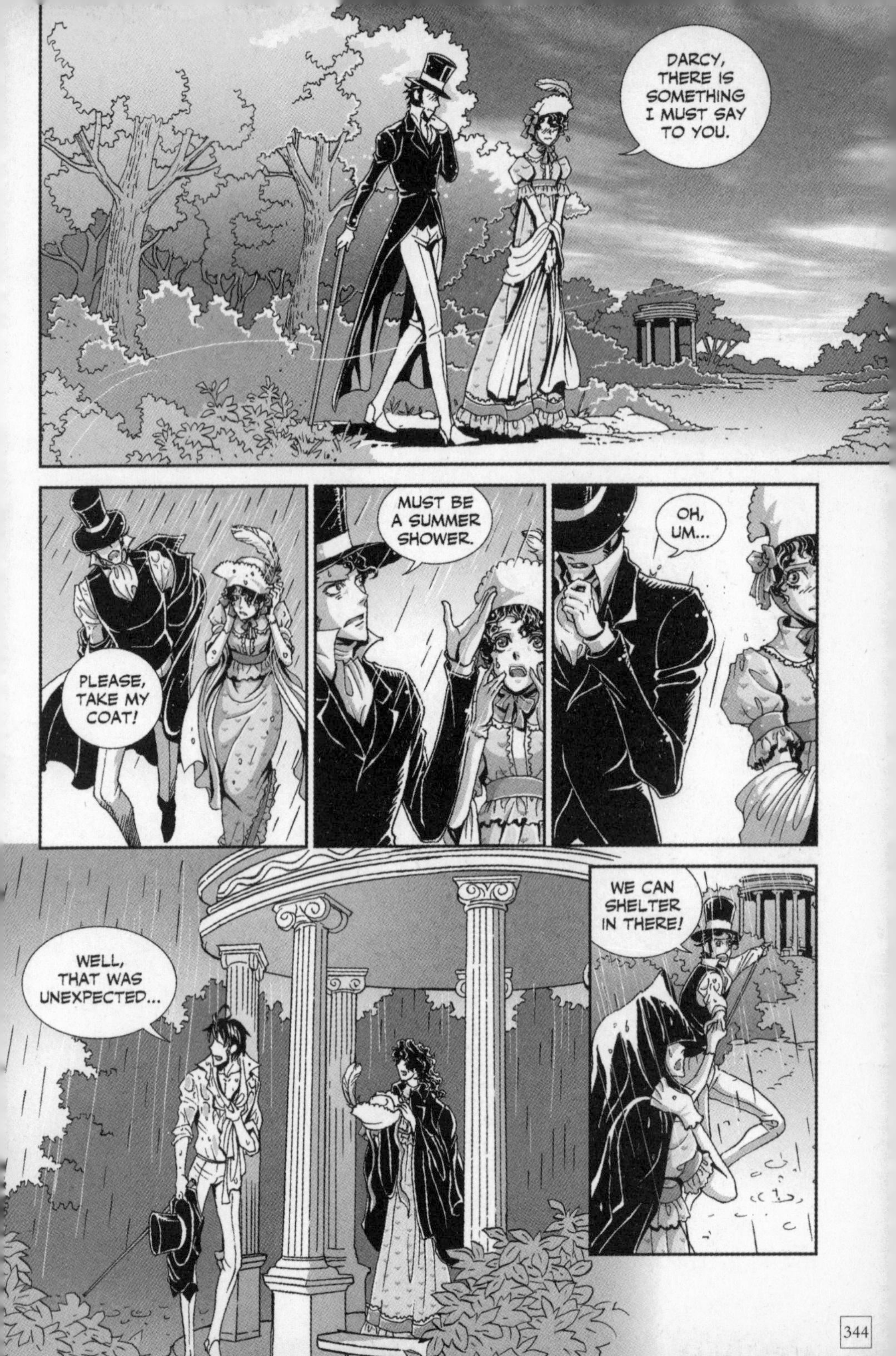
DARCY, THERE IS SOMETHING I MUST SAY TO YOU.
OH, UM...
MUST BE A SUMMER SHOWER.
PLEASE, TAKE MY COAT!
WE CAN SHELTER IN THERE!
WELL, THAT WAS UNEXPECTED...

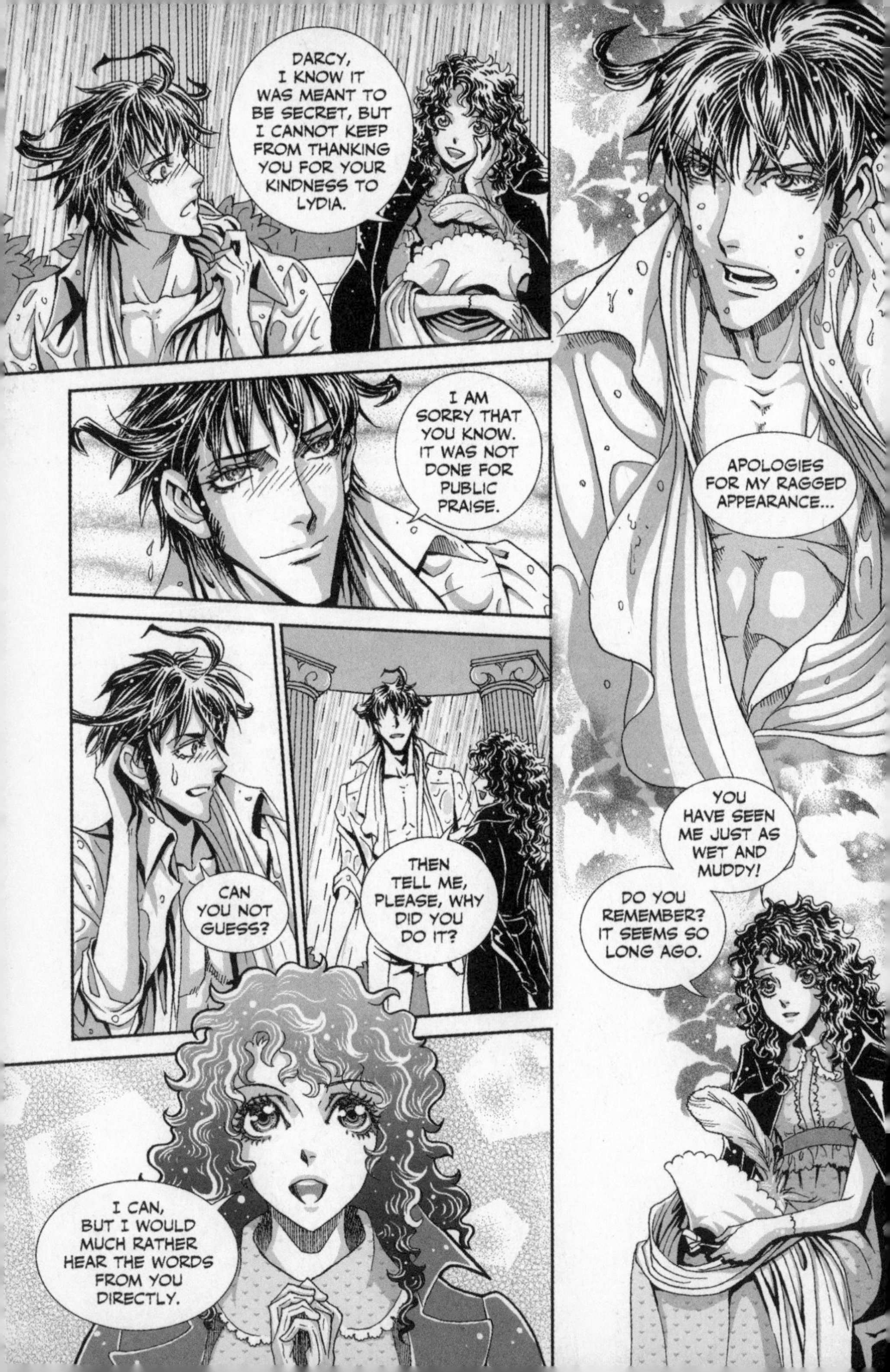
APOLOGIES FOR MY RAGGED APPEARANCE...
YOU HAVE SEEN ME JUST AS WET AND MUDDY!
DO YOU REMEMBER? IT SEEMS SO LONG AGO.
DARCY, I KNOW IT WAS MEANT TO BE SECRET, BUT I CANNOT KEEP FROM THANKING YOU FOR YOUR KINDNESS TO LYDIA.
I AM SORRY THAT YOU KNOW. IT WAS NOT DONE FOR PUBLIC PRAISE.
THEN TELL ME, PLEASE, WHY DID YOU DO IT?
CAN YOU NOT GUESS?
I CAN, BUT I WOULD MUCH RATHER HEAR THE WORDS FROM YOU DIRECTLY.

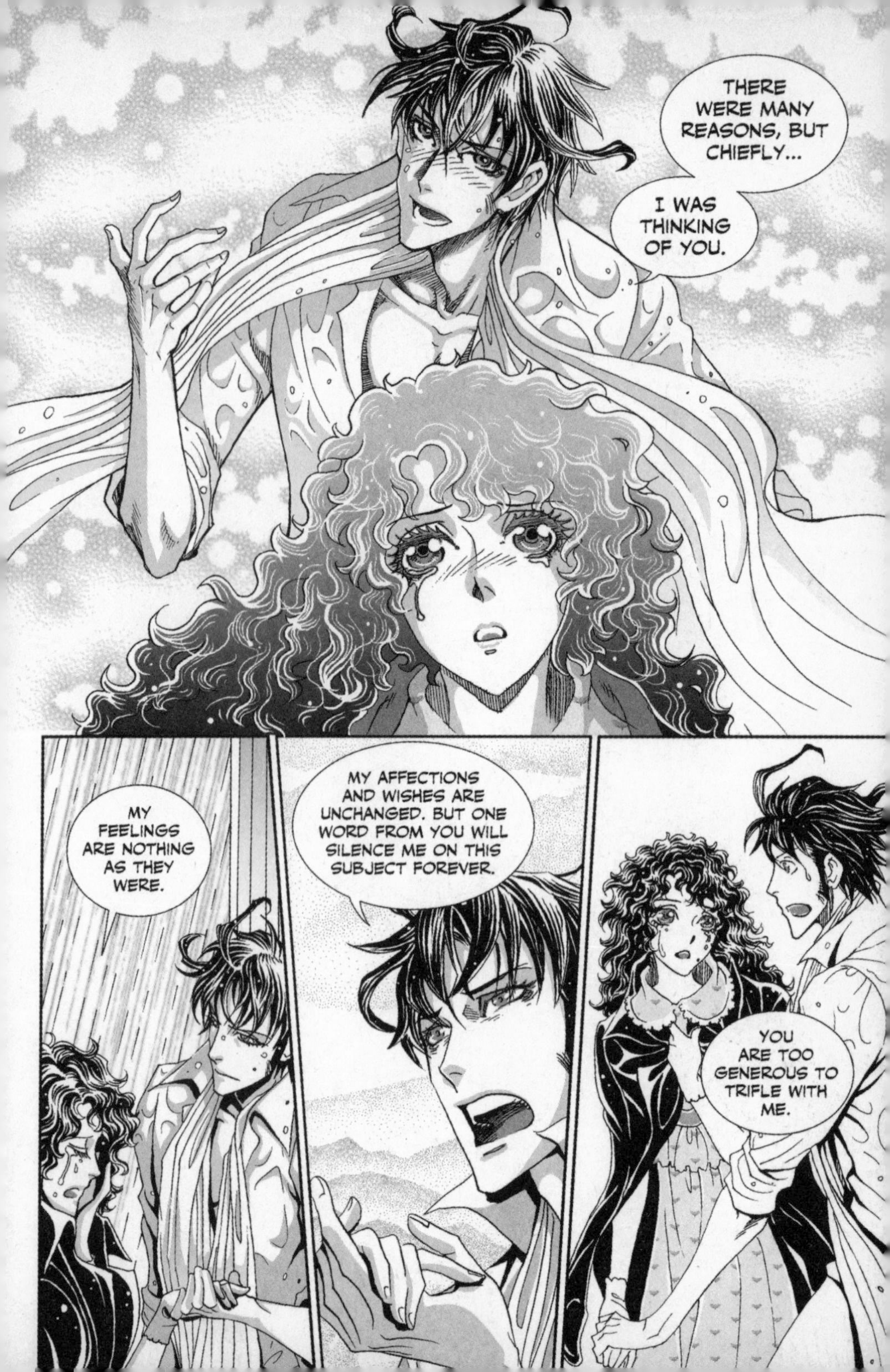
THERE WERE MANY REASONS, BUT CHIEFLY...
I WAS THINKING OF YOU.
YOU ARE TOO GENEROUS TO TRIFLE WITH ME.
MY AFFECTIONS AND WISHES ARE UNCHANGED. BUT ONE WORD FROM YOU WILL SILENCE ME ON THIS SUBJECT FOREVER.
MY FEELINGS ARE NOTHING AS THEY WERE.

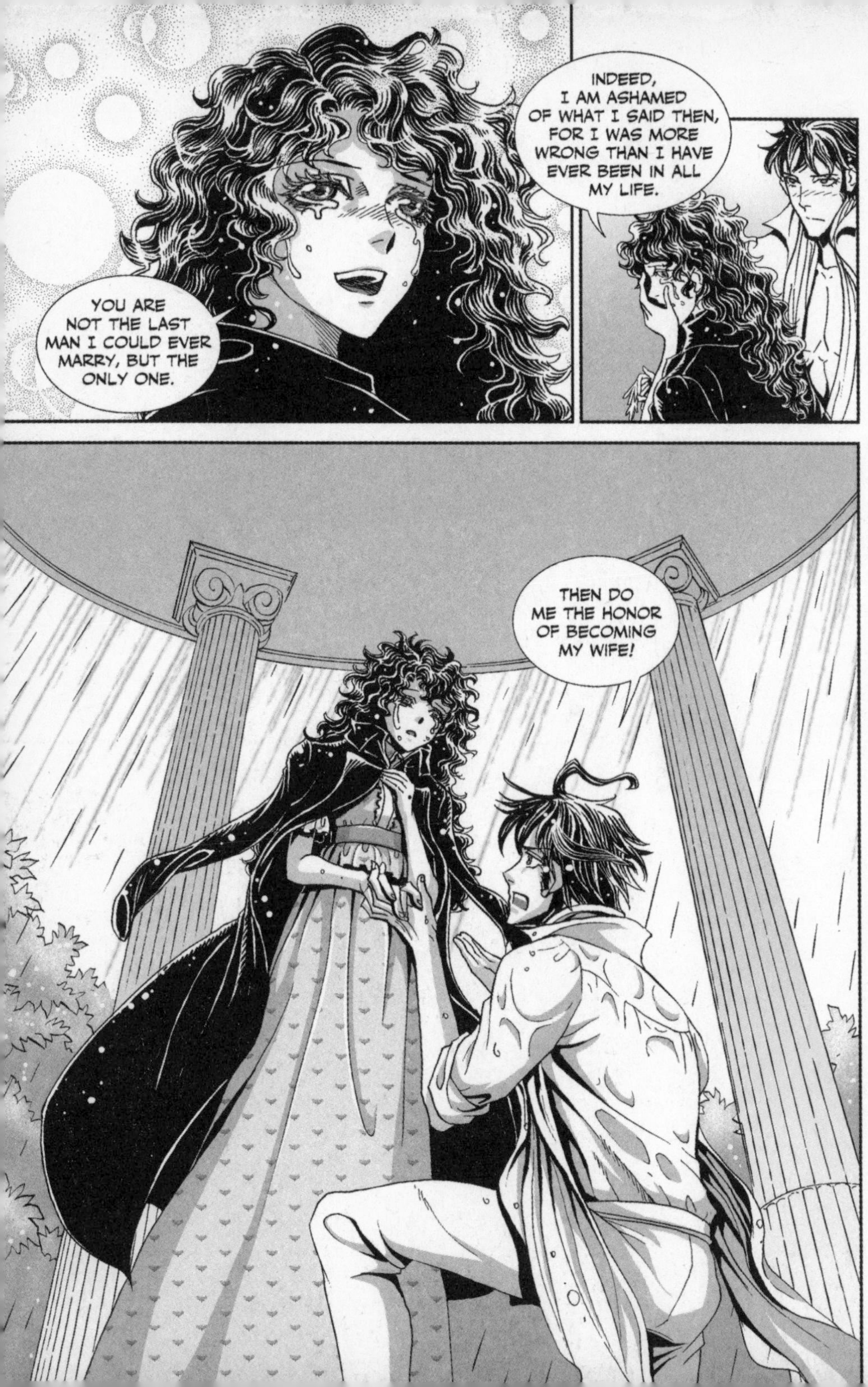
INDEED, I AM ASHAMED OF WHAT I SAID THEN, FOR I WAS MORE WRONG THAN I HAVE EVER BEEN IN ALL MY LIFE.
YOU ARE NOT THE LAST MAN I COULD EVER MARRY, BUT THE ONLY ONE.
THEN DO ME THE HONOR OF BECOMING MY WIFE!

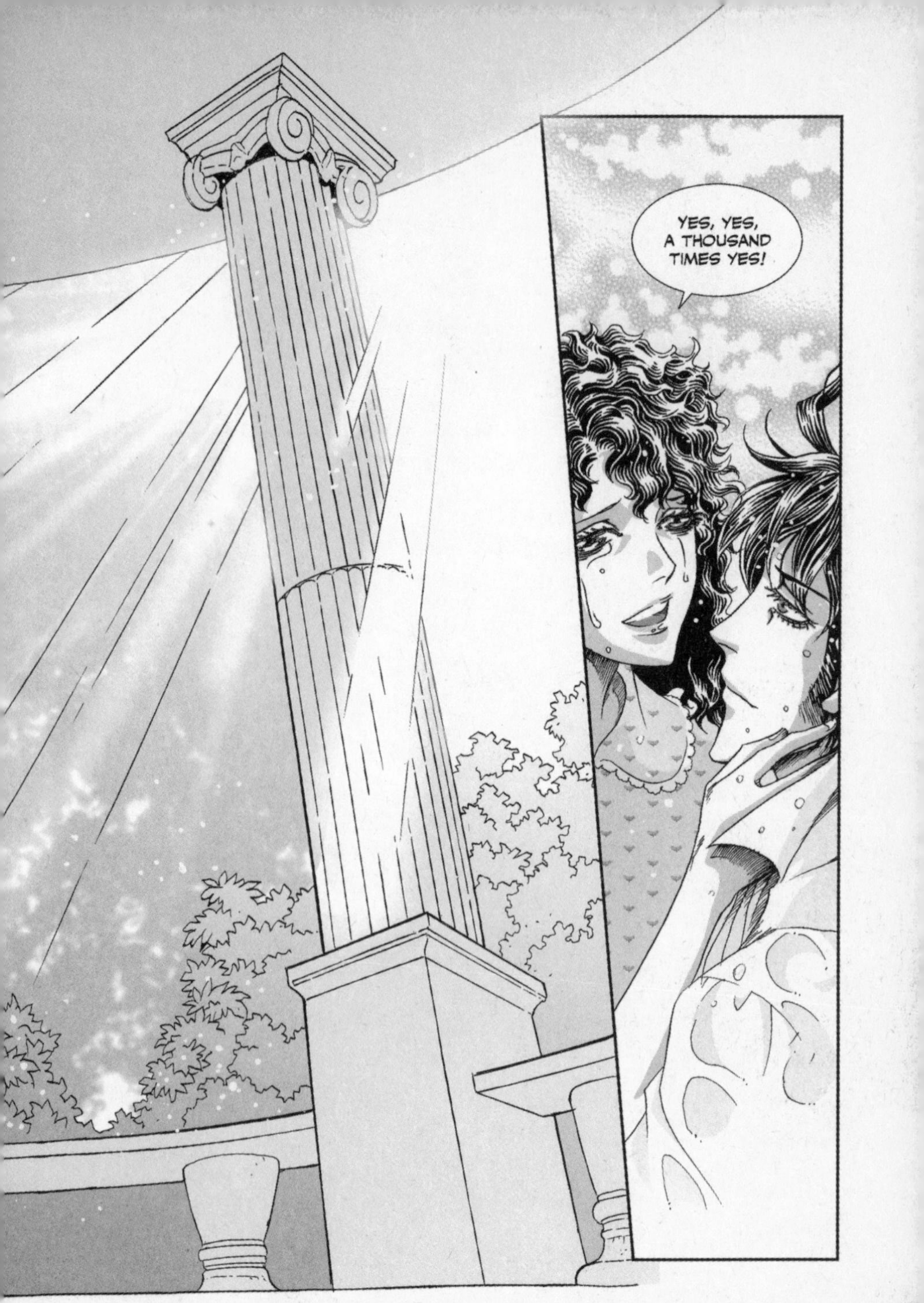
YES, YES, A THOUSAND TIMES YES!

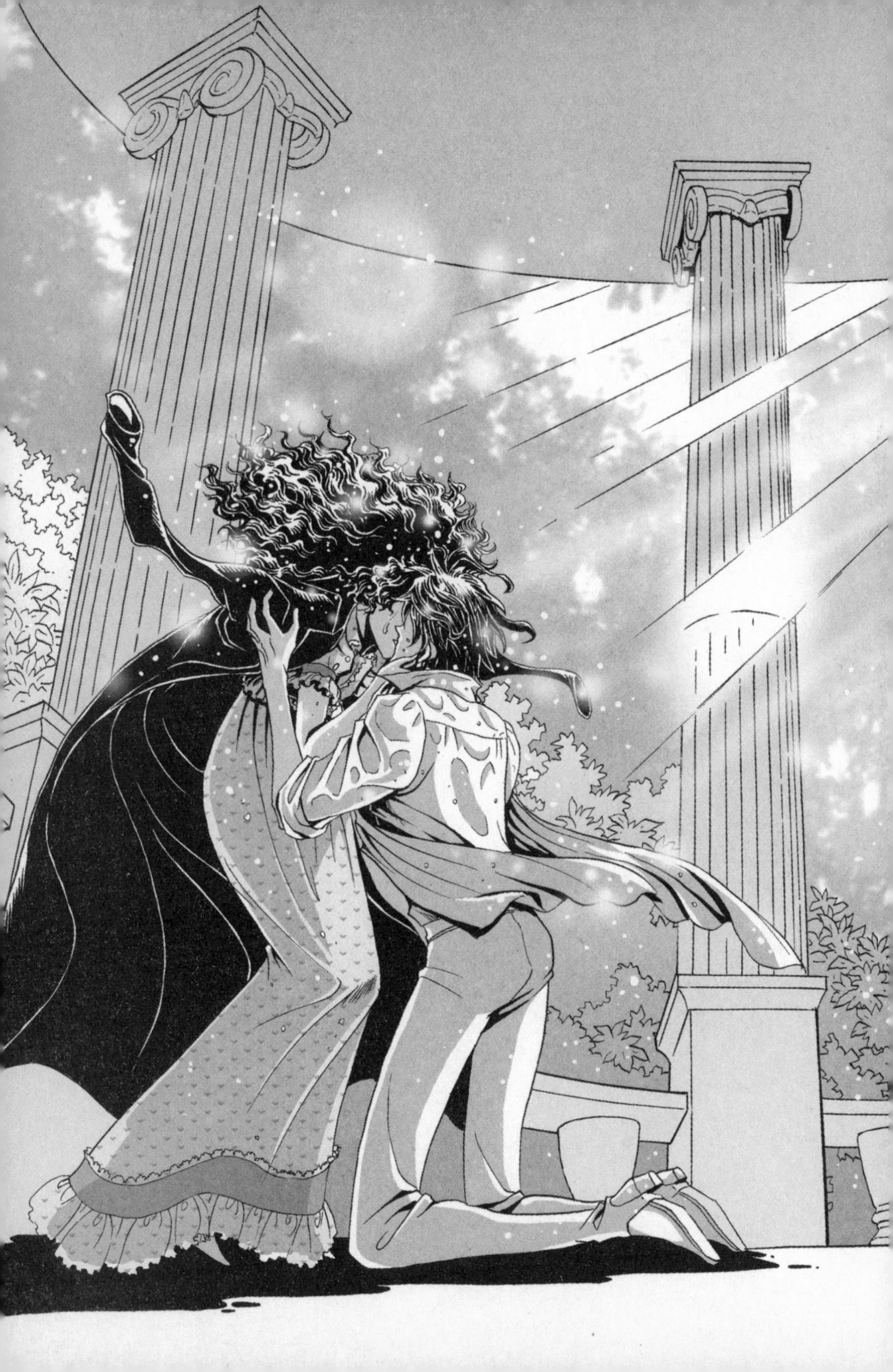

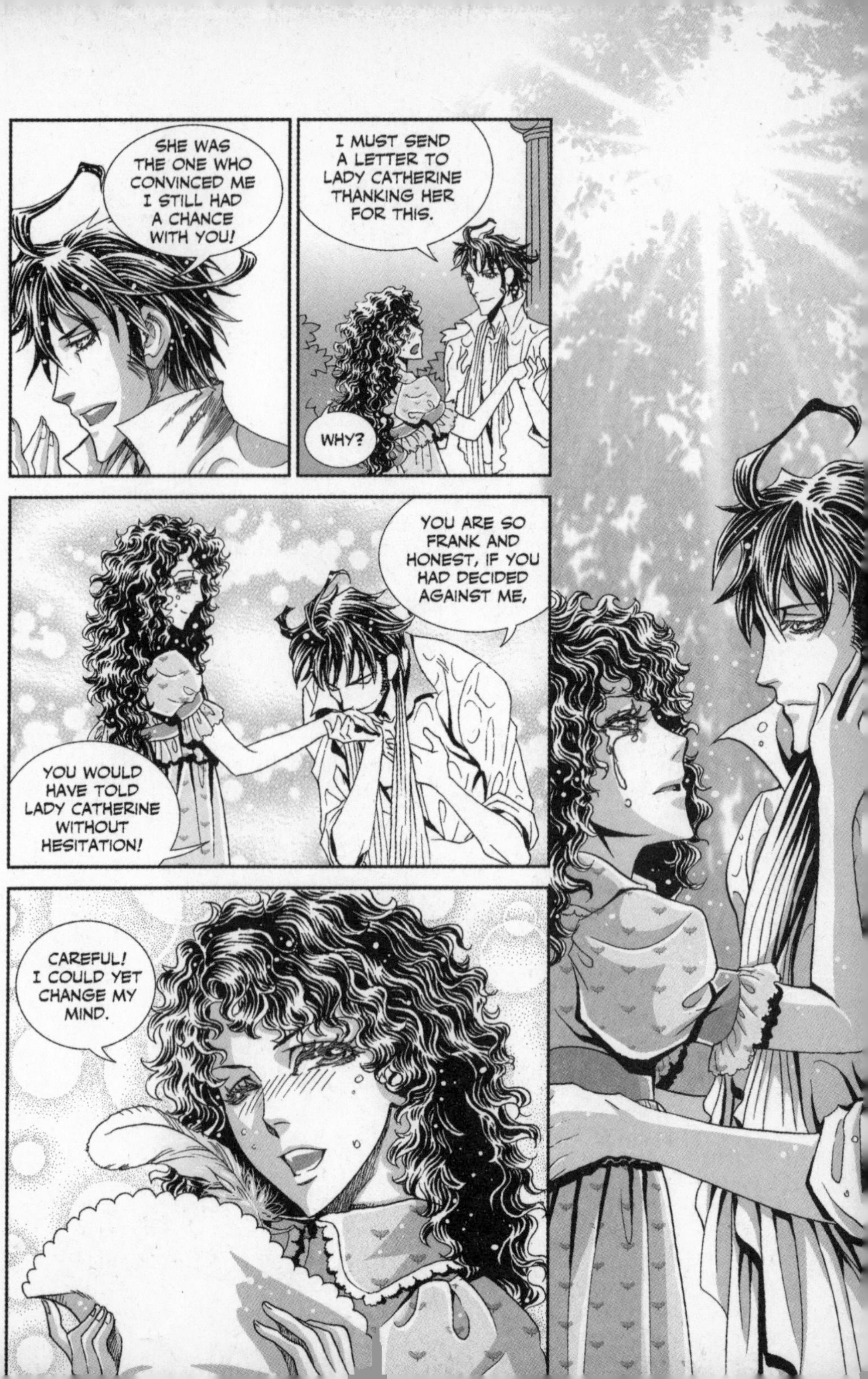
I MUST SEND A LETTER TO LADY CATHERINE THANKING HER FOR THIS.
WHY?
SHE WAS THE ONE WHO CONVINCED ME I STILL HAD A CHANCE WITH YOU!
YOU ARE SO FRANK AND HONEST, IF YOU HAD DECIDED AGAINST ME,
YOU WOULD HAVE TOLD LADY CATHERINE WITHOUT HESITATION!
CAREFUL! I COULD YET CHANGE MY MIND.

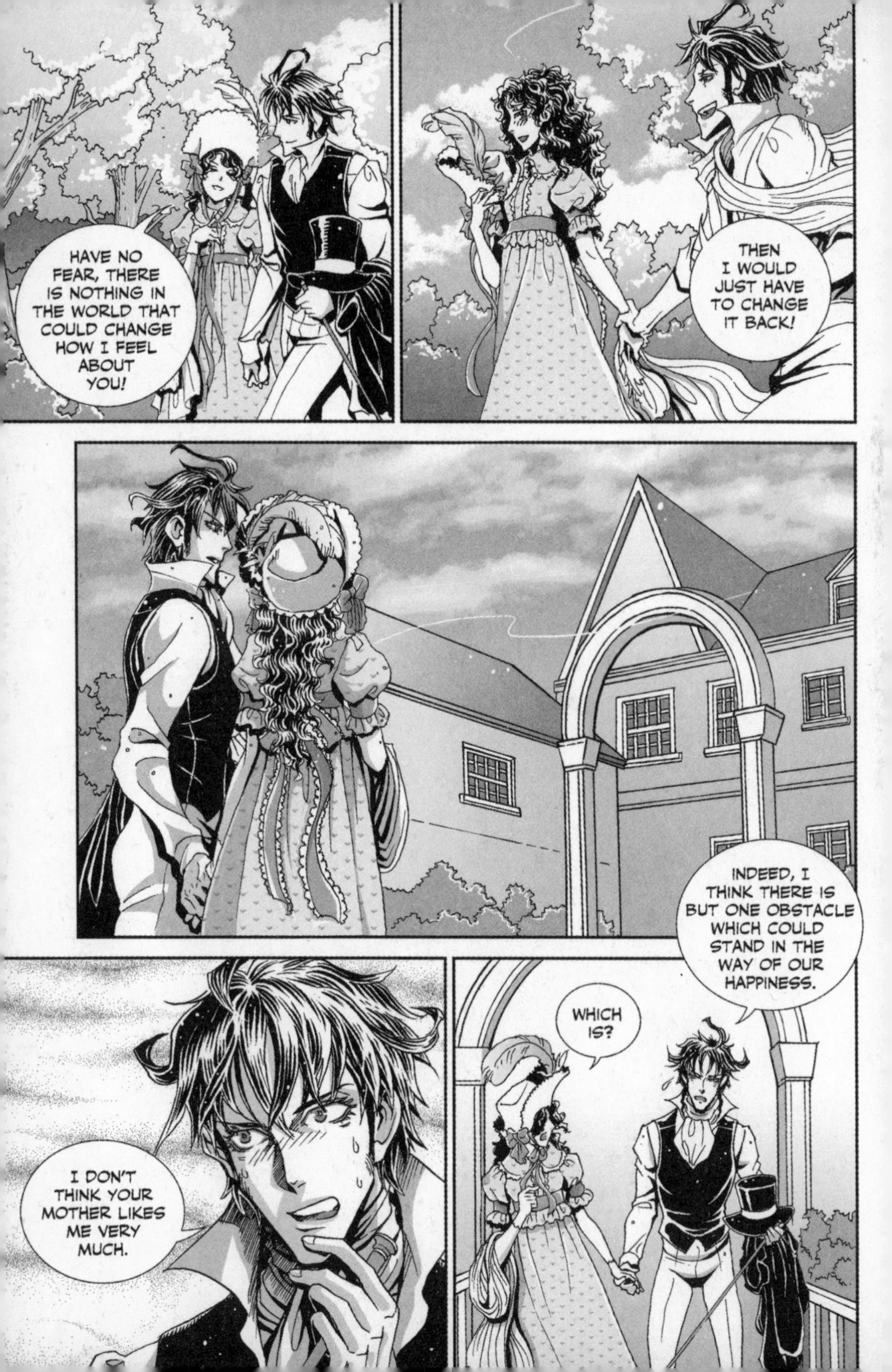
THEN I WOULD JUST HAVE TO CHANGE IT BACK!
HAVE NO FEAR, THERE IS NOTHING IN THE WORLD THAT COULD CHANGE HOW I FEEL ABOUT YOU!
INDEED, I THINK THERE IS BUT ONE OBSTACLE WHICH COULD STAND IN THE WAY OF OUR HAPPINESS.
WHICH IS?
I DON'T THINK YOUR MOTHER LIKES ME VERY MUCH.

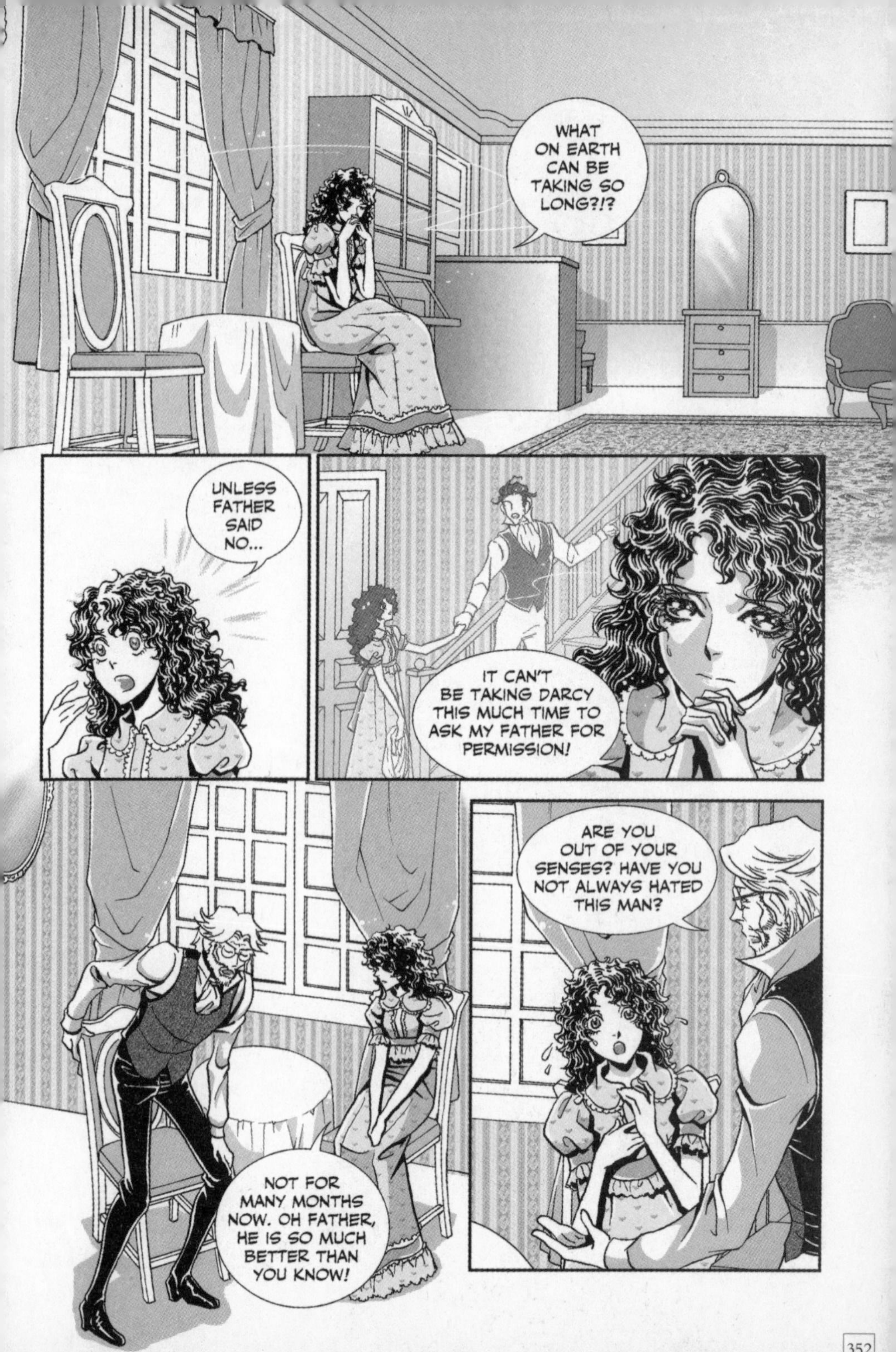
WHAT ON EARTH CAN BE TAKING SO LONG?!?
IT CAN'T BE TAKING DARCY THIS MUCH TIME TO ASK MY FATHER FOR PERMISSION!
UNLESS FATHER SAID NO...
ARE YOU OUT OF YOUR SENSES? HAVE YOU NOT ALWAYS HATED THIS MAN?
NOT FOR MANY MONTHS NOW. OH FATHER, HE IS SO MUCH BETTER THAN YOU KNOW!

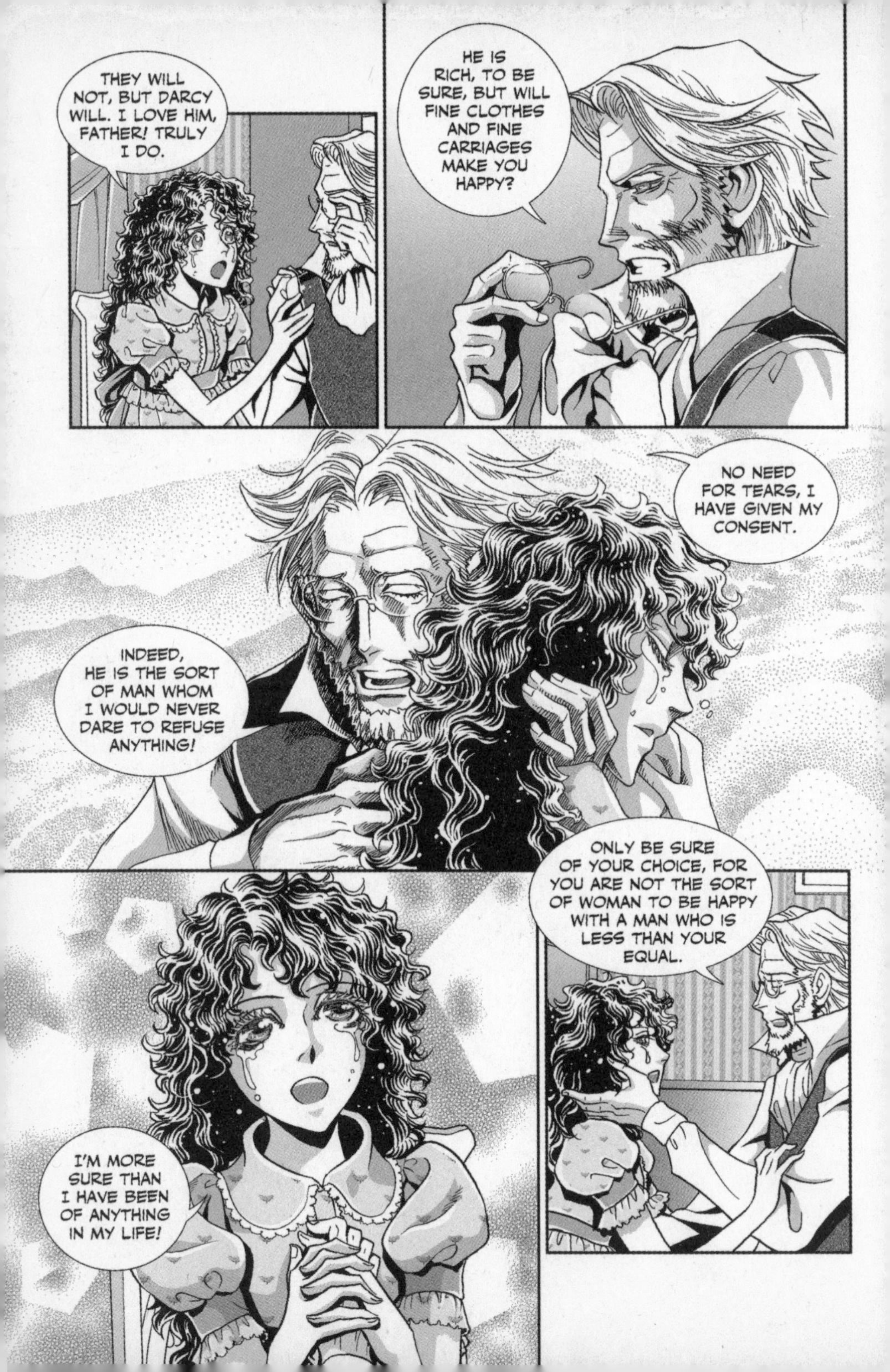
HE IS RICH, TO BE SURE, BUT WILL FINE CLOTHES AND FINE CARRIAGES MAKE YOU HAPPY?
THEY WILL NOT, BUT DARCY WILL. I LOVE HIM, FATHER! TRULY I DO.
NO NEED FOR TEARS, I HAVE GIVEN MY CONSENT.
INDEED, HE IS THE SORT OF MAN WHOM I WOULD NEVER DARE TO REFUSE ANYTHING!
ONLY BE SURE OF YOUR CHOICE, FOR YOU ARE NOT THE SORT OF WOMAN TO BE HAPPY WITH A MAN WHO IS LESS THAN YOUR EQUAL.
I'M MORE SURE THAN I HAVE BEEN OF ANYTHING IN MY LIFE!

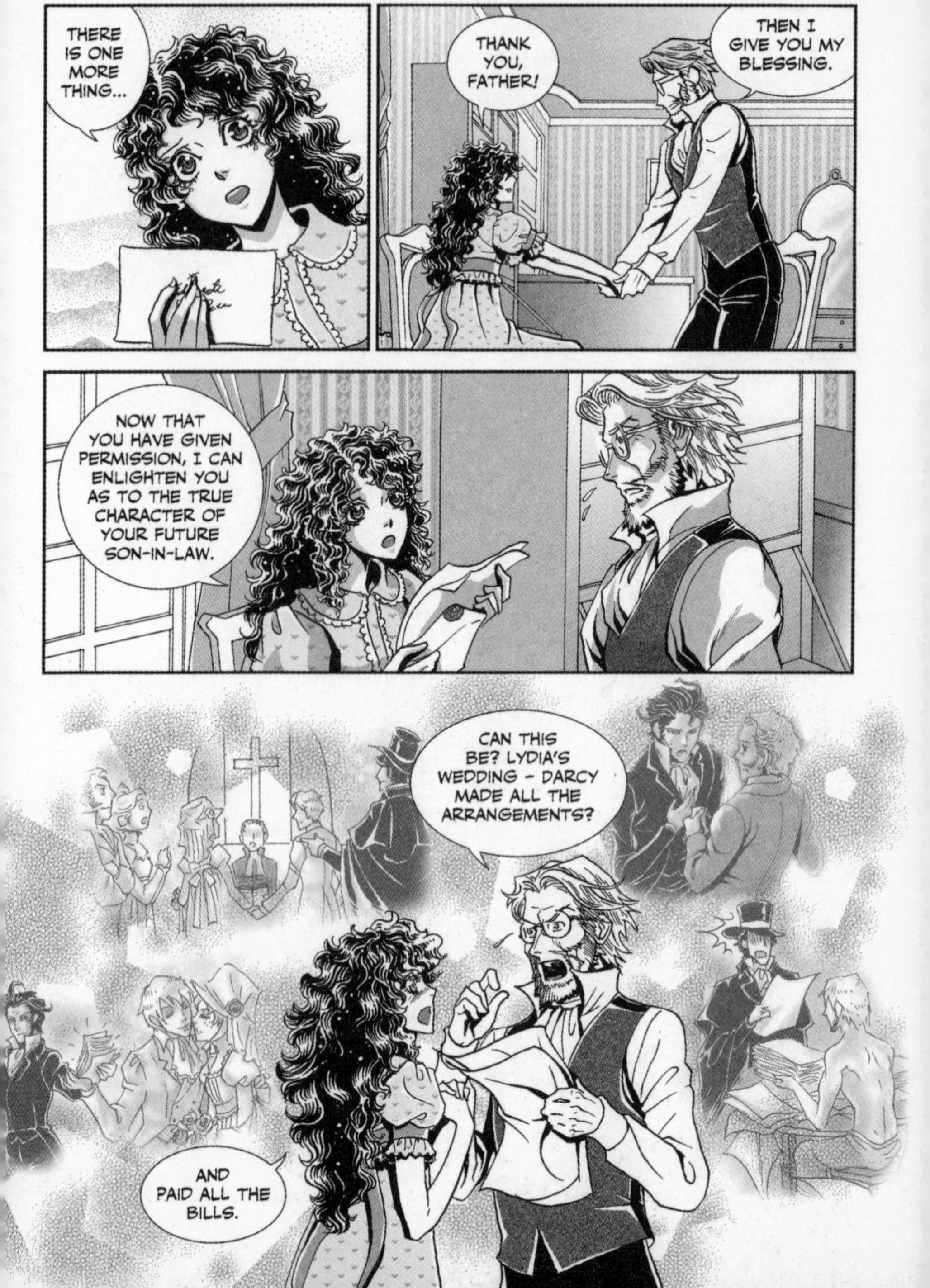
THEN I GIVE YOU MY BLESSING.
THANK YOU, FATHER!
THERE IS ONE MORE THING...
NOW THAT YOU HAVE GIVEN PERMISSION, I CAN ENLIGHTEN YOU AS TO THE TRUE CHARACTER OF YOUR FUTURE SON-IN-LAW.
CAN THIS BE? LYDIA'S WEDDING – DARCY MADE ALL THE ARRANGEMENTS?
AND PAID ALL THE BILLS.

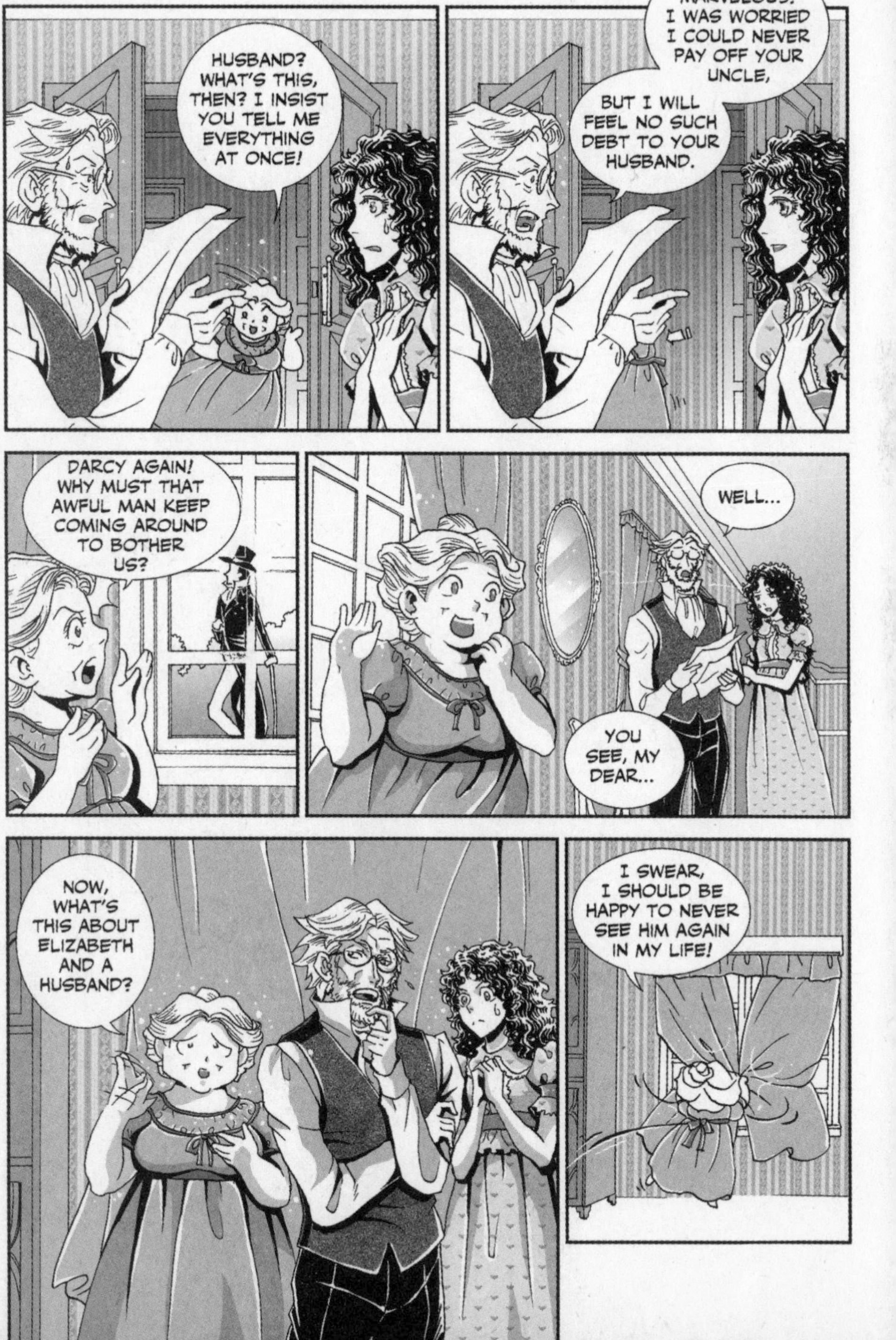
HOW MARVELOUS! I WAS WORRIED I COULD NEVER PAY OFF YOUR UNCLE,
BUT I WILL FEEL NO SUCH DEBT TO YOUR HUSBAND.
HUSBAND? WHAT'S THIS, THEN? I INSIST YOU TELL ME EVERYTHING AT ONCE!
WELL...
YOU SEE, MY DEAR...
DARCY AGAIN! WHY MUST THAT AWFUL MAN KEEP COMING AROUND TO BOTHER US?
I SWEAR, I SHOULD BE HAPPY TO NEVER SEE HIM AGAIN IN MY LIFE!
NOW, WHAT'S THIS ABOUT ELIZABETH AND A HUSBAND?

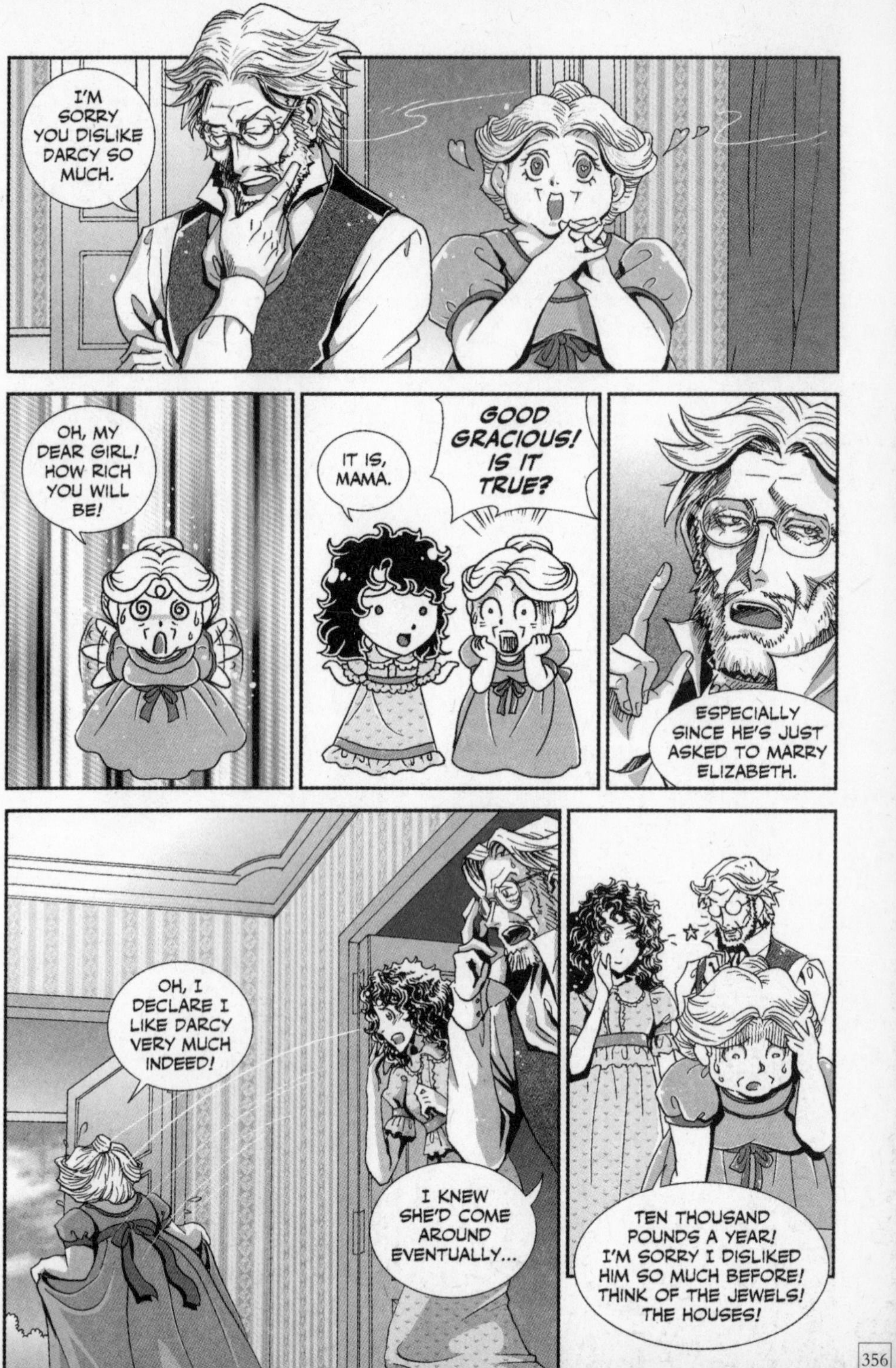
I'M SORRY YOU DISLIKE DARCY SO MUCH.
ESPECIALLY SINCE HE'S JUST ASKED TO MARRY ELIZABETH.
GOOD GRACIOUS! IS IT TRUE?
IT IS, MAMA.
OH, MY DEAR GIRL! HOW RICH YOU WILL BE!
TEN THOUSAND POUNDS A YEAR! I'M SORRY I DISLIKED HIM SO MUCH BEFORE! THINK OF THE JEWELS! THE HOUSES!
OH, I DECLARE I LIKE DARCY VERY MUCH INDEED!
I KNEW SHE'D COME AROUND EVENTUALLY...

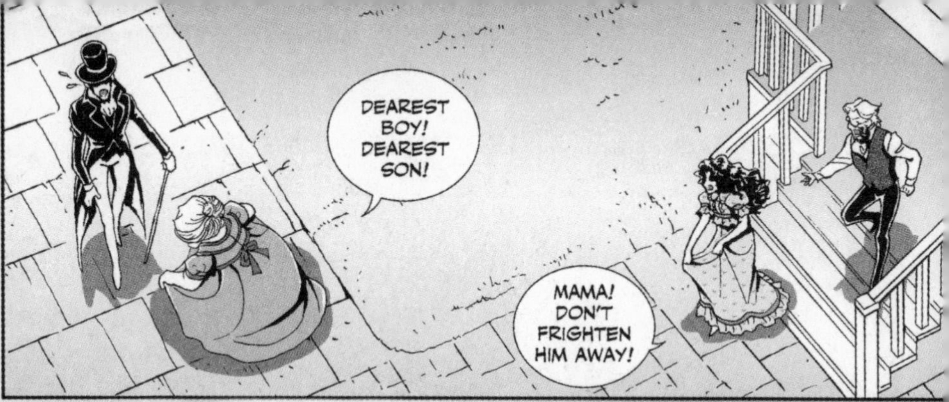
DEAREST BOY! DEAREST SON!
MAMA! DON'T FRIGHTEN HIM AWAY!

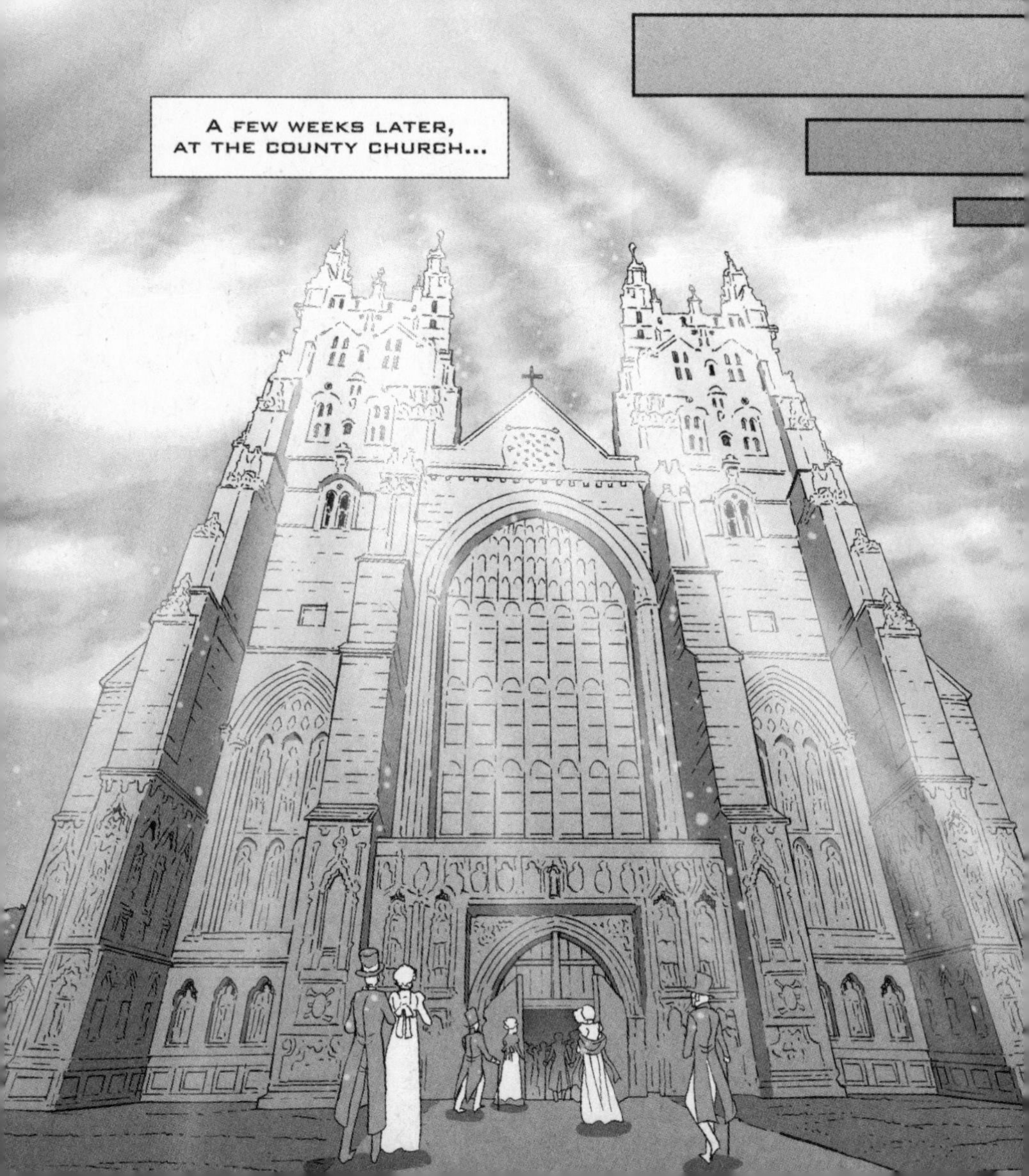
A FEW WEEKS LATER, AT THE COUNTY CHURCH...

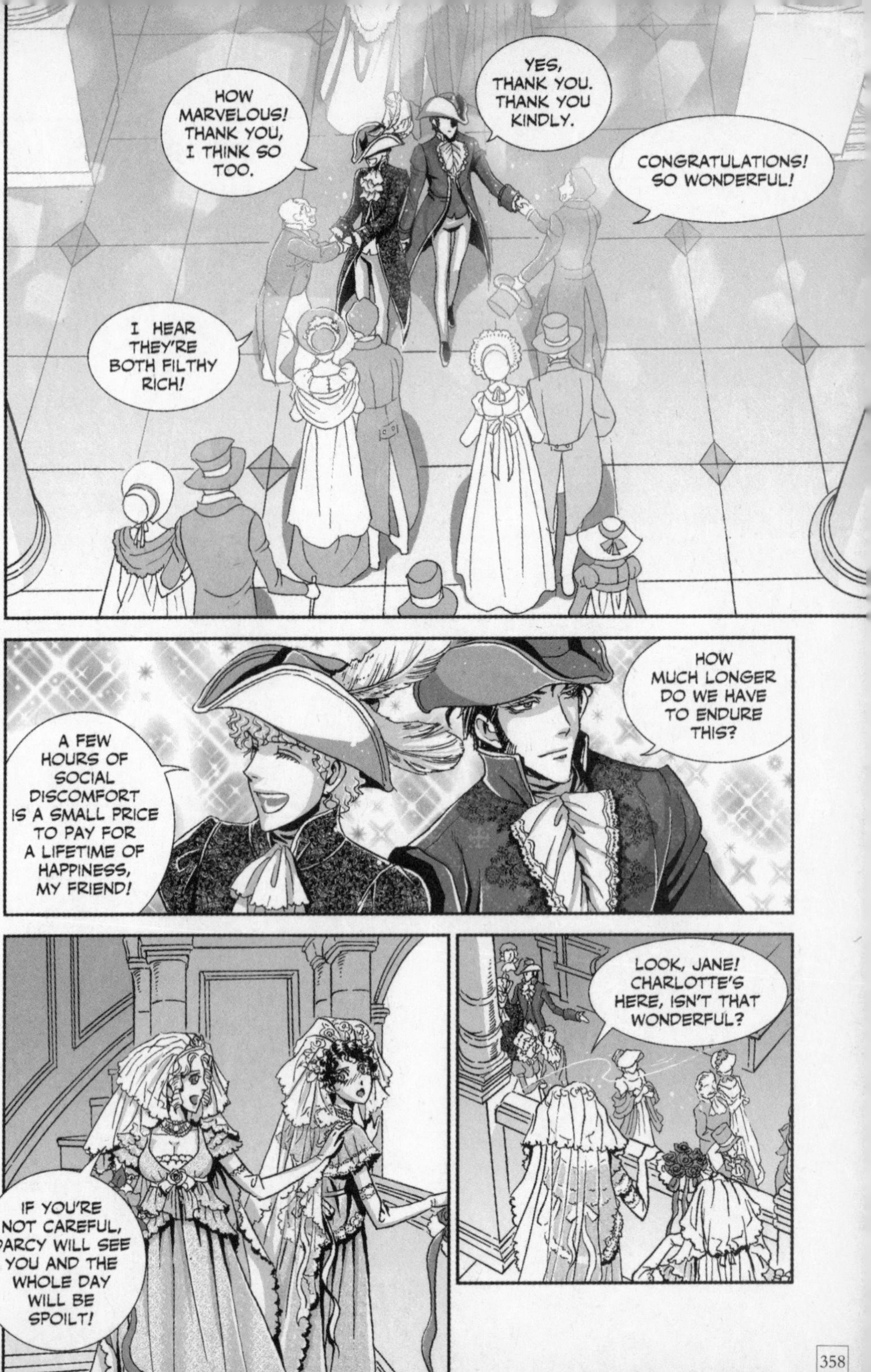
YES, THANK YOU. THANK YOU KINDLY.
CONGRATULATIONS! SO WONDERFUL!
HOW MARVELOUS! THANK YOU, I THINK SO TOO.
I HEAR THEY'RE BOTH FILTHY RICH!
HOW MUCH LONGER DO WE HAVE TO ENDURE THIS?
A FEW HOURS OF SOCIAL DISCOMFORT IS A SMALL PRICE TO PAY FOR A LIFETIME OF HAPPINESS, MY FRIEND!
LOOK, JANE! CHARLOTTE'S HERE, ISN'T THAT WONDERFUL?
IF YOU'RE NOT CAREFUL, DARCY WILL SEE YOU AND THE WHOLE DAY WILL BE SPOILT!

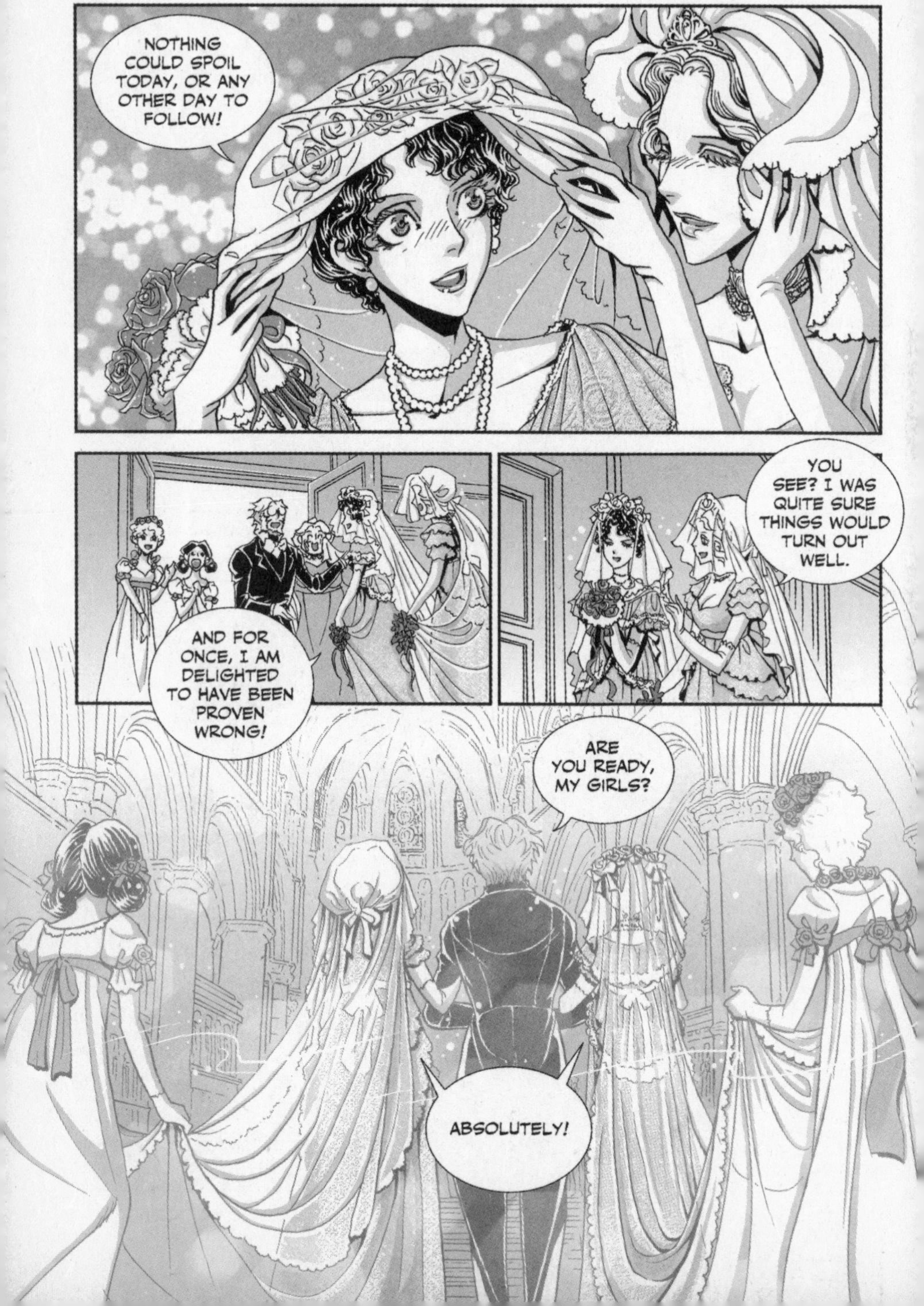
NOTHING COULD SPOIL TODAY, OR ANY OTHER DAY TO FOLLOW!
YOU SEE? I WAS QUITE SURE THINGS WOULD TURN OUT WELL.
AND FOR ONCE, I AM DELIGHTED TO HAVE BEEN PROVEN WRONG!
ARE YOU READY, MY GIRLS?
ABSOLUTELY!

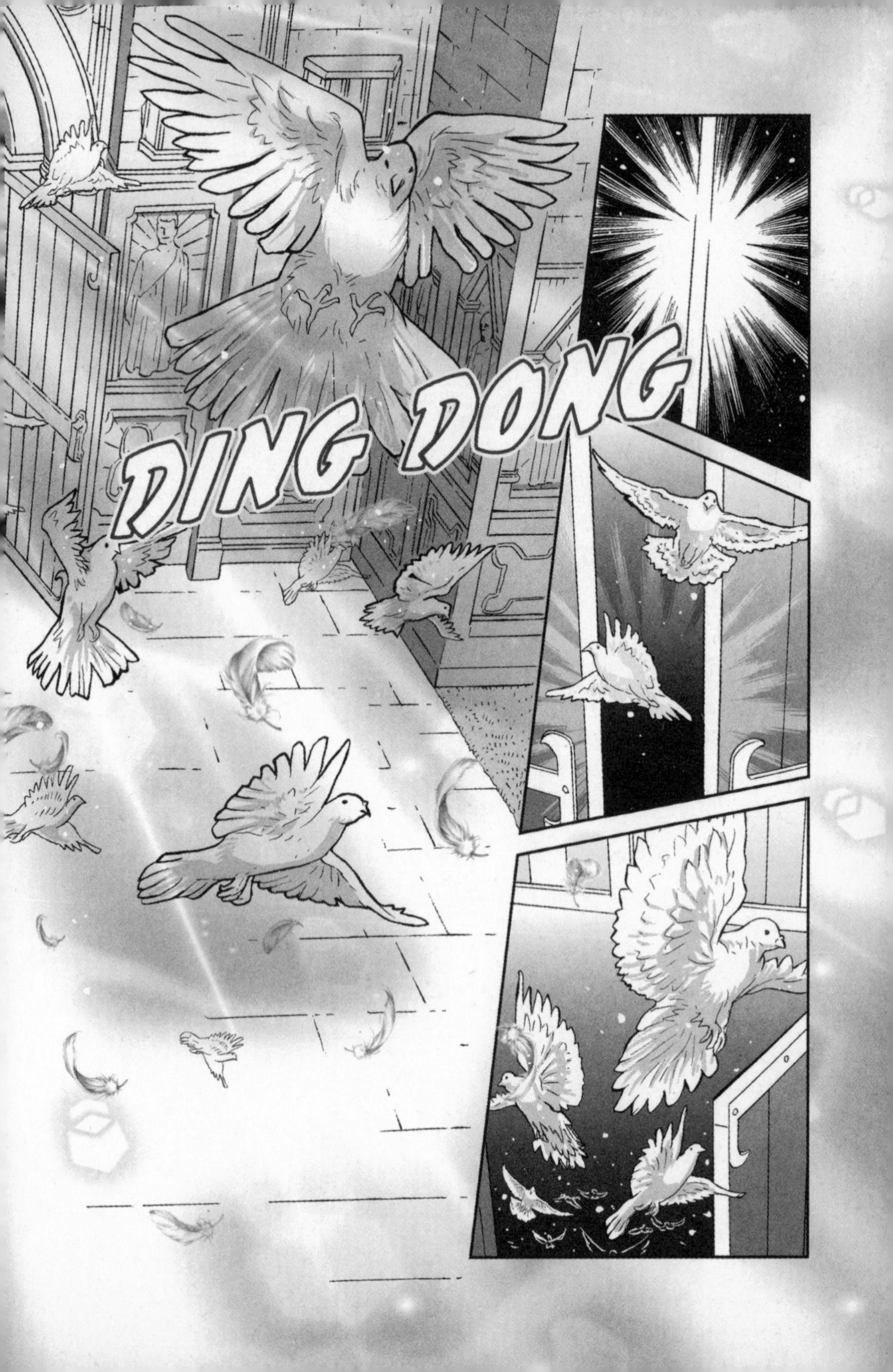
DING DONG

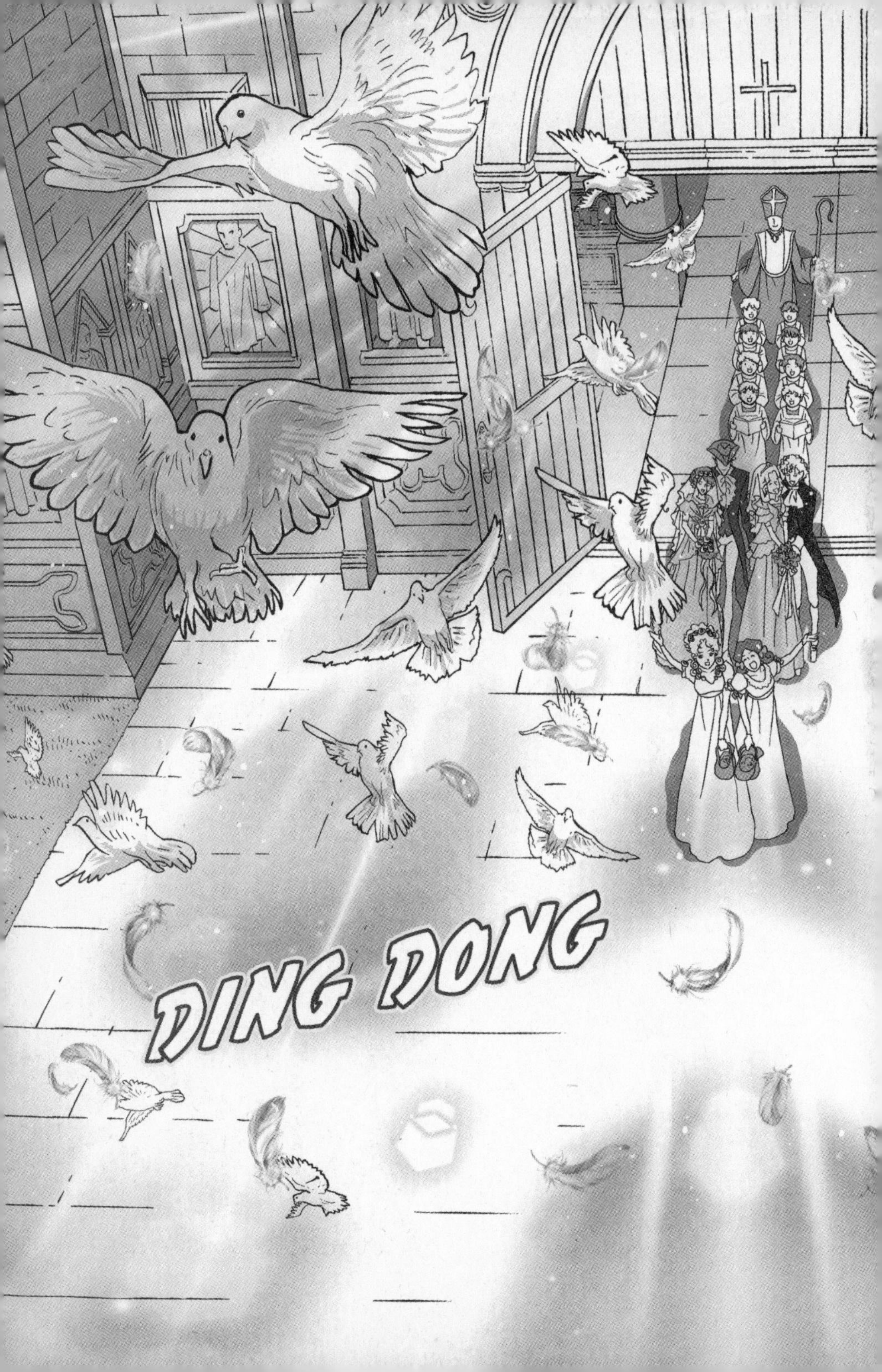
DING DONG

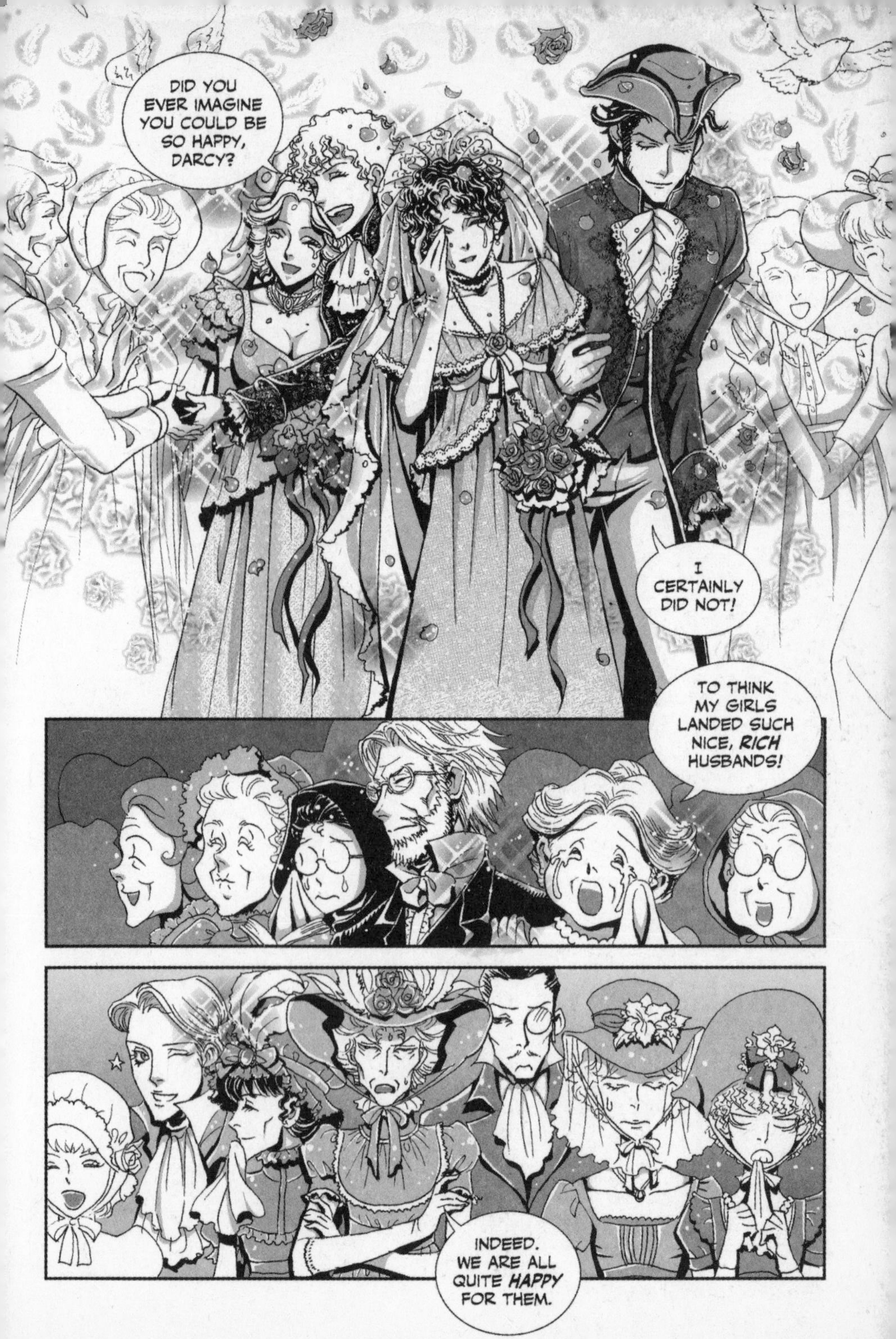
DID YOU EVER IMAGINE YOU COULD BE SO HAPPY, DARCY?
I CERTAINLY DID NOT!
TO THINK MY GIRLS LANDED SUCH NICE, *RICH* HUSBANDS!
INDEED. WE ARE ALL QUITE *HAPPY* FOR THEM.

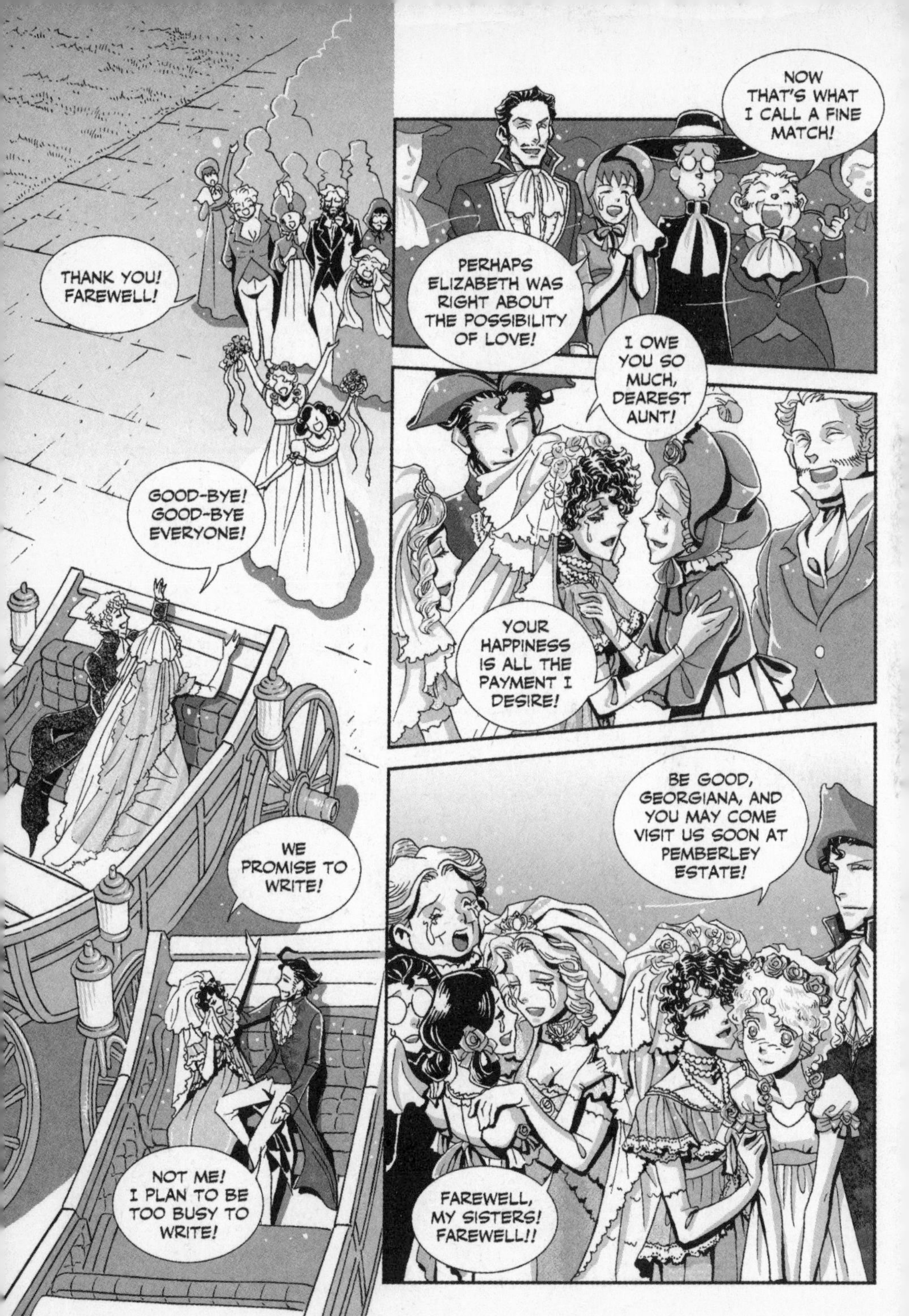
NOW THAT'S WHAT I CALL A FINE MATCH!
PERHAPS ELIZABETH WAS RIGHT ABOUT THE POSSIBILITY OF LOVE!
I OWE YOU SO MUCH, DEAREST AUNT!
YOUR HAPPINESS IS ALL THE PAYMENT I DESIRE!
BE GOOD, GEORGIANA, AND YOU MAY COME VISIT US SOON AT PEMBERLEY ESTATE!
FAREWELL, MY SISTERS! FAREWELL!!
THANK YOU! FAREWELL!
GOOD-BYE! GOOD-BYE EVERYONE!
WE PROMISE TO WRITE!
NOT ME! I PLAN TO BE TOO BUSY TO WRITE!

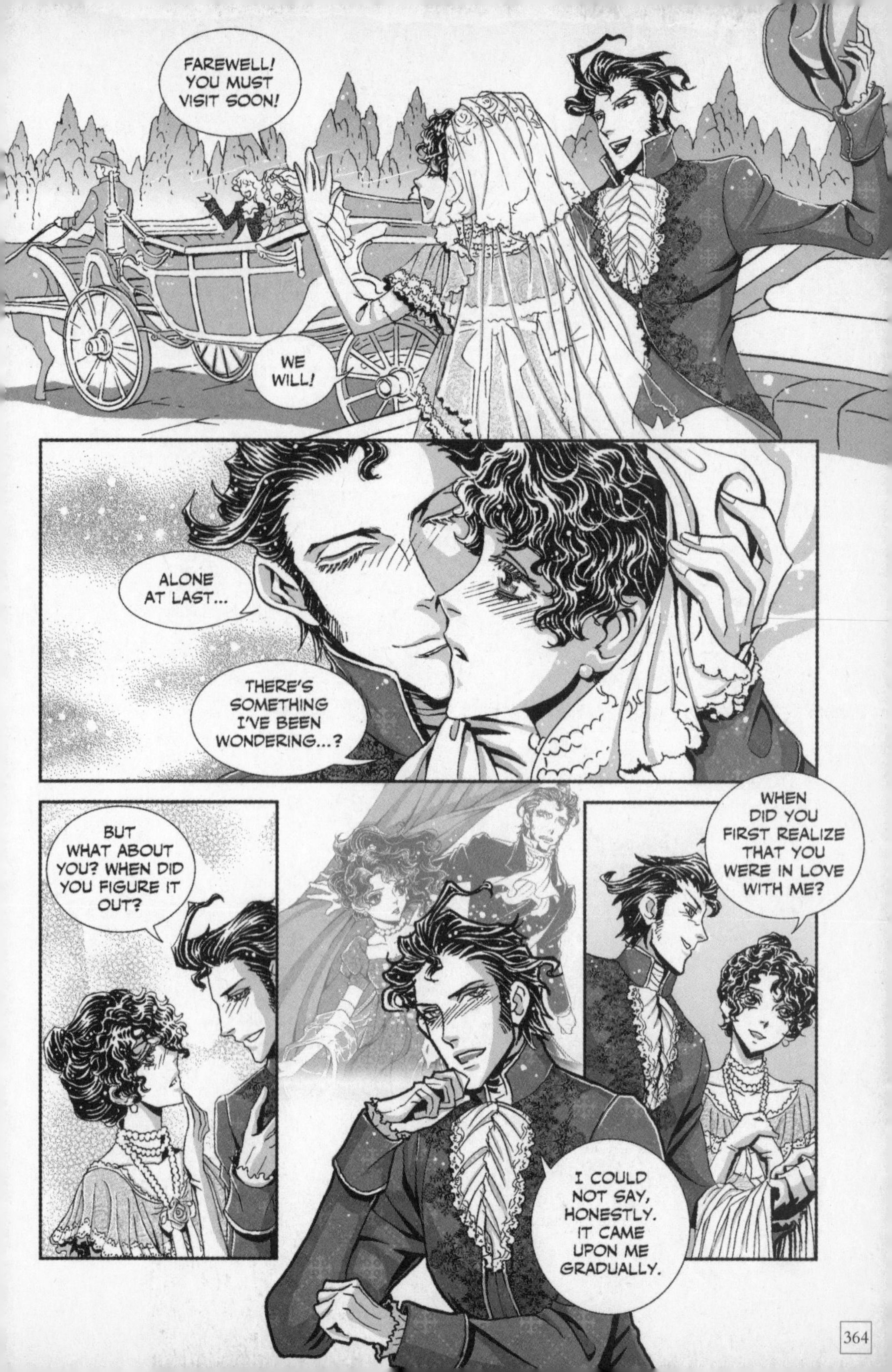
FAREWELL! YOU MUST VISIT SOON!
WE WILL!
ALONE AT LAST...
THERE'S SOMETHING I'VE BEEN WONDERING...?
WHEN DID YOU FIRST REALIZE THAT YOU WERE IN LOVE WITH ME?
I COULD NOT SAY, HONESTLY. IT CAME UPON ME GRADUALLY.
BUT WHAT ABOUT YOU? WHEN DID YOU FIGURE IT OUT?

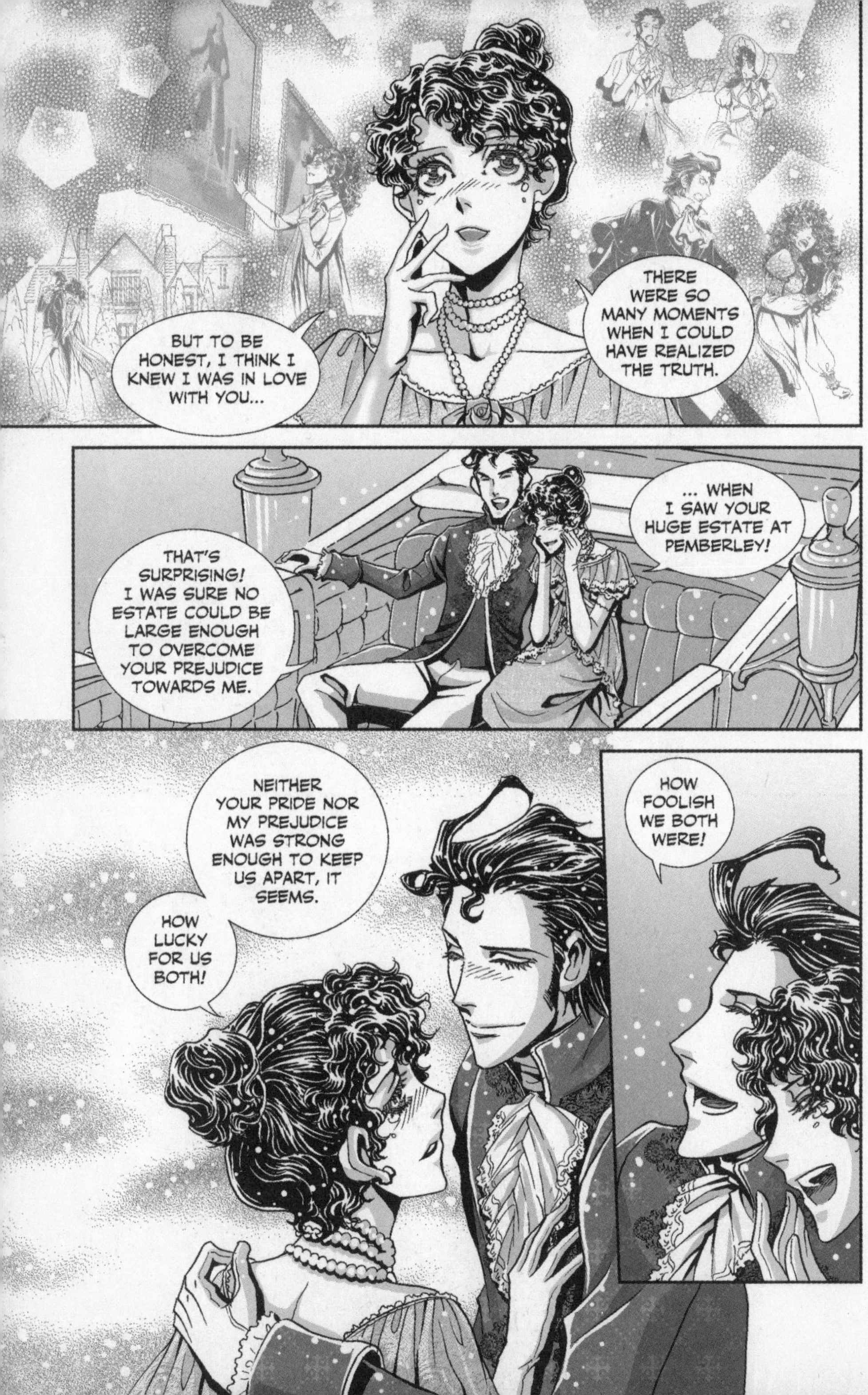
THERE WERE SO MANY MOMENTS WHEN I COULD HAVE REALIZED THE TRUTH.
BUT TO BE HONEST, I THINK I KNEW I WAS IN LOVE WITH YOU...
... WHEN I SAW YOUR HUGE ESTATE AT PEMBERLEY!
THAT'S SURPRISING! I WAS SURE NO ESTATE COULD BE LARGE ENOUGH TO OVERCOME YOUR PREJUDICE TOWARDS ME.
HOW FOOLISH WE BOTH WERE!
NEITHER YOUR PRIDE NOR MY PREJUDICE WAS STRONG ENOUGH TO KEEP US APART, IT SEEMS.
HOW LUCKY FOR US BOTH!

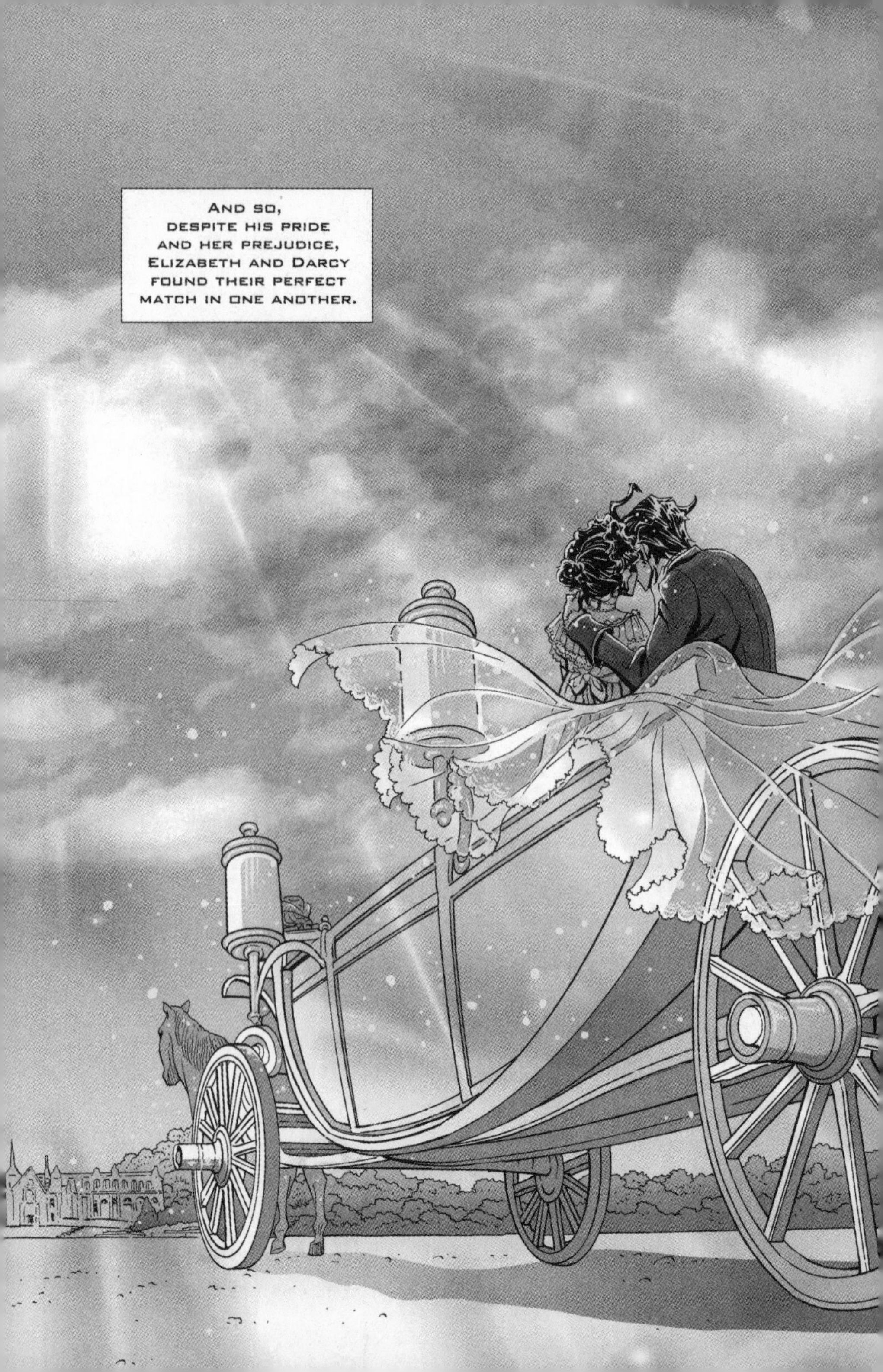
AND SO, DESPITE HIS PRIDE AND HER PREJUDICE, ELIZABETH AND DARCY FOUND THEIR PERFECT MATCH IN ONE ANOTHER.

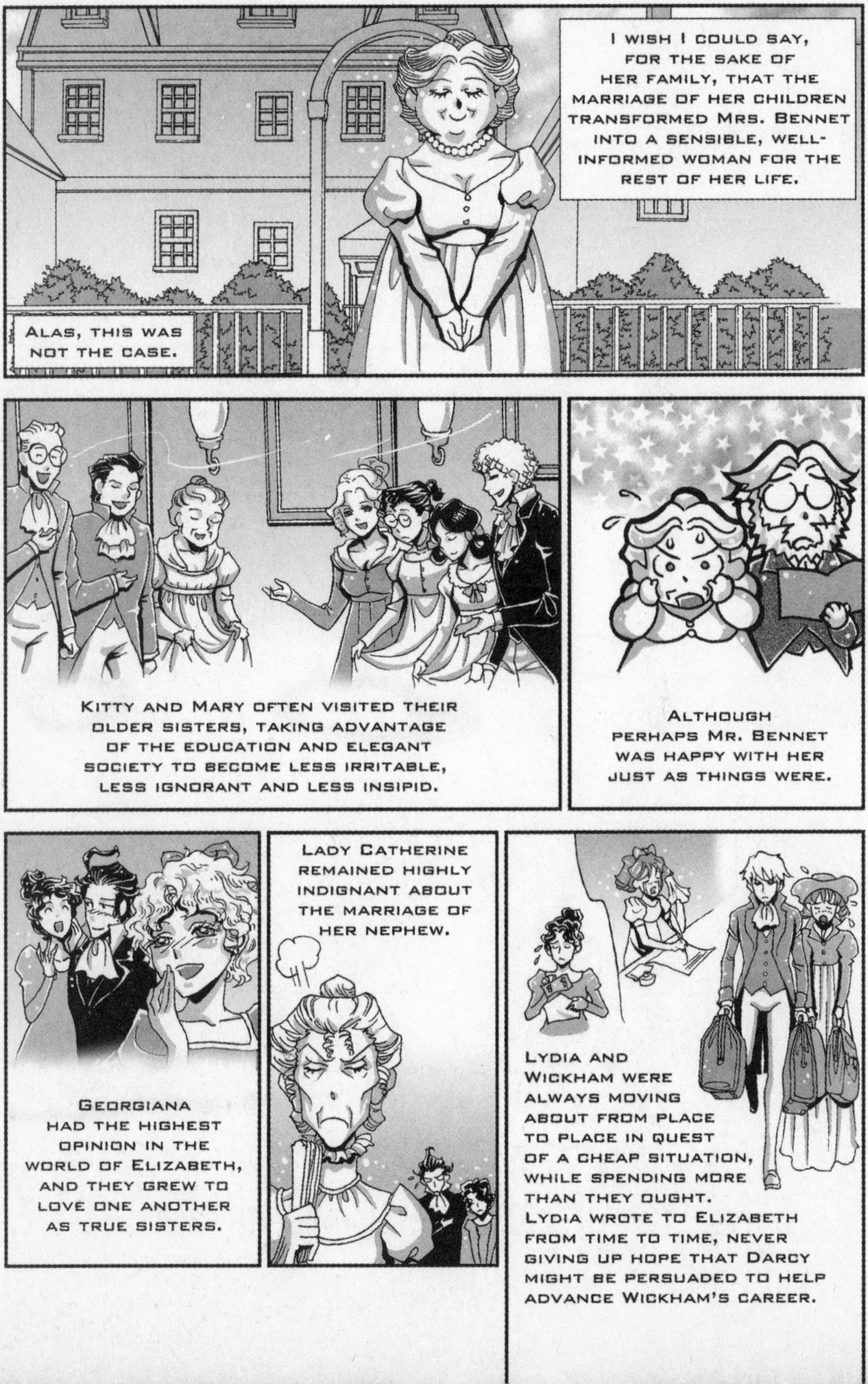
I WISH I COULD SAY, FOR THE SAKE OF HER FAMILY, THAT THE MARRIAGE OF HER CHILDREN TRANSFORMED MRS. BENNET INTO A SENSIBLE, WELL-INFORMED WOMAN FOR THE REST OF HER LIFE.
ALAS, THIS WAS NOT THE CASE.
ALTHOUGH PERHAPS MR. BENNET WAS HAPPY WITH HER JUST AS THINGS WERE.
KITTY AND MARY OFTEN VISITED THEIR OLDER SISTERS, TAKING ADVANTAGE OF THE EDUCATION AND ELEGANT SOCIETY TO BECOME LESS IRRITABLE, LESS IGNORANT AND LESS INSIPID.
LYDIA AND WICKHAM WERE ALWAYS MOVING ABOUT FROM PLACE TO PLACE IN QUEST OF A CHEAP SITUATION, WHILE SPENDING MORE THAN THEY OUGHT. LYDIA WROTE TO ELIZABETH FROM TIME TO TIME, NEVER GIVING UP HOPE THAT DARCY MIGHT BE PERSUADED TO HELP ADVANCE WICKHAM'S CAREER.
LADY CATHERINE REMAINED HIGHLY INDIGNANT ABOUT THE MARRIAGE OF HER NEPHEW.
GEORGIANA HAD THE HIGHEST OPINION IN THE WORLD OF ELIZABETH, AND THEY GREW TO LOVE ONE ANOTHER AS TRUE SISTERS.

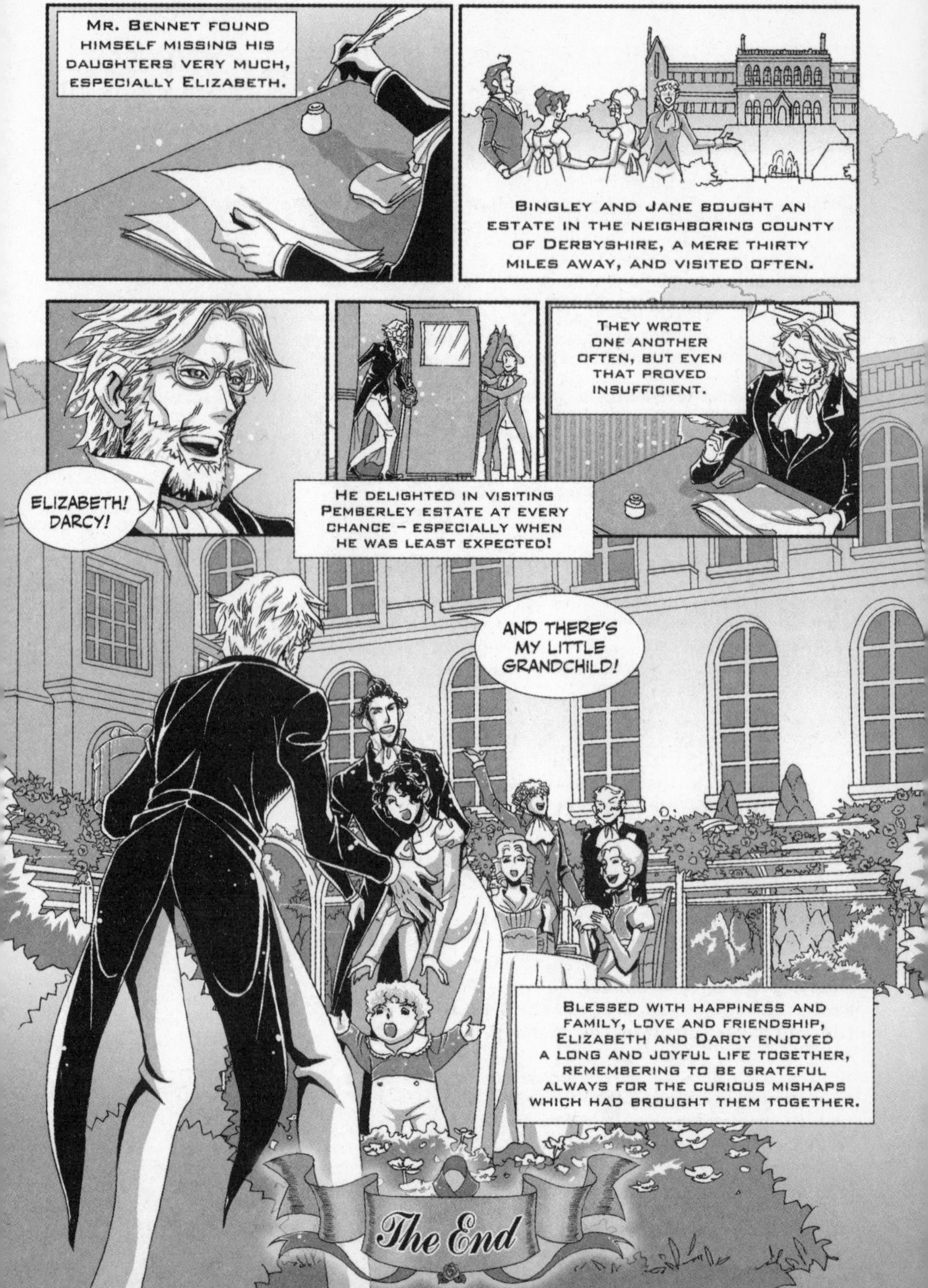

BINGLEY AND JANE BOUGHT AN ESTATE IN THE NEIGHBORING COUNTY OF DERBYSHIRE, A MERE THIRTY MILES AWAY, AND VISITED OFTEN.
MR. BENNET FOUND HIMSELF MISSING HIS DAUGHTERS VERY MUCH, ESPECIALLY ELIZABETH.
THEY WROTE ONE ANOTHER OFTEN, BUT EVEN THAT PROVED INSUFFICIENT.
HE DELIGHTED IN VISITING PEMBERLEY ESTATE AT EVERY CHANCE – ESPECIALLY WHEN HE WAS LEAST EXPECTED!
ELIZABETH! DARCY!
AND THERE'S MY LITTLE GRANDCHILD!
BLESSED WITH HAPPINESS AND FAMILY, LOVE AND FRIENDSHIP, ELIZABETH AND DARCY ENJOYED A LONG AND JOYFUL LIFE TOGETHER, REMEMBERING TO BE GRATEFUL ALWAYS FOR THE CURIOUS MISHAPS WHICH HAD BROUGHT THEM TOGETHER.
The End

As a life-long Jane Austen fan, I was both thrilled and terrified at the prospect of adapting her best-known work to a graphic novel format. Hiding within the apparent simplicity of Austen's plots is a complex understanding of human nature, one that I think still applies in so many ways – even to the high school dating scene! Imagine snubbing the plain girl who turns into a hottie over the summer holidays, and realizing how hard it will be to make up for your mistake... or keeping a nasty secret about your ex, only to be torn when your best friend starts dating him.

Clothing styles – and women's rights – have changed a lot in the last two centuries, but the challenges of human relationships remain as constant as Darcy's affection for Elizabeth. I hope this new adaptation, with its beautiful artwork and accessible design, will help both new and repeat readers discover the wonders of Austen's writing for themselves.

I'd like to express my gratitude to Po Tse and his studio assistants for bringing their remarkable art talents to this book. Many times, when I was unsure if the scene I'd written would capture the full emotions of the characters, I was reassured by knowing that Po's visuals would make up for any lack in my script! Thanks as well to Janice Leung, who helped both with organizing this project and providing translation help when needed. Above all, many thanks to Erik Ko and Andy Hung for helping to inspire and guide this book from initial idea to final creation, and for trusting me with the opportunity to work on such a wonderful and fulfilling adaptation.

I hope you enjoy this book as much as we enjoyed creating it!

Stacy King

Afterwords from PO

Hello to my dear Janeite (Fans of Jane Austen). Glad to share my thoughts with my fellow Janeite on this section. The charming relationship between Lizzy and Mr. Darcy captivated us. From their quarrel at first sight, to how their relationship eventually developed made it very enjoyable for all of us. Who can forget Miss Austen, for she was the one who created the first "Tsundere(ツンデレ)" character on Mr. Darcy, god bless her! I had a lot of fun making this manga. I especially enjoy Mr. Darcy's character. How to express his true feelings from under his emotionless face posed an enjoyable challenge for me. How did I do on that?

I would like to thank Mr.Erik Ko and Mr.Andy Hung, for giving me the opportunity to join this project, thanks for enduring all the delays from time to time, and for helping me with making it possible for Janeite to enjoy this exquisite manga! I give my gratitude to Stacy King for the perfect adaptation of the script, great job on the script of Lizzy & Mr. Darcy --- Thanks to Mr. Tai for the great arrangment. Kuma san, CL, Ahshu & Vincent Lau (also the other helpers), thanks for creating the background and manga effects. Last but not least, to my dear Jessica, thanks for everything!! Thank you to everyone involved --- see you all next time (And please visit my online pages too)!!

My Blog : http://lemonpo.blogspot.hk/
My devaintArt gallery : http://lemonpo.deviantart.com/

Manga Classics

UDON morpheus

UDON Entertainment proudly presents: **Manga Classics**!
The finest name in adaptations of great, classic literature!

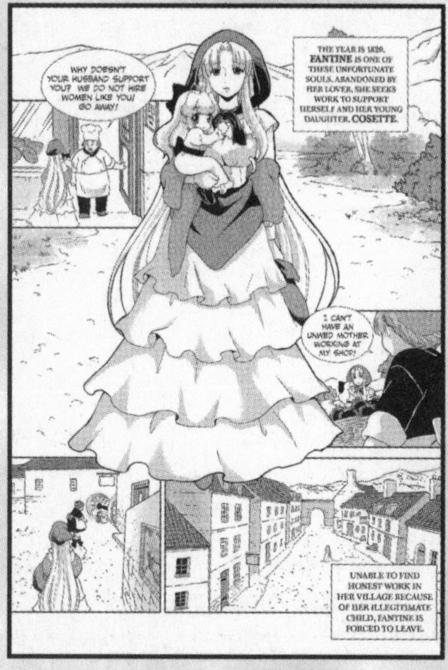

THE YEAR IS 1820. FANTINE IS ONE OF THESE UNFORTUNATE SOULS, ABANDONED BY HER LOVER. SHE SEEKS WORK TO SUPPORT HERSELF AND HER YOUNG DAUGHTER, COSETTE.
WHY DOESN'T YOUR HUSBAND SUPPORT YOU? WE DO NOT HIRE WOMEN LIKE YOU! GO AWAY!
I CAN'T HAVE AN UNWED MOTHER WORKING AT MY SHOP!
UNABLE TO FIND HONEST WORK IN HER VILLAGE BECAUSE OF HER ILLEGITIMATE CHILD, FANTINE IS FORCED TO LEAVE.

UDON is proud to bring you this very special new line of books, adapting classic literature with the same attention to detail and quality as our fantastic graphic novels, art books, and manga releases! UDON's Manga Classics is an international partnership with Asian comics and animation studio Morpheus, to bring the highest-quality adaptations of these works to the North American market!

UDON and Morpheus have worked very hard to fully realize the world of these classic works of literature. The artists have done extensive research on the settings of these works, to give the costumes and architecture a real weight and accuracy, expertly executed thanks to the studio's animation background. This high quality work has been coupled with a generous page count of over 350 pages per book, more than double the average comics-format adaptation! This allows for a more thorough, accurate, and natural adaptation of the source material, with the artists' vision given as much space as it needs to be properly realized. In short, these look and read like great commercial manga, while being faithful adaptations of literary classics!

Intended for a young adult audience, UDON's Manga Classics are just as likely to be enjoyed in the reader's free time as in the classroom . The gripping and intense story of Les Misérables and the lush shoujo art of Pride and Prejudice place them easily alongside today's bestselling popular manga, with strong and accurate adaptations that will please even the toughest teacher or librarian! UDON's Manga Classics are also a great way for adult readers to rediscover their favourite classics, or experience them for the first time!

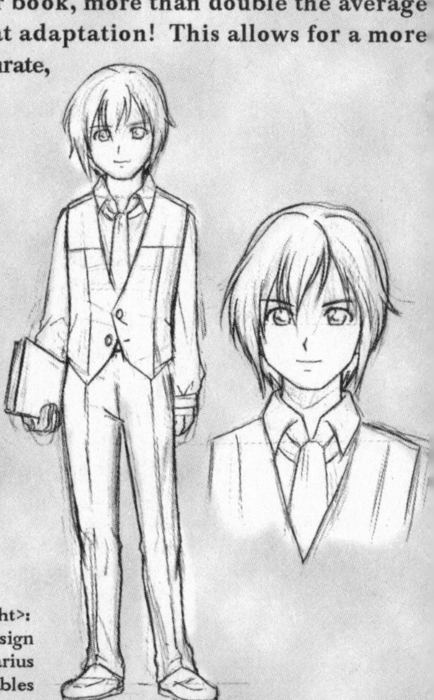

<right>:
Character Design
Sketches of Marius
from Les Misérables

Manga Classics: Victor Hugo's Les Misérables,

! WHOOPS !

This is the back of the book!

UDON's Manga Classics books follow the Japanese comic (aka Manga!) reading order. Traditional manga is read in a "reversed" format starting on the right and heading towards the left. The story begins where English readers expect to find the last page because the spine of the book is on the opposite side. Flip to the other end of the book and start reading your Manga Classics!

Pride and Prejudice
— JANE AUSTEN —
Art by: Po Tse
Story Adaptation by: Stacy King
Lettering: Morpheus Studios
Lettering Assist: Shane Law

UDON STAFF:

UDON Chief: Erik Ko
Manga Classics Group Editor: Stacy King
Senior Editor: Ash Paulsen
VP of Sales: John Shableski
Senior Producer: Long Vo
Marketing Manager: Jenny Myung
Production Manager: Janice Leung
Copy Editing Assistant: Michelle Lee
Japanese Liaison: Steven Cummings

MORPHEUS STAFF:

Morpheus Chief: Andy Hung
Production Manager: Tai
Art Assistants: Kuma, Oldman,
Roy, Ben Tsui,
Ashton, Nokman Poon,
Touyu, DORA,
Jessica, VIP 96neko,
Stoon, Mingsin Song

AGE: YOUNG ADULT 12+
BISAC Cat: FIC004000 Fiction/Classics
CGN004180 COMICS & GRAPHIC NOVELS/Manga/Romance
SUBJECT CATEGORIES: England-Fiction, Young Women-Fiction, Courtship-Fiction, Comics, Graphic Novels

Second Printing January 2016
ISBN # 978-1-927925-18-8

www.mangaclassics.com

An UDON Entertainment Production, in association with Morpheus Publishing Limited.
www.udonentertainment.com   www.morpheuspublishing.com